MW01078438

Research Methods for Criminal Justice and Criminology

"This book offers an approachable introduction to research methods with plenty of examples within the field of criminology and criminal justice. Students will benefit immensely from the critical review of various research methods and their application to criminal justice topics. Additionally, this book effectively supports instructors in facilitating classroom discussions that encourage the application of critical thinking skills."

Elias S. Nader, PhD, Assistant Professor, School of Criminal Justice,
University of Baltimore

This book explains and illustrates criminal justice research topics, including ethics in research, research design, causation, operationalization of variables, sampling, methods of data collection (including surveys), reliance on existing data, validity, and reliability. For each approach, the book addresses the procedures and issues involved, the method's strengths and drawbacks, and examples of actual research using that method. Every section begins with a brief summary of the research method. Introductory essays set the stage for students regarding the who, what, when, where, and why of each research example, and relevant discussion questions and exercises direct students to focus on the important concepts.

Research Methods for Criminal Justice and Criminology: A Text and Reader features interesting and relevant articles from leading journals, which have been expertly edited to highlight research design issues. The text offers instructors a well-rounded and convenient collection that eliminates the need to sift through journals to find articles that illustrate important precepts. All articles are recent and address issues relevant to the field today, such as immigration and crime, security post-9/11, racial profiling, and selection bias in media coverage of crime.

The book encourages classroom discussion and critical thinking and is an essential tool for undergraduate and graduate research methods courses in criminal justice, criminology, and related fields.

Christine Tartaro is Professor of Criminal Justice at Stockton University. She is an expert in corrections, suicide in correctional facilities, jail design, reentry, correctional treatment of individuals with mental illness, and criminal justice education. She has been teaching research methods since 2004, including teaching both undergraduate and graduate classes, and she writes and grades the research methods questions for her university's Master of Arts in Criminal Justice Program comprehensive exam. Prior to joining Stockton University, Tartaro worked at the New Jersey Department of Corrections, where she evaluated the state residential community release program. She has served as a research consultant to state and local correctional departments and private treatment agencies. She has been published in several journals, including *The Prison Journal, Corrections: Policy, Practice, and Research,* and *The Journal of Criminal Justice Education.* Tartaro received her PhD and MA in criminal justice from Rutgers University and her BA in history from the College of New Jersey.

Research Methods for Criminal Justice and Criminology

A Text and Reader

Christine Tartaro

Routledge
Taylor & Francis Group

NEW YORK AND LONDON

First published 2021
by Routledge
52 Vanderbilt Avenue, New York, NY 10017

and by Routledge
2 Park Square, Milton Park, Abingdon, Oxon, OX14 4RN

Routledge is an imprint of the Taylor & Francis Group, an informa business

© 2021 Christine Tartaro

The right of Christine Tartaro to be identified as author of this work has been
asserted by her in accordance with sections 77 and 78 of the Copyright, Designs and
Patents Act 1988.

All rights reserved. No part of this book may be reprinted or reproduced or utilised
in any form or by any electronic, mechanical, or other means, now known or
hereafter invented, including photocopying and recording, or in any information
storage or retrieval system, without permission in writing from the publishers.

Trademark notice: Product or corporate names may be trademarks or registered
trademarks, and are used only for identification and explanation without intent to
infringe.

Library of Congress Cataloging-in-Publication Data
Names: Tartaro, Christine, author.
Title: Research methods for criminal justice and criminology : a text and reader /
    Christine Tartaro.
Description: New York, NY : Routledge, 2021. | Includes bibliographical
    references and index.
Identifiers: LCCN 2020048814 (print) | LCCN 2020048815 (ebook) |
    ISBN 9780367509132 (hardback) | ISBN 9781003051763 (ebook)
Subjects: LCSH: Criminal justice, Administration of—Research—Methodology. |
    Criminology—Research—Methodology.
Classification: LCC HV7419.5 .T37 2021 (print) | LCC HV7419.5 (ebook) |
    DDC 364.072/1—dc23
LC record available at https://lccn.loc.gov/2020048814
LC ebook record available at https://lccn.loc.gov/2020048815

ISBN: 978-0-367-50913-2 (hbk)
ISBN: 978-0-367-50889-0 (pbk)
ISBN: 978-1-003-05176-3 (ebk)

Typeset in Goudy
by Apex CoVantage, LLC

Access the Support Material: www.routledge.com/9780367508890

To my parents, Jen, and Dena

Contents

Online Supplements

The following readings are available at www.routledge.com/9780367508890.

Preface

Why Use This Book?

I have been teaching research methods for over 15 years and have experience working with both undergraduate and graduate research methods students. I believe that students at all levels learn best when they read empirical research to reinforce the lessons included in methods textbooks. They need to see the principles of research in action to understand the strengths and weaknesses of each method. Every year, I search for an appropriate reader, and, if one is not available, I sift through dozens of articles to find good illustrations of the concepts that I plan to cover in class. The few available readers that cater specifically to criminal justice research classes include articles that are quite old and do not address many of the pressing matters in our field.

When I started this project, I had three goals. First, I wanted to provide everything necessary for teaching research methods to criminal justice and criminology students in one book. As a professor at a state university, I am mindful of the cost of tuition, fees, and textbooks, and I wanted to offer a cost-effective option. My goal was to save students money by providing everything in one book while saving professors time by giving them both a textbook and a variety of timely articles with a range of research designs. Second, I wanted the reader portion of the book to cover an array of topics in criminal justice, so students could learn about their field while simultaneously improving their ability to read and understand empirical research. The articles that I selected include a mixture of topics, including police, courts, corrections, and victimization. I specifically chose articles that address some trending subjects, such as immigration and crime, internet-based crime, racial profiling, body-worn cameras, citizen perceptions of police stops, safe injection sites, and legalization of marijuana. Third, I wanted to make assignments more manageable by editing some of the longer articles, so they are shorter while still including the essential elements of research.

I hope that you enjoy the book.

Acknowledgments

I don't think that this project would have been possible without the help and encouragement of Ellen Boyne of Routledge. Ellen and I are old friends, and when I was batting around ideas for a reader, she encouraged me and provided great advice. She, and the board members at Routledge, suggested that I go beyond my original idea of creating a reader and take the plunge into writing a textbook too. Ellen patiently answered my dozens of questions, no matter how silly they were. She was an outstanding sounding board throughout this project, and I am forever grateful to her for that. I would also like to thank Kate Taylor from Routledge for her help with organizing the final product. I am also grateful to all the wonderful scholars who permitted me to include their articles in this reader.

I have been talking about working on some sort of research methods book for almost a decade. The original plan came out of numerous dinners with Dr. Joshua Duntley, a friend and colleague. For years, we tried to find time to work together, but our schedules just never allowed it. I am grateful to him for helping me believe that I could take on something this size. I am also grateful to Dr. Deeanna Button for talking to me about her approach to teaching this subject and for sharing her assignments with me. The reading exercises sheet that I included in the instructor materials was mostly derived from my paper- and test-grading checklists, but I did adopt a few of her questions. This project gave me the opportunity to work with one of my former graduate students, Lisen Minetti. Lisen read the draft of the book, gave me valuable feedback, and helped with constructing the test bank.

Finally, I would like to thank my family and friends for politely listening to me talk about this project. Jennifer and Dena Tartaro, my parents; Abbi Erbacher; Christopher DeSantis; and Dr. Jess Bonnan-White have been very patient with my book-writing grumblings. Of course, some of the best support came from my pets, who sat next to me and even occasionally jumped on my keyboard while I worked on this. Thank you, Sully, Petey, Todd, Winston, and RayRay. If there are any typos in this book, I am blaming them. While working on this, I had to say goodbye to Templeton, Gus, and Jake, all wonderful pets whom I miss dearly.

Credits

This book and its online support material contain material previously published in the following publications. All content is reproduced with permission.

Reading 3.1

Source: Klein, J. L., Bailey, D. J. S., & Sample, L. L. (2018). Researching the registered: challenges and suggestions for researchers studying sex offender populations. *Criminal Justice Studies, 31*(2), 192–211. DOI: 10.1080/1478601X.2018.1430033. Reprinted with permission from Taylor & Francis.

Reading 3.-A

Source: Goode, E. (1999). Sex with informants as deviant behavior: an account and commentary. *Deviant Behavior, 20,* 301–324. https://doi.org/10.1080/016396299266416 Reprinted with permission from Taylor & Francis.

Reading 4.1

Source: Fallik, S. W. (2019). The methodological struggles of racial profiling research: a causal question that automobile stop data has yet to answer. *Criminal Justice Studies, 32*(1), 32–49. DOI: 10.1080/1478601X.2018.1558057. Reprinted with permission from Taylor & Francis.

Reading 4.2

Kochel, T. R. & Weisburd, D. (2019). The Impact of Hot Spots Policing on Collective Efficacy: Findings from a Randomized Field Trial. *Justice Quarterly, 36*(5), 900–928. https://doi-Org/10.1080/07418825.2018.1465579

Reading 4.3

Source: Strah, B. M., Frost, N. A., Stowell, J. I., & Taheri, S. A. (2018). Cognitive-behavioral programming and the value of failed interventions: a propensity score evaluation. *Journal of Offender Rehabilitation, 57*(1), 22–46. DOI: 10.1080/10509674.2017.1416437. Reprinted with permission from Taylor & Francis.

Reading 5.1

Source: Jakubowski, A., Kunins, H. V., Huxley-Reicher, Z., & Siegler, A. (2018). Knowledge of the 911 Good Samaritan Law and 911-calling behavior of overdose witnesses, *Substance Abuse, 39*(2), 233–238. DOI: 1080/08897077.2017.1387213. Reprinted with permission from Taylor & Francis.

Reading 5.2

Source: Patterson, C., Hogan, L., & Cox, M. (2019). A comparison between two retrospective alcohol consumption measures and the daily drinking diary method with university students. *The American Journal of Drug and Alcohol Abuse, 45*(3), 248–253. DOI: 10.1080/00952990.2018.1514617. Reprinted with permission from Taylor and Francis.

Reading 5-A

Source: Curcio, G. & Pattavina, A. (2018). Still paying for the past: examining gender differences in employment among individuals with a criminal record. *Women & Criminal Justice, 28*(5), 375–396. DOI: 10.1080/08974454.2018.1441773. Reprinted with permission from Taylor & Francis.

Reading 6.1

Source: Valcore, J. L. & Pfeffer, R. (2018). Systemic error: measuring gender in criminological research. *Criminal Justice Studies, 31*(4), 333–351. DOI: 10.1080/1478601X.2018.1499022. Reprinted with permission from Taylor & Francis.

Reading 6.2

Source: Costello, M., Rukus, J., & Hawdon, J. (2019). We don't like your type around here: regional and residential differences in exposure to online hate material targeting sexuality. *Deviant Behavior, 40*(3), 385–401. DOI: 10.1080/01639625.2018.1426266. Reprinted with permission from Taylor & Francis.

Reading 6.3

Source: Shepherd, S. M., & Anthony, T. (2018). Popping the cultural bubble of violence risk assessment tools. *The Journal of Forensic Psychiatry & Psychology, 29*(2), 211–220. DOI: 10.1080/14789949.2017.1354055. Reprinted with permission from Taylor & Francis.

Reading 6.4

Source: Ceccato, V. (2019). Fieldwork protocol as a safety inventory tool in public places. *Criminal Justice Studies, 32*(2), 165–188. DOI: 10.1080/09589236.2019.1601367. Reprinted with permission from Taylor & Francis.

Reading 7.1

Source: Adelman, R., Reid, L. W., Markle, G., Weiss, S., & Jaret, C. (2017). Urban crime rates and the changing face of immigration: evidence across four decades. *Journal of Ethnicity in Criminal Justice, 15*(1), 52–77. DOI: 10.1080/15377938.2016.1261057. Reprinted with permission from Taylor & Francis.

Reading 7.2

Source: Golladay, K. & Holtfreter, K. (2017). The consequences of identity theft victimization: an examination of emotional and physical health outcomes. *Victims & Offenders, 12*(5), 741–760. https://doi.org/10.1080/15564886.2016.1177766. Reprinted with permission from Taylor & Francis.

Reading 7.2

Source: Golladay, K. & Holtfreter, K. (2017). The consequences of identity theft victimization: an examination of emotional and physical health outcomes. *Victims & Offenders, 12*(5), 741–760. https://doi.org/10.1080/15564886.2016.1177766. Reprinted with permission from Taylor & Francis.

Reading 8.1

Source: Maeder, E. M., Yamamoto, S., & McManus, L. A. (2018). Methodology matters: comparing sample types and data collection methods in a juror decision-making study on the influence of defendant race. *Psychology, Crime, & Law, 24*(7), 687–702. DOI: 10.1080/1068316X.2017.1409895. Reprinted with permission from Taylor & Francis.

Reading 8.2

Source: Roth, J., Lee, Seungmug, & Joo, J. (2018). The effective of community-level alarm ownership on burglary rates. *Journal of Applied Security Research, 13*(2), 160–171. DOI: 10.1080/19361610/2018.1422360. Reprinted with permission from Taylor and Francis.

Reading 8.3

Source: Mowder, D., Lutze, F., & Namgung, H. (2018). Ayúdame! Who can help me? the help-seeking decisions of battered undocumented Latinas. *Journal of Ethnicity in Criminal Justice, 16*(3), 205–224. DOI: 10.1080/15377938.2018.1498818. Source: Reprinted with permission from Taylor & Francis.

Reading 8-A

Source: Upshur, C. C., Jenkins, D., Weinreb, L., Gelberg, L., & Orvek, E. A. (2018). Homeless women's service use, barriers, and motivation for participating in substance use treatment. *The American Journal of Drug and Alcohol Abuse, 44*(2), 252–262. DOI: 10.1080/00952990.2017.1357183. Reprinted with permission of Taylor & Francis.

Reading 8-B

Source: Leon, C., Cardoso, L., Mackin, S., Bock, B., & Gaeta, J. (2018). The willingness of people who inject drugs in Boston to use a supervised injection facility. *Substance Abuse, 39*(1), 95–101. DOI: 10.1080/08897077.2017.1365804. Reprinted with permission from Taylor & Francis.

Reading 9.1

Source: Boivin, R., Gendron, A., Faubert, C., & Poulin, B. (2017). The malleability of attitudes toward the police: immediate effects of the viewing of police use of force videos. *Police Practice & Research, 18*(4), 366–375. https://doi-org.ezproxy.stockton.edu/10.1080/15614263.2016.1230063. Reprinted with permission from Taylor and Francis.

Reading 9.2

Source: Kalyal, H. (2019). "Well, there's a more scientific way to do it!": factors influencing receptivity to evidence-based practices in police organizations. *Police Practice and Research*, DOI: 10.1080/15614263.2019.1608548. Reprinted with permission from Taylor & Francis.

Reading 9-A

Source: Biggar, R. W., Forsyth, C. J., Chen, J., & Burstein, K. (2017). The Poly-Drug User: Examining Associations between Drugs Used by Adolescents. *Deviant Behavior, 38*(10), 1186–1196. https://doi-org.ezproxy.stockton.edu/10.1080/01639625.2016.1246022. Reprinted with permission from Taylor & Francis.

Reading 9-B

Source: Rajakaruna, N., Henry, P. J., Cutler, A., & Fairman, G. (2017). Ensuring the validity of police use of force training. *Police Practice & Research, 18*(5), 507–521. https://doi-org.ezproxy.stockton.edu/10.1080/15614263.2016.1268959. Reprinted with permission from Taylor & Francis.

Reading 10.1

Source: Pawson, M. & Kelly, B. C. (2014). Consumption and community: the subcultural contexts of disparatemarijuana practices in jam band and hip-hop scenes. *Deviant Behavior, 35*, 347–363. https://doi.org/10.1080/01639625.2013.848127. Reprinted with permission from Taylor & Francis.

Reading 10-A

Source: Lavin, M. F. (2017). She got herself there: narrative resistance in the drug discourse of strippers. *Deviant Behavior, 38*(3), 294–305. https://doi.org/10.1080/01639625.2016.1197002. Reprinted with permission from Taylor & Francis.

Reading 11.1

Source: Maahs, J., & Pratt, T. C. (2017). "I Hate These Little Turds!": Science, Entertainment, and the Enduring Popularity of Scared Straight Programs. *Deviant Behavior, 38*(1), 47–60. https://doi.org/10.1080/01639625.2016.1190619. Reprinted with permission from Taylor & Francis.

Reading 11.2

Source: Jennings, W. G., Fridell, L. A., Lynch, M., Jetelina, K. K., & Reingle Gonzalez, J. M. (2017). A Quasi-Experimental Evaluation of the Effects of Police Body-Worn Cameras (BWCs) on Response-to-Resistance in a Large Metropolitan Police Department. *Deviant Behavior*, 38(11), 1332–1339. DOI: 10.1108/PIJPSM-03-2017-0032. Reprinted with permission from Taylor & Francis.

Reading 11.3

Source: Proctor, S. L., Kopak, A. M., & Hoffmann, N. G. (2017). Psychometric properties of the UNCOPE:Screening for DSM-5 substance use disorder among a state juvenile justice population. *Journal of Offender Rehabilitation*, 56(7), 494–504. DOI: 10.1080/10509674.2017.1359224. Reprinted with permission from Taylor & Francis.

Reading 11.4

Source: Shaffer, D. K. (2011). Looking inside the black box of drug courts. A meta-analytic review. *Justice Quarterly*, 28(3), 493–521. DOI: 10.1080/07418825.2010.525222. Reprinted with permission from Taylor & Francis.

Reading 11-A

Source: Jeanis, M. N., & Powers, R. A. (2017). Newsworthiness of Missing Persons Cases: An Analysis of Selection Bias, Disparities in Coverage, and the Narrative Framework of News Reports. *Deviant Behavior*, 38(6), 668–683. https://doi-org.ezproxy.stockton.edu/10.1080/01639625.2016.1197618. Reprinted with permission from Taylor & Francis.

Reading 11-B

Source: Lowrey-Kinberg, B. V. (2018). Procedural justice, overaccommodation, and police authority and professionalism: results from a randomized experiment. *Police Practice & Research*, 19(2), 111–124. https://doi-org.ezproxy.stockton.edu/10.1080/15614263.2018.1418167. Reprinted with permission from Taylor & Francis.

Reading 12.1

Source: Lu, R., Willits, D., Stohr, M. K., Makin, D., Snyder, J., Lovrich, N., Meize, M., Stanton, D., Wu, G., & Hemmens, C. (2019). The cannabis effect on crime: time-series analysis of crime in Colorado and Washington state. *Justice Quarterly*, DOI: 10.1080/07418825.2019.1666903. Reprinted with permission from Taylor & Francis.

Reading 12.2

Source: Makarios, M., Lovins, L. B., Myer, A. J., & Latessa, E. (2019). Treatment integrity and recidivism among sex offenders: the relationship between CPC scores and program effectiveness. *Corrections*, 4(2), 112–125. DOI: 10.1080/23774657.2017.1389318. Reprinted with permission from Taylor & Francis.

Introduction

If you are reading this, you are probably enrolled in a research methods course. You also probably aren't thrilled about it, but it will be okay. A common knock on academics is that it lacks practical application to real life. After all, how many of us regularly use the trigonometry that we learned in high school or even in college? Don't get me wrong. I believe that there is value in trigonometry because it challenges us with higher-order thinking. Plus, I like certain types of math, but I can respect those who do not. While it might not seem so now, this class is something that you can use in your life. Knowing about research can truly help you be a better criminal justice professional and be in a stronger position to judge the evidence that people use to support their arguments.

I have had enough experience working with students that I am well aware that many dread research methods and statistics courses, and the only reason they take them is because they are mandatory. I understand the apprehension because of how challenging the classes can be. What I find frustrating is when students fail to appreciate what they stand to gain. While you might not realize it now, this class has tons of practical application to all criminal justice jobs and life outside work. This class will help you sort through what is real and what is pseudoscience, "fake news," or a fad lacking any evidence of effectiveness. This is of vital importance to your careers. You might start out in a low-level position, such as a police officer on a regular beat or a case worker for a social service agency, but you are going to want to move up in the ranks and become someone who has a hand in making decisions. When that happens, you can either move the field of criminal justice in the right direction, using evidence to inform your decisions, or you can try to use what people think of as "common sense" and advocate for something that is probably ineffective. The "common sense" approach to criminal justice policy has brought us such failures as *Scared Straight*, DARE, mandatory sentences for drug possession, and correctional boot camps.

Fortunately, our field is moving in the direction of **evidence-based practice** (EBP). That means that there is a push in criminal justice to learn about what types of interventions work, to implement only programs that work, and to discard those that are ineffective. As implausible as it may seem, this is *not* how criminal justice has operated for decades. While lamenting misguided efforts in the field of corrections, Latessa, Cullen, and Gendreau (2011) argued that what we have been doing qualifies as "**quackery**," meaning the use of interventions that are *not* based on our knowledge of what causes crime or what we know is effective in changing offender behavior. Our use of ineffective programs based on flawed premises has cost us billions of dollars and has harmed victims, communities, and even offenders.

Evidence-based practice (EBP), according to the National Institute of Corrections (NIC), involves the "objective, balanced, and responsible use of current research and the best available data to guide policy and practice decisions" (NIC, n.d., para 1). EBP specifically focuses on empirical research and prioritizes that over professional experience. Researchers contribute to EBP by producing methodologically rigorous program evaluations. Practitioners and policymakers may then use this information to guide their decisions about which policies and programs to keep, which to modify, and which to jettison. Notice that this is a two-step process that requires work from both researchers and practitioners. Many students approach research methods classes with the attitude

[handwritten note: "the power of research and why we must know how research"]

of "I am not going to be a ▓▓▓▓▓▓▓▓▓▓▓▓▓▓ t true. It might have been the case back when your ▓▓▓▓▓▓▓▓▓▓▓▓▓ but not anymore. You are probably in this class beca ▓▓▓▓▓▓▓▓▓▓▓▓ kely) or a criminal justice practitioner (more likely). ▓▓▓▓▓▓▓▓▓▓▓▓ rk in our field, you need to be part of it. To do that, y ▓▓▓▓▓▓▓▓▓▓▓▓ ve to at least have a basic understanding of research ▓▓▓▓▓▓▓▓▓▓▓▓ d information.

This book will also hel ▓▓▓▓▓▓▓▓▓▓▓▓ to more information than previous generations coul ▓▓▓▓▓▓▓▓▓▓▓▓▓, but it is also a curse. With this proliferation of information comes the creation and dissemination of misinformation. Two of today's most prominent examples of how damaging misinformation can be are vaccines and climate change. A MIT professor of geochemistry recently reviewed 11,602 scientific articles about climate change and found that, among those articles, there was a 100 percent agreement that global warming is not only real but also a product of human activity (Powell, 2017). And yet, there are people, some in high-ranking positions in government and industry, who deny the science. This has profound implications for policy.

Given the strength of corporations, lobbyists, and politicians who promote certain industries, it is likely that climate change denial would continue to exist, albeit with fewer followers, even without the availability of the internet to spread misinformation. The internet, however, has been vital to the growth of the anti-vaccine movement (Larson, 2018). There is no evidence that links vaccines to autism. None. The only research conducted by an actual scientist that linked vaccines to autism was published in 1998, but the study had to be retracted due to fraud. The lead researcher took numerous steps throughout the study to make sure that the research team would find the exact results that he was seeking in order to benefit himself financially (Sathyanarayana & Andrade, 2011). Since that retraction, there has been no research conducted by any actual professional researcher that supports the anti-vax movement, but there have been plenty of credible articles refuting the vaccine-autism link. Despite the overwhelming lack of evidence of the dangers of vaccines, misinformation continues to spread, largely through the internet. Anyone can make a website and post claims that have no basis in fact. Additionally, the internet has empowered all of us to become "researchers," and those who are unable to differentiate good sources from bad can be easily convinced with incorrect information. The spread of misinformation about vaccines has become so bad that Facebook is using pop-up windows to try to direct people conducting searches to valid sources of vaccine information, such as the World Health Organization (Howard, 2019).

With the help of this book and your professor, you should leave this class having a much better sense of what constitutes actual research. You will also learn that all research is *not* created equal, and we always have to consider how the research was conducted as we try to make sense of the findings. This will help you as you hear not only about research in criminal justice but also work on all subject matters. Research methods classes for all disciplines are remarkably similar. The ethics precautions that are necessary for each study vary. For example, in your class, you will not be reviewing the necessary steps to ethically care for lab rats or chimpanzees, as you would in biology or even psychology. The research designs and sampling considerations, however, are the same no matter the discipline. So, once you start to feel more comfortable understanding the basics of criminal justice research, you should feel more confident in being able to judge the quality of work elsewhere. That will make you a better consumer of information in all corners of life.

The Scientific Method

I am sure that you have already conducted some research on something. You had to do research to figure out which laptop or car you should buy. You probably did a good amount of research to choose a college. You have also done research to write papers for other classes. All that is good. You are better off knowing that one of your top choices of cars got an excellent crash-test rating while your other choice failed and decapitated the crash-test dummy. Reading consumer magazines and comparing laptops at a store do not involve scientific research though. This book and your class will teach you about a more systematic way of learning.

The research that is the subject of this course is based on the **scientific method**. What sets this apart from the research you did to shop for a computer is that the scientific method requires adherence to a strict set of rules. Just as with your computer, or car-buying research, we make observations, but with the scientific method, we do so in a very systematic way, with the goal of generating an *unbiased* image of the world rather than an individual's personal image (Haig, 2018; Wallace, 1971). In his classic work on the scientific method, Wallace (1971) visualized the research process as a wheel, including theory formulation, hypothesis construction, observations, and then generalization of findings (Figure 1.1). The use of a wheel as an illustration is important here, as wheels lack a clear starting point. For research, the start and end points vary depending on the method the researcher adopts. The two most common approaches in criminal justice research are deductive and inductive. The deductive method has been the favored set of steps in the natural sciences for decades, and it is commonly used in criminal justice research. The **deductive approach** starts with theory. A **theory** is an attempt to construct a plausible explanation of reality (Hagan, 2007). Researchers then use logical deduction to take theories and write **hypotheses**, or predictions of relationships between variables based on our understanding of theory (Maxfield & Babbie, 2012; Wallace, 1971). Only after those two steps are completed does the researcher determine how to

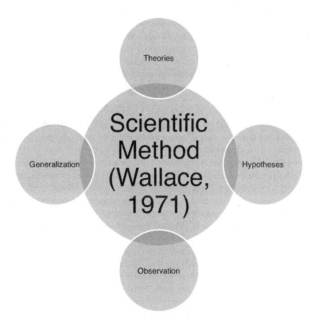

Figure 1.1 Stages of Research
Source: Wallace, W. (1971). *[...] of science in sociology*. Chicago: Aldine. P. 18

Scientific method =
requires adherence
to a strict set of
rules
(wallace 1971)

deductive approach =
starts w a theory

measure the hypotheses and conduct observations. These observations must follow specific proto-col to reduce the potential for bias. Once data have been collected, it is time to test the hypotheses. Based on the rigor of the research design, it may or may not be appropriate to generalize the findings to the wider population. Researchers using deductive reasoning would start at the top of the research wheel in Figure 1.1 and move clockwise.

Research based on inductive reasoning has a different starting point, at the bottom of the wheel and moving clockwise. Rather than beginning with a theory and then moving on to hypothesis testing, researchers taking the **inductive approach** use observations as their starting point. They seek to observe facts without any particular theory in mind. Those observations can then be used to draw conclusions and generate a theory based on the findings. These theories are known as **grounded theories** since they are based on the data that have already been col-lected (Glaser & Strauss, 1967; Maxwell, 1996). Researchers can then take that newly formed theory, generate hypotheses based on it, and go around the wheel again but with the deductive approach this time.

Qualitative and Quantitative Research

The decision of whether to approach research with inductive or deductive reasoning might be related to the kind of study the researcher is planning. Criminal justice as an academic discipline has benefitted from both quantitative and qualitative research. Quantitative research is the more common approach in criminal justice. Quantitative work tends to start with a deductive approach, with researchers using knowledge of theory to write and then test hypotheses. The primary distin-guishing characteristics of quantitative research are the use of numerical values to represent con-cepts and the quantification of results, often involving statistical procedures. Due to the rules governing statistical analysis, quantitative studies rely on large sample sizes, but to get the necessary sample size, researchers often forgo the opportunity to interact much, if at all, with potential research participants. In fact, a popular trend in criminal justice research today is to obtain access to large datasets with information collected by other researchers or practitioners and perform sophisticated statistical analysis without interacting with any of the humans who were the subject of data collection.

Qualitative research largely involves observation and long interviews of smaller groups with the goal of generating a more complete understanding of a group or subculture. Qualitative research in criminal justice draws from the work of urban anthropologists and sociologists who spend exten-sive amounts of time with and sometimes even live among those they are studying. Qualitative work could start from either the inductive or the deductive approach starting points. Unlike quantitative studies that involve testing a specific hypothesis, some qualitative studies entail collecting data first and then focusing on theory generation based on the conclusions drawn from the observations. While quantitative research follows strict data collection plans with interview schedules or data collection checklists written out and pretested prior to data collection, qualitative researchers might begin their observations while lacking any research questions (Hagan, 2007; Maxfield & Babbie, 2012).

Both qualitative and quantitative research have helped our discipline grow, and both will be necessary to help us continue to learn why people commit crime and what we can do to stop it. There are, unfortunately, professional rivalries that develop, and there are occasionally debates about the merits of both the qualitative and quantitative approaches. As I noted earlier, quantita-tive methods are more frequently used in criminal justice research. Quantitative approaches, with deductive reasoning, are synonymous with **positivism**, or the natural sciences approach to research. In the more extreme form of this approach, researchers who identify as positivists can endorse scientism and be skeptical of the value of qualitative research. Specifically, **scientism** suggests that the only research worth doing consists of concepts that are measurable, frowning upon the lack of quantitative orientation in qualitative work (Hagan, 2007; Hartley, 2011). At the other end of the research spectrum are researchers who view knowledge through the lens of **historicism**, meaning that they consider all social events as being unique and warranting chronicling. This approach avoids the quantitative practice of trying to draw generalizations from research findings and, as a result, is unscientific (Hagan, 2007).

Basic and Applied Research

There are two additional categories of social science research—basic and applied. This distinction is a carryover from the natural sciences (Hammersly, 2000). **Basic research**, also known as pure research, involves seeking information for the sake of advancing theory or our knowledge base. **Applied research** aims to solve practical problems and can be divided into two categories—program evaluation and policy analysis. Applied research, according to Maxfield and Babbie (2012), seeks links between justice policy and problems. Common types of applied research involve evaluations of criminal justice programs and policies to see what kind of impact, if any, they had on the problems that they were designed to alleviate. **Program evaluation** tends to be more focused on the past in that it answers the question of what impact the program or policy had on the problem. **Policy analysis** is more forward looking and seeks to identify possible solutions to current and future problems and then choose the best or most feasible option. Hammersly (2000) correctly noted that basic and applied research are not necessarily mutually exclusive. There have been numerous occasions when basic research work has led to practical applications, while applied research has been relevant to theory development.

Hammersly (2000) suggested that we move away from the basic/applied distinction and move toward considering social science research as either scientific or practical. Scientific inquiry, according to Hammersly,

> refers to research that is designed to contribute to a body of academic knowledge, where the immediate audience is fellow researchers—though the ultimate aim is to produce knowledge that will be a resource for anyone with interest in the relevant topic.

> (pp. 223–224)

Those engaging in scientific research rely more on the research community to evaluate the validity of their research, usually resulting in slower processes of production and dissemination of knowledge. Practical research is

> geared directly to providing information that is needed to deal with some practical problem, so that here the immediate audience for research reports is people with a practical interest in the issue; notably, but not exclusively, policymakers and occupational practitioners of the relevant kinds.

> (Hammersly, p. 224)

Practical research places an emphasis on the direct relevance of its work to current policy and practical concerns.

Whether we use the basic/applied or scientific/practical categories, it is important to appreciate the value that both types of research bring to our field and to humanity in general. Basic research may not appear to the layperson to have relevance and may be subject to criticism for appearing to be a pointless academic exercise. In fact, the late US senator William Proxmire used to mock scientists whose research he deemed lacking in relevance to the world by declaring them to be winners of the Golden Fleece award for what was, in his opinion, a waste of federal money. The negative publicity that came from Proxmire's criticism prompted some agencies to pull their grant funding from important research that Proxmire just did not understand. For example, he criticized Ohio State researchers' work on a six-legged robot and the National Institute on Alcohol Abuse's study of alcohol aggression in animals. The robotics research eventually led to the invention of computer-controlled knee joints. As for the alcohol and aggression in animals, the researchers studied animals because they could not ethically ask humans to get drunk and fight (Irion, 1988). So, while you might hear about a science project that appears to have no practical value, keep in mind that we use basic research to develop theory and learn about the world, and it is that knowledge that is the basis for development of scientific advances and social programs that benefit society. Once those advances and programs are implemented, applied or practical research can assess their effectiveness.

Steps of the Research Process

When I introduced the scientific method, I presented the wheel of research with four steps: theory, hypotheses, observations, and generalization. Now that you know a bit more about research, it is time to break down the process into more detail. I am going to do this in the order that we would follow using the deductive method.

Theory: Theories are plausible explanations of reality. Criminal justice draws on theories from multiple disciplines, including criminology, sociology, psychology, economics, biology, and business, when working to explain human behavior and the way that organizations function. Theories are used to speculate why some people commit crime while others lead law-abiding lives, why some offenders desist from crime as they grow older while others remain active in crime, and why some organizations are more efficient and effective at achieving their goals than others. Theories often form the basis of researchers' ideas for what they wish to study.

Hypotheses: A hypothesis is a clear, measurable statement that predicts a relationship between variables. Hypotheses are usually generated based on the theory that is being used as the foundation of a particular study. Someone interested in the routine activities approach, for example, might hypothesize that the proliferation of doorbell cameras and other video security devices will reduce the incidence of porch theft.

Choice of research method and data collection plan: There are a number of ways to approach social science research. The question you must ask yourself is what you are trying to learn by doing this. If you want to look at the effectiveness of an anti-truancy program, you might want to compare students who are in the new program to students subjected to the current program's rules. You might also want to compare the students and their truancy levels before and after they participated. Research methods can involve looking at one group or organization at one period in time, at multiple groups at one time, or at one or multiple groups over time.

How will you collect the data necessary to test your hypotheses? There are a wide variety of options for data collection in criminal justice. Before you decide on a data collection plan, you must first choose your **unit of analysis**. The unit of analysis is who or what you plan to study, such as individuals or organizations. Knowing that will help guide your decision on what kind of data to collect and from whom. Researchers have conducted observations; interviewed victims and offenders in person; mailed surveys to homes; called people at home; stationed themselves in public locations and asked people to participate in interviews; visited prisons, jails, or homes; or had people come to university offices for interviews or to take surveys. Computers can aid in data collection through deployment of internet-based surveys or the use of computer-assisted survey equipment that takes the place of human interviewers. Research can involve no human contact at all, through collection of records from criminal justice organizations, businesses, or social service agencies or the acquisition of publicly available data. One can even collect data by turning on the TV and analyzing the content of criminal justice documentaries and dramas. At the other end of the spectrum, research plans can involve extensive contact and interaction with research participants, through long interviews and periods spent observing their behavior.

Concepts/operationalization/measurement: Researchers begin by thinking of concepts they want to study. **Concepts** tend to be rather abstract, such as "crime," "punishment," or "recidivism." Each of these words can have a wide variety of meanings. While they are a good starting point for determining one's research agenda, researchers need to be much more specific as they get to closer to collecting the data. "Punishment" can mean a lot of different things. Do you just mean legal sanctions? If so, just criminal sanctions, or do traffic violations count too? Would you prefer to focus just on the types of punishment that constitute a loss of liberty, such as incarceration? If your focus is on the loss of liberty, what about home confinement with electronic monitoring? Research that might look pretty simple at first glance tends to become much more complex when we have to move on from concepts and determine what we will actually measure.

Take recidivism as an example. Recidivism is generally defined as reoffending, but it can be measured several different ways. It could be based on offenders' self-reported reoffending, but in that case, are you concerned with just one specific crime type or reoffending in general? Reoffending could also mean rearrest, reconviction, and/or reincarceration. It might be helpful to measure recidivism multiple ways. Research on the relationship between sex offender registration and offending among sex offenders often finds that registration is *not* associated with sex offending recidivism, but there is often a small relationship between registration and general offending (Letourneau, Levinson, Armstrong, & Zgoba, 2010; Tewksbury, Jennings, & Zgoba, 2012; Zgoba, Jennings, & Salerno, 2018), so you can see why it was important for the researchers to differentiate between different types of offending. In some of my own research, I found that diversion and reentry service participation for individuals with mental illness was not related to the chances being reincarcerated within a certain time frame, but program participation was associated with staying in the community for longer periods of time before reincarceration (Tartaro, 2015). If you use data that already exist, you may be constrained in your choices for measurement, as you are going to have to use what is there. If you are collecting your own data, you will have to make a lot of decisions about your exact plans for measuring concepts. This process is referred to as **operationalization**, which is the development of operational definitions to specify how concepts will be measured (Maxfield & Babbie, 2012). We operationalize concepts to make them variables that are measurable.

Collecting the data: Once proper ethical safeguards are in place, the next step is collecting the data. This could be as easy as downloading a preexisting dataset for secondary data analysis, or it could involve months or even years of observations and interviews.

Analysis: The necessary analysis will depend on the measurement and data collection decisions. Analysis of quantitative data will involve some statistics, but the level of sophistication will depend on the data and what is necessary to properly test the hypotheses. For qualitative projects, the focus of data analysis will likely involve coding the data into different theoretical categories and/or contextualizing the data to understand the findings in context (Maxwell, 1996).

Dissemination and application of findings: Now that the research is finished, it is time to share the results with others. If the research was conducted at the request of an agency, you will most likely provide them with a report of your findings. They may choose to use the results to make changes to their operations. Others might benefit from seeing these results, so you should consider appropriate outlets for your work. Where you share the work will depend on your preferred audience. If you would like fellow researchers to see the findings, publication in an academic journal would be the best option. If you are hoping for criminal justice practitioners to benefit from it, then a magazine or newsletter that targets professionals might be more appropriate.

Summary

This book is about research guided by the scientific method. Unlike research that you might do to figure out which restaurant to go to this weekend, the scientific method requires that researchers follow specific protocol to generate objective results. Researchers draw on theory to generate hypotheses and follow very specific protocol to generate observations in a manner that aims to reduce bias and allow for generalization of the findings to a larger group. There are multiple types of social science research, including quantitative work, that seek to find trends among large samples. Qualitative research usually aims to take an in-depth look at a small number of individuals or one group or organization. Qualitative research is less concerned with patterns and generalizations than it is with fully understanding a unique set of circumstances. Research can also be divided into basic/pure versus applied categories, with the former generating knowledge for the furtherance of the discipline. Applied research consists of program evaluation and policy analysis and focuses on a specific program or program that needs to be studied.

The exact steps one takes as part of the research process might differ depending on whether one is taking the deductive or inductive approach. With inductive, researchers begin with observations and then use those to generate a theory that can later be tested using a deductive approach. Deductive reasoning begins with theory and then moves to hypothesis generation. Following the development of hypotheses, researchers must determine who or what they are going to study and devise a research design and data collection plan. The next steps involve turning vague concepts into items that can be measured through the process of operationalization. Once we have our measurements, we can proceed with data collection and analysis. Finally, we draw conclusions and disseminate results. The rest of this book will address exactly how to take each step in the research process.

Keywords

Evidence-based practice	Quackery	Scientific method
Theory	Hypothesis	Deductive reasoning
Inductive reasoning	Positivism	Scientism
Historicism	Basic research	Applied research
Program evaluation	Policy analysis	Operationalization
Grounded theory	Unit of analysis	Concept

Discussion Questions

1. What are the steps of the scientific method? If someone is taking an inductive approach to research, what would the starting point be for that research process?
2. What are the differences between qualitative and quantitative research?
3. How can basic or scientific research ultimately impact the lives of everyday people?
4. Think of three topics in criminal justice that need more research. For these topics, come up with a question for each that you would like to answer through research.

References

Glaser, B. G., & Strauss, A. (1967). *The discovery of grounded theory: Strategies for qualitative research*. Chicago, IL: Aldine Publishing Co.

Hagan, F. (2007). *Essentials of research methods in criminal justice and criminology* (2nd ed.). Boston, MA: Pearson.

Haig, B. D. (2018). The importance of scientific method for psychological science. *Psychology, Crime, & Law*, 25(6), 527–541. https://doi.org/10.1080/1068316X.2018.1557181

Hammersly, M. (2000). Varieties of social research: A typology. *International Journal of Social Research Methodology, 3,* 221–229. https://doi.org/10.1080/13645570050083706

Hartley, R. D. (Ed.). (2011). *Snapshots of research.* Thousand Oaks, CA: Sage Publications.

Howard, J. (2019). Facebook to crack down on anti-vaccine misinformation. *CNN.* Retrieved from www.cnn.com/videos/health/2019/02/26/facebook-cracks-down-on-antivaxer-groups-cohen-harlow-nr-vpx.cnn

Irion, R. (1988). What Proxmire's Golden Fleece did for—and to—science. *The Scientist.* Retrieved from www.the-scientist.com/profession/what-proxmires-golden-fleece-did-for--and-to--science-62408

Larson, H. J. (2018). The biggest pandemic risk? Viral misinformation. *Nature, 562,* 309. https://doi.org/10.1038/d41586-018-07034-4

Latessa, E. J., Cullen, F. T., & Gendreau, P. (2011). Beyond correctional quackery: Professionalism and the possibility of effective treatment. In E. J. Latessa & A. M. Holsinger (Eds.), *Correctional contexts* (4th ed., pp. 290–300). New York, NY: Oxford University Press.

Letourneau, E., Levinson, J., Armstrong, K., & Zgoba, K. M. (2010). Failure to register as a sex offender: Is it associated with recidivism? *Justice Quarterly, 27*(3), 305–331. https://doi.org/10.1080/07418820902972399

Maxfield, M. G., & Babbie, E. (2012). *Basics of research methods for criminal justice and criminology* (3rd ed.). Belmont, CA: Thomson Wadsworth.

Maxwell, J. A. (1996). *Qualitative research design: An interactive approach.* Applied Social Research Methods Series (Vol. 41). Thousand Oaks, CA: Sage Publications.

National Institute of Corrections. (n.d.). *Evidence-based practices (EBP).* Washington, DC: United States Department of Justice, National Institute of Corrections. Retrieved from https://nicic. gov/evidence-based-practices-ebp

Powell, J. (2017). Scientists reach 100% consensus on anthropogenic global warming. *Bulletin of Science, Technology & Society, 37*(4), 183–184. https://doi.org/10.1177%2F0270467619886266

Sathyanarayana, R., & Andrade, C. (2011). The MMR vaccine and autism: Sensation, refutation, retraction, and fraud. *Indian Journal of Psychiatry, 53*(2), 95–96. https://doi.org/10.4103%2F0019-5545.82529

Tartaro, C. (2015). An evaluation of the effects of jail diversion and reentry for mentally ill offenders. *Journal of Offender Rehabilitation, 54*(2), 85–102. https://doi.org/10.1080/10509674.2015.1009966

Tewksbury, R., Jennings, W. G., & Zgoba, K. M. (2012). A longitudinal examination of sex offender recidivism prior to and following the implementation of SORN. *Behavioral Sciences and the Law, 30,* 308–328. https://doi.org/10.1002/bsl.1009

Wallace, W. (1971). *The logic of science in sociology.* Chicago: Aldine.

Zgoba, K. M., Jennings, W. G., & Salerno, L. M. (2018). Megan's law 20 years later: An empirical analysis and policy review. *Criminal Justice and Behavior, 45*(7), 1028–1046. https://doi.org/10.1177%2F0093854818771409

2 Reading and Reviewing Research

Sources of Information

We have access to so many different sources of information, but not every source is equal in its quality, accuracy, or even veracity. Knowing how to evaluate sources is a powerful tool that can not only help you learn more and excel in your classes, but it can also make you better equipped to succeed in your job and make informed decisions about other aspects of your life. Believe me when I tell you that the saying "knowledge is power" has some truth to it.

This chapter is devoted to the types of information that we might use to make decisions and the merits of each. Let me spoil it for you and tell you how it ends—research done in accordance with the scientific method is often the best source of information. This might be disappointing because research articles can be intimidating. They seem to be written in some special language, often referred to as researchese, include confusing statistical procedures, and have complicated tables. I will admit that they can also be a bit boring sometimes. The good news is that this book and your professor will teach you how to understand research.

Individual and Vicarious Experiences

None of us are blank slates, so we all acquire information based on personal experiences throughout our lives. Some of those experiences involve contact with actors in the criminal justice system, including police, court personnel, corrections staff, and even offenders. These can be powerful experiences that help shape our perceptions. For example, you thought that the campus police were rude that time they broke up the party you were attending, so based on your experience, you have concluded that police, or at least those working on campus, are disrespectful. Additionally, our views are shaped by the experiences of other people in our lives. Research has revealed that even vicarious encounters with criminal justice professionals can have a powerful impact on our opinions (Wu, Sun, & Triplett, 2009), including hearing about friends' interactions with the police or seeing viral videos of police appearing to act rudely or otherwise improperly.

What is important to understand is that these stories and individual incidents comprise what is known as **anecdotal information**, or personal stories and observations. The stories may be true, but they might be unique and not reflective of what tends to happen in most similar situations. Let's use stop-and-frisk police tactics as an example. Stop and frisk became popular because police hoped that it would help remove guns from the street, plus they would be able to find and arrest people with existing warrants. You might have a friend or relative who is a police officer who was involved in some stops during which police did find and arrest people with weapons. So, based on your friend's or family member's experience, you might be tempted to conclude that stop and frisk works. To do so would mean that you are dismissing ample empirical evidence in favor of anecdotal information. **Empirical evidence** is derived from experimentation and the scientific method process. Stop and frisk has been found to be unconstitutional, because in its application, racial minorities were being stopped at a much greater frequency than whites (Meares, 2014). Specifically, young black males were stopped in 77 of every 100 stops in New York City in 2006 (Geller & Fagan, 2010). Police departments using this tactic were not able to put up an "ends justifies the means" argument in court because research indicates that the program was not effective in achieving its goals. Out of 506,000 police stops conducted by the NYPD in 2006, fewer than 1 percent resulted in confiscation of a weapon (Geller & Fagan, 2010). The most frequent arrest resulting from stop and frisk was marijuana possession (Geller & Fagan, 2010), and given that more states are legalizing or decriminalizing marijuana each year, it is difficult to justify continued infringements on rights to confiscate small amounts of marijuana. What this means is that, overall, stop and frisk was not successful at doing what it was intended to do.

The empirical evidence here involved analysis of over half a million of these stops to see the overall results of these police-citizen interactions, whereas your friend's or relative's experiences might consist of a few arrests after stop-and-frisk encounters. Surely, we should give more weight to the review of 500,000 incidents than stories of a handful of arrests.

Media

Crime investigation, courtroom drama, and even life in prison are among the favorite subjects of television and movie directors and producers. As a criminal justice professor, I am grateful in that this generates interest in my field and encourages people to study criminal justice in college. I also find it frustrating, though, as fictitious shows often take great amounts of creative liberty, and even the nonfiction shows and documentaries can be quite misleading.

Even when the media retelling of a crime incident is correct, it can still be problematic because the coverage of crime is not proportionate to how often it occurs. Homicides receive a disproportionate amount of media coverage, and they also get different amounts of coverage depending on the race, gender, and sometimes age of the victim (Sorenson, Manz, & Berk, 1998; Schildkraut & Donley, 2012). Even true crime books, while nonfiction accounts of actual murders, are not accurate depictions of crime in society as these books focus on specific types of victims (white and affluent), usually involving unusual murder weapons (Durham, Elrod, & Kinkade, 1995), while the typical crime victim in the United States is a young, black male, and the most common murder weapon is a gun. The media has to sell newspapers and magazines or get viewers and clicks for online content, so they are motivated to give the most coverage to what they consider to be compelling stories for their audiences. The result is that the general public gets a very distorted view of crime as the least common crimes tend to get the most coverage while the most common receive little or no publicity.

The combination of reliance on anecdotal experiences and media portrayals of crime and criminal justice interventions can give people a false sense that they understand crime and the criminal justice system. The same does not happen in occupations such as astrophysics or molecular biology. If you have ever had the experience of telling someone at a party what you are studying, my guess is that you were on the receiving end of some unsolicited advice for reducing crime. These opinions are formulated and shared regardless of how much people actually know about our field. One of my most amusing professional memories is being told by a career-long toilet paper salesman that I was wrong about criminal justice reform, but not to worry because he had a three-part plan that was sure to fix the system! I cannot imagine that same person telling a rocket scientist that her planned trajectory for tomorrow's launch was incorrect and that, based on his toilet paper career, the rocket should be launched another way.

Unlike rocket science, solutions in our field often appear to be "common sense." People imagine themselves standing in a prison with a large convict yelling threats at them, and they are sure that it would "scare them straight," so that must mean that the programs that place at-risk teens in prison as a scare tactic work. Plus, they've seen it work on TV—not realizing, of course, that the footage was edited, there was no comparison group to see if any crime desistance was a part of the maturation process for the teens, and many who were portrayed in those shows admitted to continuing with criminal behavior (Maahs & Pratt, 2017). Blomberg and Lucken (2010) used the term "**illusion of knowledge**" to explain the problem of people not being aware of how their *lack* of knowledge about a subject is interfering with their ability to come up with good solutions. Fortunately, there is lots of information out there that was obtained through research. The two challenges that we face are being able to interpret research and then being able to distinguish the quality of the information.

Evaluating Sources of Information

Beyond what we personally know and what people around us are saying, we can search for other sources of information. The internet, cable television, streaming video services, and satellite radio have made the dissemination of information easier than ever. The quality and veracity of sources vary tremendously, so we all need to exercise caution and consider where and how we gather information. We can rank sources on their potential usefulness when we are conducting research.

First, we have sources created by an individual or individuals. The quality of these can vary tremendously. Anyone can create their own website, blog, or podcast. Keep in mind, just because someone wrote something and posted it on the internet, that doesn't mean that it has any credibility. Consider that person's credentials, including academic, work, and life experience. If you are doing a research paper on treatment for a specific cancer and you come across a blog written by an MD who has worked as the chief oncologist for a prestigious hospital and has a strong record of research, this could be a good source of information. I say "could" because it would be better to go with sources that were published using a process that has some quality control, and individual websites lack these safeguards. A blog or website that an individual sets up might not reveal any potential conflicts of interest that the author has, such as owning stock in the company that makes a particular drug. If the blog post is touting the effectiveness of that drug, one must ask if the author's desire to increase the stock price is influencing his or her objectivity. So the information found there might or might not be valuable. I suggest you search the name of the doctor who wrote the blog to see if you can find their research published in legitimate sources and use those articles instead. While you might find some interesting blogs written by people who have decent credentials, you will also encounter ones written by people who have no business dispensing advice to other humans. If you find a medical blog written by someone with no formal degree in medicine and, therefore, no medical license, and this person's medical experience consists of internet research and her own personal attempt at curing a disease using sauerkraut tossed in a blender (yes, this really happened!) (Gander, 2018; Morris, 2018), you might want to think twice about following any "medical" advice that you get from there.

Next, there are media outlets. Criminal justice issues are covered by hundreds, if not thousands, of media sources throughout the globe every day. Unfortunately, all have differing levels of bias and commitment to truthful and accurate reporting. In recent years, we have witnessed the proliferation of outlets designed to cater to certain groups by publishing biased and very inaccurate stories and some that frequently peddle conspiracy theories with a complete disregard for evidence. You can, and should, look to see if multiple sources are reporting on the same story. If only one or two sources have picked up what seems like very important news, you should be suspicious. There are also great websites that allow you to check the level of bias as well as the accuracy of many media outlets. I strongly suggest you visit those sites. Figure 2.1 includes helpful suggestions for evaluating types of web sources, including those run by the media.

Is your web source credible?

Pay attention to the web domain. This can tell you where your source originated.

– Colleges and universities (.edu): These are usually reliable, with attention paid to validity and reliability of the published information.
– Government or military (.gov or .mil): Generally reliable, but there are instances of these sites pushing certain political agendas. Examples are the federal government's insistence on equating marijuana with much more serious drugs and the government's scrubbing federal websites of climate change evidence.
– Company website (.com): There is a potential for bias here, as companies obviously have an interest in promoting their own products and services.
– Special interest (.org): These are mixed. Some are objective and reliable, while others seek to further their own agendas. Be careful and use some of the tips provided in this section.
– Other web domains (.com.co): Be suspicious. Some of these belong to satirical sites or ones that provide false information.

Consider the source.

– There are wonderful websites that check for bias of overall sites. Just search for media bias or fact check sites, and you will find plenty. You should do that with all media sources that you are using for the first time. You will quickly learn which to avoid. These sites often provide information on both the level and type of bias of each source and the source's commitment to accurate reporting.
– Avoid Wikipedia. It is free and online, so it is convenient. It is also written entirely by volunteers, and not necessarily qualified ones. A page covering a person or topic might be credible one day, but a prankster or someone with an ulterior motive could easily go in and change what is written at any time.

Be mindful of headlines and content.

– Be concerned when you see headlines in all capital letters. How professional does that look to you?
– Beware of inflammatory headlines that try to emotionally arouse readers. Headlines that attempt to produce anger are likely attached to stories that lack objectivity and might even be factually incorrect.
– Memes are not news! You can do better than that. If something in a meme seems intriguing, research it. Try to find corroborating information on at least two different credible websites. Never, ever rely on memes for news.
– Does the article or headline appear to be purposefully misleading?
– Can you find at least two credible sources that are reporting the same story?
– Can you find this information on fact check websites? What are those sites reporting?
– Does the article you are reading back up its assertions with either footnotes or links to supporting articles or original documents? This is very important. Credible sources include notes and hyperlinks so readers can see evidence for themselves.

Figure 2.1 Is Your Web Source Credible?

Sources: University of Maryland Global Campus (2020). *Is my source credible?* Baltimore, MD: University of Maryland Global Campus Library. https://sites.umgc.edu/library/libhow/credibility.cfm

University of Pittsburgh (2020). *Evaluating Web Resources.* Pittsburgh, PA: University of Pittsburgh Library. www.library.pitt.edu/evaluating-web-resources

Trade publications can provide a window into some of the latest topics being discussed in various disciplines. Good examples of these in criminal justice are the *FBI Law Enforcement Bulletin* published by the FBI, *American Jails* by the American Jail Association, and *Corrections Today* by the American Correctional Association. These magazines focus on articles that are of interest to criminal justice practitioners. Readers can get information about new programs and the latest trends and controversies in the field. While there are occasional pieces written by professional researchers, most of the articles are written by practitioners, for practitioners. A drawback to these publications is their lack of peer review. Potential authors submit manuscripts to the editorial boards of these magazines, so there are checks and balances not found on websites, blogs, and podcasts run by individuals, but the articles do not undergo a rigorous review of the methods used to come up with the findings.

Agency and government websites and reports can be important sources of information, particularly statistics to help measure the scope of a problem. Good examples are the FBI's Uniform Crime Reports; the United States Bureau of Justice Statistics, Substance Abuse, and Mental Health Services Administration; and the Office of Juvenile Justice and Delinquency Prevention. These sources are always excellent starting points for students and professional researchers. Some agency websites are also good sources of evaluations, policy pieces, and summaries of recent government activities. A few that come to mind are the Vera Institute of Justice, the Sentencing Project, the RAND Corporation, and the Pew Research Center. All these agencies employ professional researchers and provide information about the methods they use to collect their data.

Researchers often put their findings in book form or use the space allotted in books to review a large portion of existing research on a particular subject. Books can be very good, but books take a long time to write and publish. The latest research findings are less likely to appear in books than they are in peer-reviewed journal articles.

In the research world, the preferred source of information is **peer-reviewed** articles. Peer-reviewed journals, also known as refereed journals, are publications that use independent reviewers to assist the editor in determining whether a manuscript is appropriate for publication. Authors wishing to have their work considered submit their manuscripts to the journal editor. The editor typically conducts a quick review to confirm that the paper topic seems like it could be appropriate for that journal and does a cursory review of the research design before requesting assistance from peer reviewers, sometimes also called referees (Locke, Silverman, & Spirduso, 2009).

Editors have multiple ways of finding and choosing referees. First, journal editors are generally familiar with existing research and, therefore, know people who might be good judges of new work in that discipline. Second, editors can look at the bibliographies of the manuscripts submitted and reach out to researchers cited in the paper. A third, more recent option is that the authors themselves are asked to identify experts in the field who would be appropriate reviewers. The editor typically contacts two researchers and asks them to review a manuscript. If the reviewers agree to provide feedback, the editor sends them copies, almost always with the authors' names removed from the manuscript. This **blind peer-review** process is supposed to help reviewers make an unbiased judgment solely on the merits of the research. Revealing the names of the manuscript authors has the potential to influence reviewers. Editors and reviewers might be willing to give a manuscript written by a well-regarded scholar the benefit of the doubt and accept an otherwise borderline or unacceptable paper. On the other hand, a manuscript written by a new scholar or someone who lacks a reputation might seem less attractive, even if it is of good quality.

Peer reviewers are expected to read the manuscript and then answer a few standard questions generated by the journal. These questions usually involve whether the paper topic is appropriate for the journal, if the introduction and literature review are adequate, whether the decisions made in the research methods and statistics sections appear to be appropriate, and whether publication of this paper would provide a meaningful contribution to the discipline. Reviewers then have the following options for recommendations: accept manuscript as-is for publication, accept with minor revisions, have authors revise manuscript and resubmit it for an additional review, or reject. The editor then considers the recommendations of the two reviewers and renders a decision. If the authors are invited to revise their manuscript and resubmit it, the editor will send the newly revised manuscript to the same two reviewers, provided they are willing to review it again.

The peer-review process is designed to serve as a quality control measure to prevent substantially flawed articles from being published. Not all peer-reviewed journals are equally selective, though. Readers should be mindful of the fact that the peer-review process is no guarantee that poorly written and methodologically flawed articles will be flagged and denied publication. So, while peer-review is an extra step in the attempt at quality control, it is far from perfect. There is a webpage called Retraction Watch that reports on retractions of journal articles in a variety of fields. In Chapter 1, I mentioned the article that started the anti-vaccination scare and had to be retracted due to fraud. That article originally appeared in a highly regarded, peer-reviewed journal. *Criminology*, the flagship journal of the American Society of Criminology and one of the most highly regarded journals in criminal justice, was beset by controversy when one author from a multi-author study requested that the journal retract one of his own articles because he suspected that the findings were inaccurate. The entire research team eventually agreed to ask *Criminology* to retract the article, and other highly regarded journals in the social sciences that published work from the same authors using the same dataset have also announced their intent to retract (Chawla, 2019).

The point is that bad research does make its way to publication, even in journals that require peer review. While you would need to be very proficient in statistics to detect flaws in a few of these articles, a basic understanding of research methods will go a long way toward your being able to distinguish good research from bad. The good news is that most research results are obtained honestly and in an ethical manner, and peer-reviewed articles are considered the most appropriate sources to use when students and professionals are conducting literature reviews of their research topics.

There are steps that you can take to gauge the quality of the sources from which you are obtaining information. Locke and colleagues (2009) named four things to consider: journal selectivity, sources of funding, research or professional organization sponsorship, and reputation of the authors.

Journal Selectivity

Publishing is a requirement for most academic jobs and some professional research positions. Even if faculty are able to secure tenure, they often need to continue to publish to be promoted and be eligible for grant money and other opportunities. The term "publish or perish" describes the pressure that researchers feel to have their work seen, preferably in the most prestigious journals possible, with the goal of promoting or even saving one's career. Since so many people want or even need to publish their work, there has been a proliferation of journals as potential outlets for our work. Unfortunately, while there have been some very good journals developed by reputable publishing companies and researchers, not all journals are of equal quality, nor are all designed to be outlets to further science. Some journals are predatory.

According to 43 scholars who formed a working group to formulate a definition, **predatory journals** and publishers are "entities that prioritize self-interest at the expense of scholarship and are characterized by false or misleading information, deviation from best editorial and publication practices, a lack of transparency, and/or the use of aggressive and indiscriminate solicitation practices" (Grudniewicz et al., 2019, p. 211). The term "predatory publishers" was coined in 2010, and scholars have published checklists to encourage researchers to avoid predatory journals. These journals pose a danger because they look like legitimate scientific journals but actually lack quality checks. This means that false and misleading information may appear in what looks like a peer-reviewed scholarly journal but is not. Grudniewicz and colleagues were inspired to research predatory journals because an author's mother-in-law was fighting cancer, and the standard treatments were no longer effective. Relatives desperately looked for a way to keep fighting and were hopeful when they found an article about a promising treatment. That hope faded once the author realized that the evaluation of the treatment was published in a predatory journal, so the article was likely published without anyone vetting the quality of the work.

If there are so many reputable journals available, why would researchers publish their work in a predatory journal? One possibility is that they are unaware that the journal is predatory. Researchers get emails with invitations to submit manuscripts to journals every day, and many of these journals certainly have names that make them sound reputable, such as *Advances in Biomedicine and Pharmacy*, *British Journal of Science*, and the *International Journal of Advanced Research in Applied Science and Technology* (Scholarly Open Access, 2017). Scholars have a duty to do their homework before submitting, so not knowing that a journal is or is likely predatory is not an adequate excuse. The second reason an author might publish in a predatory journal is because they are under such pressure to have their work published, they turn to journals that will publish anything for a fee. Really, some of these journals will publish any combination of words that are submitted to them. Researchers with a sense of humor have demonstrated the lack of vetting that occurs in these predatory journals by conducting "stings" with absurd papers. One scientist wrote papers that made repeated references to Star Wars and the Force and had them accepted for publication in four "journals" that were supposed to focus on the natural sciences, not film reviews (Predatory Journals . . ., 2017). A few authors wrote the sentence "Get me off your f— mailing list" over and over again to make a ten-page paper, fit with figures and tables containing nothing but those same seven words. The "paper" was accepted and published by the *International Journal of Advanced Computer Technology* (Stromberg, 2014). Clearly, you should not trust work published in a predatory journal to be valid or reliable, as the previous stories provide evidence that some will publish absolutely anything. How can you tell if a journal is predatory? Do a simple internet search for "predatory journal list." There are a number of lists out there, including one compiled by Yale University. If you are not already familiar with a journal's reputation, check these lists first. Another option is to do an internet search of the journal name. Journals that are affiliated with established publishing companies are not predatory. Just a few examples of publishers in criminal justice are Taylor and Francis, Sage, Springer, Elsevier, and Wiley.

While information in predatory journals should always be considered suspect, articles in very prestigious journals may be of poor quality, and articles in less popular journals might be very strong and ultimately carry great weight in the field. One reason is that the large, mainstream journals may lack interest in particular topics. A great example of this is terrorism. Prior to 9/11, terrorism was considered the domain of political scientists, so little work on terrorism was being published in mainstream criminal justice journals. Another reason is that a new idea might seem too controversial or far-fetched and be rejected by the larger journals. A mentor of mine is the father of a major crime theory. The article that proposed the new theory, which has now been cited thousands of times, was initially rejected by some of the top journals.

Sources of Funding

Researchers are expected to be unbiased and focused on advancing science. Of course, since we are also human, there are times when other priorities threaten the objectivity of our work.

Conflicts of interest are "personal, financial, professional, political, or legal interests that have a significant chance of interfering with the performance of his/her ethical or legal duties" (Resnik, 2007, p. 2). Resnik argues that conflicts of interest are concerning for two reasons. First, they have the potential to impact the integrity of research. Second, they can undermine the public's trust in science.

In the medical field, two studies from the late 1990s provided good illustrations of how conflicts of interest can harm research. Earlier in this book, I mentioned that the only study to ever claim to have found evidence of a link between vaccines and autism was published in 1998 by Dr. Andrew Wakefield and colleagues. During an investigation that led to the article's retraction, it was revealed that Wakefield was secretly accepting payments from personal injury lawyers whose clients were suing the pharmaceutical companies ("A case of junk science," 2008). During another study in 1999, a young man died during a gene therapy experiment at the University of Pennsylvania. Upon investigation, the Food and Drug Administration (FDA) found that the research team withheld vital information during the informed consent phase, including the risks associated with the study and the researchers' and university's financial interest in the results. The principal investigator of the study owned 30 percent of the gene therapy company's stock, and that same company paid the university $4 million per year. The university also owned stock in the company (Resnik, 2007).

The field of criminal justice is not immune to conflicts of interest in research. Geis, Mobley, and Shichor (1999) chronicled the work of Dr. Charles Thomas from the University of Florida. Dr. Thomas became very closely affiliated with private corrections companies, particularly the Corrections Corporation of America (CCA). Dr. Thomas was frequently quoted in newspapers as an expert on private corrections, and he published articles in peer-reviewed journals on the success of private prisons. In his interviews and publications, Dr. Thomas failed to disclose his affiliation with a research center that received $400,000 from private prison companies. He also failed to disclose that he was a paid consultant for the Florida Correctional Privatization Commission or that he was being paid millions by CCA. Geis and colleagues concluded their paper about these ethical lapses with a recommendation that journals require authors to disclose any potential conflicts of interest.

It is now customary for authors submitting their manuscripts to peer-reviewed journals to have to disclose any funding that they received to conduct the research and to describe any type of possible conflict of interest. This information can then be used to make informed publication decisions.

Research or Professional Organization Sponsorship

Occasionally, a research or professional organization will choose to provide support for academic research. When I planned to survey all jails in the United States that were built using a certain design, I contacted the American Jail Association (AJA). While there had been a number of small studies done on these jails, my plan was to include hundreds of facilities in my analysis. After explaining my proposal to the president of AJA, he agreed to write a cover letter to my survey to endorse the work. This was very valuable since I was asking jail administrators to take time out of their busy schedules to do a favor for someone they never met. I have no doubt that the AJA's support of my study helped boost my credibility among jail administrators and increased the response rate to my survey. Given that AJA is a professional organization that has little involvement in research, their endorsement probably did not improve the prestige of my work in the research and academic communities. Sponsorship or support of research and professional organizations, such as the American Medical Association and the American Bar Association, can help bolster the reputation of research in the scholarly community.

Reputation of Authors

Earlier, I mentioned that the reputations of authors might influence journal editors' decisions about whether to accept a manuscript for publication. Of course, this should play some role in one's evaluation of the quality of work, but I want to caution against becoming too preoccupied with the names on the paper. New scholars who have not had enough years in the field to become "names" are producing excellent work every year. The most important consideration should be if the individuals' work has previously been flagged or retracted for ethical issues, such as conflicts of interest; if there have been questions about their objectivity; and if there have been legitimate questions about their data collection and analysis.

Elements of Published Research

Now that you know a little bit about how to judge the quality of sources, it is time to discuss what is in a typical published piece of research.

Abstract

The abstract is a very brief synopsis of the article—typically 100 to 300 words, depending on the rules governing the journal. This is a short summary of the article and is a good way for readers to see if the article matches the reader's interests and if it would be worthwhile to read the entire article. Typical abstracts are usually a paragraph, but some journals require authors to write structured abstracts. Structured abstracts are longer and include headings for each section of the paper (research background, research procedure, findings, and conclusions).

Introduction

The introduction is the authors' opportunity to introduce the topic to the reader. This section usually includes some statistics to give readers an understanding of the scope of the topic. For example, an article about children's separation from their incarcerated parents would likely begin with a review of the number of people in the United States who are incarcerated, the number of those people who have children under the age of 18, and estimates of how many children in the community have incarcerated parents. In this section, it is important to communicate to the reader why the topic needs to be studied. The writer should never exaggerate the extent of the problem though. I have received several student papers in which the authors seemed to believe that the only way the paper would be relevant is if they made it appear that their topic was a "growing problem," regardless of whether it actually was. This is a typical "rookie" mistake when learning to write about research. In just about all these instances, the students relied on hyperbole and assumptions instead of consulting and citing reputable sources of information.

Literature Review

In this section, the authors might discuss some theories related to the topic. Keeping with the example of children of incarcerated parents, it might be helpful to frame how incarceration could be detrimental to children's futures. A number of sociological and psychological theories could be used as the theoretical framework of the research.

The literature review is an opportunity for the authors to present the reader with a summary of the available research on this topic. This informs the reader about what is already known and allows the authors to highlight gaps in our current state of knowledge. After a discussion of the limitations of previous research, the authors can use the last few sentences of this section to explain the goals of their study.

Research Methods

If the research is exploratory in nature, the authors will not present any hypotheses. If the study involves hypothesis testing, the hypotheses will either appear at the end of the literature review or at the beginning of the research methods section.

Authors of research articles are expected to describe every step that they took to collect data. This includes how the sample was selected, how the concepts were operationalized to create measurable variables, the type of data collection plan used, and the time frame to collect the data. Readers should be able to understand what transpired during the data collection process, including the original plan and any issues that arose during data collection that impacted what data were ultimately available for analysis. For example, when researchers conduct surveys, they might get 1,000 responses, but once they review the responses, they may discover that many respondents dropped out halfway through the survey, and a handful wrote sarcastic or unbelievable responses, so the number of usable surveys is actually 750. It is the author's responsibility to explain all this to the readers, so they understand why there were 1,000 survey responses but only 750 usable for data analysis. Researchers conducting data collection inside a prison might initially believe that they will be able to ask for volunteers from all units but later discover that they cannot access inmates in the infirmary, and another unit is inaccessible due to lockdown. The methods section is where the researchers explain these challenges and speculate on how these changes might impact the findings.

Results

Either at the end of the research methods section or at the start of results, the researchers will explain the characteristics of the sample. If researchers sent the link to an internet survey to every chief of police in cities with at least 200,000 residents, the results section would begin by providing information about the respondents. If the unit of analysis (who or what you are studying) is the police chiefs themselves, the results section would likely begin with the demographic information, such as age, sex, education, and years of experience, of the responding chiefs. If the study's unit of analysis is the organization, and researchers sent the surveys to chiefs as representatives of the organizations, then the results section might start out with a description of the agencies, such as the number of sworn staff, demographics of staff members, and number of officers who work each shift. Next, the authors would discuss whether statistical tests revealed support for their hypotheses. Here, they could either have found the type of relationship between their independent and dependent variables that they predicted, no relationship between the variables, or a relationship between them but in the opposite direction than expected.

The results section of quantitative studies usually includes tables as well as narratives to explain what is in the tables. Depending on your understanding of statistics, you might find the tables to be helpful or confusing. The more comfortable you become with statistics, the greater your appreciation will be for tables, as they are a quick way to read the findings.

Discussion/Conclusion

The results section is simply a brief presentation of the results. It is in the discussion or conclusion section that the authors try to explain why they found what they found. In instances in which the findings are the opposite of what was expected, the discussion section is where authors will have the chance to reflect on whether they think this was a product of the way they framed the research question, collected the data, or analyzed the results or if the findings are due to some aspect of the topic that they had not previously considered. Discussion sections summarize the findings but then also try to link this work to the research conducted in the area to date. The authors will usually tie the discussion back to topics mentioned in the introduction and literature review to place the current findings into the proper context. The authors' emphasis on criminological theory and policy implications will vary, depending on the journal's focus.

Researchers often summarize the limitations of their study either in the discussion section or in the research methods section. Acknowledging the study's drawbacks is an essential part of any piece of research for three reasons. First, authors' full disclosure of the strengths and drawbacks of their work is a demonstration of scientific integrity. Second, this information can help readers understand the results in the proper context. Third, future researchers can design studies that will address these limitations.

References

Authors need to cite (give credit to) all the sources of information that they used to write the article. The reference page can be very useful to readers, so they can look up and read the articles that comprised the literature review.

How to Read/Take Notes

I have observed that one of the biggest difficulties my students experience is making sense of research articles after reading them. I want to provide some suggestions for how to take notes for two reasons. First, it will help if you can go back to your notes to see a quick summary of what you read rather than rereading the article. Second, as you spend more time studying criminal justice topics, you will amass more and more readings. How do you keep track of all of it? Here's what I do.

I have separate documents for each general subject that I study. So, if you take an introductory policing course and read articles for that, you can put your article notes in a document. Later in your academic career, you might have to revisit that subject in a more advanced class. It would be helpful to have a synopsis of what you have already read, as this will save you a lot of time. Then, as you read more, you can add more notes to this same document. This is how I have managed to keep track of notes on books, reports, and articles that I read over a decade ago. Once you set up the document, I suggest that you start your notes by putting the full APA citation of whatever you read as the first line. Next, use headings similar to what I provided in the previous section to make sure you handle information properly should you ever need it for a research paper. Remember that information provided in the introduction and literature review sections of the articles is usually not findings produced by the authors of the current article. So, if you want to write down anything interesting from the introduction or literature review, I suggest that you have it under an "intro/lit review" heading in your notes and then put a citation of the original source in your notes. That way, if you ever want to use that information, you can go look it up in the original source and cite it properly. That's important as you do not want to attribute research findings to the wrong people. You might not think it's a big deal, but believe me, it is. People want to be accurately credited for their life's work, and they also do not want to be wrongly associated with less-than-stellar research that they did not do. Plus, it hurts your credibility when someone who knows the existing research reads your work and sees you mixing up study findings and the authors who reported them.

Next, under "methodology," write a few notes about what, exactly, the researchers did. This will serve as a good reminder later after your memory of reading the article fades, and it will help you understand the results. In the results section, use bullet points to jot down a quick summary of the findings. For discussion, you can note interesting ideas that the researchers had as they attempted to explain their findings. Finally, remember to take notes on the limitations of their study. You are going to want these later, especially if you are thinking about proposing a study yourself for this class or some other course. You will want to remember how the limitations may have impacted the results, and you will want to see if you can design a study that addresses those drawbacks. If you find something particularly problematic in the article, you might want to make a very visible note to yourself. I like to put my own thoughts inside double parentheses or in all caps. Remember how I cautioned that poorly designed research gets published sometimes? I have read a few articles in which I think that the limitations are so substantial that they really call into question the results. I still take notes on those articles so I have a record of having read them (so I don't forget and then read them again some other time), and then I put a note to myself about my misgivings upon reading it.

You might look at this and think that it is a waste of time, but if you wind up studying a topic over a period of semesters or years, taking notes this way will be very valuable to you. Have you ever looked at a bibliography for an article or a book and wondered how the author could possibly keep all that information organized? Well, this is one way to do it.

Summary

We are incredibly fortunate in that more information than ever is accessible. We should all be grateful for this development, but with it comes the proliferation of sources that are biased, inaccurate, and sometimes outright deceptive. It is our responsibility, as educated individuals, to learn to be able to see through that, determine the quality of a source, and only use valid pieces of information to draw conclusions. In this chapter, I reviewed different types of sources and outlined the advantages and disadvantages of each. There are steps that we can take, such as being suspicious of outrageous stories being reported by only one or two outlets, researching the reputation of sources before using them, and considering potential conflicts of interest. When searching for sources to use in research, remember that there is a hierarchy, with peer-reviewed journal articles offering the best, but not a foolproof, outlet for objective, quality-controlled research.

In this chapter, I provided an overview of how research papers are designed and what types of information are available in each section of the articles. Research articles can be intimidating, with their specialized language, mathematical formulas, and complicated tables. The key to understanding is to break the article down by section and understand what you should gain by reading each part. It will take practice, but you should become more comfortable understanding these articles and taking notes on them throughout the class.

Keywords

Anecdotal evidence	Empirical evidence	Peer review
Blind peer review	Predatory journals	

Discussion Questions

1. Why is research in peer-reviewed journals considered among the strongest sources of information?
2. What are some of the ways that we can evaluate a story that we find in the media?
3. What are predatory journals, and why would anyone publish in them?

References

A case of junk science, conflict and hype (2008). *Nat Immunology, 9*, 1317. https://doi.org/10.1038/ni1208-1317

Blomberg, T. G., & Lucken, K. (2010). *American penology: A history of control* (2nd ed.). New York: Transaction Publishers.

Chawla, D. S. (2019). Quintet of study retractions rocks criminology community. *Science*. Retrieved from www.sciencemag.org/news/2019/11/quintet-study-retractions-rocks-criminology-community

Durham, A. M., Elrod, H. P., & Kinkade, P. T. (1995). Images of crime and justice: Murder and the "true crime" genre. *Journal of Criminal Justice, 23*(2), 143–152.

Gander, K. (2018, May 13). Woman who claims cabbage juice "cures" autism and can regrow limbs to be probed by officials. *Newsweek*. Retrieved from www.newsweek.com/jillian-mai-thi-epperly-claims-cabbage-juice-cures-autism-homosexuality-and-909737

Geis, G., Mobley, A., & Shichor, D. (1999). Private prisons, criminological research, and conflict of interest: A case study. *Crime & Delinquency, 45*(3), 372–388. https://doi.org/10.1177/0011128799045003005

Geller, A., & Fagan, J. (2010). Pot as pretext: Marijuana, race, and the new disorder in New York City street policing. *Journal of Empirical Legal Studies, 7*, 591–633. https://doi.org/10.1111/j.1740-1461.2010.01190.x

Grudniewicz, A., Moher, D., Cobey, K. D., Bryson, G. L., Cukier, S., Allen, K., . . . & Lalu, M. M. (2019). Predatory journals: No definition, no defence. *Nature, 576*, 210–212. https://doi.org/10.1038/d41586-019-03759-y

Locke, L. F., Silverman, S. J., & Spirduso, W. W. (2009). *Reading and understanding research.* (3rd ed.). Thousand Oaks, CA: Sage Publications.

Maahs, J., & Pratt, T. C. (2017). "I hate these little turds!": Science, entertainment, and the enduring popularity of scared straight programs. *Deviant Behavior, 38*(1), 47–60. https://doi.org/10.1080/01639625.2016.1190619

Meares, T. L. (2014). The law and social science of stop and frisk. *Annual Review of Law and Social Sciences, 10*, 335–352. https://doi.org/10.1146/annurev-lawsocsci-102612-134043

Morris, M. (2018, May 24). Jilly Juice recipe creator claims her concoction can regrow limbs, cure homosexuality. *Metro*. Retrieved from www.metro.us/body-and-mind/health/jilly-juice-recipe-jillian-epperly

Predatory journals hit by "Star Wars" sting (2017, July 22). *Discover*. Retrieved from www.discovermagazine.com/mind/predatory-journals-hit-by-star-wars-sting

Resnik, D. B. (2007). Conflicts of interest in scientific research related to regulation or litigation. *The Journal of Philosophy, Science, & Law, 16*(7), 1. https://doi.org/10.5840/jpsl2007722

Schildkraut, J., & Donley, A. M. (2012). Murder in black: A media distortion analysis of homicides in Baltimore in 2010. *Homicide Studies, 16*(2), 175–196. https://doi.org/10.1177/1088767912438712

Scholarly Open Access. (2017). *List of standalone journals: Potential, possible, or probably predatory scholarly open-access journals*. Retrieved from https://web.archive.org/web/20170111172309/https://scholarlyoa.com/individual-journals/

Sorenson, S. B., Manz, J. G. P., & Berk, R. A. (1998). News media coverage and the epidemiology of homicide. *American Journal of Public Health, 88*, 1510–1514. https://doi.org/10.2105/ajph.88.10.1510

Stromberg, J. (2014). "Get me off your fucking mailing list" is an actual science paper accepted by a journal. *Vox*. Retrieved from www.vox.com/2014/11/21/7259207/scientific-paper-scam

University of Maryland Global Campus. (2020). *Is my source credible?* Baltimore, MD: University of Maryland Global Campus Library. Retrieved from https://sites.umgc.edu/library/libhow/credibility.cfm

University of Pittsburgh. (2020). *Evaluating web resources*. Pittsburgh, PA: University of Pittsburgh Library. Retrieved from www.library.pitt.edu/evaluating-web-resources

Wu, Y., Sun, I. Y., & Triplett, R. A. (2009). Race, class or neighborhood context: Which matters more in measuring satisfaction with police? *Justice Quarterly, 26*, 125–156. Retrieved from https://doi.org/10.1080/07418820802119950

3 Ethics in Criminal Justice Research

As the allied countries moved through Europe and defeated the Nazis in 1945, soldiers discovered the horrors of the concentration camps. The primary purpose of the camps was to carry out the "final solution" of murdering people deemed genetically inferior and a threat to the "Aryan race." A secondary purpose of the camps was to serve as a laboratory for horrific science experiments, using non-consenting children and adults as research subjects. The research was cruel and often resulted in slow and painful deaths. Following the war, the International Military Tribunal convened trials at Nuremburg to bring those responsible to justice. One of the defenses employed by the Nazis came as a shock to ordinary Americans—the Nazis were simply doing what the Americans had been doing to prisoners for years (Cohen, 2016; Hornblum, 1998; Mitford, 1973).

As stunning at that defense may sound, the Nazis were correct. The United States has a long history of performing dangerous experiments on vulnerable populations, including prisoners and children with special needs, without adequate protections. In 1915, a doctor in Mississippi infected several inmates with pellagra, an extremely painful and potentially deadly disease (Hornblum, 1998; Oshinsky, 1996). During the American occupation of the Philippines in the early 1900s, doctors infected prisoners with cholera, killing 13 people and compensating survivors with cigars. When the United States entered World War II, prison inmates in the US "helped" the war effort by participating in medical experiments involving malaria (Hornblum, 1998). State prison inmates in Iowa were given and then cured of scurvy in the late 1960s for reasons that are unclear since scientists were already aware of the cause of and cure for that disease (Mitford, 1973).

Despite the Nazis' attempt to shift the focus to the allies' dangerous and unethical behavior, doctors who carried out the Nazi experiments were convicted and sentenced for their crimes. Outrage stemming from the Holocaust prompted government entities and some in the scientific community to take steps to prevent unethical medical experiments from being permitted in the future. The result was the **Nuremberg Code**, consisting of ten elements to protect human participants in research. A summary of the elements is as follows:

1. Voluntary consent of participants is absolutely essential.
2. The results of any experiment must be for the greater good of society.
3. Human experimentation should be based on previous animal experimentation and only after there is knowledge of the natural history of the disease.
4. Experimental procedures should avoid unnecessary physical or mental suffering.
5. No experiments should be conducted if there is reason to believe they will cause death or disability.
6. Risks taken should never be greater than the humanitarian importance of the problem to be solved.
7. Adequate facilities should be used to protect subjects.

8. Only qualified scientists should conduct experiments.
9. Subjects should be able to end their participation at any time.
10. The scientist in charge must be prepared to terminate the experiment when injury, disability, or death is likely to occur.

(Jarmusik, 2019)

Following the development of the Nuremburg Code, the World Medical Association established the **Declaration of Helsinki** in 1964. This statement outlined ethical principles for medical research involving human subjects. As with the Nuremburg Code, the writers emphasized concern for the safety of individuals and the rights of participants to receive informed consent. Section 26 of the declaration states:

> In medical research involving human subjects capable of giving informed consent, each potential subject must be adequately informed of the aims, methods, sources of funding, any possible conflicts of interest, institutional affiliations of the researcher, the anticipated benefits and potential risks of the study and the discomfort it may entail, post-study provisions and any other relevant aspects of the study. The potential subject must be informed of the right to refuse to participate in the study or to withdraw consent to participate at any time without reprisal. Special attention should be given to the specific information needs of individual potential subjects as well as to the methods used to deliver the information.
>
> (World Medical Association, 2019)

Given the medical community's apparent commitment to adopting protections for people, one might think that harmful experiments involving humans would have ceased after publication of the Nuremburg Code and the Declaration of Helsinki. Unfortunately, they continued in a few different settings, including prisons and jails. One of the longest-running and most notorious cases of using prisoners for human experimentation was chronicled by Allen Hornblum (1998) in his book *Acres of Skin*. Dr. Albert Kligman, a dermatologist with the University of Pennsylvania, set up a lab in Holmesburg Prison and ran dozens of medical experiments on inmates for two decades. Holmesburg Prison was an overcrowded, violent county jail in Pennsylvania that held both sentenced inmates and those who were still awaiting trial. Kligman originally entered the prison at the request of the facility's pharmacist, who was seeking advice on how to deal with an athlete's foot outbreak among inmates. Once there, Kligman quickly saw opportunity as he was always in search of human subjects to test new dermatology products. He quickly began to recruit participants. Unfortunately for the recruits, it appears that Kligman did not necessarily view them as humans deserving of the protections outlined in the Nuremburg and Helsinki statements. Kligman explained his reaction the first time he entered Holmesburg: "All I saw before me were acres of skin. It was like a farmer seeing a fertile field for the first time" (p. 37).

But why go through the trouble of setting up a laboratory in a jail? (Yes, I realize it was called Holmesburg *Prison*, but it largely held pretrial detainees, so it was more of a jail.) The answer is simple. Just about all of us in free society would not have willingly participated in his research. The side effects ranged from skin irritation to permanent organ damage. Since Kligman had found a seemingly endless source of human subjects, private and government entities were eager to offer him funding to conduct more and more risky experiments, even if it meant branching out to fields of medicine in which he was not qualified to practice. Kligman could not force anyone to participate, so he needed to find a group of people who were so desperate for money that they would tolerate pain and discomfort in exchange for a small reward and would refrain from asking questions about the dangers of the research. Holmesburg inmates had the choice of making $0.15 per hour on a work detail or doing the experiments for $300 to $400 per month. Remember, most of these people were in jail awaiting trial, so they could use that income to post bail or to hire a private attorney. People who were already convicted could use the money for commissary or to send home to support their families. Sentenced inmates might participate in the medical experiments with the hope of being seen as cooperative when it came time for parole consideration. Another potential benefit to participation was that inmates might be moved from the general population to a special medical experimentation wing. Some inmates who feared for their safety in the notoriously violent facility saw the experiments as the lesser of the evils, since they were able to move away from the people victimizing them. This was a population desperate for money, fearful for their safety, eager to be seen as cooperative, and with no other options to earn money or freedom. Still, the research ethics rules called for informed consent. Participants later reported that they really did not know what kinds of chemicals were involved in the studies, nor did they have an idea of the dangers and the potential short- and long-term health ramifications. When called to testify before Congress, one of the Holmesburg inmates who was a participant in the experiments explained that trying to give consent forms to inmates and expecting them to read them was the equivalent of asking them to read hieroglyphics. To make things worse, there were allegations that race played a role in the selection of participants, with minorities being given the less desirable and lower-paying projects. The Philadelphia prison system's board of trustees shut down Kligman's program in January 1974, but some of his test subjects experienced a lifetime of health problems as a result of his work (Hornblum, 1998).

Kligman's work was not an exception as doctors around the United States used prison populations for pools of human research subjects who were willing to take risks for little compensation. As an example of the cost savings associated with using inmates, Mitford (1973) interviewed a doctor who was working with prison inmates on biomedical research. The inmates were being paid $12.50 to $15 per month. Had the researchers asked financially strapped but free students to participate in that same research, the cost would have been $100 per month. Another doctor told Mitford that human prisoners were cheaper than chimpanzees, so they were especially attractive for this type of scientific research.

Kligman's actions, and those of other biomedical researchers in prisons and jails, are examples of why the United States government found the need to act on behalf of human research participants in the 1970s. Around the same time that Kligman's work was being exposed to the public, Americans learned about another extremely unethical study that had been in progress for decades. In 1932, the Public Health Service and the Tuskegee Institute recruited 600 black men, 399 of whom had syphilis, for a study to chronicle the natural progression of the disease. While the original plan was to observe participants for six months, the program continued for 40 years. During that time, researchers concealed the diagnoses from participants, mostly out of fear that they would seek treatment once it became available, thereby disrupting the natural progression of the illness. Instead, participants were left to suffer from something that became treatable decades before the study ended. The study continued until the project was exposed by the media in 1972 (Centers for Disease Control and Prevention, 2015).

In the wake of these stories, Congress passed the National Research Act, and President Nixon signed it into law in 1974. This law created the National Commission for the Protection of Human Subjects of Biomedical and Behavioral Research run by the Department of Health, Education, and Welfare (HEW) (Department of Health, Education, and Welfare, 1979). The commission worked to consider specific types of research and establish ethical guidelines for them. One of their most important documents was published in 1979 and is known as the Belmont Report. The **Belmont Report** provided researchers with a useful summary of the basic ethical principles that should guide all research involving human subjects. The first principle is **respect for persons**, meaning research participants must be treated as autonomous agents. In the case of a person with diminished autonomy, there must be protections. Autonomous persons are able to consider whether to engage in research and make decisions to protect themselves without being coerced. Second is

beneficence. Researchers must avoid harming human subjects while maximizing benefits and minimizing any possible harms. Finally, there is justice. The question of **justice** involves determining who should reap the benefits of research and who should have to bear the burdens of that work. These benefits and burdens must be equally distributed throughout society.

Harm in Social Science Research

So far, I have only discussed medical experiments, so you might be thinking to yourself right now "That's terrible, but criminologists don't do medical experiments. We can't possibly harm people in that way." Very true. However, social scientists can still hurt people or put them in harm's way with research, and there are numerous examples as evidence.

While there is still stigma and discrimination surrounding homosexuality, we have come a long way since the 1970s, when Laud Humphreys (1970) embarked on his fieldwork to learn about anonymous male-male sexual encounters, mostly involving men who lived publicly as heterosexuals. Humphreys served as a "watch queen" in bathrooms, meaning he would guard the door in exchange for being permitted to watch the men in the bathroom having sex. While there, he would secretly write down their license plate numbers, look up their information, and then visit their houses (this time with an altered physical appearance) to administer a survey on social health (a combination of socioeconomic and health factors with questions about marital relations and sex) (Humphreys, 1970). These men were unaware that they were selected for the health study due to their involvement in homosexual relations, and they were not informed or given the option to opt out of the part of the study that involved their sexual encounters. Being outed as a homosexual in the late 1960s and early 1970s would almost certainly ruin careers, livelihoods, marriages, and social standing. Humphreys published his research in a book titled *Tearoom Trade*. Critics argued that Humphreys put these men at risk without informing them of the risks and giving them the freedom to decline participation.

The **Stanford Prison Experiment** is one of the most famous psychology studies in US history. Philip Zimbardo has been criticized for several aspect of the study. Some of the problems with the research go well beyond the scope of this chapter. Of concern here are the ethical questions that surround the work. Zimbardo gathered college-age male volunteers to be randomly selected to become either inmates or corrections officers in a simulated prison. The basement of one of the academic buildings at Stanford became the "prison," and the plan was to study the dynamics between officers and inmates for two weeks. Instead, Zimbardo ended the study after six days out of concern for the inmates' psychological well-being. He became worried that the "guards" were becoming so abusive and the "prison" had become so real for the "inmates" that continuation might produce psychological harm. Later, evidence emerged showing Zimbardo actually encouraging the aggressiveness exhibited by "guards." This means that Zimbardo artificially generated what he characterized as organically occurring abusive behavior that was driving the "inmates" to the breaking point (Blum, 2018). By now, generations of psychology and criminal justice students have seen or heard the most famous video clip of the study. An "inmate" screamed about how he was losing it and needed to get out right now. The student who had that "breakdown" later reported that he did not want to participate in the research anymore but could not find any other way to be let out of the "prison." His request to be removed was denied, so he feigned distress to frighten Zimbardo into letting him go home. As we already learned in this chapter, there must be a mechanism to allow participants to withdraw from research at any time, but it does not appear that the student participants were presented with that option.

More recently, a professor of organizational behavior wanted to watch how restaurants would respond to an allegation of food poisoning from a customer. Frank Flynn, a professor at Columbia

University, sent letters to 240 restaurants, claiming that his wedding anniversary dinner was marred by a case of food poisoning (Kifner, 2001). Restaurant owners and managers reported feeling distraught; they berated and retrained staff, and some even fired employees over the alleged mishandling of food (Frumkin, 2002). Once they realized that this was all part of research, two dozen filed suit against both the university and the professor (Fried, 2004).

My point to providing all these examples is that social science research might not harm people in the same fashion as medical research, but the potential for harm exists. When we study crime, we observe people, with or without their knowledge, conduct interviews, and review criminal case files. Some of this can be harmless. A student who observes a four-way intersection and counts the number of cars that do or do not come to a full stop at the stop sign can be confident that no individual driving that day will be harmed by their "participation" in that research. People who are asked in interviews or written surveys to recount past victimization or the harm their drug addiction has caused their family and friends may experience emotional harm. A researcher who collects data on sensitive topics, such as criminal offending or non-criminal deviant behavior, can cost research participants their jobs and reputations if the data are not properly safeguarded.

Social science researchers have just as much a responsibility as our colleagues in the medical field to respect others, keep them from harm, maximize the individual and societal benefits of our research, and ensure that the risks and benefits are distributed equally across participants. There are a few steps that we can take to safeguard individuals.

Informed Consent

Informed consent is a key element in maintaining the safety of potential research participants. People should have the right to choose whether they are willing to be part of research, but they cannot make an informed decision without appropriate disclosure from the research team. By engaging with research participants in the informed consent process, researchers help ensure that potential participants maintain their autonomy and are able to deliberate and make their own decisions (Shahnazarian, Hagemann, Aburto, & Rose, 2013). The authors of the Belmont Report identified three elements of the consent process: information, comprehension, and voluntariness (Department of Health, Education, and Welfare, 1979).

Information

In most instances, individuals are to be informed about several elements of the research process before they are asked to consent to involvement. Standard information to be shared includes the identity of the researcher(s) and their professional affiliations, the research procedure itself, any information about potential risks and benefits, the voluntariness of the project, the length of the project, and confirmation that the individuals are permitted to withdraw at any time. They should also be given the chance to ask questions. There are times, however, when disclosure of some of the aforementioned elements could actually damage the validity of the research. Only then should one consider deviating from the standard consent rules. The Department of Health, Education, and Welfare (1979) identified three criteria that must be present to justify a deviation from common informed consent:

> (1) Incomplete disclosure is truly necessary to accomplish the goals of the research, (2) there are no undisclosed risks to subjects that are more than minimal, and (3) there is an adequate plan for debriefing subjects, when appropriate, and for dissemination of research results to them.

> (p. 7)

Comprehension

Including all the necessary elements seems like a straightforward enough task, but the target population for a particular study may complicate matters. In criminal justice, we study people from all walks of life, including highly educated judges, attorneys, and criminal justice administrators. Setting up informed consent for these individuals is easy in that there are no concerns about their ability to understand verbal or written information. The same cannot be said for potential research participants who are offenders, inmates, or homeless individuals. It is the researcher's responsibility to frame informed consent in a way that they can understand. If the researcher is using a consent form, then it needs to be written to match the reading and comprehension level of the participant. In the case of offenders, that is usually a fourth- to sixth-grade reading level. Another potential concern is whether the participants speak or read English, and if so, how well. If potential respondents speak and read in other languages, you will need to be able to communicate the consent information in the appropriate language. What if there is a severe developmental or psychological impairment? It may be appropriate to designate a third party, such as a social worker, to act as an advocate, observe the research, and help individuals who may have difficulty comprehending the consent (Department of Health, Education, and Welfare, 1979).

Voluntariness

Are the people being asked for their consent truly free to give it? The HEW (1979) identified two different elements that can hinder voluntary consent. The first is coercion, meaning that there is a threat of harm for failure to comply. In the early 2010s, journalists reported that California was performing sterilizations of female prisoners in a state prison. While some women were pleased to have gotten this medical procedure while in prison, others reported feeling violated and argued that they were coerced into consenting. Some complained that their status as prisoners made it difficult for them to say no to any request or recommendation coming from those holding positions of authority. Others claimed that they were only asked for consent after being sedated (Chappell, 2013). The second threat to voluntariness is undue influence. This involves the offer of an excessive or improper reward or some other overture to encourage compliance. The reward might seem appropriate at first glance, but if the population happens to be especially vulnerable, it could be inappropriate viewed in that light. As I noted earlier, inmates in Holmesburg Prison were frequent research subjects because the financial rewards were too small to induce anyone from the general public to participate. How much money would it take to convince you to have a fingernail removed? Inmates in Holmesburg did it for $50 (Hornblum, 1998). With inflation, that would be about $325 today.

In criminal justice, we frequently encounter individuals whose ability to consent is questionable. For example, juveniles are legally incapable of consenting on their own. Research involving juveniles must include consent from a parent or guardian in most cases. In the juvenile corrections setting, consent can come from someone from the administration who is designated as the person responsible. For homeless juveniles or those from homes in which it does not seem feasible to be able to contact and communicate with a parent, an advocate such as a social worker can be assigned to consider the children's best interest. Juveniles are usually asked for their assent to participate in research. Research involving juveniles and the protocols necessary to protect them are determined on a case-by-case basis by Institutional Review Boards. Institutional Review Boards consider the risks of the research, the potential of the research helping children, and the ages and maturity of the particular individuals who are going to be involved in the study (United States Department of Health and Human Services, 2018). Both prisoners and juveniles are considered vulnerable populations that require extra protections when they are asked to participate in research.

The Informed Consent Process

Researchers can communicate the elements of informed consent in a variety of ways. One of the most common is to put this information in writing for people to consider. Participants can communicate their consent on written forms a few different ways. One option is to leave a space for the individual to check "yes" or "no" and then provide a signature. There will be times, however, where the consent form is part of an anonymous survey, so a signature would run counter to the promise of anonymity. In that case, participants might be asked to check a box indicating "yes" or "no," or the instructions might state that they should fill out the survey if they consent or refrain from starting if they do not consent. If the research is being conducted over the phone or with a population that might have difficulty reading, then the researcher can deliver the consent information orally and ask for verbal consent.

Shahnazarian and colleagues (2013) describe informed consent as a process that must be considered throughout the study. Research participants may have second thoughts after providing consent. People may begin to participate in the research but then become anxious, fearful, sad, or even bored and decide to terminate involvement. Everyone must always feel that they are free to withdraw from participation at any time.

Consent is not necessary for every social science research project. If a researcher is counting cars at a four-way intersection, that person would certainly not be expected to knock on the car windows and ask for permission to watch the car go through the intersection. If you are working with the local police station and agree to analyze their recent calls for service or arrest data, you are not expected to track down the people who called the police or got arrested to get their consent. Instructors who survey their classes as part of the course's educational process do not need to get student consent unless the survey is going to be used in published research later.

Institutional Review Boards

Institutional Review Boards (IRBs) were created in response to unethical research practices in both the biomedical and behavioral fields. These exist not only in the United States but also in over 80 other countries. The boards typically consist of people with research backgrounds who are expected to independently evaluate research proposals to safeguard human subjects. IRB review is mandatory for funding proposals submitted to a number of federal agencies, including the Department of Health and Human Services (Grady, 2015). Colleges and universities typically have their own IRBs since professors are often active in research and apply for funding from federal agencies that require IRB review.

All research that involves human subjects is expected to go through some level of IRB review, either exempt, expedited, or full review. Exempt proposals involving humans should still go through the IRB so the board can confirm that the research should be exempt from review. How do researchers decide if something should go through IRB? The Department of Health and Human Services (DHHS) Office for Human Research Protections has very useful flowcharts on their website to guide researchers in decision-making (Office for Human Research Protections, 2016). Research that involves obtaining information about living individuals, has an intervention or degree of interaction with people, and includes private information should generally be reviewed by an IRB. The proposal must receive some level of review if it is eligible for DHHS funding. Examples of exempt research involve teacher activities that include collecting data from students as part of the educational process, use of certain types of already-existing data, use of publicly available data, and doing research that involves no harm to individuals should the data become public. A colleague and I did auto theft research involving a review of police records with just the date and location of auto thefts. We visited the sites of the reported thefts to record physical characteristics (lighting, traffic flow, etc.) of each area. This is an example of research that was eligible for exemption. We did not have any contact with humans involved in the theft, and our data records included no information about any individuals (Levy & Tartaro, 2010a, 2010b). Research proposals that have already been approved by an IRB and have continued past their expiration date are generally eligible for expedited review, as are previously approved proposals that require minor changes (Office for Human Research Protections, 2016). Other projects could be eligible for expedited review if there is going to be data collected directly from humans but the potential for harm is low. Research that involves collection of sensitive data that, if disclosed, could be harmful to people requires a full board review. Any research that has the potential to physically or mentally harm someone, even if that harm means having to relive bad memories, needs full IRB review.

Some Ethical Dilemmas

Confidentiality and Anonymity

People who choose to participate in research deserve protection. Fortunately, we do not have the concerns that medical researchers have about causing physical harm. We do, however, use agency records to look up criminal records and drug treatment participation, and we ask people to self-report their victimizations and even their own criminal activities. Their willingness to assist researchers by participating in a study should never come back to harm them. One of the ways that we provide protection is through the promise of either anonymity or confidentiality. These are two very different concepts. **Anonymity** means that that no one, including the researcher, will be able to look at the data and identify the individuals attached to that information. Anonymity can be achieved through distributing surveys and expressly asking for people *not* to include their names or any other unique identifiers, such as a student identification number. For research involving agency or organizational records, the agency could de-identify cases before sending the dataset to the researcher by removing names and any other identifying information. **Confidentiality** is different, in that the research team has access to information that allows them to connect surveys or other information to individuals. When researchers promise that information will remain confidential, they are saying that they will not show anyone copies of the surveys with the names still attached, share the dataset with identifying information still included, or write reports that identify any individuals.

While it is extremely rare, law enforcement can request or demand to see a researcher's notes and other files pertaining to the project. When this happens, the researcher seldom has any type of protection. Researchers are not provided the same protection as attorneys and members of clergy, who are exempt from having to provide information on clients and parishioners. The only protection available for researchers is a **certificate of confidentiality** (COC), available through the federal government. The COC is available only for select projects funded through the National Institute of Health or the Department of Health and Human Services or non–federally funded projects at the discretion of these agencies (National Institutes of Health, 2019). Most researchers lack these certificates. This means that, if they are doing research and are promising confidentiality, there might come a time when they are faced with having to break that promise and cooperate with law enforcement or keep the promise and face legal repercussions. Again, this is rare, but it is something that researchers need to consider before they embark on data collection.

During the data collection process, researchers must make sure that the data are being collected and handled in a way that allows them to maintain whatever protections they promised the participants. If the promise was anonymity, then no identifying information should appear with the data. For confidentiality, interviews must be done in a setting that provides a degree of privacy. If people are being asked to fill out a survey that needs to remain confidential, respondents must be given instructions for how to return it to the researcher safely. If the researcher is not physically present to collect surveys upon completion, one option is for respondents to place their completed forms in envelopes, seal them, and then sign their names over the seal to deter tampering. Another option is for the researcher to leave a locked box in a location, such as a police station for a policing survey, where officers can drop off their completed forms. The forms will remain secure in the box since the researcher is the only person with the key.

Once researchers collect data, they must make sure that they remain secure and out of reach of others. IRBs require researchers to explain how they will handle sensitive information once they receive it. Paper copies that have identifying information and sensitive items must be kept under two sets of lock and key at all times. In my case, that means I have a filing cabinet in my office, and I have the only key to it. The custodial staff and campus police can get into my office at any time, but the files are still protected because they are in the locked filing cabinet. If there are sensitive files with identifying information on a computer, the computer must be password protected. Whenever possible, researchers should work to de-identify datasets, meaning that as soon as individual names and any corresponding identification numbers are no longer needed, they should be removed. Failure to take these steps after data have been collected could result in researchers breaking their promise of confidentiality or anonymity.

Compensating Participants

Another potential ethical dilemma pertains to offering to pay research participants for their time. If someone has ever asked you to fill out a survey or do an interview, your first thought was likely about how much time this was going to take and what an inconvenience this would be. To encourage people to participate and thank them for their time, researchers will sometimes provide some form of renumeration, such as a gift card or cash, in exchange for participation. There are a few ethical concerns here. First, we want to make sure that we are not tempting people so much with a reward that they become willing to take on a serious risk. For an example of this, review the section on the medical experiments at Holmesburg Prison. Those individuals were so desperate to make bail or earn money to hire an attorney that they were willing to engage in painful medical experiments. While it is acceptable to provide participants with renumeration, the money should not be so much that it would have undue influence on decision-making. The money should be enough to adequately express the researcher's appreciation and show respect for the individual's time. Second, given the populations that we often interact with in criminal justice, there is worry about what the participants will do with that money. One common concern is that the money will go toward buying drugs and alcohol. A possible way around this is to provide gift cards instead of cash. When I conducted interviews of family and friends of inmates in the lobbies of two different jails, I wanted to provide some renumeration to encourage participation and thank people for their time. In order to avoid the two ethical concerns listed here, I used my grant to purchase several small ($5) gift cards for a local convenience store chain. The facilities were in New Jersey, and the convenience stores here do not even sell alcohol, so the worst that could happen would be that the cards would be used to purchase tobacco or caffeine.

Researchers often also try to show their appreciation and respect for participants by informally doing small favors. This is different from the financial renumeration that I discussed in the previous paragraph, as that type of compensation is much more formal and spelled out as researchers are obtaining consent. Researchers have provided transportation to people who needed a ride and helped people fill out job applications (Wright, Decker, Redfern, & Smith, 1992). Others have allowed people to use their phones (Adler, 1993) and done other small but legal favors. When I was conducting interviews in the lobby of a jail, family and friends would often approach a machine that allowed them to put money on inmates' accounts. Older, less technologically savvy people often found it confusing, so whenever I was not in the middle of an interview, I always got up to help people use the machine. There have also been times when I have conducted interviews with inmates and let the interview go on a bit longer even after I had collected all the information I wanted when I sensed that the individual just wanted to chat with someone from the outside for a few minutes. I decided that, out of respect for the time that they just gave me, I could spare a little bit of my time.

Plagiarism

This entire chapter has focused on ethical issues that may pose risks to human research participants (I always feel uncomfortable calling them "subjects"), but in research, there is one more ethical concern that we need to consider. This one could arise regardless of whether the project involves human participants, and it can be problematic even with work that does not adhere to the scientific method. **Plagiarism** consists of passing someone else's work off as one's own and is considered a very serious offense among academics and writers. Plagiarism is considered problematic because it consists of two offenses: theft and fraud. It is theft because you are taking work from someone else, and it is fraud because you are claiming to be the author of such work. Let me explain why this is a big deal. Whether it is in a college class or at your job, if you are expected to produce some sort of report or brief, you are going to be evaluated on the quality of that product. Professors will want to grade you on not just the quality of the thoughts/facts but also on the clarity of the writing. The same goes for your work supervisor. If you take a sentence that someone else wrote and then put it into your work without properly attributing that sentence, you are stealing from the original author and letting everyone assume that you took the time and effort to construct that sentence yourself. Without proper attribution, you are also making it look like you came up with an idea or produced some research findings when, in fact, someone else did.

You might be thinking that you can ignore this section because you are very ethical and would never do something like this. What you need to understand is that plagiarism can take on many forms, and it is very easy to plagiarize without even realizing it. The problem is that "I did not realize I was doing something wrong" stopped becoming an adequate excuse back in high school because we teach you, at multiple points in time, how to avoid plagiarism in college. Let this serve as one more of those teaching moments.

The primary tools to protect you against plagiarism are paraphrasing and proper citations. I will revisit these after I discuss the types of plagiarism.

Examples of intentional plagiarism:

- Purchasing a paper from a paper mill
- Taking a friend/relative's work and handing it in as your own
- Copying and pasting statements/sentences/paragraphs from websites, articles, books, or any other source that you did not write

Examples of unintended plagiarism:

- Copying entire statements/sentences from sources and then failing to properly cite them
- Using any idea or fact from another source and then failing to cite it

Here are some important rules to remember:

- *There is a difference between a quotation and plagiarism.* I have had students say to me, "Well, I just used the sentences from the sources I read because they stated it so well that I just could not think of a better way to write it." Unless your professor forbids it, it is usually acceptable to have a (very) few quotations in your paper. There might, indeed, be something that would best be communicated in the words of the original author, and you will see a few examples of me quoting other authors in this book. These quotations are acceptable because I am citing them properly and acknowledging that they are not my words. Whenever I take the exact words of others, I put quotation marks around them, and I either introduce or end the sentence by attributing them to the proper authors. Since we are in the social sciences, we like to use the American Psychological Association (APA) citation standards, which call for (1) identification of the author(s), (2) year of publication, and (3) page numbers when available for every quotation. Failure to include the quotation marks along with a proper citation turns a quotation into plagiarism. One other way that quotations could be problematic and detrimental to your grade or job performance is if you use them excessively. Remember, you are being judged on *your* writing, not your ability to copy and paste other people's work and insert quotation marks. If that is what you turn in, how can anyone grade your writing?

- *Paraphrase*: Since we just established that only small numbers of quotations are acceptable, that means that you must learn to paraphrase others' work. You read sources to learn about the topic for your paper, and then you have to communicate your newly acquired knowledge in your paper in your own words. One good suggestion would be to read a section of an article, put it down, and then type up a quick summary, in your own words, of what you just read. That way, your notes that you use to write your paper will already be in your own words. This will prevent you from taking someone else's sentences and attributing them to your own work.
- *Remember to cite what you paraphrase*: It is an excellent first step that you put your notes in your own words. That does not mean, however, that you now own that information. You learned new facts, and you might have gotten a few ideas that are not yours. Any time you are going to write about something that is not common knowledge that you just took from something you read (or even saw or heard because you have to cite videos and audio recordings too), you must properly cite it in your paper, or else it is plagiarism. For paraphrased items, APA style requires us to note the authors' last names and the publication year in the paragraph where we are using the information.

There is much more to learn about the specifics of when, where, and how to cite sources, and that is beyond the scope of this book. Your college or university's website is likely an excellent resource for learning about plagiarism and how to avoid it. There are very good books that also show students not only how to cite properly but also how to navigate all the tricky aspects of writing, such as grammar and punctuation. Let me be clear that, given your level of education, it is now your responsibility to understand plagiarism and how to avoid it. Of course, see your professor, a librarian, or a writing tutor with specific questions.

Summary

It is unfortunate that the history of research has been marred by horrific events. The lack of ethical standards and sheer disrespect for fellow humans prompted people to commit acts of unbelievable cruelty in the name of science. After decades of disturbing examples of harmful medical research, several countries' governments and even international groups established regulations to police the research community. In the United States, the Belmont Report helped provide general standards for the protection of human subjects. Universities, hospitals, and other institutions that often sponsor research have created their own Institutional Review Boards that are responsible for oversight of their employees' research involving humans.

In the social sciences, we do study aspects of people's lives that can prove harmful. We are interested in deviant behavior, criminal offending, and victimization. This research can be harmful in multiple ways. First, asking people to recall some of the darkest moments of their lives can make them relive the emotions, including guilt, shame, and sadness, that are associated with that period of time. Second, if others were to find out about the research participants' criminal records, drug use behavior, transactions with sex workers, stealing from employers, or any other illegal or unethical behavior that we are measuring, the consequences could be very severe. People can lose their jobs and even get into legal trouble, just because they tried to help a researcher. For these reasons, we have to make protection of our participants a top priority.

Keywords

Nuremberg Code	Declaration of Helsinki	Belmont Report
Respect for persons	Beneficence	Justice
Tearoom Trade	Stanford Prison Experiment	Informed consent
Institutional Review Board (IRB)	Anonymity	Confidentiality
Certificate of confidentiality	Plagiarism	

Discussion Questions

1. Consider the Holmesburg Prison experiments. In what ways did the researchers violate the principles in the Belmont Report, the Nuremburg Codes, and the Helsinki Declaration?
2. What steps could Zimbardo have taken to make the Stanford Prison Experiment more ethically viable by today's research standards?
3. Imagine that you are going to give your fellow students a survey about their participation in off-campus parties where alcohol and/or illegal drugs are served.

    a. What elements need to be in the consent form for this?
    b. What are the potential risks to participants?
    c. Devise a plan for how you will distribute, collect, and store the data in a way that will be acceptable to your school's IRB.

References

Adler, P. A. (1993). *Wheeling & dealing: An ethnography of upper-level drug dealing and smuggling community* (2nd ed.). New York, NY: Columbia University Press.

Blum, B. (2018). The lifespan of a lie. *Medium.* Retrieved from https://medium.com/s/trustissues/the-lifespan-of-a-lie-d869212b1f62

Centers for Disease Control and Prevention. (2015). *U.S. Public Health Service syphilis study at Tuskegee.* Retrieved from www.cdc.gov/tuskegee/timeline.htm

Cohen, A. (2016). *Imbeciles.* New York, NY: Penguin Press.

Department of Health, Education, and Welfare. (1979) *The Belmont Report: Ethical principles and guidelines for the protection of human subjects of research.* Bethesda, MD: The National Commission for the Protection of Human Subjects of Biomedical and Behavioral Research.

Fried, J. P. (2004). No stomach pills, but many legal bills. *New York Times.* Retrieved from www.nytimes.com/2004/02/08/nyregion/following-up.html

Frumkin, P. (2002). Ten operators sue Columbia U., professor over letters. *Nation's Restaurant News, 36*(2), 1.

Grady, C. (2015). Institutional Review Boards: Purpose and challenges. *Chest, 148*(5), 1148–1155.

Hornblum, A. M. (1998). *Acres of skin.* New York: Routledge.

Humphreys, L. (1970). *Tearoom trade: Interpersonal sex in public places.* Hawthorne, NY: Aldine Publishing Company.

Jarmusik, N. (2019). *The Nuremberg code and its impact on clinical research*. IMARC Research, Inc. Retrieved from www.imarcresearch.com/blog/bid/359393/nuremberg-code-1947

Kifner, J. (2001). Scholar sets off gastronomic false alarm. *New York Times*. Retrieved from www.nytimes.com/2001/09/08/nyregion/scholar-sets-off-gastronomic-false-alarm.html

Mitford, J. (1973). *Kind and usual punishment: The prison business*. New York, NY: Alfred A. Knopf.

National Institutes of Health. (2019). *Certificates of Confidentiality (CoC)—human subjects*. Washington, DC: U.S. Department of Health and Human Services.

Office for Human Research Protections. (2016). *Human subjects regulations decision charts*. Rockville, MD: United States Department of Health and Human Services, Office for Human Research Protections. Retrieved from www.hhs.gov/ohrp/regulations-and-policy/decision-charts/index.html#c1

Oshinsky, D. M. (1996). *"Worse than slavery": Parchman Farm and the ordeal of Jim Crow justice*. New York: Simon and Schuster.

Shahnazarian, D., Hagemann, J., Aburto, M., & Rose, S. (2013). *Informed consent in human subjects research*. Los Angeles, CA: University of Southern California Office for the Protection of Research Subjects.

United States Department of Health and Human Services. (2018). *Electronic code of federal regulations part 46—Protection of human subjects*. Retrieved from www.ecfr.gov/cgi-bin/retrieveECFR?gp=&SID=83cd09e1c0f5c6937cd9d7513160fc3f&pitd=20180719&n=pt45.1.46&r=PART&ty=HTML#se45.1.46_1408

World Medical Association. (2019). *WMA declaration of Helsinki—ethical principles for medical research involving human subjects*. Retrieved from www.wma.net/policies-post/wma-declaration-of-helsinki-ethical-principles-for-medical-research-involving-human-subjects/

Wright, R., Decker, S. H., Redfern, A. K., & Smith, D. L. (1992). A snowball's chance in hell: Doing fieldwork with active residential burglars. *Journal of Research in Crime and Delinquency, 29*, 148–161. https://doi.org/10.1177/0022427892029002003

Reading 3.1   Researching the Registered

Sex offender research carries unique challenges, as this tends to be a difficult-to-reach population. There are potential ethical issues whenever researchers contact potential respondents. As researchers, we work with our IRBs to try to anticipate ethical concerns that may arise using our own common sense and our understanding of the ethical rules. We can also benefit from learning about what other researchers encountered when they did research similar to ours. Klein, Baily, and Sample (2018) worked with their IRB and tried to anticipate ethical problems that might emanate from their research plans, but they still had some unanticipated ethical challenges that necessitated changes to their protocols. The authors share their experiences with making ethically appropriate adjustments to their research protocol. They also address the important topic of how to take steps to keep the researchers themselves physically safe and to care for their psychological well-being.

Researching the Registered: Challenges and Suggestions for Researchers Studying Sex Offender Populations

Jennifer L. Klein, Danielle J. S. Bailey, and Lisa L. Sample

Introduction

Public interest in sexual victimization has remained relatively consistent over time (Burchfield, Sample, & Lytle, 2014), which has led scholars to investigate the causes of sexual offending (Lussier, Blokland, Mathesius, Pardini, & Loeber, 2013; Mathesius & Lussier, 2014), the influence of law on sexual offending rates (Sandler, Freeman, & Socia, 2008; Tewksbury & Jennings, 2010; Vasquez, Maddan, & Walker, 2008), and desistance from sexual violence (Göbbels, Ward, & Willis, 2012; Kruttschnitt, Uggen, & Shelton, 2000; Lussier, Corrado, & McCuish, 2016). To the degree that sexual offending or its decline involves dynamic situational and environmental factors that evolve over time (Beauregard & Leclerc, 2007), we must directly ask registrants about their environments, relationships, routine activities, cognitive processes, and decision-making points while living in the community as officially labeled 'sex offenders.' Given the negative social stigma and experiences associated with the 'sex offender' label in society (Evans & Cubellis, 2015; Tewksbury, 2011), it can be difficult to find willing offenders in communities to participate in research studies, which leaves us to assume how laws affect behavior, how sex offender labels affect routine activities, and how registrants cope with 'sex offender' identities. This paper highlights challenges in conducting research with community sex offenders, particularly those no longer on probation or parole. Specifically, we examine what types of information and experiences scholars can expect when working with these subjects. What follows is a discussion of four specific challenges that occur when gathering data from community sex offender samples, and some suggestions for overcoming these challenges.

Background

Why Are Registered Sex Offenders a Unique Population to Study?

Convicted sex offenders are the most visible criminal offenders in society, yet they are one of the most difficult populations to research. In large part, sex offender registration and community notification (SORN) laws are responsible for this quagmire. In the early 1990s, the first legislative expansions to sex offender supervision laws occurred with the Jacob Wetterling Act of 1994, which established the modern day sex offender registry and required that law enforcement be privy to offenders' personal information (42 U.S.C. 14071). 'Megan's Law' expanded legislative efforts and established community notification policies allowing for public disclosure of registrants' personal information (42 U.S.C. 13701), which typically includes addresses, vehicle descriptions and license plate numbers, pictures of registrants, any identifiable marks or tattoos, and in some states, even their shoe size. These efforts were meant to publicly identify sex offenders and 'would, hypothetically, warn parents of an apparent risk nearby and they would be able to protect their children from such threats' (Ackerman, Sacks, & Osier, 2013, p. 30).

The passage of the Adam Walsh Act of 2006 further expanded legislative efforts to increase the duration of sex offender registration, mandate juvenile sex offender registration, and increased failure to register offenses to felony status (42 U.S.C. 16911). The Adam Walsh Act substantially impacted the number of offenders on state registries by lengthening registration periods, and by requiring new offenders to comply with SORN legislation when they were not required to in the past. With the inevitability that SORN laws will not disappear any time soon, registered sex offenders must comply with SORN requirements while possibly experiencing a variety of unintended consequences resulting from these legislative efforts.

Researchers suggest that the results of sex offender laws include challenges with unemployment (Brown, Spencer, & Deakin, 2007; Kruttschnitt et al., 2000; Levenson & Tewksbury, 2009), homelessness (Levenson & Tewksbury, 2009; Socia, Levenson, Ackerman, & Harris, 2015), and stigmatization and harassment (Burchfield & Mingus, 2008; Klein, Rukus, & Zambrana, 2012; Klein, Tolson, & Collins, 2014; Levenson, D'Amora, & Hern, 2007; Tewksbury, 2004, 2005; Zevitz, Crim, & Farkas, 2000) for registrants. These unintended consequences continue to result in detrimental effects for offenders and are often unresolved because the community protection aspects of SORN legislation are given higher priority over individual rights of offenders. As a consequence, these laws have contributed to an almost permanent sense of paranoia among registrants

concerning non-registered populations in society (Malinen, Willis, & Johnston, 2014). Moreover, these laws often function as public expressions for the disdain, disgust, and need for banishment of people exhibiting sex offending behaviors (Tolson & Klein, 2015). Given that research suggests a stressful post-conviction life increases the likelihood of recidivism (Colorado Department of Public Safety, 2004; Lasher & McGrath, 2012; Levenson, 2007; Tewksbury & Zgoba, 2010), unintended consequences of SORN legislation run counterintuitive to the goals of such regulations: reductions of sex offender recidivism and increases in community safety.

Given the many challenges that registered sex offenders may face in post-conviction life, it is important for continued research on this offender population. However, that is not an easy task for researchers for a variety of reasons, including the social and/or geographic isolation of offenders within their communities, offenders' distrust of unregistered populations, and concern over the possible legal ramifications of participating in a research study (Medlicott, 2004; Scheper-Hughes, 2004; Waldram, 2007). The goal of this paper is to help sex offender researchers consider the challenges they may face while studying sex offenders in communities. We examine researcher experiences associated with collecting data from sex offender and sex offender family member samples in three different states. In all three studies, the researchers encountered unanticipated challenges from the participants, including the addition of unsolicited data, and logistical challenges to the studies. This manuscript highlights four challenges that researchers may encounter when studying sex offender populations and provides recommendations for overcoming each.

Gathering Data From Registered Sex Offenders in the Community

There has been much discussion and debate over the best way to conduct ethically sensitive research with populations in communities (Dickson-Swift, James, Kippen, & Liamputtong, 2007; Orb, Eisenhauer, & Wynaden, 2001). Surveys provide anonymity for subjects, but often force participants' thoughts and emotions into predetermined categories and usually create low response rates (Maxfield & Babbie, 2015; Zaller & Feldman, 1992). Moreover, survey responses result from several cognitive processes (Blair & Burton, 1987) that often reflect whatever is on the mind of subjects at one moment in time (Zaller & Feldman, 1992) which is likely to change as life circumstances do. Open-ended questions on surveys allow some freedom in responses, but often require different types of analyses such as concept mapping rather than traditional narrative analyses (Jackson & Trochim, 2002). Qualitative interviews can capture a wealth of deep, in-depth personal data that allows researchers to recognize stages or processes germane to offending, but samples are seldom drawn at random and the total number of subjects often prevents generalization of the information uncovered (Adelman, Jenkins, & Kemmis, 1980; Burck, 2005; Johnson & Waterfield, 2004; Myers, 2000; Sandelowski, 2000). Johnson and Waterfield (2004) suggest the skepticism of qualitative research can be overcome by using triangulation techniques, multiple coders, audit trails and respondent validation, and addressing reflexivity. As Myers (2000) reminds us, the goals of the study should always be taken into account when choosing data gathering techniques and judging the scientific rigor and quality of research methodologies. We must also keep in mind that generalizability is not the only scientific goal of research.

As is common with all research involving direct contact with subjects, researchers examining sex offender populations experience issues in developing rapport with subjects, using self-disclosure techniques, and experiencing feelings of guilt and vulnerability (Dickson-Swift et al., 2007). In order to gain substantive data from sex offender samples, it is particularly important to establish credibility and rapport with the participants in order to break through their levels of distrust. We have found that no matter the methodological approach, sex offender participants have the desire to have their voices heard and will actively participate in both quantitative surveys and qualitative interviews when

they believe it is safe for them to do so. To date, we have conducted three studies across three states, using three different methodological approaches, and have had similar experiences while gathering qualitative and quantitative data, which is surprising given the diversity in sex offender populations, state laws, and research approaches.

Nebraska

In Nebraska, we undertook a qualitative project involving interviews with registered sex offenders who were currently living in the community. Research participation invitations were mailed to all registered citizens within the state of Nebraska, approximately 3300 individuals at the time of the research. Given the concerns about low response rates (10–15%) among previous sex offender samples (Tewksbury, 2005; Tewksbury & Lees, 2006) and the invasive nature of the research interviews, the researchers decided to coordinate with a local sex offender advocacy group in order to promote the study. The researchers had a prior working relationship with this advocacy group, and it was believed that this coordination would help provide reassurance to potential participants and presumably improve response rates. It also should be noted that most states have similar sex offender advocacy organizations trying to achieve legal reforms.

The invitations requested that the individual participate in a qualitative interview with the researchers to discuss what life was like under SORN laws. Interviews were conducted in person, over the phone, and through email to ensure that subjects could participate regardless of their geographic location, transportation availability, possible internet restrictions, and physical health. Interviews were expected to last approximately one hour, with follow-up interviews scheduled on an as-needed basis.

We received phone calls and emails from over 300 potential participants requesting to be a part of the research study in less than two weeks. As of 2016, 140 offenders had completed an initial interview. Follow up interviews with these participants have been subject initiated, occur an average of 1.3 times a year, and have been ongoing since as early as 2009. While the original study was designed for registered sex offenders only, the scope of the project was altered to include sex offender family members as well (N = 40), after several offenders brought their spouses and/or parents to the interviews with them. Although the study was officially concluded with the Institutional Review Board (IRB) in May 2017, several participants continue to provide unsolicited data regarding their progress and post-conviction life events, as the interviews seemed to hold some therapeutic value for offenders and their family members.

Texas

In Texas, we undertook a mixed methods project involving surveys with registered sex offenders and their family members. As with the Nebraska study, this project was completed with support from a sex offender advocacy group that helped promote the study by allowing us to distribute paper surveys during their annual conference. This study utilized dual surveys: one geared toward registrants and the other toward family members of registrants. Fifty-two hard copy surveys were completed at the conference: 29 sex offenders and 23 family members. After the conference, data collection continued with surveys being completed online (for those able to access the internet) and in hard-copy form (for those not permitted to access the internet). This continued collection resulted in an additional 80 registrant surveys, and 93 family member surveys. Through the use of the two solicitations, the project yielded 233 total participants: 109 male sex offenders and 116 male and female family members.

Florida

The third research study took place in Florida. We collected quantitative data through the use of mail surveys, but focused exclusively on registered female sex offenders. The Florida Department of Law Enforcement provided a list of all female sex offenders registered in Florida as of March 2010. After removing 415 offenders

due to incarceration, deportation, having an out-of-state address, abscondsion, or deregistration, an informed consent, quantitative survey, and return postage were sent out to 569 female sex offenders living in Florida. By December 2010, 106 surveys were returned resulting in a response rate of 18.6%, which is suitable for a mail out survey (Collwell, Miller, Miller, & Lyons, 2006), and is in line with previous studies of female sex offenders (Tewksbury, 2004, 2005; Vandiver & Walker, 2002).

This research was not affiliated with any other type of intermediary organization such as a sex offender advocacy group. This study differs significantly from the Nebraska and Texas studies in that the participants were cold-called and were asked to participate in a study of which they had no prior knowledge.

Challenges in Researching Sex Offender Populations Irrespective of State-Specific Laws

Based on the three research studies described above, we have identified four major challenges to researching sex offender populations. They include the submission of unsolicited data from participants, overcoming the distrust of your participants, self-protection of researchers' emotions and how to navigate and end relationships with their participants, and how to protect participants from emotional risks. We provide recommendations for future research in discussing each of these four challenges.

Challenge #1: Unsolicited Data and Contact

Across all three studies, one common theme was the provision of unsolicited data by sex offender and sex offender family member participants. Regardless of the method of initial contact, participants quickly responded with questions and information exceeding the scope of the study's purpose and the approved data collection by IRB. In Nebraska, initial contacts were intended to be used for interview scheduling purposes only, but the initial calls themselves became a source of unsolicited qualitative data. The study invitation provided the phone number of the department's front desk, staffed by an office administrator, with the expectation that these calls would be directed to the appropriate researchers' voicemails. However, we found that many of the respondents began telling their story to the first person who picked up the phone, even if it was not approved IRB study personnel. In these cases, the office administrator would try to take notes about the respondent's story, but would also repeatedly request that they discuss the matter with study staff. Eventually, the office administrator requested that we stop providing the main department number, as the volume and length of the calls were becoming disruptive to the office.

In Texas and Florida, participants provided unrequested qualitative data which was returned in person (at the Texas conference), via email or in hard-copy form through the mail (both states) when individuals returned their surveys. At the advocacy group's conference in Texas, the offenders and their family members usually engaged in personal conversations when requesting or submitting a survey. These personal conversations usually included an unprovoked synopsis of the crime and subsequent conviction. However, the most common type of unsolicited data from these studies occurred as qualitative information provided on quantitative measures. Respondents in both the Texas and the Florida studies included marginal comments about their experiences and personal situations when completing the quantitative, close-ended portions of the survey. Their comments were usually an attempt to explain situational factors that extended beyond the scope of the question, or to give more details that respondents felt were important for the researcher to know. For example, one respondent in the Texas survey provided marginal comments on nearly every question included in the quantitative survey. In all, we received 38 pieces of participant initiated qualitative datum from the Florida study and 32 pieces from the Texas study. These data were smaller in size than the amount of unsolicited data collected in the Nebraska study, a disparity we believe stems from the use of qualitative data versus

quantitative data, but in all three cases participants provided information that went beyond the original scope of the study.

Another source of unsolicited data occurred through the inclusion of additional participants. In Nebraska, registered offenders began including their family members, most commonly their spouses and/or parents, in order to provide context to their experiences during their interviews. Oftentimes this addition was unexpected; the researcher would schedule an interview with registrants themselves but then a spouse or parent would arrive with the offender for the interview. This occurred with face-to-face interviews as well as phone interviews. Phone interviews were often put onto speaker on the respondent's side so another family member could participate. Since the original IRB application was designed for interviews with registrants only, a change of protocol had to be submitted to the university IRB board so that the additional participants could be included in the study results.

The last form of unsolicited data occurred in all three studies, and was provided in the form of unsolicited emails and phone calls to the researcher. Both the Texas and the Florida studies were intended to be purely quantitative, but some participants reached out via email or phone to share more of their story with the researchers. Sometimes these emails were meant to provide further context to family members' stories, or to thank the researcher for taking an interest in this population. However, occasionally participants sent emails expressing their anger toward the registry system and toward us as researchers, for not taking into account absolutely everything that was important to the participant as an individual. For example, one male registrant in Texas sent two emails thoroughly discussing the 'emasculating nature of the registry' and spoke on several occasions about how another man (his parole officer) would be in charge of all household decisions for him. He states,

> Here is an example, say your husband, being on the registry, has to get approval/permission from another man (parole officer, PO) on making major house hold decisions, how does your husband look

to you in your eyesight? Say you wanted to have a second honey moon in San Antonio River Walk, but your husband has to get permission from another man, PO, to take you. Again, how does your husband look to you in your eyesight?

(Participant #1, June 14, 2017)[1]

I Have a Unique Story

Across all three studies, we saw several reoccurring reasons for why participants would submit unsolicited data. One of the most common reasons rested in the idea that each individual participant believed that they had a unique story, an important story, or one that we had never heard before. Frequently emphasized was the notion that 'My story is different.' Participants were adamant that their story was not the typical sex offense as portrayed by the media. These individuals claimed that they were not predatory in nature, that the charges were fabricated, or that there was a consensual relationship (statutory rape). Even those who did take responsibility for their sexual offenses usually included justification by providing some sort of mitigating statement.

The Innocent Sex Offender

Across the three studies, some participants maintained their innocence in stating that 'I didn't do it,' or that 'Someone set me up.' This 'othering' set them apart from most sex offenders on the registry, for example, the ones that should really be there. In all three studies, some participants claimed that the charges were the result of a jealous, angry, or vengeful partner. For example, a common story was that of a former partner who, while going through divorce proceedings, called the police and alleged that the participant sexually abused her own child(ren). Other participants reported that they were incapable of committing a sexual offense due to drinking or drug use, or maintained that the victim made false allegations against them. Participants used the research study as an opportunity to voice their stories to individuals (the researchers), who were perceived as credible allies or advocates. Additionally, these interactions often resulted in a request for legal assistance to help participants be removed from the registry. In the Florida study, the researcher's home department included the word Law in the title. Multiple participants assumed that the researcher was an attorney and could provide free legal assistance in their cases.

Recommendations in Handling Unsolicited Data and Contact

Using Mixed Methodological Approaches

Stigmatized individuals, like registered sex offenders and their family members, desire to be heard and have opportunities to tell their stories. Emailing the researchers, making phone calls, and mailing letters or newspaper clippings allows these individuals to tell their stories and share information pertinent to them outside the limited confines of an IRB approved quantitative survey or a guided qualitative interview. This suggests that the best methodological approach to studying sex offenders is a mixed-methods approach that incorporates both quantitative surveys and qualitative interviews, or at the very least, an outlet for sex offenders to include qualitative information. From the three studies conducted in Nebraska, Texas, and Florida, it has become clear that sex offenders have more to say than what can be included contained within close-ended surveys. The qualitative expansion allows for the gathering of in-depth information, while still allowing for the collection of larger sample sizes necessary to complete qualitative analyses.

Organization and Filing Strategies

One of the simplest ways to prepare for unsolicited data is to recognize that you will most likely experience this situation if you choose to work sex offender populations. Before the study begins, make a plan for how to store and analyze unsolicited data. For example, you can create shared folders to store all supplementary email contacts, or you can dedicate a file cabinet to mailed letters, articles, and other hard-copy supplements you receive. Organization is particularly important if you are working with a research team, as some participants may contact the entire team while others will reach out to only one researcher. Developing a system of organization where you determine, before the study begins, how to record unsolicited data will help you maintain a consistent approach throughout the study and ensure that you can use all available data when preparing your research findings.

IRB Approval

While we all learned early in our careers the importance of obtaining approval from the universities' IRB prior to data collection, this point must be discussed more thoroughly within the context of receiving unsolicited data. IRB protections allow the researcher to collect data from participants without worrying about legal threats, or about infringing on the rights of the participants. In all three studies, we gained approval from their respective IRB boards to complete either a quantitative mail-out survey (Florida), qualitative interviews (Nebraska), or a quantitative paper and internet survey (Texas). At no point did we address the possibility that there may be unsolicited data collected from the participants who wanted to expand on their responses. Once these responses started arriving, we had to contact their respective IRBs to inquire about changing initial protocols. In the case of Nebraska, we obtained IRB approval for not only unsolicited information beyond that listed in the initial protocol but also obtained approval to use subject initiated follow-ups that extended beyond our request for only one follow-up interview. In fact, after five years of study, the Nebraska IRB asked us to close the official protocol because the study had extended to the point where our conversations with offenders in the community were seen as providing a community service and beyond the definition of 'research' found in the Common Rule.

Challenge #2: Distrust

People are typically willing to share their experiences provided that trust is achieved between participants and researchers and if participants feel they are within the context of perceived safe spaces (Waldram, 2007). The media and the public nature of sex offender registries play a role in stigmatizing registrants as impulsive, predatory monsters who will inevitably reoffend (Klein, 2016), and the Adam Walsh Act of 2006 substantially increased the time period many offenders must be on the registry. This long-term, chronic stigmatization encourages sexual offenders to self-isolate and work to hide their identities, creating difficulties for researchers trying to interview or survey them (Monahan, Marolla, & Bromley, 2005; Waldram, 2007). To overcome distrust and encourage study participation, it is imperative for researchers to establish credibility with sex offender populations. This may occur by obtaining the support of a sex offender advocacy group, or by making repeated, but non-harassing, attempts to communicate with offenders. Researchers must establish themselves as scholars and members of the academy, not as state-associated researchers or psychologists. Registered sex offenders, like other felony offenders, are distrustful of state sponsored research that studies them for their own perceived enjoyment (Medlicott, 2004; Scheper-Hughes, 2004; Waldram, 2007). Some may feel threatened by researchers, if the researcher tries to cold call the offender to invite their participation in a quantitative survey or qualitative interview.

In addition to participants' distrust of researchers, scholars may also face bias in the opposite direction. Pre-existing biases are human nature (Ross, 1977) and often scholars may be skeptical of the information they receive from criminals (Webb, Katz, & Decker, 2006). Given that friendly behaviors by sex offenders are often viewed as grooming and manipulative (Payne & DeMichele, 2008), researchers working with the sex offender populations may be particularly disinclined to trust offenders' stories. This distrust can create challenges in building rapport, thus further limiting subject disclosure and trust.

Accessing Registrant Information and Subsequent Paranoia

In our experience, there will always be study participants who become concerned about your ability to find their personal information and to contact them. In all three studies, we encountered participants who demanded information about the researchers' credentials and the purpose of the study. In the Texas study, the advocacy group requested we formally present our credentials, including our schooling, work experience, and prior research, in order to establish credibility with potential participants. In Nebraska, the advocacy group provided a letter reassuring participants about some of this information, but we still received angry phone calls about our contacts. As this is a stigmatized population with trust issues, it is imperative that the researcher take whatever steps are necessary to alleviate any concerns that the participants, or advocacy groups, may have before the study commences.

Trust issues in this population also affected participants' feelings about our initial contacts. We found it surprising that multiple individuals in the Nebraska and Florida studies expressed confusion over our ability to find and use their addresses. Both of these studies involved mailed out materials, and addresses were collected from the publicly available state sex offender registry. Even though anyone has access to this information, we had several participants who became confused and upset by our ability to track down their addresses. We are unsure why this confusion occurred, but given the recurrence of this reaction in two states, this may be common experience for researchers working with sex offender populations.

Recommendations to Overcome Distrust of Both Parties

Consider Working With Local Community Groups

Thanks to public registries, registered sex offenders are easy to find but difficult to recruit for studies. Registered sex offenders and their family members value their privacy, and some potential participants will not respond to any researcher requests to participate in research study. They may feel as though they will be sanctioned by the state if they participate, a worry exhibited by participants in both Florida and Nebraska. Others may feel as though the researcher is a representative of the state, who

is trying to further harass the offender. This population is often distrustful of outsiders, and typically do not respond to cold calls. Because of this distrust, it is helpful to have an advocacy group act as an intermediary to help in reaching out to this offender group. This was done with great success in both the Nebraska and Texas studies. However, as shown by the Florida study, it is not necessary for this to occur but you might meet more resistance without an intermediary present.

One limitation of working with advocacy groups is the potential increase in selection bias. While advocacy groups can certainly aid the researcher in making initial contact with registered sex offenders, they may only be able to link researchers with members of their organization, lending to biased sampling. Given the public advocacy role of these organizations, those offenders who participate in an advocacy group are not necessarily representative of the total population of sex offenders. However, having the group's support does offer an additional level of legitimacy to researchers, thus allowing sex offenders to trust them more than if researchers were to cold call participants. Furthermore, having the legitimate backing of the advocacy group will hopefully limit the participants in any threats or complaints made against researchers.

Be Prepared for Threats of Lawsuits and Complaints

We discussed previously how registered sex offenders participating in research studies will often reach out to the researchers to provide additional, unsolicited information. However, this is not always a positive occurrence. Given the stigma of this population, many of the offenders we contacted were distrustful of the researchers' intent. In Nebraska and Florida, the initial mailing led to several threatening phone calls by respondents who were upset about our use of their home address, even though the addresses were obtained from the public sex offender registry. A few of the respondents threatened legal action against the researchers and the university if the contact did not cease immediately. Some respondents also contacted the department chair to further voice their aggravation with the research solicitation. In the end, no actions were taken against the university or researchers. Had legal action been taken, we were confident that we had abided by the conditions of the study as approved by the university's IRB and were therefore protected from legal liability. But we advise researchers studying registrant populations to consider consultation with a legal department prior to data collection, as there are laws prohibiting the harassment of convicted sex offenders that may create legal hazards for researchers.

Criminal populations are often distrustful of scholarly research and those conducting the surveying or interviewing, likely for good reason. Historically, criminal samples have been experimented on, subjected to harsh conditions, or mistreated by scientists (Blue, 2009; Lerner, 2007). This is particularly true for convicted and registered sex offenders who are publicly shamed and stigmatized by SORN laws, whose addresses are released to the public, and maps are often displayed to their homes. Credibility can be established through more frequent interactions between researchers and subjects, with the scholars indicating they are willing to listen to or read narratives without expressing judgment, and by conducting themselves as objective social scientists with the intentions of enhancing public safety.

Believe in Your Subjects

Scholars must come to trust the information subjects provide. Triangulating data sources, such as contact with registered offenders' significant others and family members, can help reduce the skepticism toward offender-provided data. Also, by including longitudinal data that discusses motives, life circumstances, and decision-making, scholars can judge the reliability with which subjects share experiences over time. Most importantly, scholars should understand that credibility is important not only to subjects' interactions with researchers, but also researchers' interactions with subjects.

Researchers must demonstrate they are willing to listen and understand subjects' narratives, are genuinely interested in subjects' experiences, and practice proper conversational etiquette including not interrupting subjects, looking at the faces of subjects, and respond only after verbal or non-verbal cues indicate the need to retort.

Challenge #3: Researcher Well-being

The third challenge of conducting research with registered sex offender populations relates to researchers' well-being. Regardless of whether subjects share narratives about their crimes and situations in the margins of a survey or while meeting face-to-face, registered offenders' narratives can be exhausting to read or hear and can evoke emotional responses in researchers that are forced to be hidden from subjects (Dickson-Swift, James, Kippen, & Liamputtong, 2006). Narrative research can and should change the researcher (Grafanaki, Brennan, Holmes, Tang, & Alvarez, 2007) as researchers learn more detail about the human condition. Most IRB boards will insist on safety plans for research staff when it comes to interacting with criminal populations in person, on the phone or over email. In Nebraska, although we did receive threats to sue researchers over unsolicited contact, we experienced no physical or phone confrontations with subjects. To ensure researcher staff's safety, all of our interviews were conducted at the University or in public spaces, personal phone numbers were never given to subjects, and two researchers were involved in interviews when initial contact with subjects indicated some mental illness. For instance, two interviewers were present when conducting life history interviews with a subject in Nebraska who believed every time he dialed the number seven on his phone he received a shock through his electronic monitor and when a Nebraska subject became outwardly anxious when researchers would not provide him legal advice. While IRB protocols are concerned with researchers' physical safety, less emphasis is placed on their emotional well-being.

In our experience, registrant subjects will sometimes over-share their sex crime experiences, leaving researchers with detailed sexual information about crimes. Even in the face of this information, we must strive to maintain awareness of our body language and our verbal expressions in order to ensure our subjects' continued comfort. For example, listening to a narrative about how a two-year-old child 'came on' to an adult male offender while maintaining a neutral expression and posture was mentally and emotionally exhausting. Other narratives we gathered included information about criminal convictions involving incest, molestation, fondling of children, as well as voyeurs, flashers, and people possessing child pornography. All of these can stimulate disgust that as researchers we could not share verbally or non-verbally with subjects. It took training and interview experience over time to learn to not show emotional reactions to research subjects, to not interrupt subjects as they spoke, and to avoid all non-verbal cues of disapproval (eyebrow raising, grimacing, etc.) when interacting face-to-face with subjects.

Mandatory Reporting

In Nebraska, we also encountered situations where we had to choose between our duties as scientists to ensure confidentiality and our duties as citizens, mandated to report any suspicion of ongoing child sexual abuse. Although this was not a common situation, we did encounter some information about crimes that were committed but for which subjects were not arrested, creating a question about breaking confidentiality. In this particular study, we never had to break confidentiality, since we were advised by legal that mandatory reporting required names of victims, suspected acts, and other details that we discouraged subjects from sharing. However, if we would have believed there was ongoing harm to children, we most certainly would have reported such to the police. We discussed this possibility at length in our researcher briefings, as we were all concerned about keeping the delicate balance of keeping our subject's trust but also fulfilling our legal obligations to public safety.

Anger

Beyond disgust, researchers also experience anger at subjects for a variety of reasons (Farrenkopf, 2008). The coldness with which subjects could relate their crimes as well as catching subjects in lies caused researchers to feel angry and somewhat betrayed. The advantage of qualitatively interviewing people over time is it increases the likelihood of discovering subjects' exaggerations and/or untruths. For instance, after interviewing the wife of a registrant at least twice, it was revealed by her that the current charges against her husband had not been his first. He had been apprehended and sentenced previously for possession of child pornography and had served two terms in federal prison. When trust appears to be established between subjects and researchers, the omission of information relevant to the study can make researchers feel angry and deceived. Equally likely is that through triangulation of information with official data or during interviews with family members, researchers will discover they have been given false information, or information that varies from that of law enforcement, spouses or significant others, and family members. In one example, a Nebraska registrant was interviewed, as were his wife and daughter (his victim). We had visible reactions in peer debriefings sessions (where the participants were not present) about the three very different versions of events. We were angry, disappointed, sad, and frustrated. The subject was quite contrite about his crimes, his wife was in denial that he ever committed a sex crime, and the daughter/victim clearly had not accepted apologies for her father's behavior, nor had she forgiven him for this actions as suggested by the registrant. These examples not only show the importance of triangulating sources of information but also how researchers can experience a range of emotions when receiving information directly from sex offender samples in the community either through interview or comments in the margins of surveys.

Blurring of Research Relationships

In all three studies, we learned that these subjects often perceived us more as advocates and friends rather than formal researchers. Part of this likely stems from the social isolation this population experiences (Bailey, 2017; ten Bensel & Sample, 2016), creating a need for people who will listen to their experiences in a non-judging manner, someone they can perceive as 'friends,' and who can acknowledge the difficulties of their lives as living as named 'sex offenders' in the community. The challenge that arose from these needs, however, was often a blurring of boundaries between the personal and professional. This was particular true in the Nebraska and Texas studies, where the coordination between subjects and advocacy groups created a stronger impression of partiality than was perhaps experienced in the Florida study. In both the Nebraska study and the Texas study, some of the research subjects began to see the researchers more as friends rather than professionals. We found ourselves offered shelter at sex offender–related conferences, invited out to drinks or lunch with research participants, and even in one case offered an overnight stay at a registrant's family member's house. This type of blending between the researcher role and the friend role is something commonly experienced by ethnographers, who find that living day to day with their subjects creates a stronger bond than the usual researcher to research subject bond (Taylor, 2011). Frequent subject initiated contact with researchers forced us to become intimately intertwined with the daily lives of subjects, including their daily ups and downs and their relationships, as would be found during a true ethnography study. It appears that because registrants believe no one cares about their situations, interaction with researchers who are willing to listen without outwardly demonstrating judgment or attempts to treat becomes a doorway to a perceived personal relationship by subjects that surpasses what most would consider science. This created challenges beyond those we observed for survey research.

Recommendations to Protect Researcher Well-being

Recognize Emotional Impact

One of the simplest ways to manage the challenge of researcher well-being is to remain aware of the emotional impact this type of research can have on researchers. In Nebraska, faced with 300 requests for interviews and only three primary interviewers, we tried to fit multiple interviews into a single day. We quickly learned that four interviews in a single day proved to be too much for researchers to mentally process and emotionally handle, and thereafter we limited the number of interviews or interactions with subjects in a single day. We found the same was true with written narratives. One researcher, whose role included analyzing online blogs of sex offender family members, found that it was best to limit the analysis to a single hour at a time because the emotional drain of the blog content was often just as disrupting as the emotional drain of a face to face interview. We also held regular peer debriefing sessions with our colleagues so that we could share our stories and discuss how subjects' narratives made us feel. This provided all researchers an outlet for any emotional trauma but still continued to protect the confidentiality of our subjects. Other suggestions to combat researchers' 'compassion stress' and fatigue include counseling, journal writing, and peer debriefing.

Maintain Professional Friendships

To avoid concerns over the loss of objectivity in our studies, our strategy in both Nebraska and Texas was to create and maintain 'professional friendships' with subjects, one which allows for personal information to be shared while still maintaining professional boundaries (Birch & Miller, 2000; Rossetto, 2014). This type of recommendation requires the application of emotional intelligence relating to qualitative research rather than the statistical skills of quantitative research. Although the therapeutic value of this type of research often decreases the social distance between researchers and subjects, by minimizing personal disclosure (Dickson-Swift et al., 2006), debriefing (Dickson-Swift et al., 2006), drawing back when responses become negative (Haynes, 2006), and always remembering our role as listeners, learners, and observers, not as counselors or therapists, we can keep an appropriate professional social distance between us and our subjects (Rossetto, 2014). For instance, we agreed to lunches if they were for a research-related purpose such as recruitment for the research study, discussion of future research directions, etc., but we did not accept invitations purely social in nature and always paid for our own meals.

Challenge #4: Subject Well-being

Surveys with both closed and open-ended questions, as well as interview methods, can both acknowledge and reaffirm registrants' status as 'sex offenders' in the community. When we seek out information from registrants in the community, are we further stigmatizing them or helping them find their voices? As we are ethically required to do, we must think about the effects research processes have on subjects, including sample recruitment, the sensitivity of the questions asked, and the methods by which we engage with subjects.

There are substantial differences between gathering information and facts from registrants living in the community for research purposes versus clinical interviews for treatment (Rossetto, 2014). As researchers, we approach our studies as 'data gathering' missions rather than 'treatment.' Researchers have more egalitarian rather than authoritative relationships with subjects than clinicians, and researchers are not responsible for stimulating behavior change like clinicians. With this being said, research seeking direct contact with subjects can and does have therapeutic effects for subjects beyond that found when working with secondary data (Rossetto, 2014). The sharing of stories and experiences with non-judgmental fact finding researchers is empowering for subjects, increases

their self-awareness (Weiss, 1994), helps them better understand their situations (Birch & Miller, 2000; MacKinnon, Michels, & Buckley, 2009), can change patterns of thinking (Pennebaker, 1997), and incite new perspectives and resolutions (Birch & Miller, 2000; Egan, 1994). In this way, there is some therapeutic value in soliciting information directly from subjects rather than analyzing existing data (Rossetto, 2014). As Glense and Peshkin (1992) explain, particularly during qualitative data collection researchers do not unwittingly assume the role of therapists, but can gather information in ways that are inherently therapeutic.

As mentioned above, the therapeutic value registered sex offenders can receive during research can lead to role confusion (Dickson-Swift et al., 2006; Weiss, 1994), blurring of professional boundaries (Birch & Miller, 2000; Eide & Kahn, 2008), and researchers becoming part of subjects' social control networks (Rossetto, 2014). Interactive interviewing, for instance, involves reciprocal sharing between investigators and subjects (Denzin, 2001; Ellis, Kiesinger, & Tillmann-Healy, 1997), thus often turning information into shared experiences. Subjects empowered by sharing their stories can be deeply affected when researchers are no longer willing to listen. This can be a particular problem for sex offender and sex offender family member populations, as these individuals are usually isolated from their communities and may lack other social support outlets to share their stories with (Bailey, 2017). Another concern relates to the mental health of the research participant. Although we are not clinicians, in all three studies we had interaction with individuals who appeared to express or who self-reported a mental health concern, including bi-polar disorders, manic depressive disorders, and suicidal ideation. Given that registrants in the community often have limited access to mental health care due to lack of insurance and lack of providers, it is important to recognize the impact of the research study, and its subsequent termination, on the participant in advance.

Recommendations to Protect Subject Well-Being

Remain Aware of Subjects' Mental State

As required by human subject IRB protocols, we included the name and number of a mental health agency on the consent form. However, the immediacy of our interaction with mentally ill registrants and family members required us to devise methods of dealing with symptom management in the course of an interview or other contact with the subject. For instance, non-verbal cues of crying, staring down at shoes, and avoiding eye contact often signaled depressive states during qualitative interviews. In those cases, we learned to quickly change the topic of conversation to something subjects previously indicated was a happy time or moment for them and encouraged them to restate these incidents of happiness, pride, and joy. During interviews, this did successfully change subject's affective states. Upon learning of suicidal ideation during interactions, we encouraged subjects to come back to interview the next day, or weekly, until subjects indicated they had entered a more positive mental state. Unbeknownst to researchers prior to interactions with registrants in the community, there appears to be a therapeutic value to sharing thoughts and emotions with people who subjects perceive as caring. Criminological researchers are rarely trained in counseling, so it was important to recognize signs of affective change among subjects and find ways to leave subjects more mentally healthy than when they began speaking. In most cases, the simple act of active listening, the use of non-verbal cues of empathy (head nods while subjects spoke), consoling words (e.g., that is a shame, etc.), and agreeing to meet subjects again for a follow-up interview was enough to address subjects' depressive states.

Plan When/How to End Research Relationships

It is important to consider your exit strategy when beginning research with sex offender populations in the community, especially if you are using qualitative methods. As discussed, researching this population can empower them. It is our hope that this effect lasts long after the research is complete. One way to address the challenges of withdrawing is to prepare them in advance of when the research will conclude and what services are available for them in the community. While maintaining rapport and professional boundaries, it would also be wise from time to time to remind subjects that within the next few months, researchers will no longer be able to listen to their narratives once the study ends and ask subjects who else they have in their lives to listen to their concerns, complaints, and experiences. As researchers, we should always be prepared to offer a list of therapists, organizations, and peer-to-peer support groups available in the community to pick up where researchers leave off.

There are professional counselors in the community who do work with sex offending populations, but these services often cost money that registrants do not have. A more economical solution is to look toward more informal approaches to registrant support, such as finding a peer support group, which can be found in most states through registered sex offender advocacy organizations working to reform sex offender laws. Many of these organizations can be accessed online (Bailey & Sample, 2017; ten Bensel & Sample, 2016) and are specifically interested in hearing the difficulties registrants face in communities. Through these organizations, registrants can find similarly situated people who will help them become activists if they so choose, will often listen to their concerns, and can provide them with information on opportunities in communities including employment, counseling, legal aid, etc.

Conclusions

This paper represents several years of research experiences that highlight the challenges in working with registered sex offender participants and their family members. The three research projects, both qualitative and quantitative in nature, were conducted in three states (Nebraska, Texas, and Florida) with relatively large sex offender populations. While none of those states are in full compliance with the federal Adam Walsh Act, Florida is reported to be substantively compliant (National Conference of State Legislatures [NCSL], 2014). This suggests differences in the state-by-state use of SORN laws. As no state SORN laws are exactly identical, we are presented with fifty different versions of the same legislative efforts. This makes it difficult to compare research on a state-by-state basis, and makes it difficult to compare the experiences of individuals across states. While the previously mentioned challenges and recommendations are based on Nebraska, Texas, and Florida samples other researchers may experience different difficulties in researching this offender group.

Just as state legislative efforts are different across the country, so too are the sex offender populations found in these states. Geographic differences, registration length, population sizes, political ideations, and punitive law enforcement practices may all have an effect on the experiences of the registered sex offenders living in that state. While we cannot be sure that our research experiences will be generalizable to others, it is important to continue researching this offender group. In particular, using mixed method approaches may be the most effective way of collecting data from this group. Qualitative surveys certainly allow for larger sample sizes and more comparable data points, but researchers must keep in mind that registered sex offenders rarely complete quantitative surveys without providing additional information in qualitative form as suggested by the unsolicited data collected in our three studies.

Researchers have to gain the trust of their participants in order to successfully collect data by either quantitative or qualitative means. Part of gaining that trust is through allowing participants to tell their stories, even if they are not as unique as the participant claims. Registered sex offenders do not want to be boxed in, or contained to a Likert scale response. This may be the only opportunity for some to voice their concerns, frustrations, or fears regarding life dominated by SORN legislation. At times, we must allow this group to guide the conversation themselves and speak to the experiences salient to their own lives.

Ethical Approval

All procedures performed in studies involving human participants were in accordance with the ethical standards of the institution and/or national research committee and with the 1964 Helsinki declaration and its later amendments or comparable ethical standards. This article does not contain any studies with animals performed by any of the authors.

Note

1. This quotation was taken verbatim from participant correspondence, with all typos and language uncorrected.

Discussion Questions

1. Given what the authors of this article learned, what seems to be the best type of data collection approach for collecting data from sex offenders? Why?
2. What are some of the ethical issues that arose during data collection?
3. What are some ideas to help maintain the physical safety and emotional well-being of the research staff?

References

Ackerman, A. R., Sacks, M., & Osier, L. N. (2013). The experiences of registered sex offenders with internet offender registries in three states. *Journal of Offender Rehabilitation*, *52*, 29–45.

Adam Walsh Act of 2006, Public Law No. 109–248 (2006).

Adelman, C., Jenkins, D., & Kemmis, S. (1980). Rethinking case study: Notes from the second Cambridge conference. In H. Simons (Ed.), *Towards a science of the singular* (pp. 45–61). Norwich: Center for Applied Research in Education, University of East Anglia.

Bailey, D. J. S. (2017). A life of grief: An exploration of disenfranchised grief in sex offender significant others. *American Journal of Criminal Justice*. Advance online publication. https://doi.org/10.1007/s12103-017-9416-4

Bailey, D. J. S., & Sample, L. L. (2017). An examination of a cycle of coping with strain among registered citizens' families. *Criminal Justice Studies.* Advance online publication. https://doi.org/10.1 080/1478601X.2017.1299286

Beauregard, E., & Leclerc, B. (2007). An application of the rational choice approach to the offending process of sex offenders: A closer look at the decision-making. *Sexual Abuse: A Journal of Research and Treatment, 19,* 115–133.

Birch, M., & Miller, T. (2000). Inviting intimacy: The interview as therapeutic opportunity. *International Journal of Social Research and Methodology, 3*(3), 189–202.

Blair, E., & Burton, S. (1987). Cognitive processes used by survey respondents to answer behavioral frequency questions. *Journal of Consumer Research, 14*(2), 280–288.

Blue, E. (2009). The strange career of Leo Stanley: Remaking manhood and medicine at San Quentin State Penitentiary, 1913–1951. *Pacific Historical Review, 78*(2), 210–241.

Brown, K., Spencer, J., & Deakin, J. (2007). The reintegration of sex offenders: Barriers and opportunities for employment. *The Howard Journal of Criminal Justice, 46,* 32–42.

Burchfield, K. B., & Mingus, W. (2008). Not in my neighborhood: Assessing registered sex offenders' experiences with local social capital and social control. *Criminal Justice and Behavior, 35,* 356–374.

Burchfield, K. B., Sample, L. L., & Lytle, R. (2014). Public interest in sex offenders: A perpetual panic? *Criminology, Criminal Justice Law, & Society, 15*(3), 96–117.

Burck, C. (2005). Comparing qualitative research methodologies for systemic research: The use of grounded theory, discourse analysis and narrative analysis. *Journal of Family Therapy, 27*(3), 237–262.

Collwell, L. H., Miller, H. A., Miller, R. S., & Lyons, P. M., Jr. (2006). U.S. police officers' knowledge regarding behaviors indicative of deception: Implications for eradicating erroneous beliefs through training. *Psychology, Crime & Law, 12,* 489–503.

Colorado Department of Public Safety. (2004). *Report on safety issues raised by living arrangements for and location of sex offenders in the community.* Denver, CO: Sex Offender Management Board.

Denzin, N. K. (2001). The reflexive interview and performative social science. *Qualitative Research, 1,* 23–46.

Dickson-Swift, V., James, E. L., Kippen, S., & Liamputtong, P. (2006). Blurring boundaries in qualitative health research on sensitive topics. *Qualitative Health Research, 16*(6), 853–871.

Dickson-Swift, V., James, E. L., Kippen, S., & Liamputtong, P. (2007). Doing sensitive research:

What challenges do qualitative researchers face? *Qualitative Research, 7*(3), 327–353.

Egan, G. (1994). *The skilled helper: A problem-management approach to helping.* Pacific Grove, CA: Brooks/Cole.

Eide, P., & Kahn, D. (2008). Ethical issues in the qualitative researcher—participant relationship. *Nursing Ethics, 15*(2), 199–207.

Ellis, C., Kiesinger, C. E., & Tillmann-Healy, L. M. (1997). Interactive interviewing: Talking about emotional experiences. In R. Hertz (Ed.), *Reflexivity and voice* (pp. 119–149). Thousand Oaks, CA: Sage.

Evans, D. N., & Cubellis, M. A. (2015). Coping with Stigma: How registered sex offenders manage their public identities. *American Journal of Criminal Justice, 40*(3), 593–619.

Farrenkopf, T. (2008). What happens to therapists who work with sex offenders? *Journal of Offender Rehabilitation, 18*(3–4), 217–224. https://doi.org/10.1300/J076v18n03_16

Glense, C., & Peshkin, A. (1992). *Becoming qualitative researchers: An introduction.* White Plains, NY: Longman.

Göbbels, S., Ward, T., & Willis, G. M. (2012). An integrative theory of desistance from sex offending. *Aggression and Violent Behavior, 17*(5), 453–462.

Grafanaki, S., Brennan, M., Holmes, S., Tang, K., & Alvarez, S. (2007). In search of flow in counseling and psychotherapy: Identifying the necessary ingredients of peak moments of therapy interaction. *Person-Centered & Experiential Psychotherapies, 6*(4), 240–255. https://doi.org/10.1080/14779757.2007.9688445

Jackson, K. M., & Trochim, W. M. K. (2002). Concept mapping as an alternative approach for the analysis of open-ended survey responses. *Organizational Research Methods, 5*(4), 307–336.

Jacob Wetterling Act of 1994, Public Law No. 103–322. (1994).

Johnson, R., & Waterfield, J. (2004). Making words count: The value of qualitative research. *Physiotherapy Research International, 9*(3), 121–131.

Klein, J. L. (2016). The media response to sex crime. In T. Sanders (Ed.), *The Oxford handbook on sex offences and sex offenders: Confronting and challenging the issues* (pp. 482–497). Oxford: Oxford University Press.

Klein, J. L., Rukus, J., & Zambrana, K. (2012). Do experienced behaviors lead to increased shame and strain for registered female sex offenders? *Justice Policy Journal, 9*(2), 1–35.

Klein, J. L., Tolson, D., & Collins, C. (2014). Lamenting the list: A partial test of Sherman's defiance theory as applied to female sex offenders. *Contemporary Justice Review: Issues in Criminal, Social and Restorative Justice, 17*(3), 326–345.

Kruttschnitt, C., Uggen, C., & Shelton, K. (2000). Predictors of desistance among sex offenders: The interaction of formal and informal social controls. *Justice Quarterly*, *17*, 61–87.

Lasher, M. P., & McGrath, R. J. (2012). The impact of community notification on sex offender reintegration: A quantitative review of the research literature. *International Journal of Offender Therapy and Comparative Criminology*, *56*, 6–28.

Lerner, B. H. (2007). Subjects or objects? Prisoners and human experimentation. *New England Journal of Medicine*, *356*(18), 1806–1807.

Levenson, J. S. (2007). The new scarlet letter: Sex offender policies in the 21st century. In D. Prescott (Ed.), *Applying knowledge to practice: Challenges in the treatment and supervision of sexual abuses* (pp. 21–41). Oklahoma City, OK: Wood and Barnes Publishing.

Levenson, J. S., D'Amora, D. A., & Hern, A. L. (2007). Megan's law and its impact on community re-entry for sex offenders. *Behavioral Sciences & the Law*, *25*, 587–602.

Levenson, J. S., & Tewksbury, R. (2009). Collateral damage: Family members of registered sex offenders. *American Journal of Criminal Justice*, *34*, 54–68.

Lussier, P., Blokland, A., Mathesius, J., Pardini, D., & Loeber, R. (2013). The childhood risk factors of adolescent-onset and adult-onset of sex offending: Evidence from a prospective longitudinal study. In A. Blokland & P. Lussier (Eds.), *Sex offenders: A career criminal approach* (1st ed., pp. 93–128). Hoboken, NJ: Wiley.

Lussier, P., Corrado, R. R., & McCuish, E. (2016). A criminal career study of the continuity and discontinuity of sex offending during the adolescence-adulthood transition: A prospective longitudinal study of incarcerated youth. *Justice Quarterly*, *33*(7), 1123–1153.

MacKinnon, R. A., Michels, R., & Buckley, P. J. (2009). *The psychiatric interview in clinical practice* (2nd ed.). Washington, DC: American Psychiatric Publishing.

Malinen, S., Willis, G. M., & Johnston, L. (2014). Might informative media reporting of sexual offending influence community members' attitudes towards sex offenders? *Psychology, Crime & Law*, *20*(6), 535–552.

Mathesius, J., & Lussier, P. (2014). The successful onset of sex offending: Determining the correlates of actual and official onset of sex offending. *Journal of Criminal Justice*, *42*(2), 134–144.

Maxfield, M. G., & Babbie, E. R. (2015). *Research methods for criminal justice and criminology* (7th ed.). Stamford, CT: Cengage Learning.

Medlicott, D. (2004). Condemned to artifice and prevent from becoming a pirate: How prisoners convicted of terrible crimes recognize themselves in discourse. In R. Hamilton & M. Breen (Eds.), *This thing of darkness: Perspectives on evil and human wickedness* (pp. 78–92). Amsterdam: Rodopi. Megan's Law of 1996, Public Law No. 104–145. (1996).

Monahan, B., Marolla, J., & Bromley, D. (2005). Constructing coercion: The organization of sexual assault. *Journal of Contemporary Ethnography*, *34*, 284–316.

Myers, M. (2000). Qualitative research and the generalizability question: Standing firm with proteus. *The Qualitative Report*, *4*(3), 1–12.

National Conference of State Legislatures. (2014). *Adam Walsh Child Protection and Safety Act*. Retrieved from www.ncsl.org/research/civil-and-criminal-justice/adam-walsh-child-protection-and-safety-act.aspx

Orb, A., Eisenhauer, L., & Wynaden, D. (2001). Ethics in qualitative research. *Journal of Nursing Scholarship*, *33*(1), 93–96.

Payne, B. K., & DeMichele, M. (2008). Warning: Sex offenders need to be supervised in the community. *Federal Probation*, *72*(1), 37.

Pennebaker, J. W. (1997). *Opening up: The healing power of expressing emotions*. New York, NY: Guilford.

Ross, L. (1977). The intuitive psychologist and his shortcomings: Distortions in the attribution process. In L. Berkowitz (Ed.), *Advances in experimental social psychology* (Vol. 10., pp. 173–220). New York, NY: Academic Press.

Rossetto, K. R. (2014). Qualitative research interviews: Assessing the therapeutic value and challenges. *Journal of Social and Personal Relationships*, *31*(4), 482–489.

Sandelowski, M. (2000). Whatever happened to qualitative description? *Research in Nursing & Health*, *23*(4), 334–340.

Sandler, J. C., Freeman, N. J., & Socia, K. M. (2008). Does a watched pot boil? A time-series analysis of New York State's sex offender registration and notification law. *Psychology, Public Policy and Law*, *14*(4), 284–302.

Scheper-Hughes, N. (2004). Parts unknown: Undercover ethnography of the organs-trafficking underworld. *Ethnography*, *5*, 29–73.

Socia, K. M., Levenson, J. S., Ackerman, A. R., & Harris, A. J. (2015). "Brothers under the bridge": Factors influencing the transience of registered sex offenders in Florida. *Sexual Abuse: A Journal of Research and Treatment*, *27*, 559–586.

Taylor, J. (2011). The intimate insider: Negotiating the ethics of friendship when doing insider research. *Qualitative Research*, *11*(1), 3–22.

ten Bensel, T., & Sample, L. L. (2016). Social inclusion despite exclusionary sex offense laws: How registered citizens cope with loneliness. *Criminal Justice Policy Review*. Advance online publication. https://doi.org/10.1177/0887403416675018

Tewksbury, R. (2004). Experiences and attitudes of registered female sex offenders. *Federal Probation, 68*, 30–33.

Tewksbury, R. (2005). Collateral consequences of sex offender registration. *Journal of Contemporary Criminal Justice, 21*, 67–81.

Tewksbury, R. (2011). Stigmatization of sex offenders. *Deviant Behavior, 33*(8), 606–623.

Tewksbury, R., & Jennings, W. G. (2010). Assessing the impact of sex offender registration and community notification on sex-offending trajectories. *Criminal Justice and Behavior, 37*(5), 570–582.

Tewksbury, R., & Lees, M. B. (2006). Perceptions of sex offender registration: Collateral consequences and community experiences. *Sociological Spectrum, 26*(3), 309–334.

Tewksbury, R., & Zgoba, K. M. (2010). Perceptions and coping with punishment: How registered sex offenders respond to stress, internet restrictions, and the collateral consequences of registration. *International Journal of Offender Therapy and Comparative Criminology, 54*, 537–551.

Tolson, D., & Klein, J. L. (2015). Registration, residency restrictions, and community notification: A social capital perspective on the isolation of registered sex offenders in our communities. *Journal of Human Behavior in the Social Environment, 25*, 375–390.

Vandiver, D. M., & Walker, J. T. (2002). female sex offenders: An overview and analysis of 40 cases. *Criminal Justice Review, 27*, 284–300.

Vasquez, B. E., Maddan, S., & Walker, J. T. (2008). The influence of sex offender registration and notification laws in the United States: A time-series analysis. *Crime & Delinquency, 4*(4), 175–192.

Waldram, J. B. (2007). Everybody has a story: Listening to imprisoned sexual offenders. *Qualitative Health Research, 17*, 963–970.

Webb, V. J., Katz, C., & Decker, S. H. (2006). Assessing the validity of self-reports by gang members: Results from the arrestee drug abuse monitoring program. *Crime and Delinquency, 52*(2), 232–252.

Weiss, R. S. (1994). *Learning from strangers: The art and method of qualitative interview studies*. New York, NY: The Free Press.

Zaller, J., & Feldman, S. (1992). A simple theory of the survey response: Answering questions versus revealing preferences. *American Journal of Political Science, 36*(3), 579–616.

Zevitz, R. G., Crim, D., & Farkas, M. A. (2000). Sex offender community notification: Managing high risk criminals or exacting further vengeance? *Behavioral Sciences and the Law, 18*, 375–391.

4 Causation, Experimental, and Quasi-Experimental Designs

So far, we explained how the process of research that we might do to shop for a new computer differs from the strict rules associated with empirical research following the scientific method. We now also know about ethics and research, something that we must consider at all stages of planning and implementation of our studies. At this point, we are ready to dive into an exploration of different ways to do research. One thing that will become abundantly clear very quickly is that not all research is equal when it comes to quality. Research designs each have their own strengths and weaknesses. The selection of a design impacts the types of conclusions that we will be able to draw from the findings. Then why don't we always just select the best design and do that? That is not always possible for a variety of reasons that you will appreciate by the end of this book. The important thing for you to learn is that each design has its own pros and cons. Learning this will make you so much better prepared not only to recognize what works and what does not in criminal justice, but also to evaluate the quality of research in other fields.

A great lesson of the power of comprehending research can be learned by observing the dissemination of information about COVID-19 during the 2020 pandemic. So many different groups shared claims about how it spreads, the accuracy of testing, and possible treatments. What should we believe? A good starting point would be to use what you learned about the quality of sources in Chapter 2 to begin screening items by source and author. The next step is to apply what you are going to learn in the rest of this book, but particularly in the next two chapters, to understand the quality of research. After taking these two steps, you should be able to distinguish good research from poorly designed work and flat-out pseudoscience.

The first step that we are going to take in this chapter is to learn about the difference between finding a relationship between two variables (correlation or association) and finding that a modification to one variable *causes* change to another variable. Next, I will review factors that might impact the internal validity, generalizability, and external validity of research. Finally, I will discuss a few high-quality research designs.

Correlation Versus Causation

Did you know that, as the US government's spending on science, space, and technology increases, so do suicides by hanging, strangulation, and suffocation (Figure 4.1)? It is a strong correlation too. How about another cause of death—dying due to becoming tangled in bedsheets? There is a very strong correlation between that and per capita cheese consumption (Figure 4.2) (Vigen, n.d.). What should we make of this? Many of you are entering the field of criminal justice because you want to keep people safe. These are really strong correlations, and people are dying, so should we confiscate all the cheese to keep people safe from their bedsheets? What about a return trip to the moon or a trip to Mars? Will that increase suicides in the United States? Of course not! You should not knock grilled cheese sandwiches out of strangers' hands in the name of saving lives. Additionally, I very much want us to explore space, and I am not afraid that increased exploration of space will result in a suicide epidemic here on Earth.

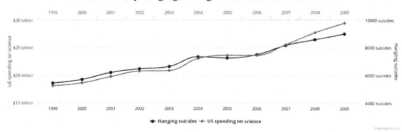

Figure 4.1 Correlation Between US Spending on Science, Space, and Technology and Suicides by Hanging, Strangulation, and Suffocation

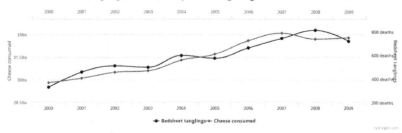

Figure 4.2 Correlation Between Per Capita Cheese Consumption and Number of People Who Died by Becoming Tangled in Their Bedsheets

How can I be so confident of that, especially when lives are at stake? One possibility is that I'm just one of those people who buys into Mark Twain's famous "There's lies, damned lies, and statistics" statement and believe that these findings are made up by some researcher with an axe to grind against space exploration and cheese. That certainly is not the case, as I also teach statistics classes and understand that the math behind these statistical findings is solid. I am confident that we will not see a rise in suicides and deaths by bedsheet because I understand that correlation does *not* equal causation. Failure to distinguish between correlation and causation is one of the biggest mistakes that people make when interpreting research results. If you want to see a great example of this, pick any news show that gives updates on recent health research. One day, coffee will be linked to increased chances of getting certain types of cancer. The next day, coffee will be linked to reduced chances of getting certain types of cancer. What gives? What they aren't telling you in that 60-second clip is that these are likely merely correlations. It doesn't mean that your morning cup of coffee is the one thing that will lead to cancer. The fact that correlation doesn't always mean that one thing causes the other is certainly good news for the ice cream industry, since there is a positive correlation between ice cream consumption and crime (Salkind, 2014). Why? Before you abstain from your favorite pint of ice cream in the name of public safety, let's learn a little about hypothesis testing.

Hypothesis Testing and the First Element of Causation—Relationships Between Two Variables

As was discussed in Chapter 1, hypotheses are predictions of relationships between variables. They are the researchers' educated guesses about what they will find when they collect and analyze data. Researchers construct hypotheses after they have considered theories and what we already know about topics in criminal justice. For example, therapeutic communities (TCs) were originally created to help veterans returning from World War II who were having difficulty adapting to civilian life (Lipton, 1998). TCs use therapeutic techniques and role playing to help individuals modify problematic behavior so they can live successfully in the community. After finding evidence that these programs were associated with positive outcomes in the military community, researchers considered what they know about learning theory and, using deductive reasoning, hypothesized that application of the TC model to drug-addicted and criminal-offending populations would be associated with reduced drug use and offending.

Hypotheses predict relationships between independent and dependent variables. **Independent variables** are known as the predictor, treatment, or cause of something and often go by the abbreviation X or IV, while **dependent variables** are thought to be the outcome or effect and go by Y or DV. **Research hypotheses** predict that there will be a relationship between the independent and dependent variables. For the TC example, our research hypothesis would be that those who complete the therapeutic community program will be less likely to recidivate, or reoffend, within one year following program completion than those who did not complete the program. In this example, the independent variable is treatment participation, while the dependent variable is recidivism. In contrast to our research hypothesis, the **null hypothesis** predicts that there is no relationship between X and Y. In other words, completion of the therapeutic community program will *not* be associated with reduced odds of recidivism. In quantitative research, we conduct statistical analysis on data to test the null hypothesis. If we find enough evidence to confidently reject the null hypothesis, we are, by default, stating that we found support for the research hypothesis. If we do *not* find evidence to reject the null hypothesis, however, we fail to reject (but do not accept!) the null hypothesis. Think of it like jury deliberations. The jury never declares the defendant innocent. Rather, they either find the person guilty or not guilty. We handle hypotheses the same way by rejecting or failing to reject the null hypothesis.

If we do decide to reject the null hypothesis and conclude that there is support for our research hypothesis, can we state that our X causes Y? Absolutely not! But why not? All we have accomplished thus far is establishing that X and Y are related. Completion of the TC program is associated with reduced recidivism. The problem is that a relationship between the independent and dependent variables is just one element of **causation**. What we accomplished by finding a relationship between X and Y is we found an association or **correlation** between the two. That is a good first step, but we are nowhere near establishing causation. Before I get to the other two requirements of causation, I want to discuss a little more about what we are accomplishing with hypothesis testing using statistics.

As I noted in Chapter 1, in quantitative research, we obtain large samples and conduct statistical analysis with the goal of seeking patterns, or what Maxfield and Babbie (2012) call regularities. Patterns or regularities reflect trends across the cases being studied and show us what is happening in most, but certainly not all, cases. Revisiting the therapeutic community example from earlier in this chapter, we will search for a pattern indicating that TC participation is associated with reduced recidivism, but even if the program is found to be helpful, there will often be exceptions and outliers. Exceptions and outliers are common in the social sciences since we are dealing with human behavior.

Here is an example that should illustrate why predicting human behavior is so much more difficult than making predictions in other fields. Pawson and Tilley (1997) highlight differences between social science research and the natural sciences and mathematics by noting that natural scientists and mathematicians can prove things. For example, we can prove that flipping a switch will always lead to the lightbulb turning on, provided that all conditions (circuitry, etc.) are correctly arranged. That is because, in the natural sciences, we know what conditions need to be present to make a lightbulb work. Mathematicians conduct **proofs** that demonstrate that there are logically guaranteed conclusions in their field. Two plus two will always equal four, and that is an absolute certainty each time someone attempts addition. Phenomena studied by social scientists are less predictable. Humans do not behave the same way as light switches and circuitry. If a dozen people are exposed to the same stressor—walking into a bedroom and finding one's spouse in bed with one's best friend—we are likely to see different reactions from each person. We can set up a rehabilitation program that is evidence based, staff it with credentialed professionals who implement that program exactly as planned, and fill it with clients who meet the admission criteria, and yet the program will rehabilitate some people but not others. The aforementioned conditions *should* lead to reduced recidivism and likely will for a substantial number of people, but it is not nearly as certain as when we flip a light switch.

Given the complexity of human behavior, our research on the outcomes of a successful rehabilitation program will provide evidence that the program improved offenders' chances of succeeding but does not present us with a 100 percent guarantee that it will address the problem we are seeking to solve. Our delinquency research indicates that children who come from poverty and unstable homes are more likely to engage in delinquency, but some students who come from such backgrounds emerge from their teenage years crime free and quite successful. So the best we can do is find evidence of regularities among a large amount of cases, or **aggregates**, rather than focusing on individual exceptions.

The decision whether to reject or fail to reject the null hypothesis is made based on probability. After collecting data, we use statistics to test our hypotheses. The tricky aspect of statistics is that we can never be 100 percent confident in our results, as there is always the possibility that any difference we are seeing between our groups is a product of a sampling error rather than an actual relationship between X and Y. Of course, researchers are always looking to minimize error, and we work to do so by careful sample selection. The possibility of error in statistics is why social scientists use less committal terms when describing their study results. Social scientists never claim that their results "prove" anything, nor do we declare that we have determined "X causes Y." If anyone is making such claims, be very suspicious.

Time Order—The Second Requirement for Causation

We did our hypothesis testing, ran our statistical analysis, and feel comfortable that we found a relationship between TC participation (our independent variable, or X) and reduced recidivism (our dependent variable, or Y). Despite all this work, we are now only one-third of the way to being able to conclude that that X causes Y. The second requirement is determining the time order between X and Y. If we are to claim that our independent variable causes a change in the dependent variable, X must come before Y in time. For our TC example, that is easy; we are looking at recidivism after people completed the program, so time order is built into the study. Unfortunately, it is not always so simple in criminal justice. Two examples that illustrate the importance of establishing the time order of X and Y are drug use and crime and home security system ownership and burglary.

There are a number of theories that seek to explain the relationship between drug use and crime. Bennett, Holloway, and Farrington (2008) identified three categories of drug-crime theories, including those that (1) suggest a direct causal connection between drug use and crime; (2) posit an indirect causal connection, meaning that other variables cause both; or (3) suggest there is no causal connection. The first group of theories suggest that either drug use causes criminal behavior or criminal behavior causes drug use. Bennett et al. (2008) reviewed and analyzed the results of 30 empirical studies of drug use and crime and found that there is a strong association between the two. The odds of offending tended to be 2.8 to 3.8 times higher for drug users than non-users, and these results varied by drug type. That is rather strong evidence of a relationship between drug use and crime, but which comes first: the drug use or the criminal behavior? Research results have been mixed, and there is currently no clear answer to this question.

Research on burglary and crime presents us with a similar dilemma. Contrary to what you might think, the research suggests that burglar alarm ownership is actually associated with greater odds of victimization (Roth, Lee, & Joo, 2018; Tseloni, Thompson, Grove, Tilley, & Farrell, 2014). What does this mean? Do burglar alarms make us *less* safe? It is difficult to tell. We know that there is a positive relationship between alarm ownership and burglary, but we do not know the time order. It could be that the presence of a burglar alarm signals to potential burglars that there are valuables worth protecting in a house, but only if the alarms were installed before the burglaries. Another possible explanation is that these houses installed the burglar alarms after they were victimized, which is why it appears that houses with burglar alarms have more burglaries. Without knowing whether the burglaries or the alarm installations occurred first, our understanding of the relationship between the two is very limited.

Accounting for All Other Possible Explanations—The Third Requirement for Causation

The third element of causation is accounting for any other possible variable that could explain the relationship between X and Y. Remember that our consumption of ice cream is related to increases in crime. Eating ice cream does not cause crime, of course. It just looks that way because there is a spurious relationship. **Spurious relationships** are those that are not genuine. What is happening here is that both X (ice cream) and Y (crime) are related to a third variable (Z)—the weather. Warmer weather prompts us to crave ice cream, but it also encourages us to change our behavior patterns and get out more. As we become more active, we leave our belongings at home, unattended, creating greater opportunity for burglary. We also interact more with other people, presenting the possibilities of assault and robbery. According to the routine activities perspective, when we have the convergence in time and space of a motivated offender, suitable target, and the absence of a capable guardian, crime is more likely to occur (Cohen & Felson, 1979). So, as the weather gets warmer and we change our routines, there is more opportunity for crime. Statisticians who check for correlations between factors such as ice cream and crime or margarine consumption and divorce rates (Vigen, n.d.) without considering other possibilities cannot assert that the correlation is equivalent to causation until all other explanations are considered. These other possibilities are called **rival causal factors** (Z), defined as any variable other than X that may be responsible for the relationship with Y. The presence of these other variables or possible rival causal factors is known as **threats to internal validity** (TIVs) (Hagan, 2007).

Threats to Internal Validity

Threats to internal validity are any factors, besides the independent variable, that exert influence on our dependent variable. We cannot conclude that X causes Y while there are other variables that are producing variation in Y. According to Cook and Campbell (1979), there are several threats to internal validity. Here is a short summary of them:

History

History refers to events external to the research that can influence the results. Imagine that you are studying a school district as it overhauls its school security procedures with the hope that it will increase both actual safety and students' perceptions of safety. You conduct a pretest of students' opinions of their safety before the administration starts to implement the changes to get a baseline. After the overhaul, you conduct the posttest and find that students are more fearful now. Did the security measures backfire? Maybe. Another possible explanation might be a historical event impacted opinions. If the pretest was administered around a time when there were no publicized school shootings, but the posttest took place within a week of a shooting that received extensive media coverage, the publicity could be what impacted students' assessment of their own safety, not the new safety measures.

Testing Effects

Testing may become more of a problem the more often respondents are asked to take the test. If people are asked to take both a pretest and a posttest, the pretest content might sensitize participants to the purpose of the study. This might increase their motivation or arouse their interest, resulting in enhanced performance on the posttest that has nothing to do with the impact of the independent variable on the dependent variable. In other words, the pretest, not the X, influenced the outcome.

Instrumentation

Instrumentation refers to a change in a data collection tool, resulting in difficulty comparing information across time. The National Crime Victimization Survey (NCVS) is the largest source of victimization data in the United States, with researchers conducting 240,000 interviews on criminal victimization each year. NVCS has been in existence since 1973, but over the years, the Bureau of Justice Statistics (BJS) has found it necessary to conduct multiple redesigns of their survey instrument. One major redesign that had a substantial impact on victimization estimates took place in 1992. BJS adjusted questions to allow for better stimulation of respondents' memories and asked additional questions to elicit more responses about sexual victimization and domestic violence. These changes resulted in increased victimization reporting. Someone who was unaware of this change might look at NCVS statistics over time and incorrectly assume that there was a substantial crime wave in the early 1990s. Fortunately, NCVS makes it very clear in their data tables that year-to-year changes during this time period likely reflect instrumentation rather than a surge in victimization (Kinderman, Lynch, & Cantor, 1997).

Statistical Regression

Inclusion of people with extremely high or low pretest scores in research will likely result in some movement of their scores toward the group mean by the second testing, regardless of the planned intervention. This is known as **statistical regression** or regression to the mean. The same goes for neighborhoods or prisons that are selected for study due to their high rates of crimes and disciplinary infractions. Farrington and Welsh (2006) found that, when selecting a high-crime area for a crime prevention initiative and using a control area with a moderate-crime rate, statistical regression accounted for about 4 percent of the crime reduction in the high-crime area from the pretest time to posttest. Grambsch (2008) studied homicide rates in states throughout the US from 1976 through 2001. Between 1981 and 1996, 25 states passed shall-issue laws that require states to issue permits to carry concealed weapons to all residents meeting certain criteria. Previous research touted these laws as producing a reduction in homicide rates. Grambsch found declines in homicides not only in states that passed shall-issue laws, but also in states that did not. In fact, those that had not passed such laws experienced greater reductions in homicide rates over the 25-year period. Grambsch concluded that the apparent relationship between shall-issue laws and declines in homicides is more of a product of regression to the mean than of substantial policy changes.

Selection (Sample) Bias

The manner in which we seek and accept participants for studies is a threat to internal validity when it produces a sample that is unlike the population from which it was drawn or when we wind up comparing groups that are nonequivalent. Comparing recidivism rates of people who were sentenced to prison to those who were sentenced to probation is problematic because there is a reason judges deemed some people to require incarceration while others were considered safe enough to be placed on community supervision. If we find that the ex-prisoners recidivated more often, it will be difficult to determine whether it was due to the harms caused by incarceration or if they were already higher-risk individuals.

Mortality

Studies that involve multiple periods of data collection or tracking people over time are likely to lose participants. This is known as **mortality**, and it can arise for numerous reasons. People who initially agreed to participate in the research might lose interest in the study and drop out. They might move out of the area, be released from incarceration, or otherwise become ineligible for continued study participation. Sometimes people also pass away. Not only does mortality make data analysis more difficult due to its impact on the sample size, but it can be especially problematic if certain types of individuals are more likely than others to withdraw or disappear. Imagine you want to study drug use and delinquency among high school students. You decide to do a panel study, which means you are going to collect data from the same group of people multiple times: in this instance, at the start of every school year. Data collection is taking place in the school, so students must be enrolled and present on the data collection days to participate. Over four years, you will lose students for a variety of reasons, but you are likely to lose more with higher involvement in drug use and delinquency as they are more likely to be suspended, be expelled, be sent to another school, or skip school. The result is that you will likely have higher mortality levels for individuals who are more involved in delinquency, resulting in a likely underestimation of drug use and criminal involvement of juveniles.

Maturation

Maturation can threaten the validity of findings when biological or psychological changes result in different performance or responses from pretest to posttest. Children become physically stronger as they enter adolescence. Teenagers become impulsive risk-takers, but that behavior changes as they transition to adulthood. Changes observed during the course of research can be a product of maturation rather than exposure to the independent variable.

Selection-Maturation Interaction

The two threats of selection bias and maturation can combine to be problematic when groups are selected unevenly, resulting in maturation impacting groups at different times. Fletcher and Tims (1992) caution that **selection-maturation** can be a problem in drug treatment evaluations as people with greater maturity and fewer psychological challenges might be more predisposed to enter and remain in treatment, introducing a factor other than treatment efficacy that can explain outcomes. A study involving juveniles would have selection-maturation problems if the experimental and comparison or control groups were different ages. The group with an average age of 17 might start changing as a result of the natural maturation process much earlier than the group with an average age of 15.

Diffusion of Treatment

For an experimental design to be carried out effectively, the control group must not be exposed to the experimental treatment stimulus. Otherwise, when comparing experimental and control groups, we are unlikely to see any difference in posttest results. In criminal justice, this has the potential to be a problem when practitioners are so hopeful or confident that a new treatment is going to be effective that they quietly start to use it with all their clients instead of leaving the control group to treatment as usual or no treatment at all. **Diffusion of the treatment** stimulus to the control group is also referred to as contamination.

Compensatory Equalization of Treatment

There may be legitimate ethical concerns about withholding treatment from a group of people, and, to combat this, it might be tempting for criminal justice professionals to provide extra services or perks to the control group, making their experiences close to or on par with those of the treatment group. During the classic **Kansas City Preventive Patrol Experiment**, researchers and the police department arranged for some parts of Kansas City to get extra police patrols (proactive beats); others were going to get normal routine patrols (control beats), while a third area would only get police attention when someone called for assistance (reactive beats). The researchers found no differences in crime rates in the three areas, nor did residents in the three beats notice differences in police behavior (Kelling, Pate, Diekman, & Brown, 1974). One drawback to the study, however, was that police officers had the discretion to engage in "patrol-initiated activity" in the control beats, and they seemed to do so very frequently, to the point that there was little difference in the observed levels of police presence in the different areas (Larson, 1975).

Compensatory Rivalry and Demoralization/Resentment

Compensatory rivalry can arise when the experimental and control groups are aware of each other's presence, and the control group attempts to outperform the experimental group or otherwise portray itself in a better light. **Demoralization** is the opposite, when members of the control group become discouraged and experience reduced productivity and morale in the face of their deprivation relative to the experimental group.

Statistical Conclusion Validity

Maxfield and Babbie (2012) define **statistical conclusion validity** as "whether we are able to determine if two variables are related" (p. 114). Statistical procedures only provide valid information if we implement them properly. One drawback to statistical tests is that they require a sufficient sample size in order to have enough "power." **Power** refers to the probability of correctly rejecting a null hypothesis. For a detailed discussion of power analysis and determining appropriate sample sizes, you should consult an introductory statistics textbook. What you should understand for now is that we can make errors when drawing conclusions based on our statistical findings, and a small sample size can increase the chance of error.

Generalizability and Threats to External Validity

If, after doing careful analysis, we are comfortable stating that we have found evidence of an actual (not spurious) relationship between X and Y, our next step is to think about whether it is appropriate to assume those results would apply to other samples or the population from which we selected our original sample. If we find support for our research hypothesis and are comfortable that our sample is representative of the population we are studying, we can generalize our findings, meaning we can assume that the pattern we witnessed in our sample also exists in the larger population. **Generalizability** is an important goal of research as we study samples with the hope learning about populations that are too expensive or time consuming for us to study.

A type of generalizability is **external validity**, or the likelihood of being able to replicate our findings if we did the same study at another time or place (Maxfield & Babbie, 2012). There are characteristics of our research designs that can impact external validity. Here is a list:

Selection Bias

This threat to internal validity could also influence external validity. If you wanted to study whether students at a specific university thought classes were rigorous enough but your sample consisted only of students in the honors program, it would be unlikely that you would get similar findings if you repeated the study with another sample of students from the same school.

Reactivity

Reactivity is individuals' awareness that they are being observed and their corresponding changes of behavior. Most people would not attempt to break into a car or a house if they knew that someone was observing them. In criminal justice research, we must be aware of the impact of our involvement in the study. In this instance, the offender's decision not to commit a crime was a product of researcher's visible presence, and if we replicated this situation without a researcher in sight, results would likely have been different.

While the presence of researchers can inhibit offenders, it can have the opposite effect on employees who feel the need to be at peak performance while being observed. The **Hawthorne Effect** refers to people behaving atypically due to their knowledge of being watched. It got its name from a study of workers at the Hawthorne Plant, where staff were suddenly much more efficient once they learned that they were being observed (Landsberger, 1958). Findings based on such changes to behavior are not generalizable to the population of factory workers, nor would they be replicated in another study where the researchers remained out of sight.

Testing Effects

This is another threat to internal validity that can also impact external validity. Participants might gain knowledge or increase their sensitivity to the topic being studied simply by being exposed to the pretest instrument. If that is the case, posttest results might be partially or completely a product of testing effects rather than a reaction to the independent variable. That means that we would not find the same results elsewhere unless we also administered a pretest. That is problematic if we are testing a new curriculum, such as a law enforcement ethics training course, that we are pilot testing with pre- and posttests now. If the plan is to then to implement the new curriculum state-wide without a corresponding research evaluation, it is imperative that the curriculum itself, and not the pretest, is what is producing the desired change.

History

History could have a far-reaching impact on the study results and the extent to which we could expect to replicate the study and find similar outcomes. If a historical event produced some or all of the observed changes in the dependent variable, we are unlikely to find the same results at another place or time absent that historical event.

Multiple Treatment Interference

In criminal justice, agencies frequently attempt multiple interventions at the same time. Inmates might be simultaneously enrolled in anger management, drug counseling, and job readiness programs and then, upon release, be placed on parole with the requirement of participation in additional programs. Police departments might consider engaging in community policing citywide, policing hot spots in certain areas, then perhaps a very specific problem-oriented policing initiative in one neighborhood. If we see that inmates were less likely to recidivate or that crime went down in the city, **multiple treatment interference** would make it difficult to determine what, exactly, contributed to our positive outcomes (Hagan, 2007).

The Importance of Replication in Research

I have used the word "replicate" a few times over the last few pages because **replication** is an important part of research, albeit time consuming and expensive. When searching for programs that work in criminal justice, it is essential that we exercise caution and refrain from rushing to change policies or adopt new programs based on just one study, even if it was quality work. The reason is that there could be something unique about that one place or time that contributed to a program's success. A recent example of the need for replication before drawing conclusions about programs is the story of Project HOPE, which originally stood for Hawaii's Opportunity Probation with Enforcement Program. As the program moved from Hawaii to the US mainland, the H was changed from "Hawaii" to "Honest." Project HOPE is a program that de-emphasizes rehabilitation and, instead, promotes swift, certain, and fair graduated sanctions for probationers with the goal of deterring negative behavior. The program was run by a very charismatic judge and evaluated by well-regarded researchers. After the researchers conducted two evaluations and reported reductions in recidivism, the researchers and the judge worked to publicize the program. Project HOPE was quickly adopted all over the United States, with 160 programs popping up in a little over a decade. Subsequent evaluations, however, have not replicated the Hawaii findings. On the contrary, replications of this program have indicated that it does not produce reductions in recidivism. Yet there are now 160 programs nationwide that have been funded and staffed using this seemingly ineffective model. What happened? We did not slowly introduce this program elsewhere, replicate the research, and wait for the findings before concluding that it worked. Instead, we assumed the findings of the Hawaii evaluations would be generalizable to everywhere else. But why weren't they? One possible reason is that the probation officers in Hawaii received cognitive-behavioral programming treatment, making them uniquely prepared to help their clients. This is something that most other probation jurisdictions do not do. Another possibility is the performance or involvement of the judge. Then, there is the flaw in the entire theory underpinning this program. Just about all the existing research on deterrence-based programs indicates that they are not effective in reducing recidivism, and that alone should have given everyone pause and encouraged replication studies before mass adoption of the program (Cullen, Pratt, Turanovic, & Butler, 2018). Replication may seem like a waste of time if a program appeals to "common sense," and there is some early evidence that it is effective. This is just one example of an ineffective criminal justice program being prematurely adopted by jurisdictions before adequate replication work was completed.

Classical Experiments

Now that we have reviewed the pitfalls of research, we are going to spend the next 1.5 chapters discussing different types of designs and learning how each fares in avoiding threats to validity. Something that you must keep in mind is that there is no perfect research design. We just do our best within the confines of what ethical rules, our budgets, and our schedules allow. Our goal is to design a study in a way that will get us closest to being able to find a causal pattern between our independent and dependent variables. To get there, we must remember the three elements of causation: (1) a relationship between X and Y, (2) X precedes Y in time, and (3) all rival causal factors (Z) are explained away. Out of all the designs we will review in this chapter and the next, the classical experiment gets us closest to our goal.

There are three characteristics that distinguish the classical experiment from other research designs (Figure 4.3). First, the participants, groups, or geographic areas being studied are divided into at least two groups—experimental and control. The **experimental group** will be exposed to whatever stimulus represents the independent variable, while the **control group** will serve as a comparison that, hopefully, differs only in that they will not be exposed to X. Second, assignment to either the experimental or control group must be handled in a way that maximizes

Classical Experiment				Quasi-Experiment		
R	O	X	O	O	X	O
R	O		O	O		O

R = Random assignment
X = Independent variable
O = observation

Figure 4.3 Classical and Quasi-experimental Designs

the chances that the two groups will be equivalent. In a classical experiment, this is achieved through random selection of participants to either the experimental or control group. While randomization does not guarantee that the groups will be equivalent, the chances of it producing similar groups grow as we increase the sample size. Third, the study must include at least one measurement of the groups before introduction of the experimental stimulus and at least one measurement after exposure. In other words, there needs to be at least one pretest to measure the dependent variable before the appearance of X and at least one posttest after X is introduced.

The goal of a classical experiment is to acquire experimental and control groups that are similar in every way that is relevant to what is being studied. Revisiting the therapeutic community example, we would seek to obtain a large sample of offenders who are somewhat similar. We would set specific inclusion and exclusion criteria with the goal of acquiring probationers with similar offending histories and criminogenic needs (personality traits, attitudes, association with delinquent peers, education levels, etc.). We could accomplish this by restricting participation to only individuals with certain criminal charges and those who scored within a specific range on a reliable and valid risk assessment test. Once we have identified a pool of eligible offenders, the probationers would be randomly assigned to either the TC program or to treatment as usual that is offered through probation services. Researchers can then look at a number of outcomes, or dependent variables, to see if there are differences between the two groups before and after treatment.

The classical experiment would allow us to (1) study whether there is a relationship between X and Y and (2) establish time order by measuring both groups before and after the experimental group is exposed to the independent variable. The third requirement for causation, controlling for all possible rival explanations, is more difficult to address.

The primary advantage to classical experiments is the degree of control the research team can have. Researchers in the natural sciences, and even psychology, are able to run classical experiments inside laboratories where they can control just about everything, including the lighting, temperature, exposure to outside information and influences, and other environmental factors. This level of control allows them to be confident that the introduction of X is truly the only difference between groups. This is an important feature because it addresses the third requirement for causality—eliminating other possible explanations for the relationship between X and Y. Of course, laboratory experiments are generally not feasible in criminal justice, as we seek to observe and measure behaviors of humans in real-world settings.

The classical experiment is a very strong research design and can help reduce or eliminate some, but not all, threats to internal validity. Maxfield and Babbie (2012) observed that mortality could continue to be a problem, despite the safeguards built into classical experimental designs, because dropout rates could be higher in the experimental or control group for a variety of reasons, including the desirability of exposure to the independent variable. Cook and Campbell (1979) note that demoralization of the control group could actually generate a spurious relationship between X and Y because the control group's dampened mood or diminished performance can create the appearance of a difference between the two groups that would incorrectly be attributed to the independent variable. For other threats, such as compensatory rivalry, compensatory equalization, and diffusion of treatment, these problems can obscure a relationship between X and Y that actually exists.

External validity is a potential problem with classical experiments, particularly those implemented in a tightly controlled environment. While those controls help enhance internal validity, they introduce a degree of artificiality into the study. That artificiality will weaken external validity, since implementation of the same study in a real-world setting will likely produce different results (Maxfield & Babbie, 2012).

Additional Experimental Designs

Solomon Four-Group Design and Factorial Design

A few designs incorporate the elements of the classical experiment—two groups, equivalence, and pre- and posttests, but take additional steps to address potential threats to validity. One of these is the **Solomon four-group design** (Figure 4.4). This can be rather cumbersome, but it serves as a check for testing bias. As the name implies, researchers randomly divide participants into four groups. The first two groups are the same as they are in the classical experiment, with both taking a pretest, followed by only one group's exposure to the independent variable, and then both groups taking the posttest. The Solomon design adds two more groups, neither of which get the pretest. Instead, one group gets exposed to the independent variable and takes the posttest, while the last group just takes the posttest. We are hypothesizing here that the two groups exposed to the experimental stimulus will have been impacted by that experience and will, therefore, have different posttest scores than the two groups that were not exposed to X. We can check to see if the pretest had any impact on the results by comparing the pretest-no stimulus-posttest group to the posttest only group. If the pretest had no impact, those two groups should be the same due to their lack of exposure to X. Additionally, posttest scores for the pretest-X-posttest and the X-posttest only groups should also be the same if there were no testing effects.

The **factorial design** is a classical experiment with an additional group added to test a second type of treatment (Figure 4.4). We could use a factorial design if we have two types of drug treatment options that we want to add as enhancements to regular probation and then test their effectiveness against that of standard probation. We could randomly assign one group of probationers to cognitive-behavioral treatment plus probation, one to medication-assisted treatment plus probation, and then the third group to standard probation conditions.

Solomon four-group design		
R O	X	O
R O		O
R	X	O
R		O
Factorial design		
R O	X_1	O
R O	X_2	O
R O		O
Equivalent groups posttest only design		
R	X	O
R		O

R = Random assignment
X = Independent variable
O = Observation

Figure 4.4 Variations of Experimental Designs

Equivalent Groups Posttest-Only Design

Pretests are not always possible, and in those instances, an equivalent-groups posttest-only design might be the only option. We can randomly assign a group of opioid-addicted individuals who are entering jail into a medication-assisted treatment program or the treatment-as-usual (counseling, Narcotics Anonymous) programs and then track participants for a period of time after release from custody and measure possible outcomes, such as recidivism, engagement in drug treatment after release from jail, or self-reported drug use after jail. The obvious drawback here is that we have no baseline or pretest data to gauge how the two groups compared on severity of drug addiction and offending history prior to the start of the treatment.

Quasi-Experiments

A **quasi-experiment** differs from the classical experimental design in that it is missing one of the three elements that characterize the classical experiment (Cook & Campbell, 1979). Random assignment of participants into treatment or control groups is not always possible, especially when researchers are dependent on an external agency to provide access to research participants. There are times, particularly during evaluation research, where it is necessary to work within the confines of agency rules or policies. When groups are selected non-randomly, we will still have an experimental group, but the control group will be referred to as a **comparison group** instead. The inability to randomly assign participants to the treatment and comparison groups has the potential to introduce a number of threats to internal validity here, including selection bias and selection-maturation interaction.

While less than ideal, quasi-experiments can be very valuable, especially when researchers take steps to match the treatment and comparison groups or use statistical controls. **Matching** involves either manually, or with statistical procedures, pairing experimental participants with comparison group members based on theoretically relevant variables. Getting back to the TC example, the criminal justice, mental health, or drug treatment agency associated with the intervention may not be in a position to allow the researchers to randomly assign people to either the TC or treatment as usual. Strah, Frost, Stowell, and Taheri (2018) faced this exact challenge when studying an in-prison cognitive-behavioral treatment (CBT) program. The corrections department's policy was that joining CBT had to be voluntary, so random assignment to treatment modality was prohibited. The researchers responded by matching program volunteers to individuals who either started the program and later dropped out or those who did not volunteer. Individuals in both groups were matched on several demographic and institutional misconduct variables to produce similar treatment and comparison groups.

An alternative to matching is to use statistical techniques to account for potential differences between the treatment and comparison groups, with the goal of isolating the effects of the treatment. A mental health agency near my university was partnering with the county jail and some police departments to offer diversion and reentry services to individuals with mental illness who were committing low-level crimes. The agency felt an ethical obligation to provide services to all who were eligible and willing to participate, so it was impossible to randomize half of those eligible into a control group. Instead, I constructed a non-equivalent comparison group by identifying people who were eligible for services but did not receive them because they either lived outside of the agency's treatment area or staff were unable to contact them. I then used multivariate statistical models to learn if program participation remained a predictor of recidivism after controlling for the demographic and legal characteristics of the two groups (Tartaro, 2015).

Interrupted time-series
O O O O O O O O O O O O X O O O O O O O O O O O O O O O

Interrupted time-series with non-equivalent comparison group
O O O O O O O O O O O O X O O O O O O O O O O O O O O O
O O O O O O O O O O O O O   O O O O O O O O O O O O O O

Interrupted time-series with treatment removal
O O O O O O X O O O O O O O O O O O O O -X O O O O O O O O

X = independent variable
O = observation

Figure 4.5 Time-Series Designs

The other type of quasi-experiment is a **time-series** (Jennings & Reingle Gonzalez, 2019; Maxfield & Babbie, 2012) (Figure 4.5). Time-series designs involve multiple data collection points. This would not be appropriate for use with the TC or CBT program example, as there would not be enough data collection points to make a time-series possible. This can be a very useful design, however, when you want to look at changes in crime patterns, such as monthly crime statistics over a period of a few years or yearly statistics over several decades. For example, Mayhew, Clarke, and Elliott (1989) conducted an **interrupted time-series.** The interruption was the introduction of the independent variable, which in this case was the helmet law with enforcement. The dependent variable was yearly rates of motorcycle theft in Germany in the 1970s and 1980s. The new law was phased in gradually. Theft rates remained stable during the phase-in period but fell sharply once police began writing tickets. Mayhew and colleagues concluded that the reduction in thefts was due to fear of being caught stealing. Most motorcycle thefts are crimes of opportunity, with someone looking for transportation committing the theft at a time and place when he or she is unlikely to be caught. Once police started to pull over and ticket motorists without helmets, stealing a bike became very risky unless one happened to be carrying around a helmet in anticipation of stealing a bike.

There are multiple variations of time-series designs, including the **interrupted non-equivalent comparison group time-series** (Figure 4.5). This would allow researchers to assess the impact of a new policing tactic on calls for service data over several months while also collecting the same type of police data from a neighboring city that is not introducing any new police initiatives (Braga, Kennedy, Waring, & Piehl, 2001). Another possibility is **interrupted time-series with treatment removal**, including several observation periods, introduction of a stimulus, more observation periods, removal of the stimulus, and then additional observation points. This design is appropriate for observing the impact of placement and then removal of crime prevention initiatives, such as such as road barriers to deter drug dealing and prostitution.

Strengths and Weaknesses of Quasi-Experimental Designs

Quasi-experimental designs are desirable in that they do provide safeguards against some threats to validity. If non-equivalent comparison groups are included, testing and instrumentation would likely impact both groups equally, as would history and maturation. Selection bias and selection-maturation remain possibilities, given the lack of equivalence between the experimental and comparison groups. As was noted earlier, it is possible to minimize the differences between the groups with matching techniques or to use statistical controls to isolate the impact of the independent variable on the dependent variable. As with classical experiments, diffusion of treatment, compensatory equalization, demoralization, and compensatory rivalry remain potential threats to validity.

Summary

This chapter covered some very important topics in research methods. I always tell my students that, if they are to walk away from my class having learned one thing, I would like it to be the elements of causality. We can only conclude that X causes Y when we find evidence that there is a relationship between X and Y, X precedes Y in time, and we can control for, or explain away, the influence of all other possible explanations. We seek evidence of associations between X and Y through hypothesis testing and accompanying statistical procedures. The results of our statistical analysis tell us whether we can reject the null hypothesis (prediction of no relationship between X and Y) or if we lack sufficient evidence to take that step. If we are able to reject the null hypothesis, we can be confident that there is an association between the independent and dependent variables, and depending on our sampling procedures, we might feel comfortable generalizing those results to the population from which we obtained our sample. Our results will reflect patterns among our sample, but they will not necessarily explain every case that was studied.

No research is perfect, and even among strong designs, there are threats to internal and external validity. Threats to internal validity are factors other than our independent variable that might impact the values of our dependent variable. Threats to external validity reduce the possibility of our finding similar results if we replicate the same study at another place or time. A goal of quantitative research is to generalize our results, meaning we feel confident that our findings would also apply to the population from which the sample was selected.

The gold standard for research designs is the classical experiment, which includes participants randomly divided into experimental and control groups. Participants are pretested prior to the introduction of the treatment stimulus, and then both groups are posttested. The goal is to generate two groups that are as similar as possible, so the only difference is that the experimental group was exposed to the independent variable while the control group was not. If the values for the dependent variable for the experimental group change from pretest to posttest, but the values for the control group remain steady, we can conclude that the independent variable is associated with the dependent variable. When conducting research, it is often difficult to find circumstances that allow for random assignment of participants into groups. It can be particularly challenging when there are clear ethical problems with denying one group of participants access to treatment or if a criminal justice agency involved in the study has strict rules about how people are assigned to treatments or punishments. For that reason, quasi-experiments with non-random assignments to experimental and comparison groups are a common and useful alternative to the classical experiment.

Keywords

Independent variable	Instrumentation	Equivalent groups posttest-only design
Null hypothesis	Mortality	
Spurious relationship	Diffusion of treatment	Matching
Proofs	Compensatory rivalry	Interrupted time-series with non-equivalent comparison group
Control group	Power	

Generalizability
Multiple treatment
interference
Dependent variable
Causation
Rival causal factors
Aggregates
History
Statistical regression
Maturation
Compensatory equalization
of treatment

Demoralization
Solomon four-group design
Quasi-experiment
Time-series
Interrupted time-series with
treatment removal
Reactivity
Replication
Research hypothesis
Correlation
Threats to internal validity
Experimental group

Testing effects
Selection (sample) bias
Selection-maturation
interaction
Kansas City Preventive Patrol
Experiment
Statistical conclusion validity
Factorial design
Comparison group
Interrupted time-series
External validity
Hawthorne effect

Discussion Questions

1. What is a spurious relationship? Besides what was mentioned in this chapter, can you think of any other relationships in the world that might be spurious?

2. Besides a relationship between X and Y, what other factors are required to determine a causal relationship between two variables?

4. If a researcher cannot put together a classical experiment due to the inability to randomize selection into the experimental and control groups, what options does the researcher have to limit the impact of non-randomization on the study's results?

5. How might changes in instrumentation impact our ability to interpret data over a period of years?

6. What are some of the drawbacks to the classical experimental design?

References

Bennett, T., Holloway, K., & Farrington, D. (2008). The statistical association between drug misuse and crime. *Aggression and Violent Behavior, 13*, 107–118. https://doi.org/10.1016/j.avb.2008.02.001

Braga, A. A., Kennedy, D. M., Waring, E. J., & Piehl, A. M. (2001). Problem-oriented policing, deterrence, and youth violence: An evaluation of Boston's youth violence. *Journal of Research in Crime and Delinquency, 38*, 195–225.

Cohen, L. E., & Felson, M. (1979). Social change and crime rate trends: A routine activity approach. *American Sociological Review, 44*(4), 588–608. https://doi.org/10.2307/2094589

Cook, T. D., & Campbell, D. T. (1979). *Quasi-experimentation: Design and analysis issues for field settings.* Chicago, IL: Rand-McNally.

Cullen, F. T., Pratt, T. C., Turanovic, J. J., & Butler, L. (2018). When bad news arrives: Project HOPE in a post-factual world. *Journal of Contemporary Criminal Justice, 34*(1), 13–34.

Farrington, D., & Welsh, B. C. (2006). How important is "regression to the mean" in area-based crime prevention research? *Crime Prevention & Community Safety, 8*, 50–60. https://doi.org/10.1057/palgrave.cpcs.8150017

Fletcher, B. W., & Tims, F. M. (1992). Methodological issues: Drug abuse treatment research in prisons and jails. In C. G. Leukfeld & F. M. Tims (Eds.), *Drug abuse treatment in prisons and jails* (pp. 246–260). Rockville, MD: National Institute on Drug Abuse.

Grambsch, P. (2008). Regression to the mean, murder rates, and shall-issue laws. *The American Statistician, 62*(4), 289–295. https://doi.org/10.1198/000313008X362446

Hagan, F. (2007). *Essentials of research methods in criminal justice and criminology* (2nd ed.). Boston, MA: Pearson.

Jennings, W. G., & Reingle Gonzalez, J. M. (2019). *Criminological and criminal justice research methods.* New York, NY: Wolters Kluwer.

Kelling, G. L., Pate, T., Diekman, D., & Brown, C. E. (1974). *The Kansas City preventive patrol experiment.* Washington, DC: The Police Foundation.

Kinderman, C., Lynch, J., & Cantor, D. (1997). *Effects of the redesign on victimization estimates.* Washington, DC: United States Department of Justice Bureau of Justice Statistics.

Landsberger, H. A. (1958). *Hawthorne revisited.* Ithaca, NY: The New York State School of Industrial and Labor Relations.

Larson, R. C. (1975). What happened to patrol operations in Kansas City? A review of the Kansas City preventive patrol experiment. *Journal of Criminal Justice, 3*, 267–297.

Lipton, D. S. (1998). Therapeutic community treatment programming in corrections. *Psychology, Crime and Law, 4*, 213–263. https://doi.org/10.1080/10683169808520010

Maxfield, M. G., & Babbie, E. (2012). *Basics of research methods for criminal justice and criminology* (3rd ed.). Belmont, CA: Thomson Wadsworth.

Mayhew, P., Clarke, R. V., & Elliott, D. (1989). Motorcycle theft, helmet legislation, and displacement. *Howard Journal of Criminal Justice, 28*, 1–8. https://doi.org/10.1111/j.1468-2311.1989.tb00631.x

Pawson, R., & Tilley, N. (1997). *Realistic evaluation.* London: Sage Publications.

Roth, J., Lee, S., & Joo, J. (2018). The effective of community-level alarm ownership on burglary rates. *Journal of Applied Security Research, 13*(2), 160–171. https://doi.org/10.1080/19361610.2018.1422360

Salkind, N. (2014). *Statistics for people who (think they) hate statistics* (5th ed.). Thousand Oaks, CA: Sage Publications.

Strah, B. M., Frost, N. A., Stowell, J. I., & Taheri, S. A. (2018). Cognitive-behavioral programming and the value of failed interventions: A propensity score evaluation. *Journal of Offender Rehabilitation, 57*(1), 22–46. https://doi.org/10.1080/10509674.2017.1416437

Tartaro, C. (2015). An evaluation of the effects of jail diversion and reentry for mentally ill offenders. *Journal of Offender Rehabilitation, 54*(2), 85–102. https://doi.org/10.1080/10509674.2015.1009966

Tseloni, A., Thompson, R., Grove, L., Tilley, N., & Farrell, G. (2014). The effectiveness of burglary security devices. *Security Journal, 30*, 646–664. https://doi.org/10.1057/sj.2014.30

Vigen, T. (n.d.). *Spurious correlations.* Retrieved from https://tylervigen.com/old-version.html

Reading 4.1   The Methodological Struggles of Racial Profiling Research

Fallick's (2019) discussion of the challenges in studying racial profiling is a terrific example of how difficult it is to establish causation in criminal justice research. Fallick rightly notes that simply asking police to self-report their motivation behind automobile stop outcomes would be the most direct way to measure possible racial animus. That, of course, has the potential to generate substantial validity issues, as officers may be unaware of their own biases. Those who are biased and are aware of it would be unlikely to disclose for social desirability reasons or for fear of jeopardizing their careers. Since plainly asking officers if racial animus causes certain behaviors while on duty would generate validity problems, the easiest and most direct way of establishing causation is not feasible. That leaves researchers searching for evidence of racial disparities through examining results of actions but not necessarily the motivations behind them. While officer-initiated traffic stops are good decision points to focus on, given the amount of discretion involved, it is still very difficult to establish all the elements of causation. Fallick's review of the existing research on racial profiling illustrates how many factors need to be considered before we can confidently state that racial profiling causes certain outcomes in police stops.

The Methodological Struggles of Racial Profiling Research: A Causal Question That Automobile Stop Data Has Yet to Answer

Seth Wyatt Fallik

Introduction

As the gatekeepers to the criminal justice system, police officers have a unique role in the administration of justice. Their enforcement practices have a ripple effect throughout the criminal justice system. Recently, however, confidence in law enforcement has been shaken in the wake of national incidents involving police use of force against racial[1] minorities in the United States of America (Newport, 2016). In the last three decades, depictions of potential racial animus have prompted data explorations of law enforcement practices. Departmental transparency, according to the President's Task Force on Twenty-first Century Policing (2015), is critical to citizen assessments of public trust and legitimacy; these analyses, therefore, are highly consequential to law enforcement (Tyler & Wakslak, 2004). Unfortunately, studies examining the differential treatment of racial minorities during automobile stops tend to find that citizen race influences officer decision-making. Researchers, notwithstanding, have reported a host of methodological issues that have inhibited them from drawing reliable causal inferences about the existence of racial profiling. Even researchers employing quantitative syntheses of this literature, such as meta-analyses, recognize that the explanatory limits of their findings are confined by the quality of available studies. Consequently, the etiology of the 'driving while Black' phenomenon, as it is also known, remains elusive, and a well of skepticism has perpetuated a divide among police and the communities they serve.

The purpose of the current study is to deconstruct this field of inquiry through a causal lens so that researchers are conscious of the methodological issues that must be contended with going forward. The topics presented in this manuscript are reoccurring issues discussed in individual racial profiling studies, but by evaluating the logical consistency of automobile stop events, assessing the relationship between citizen race and the search disposition, and observing how researchers control for exogenous influences, the current study seeks to present a succinct accounting of the causal issues that have plagued racial profiling research.

The Causal Question for Potential Data Sources

Racial profiling inquiries are a causal question at their root. They hypothesize that if law enforcement harbor implicit or explicit animus toward racial minorities, it will manifest in discriminatory outcomes. As a counterfactual model, racial profiling research asks if automobile stop outcomes would differ if officers acted absent racial animus. While the most direct measure of this causal model would seem to be officer self-reports, there are serious ethical and methodological concerns that are difficult, if not impossible, for researchers to overcome with this type of data. Racial animus, therefore, is often explored with aggregates of police-citizen encounters. In these studies, researchers must construct what constitutes equitable treatment in their analyses (Reitzel & Piquero, 2006). The selections researchers make represent statistical, rather than behavioral, differentiations; thus, *disparity*, rather than *animus*, is the preferred nomenclature in this body of literature. While the causal model for observing disparity is similar to animus, readers of this research should avoid the assumption that what is true of the whole must be true of the parts. Aggregating police-citizen encounters has allowed researchers to generalize their results among neighborhood, city, state, highway, and national samples. Unfortunately, pooled data are removed from the individualized nature of police-citizen encounters. Readers, therefore, should be cautious in making generalizations to specific officers.

The Officer Decision-Making Process in Automobile Stops

To further elaborate on the causal model found in racial profiling studies, researchers have deconstructed the officer decision-making process of automobile stop encounters. Officer-initiated decision-making points are of particular interest to racial profiling researchers because they provide measurable aspects to the 'cognitive processes that underlie [officer] discretion' (Miller, 2008, p. 127). Researchers have, therefore, strategically focused on more discretionary automobile stop outcomes in which racial disparity is most likely to be pronounced. With this in mind, there are three prominent opportunities to observe officer use of discretion within automobile stop data, including the decision to (1) initiate a stop, (2) conduct a search, and (3) apply a sanction (Schafer, Carter, Katz-Bannister, & Wells, 2006).

The decision to initiate a stop precedes all other decision-making points and researchers of this disposition typically consider the likelihood of racial minorities to be stopped by law enforcement. Researchers in these studies would ideally compare those who are stopped against the population that is not stopped to determine if there is a disparity in officer decision-making. Unfortunately, automobile stop data only reflect the former, which has forced researchers to put forth proximate, non-exact measures for the driving and/or traffic offending population. Benchmarks, as they are more commonly known, offer a solution to what has been called the 'denominator problem' (Schafer et al., 2006, p. 187). Prior research has utilized, for example, population-based and accident rate estimates, field observations, and internal benchmarks built on the pool of motorists stopped as the denominator. Identifying an appropriate benchmark has become a hotly contested debate in the racial profiling literature, due to the transient nature of the population attempting to be measured and methodological implications for each benchmark (Tillyer, Engel, & Cherauskas, 2009). Unfortunately, side-by-side comparisons of benchmark outcomes have yet to be explored in the extant literature, inhibiting discussions about their empirical strengths and weaknesses.

The second officer-initiated decision-making point occurs post-stop and is concerned with an officer's decision to search the driver, vehicle, passengers, or a combination of some or all three entities. Most research in this area asks if racial minorities are disproportionately searched by law enforcement. More discriminate efforts disaggregate searches by types and tend to focus on more discretionary search types within the search disposition (e.g. Pickerill, Mosher, & Pratt, 2009). This allows researchers to collapse similarly situated instances of officer discretion into more generalizable results with greater statistical power but does not compromise the granularity of the analyses.

The final officer-initiated decision-making point also occurs post-stop and is concerned with the sanctions issued to the citizen by the officer. The bulk of this research evaluates who is arrested by law enforcement; however, citations are the most common occurrence at this decision-making point (Langton & Durose, 2013). Other sanction-related analyses have considered more punitive or coercive outcomes, including instances of physical and verbal resistance and officer use of non-deadly and deadly force (Withrow, 2006).

Demonstrating Causality in Automobile Stops

Regardless of which disposition is being observed, establishing a causal relationship between citizen race and officer decision-making in automobile stop data hinges on three critical factors: temporal order, association, and spuriousness (Kraska & Neuman, 2012). In the sections that follow, racial profiling research is discussed among each of these factors. The current study begins by describing and assessing the logical consistency of an automobile stop's timing. The associative relationship between citizen race and the search disposition is then evaluated among systematically identified studies. An analysis of the control variables employed in each of these studies follows. Finally, the manuscript concludes by drawing attention to inherent issues in racial profiling analytical strategies and automobile stop data.

Temporal Order

Temporal order refers to the arrangement of events in time. It necessitates that a causal factor is preceded in time by the outcome. Two temporal ordering issues are prominent in the racial profiling literature. First, establishing temporal order in automobile stop data is relatively easy for post-stop dispositions. For post-stop decision-making points, officers have an opportunity to observe the race of the citizen prior to searching and sanctioning; however, establishing temporal order in stop initiation research is more difficult. Alpert, Dunham, and Smith (2007), for example, found that officers of the Miami-Dade (Florida) Police Department 'could only determine the race of the driver prior to the stop approximately 30% of the time' (p. 48). If an officer does not know the race of the driver prior to making a stop, then it cannot be the reason for the stop. In any case, stops with racial bias may be diluted by the overwhelming majority of encounters in which the citizen's race could not be determined prior to the stop.

The second temporal ordering issue affects post-stop dispositions. A stop's initiation will always be the first decision-making point in the temporal chain of events of an automobile stop because without it, there cannot be subsequent officer dispositions. Unfortunately, the temporal ordering of searches and sanctions are often not specified in automobile stop data (Withrow, 2006). This is problematic for researchers who seek to understand the larger cognitive processes that tie decision-making points together. More specifically, the temporal ordering of post-stop dispositions tells researchers something about the conditions in which the officer acted. If, for example, a suspect was arrested then searched, it suggests a less discretionary search occurred and vice versa. An inability to disentangle the temporal ordering of searches and sanctions has relegated racial profiling research to measure automobile stop data cross-sectionally, which is inconsistent with the processes that underlie officer decision-making.

Association

Once the temporal order is established, an association must be made between the hypothesized cause and effect. The cause (i.e. citizen race) and effect (i.e. disparate outcomes) in racial profiling research are fairly overt because this relationship, as was noted previously, is often on display in news media. Incidents involving the deaths of Walter Scott and Philando Castile during automobile stops have brought racial profiling to the forefront of the nation's consciousness. In fact, attitudinal research finds that minorities are more critical of police behavior and often report feelings of harassment and discrimination (Reitzel & Piquero, 2006).

Unfortunately, news media and attitudinal research only provide anecdotal associative evidence. Likewise, attitudinal research assumes that citizen feelings are a direct reflection of their contacts with law enforcement. Rather, in any given year, only about a quarter (26.6%) of the eligible driving population will encounter a police officer according to the Bureau of Justice Statistics (Langton & Durose, 2013). Though racial minorities are disproportionately found among these contacts, indirect experiences are often more salient in shaping perceptions of police. As Rosenbaum, Schuck, Costello, Hawkins, and Ring (2005) reported, vicarious knowledge is the most important predictor of citizen attitudes of law enforcement. Negative police-citizen encounters, they noted, are likely to reverberate among family, friends, and communities; thus, attitudinal research is likely to overestimate the presence of actual racial animus.

The Current Study's Selection Criteria

To better estimate the associative relationship between citizen race and officer decision-making, several studies have employed quantitative analyses of police-citizen encounters. To identify relevant research, the current study utilizes the sample of studies reviewed by Bolger (2014). In his meta-analysis of officer decision-making correlates, 60 potential studies were identified in a thorough exploration of the literature.

Association Results

The associative results from the 12 studies reviewed by Bolger (2014) and explored in the current study are presented in Figure 1.[3] When

looking at the figure in its totality, the bulk of the studies ($n = 9$, 75%) found that racial minorities are more likely to be searched during their encounters with law enforcement. Although this is consistent with the prior research, studies published in the last five years appear to be less consistent with this finding. The appearance of racial disparity and its somewhat recent dissipating effects may be attributable to the final and often most difficult to prove causal issue: spuriousness.

Spuriousness

A spurious relationship exists when two factors are associated but the relationship is non-causal because a third and unobserved factor, often referred to as a confounding factor, is responsible for the association. To establish that a relationship is nonspurious, researchers must eliminate rival explanations and/or hypotheses. Engaging in falsification, as it is also known, is a difficult task because officer decision-making is not unidimensional. In an attempt to disentangle these effects, researchers have employed a variety of analytical strategies.

Analytical Strategies and Theoretically Derived Confounding Factors

The most basic analytical strategy found among racial profiling studies are bivariate analyses. The explanatory power of bivariate analyses is limited because within unit differences may confound the results. To this point, Withrow (2006) insisted that bivariate analyses 'cannot be used to infer or predict and generally cannot account for intervening causes of police behavior' (p. 193).

Although a limitless number of factors may contribute to an officer's decision-making, the inclusion of additional variables in multivariate models is only as good as their explanatory value because the inclusion of irrelevant factors does not provide greater causal elaboration, nor does it withstand falsification challenges. Omitted influences, however, can badly bias parameter estimates and obfuscate existing but small effects. Theoretically derived confounding

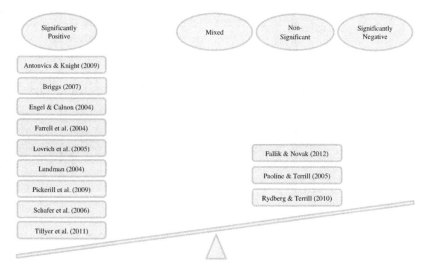

Figure 1 Associative Research Results on Racial Minority Likelihood of Being Searched

factors in racial profiling research have been organized according to their legal and extralegal influence in the extant literature (Lundman, 2004). Extralegal factors have been further distinguished into policing (i.e. officer and departmental influences), ecological, and situational typologies. Finally, driver, passenger, vehicle, and temporal characteristics of police-citizen encounters have also been differentiated among situational influences (see Figure 2).

The Current Study's Coding Scheme

To explore the prevalence of theoretically derived confounding factors, the variables employed by the studies found in Figure 1 were coded using the typologies found in Figure 2. To ensure classification consistency, variables from each of the studies were independently coded among two analysts. The initial coding procedure produced 89.3% coding agreement. Where differences were observed, analysts discussed and came to an agreement about how the items should be coded with 100% consistency.[5]

Figure 2 Organization of Confounding Factor Typologies in Racial Profiling Research

Spuriousness Results

There does not appear to be a relationship between the type or number of confounding factors included among these studies and the associative relationship found between driver race and the search disposition; however, the inclusion of control variables is sporadic (see Table 1). In fact, the racial profiling research observed in the current study employed on

Table 1 The Number of Variables Observed from Each Variable Typology Among Racial Profiling Studies Estimating the Officer Decisions to Search the Driver, Vehicle, Passengers, or a Combination of Some or All Three Entities

Article	Sample size	Race association	Policing			Extralegal		Situational				Other	Total
			Legal	Officer	Department	Ecological	Driver	Passenger	Vehicle	Temporal	Additive		
Antonovics and Knight (2009)	70,652	Positive	1	1		1	6			1			10
Briggs (2007)	9989	Positive	3			9	5				15		32
Engel and Calnon (2004)	19,277,002	Positive	7	2		2	8	1			2	2	24
Farrell, McDevitt, Bailey, Andersen, and Pierce (2004)	442,873	Positive	1			1	4	1		3			10
Lovrich et al. (2005)	1,102,529	Positive	1	2		2	8			1			14
Lundman (2004)	7034	Positive	7	4		4	9	2			7		33
Pickerill et al. (2009)	677,514	Positive	1	6		8	6			1	9		31
Schafer et al. (2006)	61,037	Positive	3				3						6
Tillyer, Klahm, and Engel (2011)	43,707	Positive	7	5		3	7	1	2	3	1		29
Fallik and Novak (2012)	4569	Non-Significant	6			1	6			1			14
Paoline and Terrill (2005)	549	Non-Significant	3	5		1	5						14
Rydberg and Terrill (2010)	3356	Non-Significant	6	6	1	1	6					1	21
Total	n = 12		46	31	1	33	73	5	2	10	34	3	

average fewer than 20 control variables ($\bar{x} =$ 19.8; not depicted) from a limited number of the nine theoretically derived typologies ($\bar{x} = 5$; not depicted). Studies from the last 5 years of the sample tended to employ a greater number of variables ($\bar{x} = 21$; not depicted) from a wider variety of the theoretically derived typologies ($\bar{x} = 5.6$; not depicted). Subsequent sections go deeper into the types and effects of variables employed in this body of research.

Legal

A legal variable was found in all of the studies listed in Table 1 (n = 12, 100.0%). Officers are legal actors influenced by legal forces, which explains why legal variables are often found in racial profiling literature (National Research Council, 2004). Accordingly, many researchers noted that the legal reason for a stop was the most important factor when attempting to understand automobile stop outcomes because the cause of the stop often dictates the scope of discretion afforded to officers (Engel, 2008).

Investigatory stops, for example, function as part of a continuing investigation and are encounters where the driver, passengers, vehicle, or combination of some or all entities is known to police. In an investigatory stop, police may encounter someone who has not violated a traffic law but fits the description of a suspect, witness, or vehicle involved in a crime. These stops are an example of proactive policing and, are, therefore, qualitatively different in their presumed presence of racial bias. Traffic stops, for example, may be presumed to be racially neutral (see the 'Temporal Order' subsection), while investigatory stops may not. Even though investigatory stops may be initiated with different knowledge of the driver's race, hypothetically, their post-stop dispositions should be absent racial disparity if selection bias, which occurs during the stops' initiation, is controlled. Unfortunately, this type of sampling error is often overlooked by many racial profiling researchers.

Perhaps equally important to the cause of the stop is the inclusion of factors relating to the offense severity and the quantity of evidence against the citizen. Engel and Calnon (2004) and Withrow (2006) report that as the severity of the offense and/or the amount of evidence of wrongdoing increases, officer discretion decreases and procedural/departmental policies become more influential on an officer's decision-making. As such, legal factors are critical to understanding officer use of discretion. Substantively, without considering the legal conditions of automobile stops, the influence of citizen race may be obscured. In Table 1, however, there is not a pattern with the presence, number, or type of legal variables employed and the associative relationship observed between citizen race and the search disposition.

Extralegal

Turning now to non-legal factors: there are three distinct types of extralegal factors (i.e. policing, ecological, and situational) identified in the racial profiling literature.

Policing

Each encounter brings together people from unique backgrounds, and policing variables suggest that these encounters may differ across officer and departmental characteristics (Batton & Kadleck, 2004).

Officer

Two thirds (n = 8, 66.7%) of the studies found in Table 1 evaluated the race, ethnicity, gender, age, years of service, and/or educational achievement of the officer involved in the search. The National Research Council (2004), on this topic, reported that officer variables tend to yield mixed, insufficient, or no influence on officer decision-making. This sentiment is echoed by the studies found in Table 1 (not depicted). Furthermore, the inclusion, number, or type of officer-related factors does not appear to influence the associative relationship observed between the driver's race and the search disposition.

Departmental

In addition to officer characteristics, differential departmental priorities may influence the types of persons encountered by law enforcement. To this point, organizational theorists posit that the actions of the individual officer are a reflection of formal and informal policing policies (Crank & Langworthy, 1992). Batton and Kadleck (2004), for example, contended that researchers should consider the department's mission as it impacts 'the time, energy, and resources allotted to various aspects of law enforcement' (p. 50). Within this context, it is highly likely that departmental tools, like 'hot spot' and 'problem-oriented' policing, will differentially impact officer deployments. In this example, disparity may result from more time spent in minority communities and not individual officer animus (Alpert et al., 2007). Departmental factors suggest that racial disparity—if it exists—is a 'blue' issue. Unfortunately, nearly all of the studies in Table 1 failed to consider departmental characteristics as a confounding influence upon officer decision-making (n = 1, 8.3%), and thus, it remains largely unclear how departmental priorities impact officer decision-making.

Ecological

Ecological factors have also been found to influence an officer's decision-making. While most of the studies found in Table 1 employed at least one ecological variable (n = 11, 91.7%), there was little consistency in the types of variables utilized, and only two variables were used in multiple studies: street type and community characteristics. Relating to street type, police-citizen encounters on highways are typically the result of a traffic violation. Alternatively, surface streets provide an extra opportunity for community engagement. As a result, researchers expect officer discretion to be different in these contexts.

Likewise, police discretion may vary based on community characteristics. The variables used to measure community contexts tend to overlap with the measures found in social disorganization and collective efficacy research (e.g.

Sampson, Raudenbush, & Earls, 1997). Unfortunately, racial profiling research has yet to fully understand how communities influence officer decision-making. Klinger (1997), for example, reported that officers working in higher crime communities are more lenient with their enforcement practices than their peers in lower crime communities. Though he attributed differences to policing factors, his ecological theory of police responses to deviance suggests that the brink of police use of authority is distinguished by community crime levels and not the racial identity of citizen who has been stopped or racial composition of the community.

While Klinger's (1997) results are somewhat racially neutral, the theory of contextual attentiveness suggests something different. Withrow (2006) reported that officers may act 'differentially attentive toward individuals or behaviors that appear inconsistent with predetermined conceptualizations' (p. 127). An officer's suspicion becomes heightened, Withrow (2006) noted, when a citizen's racial identity is inconsistent with the neighborhood context in which he or she is found. Race 'out of place' policing, as it is more commonly known, is most evident when a Caucasian citizen is encountered in a predominantly Black neighborhood or when a Black citizen is encountered in a predominantly Caucasian neighborhood. Unfortunately, the extant literature provides mixed evidence of this phenomenon (Meehan & Ponder, 2002; Novak & Chamlin, 2008). In any case, failure to include ecological factors may inflate the influence of citizen race on automobile stop dispositions. In Table 1, however, there does not appear to be a pattern between the inclusion, number, or type of ecological factors employed in racial profiling research and the associative relationship found between the driver's race and the search disposition.

Situational

The final type of extralegal variables found in the racial profiling literature are situational. Situational factors are important to officer decision-making because, like the theory of contextual attentiveness, officers may perceive some drivers, passengers, vehicles, and/or temporal factors with greater suspicion.

Driver

All of the research found in Table 1 (n = 12, 100.0%) included some demographic information on the driver being searched, including the driver's race, ethnicity, gender, and age; however, more rigorous racial profiling analyses have included the driver's socioeconomic status (SES), educational achievement, and demeanor. Similar to racial minorities, ethnic minorities, males, younger citizens, citizens of lower SES, and persons with low educational achievement tend to be overrepresented at every stage of the criminal justice system, and, as a result, the presence of these driver characteristics may independently influence officer decision-making. On the issue of driver demeanor, many researchers believe that disrespectful citizens are more likely to receive punitive sanctions during their encounters with police. The studies found in Table 1 fail to support this contention as none of the studies observing citizen demeanor (n = 3) found significant associations with the search disposition (not depicted). Furthermore, there does not appear to be a relationship between the inclusion, number, or type of driver variables and the associative relationship between the driver's race and the search disposition.

Passengers

Passengers are equally susceptible to racial profiling and require the same due diligence in data collection and analyses. More specifically, Withrow (2006) suggested that the number of occupants in the vehicle and their demographic characteristics may be as critical as driver characteristics in understanding officer decision-making. Although information about drivers is found in most racial profiling studies (see Table 1), researchers have poorly accounted for their passengers (n = 4, 33.3%). In fact, the only time that passengers were accounted for among the identified studies was if there were passengers in the vehicle at the time of the police-citizen encounter. None of the studies included demographic information for passengers, and, therefore, it remains largely unclear how passenger characteristics impact officer decision-making.

Vehicle

The vehicle transporting the driver and passengers is an outwardly visible factor vulnerable to bias according to some researchers. Batton and Kadleck (2004) asserted that vehicle characteristics, such as make, model, color, year, and modifications, may influence officer decision-making. Two vehicle factors were examined in the sample by Tillyer et al. (2011): vehicle age and the presence of a vehicle defect. The vehicle's age was unrelated to officer decision-making, but the presence of a vehicle defect increased the likelihood of a search (not depicted). Vehicle defects provide legal grounds for officers to initiate a stop if the defect poses a safety concern for motorists; however, an officer's decision to conduct a search should not be influenced by vehicle defects. Unfortunately, this finding was beyond the scope of Tillyer et al.'s (2011) objectives and was not discussed further. The overwhelming majority of these studies, however, did not estimate vehicle effects (n = 1, 8.3%), and, therefore, their influence on officer decision-making remains unknown.

Temporal

Temporal factors consider when a police-citizen encounter transpired. The only reoccurring temporal factor found in Table 1 was based on the time of day the contact took place (i.e. day vs. night). Although the majority of stops are made during daylight hours, Barnum and Perfetti (2010) reported that younger officers often work night shifts and are more likely to make arrests during their encounters with citizens. As a result, there may be a confounding organizational influence on time of day observations. Other temporal considerations found among the studies in Table 1 included the day of the week (i.e. weekday vs. weekend), enforcement quota periods, and seasonal/ weather effects (e.g. rainy vs. sunny days). Temporal factors tended to be underrepresented among the studies found in Table 1 ($n = 6$, 50.0%), which has also relegated their influence on officer decision-making unclear.

Additive Probabilities

Finally, the presence of multiple risk factors may produce stronger associative results. It may be, for example, that citizen race is a nonsignificant predictor of officer decision-making. Separately, it may be determined that citizen age does not predict officer decision-making; however, persons who are both Black and under the age of 21 may be statistically more likely to be searched. Interaction variables, or additive probabilities as they are also known, demonstrate the complexity of police-citizen encounters. Interactive factors were utilized in five (41.7%) of the studies found in Table 1. Every study that considered additive probabilities combined driver race with other driver risk factors, such as age and gender. The inclusion of interaction variables tended to increase the likelihood of a significant associative result between the driver's race and the search disposition; however, this was not an absolute finding among the sampled studies and, therefore, warrants further exploration.

Discussion

National media coverage of police use of force against racial minorities has caused many to question the efficacy of law enforcement practices. To assuage fears of racial profiling, departments across the nation began collecting and disseminating explorations into law enforcement practices. Unfortunately, quantitative inquiries into automobile stop data have been plagued by methodological issues. This has done little to reassure citizens that law enforcement decision-making is transparent and procedurally fair. To inform the next generation of racial profiling scholarship, the current study deconstructed this body of literature through a causal lens. The causal question of racial profiling was first contextualized as disparity among aggregates of police-citizen encounters. Among potential data sources, researchers have further honed their efforts onto three officer-initiated and highly discretionary decision-making points in automobile stop encounters, including the decision to (1) initiate a stop, (2) conduct a search, and (3) apply a sanction.

This manuscript then presented these dispositions among the three criteria of causality: temporal order, association, and spuriousness. The logical consistency of two temporal ordering issues was discussed. First, many officers do not know the racial identity of the persons they have stopped (Alpert et al., 2007). Citizen race, therefore, is temporally inconsistent with research aimed at an officer's decision to initiate an automobile stop. Additionally, Withrow (2006) reported that the temporal ordering of the search and sanction dispositions are rarely specified in automobile stop data. This has relegated racial profiling research to being measured cross-sectionally, which is inconsistent with the officer decision-making process. The second criteria of causality (i.e. association) was distinguished in the current study from news media incidents and attitudinal research by evaluating the associative relationship between citizen race and the search disposition among systematically identified studies. Three-quarters of the studies sampled ($n = 9$, 75.0%) found that racial minorities were more likely to be searched by police (see Figure 1), but this relationship has somewhat dissipated among more contemporary studies due to the inclusion of a growing number and variety of theoretically derived confounding factors (see Table 1). Although studies published in the last half decade of the sample appear to be doing a better job at combating spuriousness, independent coding of theoretically derived confounding factors found that their inclusion in multivariate models is erratic as departmental, passenger, vehicle, and temporal considerations were nearly non-existent among the sampled studies.

Inherent Barriers and Policy Implications

Based on these results and a reading of the available empirical literature, two barriers are inhibiting a greater understanding of the etiology of the racial profiling phenomenon: (1) narrowly constructed analytical strategies and (2) static secondary data analyses.

Narrowly Constructed Analytical Strategies

Although the prior racial profiling literature has contributed greatly to initial understandings of the etiology of officer decision-making, we now know that their analytical strategies produce poor causal validity. Researchers, for example, have employed several benchmarks to estimate the driving and/or traffic offending population, but none have compared how they impact automobile stop dispositions. Furthermore, studies employing multivariate modeling techniques have weakly attempted to eliminate spuriousness. Where suitable controls are lacking, recent innovations in causal effect estimations, such as propensity score matching, weighting, marginal meaning weighting, and instrumental variable estimators have been neglected by researchers. Even when adequate controls exist, many studies have not observed between unit differences in organizational and community characteristics, as is proposed by organizational theorists and the theory of contextual attentiveness. This is unfortunate, given the availability of hierarchical modeling techniques that can account for these structural relationships.

Researchers have also been remiss in modeling the decision-making process. This is problematic because cross-sectional observations of officer decision-making may be misleading. Novak (2004), for example, found that minority drivers were more likely to be stopped by police but were no more likely to be sanctioned. Given the previous temporal ordering discussion and null findings with regards to the sanction disposition, Novak (2004) could have dismissed racial disparity among these police-citizen encounters; however, by considering these dispositions together, he was able to draw anecdotal conclusions about the officer decision-making process. Novak (2004) hypothesized that officers use minor traffic violations as a pretext to stop racial minorities more frequently, but with few stops producing legal grounds for a formal sanction, many racial minorities are released with only a warning.

The conclusion to be drawn from Novak (2004) is that post-stop dispositions always involve some selection bias, whereby the population that is searched or sanctioned is always preselected to be stopped. Although citizen race may not directly influence a stop's initiation, it may be confounded in other factors that do. Modeling the decision-making process, therefore, requires researchers to collect data that distinguishes the temporal order of post-stop dispositions and allows them to estimate selection bias that can occur during a stop's initiation. Selection and structural equation modeling can be used to control for such biases, whereby officer decision-making points are controlled and/or measured simultaneously. Unfortunately, the decision-making process has yet to be modeled in racial profiling research.

Static Secondary Data Analyses

In addition to narrowly constructed analytical strategies, racial profiling researchers typically make use of data that are collected by law enforcement for other purposes. Researchers select available data for a variety of reasons, including the lack of resources to conduct original data collection. The problem with this custom is that available data do not directly address the research questions being proposed by racial profiling researchers and, thus, are limited in their ability to engage in falsification. Given this predicament, much of the aforementioned racial profiling research suffers from specification error, which 'is a term used to describe situations in which multivariate models are misspecified due to . . . [the] inclusion of erroneous variables and/or the exclusion of unobserved variables' (Engel, 2008, p. 11).

For our purposes, specification error causes two issues. First and foremost, it threatens our ability to draw associative inferences about race and officer decision-making because the observed associative relationships may be due to one of the many unobserved theoretically derived confounding factors discussed in Figure 2. Furthermore, specification error impacts statistical conclusion validity. When theoretically derived confounding factors are omitted from multivariate models, the weight of observed factors is likely inflated by unexplained variance. Most of the multivariate models in Figure 1, for example, had goodness of fit indices that fell far below chance (not depicted).

Perhaps the most concerning element of racial profiling's academic-practitioner arrangements is the lack of adjustment. Simply put, knowledge of the etiology of officer decision-making has outgrown available data collection methods, yet many data collection strategies have not evolved. A push needs to be made to make use of our existing knowledge to better inform methodologically conceived and executed research studies. At a minimum, this would require evolving data collection instruments and ongoing collaborations with a host of stakeholders, including law enforcement, researchers, legislators, city/state executives, and community advocates.

Limitations and Areas of Future Research

Racial profiling researchers have an ethical responsibility to identify and communicate the explanatory limits of their findings. That burden falls equally upon these analyses. First, the discussion of automobile stop temporal ordering was nonsystematic. Temporal ordering is best assessed informally by evaluating the logical consistency of an event's timing. With regards to associative and spuriousness analyses, the studies under review in the current study were systematically analyzed but do not represent an exhaustive list of racial profiling research. This was due in part to Bolger's (2014) omission of more recent studies without sufficient statistical information. Although the exclusion of the latter studies was pertinent to his meta-analysis, this sampling criteria was beyond the scope of the current study. Nevertheless, a cursory search for omitted studies suggests that they do not differ from those that were included in Figure 1 and Table 1. Additionally, many of the omitted studies that lacked sufficient statistical information would have been excluded in the current study because they were not multivariate

analyses, which was critical to assessing how researchers have eliminated rival hypotheses. Finally, it may be more appropriate for conclusions based on the stop initiation and sanction dispositions to be drawn from additional research that explores association and spuriousness results among those outcomes. Neighborhood characteristics, for example, may be of critical importance during the initiation of a stop but inconsequential to post-stop dispositions. This will allow scholars to triangulate their results among a host of findings and better inform our understandings of racial profiling.

Conclusion

The answer to the causal question of racial profiling remains largely elusive because researchers have failed to make a causal connection between citizen race and officer decision-making. While automobile stop data has been able to establish some consistency in the associative relationship between citizen race and officer decision-making, temporal order and spuriousness issues continue to plague racial profiling research. More specifically, stop initiation research tends to be temporally inconsistent with officer decision-making, and post-stop dispositions are rarely specified in automobile stop data. Additionally, specification error has constrained our ability to fully engage in falsification, as researchers rarely estimate departmental, passenger, vehicle, and temporal factors that can influence officer decision-making. Narrowly constructed analytical strategies and a heavy reliance on static secondary data analyses continue to perpetuate these issues. In order to advance this field of inquiry, researchers should engage in primary data collection and work with stakeholders to amend current data collection procedures based on existing knowledge of officer decision-making. Furthermore, researchers should explore recent statistical innovations in their analytical strategies. Addressing these methodological issues will advance our understandings of racial profiling, ground our theoretical understandings of the driving while Black phenomenon in reality, and provide citizens with the procedural justice transparency that they demand.

Discussion Questions

1. Discuss the three elements of causation and why it is difficult for researchers to find causation when they study vehicle stops.
2. Explain the differences found in the earlier versus more recent racial profiling studies. What methodological issues might explain these differences?
3. Which rival causal factors in racial profiling research seem to be the ones with the most empirical support?

References

Alpert, G., Dunham, R., & Smith, M. (2007). Investigating racial profiling by the Miami-Dade police department: A multimethod approach. *Criminology and Public Policy*, 6(1), 25–56.

Antonovics, K., & Knight, B. (2009). A new look at racial profiling: Evidence from the Boston police department. *The Review of Economics and Statistics*, 91(1), 163–177.

Barnum, C., & Perfetti, R. (2010). Race-sensitive choices by police officers in traffic stop encounters. *Police Quarterly*, 13(2), 180–208.

Batton, C., & Kadleck, C. (2004). Theoretical and methodological issues in racial profiling research. *Police Quarterly*, 7(1), 30–64.

Bolger, C. (2014). *Consistency or discord0064: A meta-analysis of police officer decisions to search and use force.* Doctoral dissertation at Cincinnati University.

Briggs, S. (2007). *People and places: An examination of searches during traffic stops in Minneapolis.* Doctoral dissertation at the University of Nebraska—Omaha.

Crank, J., & Langworthy, R. (1992). An institutional perspective of police. *Journal of Criminal Law and Criminology*, 83(2), 338–363.

Engel, R. (2008). A critique of the "outcome test" in racial profiling. *Justice Quarterly*, 25(1), 1–35.

Engel, R., & Calnon, J. (2004). Examining the influence of driver's characteristics during traffic stops with police: Results from a national survey. *Justice Quarterly*, 21(1), 49–90.

Fallik, S., & Novak, K. (2012). The decision to search: Is race or ethnicity important? *Journal of Contemporary Criminal Justice*, 28(2), 146–165.

Farrell, A., McDevitt, J., Bailey, L., Andersen, C., & Pierce, E. (2004). *Massachusetts racial and gender profiling final report.* Boston, MA: Institute on Race and Justice, Northeastern University.

Klinger, D. (1997). Negotiating order in police work: An ecological theory of police response to deviance. *Criminology*, 35, 277–306.

Kraska, P., & Neuman, L. (2012). *Criminal justice and criminology research methods* (2nd ed.). Upper Saddle River, NJ: Pearson Education, Inc.

Langton, L., & Durose, M. (2013). *Police behavior during traffic and street stops, 2011.* Washington, DC: Bureau of Justice Statistics.

Lundman, R. (2004). Driver race, ethnicity, and gender and citizen reports of vehicle searches by police and vehicle search hits: Toward a triangulated scholarly understanding. *The Journal of Criminal Law and Criminology*, 94(2), 309–350.

Meehan, A., & Ponder, M. (2002). Race and place: The ecology of racial profiling African American motorists. *Justice Quarterly*, 19(3), 399–430.

Miller, K. (2008). Police stops, pretext, and racial profiling: Explaining warning and ticket stops using citizen self-reports. *Journal of Ethnicity in Criminal Justice*, 6(2), 123–149.

National Research Council. (2004). *Fairness and effectiveness in policing.* Washington, DC: National Academies Press.

Newport, F. (2016). *Public opinion context: Americans, race and police.* Washington, DC: Gallup Organization.

Novak, K. (2004). Disparity and racial profiling in traffic enforcement. *Police Quarterly*, 7(1), 65–96.

Novak, K., & Chamlin, M. (2008). Racial threat, suspicion, and police behavior: The impact of race and place in traffic enforcement. *Crime and Delinquency*, 58(2), 275–300.

Paoline, E., & Terrill, W. (2005). The impact of police culture on traffic stop searches: An analysis of attitudes and behavior. *Policing*, 28(3), 455–472.

Pickerill, M., Mosher, C., & Pratt, T. (2009). Search and seizure, racial profiling, and traffic stops: A disparate impact framework. *Law and Policy*, 31(1), 1–30.

The President's Task-Force on 21st century policing. (2015). Washington, DC: Office of Community Oriented Policing and Services.

Reitzel, J., & Piquero, A. (2006). Does it exist? Studying citizens' attitudes of racial profiling. *Police Quarterly*, 9(2), 161–183.

Riksheim, E., & Chermak, S. (1993). Causes of police behavior revisited. *Journal of Criminal Justice*, 21(4), 353–382.

Rosenbaum, D., Schuck, A., Costello, S., Hawkins, D., & Ring, M. (2005). Attitudes toward the police: The effects of direct and vicarious experience. *Police Quarterly*, 8(3), 343–365.

Rydberg, J., & Terrill, W. (2010). The effect of higher education on police behavior. *Police Quarterly*, 13(1), 92–120.

Sampson, R., Raudenbush, S., & Earls, F. (1997). Neighborhoods and violent crime: A multilevel study of collective efficacy. *Science*, 277(5328), 918–924.

Schafer, J., Carter, D., Katz-Bannister, A., & Wells, W. (2006). Decision making in traffic stop encounters: A multivariate analysis of police behavior. *Police Quarterly, 9*(2), 184–209.

Sherman, L. (1980). Causes of police behavior: The current state of quantitative research. *Journal of Research in Crime & Delinquency, 17*(1), 69–100.

Tillyer, R., Engel, R., & Cherauskas, J. (2009). Best practices in vehicle stop data collection and analysis. *Policing, 33*(1), 69–92.

Tillyer, R., Klahm, C., & Engel, R. (2011). The discretion to search: A multilevel examination of driver demographics and officer characteristics. *Journal of Contemporary Criminal Justice, 28*(2), 184–205.

Tyler, T., & Wakslak, C. (2004). Profiling and police legitimacy: Procedural justice, attributions of motive, and acceptance of police authority. *Criminology, 42*(2), 253–281.

Withrow, B. (2006). *Racial profiling: From rhetoric to reason.* Upper Saddle River, NJ: Pearson Prentice Hall.

Reading 4.2   The Impact of Hot Spots Policing on Collective Efficacy

Over the past 50 years, researchers have reported that certain policing tactics have the potential to impact crime and social control in neighborhoods. For decades, we have known that hot spots policing, in which officers identify high-crime locations and conduct saturation patrols of those areas, can reduce crime and disorder. Kochel and Weisburd (2019) took hot spot policing research a step further by studying whether the type of policing conducted at hot spots—directed patrol or problem-solving—would produce better results than traditional policing methods. Directed patrol of hot spots involves a greater visible police presence in areas. Problem-solving, or problem-oriented policing, is a police response that encourages officers to use their own knowledge of the community's problems and feedback from the community members themselves to come up with creative solutions to each area's unique challenges. Kochel and Weisburd's (2019) classical experiment uses multiple measures to assess the extent to which policing practices are associated with crime levels and residents' feelings about police performance. The results were rather surprising, so this article contains a good discussion about the extent to which implementation of the treatment stimulus might have impacted the findings. If you have difficulty understanding the section about construct validity and how it is relevant to the paper, you might want to skip ahead to Chapter 6 for a quick review.

The Impact of Hot Spots Policing on Collective Efficacy: Findings From a Randomized Field Trial

Tammy Rinehart Kochel and David Weisburd

Tammy Rinehart Kochel, PhD, is Associate Professor and Graduate Director for Criminology and Criminal Justice at Southern Illinois University Carbondale. She conducts research on policing and communities, examining public perceptions of police and how policing strategies and behaviors may influence those views. Her focus addresses the factors that promote and the consequences of police legitimacy and procedural justice. She also examines the effectiveness of policing strategies on crime, with an emphasis on targeted approaches such as problem-solving, hot spots policing, and focused deterrence. David Weisburd is Distinguished Professor of Criminology, Law and Society at George Mason University, and Walter E. Meyer Professor of Law and Criminal Justice at the Hebrew University. His key research interests are in crime and place and policing, though he has studied a broad range of topics in his career. He received the Stockholm Prize in Criminology in 2010, the Sutherland Prize from the American Society of Criminology in 2015, and the August Vollmer Award from the American Society of Criminology in 2017. Correspondence to: Tammy Rinehart Kochel, Southern Illinois University, Carbondale, IL, USA. Email: tkochel@siu.edu

Over the last two decades, hot spots policing has emerged as one of the most widely used evidence-based practices in policing (Sherman & Weisburd, 1995; Weisburd & Telep, 2014). It has been widely recognized as an effective approach for reducing crime and disorder, and reviews over the last decade by the National Academy of Sciences (Skogan & Frydl, 2004; Weisburd & Magmundar, 2017) and the Campbell Collaboration (Braga, Papachristos, & Hureau, 2012) have concluded that hot spots policing approaches of different types can be an effective police response to crime at hot spots and that crime reductions do not lead to displacement to nearby areas (Weisburd et al., 2006). However, while much is known about crime control impacts of hot spots policing, we know little about its impacts on the community's ability to develop informal social controls.

Does hot spots policing help strengthen communities in their own efforts and their own capacity to address or control crime and disorder, indirectly reducing crime by promoting or supporting neighborhood collective efficacy? Collective efficacy is not only a well-documented protective factor against crime, it also has been shown to mediate risk factors such as concentrated disadvantage (Mazerolle, Wickes, & McBroom, 2010; Sampson & Raudenbush, 1999). If police can develop strategies that assist neighborhoods in developing stronger collective efficacy, especially disadvantaged neighborhoods where crime concentrates and collective efficacy struggles to form, this would serve as an efficient new tool for police to use for crime prevention.

Our study investigates whether hot spots policing approaches promote collective efficacy in disadvantaged, high-crime contexts. We apply an experimental design to examine a collaborative problem-solving versus a directed patrol (police presence) approach relative to standard policing practices in 71 residential crime hot spots.

Collective Efficacy

Collective efficacy is a social condition that arises in communities or neighborhoods that contain an interdependent network of people who feel a sense of community, shared ownership, and trust in one another. Collective efficacy is the product of a bond between neighbors that is based upon shared values and goals, derived from a common social situation and context with common adversaries (Sampson, Raudenbush, & Earls, 1997). While initially portrayed more as a product of friendship networks, subsequent research has shown that engagement rather than friendship can be sufficient (Bellair, 1997; Sampson, 2008). Social interaction, communication, and shared experiences, and sometimes also personal ties and

friendships, create shared expectations among residents for what behaviors and norms are acceptable versus not appropriate in the neighborhood. Residents willingly promote behaviors expected to produce social order and exert informal social control against circumstances and individuals whose actions work against that order. Residents may also develop an expectation that other neighbors will also exert influence and control in an effort to support the behavioral expectations needed to achieve social order (Coleman, 1988).

Examples of informal social control behaviors include taking action to deal with kids skipping school and hanging out on neighborhood streets, fights, questioning strangers, cleaning up disorder, watching neighbors' homes while they are gone, and similar activities. Pattillo (1998) found that neighborhood ties are associated with residents directly intervening with problems. However, the nature of that intervention (e.g., collective supervision of young children versus teens versus calling police) might vary based on the nature of the social ties (Carr, 2003).

Past research on collective efficacy consistently shows that more collective efficacy in an area is associated with less crime and disorder in the area. This finding has been robust across different contexts (Kochel, Parks, & Mastrofski, 2013; Mazerolle et al., 2010; Sampson & Raudenbush, 1999; Sampson et al., 1997). Furthermore, collective efficacy can mediate the relationship between disadvantage and crime (Browning, Dietz, & Feinberg, 2004; Sampson & Raudenbush, 1999). Of course, it can also be difficult to engender in socially disadvantaged areas because people living in socially disadvantaged contexts tend to be highly mobile, and racial and ethnic heterogeneity or language barriers in these contexts can make communication and spending time together challenging, and these conditions tend to persist in high crime places. In areas with much physical disorder, past research has found it is difficult for social cohesion to thrive (Markowitz, Bellair, Liska, & LIU, 2001). Furthermore, people living in high crime areas tend to be aware of their vulnerability (Kershaw et al., 2000), and feeling at risk for victimization, experiencing it (May & Dunaway, 2000), or being witness to it (Johnston, 2001) promotes fear, and fear can lead to withdrawal. Thus, it is important to consider whether crime control programs of the police also help communities, especially disadvantaged communities, develop collective efficacy (Kubrin & Weitzer, 2003; Sampson, 2002) such that informal social control may be applied to address a variety of problem behaviors (Wickes, Hipp, Sargeant, & Homel, 2013).

The Cooperation Hypothesis and Collective Efficacy

We draw from collective efficacy theory and the cooperation hypothesis to outline the conceptual process of how neighborhoods may develop collective efficacy and the mechanisms through which police may help foster it (Scott, 2002). For collective efficacy to develop, the theory suggests that people must interact with one another and recognize their shared situation and interests in social order for the area. Also, residents must develop a common understanding of what behaviors support that social order and which activities and conditions are not acceptable. Finally, individuals must feel a duty and follow through to take action to socialize people to those expectations by exerting informal social control.

We recognize that police could develop specific programs to increase collective efficacy in the community. We sought, however, to ask a different question. Our work does not examine whether the police "can" increase collective efficacy in the community if they focus themselves on that task. Rather we are interested in whether a widely applied and proven crime control strategy enhances collective efficacy as a secondary outcome.

The cooperation hypothesis asserts that when police are a more capable and supportive resource to neighborhoods, residents will be more inclined to take collective action to address problems (Skogan, 1989). Some scholars would advocate that, in fact, parochial efforts to exert social control cannot function effectively without police (and other local

organizations' support). Upon conducting a literature review on the topic, (Gau, 2014, p. 215) concluded that "Informal controls realize their full potential only when forces of extra-neighborhood controls are strongly and actively engaged with the community and its inhabitants." For example, Carr (2003) found that for residents to be able to actively engage in enforcing community social norms, residents needed to trust that police would be able to arrive quickly and effectively address the problem. Silver and Miller (2004) also suggest that when police are seen as a responsive and available resource to the community, residents will be more empowered to address inappropriate behaviors in the neighborhood. Likewise, Kubrin and Weitzer's (2003) study suggests that when police are not seen as a resource or viewed as unresponsive, residents may feel it is too risky to directly intervene. Furthermore, calling the police has sometimes been treated as a form of informal social control (Carr, 2003; Carr, Napolitano, & Keating, 2007).

Our point is that police may support neighborhood efforts to engage in informal social control behaviors by signaling and reinforcing informal norms affirming residents' efforts at informal social control (Kochel, 2012; LaFree, 1998) or providing an environment whereby residents feel safe enough to take action—empowering residents to exert informal social control (Kochel et al., 2013). For example, police presence in the area, while demonstrating effective and procedurally just behaviors, may reduce fear and embolden residents. Police taking action or choosing not to officially act when that behavior reinforces local behavioral norms (e.g., focusing on drinking in public, blight issues, or speeding or using informal strategies to reduce truancy) may supplement and reinforce residents' ongoing informal social control efforts.

Empirical Evidence

Available research supports two primary mechanisms through which police may contribute, albeit the findings are not conclusive. First, police presence may help reduce fear of crime and thus reduce the risk of withdrawal and subsequent lack of informal social control (Johnston, 2001; Moore & Trojanowicz, 1988; Morenoff, Sampson, & Raudenbush, 2001; Trojanowicz & Baldwin, 1982; Silverman & Della-Giustina, 2001). A systematic literature review conducted by Zhao, Schneider, and Thurman (2002) supports that police presence is associated with less fear, with the largest fear reductions for proactive policing and community policing strategies versus other forms of police presence. Several studies also found a direct link between police presence or accessibility and forms of informal social control. Scott (2002) found that residents' perceptions of police accessibility across different levels of the police organization were positively related to social capital in the neighborhood. Ferguson and Mindel (2007) found a positive relationship between police presence and residents' attendance at community meetings/participation in neighborhood watch. However, Renauer (2007) found the opposite to be true—in his study, more frequent police attendance at neighborhood association meetings was associated with diminished informal social control—he contemplated whether this backfire effect may have been because police actions disempowered rather than empowered residents. Furthermore, Sargeant, Wickes, and Mazerolle's (2013) in-depth interviews with residents living in a high crime, low income, and low collective efficacy neighborhood in Australia suggested that a strong police *enforcement* presence in an area could increase the proportion of negative interactions between the police and the public. Residents there reported that experiencing negative encounters diminishes police legitimacy and discourages them from intervening in community problems. Thus, what police do while present in a community may affect the impact on informal social control and collective efficacy outcomes.

Second, research seems to suggest that confidence and trust in the capacity of police to support the local community efforts to promote social order by delivering quality and effective services may help promote some aspects of collective efficacy. Views about the legitimacy of police may also be important. Silver and Miller (2004), Tyler and Fagan (2008) and Wells, Schafer, Varano, and Bynum (2006) found that higher satisfaction with police was associated with more informal social control and an increased willingness among residents to address neighborhood problems. Similarly, Warner (2014) found that faith in police was positively associated with informal social control behaviors, while Tyler and Fagan (2008) found that police legitimacy contributed to residents' willingness to help the community. Renauer (2007) found that a related measure, trust in police motives, also promotes informal social control.

More recently, Sargeant (2015) and Sargeant et al. (2013) found that people are more willing to intervene when they see police as effective and legitimate. Even in a developing nation, Kochel (2012, 2013) found that communities that reported that police delivered quality and competent police services and had lower levels of police misconduct reported more collective efficacy and less crime. The only study we found that uses longitudinal data to study these neighborhood processes, Kochel (2017), found that over time, greater police competence is associated with greater neighborhood collective efficacy and also that more collectively efficacious neighborhoods reported subsequently higher levels of police competence—documenting a reciprocal relationship. These studies suggest that police actions that build confidence in their effectiveness and legitimacy should promote collective efficacy. However, the findings report on residents' opinions or on associations between residents' views and do not benefit from the rigors of an experimental test. It is important to be able to examine these effects more definitively.

One key issue in our study is whether the impacts hypothesized more generally would apply to a police intervention that is focused on specific streets or a portion of an apartment complex. Some scholars have argued that neighborhood mechanisms are not relevant to micro geographic units, such as those that are the focus of hot spots policing. Sherman, Gartin, and Buerger (1989, p. 30), for example, argue that "[t]raditional collectivity theories may be appropriate for explaining community-level variation, but they seem inappropriate for small, publicly visible places with highly transient populations."

More recently, scholars have been able to explore the relevance of mechanisms of informal social controls at the street segment level. Weisburd, Groff, and Yang (2014), for example, find that collective efficacy, as measured by the frequency of voting behavior, is strongly related to crime at hot spots. In a more recent study, Wooditch, Weisburd, and White (2016) find that levels of trust and willingness to intervene differ significantly between high crime and low crime streets. Weisburd et al. (2014) argue that the geographies of crime hot spots may be seen in many cases as small-scale communities. For example, Taylor (1997, 1998) argues that such micro geographic units function as "behavior settings" (Wicker, 1987, p. 614). They have many of the traits of communities that have been seen as crucial to social disorganization theory, in that these physical units function also as social units with specific routines (Weisburd, Groff, & Yang, 2012).

In our study we compare two common approaches to hot spots policing—problem-solving and directed patrol—to a standard policing condition. We assert that each of these strategies would theoretically affect different parts of the collective efficacy-building process. Thus, they may be expected to produce different types and levels of success at promoting collective efficacy or its components—social cohesion and informal social control.

Expected Contribution of the Different Policing Approaches

Problem-solving in hot spots draws from routine activities theory and aims to investigate and understand the specific nature of the crime problem in order to develop tailored response strategies designed to reduce the opportunities for crime to occur in that location (Schmerler, Perkins, Phillips, Rinehart, & Townsend, 2006). Routine activities theory suggests that in order for a crime to occur, motivated offenders must encounter suitable targets in a location with

insufficient guardianship. Thus, when police implement problem-solving strategies, they seek to address at least one of these three components—potential offender, target, or location—often in collaboration with relevant stakeholders. When conducted in partnership with members of the neighborhood, police efforts at problem-solving may provide an opportunity for residents to interact with each other and facilitate social cohesion (Scott, 2002; Skogan & Hartnett, 1997). This should build a sense of connection to neighbors and to the neighborhood. Problem-solving may reveal potential threats to safety in the neighborhood to residents, which could unite residents in their shared fate. Finally, problem-solving should lead to situational responses that could reduce opportunities for crime—empowering residents to take collective action. Problem-solving in hot spots would appear to have the potential both to promote social cohesion among residents and to encourage informal social control.

Directed patrol in hot spots historically has entailed increasing police presence and visibility with a goal of deterring would-be criminals by increasing the risk of detection and punishment (Telep, Mitchell, & Weisburd, 2014). Generally, officers are not asked to perform a specific activity while present (e.g., traffic enforcement, pedestrian checks). No prior study that we are aware of has carefully logged what specific activities have been conducted. Only one previously published directed patrol experiment specified the nature of the directed patrol activities, and that was to conduct foot patrol (Ratcliffe, Taniguchi, Groff, & Wood, 2011). With limited knowledge about the nature of police presence during directed patrol efforts, our expectation for the impact of directed patrol on collective efficacy was that as long as activities are not limited to overt enforcement activities, the increased police presence and visibility provided by directed patrol strategies in hot spots may reassure residents of safety, allowing them to more freely engage in their own informal social control behaviors. Conversely, heavy enforcement during directed patrol could generate fear and withdrawal and so may reduce collective efficacy.

Study Site

Our experiment was conducted in St. Louis County, MO, in 2012–2013. Covering more than 500 square miles, with over one million residents, the county is the 34th largest in the US and contains 17% of the state's population (St. Louis County Department of Planning, 2013b).

From 2011 to 2012, the poverty rate increased to 9.7 percent, and the county had 24 high poverty census tracts, meaning 20 to 40 percent of residents live in poverty. Both crime and poverty are concentrated geographically. In St. Louis County, poverty is concentrated in North St. Louis County. Most of the high-poverty census tracts are located there, and additionally, within North County, two census tracts are considered extreme-poverty areas, containing more than 40 percent of residents living in poverty (St. Louis County Department of Planning, 2013a).

Our hot spots analysis, described below, identified 71 crime hot spots, two-thirds of which are situated in the North County area. Project hot spots account for 0.25 percent of the residential areas in St. Louis County and 10.6 percent of the Part I and II crimes in residential areas. Places where disadvantage and crime concentrate are the types of places that typically lack collective efficacy and where collective efficacy is difficult to foster. Yet, it is in these places where increasing informal social control and collective efficacy could potentially have the greatest impact.

Methods

Hot Spot Selection

To identify crime hot spots, a crime analyst examined Part I and Part II crime incidents between December 2010 and November 2011 using kernel density with Roberts Cross and Getis Ord GI* (Ord & Getis, 1995) to identify spatial clustering of incidents and then also assessing counts at street segments to verify crime concentrations in residential areas over which SLCPD had primary patrol jurisdiction.[1]

We identified areas with at least 40 addresses to ensure a sufficient population to reliably assess public perceptions. To ensure treatment integrity, the polygons that represented the hot spots were not permitted to share a common side, meaning we did not want to permit contamination from one hot spot to another because residents might observe a treatment or experience a treatment happening in a different hot spot. Before final selection of the hot spots, the primary author and the police liaison visited the hot spots that were in close geographic proximity to examine whether someone standing in one hot spot might reasonably see or experience the treatment of a nearby hot spot—eliminating any conflicting hot spots or altering boundaries (e.g., keeping a residential block in between). Seventy-one hot spots are included in the study.

Project hot spots average .01 square miles, equivalent to about four city blocks, although the area is suburban, and so in general, hot spots do not lie on grids like inner-city hot spots often do. Two-thirds of hot spots are located in multi-family housing areas. At baseline (2011), sites averaged 31 crime incidents in a year, ranging from 8 to 115 incidents. Calls for service ranged from 73 to 904, with a median of 203 and a mean of 247 (the hot spot with 904 calls is an outlier). Common crime problems included assault, vandalism, burglary, drugs, and larceny.

Treatment

The experiment compared problem-solving (PS) and directed patrol (DP) treatments to standard police practices (SPP). Police resources allowed us to implement treatment in 40 hot spots: 20 PS and 20 DP sites. The remaining 31 hot spots were allocated as control/SPP sites. As most of the hot spots were located in the North County precinct (one of seven precincts), in order to ensure that sufficient police resources were available to adequately conduct the treatment, we first blocked on North County, and then we randomly assigned treatment status. To protect treatment integrity, we did not identify the locations of hot spots assigned to SPP to officers. Thus, all identified areas received typical police practices (e.g., responding to calls for service, routine preventive patrol, traffic enforcement), and the 40 treatment sites received the additional assigned police strategy (DP or PS) on top of SPP for a five-month treatment period lasting June through October 2012. Past hot spots studies have varied considerably in the length of the treatment period. We identified a broad range from about 90 days (Taylor, Koper, & Woods, 2011) to 15 months (Weisburd & Green, 1995). We identified a 5-month period because we wanted to ensure that residents would be likely to see the directed patrols and thus chose warmer months, following the baseline survey, for the treatment period. A shorter time frame would have been difficult for the sites implementing problem-solving. A longer time frame would have been difficult for officers implementing directed patrols. In fact, after about 4.5 months, officer fatigue led to declines in extra patrols. Future research examining whether the length of treatment produces differences in impact would be helpful.

Problem-Solving

The PS treatment applied the SARA model of problem-solving (see Schmerler et al., 2006). Supervisors assigned specific officers to the 20 PS sites. Assigned officers and a full-time crime analyst dedicated to the project received three days of training, a booster training session one month into treatment, and access to consultation throughout treatment. Officers were instructed to partner with at least one stakeholder to address at least one neighborhood crime or disorder problem and to tie response strategies to what they learned about the conditions contributing to the identified problem(s). Many officers selected property crimes (45% of problems worked)—burglary, theft of or from vehicles, and larceny—but some focused on violent crimes (18%)—domestic violence, assault, drug and gang problems, quality of life concerns (15%), and repeat address issues (15%)—often problems with juveniles or burglar alarms. Across the 20 sites, analysis activities included examining incident and calls for service data; officers conducting resident surveys door to door;

in-person and video observation of the problem areas at different times of day; Crime Prevention through Environmental Design assessments; interviews and discussion with property managers, landlords, utility companies, a railroad company, maintenance personnel, school personnel, parents, residents, and confidential informants; attending community events to talk informally with residents; reviewing tax records to discern ownership of vacant properties; and reviewing gang databases.

Although officers employed strategies that were appropriate and tailored to the identified problems, many did not include resident engagement. Strategies included securing vacant residences; removing abandoned vehicles, trash, and overgrowth; repairing fencing and addressing other property security features—lighting and locking; instituting trespassing policies and other tenant policies; increasing communication with a variety of agencies; gang presentation to staff at a local school; identifying and stopping a stolen-property fencing operation; enforcing ordinances; securing access to utility boxes and air conditioning units; installing and monitoring security cameras; redirecting students to alternative pathways home from school; coordinating with an alarm company to fix a malfunction; and assessing fines for repeat false alarm violations, among others. Only a few sites provided the conditions outlined by approaches 2 and 3. For example, in three sites officers distributed informational materials to residents about theft of and from vehicles in the parking lots and offered strategies to limit the thefts to apartment residents. In one of these locations, a sign was also posted in the parking lot. A similar educational strategy was used in a fourth location to advise residents about residential burglary and burglary prevention. In still another location, the officer spoke to residents and conducted CPTED assessments of their homes. In spite of only about one-quarter of problem-solving sites involving providing residents information about problems and/or target hardening information, conceivably, many of the strategies may have promoted informal social control when they proved effective at reducing crime and disorder and increasing security, consistent with the cooperation hypothesis.

Directed Patrol

DP applied a general deterrence approach and aimed to double officers' time spent at the location. We used automated vehicle location (AVL) data to document time spent at baseline and weekly during the treatment to assess treatment integrity. On average, officers spent 2.25 hours per week at each hot spot in the seven weeks preceding treatment and 3.26 hours per week at each hot spot during treatment—approximately a 45 percent increase in time spent by officers. Officers did spend more time in DP locations than elsewhere and compared to baseline, albeit time spent was not doubled throughout the treatment period.

Following the Koper Curve (Koper, 1995; Telep et al., 2014), officers were asked to implement 11-to-15-minute extra patrols. In practice, 41 percent of extra patrols lasted between 11 and15 minutes, and the median length was just over 14 minutes.

The goal of directed patrol was to increase officer presence—thus, officers were not obligated to perform specific tasks during their extra patrols. Even so, we arranged a procedure with dispatchers and officers to record time spent and officer activities. Assessment of the activities revealed that there was not an enforcement orientation to directed patrol. Officer-recorded activities show that officers tended to conduct roving (37% of activities) or stationary patrols (16%) and sometimes completed reports (13%); less frequently, they conducted vehicle enforcement (9%), foot patrol (5%), or pedestrian stops (2%); conversed with residents (6%); sat car to car (6%); and other miscellaneous activities (6%). While doing DP, officers recorded talking to 247 citizens outside a traffic or pedestrian stop. Officers' activity notes suggested that they spoke to juveniles, property management personnel, and residents in general regarding problems in the area or just making brief, casual conversation. In some cases, officers initiated contact, and at times, citizens approached them while conducting stationary or roving patrols. With the additional time spent at the locations, officers seemed to default to doing "more" of what they typically did.

Standard Police Practice/Control

Officers were not informed about the locations of the SPP hot spots. No special treatment was provided to these locations, and policing activity continued as usual, generally consisting of response to calls for service and routine preventative patrols.

Community Survey

Using address data provided by SLCPD, we randomly sampled addresses in each hot spot using a random number generator and surveyed adult residents who answered the door. We attempted to survey the same residents across all three waves, although we permitted address-level substitution when individuals at later waves lived at the address with the initial respondent (e.g., spouse, child, roommate, parent), and the original respondent was not available and, to deal with potential attrition, supplemented later waves with additional randomly sampled addresses from each hot spot using a random number generator, excluding addresses that were deemed invalid or vacant at prior waves. Thus, residents were sampled one to three times using the same survey questionnaire across waves and treatment types. Baseline was conducted in March through May 2012. Short-term impact was collected between November 2012 and January 2013. Long-term impact was collected in May through July 2013.[2]

Variables

We assess the impact on collective efficacy by examining the relative effects of the two hot spots policing approaches (vs SPP) on the components of collective efficacy: informal social control and social cohesion and separately assessing the impact on a combined measure of collective efficacy. Thus, the analyses contain three dependent variables. We conducted a confirmatory factor analysis with the two components and found good model fit (CFA = .994, TLI = .992, RMSEA = .035, WRMR = 1.027). The latent measure for social cohesion (α = .8321) is composed of four indicators reflecting residents' level of agreement or disagreement that residents in the area (1) are a close-knit community, (2) are willing to help each other, (3) share the same values, and (4) interact with one another. The latent measure for informal social control (α = .7702) is also composed of four indicators reflecting residents' level of agreement or disagreement that residents in the area would (1) do something if children were spray-painting graffiti on a local building, (2) do something if a group of children were skipping school and hanging out on a local corner, (3) break up a fight happening in front of a house or business in the area, and (4) report a violent crime that they saw. The two measures are correlated at r = .548. Historically, scholars have combined these two constructs into one integrated scale (Gibson, Zhao, Lovrich, & Gaffney, 2002; Morenoff et al., 2001; Sampson & Raudenbush, 1999; Sampson et al., 1997), and so we have also created an integrated collective

efficacy scale (α = .8246) by averaging across all the non-missing indicators for each case. With limited missing data (less than 10%) and good reliability, we also opted to convert these variables to more easily interpretable percent of maximum possible (POMP) scores, which have a range of 0 to 100, like the percentages one may have on a test. The formula is:

$$POMP = \frac{(\text{Observed minus the Minimum in the scale})}{(\text{Maximum minus Minimum scale score})} \times 100$$

Results

Table 1 provides the results of the mixed effect regression models, and Figure 1 graphs the predicted margins based on those models. The results show that residents living in the PS areas

Table 1 Mixed Effect Regression with Three Dependent Variables

	Model 1		Model 2 Informal social		Model 3	
	Social cohesion (n = 2794)		Control (n = 2745)		Collective efficacy (n = 2796)	
Fixed effects	b	Robust s.e.	b	Robust s.e.	b	Robust s.e.
intercept	50.575**	(6.433)	56.541**	(6.130)	53.340**	(6.140)
Wave 2 (vs W1)	0.537	(1.314)	3.680*	(1.455)	1.833	(1.458)
Wave 3 (vs W1)	−1.250	(0.845)	1.734	(1.455)	−0.281	(1.289)
PS (vs SPP)	−2.594	(3.647)	−3.740	(3.101)	−3.198	(3.638)
DP (vs SPP)	−3.439**	(0.638)	−5.968**	(0.720)	−4.507**	(0.001)
Wave 2 x PS (vs W2xSPP)	−1.324	(1.251)	−1.866	(1.073)	−1.530	(1.093)
Wave 2 x DP (vs W2xSPP)	−0.784	(1.892)	2.778**	(0.201)	0.949	(0.836)
Wave 3 x PS (vs W3xSPP)	3.359	(2.920)	2.345*	(0.982)	2.997	(2.471)
Wave 3 x DP (vs W3xSPP)	2.417**	(0.652)	7.584**	(1.961)	4.779**	(0.853)
Black (vs not black)	2.737**	(0.932)	5.046**	(0.187)	4.398**	(0.227)
Own (vs rent)	−0.248	(1.851)	1.054	(0.069)	0.270	(1.172)
Random Effects	σ^2	s.e.	σ^2	s.e.	σ^2	s.e.
North County	21.0911	(0.383)	18.842	(0.667)	20.379	(0.577)
Hot spot	25.666	(4.184)	26.566	(3.131)	23.190	(4.466)
Address	132.137	(78.676)	105.490	(22.684)	101.063	(26.719)
Person	286.594	(94.325)	233.460	(7.855)	201.056	(35.428)
Residual	355.385	(19.342)	426.145	(76.087)	241.863	(28.325)

*$p \leq .05$; **$p \leq .01$

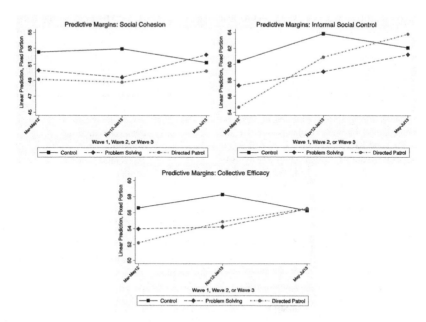

Figure 1 Predicted Margins

did not hold significantly different views than the control group residents at baseline on these outcomes (social cohesion $b = -2.594$, informal social control $b = -3.740$, collective efficacy $b = -3.198$). However, DP areas had significantly lower assessments of social cohesion ($b = -3.439$), informal social control ($b = -5.968$), and collective efficacy ($b = -4.507$) than the control group (SPP) at baseline. The main effects in the model control for baseline differences. Examining the other control measures, across all three outcomes, African American residents had more positive assessments than non-black residents for each of the outcomes (social cohesion $b = 2.737$, informal social control $b = 5.046$, collective efficacy $b = 4.398$).

Examining the treatment effect, in the short term, residents of DP areas showed significant improvements over residents receiving SPP in informal social control ($b = 2.778$). In the period immediately following treatment, DP area residents' assessments of informal social

control increased about 17 percent from baseline (The equivalent of improving from a test score of F to a D. Both residents of PS and DP areas saw significant informal social control improvements in the long term relative to residents in the SPP areas (PS $b = 2.345$, DP $b = 7.584$). DP area residents' assessments improved an additional 5 percent above what they reported immediately following treatment, while residents of PS areas showed an improvement in the long term of about 7 percent relative to baseline assessments. There was no significant difference among residents of SPP areas of assessments of informal social control in the long term relative to baseline.

Additionally, residents of DP areas saw modest but statistically significant improvements in the long term for social cohesion ($b = 2.737$; a 2% increase relative to baseline) while social cohesion among residents in SPP showed a modest 2.5 percent decline in the long term relative to baseline. Collective efficacy is a combined measure of the two components; thus it is no surprise that we see those benefits only among DP residents in the long term (b = 4.779) since that is when and where social cohesion showed significant improvement relative to SPP residents.

Discussion and Conclusions

We can conclude from these findings that hot spots policing strategies can impact on collective efficacy in a micro area, especially on residents' willingness to engage in informal social control behaviors. The results provide support for the cooperation hypothesis in that when police implemented hot spots policing strategies that reduced crime in the area—although it was not the focus of the study, we did examine the crime impact of the DP and PS approaches in a prior paper, noting a 5 percent decline in calls for service within DP areas during the treatment period relative to baseline, a 7 percent decline in calls for service in PS areas compared to baseline, and no change in the SPP areas (Kochel, Burruss, & Weisburd, 2015)—residents were more inclined to take action to address problems (Hunter, 1985; Skogan, 1989; Bursik & Grasmick, 1993; Carr, 2003; Silver & Miller, 2004). Our rigorous test of this potential secondary outcome suggests what several past correlational studies have reported: that faith in the capabilities and competence of police and the effectiveness of police at reducing crime can improve informal social control (Kochel, 2012, 2017; Sargeant, 2015; Sargeant et al., 2013; Warner, 2014).

The largest improvements were among hot spot residents receiving DP. Residents from areas receiving DP reported both short- and long-term improvements in informal social control over residents from SPP areas, whereas residents from areas receiving the PS strategy realized significant improvements over residents of SPP areas only in the long term. This is in some sense a surprising finding given prior arguments that problem-solving will increase community cohesion and informal social controls, (e.g., Braga, McDevitt, & Pierce, 2006; Braga & Weisburd, 2010). We suspect our findings may

reflect the content of problem-solving efforts in our study.

Braga (2002) and Braga and Weisburd (2010) focus on what may be called community problem-solving, or efforts that specifically look to involve the community in problem-solving efforts. In our study, we could identify only few cases where officers in the problem-solving areas truly engaged residents. Accordingly, they did not provide opportunities for residents to interact with one another. Without this engagement, there is no reason to expect a PS strategy in hot spots to improve social cohesion. A future test of PS in hot spots as a facilitator of collective efficacy should place emphasis on engaging residents actively in the effort.

Furthermore, only a few officers implementing PS in hot spots incorporated responses that provided information to residents about the nature of the problems in the area. Providing evidence about the prevalence of crime problems highlights potential threats to residents, instilling the realization of a common adversary and need for safety—promoting a sense of oneness or shared fate and need for parochial action. In the few sites that took this approach, officers also tended to outline response strategies to target harden vehicles or residences. Providing crime prevention information has the capacity to instill knowledge in residents about the tools needed for effective parochial action. However, the nature of the responses outlined for the problems addressed in PS areas (e.g., posting signs or distributing fliers telling residents to lock vehicles and not leave valuables in the vehicle, in an effort to reduce theft from vehicles) was to be implemented by individuals and did not require collective action.

Although the recommended behaviors were appropriate to reduce the opportunity for crimes in the area, they would not be expected to impact parochial informal social control behaviors. Thus, while PS was hypothesized to possibly promote social cohesion and provide tools for effective collective informal social control behaviors, it was primarily police analysis and action in partnership with non-residents that provided for crime control. This may explain why the impact in PS areas was on informal social control only and was not realized until six to nine months after the officers' PS efforts concluded. It appeared to be the case that following the reductions in crime in the short term—that is, when residents improved their informal social control efforts—was consistent with the cooperation hypothesis. Police, by demonstrating their crime control effectiveness and by providing an environment whereby residents can feel safe enough to take action, can facilitate residents engaging in informal social control.

Residents from DP areas report significant improvements in informal social control more quickly—in the short term, relative to residents of control areas. In the long term, the benefits to informal social control persist in areas treated with DP and extend to social cohesion and thus collective efficacy. These results also provide support for the cooperation hypothesis. Parochial efforts are bolstered by support from reliable police. Police spending considerably more time in small geographic areas, not just to practice enforcement activity, but also to talk to residents; check abandoned buildings; and just be frequently, readily, and visibly available may convey to residents that police are a capable and supportive resource to the neighborhood. These actions on the part of police demonstrate to residents the capacity of the neighborhood to garner this resource. Recall findings by Carr (2003) and Silver and Miller (2004), both of whom found that residents need to see police as responsive and to be able to trust that police would arrive quickly and effectively address the problem in order to empower residents to address inappropriate behaviors in the neighborhood. These results are also consistent with other past research that found an association between police presence and accessibility and informal social control (Ferguson & Mindel, 2007; Scott, 2002). It would seem that DP strategies with limited enforcement actions (see Sargeant et al., 2013), perhaps especially those that include foot patrol over merely vehicle patrols (Salmi, Grönroos, & Keskinen, 2004), focused on crime hot spots can instill confidence in police responsiveness to the community, are a resource accessible to that community, and can reinforce local behavioral norms in the

course of officers conversing with people and conducting stops or other actions in support of local norms and laws.

The improvements may in part (we think in small part) be because of the impact of the increased police presence on residents' fear of victimization risk in the neighborhood. We conducted a *post hoc* assessment using the same mixed effect regression analysis examining the impact of each treatment relative to the SPP condition in the short- and long-term effects ($\alpha = .737$). In the short term, the DP residents reported that concerns about victimization risk were slightly abated relative to their counterparts receiving SPP ($b = -1.893$, $p < .001$). Across the groups, residents, on average, reported increased victimization risk between time 1 and time 2 ($b = 3.995$, $p < .001$), but the increase was depressed among DP residents.

The timing of the impact of DP on informal social control and social cohesion is interesting. Increasing police presence through DP first benefited informal social control in the short term and then social cohesion in the long term. Perhaps in high-crime places, police presence and assistance (particularly when it is not enforcement oriented, as in this study) emboldens people to take action. Then, once residents are engaged in self-policing, they can begin to feel comfortable enough dropping the anonymity and getting to know each other and spending time together. The findings here support claims by Gau (2014) and Wickes and colleagues (2013) that the components of collective efficacy should be treated as distinct. However, our study does not suggest—contrary to Gau—that social cohesion predicts informal social control. We point out that her study was based on a survey of residents at a single point in time, without the capacity to distinguish causal order. It may be the case that in some places, where the levels of crime are high, building relations among and spending time with residents may follow the intervention by police, and subsequently, residents' informal social control behaviors can give rise to improved confidence in others' intentions in the neighborhood, which can promote trust and encourage interaction.

From our findings we conclude that police may be able to impact neighborhood capacity for collective efficacy. We believe it is reasonably the case that different strategies may be needed in different neighborhoods. In high crime neighborhoods, hot spots policing, particularly in the form of directed patrol, may be able to promote residents' assessments that police are an accessible and reliable resource, capable and willing to co-produce social order with them. The consequence of this and modest effects on perceived victimization risk appear sufficient to motivate informal social control efforts and ultimately to also improve social cohesion. Thus, given that hot spots policing has demonstrated effectiveness against crime (Braga et al., 2012) without long-term harm to public perceptions of police (Kochel & Weisburd, 2017), the further benefit to collective efficacy presents a strong case for its widespread use by police to improve neighborhoods.

We caution that our study does have several limitations. First, our primary goal of the experiment was to examine the varied nature of the hot spots strategies on the public's perceptions of police. We did not aim to develop hot spots strategies to improve collective efficacy, but rather asked if that might be a by-product of the different types of strategies in the hot spots relative to routine policing. Also, the nature of implementation of the PS and DP strategies varied considerably across sites. In the areas receiving PS, especially, it is reasonable to expect that more collaboration between residents and police to identify, understand, and address problems may be a basis for improved social cohesion and more rapid improvement of informal social control. This study alone is insufficient to make claims that DP in hot spots can do a better job of facilitating collective efficacy and its components than PS strategies would. Yet we advocate that these findings are an important first step in explaining how different policing strategies in high-crime areas may be able to provide an impetus for residents to engage in informal social control and improve parochialism—another avenue to crime prevention and improved communities.

Disclosure Statement

No potential conflict of interest was reported by the authors.

Funding

This project was supported by the National Institute of Justice, Office of Justice Programs, US Department of Justice [grant number 2011-IJ-CX-0007]. The opinions, findings, and conclusions or recommendations expressed in this publication/program/exhibition are those of the author(s) and do not necessarily reflect those of the Department of Justice.

Discussion Questions

1. How might the police officers' implementation of each type of policing intervention explain the results reported in this study?
2. Besides the use of police reports and community surveys, think about other ways of measuring the outcomes of this study. Can you think of any additional outcomes that might have been helpful in understanding the relationship between policing practices and crime and neighborhood satisfaction?
3. Why do we think that collective efficacy might help to reduce crime?

Notes

1. The police agency elected to use Part 1 and Part 2 incidents and not to solely focus on violent crime or prioritize a specific type of crime. The choice appeared to be motivated by a desire to deal with problems that were common as well as problems that were very serious, thus reflecting a sense of equity.
2. Cooperation rates were very similar across the three treatment groups at each wave. (At baseline, the range is 35.25% for PS to 38.39% for SPP. At wave 2, the range is 38.31% for SPP to 39.83% for DP. At wave 3, the range is 43.48% for PS to 46.0% for DP.)

References

Bellair, P. E. (1997). Social interaction and community crime: Examining the importance of neighbor networks. *Criminology, 35*(4), 677–704.

Bellair, P. E., & Browning, C. R. (2010). Contemporary disorganization research: An assessment and further test of the systemic model of neighborhood crime. *Journal of Research in Crime and Delinquency*, 47(4), 496–521.

Braga, A. A. (2002). *Problem-oriented policing and crime prevention*. New York: Criminal Justice Press Monsey.

Braga, A. A., McDevitt, J., & Pierce, G. L. (2006). Understanding and preventing gang violence: Problem analysis and response development in Lowell, Massachusetts. *Police Quarterly*, 9(1), 20–46. https://doi.org/10.1177/1098611104264497

Braga, A. A., Papachristos, A., & Hureau, D. (2012). Hot spots policing effects on crime. *Campbell Systematic Reviews*, 8(8), 1–96.

Braga, A. A., & Weisburd, D. (2010). *Policing problem places: Crime hot spots and effective prevention*. Oxford: Oxford University Press.

Browning, C. R., Dietz, R. D., & Feinberg, S. L. (2004). The paradox of social organization: Networks, collective efficacy, and violent crime in urban neighborhoods. *Social Forces*, 83(2), 503–534. https://doi.org/10.1353/sof.2005.0006

Bursik, R. J., Jr., & Grasmick, H. G. (1993). *Neighborhoods and crime: The dimensions of effective community control*. New York, NY: Lexington Books.

Carr, P. J. (2003). The new parochialism: The implications of the beltway case for arguments concerning informal social control1. *American Journal of Sociology*, 108(6), 1249–1291.

Carr, P. J., Napolitano, L., & Keating, J. (2007). We never call the cops and here is why: A qualitative examination of legal cynicism in three Philadelphia neighborhoods. *Criminology*, 45(2), 445–480.

Chermak, S., McGarrell, E. F., & Weiss, A. (2001). Citizens' perceptions of aggressive traffic enforcement strategies. *Justice Quarterly*, 18(2), 365–391.

Cohen, P., Cohen, J., Aiken, L. S., & West, S. G. (1999). The problem of units and the circumstance for POMP. *Multivariate Behavioral Research*, 34(3), 315–346.

Coleman, J. S. (1988). Social capital in the creation of human capital. *American Journal of Sociology*, 94, S95–S120.

Cook, T. D., & Campbell, D. T. (1979). *Quasi-experimentation: Design and analysis issues for field settings*. Chicago, IL: Rand McNally.

De Leeuw, E., & de Heer, W. (2002). Trends in household survey nonresponse: A longitudinal and international comparison. In R. M. Groves, D. A. Dillman, J. L. Eltinge, & R. J. A. Little (Eds.), *Survey nonresponse* (pp. 41–54). New York, NY: Wiley.

Efron, B. (1971). Forcing a sequential experiment to be balanced. *Biometrika*, 58, 403–417.

Ferguson, K. M., & Mindel, C. H. (2007). Modeling fear of crime in Dallas neighborhoods: A test of social capital theory. *Crime â Delinquency*, 53(2), 322–349. https://doi.org/10.1177/0011128705285039

Gau, J. M. (2014). Unpacking collective efficacy: The relationship between social cohesion and informal social control. *Criminal Justice Studies*, 27(2), 210–225. https://doi.org/10.1080/1478601X.2014.885903

Gelman, A., & Hill, J. (2007). *Data analysis using regression and multilevel/hierarchical models*. New York, NY: Cambridge University Press.

Gibson, C. L., Zhao, J., Lovrich, N. P., & Gaffney, M. J. (2002). Social integration, individual perceptions of collective efficacy, and fear of crime in three cities. *Justice Quarterly*, 19(3), 537–564.

Gill, C., Weisburd, D., Telep, C. W., Vitter, Z., & Bennett, T. (2014). Community-oriented policing to reduce crime, disorder and fear and increase satisfaction and legitimacy among citizens: A systematic review. *Journal of Experimental Criminology*, 10(4), 399–428.

Groves, R. M., & Couper, M. P. (1998). *Non-response in household interview surveys*. New York, NY: John Wiley and Sons.

Gueorguieva, R., & Krystal, J. H. (2004). Move over ANOVA: Progress in analyzing repeated-measures data and its reflection in papers. *Archives of General Psychiatry*, 61, 310–317.

Hinkle, J. C., Weisburd, D., Famega, C., & Ready, J. (2013). The problem is not just sample size: The consequences of low base rates in policing experiments in smaller cities. *Evaluation Review*, 37(3–4), 213–238. https://doi.org/10.1177/0193841X13519799

Hsu, L. M. (1989). Methodological contributions to clinical research: Random sampling, randomization, and equivalence of contrasted groups in psychotherapy outcome research. *Journal of Consulting and Clinical Psychology*, 57(1), 131–137.

Hunter, A. (1985). *Private, parochial and public social orders: The problem of crime and incivility in urban communities* (pp. 230–242). The Challenge of Social Control: Citizenship and Institution Building in Modern Society.

Johnston, L. (2001). Crime, fear and civil policing. *Urban Studies (Routledge)*, 38(5/6), 959–976. https://doi.org/10.1080/00420980120046635

Keeter, S., Miller, C., Kohut, A., Groves, R., & Presser, S. (2000). Consequences of reducing nonresponse in a national telephone survey. *Public Opinion Quarterly*, 64, 125–148.

Kershaw, C., Budd, T., Kinshott, G., Mattinson, J., Mayhew, P., & Myhill, A. (2000). The 2000 British crime survey England and Wales. *Statistical Bulletin-Home Office Research Development And Statistics Directorate*.

Kochel, T. R. (2012). Can police legitimacy promote collective efficacy? *Justice Quarterly*, 29(3), 384–419. https://doi.org/10.1080/07418825.2011.561805

Kochel, T. R. (2013). Robustness of collective efficacy on crime in a developing nation: Association with crime reduction compared to police services. *Journal of Crime and Justice*, 36(3), 334–352. https://doi.org/10.1080/0735648X.2012.698102

Kochel, T. R. (2017). Explaining racial differences in Ferguson's impact on local residents' trust and perceived legitimacy: Policy implications for police. *Criminal Justice Policy Review*, online first. https://doi.org/10.1177/0887403416684923

Kochel, T. R., Burruss, G., & Weisburd, D. (2015). *St Louis County Hot Spots in Residential Areas (SCHIRA) Final Report: Assessing the effects of hot spots policing strategies on police legitimacy, crime and collective efficacy*. Washington, DC: U.S. Department of Justice, National Institute of Justice.

Kochel, T. R., Parks, R., & Mastrofski, S. D. (2013). Examining police effectiveness as a precursor to legitimacy and cooperation with police. *Justice Quarterly*, 30(5), 895–925.

Kochel, T. R., & Weisburd, D. (2017). Assessing community consequences of implementing hot spots policing in residential areas: Findings from a randomized field trial. *Journal of Experimental Criminology*, 13(2), 143–170. https://doi.org/10.1007/s11292-017-9283-5

Koper, C. S. (1995). Just enough police presence: Reducing crime and disorderly behavior by optimizing patrol time in crime hot spots. *Justice Quarterly*, 12(4), 649–672.

Kubrin, C. E., & Weitzer, R. (2003). New directions in social disorganization theory. *Journal of Research in Crime and Delinquency*, 40(4), 374–402. https://doi.org/10.1177/0022427803256238

LaFree, G. (1998). *Losing legitimacy: Street crime and the decline of social institutions in America*. Boulder, CO: Westview Press, Inc.

Markowitz, F. E., Bellair, P. E., Liska, A. E., & Liu, J. (2001). Extending social disorganization theory: Modeling the relationships between cohesion, disorder, and fear*. *Criminology*, 39(2), 293–331.

May, D. C., & Dunaway, R. G. (2000). Predictors of fear of criminal victimization at school among adolescents. *Sociological Spectrum*, 20(2), 149–168.

Mazerolle, L., Bennett, S., Antrobus, E., & Eggins, E. (2012). Procedural justice, routine encounters and citizen perceptions of polie: main findings from the Queensland Community Engagement Trial (QCET). *Journal of Experimental Criminology*, 8(4), 343–367. https://doi.org/10.1007/s11292-012-9160-1

Mazerolle, L., Wickes, R., & McBroom, J. (2010). Community variations in violence: The role of social ties and collective efficacy in comparative context. *Journal of Research in Crime and Delinquency*, 47(1), 3–30. https://doi.org/10.1177/0022427809348898

Mohadjer, L., & Choudhry, G. H. (2002). Adjusting for missing data in low-income surveys. In M. Ver Ploeg, R. A. Moffitt, & C. F. Citro (Eds.), *Studies of welfare populations: Data collection and research issues* (pp. 129–156). Washington, DC: National Academies Press.

Moore, M. H., & Trojanowicz, R. C. (1988). *Policing and the fear of crime*. US Department of Justice, National Institute of Justice Washington, DC. Retrieved from www.ncjrs.gov/pdffiles1/nij/111459.pdf

Morenoff, J. D., Sampson, R. J., & Raudenbush, S. W. (2001). Neighborhood inequality, collective efficacy, and the spatial dynamics of urban violence. *Criminology*, 39(3), 517–558. https://doi.org/10.1111/j.1745-9125.2001.tb00932.x

Oberwittler, D., & Wikström, P. O. H. (2009). Why small is better: Advancing the study of the role of behavioral contexts in crime causation. In D. Weisburd, W. Bernasco, & G. J. Bruinsma (Eds.), *Putting crime in its place* (pp. 35–60). New York, NY: Springer.

Ord, J. K., & Getis, A. (1995). Local spatial autocorrelation statistics: Distributional issues and an application. *Geographics Analysis*, 27(4), 286–306.

Pashea, J. J. J., & Kochel, T. R. (2016). Face-to-face surveys in high crime areas: Balancing respondent cooperation and interviewer safety. *Journal of Criminal Justice Education*, 27(1), 95–120.

Pattillo, M. E. (1998). Sweet mothers and gangbangers: Managing crime in a black middle-class neighborhood. *Social Forces*, 76(3), 747–774. https://doi.org/10.1093/sf/76.3.747

Pickett, J. T. (2017). Methodological myths and the role of appeals in criminal justice journals: The case of nonresponse bias. *ACJS Today, Summer 2017*, XLII(3), 61–69.

Ratcliffe, J. H., Taniguchi, T., Groff, E. R., & Wood, J. D. (2011). The Philadelphia foot patrol experiment: A randomized controlled trial of police patrol effectiveness in violent crime hotspots. *Criminology*, 49(3), 795–831.

Renauer, B. C. (2007). Is neighborhood policing related to informal social control? *Policing: An International Journal of Police Strategies & Management*, 30(1), 61–81. https://doi.org/10.1108/13639510710725622

Salmi, S., Grönroos, M., & Keskinen, E. (2004). The role of police visibility in fear of crime in Finland. *Policing: An International Journal*, 27(4), 573–591. https://doi.org/10.1108/13639510410566280

Sampson, R. J. (2002). Transcending tradition: New directions in community research, Chicago style. *Criminology*, 40(2), 213–230. https://doi.org/10.1111/j.1745-9125.2002.tb00955.x

Sampson, R. J. (2008). Collective efficacy theory: Lessons learned and directions for future inquiry. *Taking Stock: The Status of Criminological Theory, 15*, 149–167.

Sampson, R. J., & Raudenbush, S. W. (1999). Systematic social observation of public spaces: A new look at disorder in urban neighborhoods. *American Journal of Sociology, 105*(3), 603–651. https://doi.org/10.1086/210356

Sampson, R. J., Raudenbush, S. W., & Earls, F. (1997). Neighborhoods and violent crime: A multilevel study of collective efficacy. *Science, 277*(5328), 918–924. https://doi.org/10.1126/science.277.5328.918

Sargeant, E. (2015). Policing and collective efficacy: The relative importance of police effectiveness, procedural justice and the obligation to obey police. *Policing and Society*, 1–14. https://doi.org/10.1080/10439463.2015.1122008

Sargeant, E., Wickes, R., & Mazerolle, L. (2013). Policing community problems: Exploring the role of formal social control in shaping collective efficacy. *Australian ā New Zealand Journal of Criminology, 46*(1), 70–87. https://doi.org/10.1177/0004865812470118

Scherbaum, C. A., & Ferreter, J. M. (2009). Estimating statistical power and required sample sizes for organizational research using multilevel modeling. *Organizational Research Methods, 12*(2), 347–367.

Schmerler, K., Perkins, M., Phillips, S., Rinehart, T., & Townsend, M. (2006). *A guide to reducing crime and disorder through problem-solving partnerships.* US Department of Justice, Office of Community Oriented Policing Services. Retrieved from www.popcenter.org/problems/robbery_taxis/PDFs/cops.pdf

Scott, J. D. (2002). Assessing the relationship between police-community coproduction and neighborhood-level social capital. *Journal of Contemporary Criminal Justice, 18*(2), 147–166.

Sherman, L. W., Gartin, P. R., & Buerger, M. E. (1989). Hot spots of predatory crime: Routine activities and the criminology of place. *Criminology, 27*(1), 27–56.

Sherman, L. W., & Weisburd, D. (1995). General deterrent effects of police patrol in crime "hot spots": A randomized, controlled trial. *Justice Quarterly, 12*(4), 625–648.

Silver, E., & Miller, L. L. (2004). Sources of informal social control in Chicago neighborhoods. *Criminology, 42*(3), 551–584. https://doi.org/10.1111/j.1745-9125.2004.tb00529.x

Silverman, E. B., & Della-Giustina, J.-A. (2001). Urban policing and the fear of crime. *Urban Studies, 38*(5–6), 941–957. https://doi.org/10.1080/00420980123458

Skogan, W. G. (1989). Communities, crime, and neighborhood organization. *Crime Delinquency, 35*(3), 437–457. https://doi.org/10.1177/0011128789035003008

Skogan, W. G., & Frydl, K. (2004). *Fairness and effectiveness in policing: The evidence.* Washington, DC: National Academies Press.

Skogan, W. G., & Hartnett, S. M. (1997). *Community policing, Chicago style.* New York, NY: Oxford University Press.

St. Louis County Department of Planning. (2013a). *Meeting the challenges of concentrated poverty in St Louis County, Missouri: Policy Brief.* Clayton, MO: St. Louis County.

St. Louis County Department of Planning. (2013b). *St Louis County, Missouri 2007–2012 Factbook.* Clayton, MO: St. Louis County.

Taylor, R. B. (1997). Social order and disorder of street blocks and neighborhoods: Ecology, microecology, and the systemic model of social disorganization. *Journal of Research in Crime and Delinquency, 34*(1), 113–155.

Taylor, R. B. (1998). Crime and small-scale places: What we know, what we can prevent, and what else we need to know. In *Crime and place: Plenary papers of the 1997 Conference on Criminal Justice Research and Evaluation* (pp. 1–22). Washington, DC: National Institute of Justice. Retrieved from www.politieacademie.nl/kennisenonderzoek/kennis/mediatheek/PDF/00-13878.pdf#page=7

Taylor, R. B., Koper, C. S., & Woods, D. J. (2011). A randomized controlled trial of different policing strategies at hot spots of violent crime. *Journal of Experimental Criminology, 7*, 149–181.

Telep, C. W., Mitchell, R. J., & Weisburd, D. (2014). How much time should the police spend at crime hot spots? Answers from a police agency directed randomized field trial in Sacramento. *Justice Quarterly, 31*(5), 905–933. https://doi.org/10.1080/07418825.2012.710645

Trojanowicz, R. C., & Baldwin, R. (1982). *An evaluation of the neighborhood foot patrol program in Flint.* Michigan: Michigan State University East Lansing. Retrieved from www.ncjrs.gov/App/abstractdb/AbstractDBDetails.aspx?id=96565

Tyler, T., & Fagan, J. (2008). Legitimacy and cooperation: Why do people help the police fight crime in their communities? *Ohio State Journal of Criminal Law, 6*, 231–275.

Warner, B. D. (2014). Neighborhood factors related to the likelihood of successful informal social control efforts. *Journal of Criminal Justice, 42*(5), 421–430.

Weisburd, D., Davis, M., & Gill, C. (2015). Increasing collective efficacy and social capital at crime hot spots: New crime control tools for police. *Policing,*

9(3), 265–274. https://doi.org/10.1093/police/pav019

Weisburd, D., & Green, L. (1995). Policing drug hot spots: The Jersey City drug market analysis experiment. *Justice Quarterly, 12,* 711–735.

Weisburd, D., Groff, E. R., & Yang, S.-M. (2012). *The criminology of place: Street segments and our understanding of the crime problem.* New York, NY: Oxford University Press.

Weisburd, D., Groff, E. R., & Yang, S.-M. (2014). Understanding and controlling hot spots of crime: The importance of formal and informal social controls. *Prevention Science, 15*(1), 31–43. https://doi.org/10.1007/s11121-012-0351-9

Weisburd, D., Hinkle, J. C., Famega, C., & Ready, J. (2011). The possible "backfire" effects of hot spots policing: An experimental assessment of impacts on legitimacy, fear and collective efficacy. *Journal of Experimental Criminology, 7*(4), 297–320.

Weisburd, D., & Magmundar, M. K. (2017). *Proactive policing: Effects on crime and communities.* Washington, DC: National Academies Press.

Weisburd, D., & Telep, C. W. (2014). Hot spots policing what we know and what we need to know. *Journal of Contemporary Criminal Justice, 30*(2), 200–220.

Weisburd, D., Wyckoff, L. A., Ready, J., Eck, J. E., Hinkle, J. C., & Gajewski, F. (2006). Does crime just move around the corner? A controlled study of spatial displacement and diffusion of crime control benefits. *Criminology, 44*(3), 549–592.

Weiss, C., & Bailar, B. A. (2002). High response rates for low-income population in-person surveys. In M. Ver Ploeg, R. A. Moffitt, & C. F. Citro (Eds.), *Studies of welfare populations: Data collection and research issues* (pp. 86–104). Washington, DC: National Academies Press.

Wells, W., Schafer, J. A., Varano, S. P., & Bynum, T. S. (2006). Neighborhood residents' production of order: The effects of collective efficacy on responses to neighborhood problems. *Crime Delinquency, 52*(4), 523–550.

Wicker, A. W. (1987). Behavior settings reconsidered: Temporal stages, resources, internal dynamics, context. *Handbook of Environmental Psychology, 1,* 613–653.

Wickes, R., Hipp, J. R., Sargeant, E., & Homel, R. (2013). Collective efficacy as a task specific process: Examining the relationship between social ties, neighborhood cohesion and the capacity to respond to violence, delinquency and civic problems. *American Journal of Community Psychology, 52*(1–2), 115–127.

Wooditch, A., Weisburd, D., & White, C. (2016). *Collective efficacy in hot spots of crime.* Paper presented at the 68th Annual Meeting of the American Society of Criminology's, New Orleans, LA.

Wu, L. (2009). *Mixed effects models for complex data.* Boca Raton, FL: CRC Press.

Zhao, J. "Soloman," Schneider, M., & Thurman, Q. (2002). The effect of police presence on public fear reduction and satisfaction: A review of the literature. *The Justice Professional, 15*(3), 273–299. https://doi.org/10.1080/088843102 1000049471

Reading 4.3   Cognitive-Behavioral Programming and the Value of Failed Interventions

Corrections researchers recommend that interventions follow the risk-needs-responsivity (RNR) model. Programs that adhere to the RNR model target high-risk offenders for treatment, address needs that are known to be associated with reoffending, and provide interventions that have been found to be effective. Cognitive behavioral treatment (CBT) has been recognized in the scholarly literature as a program that can have significant impacts on recidivism. Little research has been conducted on whether CBT is associated with changes in in-prison misconduct, and most of the literature that does exist includes studies with non-equivalent comparison groups. As is common in program evaluation, Strah et al. (2018) encountered the challenge of being unable to randomly assign prisoners to either the CBT intervention or treatment as usual because treatment participation was voluntary. The researchers used propensity scores matching to make the groups much more comparable. Not only does this article provide readers with a good example of a quasi-experiment, but it also highlights a number of issues researchers must face while conducting program evaluation.

Cognitive-Behavioral Programming and the Value of Failed Interventions: A Propensity Score Evaluation

Beck M. Strah, Natasha A. Frost, Jacob I. Stowell, and Sema A. Taheri

While much research assessing the efficacy of correctional programming focuses on post-release recidivism, inmate behavior while incarcerated is an important outcome that might also be affected by institutional programming. Inmate misconduct takes shape in many different forms throughout prisons, from minor infractions (e.g., unexcused absence from work, failing to keep one's quarters in accordance with facility standards) to major disciplinary infractions (e.g., theft, escape) and ongoing crime and violence (e.g., assaults, sexual assaults, homicide). Recent scholarship indicates that recidivism is significantly more common amongst inmates who engage in misconduct (Cochran et al., 2014). Moreover, misconduct represents a serious and salient problem for correctional administration. Even minor acts of misconduct can disrupt the day-to-day operations within prison facilities, compromising correctional ideals of providing a safe, secure, and humane environment for staff and inmates. Failure to control or respond to misconduct can similarly jeopardize these goals (Lovell & Jemelka, 1996; Walters, 1999).

Prison administrators struggle with this concern, as there is no clear consensus on the best practices for attenuating misconduct. However, prison programs employing cognitive behavioral therapy (CBT) have embraced it as a means of reducing misconduct within prisons and later criminal involvement (MacKenzie, 2006). CBT is rooted in the assumption that cognitive processes affect subsequent behaviors. According to the guiding theory, cognitive thinking patterns can be modified by recognizing and monitoring these processes and teaching the individual to avoid maladaptive thoughts while promoting behavioral change (Wilson et al., 2005). In the literature, prison programs designed on cognitive-behavioral principles have demonstrated promising outcomes in their ability to modify inmate behaviors (French & Gendreau, 2006; Lowenkamp et al., 2006; Morgan & Flora, 2002; Walters, 1999).

However, the existing body of research on these programs is not yet developed enough to generalize even the most promising findings. Though corrections literature often provides support and arguments for "what works" in prison interventions, few articles reporting null or negative results of prison programming are ever published (Gerber & Malhotra, 2008). Due to publication bias toward positive results, the canon of published research predominantly reflects the results of successful programming, while often neglecting to pass on the lessons learned from studies with ineffective or harmful results (Pratt, 2002; Rosenthal, 1979). Moreover, among the studies of CBT that have been published, many have used problematic research designs (e.g., small sample sizes, limited statistical controls, selection bias) and found only small, though significant, treatment effects (see, e.g., Allen et al., 2001; Welsh et al., 2007).

In this article, we demonstrate that our knowledge of CBT programming from previous evaluation research may be incomplete, and the benefits of CBT programming may not be shared universally. We employed propensity score matching (PSM), a quasi-experimental statistical technique, to assess the effect of cognitive-behavioral programming offered in a therapeutic community setting on misconduct. The analysis demonstrates that treatment effects initially observed between groups disappear after PSM, suggesting that these were a product of selection effects.

Prison Misconduct

The available correctional research has identified several risk factors associated with prison misconduct. Individual-level factors predicting increased probabilities of prison misconduct include: gender (Goetting & Howsen, 1986; Kuanliang & Sorensen, 2008), age (Steiner et al., 2014; Trulson et al., 2010), offense type (Sorensen & Cunningham, 2010; Sorensen & Davis, 2011), childhood delinquency (DeLisi et al., 2010; Meade & Steiner, 2013; Trulson, 2007; Trulson et al., 2010), criminal history (Cunningham & Sorensen, 2007; DeLisi, 2003; Steiner et al., 2014; Wooldredge et al., 2001),

early life trauma (DeLisi et al., 2011), mental health issues (Kuanliang & Sorensen, 2008; Steiner et al., 2014), gang affiliation (Sorensen & Cunningham, 2010; Trulson et al., 2010), prior substance abuse (Jiang, 2005; Steiner & Wooldredge, 2008; Steiner et al., 2014; Trulson et al., 2010), few or inconsistent visitations (Cochran, 2012; Cochran & Mears, 2013), time served (DeLisi et al., 2011; Steiner & Wooldredge, 2013), shorter sentence length (Gover et al., 2008; Sorensen & Cunningham, 2010), and misconduct during prior incarcerations (Cunningham & Sorensen, 2007; Drury & DeLisi, 2010; Steiner et al., 2014).

Extant research suggests that inmate participation in prison programming may affect in-prison behavior, with studies reporting fewer instances of misconduct following various program interventions (Adams et al., 1994; Camp et al., 2008; Lahm, 2009; Langan & Pelissier, 2001). Further, Andrews et al. (1990) suggest that programming may even reduce incidents of misconduct by as much as 17 percent, when programs are appropriately tailored to the needs of inmate populations. As a result, correctional administrators have sometimes endorsed programming as a tool for maintaining order within the prison (Gendreau & Keyes, 2001).

What Works in Corrections?

With the decline in penal welfarism in the 1970s, prison programs have become fewer in number, offering fewer opportunities for treatment, self-improvement, and rehabilitation in inmate populations (O'Malley, 2010; Travis, 2005). In spite of this, contemporary research suggests that correctional programming may offer positive outcomes for inmates, evidenced by reductions in prison misconduct and recidivism (French & Gendreau, 2006; Latessa & Holsinger, 1998; Morgan & Flora, 2002).

However, not all treatment interventions are effective; many fail to rehabilitate, and some have even been associated with increases in recidivism (Bonta et al., 2000; Wilson and Davis, 2006; Welsh et al., 2007). Prior to adopting treatment interventions, correctional administrators often look to the strengths, theoretical foundations, and previous implementations to assess the likely effectiveness of particular types of programs.

Treatment literature suggests that the most prominent positive outcomes occur when prison interventions rely on Bonta and Andrews's (2007) risk-need-responsivity (RNR) model of offender treatment and rehabilitation. First, the risk principle emphasizes that offender risk should be determined through the use of validated actuarial instrumentation, rather than a basis of professional judgment. Following this, offenders who are assessed to be at the highest risk of recidivism should be those most often targeted for treatment (Gendreau, 1996; Polaschek, 2012). Second, treatments should be structured to address criminogenic needs, which are defined as dynamic characteristics associated with reoffending such as substance abuse, antisocial associates, and antisocial attitudes and values (Andrews et al., 2011). Finally, the principle of responsivity proposes that rehabilitative interventions should be tailored to accommodate different learning styles, motivations, abilities, and strengths of all participating offenders (Bonta & Andrews, 2007). To meet the standards of responsivity, group treatments like CBT should be administered in a way that will serve diverse offending populations (Andrews et al., 2011).

CBT assumes that changes in the cognitive process will affect behavioral change (Dobson & Khatri, 2000), and encourages subjects to address maladaptive thinking patterns, and teaches ways to prevent these thoughts from manifesting into antisocial behaviors (Bahr et al., 2012, Baro, 1999; Wilson et al., 2005). In a meta-analysis assessing 68 correctional treatment programs for their effectiveness in reducing misconduct, French and Gendreau (2006) found that behavior-based programming presented the strongest effects in reducing inmate misconduct ($r = .26$), relative to the effects presented by nonbehavioral ($r = .10$), or educational/vocational programs ($r = .02$). However, reductions in misconduct were mediated by the therapeutic integrity of the programming, as well as the number of criminogenic needs targeted by the program. In other words, the

effectiveness of behavioral programming such as CBT is largely contingent upon how closely the RNR principles are followed in program implementation.

CBT Programs and Prison Misconduct

A growing body of research has established that CBT is capable of affecting behavioral change across varying modalities of prison programming. Attenuated rates of prison misconduct have been observed after inmate participation in lifestyle change programs (Walters, 1999), substance abuse treatments (Innes, 1997), residential CBT facilities (Prendergast et al., 2001), group psychotherapy (Morgan & Flora, 2002), and cognitive restructuring programs (Baro, 1999). CBT programs have also demonstrated statistically significant outcomes across offender types, decreasing rates of misconduct and recidivism amongst populations of men and women (Clark, 2011; Duwe & Clark, 2015; Spiropoulos et al., 2005), juvenile and adult offenders (Clark, 2011), gang members (Di Placido et al., 2006), sex offenders (Macgregor, 2008; MacKenzie, 2006), drug offenders (Bahr et al., 2012; McMurran, 2007), and violent offenders (Clark, 2011).

Throughout the treatment literature, CBT research has often addressed program effects on recidivism. Of these studies, results have often indicated substantial decreases in offending following program completion (Bahr et al., 2012; Duwe & Clark, 2015; Spiropoulos et al., 2005; Wilson et al., 2005). CBT-based programming is intended to affect offender cognition in the long term, reducing offending behaviors during incarceration and following release (French & Gendreau, 2006). However, CBT's effects on recidivism are more often studied than misconduct outcomes, which remain underrepresented within the literature.

Of the limited scholarship addressing CBT-based program effects on misconduct, some of the nonexperimental research has offered promising results. Comparing inmate behaviors between TCs and the general population, both Lowe (1992) and Dietz et al. (2003) observed lower levels of institutional disorder amongst inmates currently undergoing substance abuse treatment in a TC. In studies examining the behavioral effects of less intensive CBT programming, Walters (1999) and Baro (1999) have reported similar results; following CBT, program graduates accrued disciplinary reports at significantly lower rates than their peers within the comparison groups. Though these results offer a positive outlook on the promise of CBT and TC programs, they should be interpreted with caution, as each of these studies are based on simple comparisons between groups. These studies did not include important statistical controls to ensure the groups were sufficiently similar prior to treatment; in other words, the results cannot identify the individual factors contributing to these outcomes.

Recognizing the statistical limitations of prior CBT and misconduct studies, Welsh et al. (2007) used a generalized linear modeling technique to examine the effects of a TC targeting substance abuse and addiction in five Pennsylvania prisons. Results showed that rates of misconduct were significantly lower for the TC group than the comparison group, though within-participant testing failed to indicate any reduction in misconduct over time, for either group. While this study embraces a more sophisticated statistical technique to study CBT effects on misconduct, selection bias may still have presented a critical issue. In this study, the authors note several inherent differences between the TC and comparison groups; however, no matching techniques were used to minimize the potential for a selection effect.

When selecting inmates for program intervention by their individual characteristics, (i.e., risk and criminogenic need), treatment and control groups may differ systematically in ways associated with treatment outcomes (Farrington, 2003b). By handpicking treatment subjects through selective criteria, researchers and program administrators introduce bias to the social processes that occur in programming that might obscure "true" program effects (Winship & Mare, 1992). Randomized experiments have long been recognized as a "gold standard" for evaluating programs, eliminating potential for selection bias through random sampling (Farrington, 2003a, p. 218). However, due to difficulties in implementation, experimental methodologies are often neither feasible nor ethical for program evaluations, especially prison-based treatment programs (Clear, 2010). Quasi-experimental designs are often the next best alternative when true experimental designs cannot be employed for practical or ethical reasons.

The Current Study

The current study tests the hypothesis that completion of CBT programming reduces the likelihood of inmates receiving disciplinary reports for behavioral misconduct. This evaluation employs propensity score matching, a quasi-experimental matching technique for controlling for differences between treatment groups to reduce model inefficiency and bias (Imai & Van Dyk, 2004). Given the scarcity of research on the topic and the limitations of selection bias in most previous studies, the present study attempts to draw attention to the critical importance of using rigorous analytic techniques in program evaluation. The study explicitly considers the issue of selectivity, which research has shown to be vital for methodological and substantive reasons (Berk, 1983; Farrington, 2003b; Heckman et al., 1998; Winship & Mare, 1992).

Research Setting

Data were collected on an inmate population at a correctional facility in a northeastern state that houses an average population of 700 misdemeanor and low-level felony offenders. To facilitate reentry processes, the prison offers a number of programs to assist inmates as they complete their sentences and prepare to return to their respective communities. Similar to CBT programs evaluated in previous studies, these interventions are designed to address criminogenic needs (e.g., substance use, attitudes, values) and prevent future acts of offending (Baro, 1999; Innes, 1997; Walters, 1999). The institution addresses inmate needs through a wide variety of program options, including educational, vocational learning, and behavioral treatment (e.g., Thinking for a Change, sex offender treatment, anger management). In addition, the intensive treatment unit (ITU) acts as a specialized housing unit designated as a TC for substance abuse treatment. We focused on the ITU, given its focus on delivering cognitive behavioral programming in a therapeutic community setting.

ITU programming takes place over a 60-day period in a single housing unit at the prison. ITU participants are housed together in a 63-bed dormitory-style unit staffed by correctional officers, clinicians, counselors, caseworkers, and program facilitators. At intake, classification staff recommend inmates for ITU placement using both objective and subjective criteria of risk and need. ITU housing is voluntary in that offenders have to be willing to engage in the programming if recommended for the ITU. Because inmates elect to participate in ITU, the treatment assignment is not random. Once housed in ITU, program participation is mandatory as a condition of residing in the therapeutic community setting. ITU delivers a structured constellation of cognitive behavioral programming in an intensive treatment environment, requiring the active involvement of all inmate participants.

Data and Methodology

Data were collected for all sentenced offenders (N = 638) incarcerated at the corrections facility on August 1, 2011, and May 1, 2013. Each inmate's movement through housing units and program participation was tracked from their initial commitment date through July 1, 2015, by which time all but one had been released. Official inmate data was acquired from an inmate tracking system and through a Criminal Offender Record Information (CORI) request. An array of demographic and offense-related data were collected and coded, including age, race, ethnicity, current offense, prior criminal history (arraignments, convictions, and incarcerations), and sentence length. Data pertaining to program participation were collected from the daily attendance reports prepared by programming directors, and disciplinary reports were collected from the facility's administrative database.

Treatment

For evaluation purposes, inmates were separated into treatment and control groups, based upon their completion of ITU programming. Our goal in this study was to measure for behavioral changes following program completion, so graduation from ITU was used as a treatment indicator. Of the 638 inmates within the sample, 156 (24.5%) had fully completed the ITU coursework and graduated from the treatment program. The control group ($n = 482$, 75.5%) includes subjects who failed to complete the full course of ITU programming (n = 120), as well as ITU nonparticipants (n = 362). For these inmates, a counterfactual graduation date was generated to approximate the time ITU graduates spent in programming and allow comparisons in prison misconduct after treatment. First, we calculated the average number of days passed between the initial booking date and ITU graduation ($\overline{X} = 137$; $SD = 80$) for ITU graduates, which ranged between 47 and 478. This number was added to the initial booking date of each subject in the control group to create a "faux" graduation date, allowing for an equivalent misconduct consideration period for all sampled inmates. Within the context of the research, this date was utilized to compare treatment and control subjects on misconduct for the period between graduation and release.

Matching Variables

Demographic and institutional variables associated with misconduct were used as control variables in matching (see, e.g., Cunningham & Sorensen, 2007; Gendreau et al., 1997; Kuanliang & Sorensen, 2008). Matched covariates include age, race, cohort group, sentence length, offense type, number of prior convictions, and initial classification scores.

Demographic Variables

Inmate age is reported in years, ranging from 18–75 (M = 34.1, SD = 11.4). A Mann Whitney U test indicates that ITU graduates (M = 37.3, SD = 10.3) are significantly older than inmates comprising the control group

($M = 33.0$, $SD = 11.6$, $p < .0001$). Race/ethnicity was included as a demographic control, dichotomized to represent each racial group included for analysis ($0 =$ no, $1 =$ yes). The majority of inmates identified as non-Hispanic White ($n = 441$, 69.1%), though non-Hispanic Black inmates comprised approximately one fifth of the sample ($n = 137$, 21.5%). The "other" (including unknown, Asian, Native American, and Pacific Islander) made up the reference group for statistical modeling ($n = 14$, 2.2%). Though relatively few inmates were identified as Hispanic ($n = 50$, 7.8%), this covariate was also included for analysis. As only male inmates are housed within the facility, gender was not included as a control variable in this study.

A dichotomous variable indicating the data collection period was also included to control for any potential cohort effects (2011 $= 0$; 2013 $= 1$). Each cohort comprised approximately half of the inmate sample (2011: $n = 341$, 53.4%; 2013: $n = 297$, 46.6%). As of December 31, 2014, all offenders of the 2011 cohort have been released. With the exception of one offender, every inmate in the 2013 cohort (99.7%) has been released as of July 1, 2015.

Offending Characteristics

Each inmate's current offense is categorically represented as property (27.3%), personal (26.5%), drug (15.4%), and other (30.8%). Within the data, inmates are categorized by only their most serious current offense at the time of sentencing. The "other" category comprises offenses such as possession of a firearm without a license, sex offenses, OUI, and resisting arrest. Three dichotomous variables were created ($1 =$ yes, $0 =$ no) to represent each offense type (personal, property, drug). Other offenses were the reference category.

The majority of sampled inmates had been previously convicted of an offense ($n = 547$, 85.3%). Within the study sample, the number of prior convictions ranged from 0–120, with an average of 7.4 prior convictions. A Mann-Whitney U test indicates that ITU graduates were significantly more likely to have prior convictions ($M = 9.48$, $SD = 8.44$) than inmates

who did not graduate from ITU ($M = 6.72$, $SD = 9.21$; $p < .0001$). Prior convictions were categorized as a continuous variable, organized by offense type: personal, property, drug, and other. Other offenses were again used as a reference category. Sentence length, expressed in months, ranged from 1–167 months in prison ($M = 15.9$, $SD = 19.4$). ITU graduates were sentenced to significantly longer terms ($M = 15.9$, $SD = 8.9$, $p < .0001$) than the control group ($M = 15.8$, $SD = 21.7$). As the participating facility does not traditionally incarcerate offenders for a period greater than 30 months unless they are serving consecutive shorter sentences, offenders serving sentences longer than 2.5 years comprised a small segment of the sample ($n = 54$, 8.5%).

Initial Classification

Upon entry to the prison facility, inmates were assessed during classification using the Jail Inmate Classification System (JICS). JICS scores assign a level of risk to each inmate, ranging from 1 (high risk) to 8 (very low risk). Scores are based on institutional risk factors (e.g., escape attempts, gang involvement), current charge(s), offending history, and special needs for accommodation (e.g., protective custody, medical issues, handicapped/disabled). Whereas inmates with high JICS scores (low risk) are typically assigned to minimum-security housing, inmates with low JICS scores (high risk) are likely to be placed in restrictive housing, with limited options for programming or recreation. As a classification tool, as opposed to an assessment tool, the JICS score serves only as a metric to denote an institutional risk; this classification does not explicitly assess an inmate's risk of reoffending. At initial classification, a majority of the sample was classified at levels of medium risk. More than half of the inmate sample received an initial JICS score of 4 ($n = 328$, 51.3%), followed by scores of 3 ($n = 157$, 24.6%), and 7 ($n = 57$, 8.9%).[8] On average, treatment subjects were classified at the same risk level as those in the control group. Extremes were uncommonly observed within the sample; only 1 inmate was classified as a 1 (very high risk), and 24 were classified as an 8 (very low risk).

Initial JICS scores are specified as a count variable in analysis.

Dependent Variable

Disciplinary reports, the official record of inmate misconduct, represent the outcome variable in the current analysis. Disciplinary reports are incurred as a consequence of an inmate's failure to comply with rules enforced by the prison facility and are issued at the discretion of the staff member on duty. Prior to analysis, a significant disparity was observed in the number of disciplinary reports between groups. Following graduation, treated inmates accrued a total of 20 disciplinary reports (M = 0.11, SD = 0.31), whereas the control group incurred a significantly greater (p < .0001) total of 136 (M = 0.18, SD = 0.39). On an individual level, the majority of sampled inmates were not formally cited for misconduct, (n = 532, 83.4%) though this, too, varied significantly (p < .0001) between treatment (n = 139, 89.1%) and control (n = 387, 78.0%) groups.

Four outcome measures of inmate misconduct were used for analysis, each operationalized as a dichotomous variable (0 = no, 1 = yes). The first measure identifies whether the inmate had incurred any disciplinary reports following graduation from ITU programming or, in the case of the control group, the faux graduation date. Using a criteria established by Steiner and Wooldredge (2013), the three remaining outcomes were categorically based on the type of post-ITU misconduct for which the inmate was cited. These outcomes are classified as alcohol/substance-related (n = 45), violent (n = 62), and other nonviolent (n = 49) misconduct.

Analytic Strategy

To assess the effect of the intensive treatment programming on misconduct, we employed propensity score matching (PSM), a quasi-experimental modeling technique intended to overcome limitations of selection bias (Franklin, 2015; Langan & Pelissier, 2001). As Cochran et al. (2014) have explained, the primary goal of PSM is to create balance. To achieve balance, PSM utilizes a data reduction technique, allowing researchers to match individual subjects between treatment and control groups on a number of observed covariates (Rosenbaum & Rubin, 1983). When covariate balance has been achieved, observable pre-existing differences between treatment and control groups are minimized—reducing selection bias, and allowing for a more representative outcome in the estimated treatment effects (Stuart, 2010). In the context of the current study, PSM is used to predict potential outcomes of treatment, which are estimated as the difference in misconduct between subjects of the treatment group and their matched subjects in the control group.

Findings

Prior to matching, considerable covariate imbalance was observed between the treatment and control groups on several covariates. In comparison to the control group, inmates graduating ITU were significantly more likely to be non-Hispanic White, older, and previously convicted for a property or drug offense. Inmates comprising the control group were more likely to self-identify as Black, Hispanic, or other and were significantly more likely to have obtained a disciplinary report prior to their counterfactual graduation date.

Matching with replacement, 113 control propensity scores (PSs) were matched to 154 PSs in the treatment group. Prior to matching, the treatment group exhibited a significantly lower likelihood (p < .0001) of receiving a disciplinary report (10.9%) than the control group (22.0%). After matching, a negative and non-significant difference was observed between treatment and control groups in their likelihood of receiving a disciplinary report. This change is expressed through the average treatment effect (ATE), a statistic illustrating the expected treatment effects for ITU completion. Matching with one nearest neighbor, the ATE for general misconduct was estimated at -0.038, though this result did not reach statistical significance at a .05 level (p = .398). Substantively, this finding indicates that ITU graduates received fewer disciplinary reports, though effects were marginal and indistinguishable from the comparison group.

By employing PSM to achieve covariate balance, group differences in misconduct were reduced to a level of nonsignificance, suggesting that previously observed differences between groups can likely be attributed to the presence of selection effects. Effectively, these results call into question the findings of studies that have evaluated correctional programming effectiveness using less sophisticated methods while highlighting the importance of applying quasi-experimental designs when experimental designs are not possible.

Discussion

The current research contributes to scholarship by testing a CBT-based substance abuse program delivered in an intensive treatment unit (a TC) for its efficacy in reducing inmate misconduct. CBT treatments are generally intended to make offenders cognizant of maladaptive thought patterns, then altering these thought patterns to result in positive behavioral changes, which should be measurable as treatment outcomes. Analysis results did not support the hypothesis that CBT program completion will reduce the likelihood of inmates incurring disciplinary reports. Findings indicated that inmates who completed ITU programming experienced no significant change in accrual of disciplinary reports compared to the control group. This outcome runs contrary to most previous research, which posits that inmate misconduct may be significantly reduced as a treatment effect of CBT interventions (Baro, 1999; Di Placido et al., 2006; Langan & Pelissier, 2001; Walters, 1999).

So, why did the ITU prove ineffective at reducing misconduct? Three distinct possibilities present themselves as plausible explanations: (a) the CBT-based treatment approach of ITU programming was ineffective (i.e., theory failure); (b) the ITU programming lacked the program integrity to make the treatments effective (i.e., implementation failure); and (c) participant selection was not properly guided by RNR principles (i.e., implementation failure).

The first possibility presents an obvious conclusion from the null findings: the treatment did not work because the underlying program theory (CBT) was flawed in the context of influencing prison misconduct. Though prior evaluations of prison CBT programs have generally offered positive behavioral outcomes, many did not consider the potential for selection effect (Bahr et al., 2012; Dietz et al., 2003; Innes, 1997; Lowe, 1992; Morgan & Flora, 2002; Walters, 1999), and only one has used quasi-experimental methods to minimize selection bias from the model (Langan & Pelissier, 2001). While the current study found no visible treatment effects of CBT programming, these null findings may still offer value to program administrators. By using PSM and other quasi-experimental methods to evaluate program offerings, prison and program administrators may better ascertain the causal effects of treatment with mitigated influence from selection bias. In this context, we gain a greater understanding of the implementations in which CBT is most likely to be effective, promoting new theoretical insights for practice.

As a second possibility, ITU may have lacked the program integrity necessary to influence participants as intended by the treatment model. This principle of program integrity suggests that programs offer greater effectiveness when rooted in sound criminological theory or evidence-based practices (Lowenkamp & Latessa, 2005; Lowenkamp et al., 2010). Though ITU functions through a constellation of CBT programs, only two of these offerings, Thinking for a Change, and Living in Balance, are evidence-based interventions (Landenberger & Lipsey, 2005; Lowenkamp et al., 2009). Other CBT programs included in the ITU framework (e.g., Science of Addiction, 12 Steps) have not yet been subject to rigorous empirical inquiry or validation; their effectiveness and fidelity to treatment theory remain unknown.

Although Thinking for a Change is designed for small groups of 8–12 offenders, the ITU model of this program included up to 15 participants. As the Project Greenlight evaluation demonstrated over a decade ago, these adaptations in program delivery can result in unintended compromises in treatment effects (see, e.g., Wilson & Davis, 2006; Wilson & Zozula, 2012). Thus, by offering a mixed bag of interventions, with modifications that could impact program fidelity, program administrators may actually be working against themselves, producing null or iatrogenic effects under the guise of rehabilitation (Duwe & Clark, 2015).

A third possible explanation for null effects is that ITU may not have followed the principles of the RNR model closely enough to be effective in practice. While the first two explanations focused on ineffective theory and implementation, this explanation posits a failure in the selection of ITU participants. Post-analysis discussions with facility administration revealed inmates between medium (4) and very low risk (8) were targeted for ITU placement; higher risk categories (1–3) were not eligible for this form of programming unless an administrative override was provided, due to the dormitory-style setting of the treatment community.[14] To this end, program administrators may have inadvertently circumvented the principles of risk, need, and responsivity in their selection of ITU participants.

By prioritizing medium- and low-risk offenders for ITU placement, treatment effects are likely to be attenuated. While these offenders are already noted as the least likely to engage in criminal or infractionary behavior, high-risk offenders can potentially reap the most benefits from treatment and should be distinguished as a primary focus for future iterations of ITU programming (Lowenkamp et al., 2006; Wilson & Zozula, 2012). If a number of ITU graduates did experience a treatment effect, it is possible that this result was simply "washed out"; that is, some offenders may have experienced treatment utility, though these effects were attenuated by the lack of effects amongst the greater number of inmates who did not need the treatment.

Several limitations with this study are worth noting. For one, official data was used as the measure of prison misconduct (the dependent variable), and these data measure only an institutional response to observed misconduct. Whereas inmates may engage in many unobserved acts of misconduct, only detected acts are subject to staff involvement and subsequent disciplinary action. Moreover, the issuing of disciplinary reports is a highly discretionary process. Given that misconduct would result in ejection from the treatment unit, it is entirely possible that discretion would err against writing an offender up in a therapeutic community setting within a prison. Self-reported misconduct may further elucidate treatment outcomes in future studies.

Second, the effectiveness of ITU programming was tested amongst a sample of male inmates, incarcerated for relatively low-level offenses in a northeastern correctional facility. As a result, it is unknown if the results of the ITU intervention are generalizable to dissimilar inmate populations (e.g., female offenders, felony offenders convicted of more serious offenses). Finally, the analysis is also limited by the inmate characteristics that were not observed within the official data. Valuable predictors may include gang membership, misconduct during prior incarcerations, and offender attitudes toward ITU programming. Although ITU is primarily designed to deliver substance abuse programming, classification data did not indicate if subjects had ever experienced addiction problems or participated in other modalities of CBT or substance abuse treatment. Thus, the data are limited in their ability to capture individual criminogenic needs that could indicate which offenders are in greatest need of therapeutic intervention.

Implications for Research and Policy

Although null treatment effects were observed, the quasi-experimental methodology effectively achieved balance between treatment and control groups, minimizing selection effects. While randomized experiments are unequaled in their utility to evaluate social programs (King & Nielsen, 2015; Shadish, 2013), propensity score matching may offer a viable alternative for treatment contexts wherein random assignment is impractical or unethical for use (Apel & Sweeten, 2010; Stuart, 2010). As random assignment was not possible in the current study, PSM was utilized as a "next best" substitute for experimental design.

However, non-random assignment highlights a larger concern for the methodological standards of program evaluations. As randomization is a luxury rarely afforded within prison research, threats to internal validity (e.g., selection effects) are ubiquitous and need to be properly addressed in research (Berk, 1983; Langan & Pelissier, 2001; Mears & Bales, 2009). Though nonexperimental methodologies are commonly utilized to examine program effects, these analyses are restricted in their ability to control for selection bias, thus severely limiting their evaluative utility (Baro, 1999; Walters, 1999). As demonstrated in the current study, PSM directly addresses this issue, creating covariate balance between groups to disentangle the effects of ITU treatment from pre-existing differences between treatment and control groups (Franklin, 2015). Although statistical modeling techniques still fall short of experimental designs, null results generated using quasi-experimental techniques may be of greater value than positive results generated through nonexperimental analyses using unmatched control or comparison groups. Future research in correctional programming should be extremely mindful of this issue, employing quasi-experimental methods such as propensity score matching and, whenever possible, true experimental designs for evaluation.

Though results fail to offer support for CBT program effects on misconduct, this finding alone is important to furthering evidence-based practices. Whereas past CBT studies have generally shown positive outcomes, few studies presenting null or negative results of prison interventions have made their way to publication (Franco et al., 2014; Gerber & Malhotra, 2008; McCord, 2003; Welsh et al., 2007). This dearth of scholarship reflecting null effects is understood as a result of publication biases, whereby publication decisions are ultimately determined by the "direction of the significance of the findings" (Dickersin, 1990, p. 1385).

The "what works" literature is based on a fraction of all the research conducted, with a bias toward studies reporting (usually positive) effects (Gerber & Malhotra, 2008). Whereas authors frequently report and submit findings of

program successes, a majority of failed evaluations are never even written up and published, due to common belief that "null results have no publication potential" even if the findings may offer value in themselves (Franco et al., 2014, p. 8). However, a body of knowledge based almost exclusively upon the achieving of statistical significance may not accurately represent the overall findings of research being conducted (Gerber & Malhotra, 2008). Moreover, because many of these evaluations are conducted at the request of correctional administrators who would rather not publicize the perceived failures of the programming, they are often not ever made publicly available. In effect, the multiple biases toward significant (and positive) program effects substantially narrows the value of our what works knowledge base and limits our ability to refine program delivery through ignoring the valuable lessons that could be garnered from programs that failed to produce their intended effects (Zane et al., 2016).

Discussion Questions

1. According to the authors, how has the selection of research design impacted the findings of studies evaluating CBT programs' impact on prison misconduct?

2. Why was it important to use matching for the two groups? How might the result have been different had the researchers not matched them?

3. There are a number of reasons the researchers found this program to be ineffective. Discuss the possible reasons and consider which explanation you find the most plausible.

References

Adams, K., Bennett, K. J., Flanagan, T. J., Marquart, J. W., Cuvelier, S. J., Fritsch, E., . . . & Burton, V. S. (1994). A large-scale multidimensional test of the effect of prison education programs on offenders' behavior. The Prison Journal, 74(4), 433–449. https://doi.org/10.1177/0032855594074004004

Allen, L. C., MacKenzie, D. L., & Hickman, L. J. (2001). The effectiveness of cognitive behavioral treatment for adult offenders: A methodological, quality-based review. *International Journal of Offender Therapy and Comparative Criminology*, *45*(4), 498–514. https://doi.org/10.1177/0306624x01454009

Andrews, D. A., Bonta, J., & Wormith, J. S. (2011). The risk-need-responsivity (RNR) model does adding the good lives model contribute to effective crime prevention? *Criminal Justice and Behavior*, *38*(7), 735–755. https://doi.org/10.1177/0093854811406356

Andrews, D. A., Zinger, I., Hoge, R. D., Bonta, J., Gendreau, P., & Cullen, F. T. (1990). A human science approach or more punishment and pessimism: A rejoinder to Lab and Whitehead. *Criminology*, *28*(3), 419–430. https://doi.org/10.1111/j.1745-9125.1990.tb01332.x

Antonowicz, D. H., & Ross, R. R. (1994). Essential components of successful rehabilitation programs for offenders. *International Journal of Offender Therapy and Comparative Criminology*, *38*(2), 97–104. https://doi.org/10.1177/0306624x9403800202

Apel, R. J., & Sweeten, G. (2010). Propensity score matching in criminology and criminal justice. In *Handbook of quantitative criminology* (pp. 543–562). New York, NY: Springer.

Bahr, S. J., Masters, A. L., & Taylor, B. M. (2012). What works in substance abuse treatment programs for offenders? *The Prison Journal*, *92*(2), 155–174. https://doi.org/10.1177/0032885512438836

Baro, A. L. (1999). Effects of a cognitive restructuring program on inmate institutional behavior. *Criminal Justice and Behavior*, *26*(4), 466–484. https://doi.org/10.1177/0093854899026004004

Berk, R. A. (1983). An introduction to sample selection bias in sociological data. *American Sociological Review*, *48*(3), 386–398. https://doi.org/10.2307/2095230

Bonta, J., & Andrews, D. A. (2007). Risk-need-responsivity model for offender assessment and rehabilitation. *Rehabilitation*, *6*, 1–22.

Bonta, J., Wallace-Capretta, S., & Rooney, J. (2000). A quasi-experimental evaluation of an intensive rehabilitation supervision program. *Criminal Justice and Behavior*, *27*(3), 312–329. https://doi.org/10.1177/0093854800027003003

Camp, S. D., Daggett, D. M., Kwon, O., & Klein-Saffran, J. (2008). The effect of faith program participation on prison misconduct: The life connections program. *Journal of Criminal Justice*, *36*(5), 389–395. https://doi.org/10.1016/j.jcrimjus.2008.07.004

Clark, P. M. (2011). An evidence-based intervention for offenders. *Corrections Today*, *73*(1), 62–64.

Clear, T. R. (2010). Policy and evidence: The challenge to the American Society of Criminology: 2009 presidential address to the American Society of Criminology. *Criminology*, *48*, 1–25. https://doi.org/10.1111/j.1745-9125.2010.00178.x

Cochran, J. C. (2012). The ties that bind or the ties that break: Examining the relationship between visitation and prisoner misconduct. *Journal of Criminal Justice*, *40*(5), 433–440. https://doi.org/10.1016/j.jcrimjus.2012.06.001

Cochran, J. C., & Mears, D. P. (2013). Social isolation and inmate behavior: A conceptual framework for theorizing prison visitation and guiding and assessing research. *Journal of Criminal Justice*, *41*(4), 252–261. https://doi.org/10.1016/j.jcrimjus.2013.05.001

Cochran, J. C., Mears, D. P., Bales, W. D., & Stewart, E. A. (2014). Does inmate behavior affect post-release offending? Investigating the misconduct-recidivism relationship among youth and adults. *Justice Quarterly*, *31*(6), 1044–1073. https://doi.org/10.1080/07418825.2012.736526

Cunningham, M. D., & Sorensen, J. R. (2007). Predictive factors for violent misconduct in close custody. *The Prison Journal*, *87*(2), 241–253. https://doi.org/10.1177/0032885507303752

Dehejia, R. H., & Wahba, S. (2002). Propensity score-matching methods for nonexperimental causal studies. *Review of Economics and Statistics*, *84*(1), 151–161. https://doi.org/10.1162/003465302317331982

DeLisi, M. (2003). Criminal careers behind bars. *Behavioral Sciences & the Law*, *21*(5), 653–669. https://doi.org/10.1002/bsl.531

DeLisi, M., Drury, A. J., Kosloski, A. E., Caudill, J. W., Conis, P. J., Anderson, C. A., . . . & Beaver, K. M. (2010). The cycle of violence behind bars: Traumatization and institutional misconduct among juvenile delinquents in confinement. *Youth Violence and Juvenile Justice*, *8*(2), 107–121. https://doi.org/10.1177/1541204009349399

DeLisi, M., Trulson, C. R., Marquart, J. W., Drury A. J., & Kosloski, A. J. (2011). Inside the prison black box: Toward a life course importation model of inmate behavior. *International Journal of Offender Therapy and Comparative Criminology*, *55*, 1186–1207. https://doi.org/10.1177/0306624x11383956

Dickersin, K. (1990). The existence of publication bias and risk factors for its occurrence. *Jama*, *263*(10), 1385–1389. https://doi.org/10.1001/jama.263.10.1385

Dietz, E. F., O'Connell, D. J., & Scarpitti, F. R. (2003). Therapeutic communities and prison management: An examination of the effects of operating an in-prison therapeutic community on levels of institutional disorder. *International Journal of Offender Therapy and Comparative Criminology*, *47*(2), 210–223. https://doi.org/10.1177/0306624x03251088

Di Placido, C., Simon, T. L., Witte, T. D., Gu, D., & Wong, S. C. (2006). Treatment of gang members can reduce recidivism and institutional misconduct. *Law and Human Behavior*, 30(1), 93. https://doi.org/10.1007/s10979-006-9003-6

Dobson, K. S., & Khatri, N. (2000). Cognitive therapy: Looking backward, looking forward. *Journal of Clinical Psychology*, 56(7), 907–923. https://doi.org/10.1002/1097-4679(200007)56:7<907::aid-jclp9>3.0.co;2-i

Drury, A. J., & DeLisi, M. (2010). The past is prologue: Prior adjustment to prison and institutional misconduct. *The Prison Journal*, 90(3), 331–352. https://doi.org/10.1177/0032885510375676

Duwe, G., & Clark, V. (2015). Importance of program integrity. *Criminology & Public Policy*, 14(2), 301–328. https://doi.org/10.1111/1745-9133.12123

Farrington, D. P. (2003a). A short history of randomized experiments in criminology a meager feast. *Evaluation Review*, 27(3), 218–227. https://doi.org/10.1177/0193841x03027003002

Farrington, D. P. (2003b). Methodological quality standards for evaluation research. *The Annals of the American Academy of Political and Social Science*, 587(1), 49–68. https://doi.org/10.1177/0002716202250789

Franco, A., Malhotra, N., & Simonovits, G. (2014). Publication bias in the social sciences: Unlocking the file drawer. *Science*, 345(6203), 1502–1505. https://doi.org/10.1126/science.1255484

Franklin, T. W. (2015). Race and ethnicity effects in federal sentencing: A propensity score analysis. *Justice Quarterly*, 32(4), 653–679. https://doi.org/10.1080/07418825.2013.790990

French, S. A., & Gendreau, P. (2006). Reducing prison misconducts: What works! *Criminal Justice and Behavior*, 33(2), 185–218. https://doi.org/10.1177/0093854805284406

Gendreau, P. (1996). Offender rehabilitation: What we know and what needs to be done. *Criminal Justice and Behavior*, 23(1), 144–161. https://doi.org/10.1177/0093854896023001010

Gendreau, P., Goggin, C. E., & Law, M. A. (1997). Predicting prison misconducts. *Criminal Justice and behavior*, 24(4), 414–431. https://doi.org/10.1177/0093854897024004002

Gendreau, P., & Keyes, D. (2001). Making prisons safer and more humane environments. *Canadian Journal of Criminology*, 43, 123.

Gerber, A. S., & Malhotra, N. (2008). Publication bias in empirical sociological research: Do arbitrary significance levels distort published results? *Sociological Methods & Research*, 37(1), 3–30. https://doi.org/10.1177/0049124108318973

Goetting, A., & Howsen, R. M. (1986). Correlates of prisoner misconduct. *Journal of Quantitative Criminology*, 2(1), 49–67. https://doi.org/10.1007/bf01064595

Gover, A. R., Pérez, D. M., & Jennings, W. G. (2008). Gender differences in factors contributing to institutional misconduct. *The Prison Journal*, 88(3), 378–403. https://doi.org/10.1177/0032885508322453

Heckman, J., Ichimura, H., Smith, J., & Todd, P. (1998). Characterizing selection bias using experimental data. *Econometrica*, 66(5), 1017–1098. https://doi.org/10.2307/2999630

Imai, K., & Van Dyk, D. A. (2004). Causal inference with general treatment regimens: Generalizing the propensity score. *Journal of the American Statistical Association*, 99(467), 854–866. https://doi.org/10.1198/016214504000001187

Innes, C. A. (1997). Patterns of misconduct in the federal prison system. *Criminal Justice Review*, 22(2), 157–174. https://doi.org/10.1177/073401689702200203

Jiang, S. (2005). Impact of drug use on inmate misconduct: A multilevel analysis. *Journal of Criminal Justice*, 33(2), 153–163. https://doi.org/10.1016/j.jcrimjus.2004.12.007

King, G., & Nielsen, R. (2015). *Why propensity scores should not be used for matching*. Working Paper. Retrieved from http://gking.harvard.edu/publications/why-propensity-scores-should-not-be-used-formatching

Kuanliang, A., & Sorensen, J. (2008). Predictors of self-reported prison misconduct. *Criminal Justice Studies*, 21(1), 27–35. https://doi.org/10.1080/14786010801972662

Lahm, K. F. (2009). Educational participation and inmate misconduct. *Journal of Offender Rehabilitation*, 48(1), 37–52. https://doi.org/10.1080/10509670802572235

Landenberger, N. A., & Lipsey, M. W. (2005). The positive effects of cognitive—behavioral programs for offenders: A meta-analysis of factors associated with effective treatment. *Journal of Experimental Criminology*, 1(4), 451–476. https://doi.org/10.1007/s11292-005-3541-7

Langan, N. P., & Pelissier, B. M. (2001). The effect of drug treatment on inmate misconduct in federal prisons. *Journal of Offender Rehabilitation*, 34(2), 21–30. https://doi.org/10.1300/j076v34n02_02

Latessa, E. J., & Holsinger, A. (1998). The importance of evaluating correctional programs: Assessing outcome and quality. *Corrections Management Quarterly*, 2, 22–29.

Lovell, D., & Jemelka, R. (1996). When inmates misbehave: The costs of discipline. *The Prison Journal*, 76(2), 165–179. https://doi.org/10.1177/0032855596076002004

Lowe, L. (1992). *A process evaluation of the R.J. Donovan correctional facility Amity RighTurn Substance Abuse Program: July 1, 1990—September 30, 1991*. Sacramento, CA: Department of Corrections, Office of Substance Abuse Programs.

Lowenkamp, C. T., Flores, A. W., Holsinger, A. M., Makarios, M. D., & Latessa, E. J. (2010). Intensive supervision programs: Does program philosophy and the principles of effective intervention matter? *Journal of Criminal Justice, 38*(4), 368–375. https://doi.org/10.1016/j.jcrimjus.2010.04.004

Lowenkamp, C. T., Hubbard, D., Makarios, M. D., & Latessa, E. J. (2009). A quasi-experimental evaluation of thinking for a change a "real-world" application. *Criminal Justice and Behavior, 36*(2), 137–146. https://doi.org/10.1177/0093854808328230

Lowenkamp, C. T., & Latessa, E. J. (2005). Developing successful reentry programs: Lessons learned from the "what works" research. *Corrections Today, 67*(2), 72–77.

Lowenkamp, C. T., Latessa, E. J., & Smith, P. (2006). Does correctional program quality really matter? The impact of adhering to the principles of effective intervention 2006. *Federal Probation, 5,* 201–220.

Macgregor, S. (2008). *Sex offender treatment programs: Effectiveness of prison and community based programs in Australia and New Zealand.* Canberra, Australia: Indigenous Justice Clearinghouse.

MacKenzie, D. L. (2006). *What works in corrections: Reducing the criminal activities of offenders and delinquents.* Cambridge: Cambridge University Press.

McCord, J. (2003). Cures that harm: Unanticipated outcomes of crime prevention programs. *The Annals of the American Academy of Political and Social Science, 587*(1), 16–30. https://doi.org/10.1177/0002716202250781.

McMurran, M. (2007). What works in substance misuse treatments for offenders? *Criminal Behaviour and Mental Health, 17*(4), 225–233. https://doi.org/10.1002/cbm.662

Meade, B., & Steiner, B. (2013). The effects of exposure to violence on inmate maladjustment. *Criminal Justice and Behavior, 40*(11), 1228–1249. https://doi.org/10.1177/0093854813495392

Mears, D. P., & Bales, W. D. (2009). Supermax incarceration and recidivism. *Criminology, 47*(4), 1131–1166.

Morgan, R. D., & Flora, D. B. (2002). Group psychotherapy with incarcerated offenders: A research synthesis. *Group Dynamics: Theory, Research, and Practice, 6*(3), 203. https://doi.org/10.1037/1089-2699.6.3.203

Nielsen, A. L., Scarpitti, F. R., & Inciardi, J. A. (1996). Integrating the therapeutic community and work release for drug-involved offenders: The CREST program. *Journal of Substance Abuse Treatment, 13*(4), 349–358. https://doi.org/10.1016/s0740-5472(96)00112-2

O'Malley, P. (2010). *Crime and risk.* London: SAGE Publications.

Pan, H., Scarpitti, F. R., Inciardi, J. A., & Lockwood, D. (1993). Some considerations on therapeutic communities in corrections. In J. A. Inciardi (Ed.), *Drug treatment and criminal justice* (Vol. 27, pp. 30–43). Newbury Park, CA: SAGE Publications.

Polaschek, D. L. (2012). An appraisal of the risk-need-responsivity (RNR) model of offender rehabilitation and its application in correctional treatment. *Legal and Criminological Psychology, 17*(1), 1–17. https://doi.org/10.1111/j.2044-8333.2011.02038.x

Pratt, T. C. (2002). Meta-analysis and its discontents: Treatment destruction techniques revisited. *Journal of Offender Rehabilitation, 35*(1), 23–40. https://doi.org/10.1300/j076v35n01_02

Prendergast, M., Farabee, D., & Cartier, J. (2001). The impact of in-prison therapeutic community programs on prison management. *Journal of Offender Rehabilitation, 32*(3), 63–78. https://doi.org/10.1300/j076v32n03_05

Rosenbaum, P. R., & Rubin, D. B. (1983). The central role of the propensity score in observational studies for causal effects. *Biometrika, 70*(1), 41–55. https://doi.org/10.2307/2335942

Rosenbaum, P. R., & Rubin, D. B. (1985). Constructing a control group using multivariate matched sampling methods that incorporate the propensity score. *The American Statistician, 39*(1), 33–38. https://doi.org/10.1080/00031305.1985.10479383

Rosenthal, R. (1979). The "file drawer problem" and tolerance for null results. *Psychological Bulletin, 86*(3), 638–641. https://doi.org/10.1037/0033-2909.86.3.638

Shadish, W. R. (2013). Propensity score analysis: Promise, reality and irrational exuberance. *Journal of Experimental Criminology, 9*(2), 129–144. https://doi.org/10.1007/s11292-012-9166-8

Sorensen, J., & Cunningham, M. D. (2010). Conviction offense and prison violence: A comparative study of murderers and other offenders. *Crime & Delinquency, 56*(1), 103–125. https://doi.org/10.1177/0011128707307175

Sorensen, J., & Davis, J. (2011). Violent criminals locked up: Examining the effect of incarceration on behavioral continuity. *Journal of Criminal Justice, 39*(2), 151–158. https://doi.org/10.1016/j.jcrimjus.2011.01.003

Spiropoulos, G. V., Spruance, L., Van Voorhis, P., & Schmitt, M. M. (2005). Pathfinders and problem solving: Comparative effects of two cognitive-behavioral programs among men and women offenders in community and prison. *Journal of Offender Rehabilitation, 42*(2), 69–94. https://doi.org/10.1300/j076v42n02_05

Steiner, B., Butler, H. D., & Ellison, J. M. (2014). Causes and correlates of prison inmate misconduct: A systematic review of the evidence. *Journal of Criminal Justice, 42*(6), 462–470. https://doi.org/10.1016/j.jcrimjus.2014.08.001

Steiner, B., & Wooldredge, J. (2008). Inmate versus environmental effects on prison rule violations. *Criminal Justice and Behavior*, 35(4), 438–456. https://doi.org/10.1177/0093854807312787

Steiner, B., & Wooldredge, J. (2013). Implications of different outcome measures for an understanding of inmate misconduct. *Crime & Delinquency*, 59(8), 1234–1262. https://doi.org/10.1177/0011128709335151

Stuart, E. A. (2010). Matching methods for causal inference: A review and a look forward. *Statistical Science: A Review Journal of the Institute of Mathematical Statistics*, 25(1), 1–28. https://doi.org/10.1214/09-sts313

Travis, J. (2005). *But they all come back: Facing the challenges of prisoner reentry*. Washington, DC: The Urban Institute.

Trulson, C. R. (2007). Determinants of disruption: Institutional misconduct among state-committed delinquents. *Youth Violence and Juvenile Justice*, 5(1), 7–34. https://doi.org/10.1177/1541204006295162

Trulson, C. R., DeLisi, M., Caudill, J. W., Belshaw, S., & Marquart, J. W. (2010). Delinquent careers behind bars. *Criminal Justice Review*, 35(2), 200–219. https://doi.org/10.1177/0734016809360326

Walters, G. D. (1999). Short-term outcome of inmates participating in the lifestyle change program. *Criminal Justice and Behavior*, 26(3), 322–337. https://doi.org/10.1177/0093854899026003003

Welsh, W. N., McGrain, P., Salamatin, N., & Zajac, G. (2007). The effects of prison drug treatment on inmate misconduct: A repeated measures analysis. *Criminal Justice and Behavior*, 34(5), 600–615. https://doi.org/10.1177/0093854806296897

Wilson, D. B., Bouffard, L. A., & MacKenzie, D. L. (2005). A quantitative review of structured, group-oriented, cognitive-behavioral programs for offenders. *Criminal Justice and Behavior*, 32(2), 172–204. https://doi.org/10.1177/0093854804272889

Wilson, J. A., & Davis, R. C. (2006). Good intentions meet hard realities: An evaluation of the project greenlight reentry program. *Criminology & Public Policy*, 5(2), 303–338. https://doi.org/10.1111/j.1745-9133.2006.00380.x

Wilson, J. A., & Zozula, C. (2012). Risk, recidivism, and (re)habilitation: Another look at Project Greenlight. *The Prison Journal*, 92(2), 203–230. https://doi.org/10.1177/0032885512438870

Winship, C., & Mare, R. D. (1992). Models for sample selection bias. *Annual Review of Sociology*, 1992(18), 327–350. https://doi.org/10.1146/annurev.so.18.080192.001551

Wooldredge, J., Griffin, T., & Pratt, T. (2001). Considering hierarchical models for research on inmate behavior: Predicting misconduct with multilevel data. *Justice Quarterly*, 18(1), 203–231. https://doi.org/10.1080/07418820100094871

Zane, S. N., Welsh, B. C., & Zimmerman, G. M. (2016). Examining the iatrogenic effects of the Cambridge-Somerville youth study: Existing explanations and new appraisals. *British Journal of Criminology*, 56(1), 141–160. https://doi.org/10.1093/bjc/azv033

5   Pre-Experimental, Longitudinal, and Cross-Sectional Designs

Classical and quasi-experiments are ideal when evaluating the effectiveness of a program. Those designs allow us to safeguard the study against several threats to internal validity. There are, however, circumstances in which experimental designs are not possible or are not appropriate for what we are looking to research. That is why there are a variety of other designs available for consideration. In this chapter, I will describe three different types of studies: pre-experimental, longitudinal, and cross-sectional designs.

Pre-Experimental Designs

Ideally, we would like to utilize the most rigorous methodology every time we engage in research. The reality is that, since criminal justice research takes place in the real world, we are often forced to modify our plans to fit the situation at hand. Sometimes, that means that the only available option for a program evaluation might be a **pre-experimental design**. Whereas quasi-experiments lack one of the three requirements of a classical experiment, pre-experimental designs lack two of the three elements. So here we get designs that not only lack randomization of participants into experimental and control groups but also might not even have a comparison group or pretest data.

One-Group Before-After Design

A common pre-experimental design is the **one-group before-after design**, which allows us to make comparisons before and after the introduction of the independent variable. Stauss, Sparks, Thomas, and Grant (2018) evaluated a program that aimed to help incarcerated mothers work on their communication skills while also bonding with their children. A state prison for women offered a voluntary letter-writing program for mothers of minor children. Researchers evaluated the women's progress on dealing with parenting stress by conducting interviews and comparing their pretest and posttest scores on a parenting stress survey. In this instance, the researchers either lacked access to prisoners who were not involved in the program, or they did not feel that they would be able to encourage those receiving no such programming to sit through the interviews and take the survey twice. The findings of these types of studies do hold some value. Stauss and colleagues reported posttest scores that indicated reduced parental stress compared to the pretest results. Participants also reported in the interviews that the program helped them work on becoming more empathetic mothers, increased their confidence, and allowed them to have a more positive view of themselves as parents. This type of evaluation is worthwhile, in that it helps us establish a relationship between X (the classes) and Y (parenting stress), and it provides evidence that the introduction of X preceded the observed changes in Y. The design does not, however, address a number of potential threats to internal validity, including maturation. Without a comparison group, we cannot tell if the changes observed in the participants would have occurred absent the intervention.

Pre-experimental designs

One-group before-after design		
O	X	O
Two-group posttest only design		
	X	O
	X	O
One-group posttest only design		
	X	O

X = Independent variable
O = Observation

Figure 5.1 Pre-experimental Designs

One- and Two-Group Posttest-Only Designs

The **two-group posttest-only design** addresses the problem of lacking a comparison group, but a significant drawback is the lack of a pretest to tell us whether the two groups were similar or different before introduction of the independent variable. The **one-group posttest-only design** has the most limitations of any of the plans we have discussed thus far, with no comparison group and no data to indicate where the treatment group was at baseline before being exposed to the independent variable. There are occasions, however, when this is the only feasible option. Early in my career, I received a frantic phone call from a criminal justice agency. They had been implementing a three-year grant-funded program for the past two years and nine months. The problem was that one of the grant stipulations was they had to have an outside researcher evaluate the program. While they attempted to contract with another researcher at the outset of the project, that deal fell through, and the agency was now desperate to find someone who would step in at the last minute to do an evaluation. I agreed to help with the understanding that I was coming in too late to monitor the data collection process and could not ensure the quality of what I would be able to produce. The practitioner who called me was confident that all would be well because the person responsible for implementing the program had been distributing pre- and posttests all along. Unfortunately, that was only partially correct. There were no pretests. The program consisted of a series of twelve-week sessions with a different group of juveniles each time. When I came on board, I asked for what I expected to be piles of pre- and post-tests, but I only received the latter. Consequently, I had no choice but to explain to the grant agency that a one-group posttest-only design was the only possible option. I submitted a report but made it clear I could not make any statements regarding the efficacy of the program since I had no idea if the participants changed from the beginning of the program to the end. Even if I had the pretests and been able to do a one-group before-after design, I would have had to note that any changes seen in the juveniles might have been a case of maturation rather than program effectiveness, since I also lacked a comparison group.

Longitudinal Designs

You have already learned about some **longitudinal designs**. Classical and quasi-experiments and one-group before-after methods involve data collection at multiple points in time. Time-series studies include several data collection points over a period of weeks, months, or years. In this section, I am going to describe a few additional design types that require multiple waves of data collection.

Trend Studies

Trend studies are exactly what they sound like in that they examine trends in populations over time. A review of the FBI's **Uniform Crime Reports** (UCR) homicide statistics over a 30-year period would give us a good overview of homicide trends in the United States. More and more states are enacting criminal justice reform, with one of the targets of reform being reduction of pretrial incarceration. States are working to limit the use of pretrial incarceration based on fairness, as being released on bail is often more of a matter of a person's wealth than an assessment of the person's threat to the community. As states enact bail reform, citizens are concerned with whether the decision to grant pretrial release will produce increases in crime in the community. Criminal justice practitioners share the community's concern about crime, but they are also keeping a close eye on the jail population sizes as bail reform efforts aim to substantially reduce incarceration. Trend studies can help us monitor both the community crime rates and the jail population statistics over time.

Panel Studies

Panel studies are a type of longitudinal design that involves repeatedly collecting data on the same individuals over time. Examples of large-scale panel designs are the **National Youth Survey** (NYS) and the **National Crime Victimization Survey**. NCVS collects victimization data at the household level from all persons 12 and older residing in each selected home. Once a house is selected, it remains part of their study for three years. The first interview is conducted in person, and then the majority of the subsequent six interviews (at six-month intervals) are completed via telephone (United States Bureau of Justice Statistics, n.d.). The **Communities that Care Youth Survey** is another example of a panel study. The surveys were part of a program aimed at reducing health and behavioral problems among children and adolescents. For data collection, researchers tracked 4,407 students, half of whom were part of the Communities that Care Program and half of whom were in the control group, and surveyed the same students each year, starting when they were in the fifth grade (Communities that Care Plus, n.d.).

Cohort Studies

Cohort studies involve following people who are grouped together. While cohorts are often age groups, they can be categorized in other ways, such as by grade in school or police academy class. Perhaps the most famous cohort study in our discipline was the **Philadelphia Birth Cohort Study** conducted by Marvin Wolfgang, Robert Figlio, and Thorsten Sellin (1972) and published in *Delinquency in a Birth Cohort*. Wolfgang and colleagues identified 9,945 males born in Philadelphia in 1945 and used police records to trace their delinquent activity from their tenth through eighteenth birthdays. Their work was groundbreaking, in that they discovered that a very small proportion (6 percent of the entire cohort) was responsible for over half the entire cohort's criminal offending and nearly three-quarters of serious offending. Several years later, Wolfgang, Figlio, and Sellin (1987) followed up this work by continuing to track 10 percent of the original Philadelphia sample through the age of 30. This research taught us that a small percentage of the population is responsible for a disproportionate amount of crime, and, contrary to what was conventional wisdom at the time, offenders generally do *not* specialize in a particular type of criminal behavior.

Accelerated or Intensive Longitudinal Designs

The **Monitoring the Future** (MTF) Survey, which surveys eighth, tenth, and twelfth graders, college students, and young adults, is another example of a cohort design. By looking at all these different age groups at once, MTF provides us with indicators of age effects, cohort effects, environmental effects (high school, college, employment), and change in years across all included age groups (Monitoring the Future, n.d.). This use of multiple cohorts at the same time is known a cohort-sequential longitudinal design or an **accelerated** or **intensive longitudinal design.** Unlike traditional cohort designs, which take years to generate results, these accelerated designs provide information in a much shorter time (Galbraith, Bowden, & Mander, 2017). Intensive longitudinal designs can include frequent measurements of the same participants or repeated use of cross-sectional data for the same population or crime type (Jennings & Reingle Gonzalez, 2019).

Potential Drawbacks to Longitudinal Designs

Longitudinal studies have numerous strengths, with the prominent one being establishing time order between the independent and dependent variables, a requirement for causation. An important disadvantage is that any research that involves multiple data collection periods over time is also going to be susceptible to some threats to validity. For example, instrumentation, or a change in the way the data are being collected and recorded, must be closely monitored throughout the study. Data collection practices change for various reasons, including adjustments to the way we are asking questions and how data are being input into databases. Attrition, also known in research as mortality, is likely in any study that takes place over time. Researchers may need to consider selecting a larger sample size than what will ultimately be needed for analysis to account for attrition. Of course, if group attrition occurs in non-random fashion, what will be left is a sample that no longer resembles the study population. Incentives to maintain participation, such as a small renumeration at each wave of data collection, might help reduce attrition.

Cross-Sectional Designs

Cross-sectional designs involve just one wave of data collection. The FBI's Uniform Crime Reports (UCR) and National Incident Based Reporting System (NIBRS) are both examples of cross-sectional studies. The National Crime Victimization Survey is a panel design, but just one wave of data collection for that project is considered cross-sectional. Cross-sectional studies are good options whenever we need to learn about something quickly, and they can provide very good descriptive data. As the country deals with the opioid epidemic, some cities are looking to open supervised injection facilities as a harm-reduction measure. One question that policymakers have is whether drug users would be willing to use them. Leon, Cardoso, Mackin, Bock, and Gaeta (2018) used a cross-sectional design to survey a sample of drug users in the Boston area to learn how likely they would be to use such facilities and, if not, why. This descriptive data can help city officials and rehabilitation agency coordinators design injection sites that are most likely to be used by drug-addicted city residents.

Cross-sectional designs are not hampered by attrition problems, nor are changes in instrumentation over time a concern. What we do lose here is the ability to learn about time order. We might be able to find that there is a relationship between an independent and a dependent variable, but we will not know if the change in Y preceded or followed the introduction of X. As I noted in previous chapters, research on home security systems has been hampered by this problem. Do burglar alarms prevent burglaries? It is difficult to tell with cross-sectional research. Cross-sectional research only helps us establish that there is some sort of relationship between alarm ownership and burglaries, but not whether the alarm installation came before or after the break-in.

Approximating Longitudinal Designs With Cross-Sectional Data

Since longitudinal studies are time consuming and expensive, researchers may attempt to use cross-sectional designs in a way that can allow us to get a picture of what interests us over time.

Retrospective Studies

A common way of approaching crime and victimization research is to ask participants to recall past events. Individuals might be asked to keep diaries to record their recent alcohol or drug consumption. Women who have been in abusive relationships are interviewed about their experiences and reasons they choose informal or formal avenues of assistance. Adults can be asked to recall their juvenile offending patterns and the age at which they became involved in delinquency. Researchers can also search official records to learn about recidivism of a sample of people who completed a rehabilitation program one year ago.

Researchers refer to cross-sectional designs that involve use of data sources to examine past behavior as **retrospective designs**. Degenardt, Gisev, Trevena, and colleagues (2013) obtained the records of all clients of opioid-substitution therapy treatment centers in part of Australia. They then used that information to conduct data linkages with other databases in the country to research these individuals' criminal activity starting at the age of ten. Carr, Baker, and Cassidy (2016) conducted a retrospective quasi-experiment of offenders with mental illness who went to a specialized day reporting center over a five-year period and compared them to a similar group of probationers. The outcome of interest here was recidivism, measured as new convictions. The researchers constructed a comparison group based on their knowledge of the characteristics of the experimental group, and then they searched non-public agency records for conviction data. In both these examples, the researchers were able to use databases to get a picture of participants' criminal offending over time, even though they were collecting the data at one time period. Such retrospective work is sometimes used in program evaluation when researchers are not brought in to study the effectiveness of a program until well after the program started. Keep in mind, though, that this type of research is susceptible to instrumentation problems. While the researcher is collecting the data at one time, the agency records were collected over a period of years, and the data collection procedures could have changed during that time.

Retrospective designs are much quicker to implement than prospective designs. For retrospective designs, we ask people to recall past events, sometimes years preceding the survey. **Prospective designs** involve starting with a sample and then observing them or asking them to self-report as time progresses. An example of a retrospective study would be to ask 25-year-old men to tell us the age at which they first drank alcohol. For a prospective study, we might identify a sample of 10-year-old boys and then interview them every 2 to 3 years until they turn 25. During those interviews, we would ask them if they have had alcohol since the last study period. The latter study is clearly going to be more expensive and take 15 years, so the retrospective design is advantageous in terms of time and money.

The downside is that, when we rely on individuals to recall events, there is always the possibility that they will not be forthcoming or will forget about an incident, or their memory will not be an accurate representation of what really occurred. When we ask people to recall events, even if they do remember something happening, there is the possibility of telescoping. **Telescoping** involves placing events into an improper time frame. In other words, something happened 14 months ago (outside the time frame of the survey question), but the respondent mistakenly reports that it occurred 9 months ago (within the survey time frame). More trivial events are also less likely to remain in our memories. Emiko, Herrenkohl, Huang, and Witney (2004) analyzed data from the **Lehigh Longitudinal Study**, a research project that involved data collection of prospective parental reports of child maltreatment as well as retrospective reports from those parents' children. When comparing the prospective and retrospective measures, the authors found that two-thirds of adolescents whose parents prospectively reported child abuse retrospectively reported that same abuse. The retrospective accounts were associated with substantial underreporting of abuse.

The **Cambridge Study in Delinquent Development** is a prospective longitudinal survey of 411 males from London who were first contacted when they were 8 to 9 years old in the early 1960s. Researchers then interviewed the boys again at ages 10, 14, 16, 18, 21, 25, and 32. Since this was a prospective design, researchers were able to ask questions about the onset of criminal behavior. As the respondents aged, they were also asked to retrospectively report on juvenile offending patterns. Their findings revealed that retrospective studies are not necessarily an adequate substitution for prospective designs. Nearly 90 percent of the males interviewed at age 32 failed to report at least one offense that they reported when they were juveniles. The lack of reporting differed by offense type, with respondents much more likely to forget or otherwise neglect to mention less serious offenses. Retrospective reporting was especially problematic for people with serious substance use problems, which should not be surprising given the impact that substance use has on memory. The retrospective interviews were also less useful for identifying the age at which people began offending as juveniles or young adults (Kazemian & Farrington, 2005). When should we use retrospective designs to collect self-reported data? Kazemian and Farrington concluded that data collected retrospectively tends to be more valid and reliable when used to measure more serious offending and more memorable events, as more trivial incidents are likely to be lost with time.

Summary

Pre-experimental designs lack two of the three elements of classical experiments. Not only are these designs missing random assignment of individuals into treatment and control groups, but some lack a comparison group. Pre-experimental designs may also fail to utilize pretest measurements. These studies are limited in what they can tell us about what is being studied because they fail to address numerous threats to internal validity. They might be the only options available for researchers due to data or program access constraints.

The primary strengths of longitudinal designs are their ability to establish time order between X and Y and to study phenomena over time. Some vitally important data have come from longitudinal studies, including data collected as part of the Cambridge Study in Delinquent Development and the Philadelphia Birth Cohort Study. Of course, significant barriers to longitudinal research are the time and money that it takes to complete. It is difficult to secure funding and to wait years, or even decades, to collect all the desired data. That is why cross-sectional retrospective research is an attractive alternative to prospective panel or cohort designs. Of course, anything that is an easier and cheaper alternative comes with limitations, and retrospective designs have been found to produce underestimations of offending and victimization incidents compared to prospective work designed to measure the same variables.

Keywords

Pre-experimental design
One-group posttest-only design
Panel study
Philadelphia Birth Cohort Study
Cross-sectional design
Telescoping

One-group before-after design
Longitudinal design
Communities that Care Youth Survey
Monitoring the Future (MTF)
Retrospective design
Lehigh Longitudinal Study
Two-group posttest-only design

Trend study
Cohort studies
Accelerated/intensive longitudinal design
Prospective design
Cambridge Study in Delinquent Development

Discussion Questions

1. How do trend studies, panel studies, and cohort design differ from each other?
2. What are the advantages and disadvantages of using a prospective design instead of retrospective?
3. What threats to internal validity might be present with a two-group posttest-only design?

References

Carr, W. A., Baker, A. B., & Cassidy, J. J. (2016). Reducing criminal recidivism with an enhanced day reporting center for probationers with mental illness. *Journal of Offender Rehabilitation, 55*, 95–112. https://doi.org/10.1080/10509674.2015.1124958

Communities that Care Plus. (n.d.). *Research and results*. Seattle, WA: University of Washington. Retrieved from www.communitiesthatcare.net/research-results/

Degenhardt, L., Gisev, N., Trevena, J., Larney, S., Kimber, J., Burns, L., . . . & Weatherburn, D. (2013). Engagement with the criminal justice system among opioid-dependent people: A retrospective cohort study. *Addiction, 108*, 2152–2165. https://doi.org/10.1111/add.12324

Emiko, T., Herrenkohl, T. I., Huang, B., & Whitney, S. D. (2004). Measuring child maltreatment: A comparison of prospective parent reports and retrospective adolescent reports. *American Journal of Orthopsychiatry, 74*(4), 424–435. https://doi.org/10.1037/0002-9432.74.4.424

Galbraith, S., Bowden, J., & Mander, A. (2017). Accelerated longitudinal designs: An overview of modeling, power, costs, and handling of missing data. *Statistical Methods in Medical Research, 26*(1), 374–398. https://doi.org/10.1177/0962280214547150

Jennings, W. G., & Reingle Gonzalez, J. M. (2019). *Criminological and criminal justice research methods*. New York, NY: Wolters Kluwer.

Kazemian, L., & Farrington, D. P. (2005). Comparing the validity of prospective, retrospective, and official onset for different offending categories. *Journal of Quantitative Criminology, 21*(2), 127–147.

Leon, C., Cardoso, L., Mackin, S., Bock, B., & Gaeta, J. (2018). The willingness of people who inject drugs in Boston to use a supervised injection facility. *Substance Abuse, 39*(1), 95–101. https://doi.org/10.1080/08897077.2017.1365804

Monitoring the Future. (n.d.). Retrieved from http://monitoringthefuture.org/purpose.html#Design

Stauss, K., Sparks, L., Thomas, J., & Grant, K. (2018). Letters to children: Findings of a program to enhance communication of incarcerated mothers and their children. *Corrections, 3*(4), 225–247. https://doi.org/10.1080/23774657.2017.1381054

United States Bureau of Justice Statistics. (n.d.). *National crime victimization survey methodology*. Washington, DC: United States Department of Justice Bureau of Justice Statistics. Retrieved from www.bjs.gov/developer/ncvs/methodology.cfm

Wolfgang, M. E., Figlio, R. M., & Sellin, T. (1972). *Delinquency in a birth cohort*. Chicago: University of Chicago Press.

Wolfgang, M. E., Figlio, R. M., & Sellin, T. (1987). *From boy to man, from delinquency to crime*. Chicago: University of Chicago Press.

Reading 5.1   Knowledge of the 911 Good Samaritan Law and 911-Calling Behavior of Overdose Witnesses

Professionals from the medical, social service, and criminal justice fields are all searching for ways to mitigate the harm of the opioid epidemic. As Jakubowski, Kunins, Huxley-Reicher, and Siegler (2018) note in the introduction to their article, opioids are involved in the majority of overdose deaths. Interventions at the time of opioid overdose have the potential to save lives, but a challenge is that the people most likely to be present at an overdose incident are also addicted to opioids. Jakubowski and colleagues conducted a program evaluation of a training that educates syringe exchange clients about seeking help in the event that they witness an overdose. Following the instruction about Good Samaritan laws (GSLs), the researchers conducted periodic follow-up interviews with the cohorts to see if they retained what they had learned and used the information to seek help for someone experiencing an overdose.

Knowledge of the 911 Good Samaritan Law and 911-Calling Behavior of Overdose Witnesses

Andrea Jakubowski, Hillary V. Kunins, Zina Huxley-Reicher, and Anne Siegler

Introduction

Drug overdose deaths in the United States continue to rise, nearly tripling between 1999 and 2014.[1] In 2014, 61% of overdose deaths involved opioids.[1] Most fatal overdoses are witnessed, presenting an opportunity for life-saving medical intervention, such as calling 911 for emergency medical service.[2] However, barriers to calling 911 are well documented among users of illicit drugs, with fear of police involvement and arrest of primary concern.[2-8] Rates of 911 calling for fatal overdose have been reported to range from 15% to 72%, indicating that emergency medical services are underutilized.[9,10]

In response to the opioid overdose epidemic, 36 states in the United States have passed 911 Good Samaritan laws (GSLs).[11] These laws provide legal protection for overdose victims and bystanders who call 911, although they vary in their specific criminal protections for drug possession, drug paraphernalia, and parole or probation violation.

Although the intent of GSLs is to increase 911 calls in overdose events, little is known about the effect of these laws on 911-calling behaviors of overdose witnesses. One survey showed that after receiving GSL information, drug users reported they would be more likely to call 911 if they were to witness an overdose,[12] but no studies have documented an association between 911-calling behavior and knowledge of GSLs.

Educating individuals about GSLs is a key component of opioid overdose prevention training (OPT) curricula. OPTs are designed to teach people who use drugs and those in their social networks to recognize the signs of an overdose and respond by calling 911 and administering rescue breathing and naloxone, a medication that reverses the effects of opioid overdose.

In this prospective longitudinal study of the impact of OPT on behaviors associated with witnessed overdoses, we sought to determine the relationship between participant knowledge of the New York state GSL and 911 calling in response to overdose events. We hypothesized that correct knowledge of the GSL would be associated with 911 calling. Based on prior studies and a priori hypotheses, we also examined whether other event characteristics are associated with 911 calling, including overdose event location and participant receipt of public benefits or residence in public housing.

Methods

Study Design

We conducted a prospective cohort study of trained overdose responders. Study participants were recruited following OPTs at six syringe exchange programs in New York City between June and September of 2013. OPT recipients were recruited immediately following completion of training. Exclusion criteria were age less than 18 years, inability to complete an oral survey in Spanish or English, residence outside the city in which the study was conducted, and no contact information for follow-up interviews. The study was approved by the New York City Department of Health and Mental Hygiene Institutional Review Board. Participants provided written informed consent.

Trained researchers conducted in-person or phone surveys immediately after OPT (baseline) and at 3, 6, and 12 months according to standardized protocols using a close-ended questionnaire. We attempted to reach participants in person and by mail, phone, and text message up to 3 months after the 3-month follow-up date, up to 6 months after the 6-month follow-up date, and up to 3 months after the 12-month date of the last participant enrolled for the 12-month follow-up. For surveys administered after 12 months, outcomes were included only if they occurred within two weeks of the participant's 12-month follow-up date.

Measures

Characteristics of Study Participants

All participant characteristics were self-reported at baseline. Demographic characteristics included race/ethnicity (non-Hispanic white, non-Hispanic black, Hispanic, and other), gender (male or female, with transgender categorized according to the participant's self-identified gender), and education (less than high school, grade 12 or General Educational Development [GED], at least some college). Participant age was collected as a continuous variable and then collapsed into five age groups (21–24, 25–34, 35–44, 45–54, 55+). Criminal justice involvement was defined as any criminal justice involvement in the last 12 months (having been arrested, on probation, or on parole) or none. Current receipt of public benefits was defined as any federal or state benefits, including social security, public assistance, Supplemental Nutrition Assistance Program (SNAP), Home Energy Assistance Program (HEAP), and HIV/AIDS Service Administration (HASA) or none. Housing status was defined as stable permanent, temporary, or unstable, based on United States Department of Housing and Urban Development definitions.[13] Stable permanent housing included living in one's own home or apartment. Temporary housing included living in a single room occupancy hotel, transitional housing, a treatment facility, or a family member's or friend's home. Unstable housing was defined as living on the street or in a shelter. Substances used 30 days prior to baseline included licit substances (prescription painkillers, benzodiazepines, methadone, buprenorphine, and alcohol) and illicit substances (heroin and crack/cocaine). No distinction was made between prescribed and nonprescribed use of benzodiazepines, methadone, or buprenorphine. Injecting in the last year (always, sometimes, rarely, and never) was collapsed into a dichotomous variable (any or none). Participants reported current participation in an opioid treatment program (OTP) and participation in a syringe exchange program (SEP). We also measured any lifetime personal experience of an overdose event and total number of lifetime witnessed overdose events.

Independent Variables

GOOD SAMARITAN LAW (GSL) KNOWLEDGE AT TIME OF EVENT

New York state's GSL, passed in 2011, protects the 911 caller and the overdose victim from charge and prosecution for possession of up to eight ounces of a controlled substance, alcohol consumption for underage drinkers, any amount of marijuana, paraphernalia offenses, and sharing drugs.[14] To develop the question about knowledge of the GSL, we consulted with policy experts and then performed cognitive pretesting on the question. Immediately following OPT and at 3-, 6-, and 12-month follow-ups, participants were asked, "Let's say you have drugs on you, you see someone overdose, and you call 911. Do you think it would be legal or illegal for the police to prosecute you for your drugs, or are you not sure?" Participants responded "legal," "illegal," or "don't know/not sure." Participant responses were categorized as correct, incorrect, or unknown. "Illegal" was categorized as correct knowledge of the GSL, and "legal" was categorized as incorrect knowledge of the law. The correct answer to the question was explained to the participant, regardless of response, so participants were reeducated about the GSL at 3-, 6-, and 12-month follow-ups.

OVERDOSE EVENT CHARACTERISTICS

All characteristics of overdose events were reported by study participants who witnessed an overdose. Overdose event characteristics included victim gender (male, female, and transgender), relationship to overdose victim (relative, friend, acquaintance and/or drug-using associate, and stranger), and overdose location (by New York City borough determined by ZIP code or cross street of reported overdose). Overdose setting was categorized as public (abandoned building, public bathroom, roof, stairway/lobby/elevator, street/park/outside, and subway/bus/car), semiprivate (drug treatment program, hotel, syringe exchange program, shelter, and shooting gallery), and private (participant's home, overdose victim's home, someone else's home, supportive housing, and single room occupancy [SRO]). Naloxone administration at overdose event was categorized dichotomously; an affirmative response included either participant or another bystander administration of naloxone.

Dependent Variables

Witnessing an Overdose

Three, six, and twelve months after OPT, participants were asked how many overdoses they had witnessed since their last interview, followed by a series of questions about their response to each overdose. An overdose event was defined as witnessing an individual who "is unresponsive or cannot be woken up, collapses, has blue skin color, difficulty breathing, loses

consciousness or dies while using drugs." This analysis includes only participants who witnessed at least one overdose after OPT.

911 Calling

For each witnessed overdose, participants were asked, "Were you able to call 911 during the overdose?" If they were unable to call, they were asked "What's the main reason you didn't call 911?" Predefined field-coded responses included someone else called 911, I didn't have a phone on me, fear of police/arrest, fear of losing my housing, fear of violating probation/parole, fear of losing my kids, phone was dead/out of minutes, no phone signal, and the person who overdosed woke up. After asking why the participant did not call 911, participants were asked if anyone else called. Events were classified into "911 called," defined as either the participant or another bystander calling 911, and "911 not called," defined as neither the participant nor another bystander calling 911.

Statistical Analysis

We describe baseline demographic characteristics of study participants who witnessed one or more overdose within 12 months of OPT and knowledge of the GSL at baseline and 3-, 6-, and 12-month follow-ups. Participants who completed a survey but did not respond to the Good Samaritan question and participants who did not complete a follow-up survey were excluded from this analysis.

Bivariable frequencies were used to compare characteristics of overdose events in which 911 was called with events in which 911 was not called. Odds ratios (ORs) and 95% confidence intervals (CIs) were calculated to assess for associations between overdose characteristics and 911 calling. Generalized linear models were used to test association between GSL knowledge of participant and whether 911 was called by any bystander. Logistic regression was performed using the PROC GENMOD model statement in SAS (SAS Institute, Cary, NC) to account for nonindependence among overdose events witnessed by the same individual. We included in multivariable analysis variables significant at the $P < .05$ level in bivariable analysis and excluded variables that met criteria for confounding.[15]

We also adjusted the final model for witness age, gender, and race. We used a first-order autoregressive covariance structure due to correlation of model residuals in repeated measures. Analyses were carried out using SPSS 22 (IBM, Armonk, NY) and SAS 9.2.

Results

Sample Description

Of the 675 individuals trained in overdose prevention at selected programs during the study period, 429 (64%) were approached to participate in the study, and 351 (52%) agreed to enroll. Overall, 299 (85%) completed at least one follow-up survey in the 12-month period. Of the 299, 128 (43%) had witnessed one or more overdoses since baseline, constituting our analytic sample for this report. See Table 1 for descriptive statistics of the 128 participants.

Number of Overdoses Witnessed at 12 Months

The total number of overdose events witnessed by 128 participants was 326. Two thirds (66%) witnessed more than one overdose (range: 1–14): 31% witnessed two, 18% witnessed three, and 16% witnessed four or more. In five (1.5%) events, the witness reported that the victim did not survive.[16]

Knowledge of Good Samaritan Law Over Time

The proportion of participants with correct knowledge of the GSL increased over time. The proportion with correct knowledge was 43% (n = 55) immediately after completing OPT, 55% (n = 61) at 3 months, 75% (n = 85) at 6 months, and 78% (n = 94) at 12 months. Incorrect knowledge declined over time, with 40% (n = 51) having incorrect knowledge immediately after OPT, 31% (n = 34) at 3 months, 17% (n = 19) at 6 months, and 12% (n = 15) at 12-month follow-up. The percentage that reported "don't know/not sure" did not change over time, with 9% (n = 12) of participants responding "don't know/not sure" at

baseline and 11% (n = 13) responding "don't know/not sure" at 12-month follow-up.

911 Calling

Information is available on 316 overdose events witnessed over the course of 12 months by 128 individuals (Table 2). In 272 events (86% of events with information; 83% of all overdose events), 911 was called by either the participant or another witness as previously reported.[16] The most common reasons participants reported not calling 911 (n = 139) were someone else called 911 (n = 89), the victim woke up (n = 31), and fear of arrest/police (n = 9).

In the events in which the overdose witness had correct knowledge of the GSL at the time of the event, the unadjusted odds of 911 being called were over 3 times greater than when the witness had incorrect knowledge of the GSL (OR = 3.3, 95% CI: 1.4–7.5). In events in which the overdose witness responded they were unsure of the GSL, the unadjusted odds of 911 being called were 7.5 times greater than when the witness had incorrect knowledge of the GSL (95% CI: 1.5–37.8). The odds of 911 being called for a relative were significantly lower than for a stranger (OR = 0.2, 95% CI: 0.1–0.6). There was no association between naloxone administration (OR = 1.8, 95% CI: 0.9–3.6) and 911 calling.

In the multivariable model, overdose witnesses with correct knowledge or who were unsure remained more likely to call 911 than witnesses with incorrect knowledge (adjusted OR [AOR] = 3.6 correct knowledge, 95% CI: 1.4–9.4; AOR unsure = 5.9, 95% CI: 1.8–20.1). Overdose setting was also independently associated with 911 calling: witnesses were less likely to call 911 for overdoses that took place in private settings compared with public settings (AOR = 0.2, 95% CI: 0.1–0.6). We could not include witness relationship to the victim in the multivariable model due to its collinearity with overdose setting.

Discussion

In our study, both correct GSL knowledge and no knowledge as compared with incorrect knowledge were associated with 911 calling during an

Table 1 Baseline Characteristics of Participants Who Witnessed an Overdose Within 12 Months of Overdose (OD) Prevention Training

	Total n (%)
Total participants who witnessed OD	128 (100)
Race	
White, non-Hispanic	15 (11.7)
Black, non-Hispanic	44 (34.4)
Hispanic	63 (49.2)
Other	6 (4.7)
Gender	
Male	86 (67.2)
Female	42 (32.8)
Age	
21–24	2 (1.6)
25–34	16 (12.5)
35–44	24 (18.8)
45–54	56 (43.8)
55+	30 (23.4)
Education	
Less than high school	41 (32.0)
Grade 12 or GED	45 (35.2)
Some college	42 (32.8)
Criminal justice involvement	47 (36.7)
Receives public benefits	108 (84.4)
Housing status	
Unstable[a]	24 (19.1)
Temporary[b]	63 (50.0)
Stable permanent[c]	39 (31.0)
Substances used in study period	
Licit[0]	
Prescription painkillers	75 (58.6)
Benzodiazepines	72 (56.3)
Methadone	99 (77.3)
Buprenorphine	15 (11.7)
Alcohol	70 (54.7)
Illicit	
Heroin	65 (50.8)
Crack/cocaine	54 (42.2)
Injected drugs in year prior to baseline	52 (40.6)
Participant in opioid treatment program	84 (65.6)
Participant in syringe exchange program	82 (64.1)
Participant experienced OD in lifetime	55 (43.0)
Lifetime mean number of ODs witnessed (SD)	11.4 (25.1)

a Unstable was defined as living on the street or in a shelter. b Temporary collapsed single room occupancy hotel, transitional housing, treatment facility, and family member's or friend's home.
c Stable permanent was defined as participant's own home or apartment.
d No distinction was made between prescribed and non-prescribed use.

overdose event, independent of race, age, and gender of the witness and overdose setting. To our knowledge, this is the first study to investigate the relationship between GSL knowledge and 911 calling and to highlight the potential impact of a GSL to reduce overdose mortality.

Furthermore, our finding that knowledge of the GSL increased over time has important implications for overdose prevention training. Our study protocol of reinforcing correct knowledge and correcting misinformation at each follow-up suggests that refresher trainings and repeated exposure to information about the GSL can help OPT participants retain and increase their knowledge of the law and, importantly, dispel misconceptions that can prevent overdose witnesses from calling 911.

Our findings, however, demonstrate that there are still serious barriers preventing witnesses from calling 911. Overdose witnesses were less likely to call 911 when the overdose happened in a private setting, consistent with other reports.[8] This finding is particularly concerning given that previous studies have shown that between 28% and 83% of unintentional opioid overdose deaths occur in private settings.[3,10,17,18]

We hypothesize that a common reason witnesses were less likely to call 911 in a private setting was fear of police involvement and/or arrest at someone's home. Participants may be reluctant to endanger friends and family members in their home with arrest and fear of losing housing if drugs are found on their property by law enforcement.

Similarly, the finding that 911 was less likely to be called when the overdose victim was a witness's relative than when the victim was a stranger may be the result of fear of exposing a relative to legal risks. Both findings suggest that, despite the protections afforded by the GSL, participants with personal connections to the setting or victim are reluctant to engage help. Additional work is needed to address the real and perceived consequences for Good Samaritans in order to further encourage help-seeking behaviors.

We report rates of 911 calling that were at the high end of the range previously reported for fatal and nonfatal overdoses (15%–72%).[2,7,8,10,16] One explanation for our finding of high 911-calling rates may be that most other reports

Table 2 Factors Associated with 911 Calling at Witnessed Overdose (OD) Events

	Total n (%)	911 called, n (%)	OR (95% CI)[a]	AOR[b]
Total witnessed OD events	316 (100)	272 (100)		
Gender of OD victim				
Male	230 (72.8)	201 (73.9)	ref	
Female	84 (26.6)	69 (25.4)	0.80 (0.5–1.4)	
Transgender	2 (0.6)	2 (0.7)	–	
OD location[c]				
Area of city 1[d]	180 (58.4)	155 (57.0)	ref	
Area of city 2	92 (29.9)	79 (29.0)	1.1 (0.3–3.9)	
Area of city 3	36 (11.7)	31 (11.4)	1.25 (0.2–8.6)	
OD setting				
Public	170 (54.0)	158 (58.1)	ref	ref
Semi-private	53 (16.8)	49 (18.0)	0.6 (0.2–1.9)	0.5 (0.2–1.4)
Private	92 (29.2)	64 (23.5)	0.2 (0.1–0.5)	0.2 (0.1–0.6)
Witness relationship to OD victim				
Relative	19 (6.0)	12 (4.4)	0.2 (0.1–0.6)	
Friend	115 (36.5)	96 (35.3)	0.9 (0.4–2.5)	
Acquaintance/drug-using associate	97 (30.8)	87 (32.0)	1.5 (0.4–5.1)	
Stranger	84 (26.7)	76 (27.9)	ref	
Naloxone given at event	241 (77.2)	210 (77.2)	1.8 (0.9–3.6)	
Witness Good Samaritan knowledge at time of event[e]				
Correct	212 (67.5)	189 (69.5)	3.3 (1.4–7.5)	3.6 (1.4–9.4)
Incorrect	55 (17.5)	41 (15.1)	ref	ref
Don't know/not sure	47 (15.0)	41 (15.1)	7.5 (1.5–37.8)	5.9 (1.8–20.1)
Witness participant in syringe exchange program	226 (71.5)	189 (69.5)	0.4 (0.1–1.1)	
Witness participant in opioid treatment program	182 (57.6)	153 (56.3)	0.8 (0.3–2.2)	
Witness race				
White, non-Hispanic	33 (10.4)	25 (9.2)	0.6 (0.2–1.8)	0.6 (0.2–2.6)
Black, non-Hispanic	107 (33.9)	102 (37.5)	3.6 (1.0–12.7)	3.1 (1.0–9.8)
Hispanic	156 (49.4)	126 (46.3)	ref	ref
Other	20 (6.3)	19 (7.0)	–	–
Witness gender				
Male	234 (74.1)	199 (73.2)	ref	ref
Female	82 (25.9)	73 (26.8)	0.72 (0.3–1.9)	1.9 (0.6–5.9)
Witness age (ean, SD)	47.8 (9.6)	47.9 (9.4)	1.0 (1.0–1.1)	1.0 (1.0–1.1)

[a] Odds Ratio. 95% CI: 95% Confidence Interval. ORs model events where 911 was called vs. those where 911 was not. OR >1 indicates greater odds of 911 being called.

b Final model adjusts for GSL knowledge, age, gender, race of witness, and OD setting.

[c] n = 308.

[d] Area of city is blinded.

[e] n = 314. Two events in which GSL knowledge was missing were excluded from this analysis.

studied participants who had not completed OPT. OPT typically includes 911 calling as part of the training. We are only aware of one small study that assessed 911 calling specifically among participants trained in overdose prevention. In that study, the overall 911-calling rate was 43%.[4] Another study showed that injection drug users who received information on how to respond to overdose solely from lay sources were less likely to call 911 than those who had received no information about how to respond to an overdose.[5] Those who received information from medical or social services were less likely to delay calling 911 and less likely to use ineffective methods to try to resuscitate the overdose victim.[5] Given these prior findings, it is plausible that completion of OPT contributed to our participants calling 911 at such high rates.

Finally, we found no association between naloxone administration and 911 calling, which may allay concerns that naloxone distribution could inadvertently cause harm by decreasing 911 calling. We found that in the great majority of overdose events, naloxone is administered and 911 is called. This finding, along with other research showing that drug users do not engage in riskier drug use behavior after receiving take-home naloxone, shows that naloxone's benefits far outweigh its theoretical risks.[19]

A strength of our study is that, to our knowledge, it is one of the largest prospective studies of overdose prevention training recipients and the only study to assess the association between knowledge of GSLs and 911-calling behavior. Our high rate of follow-up achieved with an often transient and difficult to reach population is another strength of our study.

Our findings are subject to several limitations. Since our study is based on self-report, participants could overreport positive responses to overdose, including naloxone administration and 911 calling. In order to address this limitation, we administered surveys in relative privacy and did not offer incentives for witnessing overdoses or responding to them in any particular way. Another limitation is that our protocol of reeducating participants about the GSL at each follow-up did not allow us to assess knowledge retention over longer periods of time. However, we felt that it would be unethical not to supply the participant with the correct answer.

In conclusion, this is the first study to demonstrate a relationship between knowledge of the GSL and 911 calling during overdose events. Our work highlights the importance of educating people at risk of witnessing overdose about

GSLs. Having correct knowledge about the GSL was associated with use of emergency medical care for individuals who experience an overdose and may be an important strategy to reduce overdose fatalities nationally. For states that have not yet passed GSLs, our research provides evidence that passage of GSLs may promote seeking help for an overdose victim and help reduce opioid overdose–related mortality.

Discussion Questions

1. What kind of longitudinal design did the researchers use? How did they collect data, and over what period of time did they do it?
2. The researchers could have only checked in with the participants once after they completed the curriculum, but they chose a different strategy. What additional information were they able to gain due to that decision?
3. If you were in charge of this training program, what, if anything, would you change, given these results?

References

[1] Rudd, RA, Aleshire N, Zibbell JE, et al. Increases in drug and opioid overdose deaths—United States, 2000–2014. *MMWR Morb Mortal Wkly Rep.* 2016;64:1378–1382. https://doi.org/10.15585/mmwr.mm6450a3. PMID:26720857

[2] Baca CT, Grant KJ. What heroin users tell us about overdose. *J Addict Dis.* 2007;26:63–68. https://doi.org/10.1300/J069v26n04_08. PMID:18032233

[3] Davidson PJ, McLean RL, Kral AH, et al. Fatal heroin-related overdose in San Francisco, 1997–2000: A case for targeted intervention. *J Urban Health.* 2003;80:261–273. https://doi.org/10.1093/jurban/jtg029. PMID:12791802

[4] Lankenau SE, Wagner KD, Silva K, et al. Injection drug users trained by overdose prevention programs: Responses to witnessed overdoses. *J Community Health.* 2013;38:133–141. https://doi.org/10.1007/s10900-012-9591-7. PMID:22847602

[5] Pollini RA, McCall L, Mehta SH, et al. Response to overdose among injection drug users. *Am J Prev Med.* 2006;31:261–264. https://doi.org/10.1016/j.amepre.2006.04.002. PMID:16905039

[6] Sherman SG, Gann DS, Scott G, et al. A qualitative study of overdose responses among Chicago IDUs. *Harm Reduct J.* 2008;5:2. https://doi.org/10.1186/1477-7517-5-2. PMID:18218071

[7] Tobin KE, Davey MA, Latkin CA. Calling emergency medical services during drug overdose: An examination of individual, social and setting correlates. *Addiction*. 2005;100:397–404. https://doi.org/10.1111/j.1360-0443.2005.00975.x. PMID:15733253

[8] Tracy M, Piper TM, Ompad D, et al. Circumstances of witnessed drug overdose in New York City: implications for intervention. *Drug Alcohol Depend*. 2005;79:181–190. https://doi.org/10.1016/j.drugalcdep.2005.01.010. PMID:16002027

[9] Levy B, Spelke B, Paulozzi LJ, et al. Recognition and response to opioid overdose deaths–New Mexico, 2012. *Drug Alcohol Depend*. 2016;167:29–35. https://doi.org/10.1016/j.drugalcdep.2016.07.011

[10] Darke S, Ross J, Zador D, et al. Heroin-related deaths in New South Wales, Australia, 1992–1996. *Drug Alcohol Depend*. 2000;60:141–150. https://doi.org/10.1016/S0376-8716(99)00147-7. PMID:10940541

[11] Atlas Law. *The Policy Surveillance Portal*. Good Samaritan Overdose Prevention Laws Map. www.lawatlas.org/query?dataset=good-samaritan-overdose-laws. Accessed December 29, 2016.

[12] Banta-Green, CJ, Kuszler PC, Coffin PO, et al. *Washington's 911 Good Samaritan Drug Overdose Law–Initial Evaluation Results*. Seattle, WA: Alcohol & Drug Abuse Institute, University of Washington; 2011. http://adai.uw.edu/pubs/infobriefs/ADAI-IB-2011-05.pdf. Accessed December 29, 2016.

[13] Homeless Emergency Assistance and Rapid Transition to Housing Act of 2009, Pub. L. No. 111–122, 1664 Stat. 123, codified as amended at 42 U.S.C. §1003.

[14] Witness or victim of drug or alcohol overdose, N.Y. Penal Law §220.78.

[15] Hernán MA, Hernán, AM. Confounding—structure. In: *Wiley Stats-Ref: Statistics Reference Online*. Chichester: John Wiley & Sons; 2014. https://doi.org/10.1002/9781118445112.stat03729

[16] Siegler A, Huxley-Reicher Maldjian L, Jordan R, et al. Naloxone use among opioid overdose rescue trainees in New York City: A longitudinal cohort study. *Drug Alcohol Depend*. 2017;179:124–130. https://doi.org/10.1016/j.drugalcdep.2017.06.029

[17] Cerdá M, Ransome Y, Keyes KM, et al. Prescription opioid mortality trends in New York City, 1990–2006: Examining the emergence of an epidemic. *Drug Alcohol Depend*. 2013;132:53–62. https://doi.org/10.1016/j.drugalcdep.2012.12.027. PMID:23357743

[18] Siegler A, Tuazon E, Bradley O'Brien D, et al. Unintentional opioid overdose deaths in New York City, 2005–2010: A place-based approach to reduce risk. *Int J Drug Policy*. 2014;25:569–574. https://doi.org/10.1016/j.drugpo.2013.10.015. PMID:24412006

[19] Jones JD, Campbell A, Metz VE, et al. No evidence of compensatory drug use risk behavior among heroin users after receiving take-home naloxone. *Addict Behav*. 2017;71:104–106. https://doi.org/10.1016/j.addbeh.2017.03.008. PMID:28325710

Reading 5.2   A Comparison Between Two Retrospective Alcohol Consumption Measures and the Daily Drinking Diary Method With University Students

Repeated alcohol consumption among specific individuals is nearly impossible to observe as, drinking can occur in multiple locations at any time of the day. The most practical way to capture such data is to rely on people to self-report their drinking. As Patterson, Hogan, and Cox (2019) discovered, not every self-report method is equally valid and reliable. Researchers continue to search for measures that are easy for respondents to use but still provide accurate estimates of daily drinking habits. Patterson and colleagues compared three different ways to measure drinking habits retrospectively. Each measure required respondents to catalog their drinking habits differently. This article is an excellent example of how the decisions we make when collecting data have an impact on the results that we find.

A Comparison Between Two Retrospective Alcohol Consumption Measures and the Daily Drinking Diary Method With University Students

Chris Patterson, Lee Hogan, and Miles Cox

Recent epidemiological evidence has identified that as little as one heavy-drinking episode per week increases a person's chances of dying from a long-term illness (1). Considering the significant risks and consequences posed by excessive alcohol consumption, accurate alcohol consumption measurement is essential (2).

The most widely used method of assessing and evaluating alcohol consumption is self-report. This is because it: (a) is less intrusive and easier and cheaper to administer and interpret than alternative methods (i.e., biochemical), (b) provides detailed information that can be used to identify alcohol misuse and dependency, and (c) has consistently been shown to be a reliable and valid method of measuring alcohol consumption (3). There are three main categories of self-report measures: (1) retrospective, summary measures; (2) retrospective, daily drinking measures; and (3) concurrent, daily drinking measures. Retrospective summary measures (e.g., quantity-frequency measures) require respondents to report their average quantity of alcohol consumed on a drinking occasion and average frequency of drinking occasions for a specified period in the past. These quantity and frequency estimates are then multiplied together to calculate total alcohol consumption (4).

The earlier, more simplistic QF measures were criticized for being unable to identify the variability of a person's drinking (5). For instance, they were unable to distinguish between different drinking patterns when the total number of units consumed was the same: (a) drinking two units of alcohol on each day of the week, (b) drinking seven units twice a week, and (c) drinking fourteen units once a week. Information about drinking pattern variability is essential, especially considering the unique risks associated with particular drinking patterns, such as heavy drinking (6). In response to this criticism, researchers (7) designed more sophisticated QF measures that could classify respondents' drinking (e.g., abstainer, light, moderate, and heavy).

Quantity-frequency measures have been consistently shown to produce reduced estimates of alcohol consumption and to be poor at distinguishing different drinking patterns, compared to daily drinking measures (8–10). For example, in Flegal's study (10), 31% of heavy drinkers—identified by a daily drinking measure—were classified as moderate drinkers by the QF method. Similarly, in Redman et al.'s study (9), the QF method failed to detect 78% of heavy drinkers identified by a daily drinking measure.

Fitzgerald and Mulford (8) managed to quantify the QF method's insensitivity for capturing atypical drinking. Participants in Fitzgerald and Mulford's study (8) were asked to complete a standard QF measure (i.e., reporting their typical drinking pattern) and then separately asked to report any atypical drinking. The addition of atypical drinking questions resulted in 35% of participants reporting more drinking, thus increasing the total alcohol consumption estimate by 14%. Adapted QF measures (which also ask respondents to report atypical and heavy drinking) have been found to produce estimates of alcohol consumed that are similar to those obtained from concurrent drinking records (11).

The Timeline Followback (TLFB) (i.e., retrospective, daily drinking) is widely accepted as the gold standard alcohol consumption measure. This is because it can capture detailed information about people's drinking behavior, including drinking pattern and variability (12). Moreover, the reliability and validity of drinking data captured by the TLFB have been shown to be high (13).

Clinicians favor the TLFB because its data can be reviewed to help identify individuals' triggers to use, high-risk situations, and relapse periods and increase individuals' motivation and commitment to change (14). As a product of the precision with which the TLFB captures alcohol consumption, however, the TLFB's administration is more time consuming and more demanding than other measures (i.e., QF measures). The TLFB may, therefore, be unsuitable in time-limited situations where precise information is not required: for example, some survey studies. Survey studies that have used the TLFB have reported high rates of attrition (15).

Concurrent daily drinking measures require respondents to make concurrent, detailed records of their daily alcohol consumption (e.g., recording amount, frequency, mood, and urges). This approach has been used extensively to monitor different behaviors in clinical settings (16). Many researchers believe that the Daily Drinking Diary (DDD) method produces the most accurate reports of alcohol consumption as respondents are less likely to misreport their consumption as a consequence of forgetting (17). As a result of its increased accuracy, the DDD method often produces higher estimates of drinking frequency in studies.

This concurrent daily drinking method is recommended to researchers and clinicians who require precise information about the frequency of alcohol consumption (12). Additionally, researchers and clinicians may ask their clients to keep a daily record of their drinking during treatment. Clients might also be asked to record other variables such as their mood at the time of drinking. This information can be used to identify the antecedents to their drinking; for example, a person might consume alcohol as a means of avoiding unwanted emotional experiences, such as anxiety. DDD data can also be used to track a client's progress during treatment.

It is important to consider that the DDD method has a number of limitations. First, individuals might not adhere to self-monitoring instructions (18). Second, the DDD method cannot be used to gather information about pretreatment alcohol consumption. In cases in which pretreatment drinking information is required, researchers and clinicians would have to use a retrospective measure (12). Third, respondents tend to reduce their drinking as a product of recording their alcohol consumption concurrently (i.e., recording one's own drinking is reactive). For instance, when DDDs have been used as control or waiting conditions in clinical trials, significant reductions in alcohol consumption have been reported (19). Reactivity, however, can be beneficial in clinical settings, where the aim of treatment is to reduce alcohol consumption and change harmful drinking patterns.

This study aimed to compare the accuracy of two retrospective alcohol consumption measures, the Timeline Followback (TLFB) and the Typical and Atypical Drinking Diary (TADD) to an assessment of alcohol consumption captured concurrently in Daily Drinking Diaries (DDD) during a 28-day period. The administration of the retrospective drinking questionnaires was to be delayed for a further 28 days after the completion of the diaries in order to prevent the easier recall of estimates following the daily diary procedure. Comparisons of drinking estimates would focus on three aspects of drinking behavior: (a) the total amount of alcohol consumed, (b) the total number of drinking days, and (c) the total number of heavy drinking episodes. There is a strong body of evidence indicating that the DDD method provides the most accurate record of alcohol consumption. It was hypothesized that the gold standard TLFB would provide the most accurate retrospective estimates of alcohol consumption. If the TADD was found to produce estimates that were as accurate, or more accurate, than those provided by the TLFB, this would offer certain advantages to professionals within the field. There would then be evidence that the self-administered and easy to administer TADD can produce reliable and valid estimates of total alcohol consumption, drinking patterns, and drinking variability.

Method

Participants

Out of the 75 psychology undergraduates who initially volunteered to participate in this study, 43 managed to complete the study and provide valid data: 34 females (79.1%) and 9 males (21.9%), whose ages ranged from 18 to 46 years ($M = 20.8$, SD = 5.1). Twenty participants were first-year students (46.5%), 21 were second-year students (48.8%), and 2 were third-year students (4.7%). The majority of participants identified themselves as White (76.7%), while the remainder identified themselves as Asian (23.3%). There were 33 British students (76.7%), 5 from other European countries (11.2%) and 5 from Asia (11.2%). Participation in this study was rewarded with course credit, as well as tickets for a prize draw where monetary prizes could be won: participants who provided all the necessary data gained the maximum number of tickets. The School of Psychology's ethics committee approved this study prior to its commencement.

Procedure

Participants met with the investigator in a quiet experimental room in groups of five or less ($M = 2.41$, $SD = 1.40$), between 25 and 33 days ($M = 28.20$, $SD = 3.34$) after the start of the second semester. Participants were required to read the participant information sheet and provide their informed consent before commencing this study. Participants were then provided with their first drinking diary and instructed on how to complete the diary correctly (see DDD section).

As agreed, participants met with the investigator for ten minutes once a week for four weeks. During these meetings, participants handed over their completed diaries and received new diaries. If participants completed their diaries correctly, they were praised. If they completed their diaries incorrectly, they were given extra instruction.

Between 28 and 41 days after completing the DDD ($M = 34.02$, $SD = 3.96$), participants met with the investigator, in groups of six or less ($M = 2.38$, $SD = 1.52$), for approximately 30 minutes. Participants filled in a demographics form and then estimated their alcohol consumption for the period of time that they recorded their drinking using the DDD (i.e., a time period that was approximately 56 days to 28 days previously) using two retrospective measures: the TADD and TLFB (in that order). Subsequently, participants were debriefed, thanked, and dismissed. A prize draw was conducted when data collection was complete.

Instruments

DDD

The DDD is a method of concurrently recording alcohol consumption information. The DDD method has been used widely in research validating retrospective alcohol consumption measures. In this study, participants recorded their daily alcohol consumption for 28 consecutive days, detailing the alcohol percentages, volumes, and quantities of beverages consumed: this information enabled the calculation of units. Participants recorded their alcohol consumption the day after it had occurred in a seven-day diary created specifically for this study. They submitted each of their four weekly diaries directly to one of the researchers. Due to its not being a standardized alcohol consumption measure, the DDD does not have any psychometric properties to report.

TADD

The six-item TADD was developed by Hogan (20) as a method of retrospectively estimating alcohol consumption and drinking patterns for a specified time period. It can also calculate peak blood-alcohol concentration (BAC) for each drinking session if required (21). The TADD comprises two weekly diaries: one for *typical* weeks and the other for *atypical* weeks (21) (i.e., heavier or lighter drinking weeks). In the typical drinking diary section, respondents stated the types of drinks, alcohol percentages, volumes, and quantities of the beverages that they consumed for each day of a seven-day week (i.e., Monday through Sunday), and then they estimated how many weeks they drank this *typical* amount during a specified time (in this instance, four weeks). In the atypical drinking diary section, respondents provided all the same information, but for a pattern of drinking that might be an atypical week for the respondent (i.e., either greater or lesser than their *typical* weekly pattern). Again, they estimated how many weeks they drank this *atypical* amount during the four weeks of the drinking diary period. Typical beverage sizes and their alcohol content were shown in an accompanying table, to aid recall. Hogan (20) reported a Cronbach's alpha, a measure of internal consistency (reliability), of .78 (n = 170) for the TADD. In terms of (concurrent) validity, when compared with the TFLB, the TADD's ICC = .872 (95% CI = .677–.935) for an 84-day period.

TLFB

The TLFB (22) is a retrospective daily drinking alcohol consumption measure, which can be used to gain a detailed picture of a person's daily drinking over a specified time period. There is a robust body of evidence attesting to the TLFB's ability to produce reliable and valid estimates of alcohol consumption with a wide range of clinical and nonclinical populations (12, 22, 23). For example, the TLFB has been reported to have a Cronbach's alpha of .84 (24) and test-retest reliability ranging between r = .80–1.00 for a number of drinking variables over a 90-day interval (25).

In an interview with the investigator, who was trained to administer the TLFB, respondents used the calendar-based TLFB form to retrospectively estimate their daily drinking over a specified period of time: the 28-day period when they concurrently recorded their daily alcohol consumption using the DDD method. To aid recall, participants were provided with a sheet outlining the volume and alcohol content of the most commonly consumed beverages.

Design

This study used a within-subjects design to compare participants' reports of alcohol consumption on three instruments.

Statistical Analysis

Summary statistics (i.e., means and standard deviations) were obtained for the three alcohol consumption measures on three drinking variables: total alcohol consumption, number of drinking days, and number of heavy drinking episodes.

Intra-class correlations (ICC) were employed to establish how similar the estimates provided by the TLFB and the TADD were in comparison to those produced by the DDD. ICC used the two-way mixed subjects and absolute agreement methods. Moreover, Koo and Li's (26) guideline for reporting ICC was used. This guideline states that values less than 0.5 are 'poor,' between 0.5 and 0.75 are 'moderate,' between 0.75 and 0.9 are 'good,' and greater than 0.9 are 'excellent.'

Paired-sample t-tests were applied to ascertain whether the TLFB's and the TADD's estimates were significantly different from those yielded from the DDD.

Drinking Definitions

In this study, alcohol consumption was calculated using the UK's unitary system. According to this system, one unit is equal to 8 g or 10 mL of pure alcohol. One UK unit is equivalent to 0.56 standard drinks in the USA. Heavy drinking is referred to in the following results section. This term refers to instances when male participants consumed eight or more UK units (4.51 or more standard drinks in the USA), and female participants consumed six or more UK units in a single drinking session (3.38 or more standard drinks in the USA).

Results

Using data obtained from the concurrent DDD method, the mean weekly consumption of alcohol in UK units was 15.33 (SD = 11.10). On average, students drank alcohol on 8.83 days over the 28-day period they recorded their drinking (SD = 4.06) and drank heavily on 4.02 days (SD = 3.48). Overall, 86% of students drank heavily on at least one occasion during the 28-day period, and 46.5% drank heavily at least once per week. In Table 1, summary

Table 1 Summary Statistics of Drinking Measures for the Concurrent Daily Drinking Diary (DDD) and the Retrospective Measures of the Typical and Atypical Drinking Diary (TADD) and the Timeline Followback (TLFB)

	Total alcohol consumption	Number of drinking days	Number of heavy drinking episodes
	M (SD)	M (SD)	M (SD)
DDD	61.34 (44.39)	8.83 (4.06)	4.02 (3.48)
TADD	65.80 (43.34)	9.0 (4.05)	4.86 (4.29)
TLFB	36.39 (33.13)	5.49 (2.91)	2.51 (2.93)

Note: Total alcohol consumption is reported in terms of the number of UK alcohol units consumed.

statistics are shown for each of the three methods for assessing alcohol consumption.

Comparison of the DDD and TLFB for overall alcohol consumption had an ICC = .735 (95% CI .229–.886), which is 'moderate.' When compared, the DDD's and TADD's overall alcohol consumption estimates had an ICC = .908 (95% CI .832–.950), which is 'excellent.' With regard to estimated number of drinking days, the DDD and TLFB had an ICC = .498 (95% CI–.087 to .758), which is 'poor.' Comparison of the DDD and TADD for number of days drinking had an ICC = .886 (95% CI .789–.938), which is 'good.' The ICC between the DDD's and TLFB's estimated number of heavy drinking episodes was = .799 (95% CI .493–.907), which is 'good.' Similarly, the ICC between the DDD's and TADD's estimated number of heavy drinking episodes was = .757 (95% CI .555–.868), which is 'good.'

Paired-samples t-tests revealed no significant difference between the TADD and the DDD in terms of total alcohol consumption, t (42) = –1.16, p = .254, number of drinking days, t (42) = –0.41, p = .686, and number of heavy drinking episodes, t (42) = –1.61, p = .115. Further paired-samples t-tests demonstrated that the TLFB, in comparison to the DDD, produced significantly lower estimates of alcohol consumption, t (42) = 5.35, p t (38) = 6.07, p t (42) = 4.23, p < 001.

Discussion

This study established that it is possible to accurately estimate alcohol consumption using a retrospective alcohol consumption measure. The TADD provided highly accurate estimates of three important drinking variables: total alcohol consumption, number of drinking days, and number of heavy drinking episodes. In contrast, the TLFB significantly underestimated total alcohol consumption, number of drinking days, and number of heavy drinking episodes.

Why did the TLFB underreport actual consumption? In line with Fishburne and Brown's (27) social desirability hypothesis, students in this study might have feared that the interviewer was going to judge them negatively as the TLFB was administered in a one-to-one interview. In contrast, the TADD was completed independently without an interviewer scrutinizing the drinking estimates. It is hypothesized that this level of independence enabled respondents to describe their alcohol consumption patterns without fear of judgment.

The results from this study provide further evidence that QF measures can provide accurate retrospective estimates of alcohol consumption and drinking variability, as long as they ask questions about both typical and atypical drinking (8, 11, 28). Giving respondents a full weekly pattern of assessment for their alcohol consumption for a typical week and for an atypical week in the TADD provided sufficient range/variability to capture a reasonable estimate of actual drinking. The independent administration of the TADD gives it a greater advantage over the TLFB in terms of ease of administration and reduced burden on respondents.

A number of limitations exist in this study. For example, it is possible that the estimate of alcohol consumption using the DDD might not have accurately estimated actual consumption: the DDD was also an estimate of consumption rather than an objective independent report. The procedure of administering the TADD prior to the TLFB might have influenced the completion of the TLFB; however, it was felt that the completion of the TLFB first was highly likely to improve recall on the TADD.

The generalizability of this study's results is also limited by the study's sample size, as well as the underrepresentation of male students. While a sufficient number of individuals initially volunteered to participate in this study, a large number failed to complete it. This high rate of attrition is likely to have been associated with this study's demanding data collection procedure. If this study was to be replicated, researchers should consider replacing face-to-face contact with communication via email. The ratio of male to female students in this study was characteristic of the anecdotal underrepresentation of male psychology undergraduates. In retrospect, it

would have been beneficial if students studying other subjects were recruited to balance this ratio.

Conclusion

These results can be taken as preliminary evidence that the TADD can be a quick and easy to administer instrument that provides accurate estimates of total alcohol consumption, number of drinking episodes, and number of heavy drinking episodes. In the future, therefore, clinicians and researchers should consider using the TADD if they require accurate retrospective information about a client's total alcohol consumption and drinking variability, especially if they are time limited.

Discussion Questions

1. If the TADD and the TLFB were both retrospective consumption measures, what is the likely explanation for why they produced such different results?

2. From a research participant's standpoint, what were the pros and cons of having to fill out each of the three data collection instruments?

3. How did the fact that participants had to complete one of the forms in front of a research staff member impact those results?

References

1. Holmes J, Angus C, Buykx P, Ally A, Stone T, Meier P, Brennan A. *Mortality and morbidity risks from alcohol consumption in the UK: analyses using the Sheffield Alcohol Policy Model (v. 2.7) to inform the UK Chief Medical Officers' review of the UK lower risk drinking guidelines*. Sheffield: ScHARR, University of Sheffield; 2016.

2. Gmel G, Rehm J. Measuring alcohol consumption. *Contemp Drug Probs*. 2004;31:467. https://doi.org/10.1177/009145090403100304.

3. Del Boca FK, Noll JA. Truth or consequences: the validity of self-report data in health services research on addictions. *Addiction*. 2000 Nov 1;95(11s3):347–360. https://doi.org/10.1046/j.1360-0443.95.11s3.5.x.

4. Midanik LT. Comparing usual quantity/frequency and graduated frequency scales to assess yearly alcohol consumption: results from the 1990 US

National Alcohol Survey. *Addiction*. 1994 Apr 1;89(4):407–412.

5. Alanko T. An overview of techniques and problems in the measurement of alcohol consumption. In: Smart RG, Cappell HD, Glaser FB, et al., eds. *Research advances in alcohol and drug problems*. Boston (MA): Springer; 1984. Pp. 209–226. https://doi.org/10.1007/978-1-4613-2719-6_7.

6. Connor J. Alcohol consumption as a cause of cancer. *Addiction*. 2017 Feb 1;112(2):222–228. https://doi.org/10.1111/add.13477.

7. Polich JM, Orvis BR. *Alcohol problems: patterns and prevalence in the US air force*. Santa Monica (CA): RAND CORP; 1979 Jun.

8. Fitzgerald JL, Mulford HA. Self-report validity issues. *J Stud Alcohol*. 1987 May;48(3):207–211. https://doi.org/10.15288/jsa.1987.48.207.

9. Redman S, Sanson-Fisher RW, Wilkinson C, Fahey PP, Gibberd RW. Agreement between two measures of alcohol consumption. *J Stud Alcohol*. 1987 Mar;48(2):104–108. https://doi.org/10.15288/jsa.1987.48.104.

10. Flegal KM. Agreement between two dietary methods in the measurement of alcohol consumption. *J Stud Alcohol*. 1990;51(5):408–414. https://doi.org/10.15288/jsa.1990.51.408.

11. Wyllie A, Zhang JF, Casswell S. Comparison of six alcohol consumption measures from survey data. *Addiction*. 1994 Apr 1;89(4):425–430. https://doi.org/10.1111/j.1360-0443.1994.tb00917.x.

12. Sobell LC, Sobell MB. Alcohol consumption measures. *Assess Alcohol Prob*. 1995;2:75–99.

13. Sobell LC, Maisto SA, Sobell MB, Cooper AM. Reliability of alcohol abusers' self-reports of drinking behavior. *Behav Res Ther*. 1979 Jan 1;17(2):157–160. https://doi.org/10.1016/0005-7967(79)90025-1.

14. Sobell LC, Cunningham JA, Sobell MB, Agrawal S, Gavin DR, Leo GI, Singh KN. Fostering self-change among problem drinkers: a proactive community intervention. *Addict Behav*. 1996 Nov 1;21(6):817–833. https://doi.org/10.1016/0306-4603(96)00039-1.

15. Cunningham JA, Ansara D, Wild TC, Toneatto T, Koski-Jännes A. What is the price of perfection? The hidden costs of using detailed assessment instruments to measure alcohol consumption. *J Stud Alcohol*. 1999 Nov;60(6):756–758. https://doi.org/10.15288/jsa.1999.60.756.

16. Korotitsch WJ, Nelson-Gray RO. An overview of self-monitoring research in assessment and treatment. *Psychol Assess*. 1999 Dec;11(4):415. https://doi.org/10.1037/1040-3590.11.4.415.

17. Sobell MB, Bogardis J, Schuller R, Leo GI, Sobell LC. Is self-monitoring of alcohol consumption reactive. *Behav Assess*. 1989 Jan 1;11(4):447–458.

18. Sanchez-Craig M, Annis HM. 'Self-monitoring' and 'recall' measures of alcohol consumption: convergent validity with biochemical indices of liver function. *Alcohol Alcohol*. 1982 Dec 1;17(3):117–121.

19. Kavanagh DJ, Sitharthan T, Spilsbury G, Vignaendra S. An evaluation of brief correspondence programs for problem drinkers. *Behav Ther*. 1999 Sep 1;30(4):641–656. https://doi.org/10.1016/S0005-7894(99)80030-6.

20. Hogan LM. Developing and evaluating brief, computerised interventions for excessive drinkers [Doctoral dissertation]. Bangor: University of Wales; 2005.

21. Hogan LM. Relationships among alcohol use, emotion, motivation, and goals [Doctoral dissertation]. Bangor: University of Wales; 2008.

22. Sobell LC, Sobell MB. *Timeline follow-back*. In *Measuring alcohol consumption*. Totowa, NJ: Humana Press; 1992. Pp. 41–72.

23. Sobell LC, Sobell MB. *Alcohol Timeline Followback (TLFB)*. *Handbook of psychiatric measures B2. Handbook of psychiatric measures*. Washington, DC: American Psychiatric Association; 2000. Pp. 477–479.

24. Wennberg P, Bohman M. The timeline follow back technique: psychometric properties of a 28-day timeline for measuring alcohol consumption. *Ger J Psychiatry*. 1998;2:62–68.

25. Sobell LC, Sobell MB, Leo GI, Cancilla A. Reliability of a timeline method: assessing normal drinkers' reports of recent drinking and a comparative evaluation across several populations. *Br J Addict*. 1988 Apr;83(4):393–402.

26. Koo TK, Li MY. A guideline of selecting and reporting intraclass correlation coefficients for reliability research. *J Chiropr Med*. 2016 Jun 1;15(2):155–163. https://doi.org/10.1016/j.jcm.2016.02.012.

27. Fishburne JW, Brown JM. How do college students estimate their drinking? Comparing consumption patterns among quantity-frequency, graduated frequency, and timeline followback methods. *J Alcohol Drug Educ*. 2006 Mar 1;50(1):15.

28. Rehm J, Dawson D, Frick U, Gmel G, Roerecke M, Shield KD, Grant B. Burden of disease associated with alcohol use disorders in the United States. *Alcoholism*. 2014 Apr 1;38(4):1068–1077. https://doi.org/10.1111/acer.12331.

6 Measurement, Validity, and Reliability

Operationalization and measurement are, in my opinion, some of the more challenging aspects of research design. The reason is that we must be very careful how we ask questions because different people can visualize the same concept in different ways. This variety of interpretation can have a tremendous impact on our results, so it is necessary to make sure that we move forward with clear definitions of what we are trying to study. In this chapter, we are going to discuss the process of defining our concepts in preparation for data collection. Next, we will discuss types of variables and how they are measured. Finally, we will review validity and reliability.

From Concepts to Measurements

A starting point for coming up with an idea for research is to consider different concepts that might interest you. "Corporate crime," "rehabilitation," and "problem gambling" are examples of concepts as they are all rather vague mental images that can easily mean different things to different people. At the mention of corporate crime, one person might picture Bernie Madoff, the disgraced financier who pleaded guilty to running a multibillion-dollar Ponzi scheme. Others might think of the collapse of Enron, in which the executives sold their own stocks while illegally concealing the company's massive debts, resulting in devastating losses to investors and lower-level employees. Or you might be picturing a company that saves money by breaking environmental laws and dumps waste into our rivers and streams. All are types of corporate crime, and you can choose to study all of them or be more specific and focus just on one type. Let's pretend that you have decided to limit your work to examining just one type of corporate crime, such as stock manipulation. You would have to operationalize exactly what you mean by this specific type of corporate crime before you embark on your data collection. Your data collection plan could involve you doing a systematic literature review in which you look up instances of the specific type of offense that you identified, or you could survey individuals to get their opinions about how appropriate penalties are for such fraud. Either way, you are going to need to determine exactly what you mean by corporate crime before going any further.

Operationalization is the process of taking concepts and more concretely defining them. The end product should be measurable items that can be used for data collection. While working on operationalization, it might be useful to consider different dimensions of what you want to study. Maxfield and Babbie (2012) define **dimensions** as specifiable aspects of a concept. Going back to the example of corporate crime, Unnever, Benson, and Cullen (2008) observed that corporate crime can cause a wide range of harms to society, including financial impacts, environmental hazards (illegal dumping), and physical harm (lax adherence to building regulations that lead to structural failures). While there were multiple possible harm dimensions for corporate crime, the authors chose to measure corporate crime only as financial fraud for their study of the public opinion of sentences for corporate criminals.

Variables

As we operationalize concepts, we make them measurable by creating variables. **Variables** are simply logical groupings of attributes that vary from case to case. **Attributes** are characteristics that describe something (Maxfield & Babbie, 2012). If I were to survey my students, gender would be a variable since it describes individuals' attributes that vary, as my classes are co-ed. Something that does not change on a case-by-case basis in our study would be called a **constant**. For example, if I am surveying my students at the end of a class session, and those are the only people I am surveying, I do not need to ask them if they are college students. That would be a constant, since 100% of those being surveyed would respond affirmatively to that question. What would likely be a variable in that same survey is their year in college (freshman, sophomore, junior, senior), provided that I am not teaching either a freshman or a senior seminar. Another variable in that class would be the number of credits each student is currently attempting. Figure 6.1 includes some examples of moving from concepts to variables.

In previous chapters, I explained that independent variables are predictors that are thought to contribute to change in the value of the dependent variable. Other words that might be used to describe the independent variable are "predictor" or "cause," although we must be very careful with "cause" since it is extremely rare that we would be able to establish causation in social science research. The dependent variable is something that we think will change depending on the value of the independent variable and is also known as the "outcome" or "effect." For example, a safe prediction would be that alcohol use (the independent variable) would predict driving performance (the dependent variable). Another type of variable is a **control variable**, which is a potential alternative explanation for the outcome but is not of central interest to the current study (Jennings & Reingle Gonzalez, 2019). If we were to look at the impact of number of prior convictions on sentence severity for people convicted of burglary, our independent variable would be number of prior convictions, and the dependent variable would be incarceration sentence in months. Of course, we know that number of prior convictions is not the only factor taken into consideration for sentence length. We would want to think about the possible impact of some other factors, such as whether the person was subject to pretrial detention or the dollar value of what was stolen. Sentencing researchers have also found that extralegal factors, such as personal characteristics of defendants, may impact sentence length as well (Spohn & Holleran, 2000; Steffensmeier, Ulmer, & Kramer, 1998; Tartaro & Sedelmaier, 2009). Since human behavior is so complex, most studies today involve multivariate statistical analysis that allows researchers to test the relationship between the independent and dependent variables while also accounting for the influence of control variables.

Variables can be structured to collect data in a variety of ways. There are **open-ended questions** or items. These are either fill-in-the-blank, short answer, or long answer questions in which the survey respondent or data collector who is making observations can express their thoughts using their own words. These open-ended options help collect qualitative information. **Close-ended** items are survey questions or statements that have answer items included. These allow researchers to capture quantitative data and are helpful when the goal is to input data into a spreadsheet or database for quantitative analysis. The close-ended items allow for researchers to quickly handle **coding**, meaning that they are assigning numerical values to items. Coding facilitates data entry and analysis.

Close-ended items should be both mutually exclusive and exhaustive. **Mutually exclusive** items give respondents one, and only one, appropriate answer option. So, for a question about income, the question might be written as follows:

Concept	Operationalization	Variable(s)
Recidivism	Reincarceration within one year of release	Individual was reincarcerated within 365 days of being released from custody (yes/no).
Recidivism	Rearrest within one year of release.	Individual was re-arrested within 365 days of being released from custody (yes/no).
		Number of times individual was re-arrested within 365 days of release from custody.
Education level	Highest level of education person completed	Please indicate the highest level of education you completed:
		1. Less than high school
		2. High school/GED
		3. Some college
		4. A.A./A.S. degree
		5. B.A./B.S. degree
		6. M.A./M.S. degree
		7. Doctorate (including M.D., Ph.D., J.D., Ed.D., Psy.D.)

Figure 6.1 Operationalization of Concepts

What is your yearly household income?

1. 0 to $24,999
2. $25,000 to $49,999
3. $50,000 to $74,999
4. $75,000 to $99,999
5. $100,000+

These answer options are mutually exclusive because there is no overlap in categories. A respondent could correctly circle only one of these responses. The categories are also exhaustive because there is an option for every possible answer. No one can earn less than $0.00 each year. As for the upper range, we can continue to add categories, and if we know the groups we are surveying well enough, we can list enough categories to include the top income of all our respondents. The other option is to do just what I did here and write an open-ended category that allows for even multimillionaires to provide an accurate response. Answers to survey questions can be either **discrete**, having a finite, specific number of values, or **continuous**, meaning that they can take on any value (Kranzler, 2018).

Levels of Measurement

There are four levels of measurement for variables, starting with **nominal**. Nominal level is the most basic level of measurement in which any numbers assigned to variable attributes are for labeling purposes only. For example, if I had a survey item asking for a respondent's favorite professional sport, I might code the answer options this way:

What is your favorite professional sport?

(1) Soccer   (2) Baseball   (3) Basketball   (4) Football
(5) Golf   (6) Tennis   (7) Other

The numbers next to the sports do not rank them in level of importance, international popularity, television ratings, or anything else. They are simply for coding purposes, so when this information is input into a statistical package, such as SPSS, Mini Tab, Stata, or SAS, we can use the numbers for analysis. That is necessary, as statistical software will not run any tests when the variable attributes are input as words.

The next level is **ordinal**. Unlike nominal, ordinal-level data are rank ordered, so coding associated with items provide more information than do nominal-level variables. One drawback to ordinal ranks, however, is that they do not distinguish the precise magnitude of the difference between ranks. For example, runners who win a race are assigned first place, second place, and so on. What ordinal data do not tell us is how close the second-place finisher was to the winner and how far behind the third-place runner was. In other words, the units of measurement here (first, second, third) are not necessarily equal (Kranzler, 2018). To get that level of information, it is necessary to look at interval- and ratio-level data.

Interval-level data have equal levels of measurement, a key characteristic that is lacking with ordinal ranks. Revisiting the example of runners completing a race, if we had the times that each runner crossed the finish line, we would not only know their rank order, but we would be able to tell the exact distance between the winner, second-place finisher, third-place finisher, and so on. There would be no question whether the battle for first or second was a photo finish or if the winner easily defeated the field. We could compare the times, so we would know precisely how much faster the winner was than the competition. Interval-level data can go below zero, so a good example of data at this level would be the air temperature.

Ratio is the final level of measurement, and the only difference between interval and ratio is that interval lacks a true zero point (Kranzler, 2018). Ratio-level data can never go below zero. An example is college GPA. Try as one might, it is impossible to get below a 0.0.

The highest levels of measurement (interval and ratio) are the most informative. One can take interval- and ratio-level variables and then turn them into ordinal or nominal. If we have the times for everyone who completed the race, we can either use those exact times, rank order them (ordinal), or just label runners as having "won" or "lost" (nominal). We cannot do that in reverse, though. If you asked some friends to get you information about the race results, and all they told you was who won and who did not win, you could not then piece together who came in second or third, nor would you know how close the race was. When constructing variables, it is often advisable to collect as much specific information as possible, provided that doing so would not inconvenience the research respondents and decrease the chances of completing data collection. For example, if I was sending a survey to local jails and asking the administrator to provide an estimate of the percentage of inmates who were Latinx by checking an answer option such as 0–24%, 25–49%, etc., someone as familiar with the jail population as the warden would likely be able to answer that without having to take the time to look up the daily census. If I asked for the exact percentage of Latinx inmates, however, this would likely necessitate the respondent having to look up the information and would be more of a burden to the respondent. Besides convenience to the research participants, one other reason why a researcher might request less specific, nominal, or ordinal data would be to protect anonymity of respondents. I once supervised a student thesis on drug use in college. My student originally submitted a plan to the university's IRB to distribute an anonymous survey with some ratio-level variables, including age and college GPA, to a few criminal justice classes. The IRB required her to change the GPA question from ratio ("please provide your exact GPA on a 4-point scale") to ordinal ("please indicate if you have a GPA of 3.5 to 4.0, 3.0 to 3.49," etc.). The IRB's reasoning was that someone who knew which college courses received the survey could use the students' sex, age, and GPA answers to learn respondents' identities. For example, if there was only one 22-year-old female with a 3.97 GPA in that particular class, someone with access to the university database could determine who filled out that survey. Unmasking respondents would be much more difficult to do if the GPA variable was less specific, and the IRB determined that the risk to the participants was not worth the benefits of collecting such specific GPA information.

Scales and Indexes

Composite measures, or the combination of individual items, allow us to better measure some concepts. We can create an **index** by adding up responses to items on a survey (Jennings & Reingle Gonzalez, 2019). When Costello, Ruckus, and Hawdon (2019) sought to study individuals' exposure to online hate, they needed to measure the extent of survey respondents' media usage. The authors listed twenty-two different social media, game, photo-sharing, and instant message platforms on their survey and asked participants to check all that they used. Before analyzing the data, the researchers totaled all individual items to generate a composite variable.

In the social sciences, we often use scales to measure items. Scaling allows us to increase the level of measurement, usually from nominal to ordinal. We could ask someone if they approve of the job performed by the current governor and get a yes/no response, but we could find out more about what people think about the governor by framing the responses on a **scale**. A commonly used scale in social science is the **Likert scale**, which typically includes five to seven answer options that indicate a range of approval. Typical answer item responses are strongly disagree, disagree, neutral, agree, or strongly agree. For the example of the governor's job rating, we could use strongly approve, approve, neutral, disapprove, or strongly disapprove. Scales allow us either to use the five different points of approval for data analysis or to collapse categories to a dichotomous response with "strongly approve or approve" versus "disapprove or strongly disapprove" or add a third category of "neutral." You obviously could not, however, poll people and ask for just a yes/no or approve/disapprove response and then try to divide the responses into more detailed categories later.

Another possibility is to develop a scale with multiple survey items to capture a greater scope of content. Mental illness tends to be associated with stigma. There are a number of reasons why some people hold negative perceptions of individuals with mental illness including, but not limited to, negative stereotypes about hygiene, perceptions that it would be too difficult to carry on a meaningful relationship, and pessimism about the treatability of the illness. It would be impossible to capture all aspects of stigma with just one question, so Day, Edgren, and Eshleman (2007) created a 28-item Mental Illness Stigma Scale to capture the three aforementioned domains plus four others relating to mental illness stigma. Such composite items can serve to increase the validity of your measures, plus they make statistical analysis much easier.

Validity and Reliability

Operationalization and precise measurements of variables are essential parts of data collection, as the consistency and accuracy of your measures obviously have direct bearing on the quality of your results. **Validity** refers to accuracy or the extent to which one is measuring what was intended, and there are four ways to measure this. First, and least complicated, is **face validity**, or how well it appears that we are measuring items correctly. Simply put, on face value, does our survey or data collection checklist look appropriate? Measuring face validity tends to be an exercise in common sense (Hartley, 2011).

Content validity concerns whether the selected measurements capture the full range and meaning of the concepts in question (Hartley, 2011). Earlier in this chapter, I noted that, during the operationalization process, we might purposefully choose to measure a concept in a way that we select just one dimension of a broader topic. For example, we might choose to study only instances intention was to study all types of corporate crime but we proceed with a survey that covers only financial fraud, that survey would lack content validity.

Criterion validity involves comparison of our measure of choice with some external item to see if the two are similar. The criterion can be something that is being measured at the same time (**concurrent validity**), such as a self-report survey of current drug use and then a urine test immediately thereafter. Another example of concurrent validity would be comparison of multiple suicide screening tools that are administered simultaneously. **Predictive validity** assesses how well a measure is able to predict future performance. The SATs, ACTs, GREs, LSATs, and MCATs are used by colleges and graduate schools because they help predict students' future academic performance. In corrections, researchers have found that the Correctional Program Checklist has good predictive validity for identifying which correctional programs will reduce recidivism (Makarios, Lovins, Myer, & Latessa, 2019).

Construct validity refers to how accurately our measure reflects the theory and philosophy of what the researchers are attempting to measure (Hartley, 2011). The Kansas City Preventive Patrol Experiment was designed to test whether police patrols impacted crime by having officers spend extra time on proactive beats and less time on reactive beats. This plan was designed to test the hypothesis that enhanced officer presence would reduce crime. Researchers encountered challenges in actually testing this due to police officers using their discretion to go into and remain in the control beat locations, possibly in an effort to offer compensatory treatment (Kelling, Pate, Diekman, & Brown, 1974). This posed a threat to construct validity because the purpose of the study was to measure the impact of different police tactics, but evidence suggests that the beats were not as different as the researchers planned for them to be.

Whereas validity measures the accuracy of various measures, **reliability** addresses their consistency or stability. A good example of reliability is a bathroom scale that is consistent. Ceccato (2019) notes that it is possible to consider reliability in three different ways: across time, across different observers, and across items. Regarding reliability across time, reliable measures would produce the same results when applied to the same variables, even over time. Ceccato (2019) used the example of noise estimates for subway stations during rush hour, as the noise levels during those times should remain fairly constant from one day to another at a particular station.

For survey and interview items, the **test-retest method** can check for reliability. For example, if researchers are studying deviant behavior among college students and plan to survey first-time freshmen during welcome week and again at the end of the fall semester, it might be a good idea to find out about the students' behavior in high school. It would make sense that misbehavior in high school would predict future misbehavior in college. A helpful reliability check would be to ask students the number of times they were suspended from high school. That is likely to be a fairly memorable incident for individuals, and the number of suspensions rather than the number of days suspended is likely easier to remember. This question can be repeated during the second survey, as there is no reason for the answer to change now that the students are out of high school. Test-retest can be difficult to do, as you do not want to annoy your respondents by asking them too many identical questions multiple times.

Maintaining reliability can become problematic whenever someone's subjectivity enters into measurement and can become even more challenging when multiple researchers are involved. When multiple individuals are involved in observing, interviewing, and/or coding responses, the inter-rater reliability, also known as inter-observer reliability, must be monitored, since it is certainly possible that different people would interpret the same observation or response differently. The two best ways to ensure a high degree of **inter-rater reliability** are to conduct training and maintain good communication between researchers. When I was a graduate student at Rutgers

University, I worked as a field researcher with the Police Foundation on a study of crime and disorder in Jersey City, New Jersey. One of my duties was to conduct physical observations of street segments and fill out a data collection form that captured the amount of litter, broken glass, and drug paraphernalia in each area. Our response options were "none," "a little," "some," or "a lot," but what is "some" or "a lot" of litter? To decide, the research team had to work together, sometimes by emptying wastebaskets on the floor to simulate littler, so all researchers would interpret things similarly. Drug paraphernalia was a bit easier. After a discussion, the research team decided that we would consider one empty drug bag, crack vial, or crack vial cap on a street segment to be "a little," two to three would be "some," and four or more would be "a lot." To keep ourselves in sync, we would start our observation days by doing one street segment together, followed by a discussion to reconcile any coding differences. After that warm-up, we would go our separate ways to collect data. Every few hours, we would do another segment together to test our inter-rater reliability.

If we are giving out a survey, how do we ensure a high degree of reliability? The first step is to work very carefully on the question writing phase of research. Good operationalization is key. Every item should be worded in a way that minimizes ambiguity, so all respondents understand what is being asked. A good way to do this is to pretest whatever data collection instrument that you plan to use with a small group of people who are similar to the target population. If it is not a survey but a fieldwork protocol sheet, ask a few fellow researchers to test it and see what they think. Pretesting does not take much time, but it can be a tremendous help and cut down on both validity and reliability problems.

To test reliability across items, the **split-half method** is useful. This is a typical way of testing for reliability across items. If you have ever taken a survey in a psychology course or one that was administered by someone studying psychology, you might have noticed how it appeared that the researchers were asking you the same thing over and over again. That is because they were conducting a reliability check. The split-half technique involves surveying opinions or some other construct, splitting the survey in half (first half versus second half or even-numbered items versus odd-numbered), and then testing for internal consistency of the items designed to measure the same construct.

Mixed Methods Approaches to Address Validity and Reliability

Working to ensure reliability is important but remember that just because something is reliable does not mean that it is necessarily valid, and vice versa. Take the example of the reliable bathroom scale. It could be consistent in that it is reliably off by three pounds every time you use it. It is much less common for something to be valid while not also being reliable, but it is possible. Researchers must take steps to make sure that their measures are both valid and reliable. One way to do that is to do validity and reliability checks by using multiple methods to measure the same construct. For example, research involving self-reports could be supplemented by consulting official records. If we were surveying high school students about their behavior, self-report surveys are really the only way to capture the things that they did without getting caught by the school system or police. The downside, however, is that we don't know whether to trust those results. One way that we can get an idea of how honest people are being is by asking them about the number of suspensions or detentions that have received in the past year and then also consulting the school's disciplinary records to see if they were being truthful and/or were recalling at least some incidents correctly. A match between the two different sets of data would indicate reliability, and it would also bolster the validity of the results.

Weisburd et al. (2006) used multiple methods to study crime and disorder in two neighborhoods subject to intensive police interventions in addition to adjacent neighborhoods. The goal was to not only observe the impact of the policing intervention in the target neighborhoods but also to see if it would then lead to spatial, temporal, or tactical displacement of offending. Instead of relying exclusively on police reports and calls for service data to detect changes in offending patterns, the research team devised a plan to measure offending several different ways. For community members' perspectives on crime in the neighborhoods, they did victimization surveys via random household telephone interviews and face-to-face interviews with shopkeepers and employees who worked in the neighborhoods. Interviewers went to the police stations and county jail to interview offenders to ask about their offending patterns. Researchers were also stationed on randomly selected streets every day to observe individuals' behavior. The research team became such a fixture in the neighborhoods that prostitutes and drug dealers became comfortable engaging with customers in their presence. To detect possible changes in the cleanliness of the neighborhoods, including the presence of indicators of disorder (discarded condoms, drug paraphernalia), researchers conducted physical observations of street segments before and during the police interventions. The police data, community surveys, social observations, and physical observations provided evidence that crime decreased in the target areas without displacing to adjacent neighborhoods. To understand why offenders did not just move to other locations to commit crimes, researchers relied on data from the jail and police station interviews. The use of so many different data collection methods to study neighborhood crime substantially enhanced the validity and reliability of the data.

In Chapter 5, I discussed how Stauss, Sparks, Thomas, and Grant (2018) used a one-group before-after design to study a program for mothers in prison. For data collection, the researchers used a mixed-methods approach by both conducting interviews and administering a previously validated structured survey to measure parenting stress. The interviews addressed the drawback of structured surveys in that they fail to give respondents the opportunity to explain issues in their own words, while the surveys helped the researchers collect quantitative data using an instrument known to be valid and reliable. Both the interviews and structured surveys provided evidence that the parenting program helped reduce participants' negative emotions while increasing their confidence as parents and enhancing their communication skills.

Summary

Operationalizing concepts to produce measurable variables is a difficult process. This is the stage of research at which we will decide exactly what we plan to measure. So, if I am interested in criminological theory and want to study how levels of self-control may be related to juvenile delinquency, I must decide what I mean, precisely, by self-control. Also, what kind of delinquency do I want to study? Am I just worried about violent crimes? Do I want to include behaviors that are only illegal when people are juveniles, such as drinking alcohol, smoking tobacco, or breaking curfew? For almost all types of studies, we will need to make these decisions now, so our surveys and fieldwork protocol are clear, and anyone taking the survey or using the fieldwork instrument interprets each item the way we intended.

At this point, we will need to decide between open-ended and close-ended questions and whether we want to use a scale or an index. If you are working on any type of survey wording now, I suggest that you skip ahead to Chapter 9, since that chapter is an extension of this type of work. There are a number of already constructed and validated surveys available, so it might be possible for you to use an entire instrument or adapt one for your needs (with permission of the original authors, of course).

We must make sure that we word items for surveys and other data collection protocol in a precise manner, as this will go a long way in avoiding problems with validity and reliability. Validity reflects how accurately we are measuring what we hope to measure, while reliability is defined as the consistency or stability of an item. Just because an item or set of items has been found to be reliable, that is no guarantee that it is valid. Using a mixed-methods approach involving multiple ways of collecting data on the same construct is an effective way of addressing validity and reliability concerns.

Keywords

Dimension	Variable	Attribute
Constant	Control variable	Open-ended questions
Close-ended questions	Coding	Mutually exclusive
Exhaustive	Discrete variables	Continuous variables
Nominal level	Ordinal level	Interval level
Ratio level	Scale	Likert scale
Index	Validity	Face validity
Content validity	Criterion validity	Concurrent validity
Predictive validity	Construct validity	Reliability
Test-retest reliability	Inter-rater reliability	Split-half reliability

Discussion Questions

1. When deciding on levels of measurement for data collection, why is it usually wise to go with the higher levels of measurement?
2. Consider the concept of "recidivism." Come up with five different ways that you could operationalize it.
3. What steps can researchers take to prevent reliability problems and/or be in a position to check for reliability as they are designing a survey?

References

Ceccato, V. (2019). Fieldwork protocol as a safety inventory tool in public places. *Criminal Justice Studies*, *32*(2), 165–188. https://doi.org/10.1080/09589236.2019.1601367

Costello, M., Rukus, J., & Hawdon, J. (2019). We don't like your type around here: Regional and residential differences in exposure to online hate material targeting sexuality. *Deviant Behavior*, *40*(3), 385–401. https://doi.org/10.1080/01639625.2018.1426266

Day, E. N., Edgren, K., & Eshleman, A. (2007). Measuring stigma toward mental illness: Development and application of the mental illness stigma scale. *Journal of Applied Social Psychology*, *37*(10), 2191–2219. https://doi.org/10.1111/j.1559-1816.2007.00255.x

Hartley, R. D. (Ed.). (2011). *Snapshots of research*. Thousand Oaks, CA: Sage Publications.

Jennings, W. G., & Reingle Gonzalez, J. M. (2019). *Criminological and criminal justice research methods*. New York, NY: Wolters Kluwer.

Kelling, G. L., Pate, T., Diekman, D., & Brown, C. E. (1974). *The Kansas City preventive patrol experiment*. Washington, DC: The Police Foundation.

Kranzler, J. H. (2018). *Statistics for the terrified*. Lanham, MD: Rowman & Littlefield.

Makarios, M., Lovins, L. B., Myer, A. J., & Latessa, E. (2019). Treatment integrity and recidivism among sex offenders: The relationship between CPC scores and program effectiveness. *Corrections*, *4*(2), 112–125. https://doi.org/10.1080/23774657.2017.1389318

Maxfield, M. G., & Babbie, E. (2012). *Basics of research methods for criminal justice and criminology* (3rd ed.). Belmont, CA: Thomson Wadsworth.

Spohn, C., & Holleran, D. (2000). The imprisonment penalty paid by young, unemployed black and Hispanic male offenders. *Criminology*, *38*(1), 281–306. https://doi.org/10.1111/j.1745-9125.2000.tb00891.x

Stauss, K., Sparks, L., Thomas, J., & Grant, K. (2018). Letters to children: Findings of a program to enhance communication of incarcerated mothers and their children. *Corrections*, 3(4), 225–247. https://doi.org/10 .1080/23774657.2017.1381054

Steffensmeier, D., Ulmer, J., & Kramer, J. (1998). The interaction of race, gender, and age in criminal sentencing: The punishment cost of being young, black, and male. *Criminology*, 36(1), 763–797. https://doi. org/10.1111/j.1745-9125.1998.tb01265.x

Tartaro, C., & Sedelmaier, C. (2009). A tale of two counties: The impact of pretrial detention on later court processing decisions. *Criminal Justice Studies: A Critical Journal of Crime, Law & Society*, 22(2), 203–221. https://doi.org/10.1080/14786010902975507

Unnever, J. D., Benson, M. L., & Cullen, F. T. (2008). Public support for getting tough on corporate crime: Racial and political divides. *Journal of Research in Crime & Delinquency*, 45(2), 163–190. https://doi. org/10.1177/0022427807313707

Weisburd, D., Wyckoff, L. A., Ready, J., Eck, J. J., Hinkle, J. C., & Gajewski, F. (2006). Does crime just move around the corner? A controlled study of spatial displacement and diffusion of crime control benefits. *Criminology*, 44(3), 549–592. https://doi.org/10.1111/j.1745-9125.2006.00057.x

Reading 6.1   Systemic Error

Sex and gender are two of the most commonly used variables in criminal justice research. Until fairly recently, they were also considered among the easiest to operationalize. As our knowledge of biology has advanced and our society has become more progressive, researchers are gradually acknowledging the need to (a) fully understand that gender and sex are two separate constructs, and (b) reconsider how we operationalize these variables. Valcore and Pfeffer (2018) note that the outdated, simplified way of collecting data on sex and gender can result in the misclassification of over a million individuals. This matter is especially important for social scientists, as people who are transgender or gender nonconforming tend to be disproportionately represented in the criminal justice system, as both victims and offenders.

Systemic Error: Measuring Gender in Criminological Research

Jace L. Valcore and Rebecca Pfeffer

Gender is one of the most frequently analyzed variables in research on crime and criminal justice, yet it is measured insufficiently across most mainstream studies. The almost universal operationalization of gender as a male-female binary in criminological studies either misclassifies or excludes any transgender or gender non-conforming individuals. A 2014 study estimates that as many as 1.4 million adults in the United States identify as either transgender or gender non-conforming (Flores, Herman, Gates, & Brown, 2016). Though there is evidence that this population makes disproportionate contact with the criminal justice system (Dwyer, 2011; James et al., 2016; McCauley & Brinkley-Rubinstein, 2017), they are a population glaringly absent from traditional criminological research. This is a critical issue that must be addressed.

Evidence about the importance of gender at all levels of the criminal justice process continues to accumulate. In general, the literature contends that male and female offenders are very different in their pathways into crime, in the types of criminal activity in which they are involved, and in their needs during their time of contact with the criminal justice system and beyond (Belknap, 2007; Chesney-Lind & Shelden, 2004; Van Voorhis, Wright, Salisbury, & Bauman, 2007). This body of literature has contributed to a more nuanced understanding of the way that various experiences in childhood and adulthood can be influenced by sex or gender, such as child abuse, relationships with others, and victimization experiences. Moreover, these findings have paved the way for 'gender-responsive' programming in criminal justice institutions that acknowledge the distinct needs of both males and females who come into contact with the criminal justice system. Yet, many of these systemic improvements fall short of their potential because they are based upon an incomplete conceptualization of gender.

We argue that it is necessary to also examine patterns in the pathways to crime of transgender and genderqueer/non-binary individuals, as well as their needs once in contact with the criminal justice system. In this paper, we review the way that gender has been measured in recent mainstream criminological studies and provide suggestions for improving this practice to be more inclusive and to collect more reliable information about gender diverse populations.

Gender and Sex

Gender is a common word. Gender is a common demographic, a common variable, and a common topic for research, policy, and daily discussion. Nonetheless, gender is not commonly understood. According to Noble (2004), gender is one of many 'passionate fictions,' along with sexuality, class, race, nationality, ethnicity, and other social categories (p. 22), but it is also a fact of life, one which invades daily interactions, dictates public spaces, and directs laws, policies, and institutions. Gender is a master status, meaning that its determination will guide how one is treated, viewed, and described by others based upon arbitrarily built and painstakingly maintained stereotypes and expectations of human identity, cognition, and behavior (Allen, 2011; Worthen, 2016). In the fields of criminology and criminal justice (CCJ), biological sex (commonly misunderstood as gender) is considered to be one of the most powerful variables and strongest indicators of crime (Belknap, 2007).

Gender, despite its importance, is often oversimplified in CCJ research by reliance upon an essentialist definition that suggests it is biologically based: that genitalia, viewed as either male or female, determines gender as either man or woman (Englert & Dinkins, 2016). Biologists inform us, however, that the basis for the common conception of gender as derived from biological sex is inaccurate because sex is a spectrum that varies based upon an individual's chromosomes, hormones, gonads, genitals, and other secondary sex characteristics. The boundary between sexes is not as clear as it once seemed. High school biology students have long been taught that a typical female has XX chromosomes and female sex anatomy, and a typical male has XY chromosomes and male sex anatomy. But in between there are several conditions in which a person's sex chromosomes do not 'match' their sexual anatomy; these conditions are commonly referred to by the collective term *intersex*. There is neither a consensus within the medical community regarding the classification of intersex conditions nor a single accepted definition of sex (Van Anders et al., 2017). It is recognized, however, that every aspect of sex, including chromosomes, hormones, genitalia, and secondary characteristics like body hair, is multifaceted and widely varied (Deaux, 1985; Van Anders et al., 2017). In short, biological sex cannot be understood as a simple binary (Ainsworth, 2015) and should also not be conflated with gender, a social construct. Yet, CCJ scholars have long treated gender as a binary variable based upon invalid assumptions that sex equals gender (Cohen & Harvey, 2007).

A more nuanced understanding of gender is offered by social constructionists, theorists who maintain that gender is a performance, a socially created construct determined through interaction, presentation, and attribution (Lenning, 2009). In other words, it is not predetermined by biology; rather, individuals exert agency in their expressions of masculinity, femininity, or androgyny and their attempts to fit into the box of man, woman, both, or neither, though they are often constrained by social context and norms (West & Zimmerman, 1987). Extending this perspective, queer theorists view gender as a fluid, changeable, and complex aspect of identity that exists on a spectrum. It is neither binary nor fixed at birth (Englert & Dinkins, 2016).

Gender is a multidimensional concept. Englert and Dinkins (2016) define gender as 'a socially constructed category that reflects a set of behaviors, markers, and expectations associated with a person's biological sex and social norms concerning masculinity and femininity' (p. 4). They further explain that the construct of gender can be broken down into three distinctly measurable components: physical sex characteristics, gender identity, and gender expression/presentation.

The majority of individuals are cisgender, meaning their gender identity and/or expression aligns with their sex assigned at birth. An important and increasingly visible segment of society, however, includes people whose birth sex assignment does not readily match or conform to their gender identity or expression. These individuals do not identify as simply man or woman, but as transgender, genderqueer, gender fluid, agender, non-binary, or any other self-identification chosen to reflect gender non-conformity, i.e. gender expression that does not conform to the norms of masculinity or femininity typically applied to one's assigned sex. Many American youth today are growing up with conceptions of gender as a spectrum or continuum full of new and yet to be determined possibilities (Gevisser, 2015). Their social experiences, especially in terms of interactions with criminal justice agencies and systems, need to be acknowledged, counted, and documented by scholars in our field.

Gender in Criminology and Criminal Justice

The concept of gender was introduced as a variable in CCJ as an important means of acknowledging and addressing the existence of women in contrast to that of men, and to draw attention to the differing needs and experiences of female victims and offenders (Belknap, 2007). Many academics see the word gender in the title of an article or book, or listed as a keyword in an abstract, and recognize it to mean that the primary topic, if not the exclusive one, is women. Most often, even then, the focus is not all women, but rather cisgender, heterosexual women. It is not uncommon to find that lesbian and bisexual women, queer women, trans women, and non-binary females are discussed separately, in a different journal, or in a separate chapter, if at all. There is direct and recent evidence of this in mainstream CCJ research and discussions. For example, in the 2015 American Society of Criminology Presidential Address, entitled 'The politics, and place, of gender in research on crime,' Kruttschnitt (2016) highlighted the political nature of research regarding gender in CCJ, noted the salience of gender stereotypes, described important gender differences for victims and offenders of crime, discussed the 40-year history of feminist criminology, and called for future gender-based research to focus on areas where it can have the most significant impact. The address (13 pages single-spaced when downloaded from *Criminology*) talked about men and women, males and females, girls and boys. Kruttschnitt (2016) deserves credit for highlighting the importance of sex differences in CCJ research; nonetheless, even this important call to action did not specifically mention transgender, intersex, or any non-binary gender identity, despite acknowledging the need to account for 'multiple femininities and masculinities' in the field of CCJ (p. 13).

Transgender and Non-Binary Persons and the Criminal Justice System

Within the criminal justice system, an individual's perceived or reported gender impacts decisions regarding arrest procedures, sentencing, risk assessment, correctional housing, and treatment programming. Transgender, non-binary, and gender non-conforming persons are disproportionately involved in the criminal justice system (Grant et al., 2011). Despite increased awareness within law enforcement about gender and sexual identity, research finds that many officers still fail to recognize both overt and covert heterosexist and transphobic situations, or to take them seriously, as demonstrated by poor response times, insensitive responses by officers, or even inappropriate or abusive behavior by officers when answering calls for service (Grant et al., 2011; Stotzer, 2014; Wolff & Cokely, 2007). Beyond discriminatory responses from police officers, transgender and non-binary individuals also face inequitable treatment from judges, barriers to social services, inadequate housing options, and a lack of affirming treatment and rehabilitation programs (Buist & Stone, 2014; Grant et al., 2011).

These disparities, in turn, impact the attitudes of gender diverse persons toward law enforcement. Nearly half (46%) of the respondents who completed the National Transgender Discrimination Survey indicated that they were uncomfortable seeking assistance from the police (Grant et al., 2011), and this was echoed in the 2015 U.S. Transgender Survey in which 57% of respondents reported that they would be uncomfortable asking the police for help (James et al., 2016). Even more troubling is that 58% of respondents reported that they had been mistreated by police in the past year, in the form of either verbal harassment, physical and/or sexual assault, intentional misuse of personal pronouns, and being asked to engage in sex acts to avoid arrest. Intersectionality is certainly relevant for gender diverse populations in their reported experiences with law enforcement. A 2016 study found that transgender women of color face particularly high rates of perceived harassment from police as they report they are often stopped or arrested for 'walking while trans.' In this study, approximately a third of black trans women (33%) and multiracial trans women (30%) reported interacting with officers who assumed they were sex workers (James et al., 2016).

While vulnerable to victimization, a pervasive distrust of law enforcement results in the underreporting of experiences of victimization among members of the transgender community (Buist & Stone, 2014; Grant et al., 2011; Ritchie & Jones-Brown, 2017; Wolff & Cokely, 2007). Thus, the disproportionate contact that transgender individuals have with law enforcement tends to be in the role of perpetrators of crime. This is important because for accused perpetrators of crime, contact with police officers is only the beginning of extensive contact with the criminal justice system. For transgender or non-binary individuals accused of crime, every step of contact with the criminal justice system presents different challenges for proper gender identification and classification that can impact their physical and mental well-being (Leach, 2007; Reisner, Bailey, & Sevelius, 2014).

Sex and Gender Data Collection

The U.S. Census and other federal surveys do not currently count transgender, non-binary, or intersex persons, so it is difficult to determine the exact percentage of the population that identifies as anything other than man or woman (Grant et al., 2011). Nongovernmental sources provide the most valid information about the lives and experiences of non-heterosexual and non-cisgender people (Stotzer, 2009), and the Williams Institute provides the most recent estimate of 1.4 million transgender or gender non-conforming adults residing in the United States (Flores et al., 2016). The 2017 GLAAD[1] Accelerating Acceptance report found that 20% of millennials between the ages of 18 and 34 identify as LGBTQ (lesbian, gay, bisexual, transgender, or queer). More specifically, the study found that LGBTQ millennials are two to three times more likely to identify as transgender or a non-binary gender, such as gender fluid or agender, than LGBTQ adults age 35 and older (GLAAD, 2017). As understanding, visibility, and acceptance of gender diversity increases, criminal justice practitioners and scholars should respond, and should also be leading the way in providing the public and policy makers with relevant research and expertise (Panfil & Miller, 2014).

A major challenge for research in CCJ is the reliance on federal, state, and local data, which

often records sex or gender classification as reported on an individual's state-issued identification card. Policies to report non-binary gender identification are lacking at every jurisdictional level, though a few states have recently begun to issue IDs that recognize a third, neutral gender, including Oregon, California, Maine, Washington, and the District of Columbia (Capatides, 2018; Sanders, 2018). At the federal level, where there are not yet policies in place to count and properly recognize transgender and non-binary citizens, there is documented awareness of this population's contact with the criminal justice system and steps have been taken to address their treatment and needs. The first visible recognition was when President Barack Obama signed the Matthew Shepard and James Byrd, Jr., Hate Crime Protections Act of 2009, which designated gender identity as a protected social group, thereby identifying transgender and non-binary individuals as ones likely to become victims of bias-motivated criminal offenses. In 2012, the U.S Department of Justice (DOJ) issued regulations under the authority of the Prison Rape Elimination Act of (2003) (PREA). These regulations, known as the PREA Prison and Jail Standards (2012), specified that transgender and gender non-conforming inmates must be given specific consideration for housing, treatment, and safety. Two years later, DOJ issued a formal guidance memorandum (2014) to federal law enforcement agencies directing that they could no longer profile or target citizens based upon their gender identity. This progression of policy action is an acknowledgment of diverse genders and reflects increased societal recognition of transgender and non-binary individuals.

More recent federal policy changes have created more barriers to the identification, documentation, and protection of transgender individuals as both crime victims and offenders. The Department of Justice now allows for open discrimination against transgender citizens based on religious belief (National Center for Transgender Equality, 2018). Most recently, the Bureau of Prisons reversed policy regarding transgender inmates and will now place inmates into federal prisons based primarily upon sex assigned at birth, rather than gender identity, putting hundreds at increased risk for physical and sexual assault (Movement Advancement Project, 2016; U.S. Department of Justice, 2018).

Despite challenges imposed by rigid gender measurement in most crime data sets, select studies conducted by criminal justice researchers have utilized modern gender classification mechanisms that extend beyond the male-female dichotomy. For instance, in a qualitative study about survival sex among young people in New York City, Meredith Dank and her colleagues at the Urban Institute (2015) utilized an open-ended question about gender identification in interviews with respondents. Though the potential variation in responses may seem overwhelming to researchers accustomed to binary gender classification, this study demonstrates that it is possible to categorize responses in a manageable classification scheme. Using the responses generated from an open-ended question during semi-structured interviews with approximately 300 youth, they were able to confine responses into just seven categories: 'male', 'female', 'transgender female', 'transgender male', 'transgender other', 'queer and questioning', and 'other' (p. 13). These gender classifications allowed for much more meaningful analysis than a traditional gender classification would, particularly for this topic. Indeed, if only given the choice between male and female, 17% of their sample would have been mislabeled, leading to less reliable findings for all groups of participants. This is because when presented with no other option besides male and female, people who represent other sex or gender identities will be forced to pick one that is in fact not representative of their identity. They may defer to their sex at birth or to the gender with which they more closely currently identify (Butler, 2004), but neither is truly correct, which leaves their true gender identity unreported and skews the results for the male and female study populations.

The conflation of sex and gender, and the mismeasurement of both as binary constructs, also poses salient questions for the advancement of criminological theory. Dolliver and Rocker (2017), for example, recently compared measures of biological sex (male/female) and gender (masculine, feminine, androgynous, undifferentiated) in a test of General Strain Theory. Results showed that using gender, rather than sex, produced a stronger predictive model of deviance. This is empirical evidence for the need to accurately and consistently measure gender in order to better understand and explain crime and deviance.

This same problem presents in the secondary analysis of official data collected by criminal justice and other government agencies. Although the secondary analysis of data provided by police agencies, court systems, and correctional institutions at the local, state, and federal level provides invaluable insight into trends in the criminal justice system, most agencies do not yet have a mechanism for accounting for gender minorities. For example, in a study analyzing a year's worth of prostitution incident reports from the Houston Police Department, Pfeffer (2015) had to recode 4% of sex sellers' genders from either male or female to transgender. Although there was information recorded in the incident report that indicated that the person identified as transgender, the reporting officers could only choose between two tick boxes when reporting the suspect's gender in the incident report. Therefore, if only the official HPD data was examined, it would not indicate the presence of any transgender suspects, when in fact, at least 4% were (Pfeffer, 2015). Similarly, Richards and colleagues (2016) report that population-based studies show a small percentage of people who identify as non-binary. Though the percentages are small, when translated into raw numbers, this population is sizable, yet is misrepresented in most official data.

The present study is not the first to describe or critique the way in which CCJ research measures and discusses gender. Cohen and Harvey's (2007) study found that 60% of articles published in Criminology and Justice Quarterly from 2003–2004 utilized a measure of sex or gender. Only 1 of the 137 articles (0.07%) utilized a nonbiological measure of sex and 37% mislabeled their biological measure of sex as gender. When analyzing only the articles in which sex or gender was mentioned in the title or analysis, the incorrect conceptualization of sex as gender increased to 60.5%. Cohen and Harvey (2007) were specifically concerned with understandings of masculinity and assumptions among criminologists regarding men and crime and violence. An expansion of this inquiry to include measures of gender diversity is the goal of the current study.

The Current Study

Given contemporary sociological and biological understandings of sex and gender, previous calls by researchers to better measure gender, and the changes in law and policy that have occurred in the criminal justice system, this study provides an updated examination of the field by addressing two research questions:

(1) Do recent mainstream CCJ studies appropriately measure and operationalize the constructs of sex and gender?
(2) Do temporal patterns in recently published research indicate improvements over earlier, invalid measures of gender?

Methodology

A total of 1,629 empirical articles published in top mainstream criminology and criminal justice journals between the years 2010 and 2015 were examined using traditional content analysis techniques in order to determine how the construct of gender is defined and measured in recent CCJ research. The temporal scope of these data is based on two factors. The start date was selected because federal legislation first recognized gender identity at the end of 2009. While we understand that this would not necessarily translate into immediate changes in the operationalization of gender in research, as these definitional and resulting cultural changes take time, we believed it would be prudent to begin our observations with the year 2010 in order to view any trend changes over time. The year 2015 was selected as the ending data for data collection because it was the most recent year of journal publication at the time data collection began.

Sample

Previous studies seeking to assess the state of research in the field of CCJ have recognized and utilized eight 'elite' journals, using a variety of measures ranging from reputation to impact factors (e.g. Barranco, Jennings, May, & Wells, 2015; Kim & Hawkins, 2013; Sorensen & Pilgrim, 2002; Steiner & Schwartz, 2006; Weir & Orrick, 2013; Woodward, Webb, Griffin, & Copes, 2016). It is common for content analysis of journals to be conducted in order to determine, for example, dominant methodologies (Woodward et al., 2016), scholarly productivity (Steiner & Schwartz, 2006), measures of gender (Cohen & Harvey, 2007), and authorship trends (Tewksbury & Mustaine, 2011). These 'elite' journals include *Criminal Justice and Behavior*, *Criminology*, *Journal of Criminal Justice*, *Journal of Research in Crime & Delinquency*, *Crime & Delinquency*, *Journal of Quantitative Criminology*, *Justice Quarterly*, and the *Journal of Criminal Law and Criminology*. Our analysis includes content from seven of these eight mainstream CCJ outlets; as *Journal of Criminology and Criminal Law* primarily focuses on non-empirical legal analysis, it was not included.

Every article published in the seven aforementioned journals between 2010 and 2015 was collected and analyzed. After eliminating non-empirical articles (e.g. book reviews, commentaries), the sample size of articles for analysis was 1,629 (see Table 1).

Table 1 Sample Frequencies

Journal	Frequency (n)	Percent
Criminal Justice and Behavior	376	23.1%
Criminology	158	9.7%
Journal of Criminal Justice	366	22.5%
Journal of Research in Crime & Delinquency	136	8.3%
Crime & Delinquency	254	15.6%
Journal of Quantitative Criminology	145	8.9%
Justice Quarterly	194	11.9%
Total:	1629 (N)	100%

Coding

Each article was analyzed in order to determine 1) the methods utilized in the study (codes as quantitative, qualitative, or mixed); 2) whether gender was a focus of the study as evidenced by the inclusion of the word 'gender' either in each article's title or as a keyword; 3) how the variables sex and/or gender were conceptualized and operationalized; 4) whether transgender or non-binary identities were discussed; and 5) whether any recommendations were made by the author(s) based upon sex/gender.

Results

Similar to findings by Woodward and colleagues (2016), 88.6% of the published empirical studies in this study used quantitative methods, 5% were qualitative, and 6.4% utilized mixed methods.

Gender Definition and Operationalization in CCJ Studies

In the current sample, 913 (56%) articles included an individual-level measure for sex and/or gender. The way in which the variables were labeled and operationalized is presented in Table 2. The vast majority of published studies in the sample (94.5%) utilized a binary male/ female operationalization of sex and/or gender. Most of the studies (65.2%) had a measure labeled as 'Gender' that was incorrectly operationalized as male/female, while only 25% of studies used 'Sex' as a measure. Fourteen studies

in the sample (1.5%) operationalized gender as men/women. Fourteen studies presented measures for both sex and gender (usually in different data tables), or had a variable that was labeled as 'Sex/Gender.' Twenty-eight studies had a variable labeled Male or Female, but never specified whether it was a measure of sex or gender. Interestingly, 1% of studies offered no specific attributes and a few used both male/ female and men/women as attributes. No studies provided an attribute for transgender or non-binary gender identity.

When studies in which sex/gender were not included as measures were considered, an additional 67 articles were found that used the terms sex and gender interchangeably in describing their samples or the discussions of their data. This is a considerable concern because biological sex is not equivalent to gender (see Englert & Dinkins, 2016). Accordingly, conclusions based upon one of these distinct constructs cannot logically be applied to the other.

Only four articles in the entire sample mentioned transgender individuals or groups. Only one of the four articles, an exploration of transgender identity in a women's prison, defined and discussed transgender identity and individuals (see Sexton, Jenness, & Sumner, 2010). The second article was also published in 2010 and it misconceptualized the term *sexual orientation* by including 'transgendered.' Although well intentioned, it is important to note that the term 'transgendered' is grammatically incorrect. As the advocacy group GLAAD (n.d.) explains,

Table 2 The Operationalization of Sex/Gender in Empirical Studies

Variable	Male /Female	Attributes					Total
		Boys/Girls	Men/ Women	None	Both	Transgender /Non-binary	
Gender	595 (65.2%)	10 (1%)	14 (1.5%)	6 (< 1%)	4 (< 1%)	0	629 (68.9%)
Sex	228 (25%)	8 (< 1%)	2 (< 1%)	2 (< 1%)	0	0	240 (26.3%)
Sex/Gender	12 (1.3%)	1 (< 1%)	0	1 (< 1%)	0	0	14 (1.5%)
Unspecified	28 (3%)	1 (< 1%)	0	1 (< 1%)	0	0	30 (3.3%)
Total	863 (94.5%)	20 (2.2%)	16 (1.7%)	10 (1%)	4 (< 1%)	0	913 (100%)

The adjective transgender should never have an extraneous "-ed" tacked onto the end. An "-ed" suffix adds unnecessary length to the word and can cause tense confusion and grammatical errors. It also brings transgender into alignment with lesbian, gay, bisexual, and queer. You would not say that Elton John is "gayed" or Ellen DeGeneres is "lesbianed," therefore you would not say Chaz Bono is "transgendered."

Beyond the use of a term that is considered pejorative, trans refers to a gender identity, not a sexual orientation, which is a distinct concept (see Englert & Dinkins, 2016; GLAAD, n.d.). The third article, published in 2014, is included here simply because the title included the acronym 'LGBT.' The actual study was about anti-gay homicides, specifically, and did not include a measure of gender. The fourth article, published in 2011, included mention of transgender issues in the literature review, but did not include it as part of the study.

Discussions Regarding Gender in CCJ Studies

Our analysis found that even when gender is not of central relevance to a study's main inquiry, it is often still included as a variable in analysis. While only 6.3% (n = 103) of the articles in this study had an indication that gender was a focus of the analysis (by either listing gender as a

keyword or including it in the title of the paper, 34.4% (n = 561) included a mention of sex or gender in the discussion or limitations sections. Many of these references were simply to note that the sample of females was too small to draw conclusions, or non-existent, thus preventing generalization of the results.

Several studies similarly noted that comparisons and analyses based on gender, while missing in their study, should be attempted in future research. For example, 'Further, research in this area might also consider whether peer influences on self-control depend in part upon the sex-composition of the peer network and the sex of the target respondent.' (Meldrum, Young, & Weerman, 2012, p. 460).

Conceptions of Gender in CCJ Studies, 2010–2015

Because sociopolitical understandings of gender continue to progress, changes in measurement over time were examined in order to determine whether or not criminological research is utilizing more valid conceptions of the important social construct.

As can be seen in Figure 1, the number of articles utilizing a measure of sex or gender varies slightly year to year, but the proportion of articles misconceptualizing gender as a simple male/female dichotomy, rather than a more complex spectrum, has not decreased over

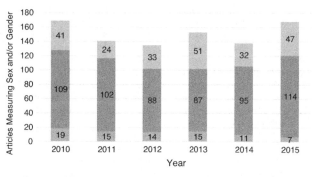

Figure 1 Measuring Sex/Gender from 2010–2015

time. Over the six-year period described here, the percentage of articles using the binary attributes of male/female to represent gender in a given year ranged from 57% in 2013 to 72% in 2011. The year 2010 had the most articles measuring gender ($n = 169$), and also had a high percentage (64.5%) of studies which attributed male/female to the variable. For every year included in this study, the majority of articles measuring gender used invalid attributes.

Discussion

This research identifies a need for improvement in the way we measure, report, and operationalize gender as a variable in criminological studies, but we do not wish to stop there. The following discussion also provides tips and methods for improvement.

Secondary Analysis in CCJ Research and Gender Classification

The vast majority of criminological research published in those CCJ journals considered 'elite' involves the use of surveys and secondary data analysis with no subject contact (Woodward et al., 2016). Field research or ethnography that would perhaps more readily allow for the observation of gender as performative, or qualitative interviews that would allow for exploration of gender presentation/expression, are comparatively rare. Woodward and colleagues' (2016) examination of research methodologies in seven top criminology and criminal justice (CCJ) journals revealed that 88.5% of published articles utilized quantitative methodologies, and among those the most common methods were utilization of secondary data-sets (39.1%) and data collection that required no contact with participants (28.8%). Primary data collection was used in just 27.8% of published studies. This heavy reliance on quantitative methods has been criticized by several scholars for the way in which it renders invisible persons and groups who do not readily fit into one of the provided check boxes (Johnson, 2014; Pfeffer, 2015) and severely limits the ability of scholars to provide valid and reliable discussions of complex topics like gender, race, and class (Cohen & Harvey, 2007). Even recent research which purports to account for gendered experiences and discusses gender non-conformity is limited by reliance upon survey data that measures gender as a binary variable indicated as male or female (e.g. Button & Worthen, 2014).

There are four primary purposes of social science, and therefore criminological research: exploration, description, explanation, and application (Maxfield & Babbie, 2015). If social scientists wish to be able to understand or explain a social problem or phenomenon, they must first be able to describe it. Gender is a social construct, a concept. As such, it requires researchers who utilize it as a variable to engage in conceptualization and operationalization (Maxfield & Babbie, 2015). As the results of this study show, it continues to be accepted within criminal justice and criminology, though, that gender can be simply treated as a binary variable, indicating male/female. Few mainstream scholars even bother to provide a justification for measuring gender this way, at least not when publishing in 'elite' journals (Cohen & Harvey, 2007). This treatment of gender has long dominated criminal justice research, programs, and policies, despite advances in the fields of biology, psychology, sociology, and many others, and despite the growing acknowledgement within U.S. society that gender is not, in fact, equivalent to sex.

The measurement of gender as male/female, therefore, lacks construct validity. If the construct of gender is understood to be performative and to include a spectrum of possibilities, then treating it as a binary variable is invalid and will produce invalid results. The attributes of male and female to the variable gender is neither a mutually exclusive nor exhaustive measure because it excludes intersex persons and ignores trans and non-binary gender identities. There is a further need to improve the common conceptualization of gender to include expression/presentation so that scholars may better understand how gender truly impacts society and individual experiences (Lenning, 2009). Toward that noble end, CCJ researchers must first cease the common reliance on invalid, binary measures of gender.

Scholars are also limited by reliance on agency records and reporting practices. At the point of initial contact with law enforcement, officers are often instructed to record the gender of suspects based on the gender as listed on their official government identification card. Therefore, this problem must be addressed at a larger structural level. It is impractical to suggest that researchers can comb through data and recode gender. A more feasible solution would be to advocate for policy changes that allow for at least a third gender category on official government documents. There is already precedent for this change, as there are now three states and Washington, DC, that recognize a third gender on state driver's licenses. Residents in Oregon, Maine, and California can select from gender options male, female, and X, which indicates that they identify as non-binary or unspecified (Capatides, 2018; O'Hara, 2017). The addition of X gender in official government data is very promising for future research in CCJ utilizing secondary datasets from government sources.

Measuring Gender in Criminology and Criminal Justice

Key to our findings in this paper is that gender minorities are underrepresented in criminal justice research. Shockingly few studies in the sample (.002%) mentioned or considered transgender persons. When gender minorities were addressed, it was often in a section on 'limitations,' or 'next steps.' Echoing this concern, in an NIJ systematic review of 34 studies about campus sexual assault published from 2000–2015, Fedina, Holmes, and Backes (2018) noted that none had included any students who identify as transgender, though they are known to be a population vulnerable to this type of victimization. Following up on this notable gap was appropriately noted as an important next step. But as this study demonstrates, a persistent relegation of the study of gender minorities to be addressed at some ambiguous time in the future can no longer be acceptable.

It must certainly be recognized that there are scholars attempting to accurately study gender and the criminal legal system but thus far, such vitally important work is overwhelmingly being submitted to and published by non-elite journals (Panfil & Miller, 2014). Anecdotally, the publishing process may also be a hindrance for scholars. For example, in a personal communication with

a leading scholar on the intersection of sexuality and criminal justice who has been the editor in chief of several journals, including one of the 'elite' journals samples in this study, we learned that mainstream journal editors and peer reviewers sometimes demand the use of the term *gender*, rather than *sex*. And we are aware of at least one scholar who reported experiences to us in which papers were desk rejected for the stated reason that the scholarship focused on transgender populations and, therefore, was not of widespread interest to mainstream scholars in the field.

The emphasis in this study was on mainstream journals and orthodox criminology because that is where the majority of students, instructors, and practitioners get their information. Mainstream CCJ research is the foundation of the most widely used textbooks, resources, and trainings, and is the basis for curriculum development and CCJ education in the United States. LGBTQ content is not widely taught and is rarely included in criminal justice courses and textbooks (Cannon & Dirks-Linhorst, 2006; Fradella, Owen, & Burke, 2009). This is important because as a discipline, we are failing to prepare students and practitioners alike for work in the criminal legal system if they are leaving our institutions without adequate understanding of sexual and gender diversity and without adequate education to identify and meet the needs of an under-served population (Cannon et al., 2014; Miller & Kim, 2012).

Other fields of study have begun to shift away from the traditional understanding of sex and gender as a parallel dichotomy. In health, for example, there has been progress toward understanding that while measuring sex is important when talking about health outcomes, it is just as important to consider the effects of social norms and expectations that come with gender identity and the role of sex in public policy (e.g., Phillips, 2005; Van Anders et al., 2017). It is important now that we advance the way we measure gender in the field of CCJ to align with modern understandings of sex and gender as non-binary and multifaceted. Fortunately, there are some feasible steps we can take to improve the way that gender is measured in research in criminology and criminal justice. Although this may seem initially daunting to researchers, some contemporary frameworks for measuring gender are already emerging.

Promising Methodologies

One general approach that has been proposed is the use of a two-step question that captures a person's current gender identity as well as their assigned sex at birth. The Center of Excellence for Transgender Health recommends first asking for 'current gender identity,' followed by a question about the respondents' 'assigned sex at birth' (Sausa, Sevelius, Keatley, Iniguez, & Reyes, 2009). Other researchers (see, e.g., Cahill & Makadon, 2014) have advocated for the same two-step process, but in the opposite order—first querying about assigned sex at birth and then current gender identity (see also Flentje, Bacca, & Cochran, 2015). The Williams Institute at UCLA published a report on best practices for identifying gender diverse respondents that similarly suggests a two-step process which distinguishes between sex and gender (GenIUSS, 2014).

As discussed above, we recognize that at present a large majority of research is secondary and relies on previously compiled datasets that may conflate sex and gender and had only a dichotomous sex/gender measure. In those cases, an acknowledgement of the limitations of such a gender measure would constitute a step in the right direction. Yet, to increase understanding of transgender and non-binary persons and their contact with the criminal justice system, CCJ studies must continue to expand and improve the measurement of gender identity. Therefore, for those collecting primary data, we recommend the utilization of a more advanced sex measure, with at the very least, an option to choose between 'male,' 'female,' and either 'X' or 'intersex,' with a text box for participants to elucidate if desired. When measuring gender, the options should ideally include, 'man,' 'woman,' 'trans man,' 'trans woman,' 'genderqueer or non-binary,' and 'different identity.' Of course, quantitative methods, the dominant methodology in mainstream CCJ research, require large and comparable sample sizes. This reason

undoubtedly contributes to our finding that transgender and non-binary study participants are often eliminated from the analyses in studies published in leading criminal justice journals.

To address this concern, we encourage quantitative researchers to consider asking respondents about gender using three distinct categories: (1) 'man/transman,' (2) 'woman/transwoman,' and (3) 'non-binary/different gender identity.' This would help reduce the erasure of people along the spectrum of gender identities while potentially preserving a sufficient number of cases in cells to meet the requirements of many statistical techniques.

Limitations and Conclusion

Although the CCJ journals analyzed here may be generally considered the leading or top journals in the field, there is certainly disagreement among scholars regarding reliance on those journals as representative of the field. For instance, Kleck and Barnes (2011) noted that many CCJ scholars publish in journals in other fields, and Rowe, McCann, and Hemmens (2017) analyzed the marginalization of legal research in CCJ journals. And although reliance on impact factors has also been critiqued (see, e.g., DeJong & George, 2018), Sorensen (2009) found that a combination of impact measures and prestige surveys can fairly reliably identify a 'rather stable hierarchy of outlets' (p. 510). With these critiques of the classification of 'elite' journals in mind, future research should examine the measurement of sex and gender in specialty journals to see if binary measures are similarly prevalent, and perhaps discover other methods of operationalizing gender. The 'cutting edge' research on gender (broadly) and LGBTQ issues in CCJ (more narrowly) is often published in specialty journals, such as *Feminist Criminology, Critical Criminology, and Women & Criminal Justice,* just to name a few. As a result, it may be that better operationalization of gender is common (or at least in increasing) in CCJ research that is published in these journals. Alternatively, these journals may be like their 'elite' counterparts insofar as they reify the status quo about the conflation of sex and gender and the mismeasure of both constructs.

Note

1   GLAAD was created as an acronym for the Gay and Lesbian Alliance Against Defamation, but the organization stopped using GLAAD as an acronym in 2013 to broaden its mission to include advocating for equality for transgender people.

Discussion Questions

1.   Explain how using dichotomous, close-ended "gender" or "sex" variables can be problematic for research.
2.   How has the widespread use of official records and secondary analysis in criminal justice research impacted the move toward more comprehensive study of gender and/or sex?
3.   How have the results of studies using more comprehensive definitions of gender and sex differed from studies that define them dichotomously?

References

Ainsworth, C. (2015, February 19). Sex redefined. *Nature, 518*, 288–291.

Allen, B. J. (2011). *Difference matters: Communicating social identity* (2nd ed.). Long Grove, IL: Waveland Press, Inc.

Barranco, R. E., Jennings, W. G., May, D. C., & Wells, M. J. (2015). What journals are the most cited in criminology and criminal justice's "big three" journals? *Journal of Criminal Justice Education, 27*(1), 1–16. https://doi.org/10.1080/10511253.2015.1065337

Baskin, D., & Sommers, I. (2015). Trajectories of exposure to community violence and mental health symptoms among serious adolescent offenders. *Criminal Justice & Behavior, 42*(6), 587–609.

Belknap, J. (2007). *The invisible woman: Gender, crime, and justice* (3rd ed.). Belmont, CA: Wadsworth/Thomson.

Buist, C. L., & Stone, C. (2014). Transgender victims and offenders: Failures of the United States criminal justice system and the necessity of queer criminology. *Critical Criminology, 22*, 35–47.

Butler, J. (1988). Performative acts and gender constitution: An essay in phenomenology and feminist theory. *Theatre Journal, 40*(4), 519–531.

Butler, J. (2004). *Undoing gender*. New York, NY: Routledge.

Button, D. M., & Worthen, M. G. (2014). General strain theory for LGBQ and SSB youth: The importance of intersectionality in the future of feminist criminology. *Feminist Criminology, 9*(4), 270–297.

Cahill, S., & Makadon, M. (2014). Sexual orientation and gender identity data collection in clinical settings and in electronic health records: A key to ending LGBT health disparities. *LGBT Health, 1*(1), 34–41.

Cannon, K. D., & Dirks-Linhorst, P. A. (2006). How will they understand if we don't teach them?: The status of criminal justice education on gay and lesbian issues. *Journal of Criminal Justice Education, 17*(2), 262–278.

Cannon, K. D., Dirks-Linhorst, P. A., Cobb, P. D., Maatita, F., Beichner, D., & Ogle, R. (2014). LGBT issues and criminal justice education. In D. Peterson & V. R. Panfil (Eds.), *Handbook of LGBT communities, crime, and justice* (pp. 261–279). New York, NY: Springer.

Capatides, C. (2018, June 11). Maine to offer third, non-binary gender option on driver's licenses, IDs. *CBS News*. Retrieved from www.cbsnews.com/news/maine-to-offer-non-binary-gender-option-on-licenses-ids/

Chesney-Lind, M., & Shelden, R. G. (2004). *Girls, delinquency, and juvenile justice* (3rd ed.). Belmont, CA: Wadsworth/Thomson.

Cohen, J. W. (2015). Criminal justice as a male enterprise. In T. L. Freiburger & C. D. Marcum (Eds.), *Women in the criminal justice system: Tracking the journey of females and crime* (pp. 31–45). Boca Raton, FL: CRC Press.

Cohen, J. W., & Harvey, P. J. (2007). Misconceptions of gender: Sex, masculinity, and the measurement of crime. *The Journal of Men's Studies, 14*(2), 223–233.

Dank, M., Yahner, J., Madden, K., Banuelos, I., Yu, L., Ritchie, A., . . . Conner, B. (2015). *Surviving the streets of New York: Experiences of LGBTQ youth, YMSM, and YWSW engaged in survival sex.* Washington, DC: Urban Institute.

Deaux, K. (1985). Sex and gender. *Annual Review of Psychology, 36*, 49–81.

DeJong, C., & St. George, S. (2018). Measuring journal prestige in criminal justice and criminology. *Journal of Criminal Justice Education, 29*(2), 290–309.

Dolliver, M. J., & Rocker, D. L. (2017). Addressing a divide in the conceptualization of the gender-crime relationship: A comparative test of gender and sex using general strain theory. *Deviant Behavior, 39*(2), 1–14. https://doi.org/10.1080/01639625.2017.1410619

Dwyer, A. E. (2011). Policing lesbian, gay, bisexual and transgender young people: A gap in the research literature. *Current Issues in Criminal Justice*, 22(3), 415–433.

Englert, P., & Dinkins, E. G. (2016). An overview of sex, gender, and sexuality. In H. F. Fradella & J. M. Sumner (Eds.), *Sex, sexuality, law, and (in)justice* (pp. 1–30). New York, NY: Routledge.

Fedina, L., Holmes, J. L., & Backes, B. L. (2018). Campus sexual assault: A systematic review of prevalence research from 2000 to 2015. *Trauma, Violence, and Abuse*, 19(1), 76–93.

Flentje, A., Bacca, C. L., & Cochran, B. N. (2015). Missing data in substance abuse research? Researchers' reporting practices of sexual orientation and gender identity. *Drug and Alcohol Dependence*, 147, 280–284.

Flores, A. R., Herman, J. L., Gates, G. J., & Brown, T. N. T. (2016). *How many adults identify as transgender in the US?* Los Angeles, CA: The Williams Institute.

Fradella, H. F., Owen, S. S., & Burke, T. W. (2009). Integrating gay, lesbian, bisexual, and transgender issues into the undergraduate criminal justice curriculum. *Journal of Criminal Justice Education*, 20(2), 127–156.

GenIUSS Group. (2014). *Best practices for asking questions to identify transgender and other gender minority respondents on population-based surveys.* Los Angeles, CA: The Williams Institute.

Gevisser, M. (2015, April 6). Engendered: Beyond the binary. *The Nation*, 233–235.

GLAAD. (2017). *Accelerating acceptance 2017.* Retrieved from www.glaad.org/publications/accelerating-acceptance-2017

GLAAD. (n.d.). *GLAAD media reference guide—Transgender.* Retrieved from www.glaad.org/reference/transgender

Grant, J. M., Mottet, L. A., Tanis, J., Harrison, J., Herman, J. L., & Keisling, M. (2011). *Injustice at every turn: A report of the National Transgender Discrimination Survey.* Washington, DC: National Center for Transgender Equality and National Gay and Lesbian Task Force.

James, S. E., Herman, J. L., Rankin, S., Keisling, M., Mottet, L., & Anafi, M. (2016). *The report of the 2015 U.S. Transgender Survey.* Washington, DC: National Center for Transgender Equality.

Johnson, D. E. (2014). When they tell you who you are: Lesbian resistance to the policing of multiple identities. In D. Peterson & V. R. Panfil (Eds.), *Handbook of LGBT communities, crime, and justice* (pp. 103–119). New York, NY: Springer.

Kim, B., & Hawkins, P. B. (2013). Who's getting cited: Representation of women and non-white scholars in major American criminology and criminal justice journals between 1986–2005. *International Journal of Criminology and Sociology*, 2, 306–321.

Kleck, G., & Barnes, J. C. (2011). Article productivity among the faculty of criminology and criminal justice doctoral programs, 2005–2009. *Journal of Criminal Justice Education*, 22(1), 43–66. https://doi.org/10.1080/10511253.2010.517650

Kruttschnitt, C. (2016). The politics, and place, of gender is research on crime. 2015 presidential address to the American society of criminology. *Criminology*, 54(1), 1–22.

Leach, D. L., II. (2007). Managing lesbian, gay, bisexual, transgender, and intersex inmates: Is your jail ready? *LJN Exchange*, 25–30.

Lenning, E. (2009). Moving beyond the binary: Exploring the dimensions of gender presentation and orientation. *International Journal of Social Inquiry*, 2(2), 39–54.

Matthew Shepard & James Byrd, Jr. Hate Crime Protections Act, Pub. L. 111–84, 123 Stat. 2835 (2009, October 28) (codified at 18 U.S.C. § 249).

Maxfield, M. G., & Babbie, E. R. (2015). *Research methods for criminal justice and criminology* (7th ed.). Stamford, CT: Cengage Learning.

McCauley, E., & Brinkley-Rubinstein, L. (2017). Institutionalization and incarceration of LGBT individuals. In K. L. Eckstrand & J. Potter (Eds.), *Trauma, resilience, and health promotion in LGBT patients* (pp. 149–161). Cham, Switzerland: Springer.

McCuish, E. C., Corrado, R. R., Hart, S. D., & DeLisi, M. (2015). The role of symptoms of psychopathy in persistent violence over the criminal career into full adulthood. *Journal of Criminal Justice*, 43(4), 345–356.

Meldrum, R. C., Young, J. T. N., & Weerman, F. M. (2012). Changes in self-control during adolescence: Investigating the influence of the adolescent peer network. *Journal of Criminal Justice*, 40(6), 452–462.

Miller, H. A., & Kim, B. (2012). Curriculum implications of anti-gay attitudes among undergraduate criminal justice majors. *Journal of Criminal Justice Education*, 23(2), 148–173.

Movement Advancement Project. (2016). Unjust: How the broken criminal justice system fails LGBT people. *Movement Advancement Project.* Retrieved from http://lgbtmap.org/policy-and-issue-analysis/criminal-justice

National Center for Transgender Equality. (2018). *The discrimination administration: Trump's record of action against transgender people.* Retrieved from https://transequality.org/the-discrimination-administration

Noble, J. B. (2004). Sons of the movement: Feminism, female masculinity and female to male (FTM) transsexual men. *Atlantis*, 29(1), 21–28.

O'Hara, M. E. (2017, June 15). Oregon becomes first state to add third gender to driver's licenses. *NBC News.* Retrieved from www.nbcnews.com/feature/nbc-out/oregon-becomes-first-state-add-third-gender-driver-s-licenses-n772891

Panfil, V., & Miller, J. (2014). Beyond the straight and narrow: The import of queer criminology for criminology and criminal justice. *The Criminologist*, 39(July/August), 1–6. Retrieved from www.asc41.com/Criminologist/2014/2014_July-Aug_Criminologist.pdf

Pfeffer, R. (2015). Hidden but not forgotten: The importance of including understudied populations in research. *Journal of Family Strengths*, 15(1). Retrieved from http://digitalcommons.library.tmc.edu/jfs/vol15/iss1/1/

Phillips, S. P. (2005). Defining and measuring gender: A social determinant of health whose time has come. *International Journal for Equity in Health*, 4(1), 11.

Prison Rape Elimination Act of 2003, Pub. L. No. 108–79, 117 Stat. 972 (2003, September 4) (codified at 42 U.S.C. § 15601 et seq.).

Prison Rape Elimination Act Prison and Jail Standards, 28 C.F.R. § 115 (2012).

Reisner, S. L., Bailey, Z., & Sevelius, J. (2014). Racial/ethnic disparities in history of incarceration, experiences of victimization, and associated heath indicators among transgender women in the U.S. *Women's Health*, 54(8), 750–767.

Richards, C., Bouman, W. P., Seal, L., Barker, M. J., Nieder, T. O., & T'Sjoen, G. (2016). Non-binary or genderqueer genders. *International Review of Psychiatry*, 28(1), 95–102.

Ritchie, A. J., & Jones-Brown, D. (2017). Policing race, gender, and sex: A review of law enforcement policies. *Women & Criminal Justice*, 27(1), 21–50.

Rowe, B. I., McCann, W. S., & Hemmens, C. (2017). Persona non grata: The marginalization of legal scholarship in criminology and criminal justice journals. *Journal of Criminal Justice Education*, 28(4), 514–541.

Ryle, R. (2018). *Questioning gender: A sociological exploration* (3rd ed.). Thousand Oaks, CA: Sage.

Sanders, L. (2018, January 9). What is gender X? New identity is accepted in these states, and Washington and Vermont could be next. *Newsweek*. Retrieved from www.newsweek.com/gender-x-new-identity-states-washington-vermont-775221

Sausa, L., Sevelius, J., Keatley, J., Iniguez, J., & Reyes, M. (2009). *Policy recommendations for inclusive data collection of trans people in HIV prevention, care & services*. San Francisco, CA: Center of Excellence for Transgender HIV Prevention, University of California San Francisco.

Sexton, L., Jenness, V., & Sumner, J. M. (2010). Where the margins meet: A demographic assessment of transgender inmates in men's prisons. *Justice Quarterly*, 27(6), 835–866.

Sorensen, J. R. (2009). An assessment of the relative impact of criminal justice and criminology journals. *Journal of Criminal Justice*, 37, 505–511.

Sorensen, J. R., & Pilgrim, R. (2002). The institutional affiliations of authors in leading criminology and criminal justice journals. *Journal of Criminal Justice*, 30, 11–18.

Steiner, B., & Schwartz, J. (2006). The scholarly productivity of institutions and their faculty in leading criminology and criminal justice journals. *Journal of Criminal Justice*, 34(4), 393–400.

Stotzer, R. L. (2009). Violence against transgender people: A review of United States data. *Aggression and Violent Behavior*, 14(3), 170–179.

Stotzer, R. L. (2014). Law enforcement and criminal justice personnel interactions with transgender people in the United States: A literature review. *Aggression and Violent Behavior*, 19(3), 263–277.

Tewksbury, R., & Mustaine, E. E. (2011). How many authors does it take to write an article? An assessment of criminology and criminal justice research article author composition. *Journal of Criminal Justice Education*, 22(1), 12–23.

Treharne, G. H. (2011). Questioning sex/gender and sexuality: Reflections on recruitment and stratification. *Gay and Lesbian Issues and Psychology*, 7(2), 132–154.

U.S. Department of Justice. (2018, May). *Federal Bureau of prisons change notice: Transgender offender manual, 5200.04 CN-1*. Retrieved from www.documentcloud.org/documents/4459297-BOP-Change-Order-Transgender-Offender-Manual-5.html

Van Anders, S. M., Schudson, Z. C., Abed, E. C., Beischel, W. J., Dibble, E. R., Gunther, O. D., . . . & Silver, E. R. (2017). Biological sex, gender, and public policy. *Policy Insights from the Behavioral and Brain Sciences*, 4(2), 194–201.

Van Voorhis, P., Wright, E. M., Salisbury, E., & Bauman, A. (2007). Women's risk factors and their contributions to existing risk/needs assessment: The current status of a gender-responsive supplement. *Criminal Justice and Behavior*, 37(3), 261–288.

Warner, D. N. (2004). Towards a queer research methodology. *Qualitative Research in Psychology*, 1(4), 321–337.

Weir, H., & Orrick, E. (2013). The most prolific female scholars in elite criminology and criminal justice journals. *Journal of Criminal Justice Education*, 24(3), 273–289.

West, C., & Zimmerman, D. H. (1987). Doing gender. *Gender & Society*, 1(2), 125–151.

Wolff, K. B., & Cokely, C. L. (2007). "To protect and to serve?": An exploration of police conduct in relation to the gay, lesbian, bisexual, and transgender community. *Sexuality and Culture*, 11(2), 1–23.

Wolff, N., Shi, J., & Schumann, B. E. (2012). Reentry preparedness among soon-to-be-released inmates and the role of time served. *Journal of Criminal Justice*, 40(5), 379–385.

Woodward, V. H., Webb, M. E., Hayden Griffin, O., & Copes, H. (2016). The current state of criminological research in the United States: An examination of research methodologies in criminology and criminal justice. *Journal of Criminal Justice Education*, 27(3), 340–361.

Worthen, M. G. F. (2016). *Sexual deviance and society: A sociological examination*. New York, NY: Routledge.

Reading 6.2   We Don't Like Your Type Around Here

The internet facilitates the spread of ideas and allows for anyone who wants to have a platform to be heard. Unfortunately, the ideas can be hateful, and the internet has generated a new way for people to be cruel to each other—cyberbullying. Cyberbullying can be attractive to would-be offenders, since they can often do it anonymously and rarely suffer any consequences for their behavior. Since members of the LGBTQ community are disproportionately likely to be victims of harassment offline, Costello, Rukus, and Hawdon (2019) suspected that they would also be attractive targets for cyberhate. Costello and colleagues used routine activities as a theoretical framework for their project, as they believed that exposure to potential offenders, target suitability, and guardianship would impact the extent to which respondents would report being victims of online hate. To test their hypotheses, they had to take the concepts outlined in routine activities and consider how to generate measurable survey items. The operationalization section of the paper provides readers with a good explanation of this work. Specifically, Costello et al. identified dimensions of the theory's three concepts and explained, in great detail, how they operationalized each of them.

We Don't Like Your Type Around Here: Regional and Residential Differences in Exposure to Online Hate Material Targeting Sexuality

Matthew Costello, Joseph Rukus, and James Hawdon

Introduction

On September 10, 2010, 18-year-old Tyler Clementi committed suicide by jumping off the George Washington Bridge. In a case that received national attention, Clementi, an openly gay student at Rutgers University, was the victim of online bullying and harassment. Clementi became the target of online ridicule when unauthorized footage of him kissing another man was streamed. On January 29, 2012, openly gay 14-year-old Rafael Morelos hanged himself. Like Clementi, Morelos was the victim of bullying—both online and offline—based on his sexual orientation. A phony Facebook page was created by one of Morelos's harassers in order to taunt and torment him.

Online hate, bullying, and harassment are growing problems that can result in a host of injurious outcomes, including diminished levels of well-being (Keipi et al. 2017) and trust (Nasi et al. 2015), acts of violence (Freilich et al. 2014; Daniels 2008), and suicide (Russell and

Joyner 2001). These negative outcomes are more likely when the hate is aimed at vulnerable populations. Anti-lesbian, gay, bisexual, transgender, questioning (LGBTQ) hate has an especially negative psychological impact on those affected because it attacks a core tenet of the target's identity and community membership (Garnets, Herek, and Levy 1990; Herek 2009; Herek and Garnets 2007; Herek, Gillis, and Cogan 1999). Therefore, understanding factors that contribute to the genesis of online hate based on sexual orientation is critical.

The ubiquity of the internet has led to a spike in the quantity of hate material online. Although the anonymity, immediacy, and global reach of the internet offer benefits that are evident, these same attributes also create avenues for hatemongers to promote their ideology and grow their ranks. It is precisely the open and egalitarian nature of the internet that renders cyberspace an ideal breeding ground for hate groups. Indeed, the dramatic increase in online hate over the past 20 years serves as stark evidence. Though the nomadic nature of hate sites makes it nearly impossible to measure the number of online groups active at any given time, there is consensus that the number is growing, and at a rapid rate (Banks 2010; Hawdon, Oksanen, and Räsänen 2014; Potok 2015).

Recent research has sought to understand correlates of exposure to, and targeting by, online hate (Costello et al. 2016; Costello, Hawdon, and Ratliff 2016; Hawdon, Oksanen, and Räsänen 2014). Much of this work has focused on online exposure and targeting broadly defined, though. Less attention has been afforded to the examination of particular types of targeting based on attributes such as sexuality, the focus of this paper. Further, this study pays particular heed to one's geographic place of residence as a potentially salient predictor of victimization. Most existing studies of cybervictimization do not consider the influence of locality; however, residence might be relevant when examining hate related to sexuality, given the opposition to lesbian, gay, bisexual, and transgender (LGBT) rights in certain parts of the country (Smith 1997). For example, public opinion polls consistently show that levels of sexual prejudice are higher amongst people living in the South and rural areas (Baunach, Burgess, and Muse 2009), and lesbian, gay, and bisexual individuals have reported higher levels of enacted sexual stigma in rural areas (Swank, Fahs, and Frost 2013).

To examine targeting of online hate based on sexual orientation, we examine the following hypotheses:

> **Hypothesis #1**: Individuals who spend more time online, or engage in antagonistic behaviors online, are more likely to be targeted by online hate based on sexual orientation.
> **Hypothesis #2**: Individuals with more robust support systems, online and offline, are less likely to be targeted by online hate based on sexual orientation.
> **Hypothesis #3**: Individuals living in the Southern region of the United States are more likely to be targeted by online hate based on sexual orientation.

> **Hypothesis #4**: Individuals living in a rural area are more likely to be targeted by online hate based on sexual orientation.

Literature Review

An Overview of Online Hate

Online hate expresses hatred of a group (see Hawdon, Oksanen, and Räsänen 2016). Although it shares similarities with cyberbullying and cyberstalking, cyberhate focuses on a collective, not individuals in isolation. Online hate can take many forms, though most commonly it expresses attitudes that demean or degrade others based on their race/ethnicity, national origin, sexual orientation, gender, gender identity, or other characteristics.

Tracking online hate is a formidable task. As hate groups build, dismantle, and move their web presence, tallying an accurate count of groups is nearly impossible. Nevertheless, the best available information suggests that online hate groups proliferated between 2000 and 2011, increasing by over 66% and peaking at over 1,000 active groups in 2011 (see Brown 2009; Cooper 2010; Potok 2015). Although down since 2011, the number of active groups increased from 892 in 2015 to 917 in 2016 (Potok 2017). Measuring online hate groups does not fully capture the universe of online hate, however. Indeed, today, the number of individuals maintaining websites or espousing hate online who are not affiliated, or only loosely affiliated, with hate groups outstrips the number of hate groups (Potok 2015).

This surge in online hate naturally translates into increased exposure to such material. Recent work found that the number of Americans between the ages of 15 and 30 who were exposed to online hate increased from 53% in 2013 to 63% in 2015 (compare Hawdon, Oksanen, and Räsänen 2015; Costello, Hawdon, and Ratliff 2016; also see Ybarra, Mitchell, and Korchmaros 2011). A more recent survey found that the number jumped to 70% in 2016 (Hawdon and Costello 2017). The rise coincides with the evolution of online interactivity, which allows for quick and easy dissemination of hate through blogs, social media platforms, and mass emails, among other conduits.

Although most people who see hate material are not noticeably harmed by it—for instance, some actively seek it out, and others scroll past it without much notice (Gerstenfeld, Grant, and Chiang 2003; McNamee, Peterson, and Peña 2010)—others are affected. In rare cases, exposure has been linked to incidences of violence (Federal Bureau of Investigation 2011; Freilich et al. 2014; The New America Foundation International Security Program 2015). But, although these cases are rare, experts are increasingly fearful that the link between hate speech and action is becoming progressively more tangible. This is especially true as concerns over conspiracy theories and fake news grow, and fringe thinking and the incitement of hate are mainstreaming (Faiola and Kirchner 2016). In addition, given the link between exposure to online hate and mood swings, anger, fear, and diminished well-being (Keipi et al. 2017; Tynes 2006; Tynes, Reynolds, and Greenfield 2004), being the target of hate based on one's sexual orientation could be especially damaging because of the destructive impact it can have on one's core identity.

Hate and the LGBTQ Community

A sizable literature examines the prevalence of hate crimes targeting members of the LGBTQ community. Herek (2009), using a national sample of gay, lesbian, and bisexual adults, found that roughly half of those examined reported experiencing verbal harassment, and approximately 20% were victims of a crime based on their sexual orientation. Other work largely echoes these results. For instance, Berrill and Herek (1992), focusing on a series of published and unpublished studies concerning LGBT-targeted hate and criminality between 1977 and 1991, found that 80% of respondents reported being verbally harassed, and 44% had been threatened. Smaller percentages reported being the victim of aggravated assault (9%), simple assault (17%), or vandalism (19%) based on their sexuality. Herek and colleagues (1999), examining lesbian, gay, and bisexual adults in

Sacramento, California, found that 13% of gay men, 7% of lesbians, 11% of bisexual men, and 5% of bisexual women had experienced a simple or aggravated assault based on their sexual orientation, whereas smaller percentages reported a sexual assault based on their sexuality.

Looking at young gay and bisexual men in the Southwest, Huebner, Rebchook, and Kegeles (2004) found that 5% of respondents reported being the victim of physical violence based on their sexuality in the past six months. A national sample of young lesbian, gay, and bisexual men showed that aggravated assault (9%), simple assault (18%), sexual assault (22%), and threats with attack (44%) were relatively common. Further, a study in New York City and surrounding areas focusing on youths who identified as sexual minorities demonstrated that 11% of respondents were subject to physical violence, 9% reported sexual assault, and 78% said they had been subject to verbal threats of harassment, all based on their sexual orientation (D'Augelli, Grossman, and Starks 2006). D'Augelli and Grossman (2001) found that older lesbian, gay, and bisexual individuals are at risk as well. Lifetime occurrence rates showed that 16% suffered physical assault, 7% were victims of sexual assault, and 29% were threatened with violence.

Social Identity Theory

All crimes have a negative impact on their victims. But incidences of hate are often argued to have a more pronounced detrimental impact on the attacked (Herek, Gillis, and Cogan 1999; Herek et al. 1997). In a comparison of victims of bias and non-bias crimes, Herek and colleagues (1999) found that lesbian and gay victims showed significantly more symptoms of depression, post-traumatic stress disorder (PTSD), anxiety, and anger, compared to victims of analogous non-bias crimes. Additionally, gay and lesbian victims viewed the world as more unsafe, had a diminished view of the goodness of others, questioned their own abilities, and were more likely to attribute their attacks to their sexual orientation, all compared to victims of non-bias crimes. Gay and lesbian victims also reported longer recovery times as their symptoms of anger, depression, and PTSD lingered for years.

Hate speech is so powerful precisely because it attacks a person for who they are. According to Social Identity Theory, our self-worth and self-determination are largely tied to our cognitive and affective bond to particular social categories (Boeckmann and Liew 2002; Tajfel and Turner 2004). A person's self-esteem, in part, is bonded to membership with a social group and how that membership is viewed by others (Luhtanen and Crocker 1992). Turner (1999) notes that social identity becomes most salient when boundaries are clearly drawn between members of a group and non-members. Hate speech does exactly that, not only drawing borders between members of a group and non-members, but also simultaneously devaluing members of the targeted group. Further, hate erodes the positive aspects of group membership, chipping away at the self-esteem derived from group membership.

According to Garnets and associates (1990), a positive self-identity is crucial for gay, lesbian, and bisexual individuals to cope with stresses that result from societal prejudices. Hate, however, can alter one's sense of self. In particular, research finds that being the victim of a hate crime causes the victim's core identity to become linked with a sense of vulnerability that naturally follows any victimization (Norris and Kaniasty 1991). This means that instead of identifying one's sexual identity with feelings of love and acceptance, victims of hate-motivated offenses instead correlate their sexuality with pain and danger (Garnets, Herek, and Levy 1990).

LGBTQ Experiences in the South and Rural Areas

Rightly or wrongly, the South is often portrayed as a region that struggles with accepting diversity. The LGBTQ civil rights movement has faced major hurdles in the South, and public opinion polls consistently show higher rates of sexual prejudice in the South (Baunach, Burgess, and Muse 2009; Herek 1994. Smith 1997; Swank, Fahs, and Frost 2013). In 2014,

the MSNBC television network commissioned a study of state LGBT climates. Examining state policies on marriage equality, adoption codes, and religious freedom restoration codes, the worst performing states were Alabama, Florida, Kentucky, Louisiana, Mississippi, Missouri, Tennessee, and Texas, all former Confederate states (MSNBC 2014). Given findings such as these, it is unsurprising that studies show verbal abuse based on sexuality is more common amongst gay men in Kentucky (Tewksbury et al. 1999).

Traditionally, sodomy laws have been the weapon of choice to use against LGBTQ individuals by criminalizing same gender sexual encounters (Leyland 2002). Even after the Supreme Court ruled that sodomy statutes were unconstitutional in *Lawrence v. Texas* (539 U.S. 186), 12 states have refused to repeal their sodomy laws from the books, 8 of which are located in the American South (Associated Press 2014). A 2014 attempt to repeal Louisiana's sodomy law in 2014 failed by a 66–27 vote in the state's House of Representatives (O'Donoghue 2014).

Since the Supreme Court decision in *Obergell v. Hodges* (576 U.S. 2015), which legalized gay marriage across the United States, Southern opposition to LGBTQ rights has intensified. Immediately following the ruling, a Kentucky county clerk, in defiance of the court, was jailed for refusing to issue marriage licenses to same-sex couples (Higdon and Somashekhar 2015). The following year North Carolina received national attention after passing HB2, which nullified local LGBTQ anti-discrimination ordinances and limited transgender bathroom use, an action criticized nationally by LGBTQ groups and many large corporations (Gordon, Price, and Peralta 2016). Recently, a movie theater in Alabama refused to show Disney's *Beauty and the Beast* because a character is openly gay (Barnes and Deb 2017). In this context, it is unsurprising that the Trevor Project, a telephone hotline for LGBT individuals contemplating suicide, receives more calls from the South than other region in the county (Trevor Project 2016).

In addition to region, research shows that locality—urban versus rural—can be an influential factor in the LGBTQ climate. The tight-knit, often religiously rooted structure of rural communities can create hostile environments for members of the LGTB community (Smith 1997). Studies have found that individuals in non-metropolitan LGBT areas experience high levels of homophobia and family estrangement that increase levels of self-isolation and guardedness about sexual orientation (Boulden 2001; Connolly and Leedy 2006; Lee and Quam 2013), a phenomenon Connolly and Leedy (2006, p. 16) refer to as "Don't ask. Don't tell."

There are numerous reasons for the feelings of unease felt by many LGBTQ rural-dwellers. Rural areas tend to prize culture homogeneity, religiosity, and "traditional" values. Urban areas tend to be hubs of newness, and thus largely disregard authoritarian morality. Urbanites are forced to respond to heterogeneous lifestyles in a way that rural residents are not. City-dwellers are also more apt to hold liberal views, be more educated, and less religious, traits associated with an acceptance of diversity, including diversity of sexual orientation (Moore and Vanneman 2003; Van Dyke, Soule, and Windom 2001). Unsurprisingly, this phenomenon results in many LGBTQ individuals migrating from rural areas to bigger cities. In urban areas, LGBTQ individuals struggling with issues of sexual orientation are able to meet other LGBTQ individuals facing similar struggles and come together for group support (Leyland 2002). However, this path is not feasible for many LGBTQ individuals who lack resources or cannot leave rural areas due to family or communal ties.

When asked about rural living, LGBTQ individuals portray it negatively, describing it as inhospitable (Barton 2010; Gray 2009; Kazyak 2011; McCarthy 2000). This leads many to hide their sexual identities and feel lonely, isolated, and fearful. Recent work by Swank and colleagues (2013) demonstrates that rural sexual minorities are more likely to face various forms of enacted stigma if they are open about their sexuality, compared to sexual minorities in similar locales who do not disclose their identity. Poon and Saewyc (2009), studying Canadian LGB adolescents, found that rural youths were more likely to be verbally teased and physically assaulted, relative to their urban counterparts. Similarly, LGB high school students in urban areas faced fewer homophobic remarks and less sexual harassment related to their sexual identity, compared to urban-dwelling students (Kosciw, Greytak, and Diaz 2009), and rural lesbian mothers are more likely to experience public harassment and rejection in relation to urban lesbian moms (Puckett et al. 2011).

Methods and Data

This study seeks to understand factors related to the targeting of online hate based on sexuality. We use logistic regression because we are analyzing a binomial dependent variable: if an individual has or has not been a target of online hate based on their sexual orientation. The effect of independent variables is reported as odds ratios, which show relative changes in the odds of an outcome when an independent variable's value is increased by one unit, holding all other effects constant.

Sample

The sample consists of 968 internet users aged 15 to 36 and was collected during the week of January 28, 2015, from demographically balanced panels of people who voluntarily agreed to participate in research surveys. Survey Sample International (SSI) recruits potential participants through permission-based techniques such as random digit dialing and banner ads. SSI sent email invitations to a sample of panel members ages 15 to 36, stratified to reflect the US population on age, gender, and geographic region. SSI provides various incentives to respondents for participating in their surveys. The ages 15 to 36 were selected because these data are from a study of exposure to online hate materials designed in part to match comparative samples from earlier research conducted in several European nations (e.g., Räsänen et al. 2016).

Demographically balanced online panels protect against bias in online surveys because screening can eliminate respondents and panelists who have previously participated (Evans and Mathur 2005; Wansink 2001). Moreover, the recruitment and selection processes, the use of pre-panel interviews, and incentives increase the validity of responses because those who volunteer to be in the panel tend to be more serious about answering the questions (see Wansink 2001).

Dependent Variable

Target of Online Hate Based on Sexual Orientation

Our dependent variable asks respondents if respondents have been the target of online hate based on their sexual orientation. Respondents were first asked, "Have you ever personally been the target of hateful or degrading material online?" Those who were victimized were asked to specify what the hateful or degrading material that targeted them pertained to. We found that 5.9% of our respondents indicated that they have been targeted because of their sexuality at some point in their life. This was one of the most common types of targeting amongst our respondents, with only targeting based on race/ethnicity, religious beliefs, and appearance being more common.

Independent Variables

Past work shows the applicability of RAT to cybercrime (Costello, Hawdon, and Ratliff 2016; Costello et al. 2016; Bossler and Holt 2009: Holt and Bossler 2013; Holtfreter, Reisig, and Pratt 2008; Leukfeldt and Yar 2016; Marcum, Higgins, and Ricketts 2010; Reyns and Henson 2015; Reyns, Henson, and Fisher 2015; van Wilsem 2011). Thus, our independent variables measure the core aspects of RAT, which are exposure to potential offenders, target suitability, and guardianship. We also control for sociodemographic characteristics, including where individuals live, in the full model.

Exposure to Online Hate

All else equal, we expect individuals who are more regularly exposed to online hate to be more likely victims. We therefore control for

online habits that affect exposure patterns. First, we asked respondents how many hours they spend online per day. The variable response set ranges from 1, "less than one hour per day," to 6, "ten or more hours per day." Respondents spend between 3 and 5 hours online per day, on average. We expect to find a positive relationship between time online and targeting, surmising that individuals who spend more time online will simply have more opportunities to be targeted.

Second, we asked respondents to tell us about their social media use. Specifically, respondents were asked to indicate whether they use a series of common platforms, including Facebook, YouTube, Twitter, Google+, Habbo, Wikipedia, MySpace, Ning, MyLife, Tumblr, Live Journal, newspaper message boards, general message boards, image boards (e.g., 4chan), instant messengers (e.g., Windows Live Messenger), online role-playing games (e.g., World of Warcraft), photo-sharing services (e.g., Instagram, Pinterest), blogs, Skype, anonymous networks (e.g., Tor), and email. The variable sums the social networking services (SNS) respondents used in the three months prior to being surveyed. Although the original variable ranged from 0 to 22, it was highly skewed. We therefore recoded the variable to range from 0, corresponding to "none," to 12, corresponding to "12 or more sites/services." Nearly 93% of the sample used 11 or fewer sites or services and recoding the variable did not influence the results in any substantive way. Like time spent online, we anticipate that individuals who use more SNS will be more apt to face- targeting by virtue of increasing exposure.

We also assess if respondents visited hostile online environments using a composite of three indicators. The factorability of all three measures demonstrated that each measure shares common variance with the other items. The first indicator asked respondents how often they see people being hateful on SNS. Responses range from 1 to 4, with 1 corresponding to "never," and 4 corresponding to "frequently." The second measure, utilizing the same scale, asked respondents how often they see people using language, images, or humor on SNS they find offensive. The third measure asked respondents if they believe people are "mostly kind" or "mostly unkind" to others on SNS, or if "it depends" on the situation. Individuals who visit hostile online environments with more regularity are hypothesized to face a greater likelihood of being targeted. Indeed, exposure to hate is a strong predictor of targeting, both online and offline (Bossler and Holt 2009; Holtfreter et al. 2010; Jennings, Piquero, and Reingle 2012).

Target Suitability

There are a number of ways that one's actions online can potentially magnify or diminish their likelihood of being a target for purveyors of hate. One way to potentially increase the likelihood of targeting is to engage in online confrontations, either in an attempt to intensify or deescalate them. We use two measures to estimate engagement in confrontations. First, we asked respondents who witnessed hate online how often they either told the person who is being offensive to stop or defended the person who is being attacked. These two items were combined into a composite indicator approximating enacting informal social control. Both measures have response sets ranging from 1, referring to "never," to 4, corresponding to "frequently." Sizable shares of respondents said they never tell hateful individuals to stop their behavior (28.3%) or defend the attacked (20.2%). Frequently intervening, either to tell the person to cease their behavior (10.2%), or by defending the target of the attacks (13.7%), was fairly uncommon. Respondents were much more likely to say that they engaged in attempts of informal social control either once in a while or sometimes. Although the attempt of the interveners in this instance is to mediate a conflict, it is possible that the intervention will, in turn, make the potential arbitrator the target of hate. By simply engaging the offender, an individual is drawing attention to themselves, thereby making themselves a potential victim (Costello, Hawdon, and Cross 2017).

Second, we assess if respondents were antagonistic online. More specifically, we asked how

often, if ever, they joined in when encountering hate online. We use a 4-point scale ranging from 1, "never," to 4, "frequently." Almost three-quarters (73%) of our sample said they never engage in this type of behavior, whereas only 3.1% said they do so frequently. Roughly 24% of respondents said they did so sometimes or once in a while. We expect more antagonistic individuals will be more likely to become targets themselves, in part as a result of engaging in a confrontation, but also because they are in virtual proximity to hateful material.

We also asked respondents if they discussed private matters online by having them rate on a 10-point scale how easy they find it to discuss private matters online when others do not know who they are. A score of 1 indicated the statement was "not very true of me," and a score of 10 indicated that it was "very true of me." Approximately 11% of respondents recorded a score of 10, and 15.3% recorded a 1. Slightly over 23% responded with a more neutral response of 5 or 6. We hypothesize that those who discuss private matters online more willingly are more likely to become targets of hate. Discussing private matters online can provide fodder for would-be haters, and thus doing so opens one to the possibility of being targeted.

Guardianship

The third aspect of RAT concentrates on social bonds that act as capable guardians. We use three measures to estimate online and offline social bonds. One measure asked respondents how close they are to an online community to which they belong. Closeness to an online community is measured on a 5-point scale. A response of 5 indicates that individuals "feel very close to an online community to which they belong," whereas a value of 1 indicates that they feel "not close at all" to such a community. Most of the survey respondents reported a moderate level of closeness to an online community, with nearly 69% reporting a score of 2, 3, or 4. Only 9.1% reported feeling very close to an online community. This item has been used in previous studies of online victimization to assess if online attachments serve as a protective factor (see

Oksanen et al. 2014). Thus, we expect individuals with stronger ties to an online community to be less likely to be targeted.

We use two measures to examine social bonds offline. The first is an index created from two measures—one concerning closeness to family, and the other regarding closeness to friends. Like our measure of closeness to an online community, this indicator uses an identical 5-point Likert scale. Over 80% of respondents reported a 4 or 5 regarding closeness to their family, and 77% responded similarly when asked about closeness to friends. Only 5% of respondents reported a 1 or 2 regarding closeness to family, whereas only 5.9% responded similarly regarding closeness to friends. Like online social bonds, we expect close family and friendship bonds to reduce the likelihood of being targeted.

Our second measure of offline guardianship is a dummy variable that indicates whether respondents lived alone as people who live alone most likely have lower levels of guardianship (Reyns, Henson, and Fisher 2016). Only 11.5% of respondents reported living alone. We expect them to have higher rates of being targeted by hate online.

Place of Residence

We use two measures to gauge respondents' place of residence to assess if residence affects their likelihood of being targeted by online hate pertaining to sexual orientation.

We control for region of the country using a dummy variable that codes 16 Southern states as 1 and all other states as 0, following the U.S. Census Bureau regional breakdown. We use a dummy variable to capture whether an individual lived in a rural locale. Rural areas are defined as open country areas with less than 50,000 residents. We hypothesize that individuals living in the South or rural areas will have a greater likelihood of being targeted by online hate related to sexual orientation. Even though the internet allows for interactions that transcend boundaries, all else being equal, individuals are more prone to interact online, positively or negatively, with those who they interact with

in the offline world (see Subrahmanyam et al. 2008; Valkenburg and Peter 2007), and these individuals will most likely be those who are in geographic proximity to them.

Sociodemographics

Finally, we control for sociodemographic variables, including gender, age, and a dummy variable for race/ethnic minority status. Although others have found that these factors are unrelated to targeting in general (see Näsi et al. 2014; Räsänen et al. 2016), it is possible that these characteristics pattern specific forms of targeting, such as that based on sexuality.

Findings

We use a two-model sequence: the first model controls for variables that proxy the three components of RAT, and the second model adds indicators for place of residence and other sociodemographic variables to the equation.

Model 1 shows that using more SNS leads to an increased likelihood of targeting based on sexuality (OR = 1.18, p < .001). In fact, respondents who report using more social networking platforms are 1.18 times as likely to be targeted. This finding aligns with expectations regarding increased internet usage and targeting. However, spending more time online does not significantly affect our outcome of interest, nor does visiting hostile online environments.

Engaging in confrontations, as hypothesized, is related to targeting as well. Interestingly, trying to enact social control online by defending others who are being targeted increases the chance that the defender will now become a target (OR = 1.76, p < .01). More precisely, defenders are 1.76 times as likely to be targeted, relative to those who do not confront hate online. Similarly, those who see hate and join in the hate are 1.55 times more likely to then become a target themselves (OR = 1.55, p < .01). These findings provide powerful evidence that both positive and negative engagement online can lead to targeting. Discussing private matters online does as well, as those who do so are 1.14 times more likely to be targeted by hate based on their sexuality (OR =1.12, p < .05). Counter to our hypotheses, we find no evidence that social bonds—either online or offline—affect targeting based on sexual orientation.

The second model demonstrates that, whereas gender, age, and minority status are unrelated to targeting based on sexuality, living in the South and living in rural areas both increase one's chances of being targeted. In fact, these are the two strongest effects in the model. Respondents in the South were nearly three times as likely to be targeted compared to individuals living in other geographic regions (OR = 2.92, p < .001). Additionally, respondents living in rural areas are more than two times as likely to be targeted based on their sexual orientation, relative to those living in the suburbs, or small, medium, or large cities (OR = 2.25, p < .05). Both of these findings align with our expectations. The results from the first model are generally parallel in the second model. There is no change in significance, and only slight change in the magnitude of effects for the RAT variables. We also tested for a possible interaction effect between living in the South and living in rural areas, positing that individuals who live in rural areas in the South might be particularly susceptible to being victimized. However, the effect was nonsignificant, and we therefore do not report it.

Discussion

Hate speech can profoundly affect those who are targeted. Past work shows that the effects of hate run the gamut from mundane to severe. Hate speech derives its power from its ability to devalue one's very identity. Not only that, but hate speech can make individuals question their lifestyle, social networks, and even cause victims to blame themselves for their victimization. These ill effects are amplified for individuals who feel ostracized, either from their family or society at large (Herek 1992), which is often the case with sexual minorities. Indeed, research has shown an unsupportive environment increases the suicide risk by 20% (Hatzenbuehler 2011).

Several of our hypotheses received at least partial support. Echoing previous findings

concerning online targeting of hate, we find that certain internet habits affect the likelihood of being the target of hate based on sexuality. We found that SNS usage, but not time online or browsing behavior, increases targeting. Being engaging or antagonistic online also increased being targeted. In fact, seeing hate and defending the attacked, seeing hate and joining in, and discussing private matters online all led to a greater likelihood of being targeted by hate based on sexual orientation. Our hypotheses regarding online and offline guardianship were not supported. Although all of the effects are in the hypothesized direction, living alone and having close bonds to family, friends, or an online community all fail to reach significance in either model. This is not entirely surprising, though, as the efficacy of guardianship in an online setting has received less support than the other elements of RAT (Bossler and Holt 2009; Choi 2008; Leukfeldt and Yar 2016; Reyns 2015).

Our third and fourth hypotheses both receive strong support: those living in the South were targeted nearly three times more as those living elsewhere, and those living in rural areas were targets of anti-LGBT online hate twice as often as those living in other locales. Both of these outcomes align with past findings showing increased rates of harassment, bullying, and violence associated with sexuality in the South and rural areas.

Several explanations could account for the regional effects found in this study, ranging from disparities in religiosity between regions to a desire to hold tight to "traditional" values in the South and rural areas. It is worthwhile evaluating these findings in the context of Contact Theory (Allport 1958; Pettigrew 1998). Contact Theory suggests that amiable relationships develop between members of majority and minority groups under certain conditions. Chief among them, intergroup contact has been found to lower intergroup prejudice (Allport 1958; Pettigrew 2005). Contact Theory is useful for explaining various types of negative attitudes toward marginalized groups (Krahé and Altwasser 2006; Lee, Farrell, and Link 2004; McClelland and Linnander 2006; Reinke et al.

2004), including gay and lesbian individuals (Herek 2000; Schope and Eliason 2000). Studies show that individuals who report knowing someone who is gay express more positive attitudes toward lesbian and gay individuals than do those who do not report such contacts (Berkman and Zinberg 1997; Herek 2000; Herek and Glunt 1993). Other work shows that having a close relationship to a sexual minority diminishes prejudice against LGBT individuals, as does having more LGBT contacts (Basow and Johnson 2000; Finlay and Walther 2003; Herek and Capitanio 1995, 1996).

Individuals residing in the South or rural areas are perhaps less likely to have numerous and intimate contacts with LGBTQ individuals. This could, in part, explain the increased rates of online victimization based on sexuality in these areas. In rural areas, and many parts of the South, this could simply be the result of sparsity. Indeed, the land-to-human ratio is high in rural areas, as well as many parts of the South. This by nature lessens all human contacts. Moreover, research shows that sexual minorities are more prone to hide their sexuality in the South and rural locales. Again, this opaqueness lessens the chance that straight individuals will knowingly have contact with a member of a sexual minority group.

Although these explanations of our findings are certainly plausible and, we believe, probable, we recognize these are contingent on an untested assumption. As the internet is truly the "worldwide web," it does not really make sense that region and residential location would influence targeting. That is, at least in nations that do not restrict access, internet sites are equally available to everyone with access to the internet regardless of their location. For region to have an effect in the online world, it is likely that online associations significantly overlap with offline associations. If this is indeed the case, individuals living in the South or in rural areas would be more likely to interact with people holding anti-LGBT attitudes both online and offline, all else being equal. Although previous research finds there is considerable overlap between offline and online networks, our data

do not allow us to establish this empirically in our sample. This is therefore a limitation of our research.

Limitations

Our study has additional limitations that merit consideration. First, our sample is limited to individuals between the ages of 15 and 36. The decision to limit our sample was strategic as research shows young people spend more time online and are therefore more likely targets of online hate. Even so, this places limits on our sample. We also face a limitation that coincides with all survey-based research. Namely, it is possible that individuals who chose to participate in our survey differ from individuals who chose not to participate. Thus, though our sample is demographically balanced, allowing for general claims to be made regarding our findings, we cannot be sure that our sampling procedure does not suffer from other biases.

Our dependent variable also has limitations. It asks respondents if they have ever been the target of online hate based on sexuality. Thus our study is correlational, which hampers our ability to make strong claims regarding causal relationships. We believe that it is certainly possible that many of our independent variables temporally precede our outcome, but we cannot know this with certainty. Finally, because our dependent variable is based on a subjective judgment, our ability to generalize our findings is limited.

Conclusions

The internet can cause great harm to vulnerable populations, but it can also be a source of great comfort. Therein lies the paradox. For those living in inhospitable environments, online communication and social networking can be a boon. They allow a person struggling with his or her identity to reach out to others experiencing similar feelings. The web opens the world so these individuals realize they are not alone; it also allows them to share coping strategies. Ybarra and associates (2015) found

LGBT youth were more likely to have online friends, and those friends are a vital link in their support systems. Yet, cyberspace can be a dangerous place. The amount of online hate is growing, and there is little reason to believe that trend will slow or reverse. Stigmatized groups are finding themselves increasingly the target of a growing population of hatemongers. As noted earlier, the consequences of this hate can be dire. This raises an important question—what, if anything, can be done to curb anti-LGBTQ hate?

There is little that the government can do to regulate hate speech online, as primacy is afforded the First Amendment in the United States (Hawdon, Oksanen, and Pekka 2016). Formal social control mechanisms, such as firewalls, antivirus programs, filtering, and blocking software, have proven ineffective at curtailing online hate as well (Bossler and Holt 2009; Fleming et al. 2006). Additionally, informal social control can, at times, have the opposite of the intended effect. Even when an individual intervenes in a situation involving hate with the intent of aiding the victim, hate is often multiplied, not dismissed. The news is not all bad, though. There is evidence that online collective efficacy, although difficult to foster in cyberspace due to the internet's impersonal and dispersed nature, can reduce online hate by sending the message to would-be haters that such behavior is not tolerated in that environment (Costello, Hawdon, and Cross 2017). Thus, the likelihood of being the target may be reduced, at least somewhat, if individuals employ strategic internet usage patterns.

Discussion Questions

1. How did the researchers operationalize each dimension of the routine activities perspective?
2. Why is it that we cannot be sure that people were victimized online *because of* their sexuality?
3. How did the researchers' sampling decisions possibly impact the results that they found?

References

Allport, Gordon. 1958. *The Nature of Prejudice*. New York: Doubleday.

Associated Press. 2014. "12 States Still Ban Sodomy a Decade after Court Ruling." Retrieved November 22, 2016 (www.usatoday.com/story/news/nation/2014/04/21/12-states-ban-sodomy-a-decade-after-court-ruling/7981025/).

Banks, James. 2010. "Regulating Hate Speech Online." *International Review of Law, Computers and Technology* 24 (3):233–239. https://doi.org/10.1080/13600869.2010.522323.

Barnes, Brooks and Sopan Deb. 2017, March 3. "An Alabama Drive-In Bans Beauty and the Beast Over Gay Character." *New York Times*. Retrieved March 18, 2017 (www.nytimes.com/2017/03/03/movies/beauty-and-the-beast-ban-alabama-drive-in-gay-character.html).

Barton, Bernadette. 2010. "Abomination' Life as a Bible-Belt Gay." *Journal of Homosexuality* 57:464–484. https://doi.org/10.1080/00918361003608558.

Basow, Susan and Kelly Johnson. 2000. "Predictors of Homophobia in Female College Students." *Sex Roles* 42:391–404. https://doi.org/10.1023/A:1007098221316.

Baunach, Dawn, Elisabeth O. Burgess, and Courtney Muse. 2009. "Southern (Dis) Comfort: Sexual Prejudice and Contact with Gay Men and Lesbians in the South." *Sociological Spectrum* 30:30–64. https://doi.org/10.1080/02732170903340893.

Berkman, Cathy S. and Gail Zinberg. 1997. "Homophobia and Heterosexism in Social Workers." *Social Work* 42 (4):319–332. https://doi.org/10.1093/sw/42.4.319.

Berrill, Kevin T. and Gregory Herek. 1992. "Primary and Secondary Victimization in Anti-Gay Hate Crimes: Official Response and Public Policy." Pp. 289–305 in *Hate Crimes: Confronting Violence against Lesbians and Gay Men*, edited by G. M. Herek and K. T. Berrill. Newbury Park, CA: Sage.

Boeckmann, Robert and Jeffrey Liew. 2002. "Hate Speech: Asian American Students' Justice Judgments and Psychological Responses." *Journal of Social Issues* 58 (2):363–381. https://doi.org/10.1111/1540-4560.00265.

Bossler, Adam and Thomas Holt. 2009. "On-Line Activities, Guardianship, and Malware Infection: An Examination of Routine Activities Theory." *International Journal of Cyber Criminology* 3:400–420.

Boulden, Walter. 2001. "Gay Men Living in a Rural Environment." *Journal of Gay and Lesbian Social Services* 12 (3/4):63–75. https://doi.org/10.1300/J041v12n03_05.

Brown, Christopher. 2009. "WWW.HATE.COM: White Supremacist Discourse on the Internet and the Construction of Whiteness Ideology." *The*

Howard Journal of Communications 20:189–208. https://doi.org/10.1080/10646170902869544.

Choi, Kyung-shick. 2008. "Computer Crime Victimization and Integrated Theory: An Empirical Assessment." International Journal of Cyber Criminology 2:308–333.

Connolly, Cathy and M. Gail Leedy. 2006. "Out in the Cowboy State: A Look at Gay and Lesbian Lives in Wyoming." Journal of Gay and Lesbian Social Services 19 (1):17–34.

Cooper, Simon Wiesenthal. 2010. Facebook, YouTube +: How Social Media Outlets Impact Digital Terrorism and Hate. Los Angeles: Simon Wiesenthal Center.

Costello, Matthew, James Hawdon, and Thomas Ratliff. 2016. "Confronting Online Extremism: The Effect of Self-Help, Collective Efficacy, and Guardianship on Being a Target for Hate Speech." Social Science Computer Review 35:587–605. https://doi.org/10.1177/0894439316666272.

Costello, Matthew, James Hawdon, and Amanda Cross. 2017. "Virtually Standing up or Standing By? Correlates of Enacting Social Control Online." International Journal of Criminology and Sociology 6:16–28.

Costello, Matthew, James Hawdon, Thomas Ratliff, and Tyler Grantham. 2016. "Who Views Online Extremism? Individual Attributes Leading to Exposure." Computers in Human Behavior 63:311–320. https://doi.org/10.1016/j.chb.2016.05.033.

D'Augelli, Anthony R. and Arnold H. Grossman. 2001. "Disclosure of Sexual Orientation, Victimization, and Mental Health among Lesbian, Gay, and Bisexual Older Adults." Journal of Interpersonal Violence 16:1008–1027. https://doi.org/10.1177/088626001016010003.

D'Augelli, Anthony R., Arnold H. Grossman, and Michael T. Starks. 2006. "Childhood Gender Atypicality, Victimization, and PTSD among Lesbian, Gay, and Bisexual Youth." Journal of Interpersonal Violence 21:1462–1482. https://doi.org/10.1177/0886260506293482.

Evans, Joel R. and Anil Mathur. 2005. "The Value of Online Surveys." Internet Research 15:195–219. https://doi.org/10.1108/10662240510590360.

Faiola, Anthony and Stephanie Kirchner. 2016, March 24. "In Germany, Right-Wing Violence Flourishing amid Surge in Online Hate." Washington Post. Retrieved November 15, 2016 (www.washingtonpost.com/world/europe/in-germany-right-wing-violence-flourishing-amid-surge-in-online-hate/2017/03/20/fc18d586-f867-11e6-aa1e5f735ee31334_story.html?utm_term=.952f62a3d3d6).

Federal Bureau of Investigation. 2011. Domestic Terrorism: Focus on Militia Extremism. Retrieved November 16, 2016 (www.fbi.gov/news/stories/2011/september/militia_092211).

Finlay, Barbara and Carol Walther. 2003. "The Relation of Religious Affiliation, Service Attendance, and Other Factors to Homophobic Attitudes among University Students." Review of Religious Research 44:370–393. https://doi.org/10.2307/3512216.

Fleming, Michele J., Shane Greentree, Dayana Cocotti-Muller, Kristy A. Elias, and Sarah Morrison. 2006. "Safety in Cyberspace: Adolescents' Safety and Exposure Online." Youth and Society 38 (2):135–154. https://doi.org/10.1177/0044118X06287858.

Freilich, Joshua D., Steven M. Chermak, Roberta Belli, Jeff Gruenewald, and William S. Parkin. 2014. "Introducing the United States Extremist Crime Database (ECDB)." Terrorism and Political Violence 26:372–384. https://doi.org/10.1080/09546553.2012.713229.

Garnets, Linda, Gregory M. Herek, and Barrie Levy. 1990. "Violence and Victimization of Lesbians and Gay Men Mental Health Consequences." Journal of Interpersonal Violence 5 (3):366–383. https://doi.org/10.1177/088626090005003010.

Gerstenfeld, Phyllis B., Diana R. Grant, and Chau-Pu Chiang. 2003. "Hate Online: A Content Analysis of Extremist Internet Sites." Analysis of Social Issues and Public Policy 3:29–44. https://doi.org/10.1111/j.1530-2415.2003.00013.x.

Gordon, Michael, Mark Price, and Katie Peralta. 2016, March 26. "Understanding HB2: North Carolina's Newest Law Solidifies State's Role in Defining Discrimination." Charlotte Observer. Retrieved October 12, 2016 (www.charlotteobserver.com/news/politics-government/article68401147.html).

Gray, Mary. 2009. Out in the Country: Youth, Media and Queer Visibility in Rural America. New York: New York University Press.

Hartzenbuehler, Mark. 2011. "The Social Environment and Suicide Attempts in Lesbian, Gay, and Bisexual Youth." Pediatrics 127 (5):896–903. https://doi.org/10.1542/peds.2010-3020.

Hawdon, James and Matthew Costello. 2017. "Status Relations and the Changing Face of Extremism in the United States since 1960." Paper presented at Les jeunes et l'incitation à la haine sur Internet: victimes, témoins, agresseurs? Comparaisons internationales. Nice, France. January 23.

Hawdon, James, Atte Oksanen, and Pekka Räsänen. 2014. "Victims of Online Hate Groups: American Youth's Exposure to Online Hate Speech." Pp. 165–82 in The Causes and Consequences of Group Violence: From Bullies to Terrorists, edited by J. Hawdon, J. Ryan, and M. Lucht. Lanham: Lexington Books.

Hawdon, James, Atte Oksanen, and Pekka Räsänen. 2015. "Online Extremism and Online Hate: Exposure among Adolescents and Young Adults in Four Nations." Nordicom-Information 37:29–37.

Hawdon, James, Atte Oksanen, and Pekka Räsänen. 2016. "Exposure to Online Hate in Four Nations: A Cross-National Consideration." *Deviant Behavior* 38 (3):254–266. https://doi.org/10.1080/01639625.2016.1196985.

Herek, Gregory M. 1992. "The Social Context of Hate Crimes: Notes on Cultural Heterosexism." Pp. 89–104 in *Hate Crimes: Confronting Violence against Lesbians and Gay Men*, edited by H. G. Herek, K. T. Berrill, and K. Berrill. Thousand Oaks, CA: Sage.

Herek, Gregory M. 1994. "Assessing Heterosexuals' Attitudes Toward Lesbians and Gay Men: A Review of Empirical Research with the ATLG Scale." Pp. 206–28 in *Psychological Perspectives on Lesbian and Gay Issues, Vol. 1. Lesbian and Gay Psychology: Theory, Research, and Clinical Applications*, edited by B. A. Greene and G. M. Herek. Thousand Oaks, CA: Sage.

Herek, Gregory M. 2000. "The Psychology of Sexual Prejudice." *Current Directions in Psychological Science* 9:19–22. https://doi.org/10.1111/1467-8721.00051.

Herek, Gregory M. 2009. "Hate Crimes and Stigma-Related Experiences among Sexual Minority Adults in the United States: Prevalence Estimates from A National Probability Sample." *Journal of Interpersonal Violence* 24 (1):54–74. https://doi.org/10.1177/0886260508316477.

Herek, Gregory M. and John P. Capitanio. 1995. "Black Heterosexuals' Attitudes toward Lesbians and Gay Men in the United States." *Journal of Sex Research* 32 (2):95–105. https://doi.org/10.1080/00224499509551780.

Herek, Gregory M. and John P. Capitanio. 1996. "Some of My Best Friends: Intergroup Contact, Concealable Stigma, and Heterosexuals' Attitudes toward Gay Men and Lesbians." *Personality and Social Psychology Bulletin* 22 (4):412–424. https://doi.org/10.1177/0146167296224007.

Herek, Gregory M. and Linda D. Garnets. 2007. "Sexual Orientation and Mental Health." *Annual Review of Clinical Psychology* 3:353–375. https://doi.org/10.1146/annurev.clinpsy.3.022806.091510.

Herek, Gregory M., J. Roy Gillis, and Jeanine C. Cogan. 1999. "Psychological Sequelae of Hate-Crime Victimization among Lesbian, Gay, and Bisexual Adults." *Journal of Consulting and Clinical Psychology* 67:945–951. https://doi.org/10.1037/0022-006X.67.6.945.

Herek, Gregory M., J. Roy Gillis, Jeanine C. Cogan, and Eric K. Glunt. 1997. "Hate Crime Victimization among Lesbian, Gay, and Bisexual Adults: Prevalence, Psychological Correlates, and Methodological Issues." *Journal of Interpersonal Violence* 12 (2):195–215. https://doi.org/10.1177/088626097012002003.

Herek, Gregory M. and Eric K. Glunt. 1993. "Interpersonal Contact and Heterosexuals' Attitudes Toward Gay Men: Results from a National Survey." *Journal of Sex Research* 30 (3):239–244. https://doi.org/10.1080/00224499309551707.

Higdon, James and Sandhya Somashekhar. 2015, September 3. "Kentucky Clerk Ordered to Jail for Refusing to Issue Gay Marriage License." *Washington Post*. Retrieved October 14, 2016 (www.washingtonpost.com/national/defiant-kentucky-clerk-could-be-found-in-contempt-thursday/2015/09/03/34e50f08-51af-11e5-9812-92d5948a40f8_story.html?utm_term=.733dc3951120).

Holtfreter, Kristy, Michael D. Reisig, Nicole Leeper Piquero, and Alex R. Piquero. 2010. "Low Self-Control and Fraud Offending, Victimization, and Their Overlap." *Criminal Justice and Behavior* 37 (2):188–203. https://doi.org/10.1177/0093854809354977.

Holtfreter, Kristy, Michael D. Reisig, and Travis Pratt. 2008. "Low Self-Control, Routine Activities, and Fraud Victimization." *Criminology* 46 (1):189–220. https://doi.org/10.1111/j.1745-9125.2008.00101.x.

Huebner, David M., Gregory M. Rebchook, and Susan M. Kegeles. 2004. "Experiences of Harassment, Discrimination, and Physical Violence among Young Gay and Bisexual Men." *American Journal of Public Health* 94 (7):1200–1203. https://doi.org/10.2105/AJPH.94.7.1200.

Jennings, Wesley G., Alex R. Piquero, and Jennifer M. Reingle. 2012. "On the Overlap between Victimization and Offending: A Review of the Literature." *Aggression and Violent Behavior* 17 (1):16–26. https://doi.org/10.1016/j.avb.2011.09.003.

Kazyak, Emily. 2011. "Disrupting Cultural Selves: Constructing Gay and Lesbian Identities in Rural Locales." *Qualitative Sociology* 34 (5):61–581.

Keipi, Teo, Atte Oksanen, James Hawdon, Matti Näsi, and Pekka Räsänen. 2017. "Harm Advocating Online Content and Subjective Well-Being: A Cross-National Study of New Risks Faced by Youth." *Journal of Risk Research* 20 (5):634–649.

Kosciw, Joseph, Emily Greytak, and Elizabeth Diaz. 2009. "Who, What, Where, When, and Why: Demographics and Ecological Factors Contributing to Hostile School Climates for Lesbian, Gay, Bisexual and Transgender Youth." *Journal of Youth and Adolescence* 30:976–988. https://doi.org/10.1007/s10964-009-9412-1.

Krahé, Barbara and Colette Altwasser. 2006. "Changing Negative Attitudes Towards Persons with Physical Disabilities: An Experimental Intervention." *Journal of Community and Applied Social Psychology* 16:59–69. https://doi.org/10.1002/casp.849.

Lee, Barrett A., Chad R. Farrell, and Bruce G. Link. 2004. "Revisiting the Contact Hypothesis: The Case of Public Exposure to Homelessness." *American Sociological Review* 69:40–63. https://doi.org/10.1177/000312240406900104.

Lee, Michael and Jean Quam. 2013. "Comparing Supports for LGBT Aging in Rural versus Urban Areas." *Journal of Gerontological Social Work* 56:112–126. https://doi.org/10.1080/01634372.2012.747580.

Leukfeldt, Eric R. and Majid Yar. 2016. "Applying Routine Activity Theory to Cybercrime: A Theoretical and Empirical Analysis." *Deviant Behavior* 37 (3):263–280. https://doi.org/10.1080/01639625.2015.1012409.

Leyland, Winston. 2002. *Out in the Castro: Desire, Promise, Activism.* San Francisco: Leyland Publications.

Luhtanen, Riia and Jennifer Crocker. 1992. "A Collective Self-Esteem Scale: Self-Evaluation of One's Social Identity." *Personality and Social Psychology Bulletin* 18 (3):302–318. https://doi.org/10.1177/0146167292183006.

Marcum, Catherine D., George E. Higgins, and Melissa L. Ricketts. 2010. "Potential Factors of Online Victimization of Youth: An Examination of Adolescent Online Behaviors Utilizing Routine Activity Theory." *Deviant Behavior* 31 (5):381–410. https://doi.org/10.1080/01639620903004903.

McCarthy, Linda. 2000. "Poppies in a Wheat Field: Exploring the Lives of Rural Lesbians." *Journal of Homosexuality* 39:75–90. https://doi.org/10.1300/J082v39n01_05.

McClelland, Katherine and Erika Linnander. 2006. "The Role of Contact and Information in Racial Attitude Change among White College Students." *Sociological Inquiry* 76:81–115. https://doi.org/10.1111/soin.2006.76.issue-1.

McNamee, Lacy G., Brittany L. Peterson, and Jorge Peña. 2010. "A Call to Educate, Participate, Invoke and Indict: Understanding the Communication of Online Hate Groups." *Communication Monographs* 77 (2):257–280. https://doi.org/10.1080/03637751003758227.

Moore, Laura M. and Reeve Vanneman. 2003. "Context Matters: Effects of the Proportion of Fundamentalists on Gender Attitudes." *Social Forces* 82:115–139. https://doi.org/10.1353/sof.2003.0099.

MSNBC. 2014. "The Best and Worst States for LGBT Equality." Retrieved October 16, 2016 (www.msnbc.com/msnbc/the-best-and-worst-states-lgbt-equality).

Näsi, Matti, Atte Oksanen, Pekka Räsänen, Teo Keipi, Emma Holkeri, and James Hawdon. 2014. "Association between Online Harassment and Exposure to Harmful Online Content: A Cross-National Comparison between the United States and Finland." *Computers in Human Behavior* 41:137–145. https://doi.org/10.1016/j.chb.2014.09.019.

Näsi, Matti, Pekka Räsänen, James Hawdon, Emma Holkeri, and Atte Oksanen. 2015. "Exposure to Online Hate Material and Social Trust Among Finnish Youth." *Information Technology & People* 28 (3):607–622. https://doi.org/10.1108/ITP-09-2014-0198.

The New America Foundation International Security Program. 2015. *Homegrown Extremists.* Retrieved October 11, 2016 (http://securitydata.newamerica.net/extremists/deadly-attacks.html).

Norris, Fran and Krzysztof Kaniasty. 1991. "The Psychological Experience of Crime: A Test of the Mediating Role of Beliefs in Explaining the Distress of Victims." *Journal of Social and Clinical Psychology* 10 (3):239–261. https://doi.org/10.1521/jscp.1991.10.3.239.

O'Donoghue, Julia. 2014, April 15. "Louisiana House Votes 27–67 to Keep Unconstitutional Anti-Sodomy Law on the Books." *The Time-Picayune.* Retrieved October 1, 2016 (www.nola.com/politics/index.ssf/2014/04/post_558.html).

Oksanen, Atte, James Hawdon, Emma Holkeri, Matti Näsi, and Pekka Räsänen. 2014. "Exposure to Online Hate among Young Social Media Users." *Sociological Studies of Children and Youth* 18:253–273.

Pettigrew, Thomas F. 1998. "Intergroup Contact Theory." *Annual Review of Psychology* 49 (1):65–85. https://doi.org/10.1146/annurev.psych.49.1.65.

Pettigrew, Thomas F. and L. R. LindaTropp. 2005. "Allport's Intergroup Contact Hypothesis: Its History and Influence." *On the Nature of Prejudice* 50:262–277.

Poon, Colleen and Elizabeth Saewyc. 2009. "Out Yonder: Sexual-Minority Adolescents in Rural Communities in British Columbia." *American Journal of Public Health* 99:118–124. https://doi.org/10.2105/AJPH.2007.122945.

Potok, Mark. 2015. "The Year in Hate and Extremism, 2010." *Intelligence Report, 141.* Retrieved December 3, 2015 (www.splcenter.org/fighting-hate/intelligence-report/2015/year-hate-and-extremism-0).

Potok, Mark. 2017 "The Year in Hate and Extremism." *Sothern Poverty Law Center Annual Intelligence Report.* Retrieved March 12, 2017 (www.splcenter.org/fighting-hate/intelligence-report/2017/year-hate-and-extremism).

Puckett, Julia, Sharon Horne, Heidi Levitt, and Teresa Reeves. 2011. "Out in the Country: Rural Sexual Minority Mothers." *Journal of Lesbian Studies* 15:176–186. https://doi.org/10.1080/10894160.2011.521101.

Race, Daniels J. 2008. "Civil Rights, and Hate Speech in the Digital Era." Pp. 129–154 in *Learning Race and Ethnicity: Youth and Digital Media*, edited by A. Everett. Cambridge, MA: The MIT Press.

Räsänen, Pekka, James Hawdon, Emma Holkeri, Teo Keipi, Matti Näsi, and Atte Oksanen. 2016. "Targets of Online Hate: Examining Determinants of Victimization among Young Finnish Facebook Users." *Violence and Victims* 31 (4):708–726. https://doi.org/10.1891/0886-6708.VV-D-14-00079.

Reinke, Rebecca R., Patrick W. Corrigan, Christoph Leonhard, Robert K. Lundin, and Mary Anne Kubiak. 2004. "Examining Two Aspects of Contact on the Stigma of Mental Illness." *Journal of Social and Clinical Psychology* 23:377–389. https://doi.org/10.1521/jscp.23.3.377.35457.

Reyns, Bradford W. 2015. "A Routine Activity Perspective on Online Victimisation: Results from the Canadian General Social Survey." *Journal of Financial Crime* 22:396–411. https://doi.org/10.1108/JFC-06-2014-0030.

Reyns, Bradford W. and Billy Henson. 2015. "The Thief with a Thousand Faces and the Victim with None: Identifying Determinants for Online Identity Theft Victimization with Routine Activity Theory." *International Journal of Offender Therapy and Comparative Criminology* 60 (10):1119–1139. https://doi.org/10.1177/0306624X15572861.

Reyns, Bradford W., Billy Henson, and Bonnie S. Fisher. 2015. "Guardians of the Cyber Galaxy an Empirical and Theoretical Analysis of the Guardianship Concept from Routine Activity Theory as It Applies to Online Forms of Victimization." *Journal of Contemporary Criminal Justice* 32 (2):148–168. https://doi.org/10.1177/1043986215621378.

Reyns, Bradford W., Billy Henson, and Bonnie S. Fisher. 2016. "Guardians of the Cyber Galaxy: An Empirical and Theoretical Analysis of the Guardianship Concept from Routine Activity Theory as It Applies to Online Forms of Victimization." *Journal of Contemporary Criminal Justice* 32 (2):148–168. https://doi.org/10.1177/1043986215621378.

Russell, Stephen T. and Kara Joyner. 2001. "Adolescent Sexual Orientation and Suicide Risk: Evidence from A National Study." *American Journal of Public Health* 91 (8):1276–1281. https://doi.org/10.2105/AJPH.91.8.1276.

Schope, Robert D. and Michele J. Eliason. 2000. "Thinking Versus Acting: Assessing the Relationship between Heterosexual Attitudes and Behaviors Toward Homosexuals." *Journal of Gay and Lesbian Social Services* 11 (4):69–92. https://doi.org/10.1300/J041v11n04_04.

Smith, James Donald. 1997. "Working with Larger Systems." Pp. 13–21 in *Rural Gays and Lesbians:* *Building on the Strength of Communities*, edited by J. Smith and R. Mancoske. New York: Haworth Press.

Subrahmanyam, Kaveri, Stephanie M. Reich, Natalia Waechter, and Guadalupe Espinoza. 2008. "Online and Offline Social Networks: Use of Social Networking Sites by Emerging Adults." *Journal of Applied Developmental Psychology* 29:420–433. https://doi.org/10.1016/j.appdev.2008.07.003.

Swank, Eric, Breanne Fahs, and David M. Frost. 2013. "Region, Social Identities, and Disclosure Practices as Predictors of Heterosexist Discrimination against Sexual Minorities in the United States." *Sociological Inquiry* 83 (2):238–258. https://doi.org/10.1111/soin.12004.

Tajfel, Henri and John C. Turner. 2004. "The Social Identity Theory of Intergroup Behavior." Pp. 276–93 in *Key Readings in Social Psychology*, edited by J. T. Jost and J. Sidanius. New York: Psychology Press.

Tewksbury, Richard, Elizabeth Grossi, Geetha Suresh, and Jeff Helms. 1999. "Hate Crimes Against Gay Men and Lesbian Women." *Humanity and Society* 23:125–142. https://doi.org/10.1177/016059769902300203.

Trevor Project. 2016. *Annual Report FY 2015*. Retrieved October 11, 2016 (www.thetrevorproject.org/site/pages/annual-report-programs).

Turner, John C. 1999. "Some Current Issues in Research on Social Identity and Self-Categorization Theories." Pp. 6–34 in *Social Identity: Context, Commitment, Content*, edited by N. Ellemers, R. Spears, and B. Doosje. Oxford: Blackwell Publishing.

Tynes, Brendesha. 2006. "Children, Adolescents, and the Culture of Hate Online." Pp. 267–289 in *Handbook of Children, Culture, and Violence*, edited by N. Dowd, D. Singer, and R. F. Wilson. New York, NY: Sage.

Tynes, Brendesha, Lindsay Reynolds, and Patricia Greenfield. 2004. "Adolescence, Race and Ethnicity on the Internet: A Comparison of Discourse in Monitored and Unmonitored Chat Rooms." *Journal of Applied Developmental Psychology* 25:667–684. https://doi.org/10.1016/j.appdev.2004.09.003.

Valkenburg, Patti and Jochen Peter. 2007. "Online Communication and Adolescent Well-Being: Testing the Stimulation Versus the Displacement Hypothesis." *Journal of Computer-Mediated Communication* 12:1169–1182. https://doi.org/10.1111/j.1083-6101.2007.00368.x.

Van Dyke, Nella, Sarah Soule, and Rebecca Windom. 2001. "The Politics of Hate: Explaining Variation in the Incidence of Anti-Gay Hate Crime." *Research in Political Sociology* 9:35–58.

van Wilsem, Johan. 2011. "Worlds Tied Together?: Online and Non-Domestic Routine Activities and Their Impact on Digital and Traditional Threat Victimization." *European Journal of Criminology* 8 (2):115–127. https://doi.org/10.1177/1477370810393156.

Wansink, Brian. 2001. "Editorial: 'The Power of Panels'." *Journal of Database Marketing and Customer Strategy Management* 8 (3):190–194. https://doi.org/10.1057/palgrave.jdm.3240034.

Ybarra, Michele L., Kimberly J. Mitchell, and Josephine D. Korchmaros. 2011. "National Trends in Exposure to and Experiences of Violence on the Internet among Children." *Pediatrics* 128 (6):1376–1386. https://doi.org/10.1542/peds.2011-0118.

Ybarra, Michele L., Kimberly J. Mitchell, Neal A. Palmer, and Sari L. Resiner. 2015. "Online Social Support as a Buffer against Online and Offline Peer and Sexual Victimization among US LGBT and Non-LGBT Youth." *Child Abuse and Neglect* 39:123–136. https://doi.org/10.1016/j.chiabu.2014.08.006.

Reading 6.3   Popping the Cultural Bubble of Violence Risk Assessment Tools

Risk assessment tools are used by many criminal justice and human services agencies because they represent an advancement in our field. Prior to the creation of such data collection methods, decisions regarding treatment, risk level, and custody level were made with clinical judgment or gut feelings. The earliest risk assessment instruments involved only the incorporation of static risk factors, meaning characteristics that are unchangeable (e.g., arrest record, incarceration history, age). More modern screening tools also measure dynamic risk factors (e.g., educational attainment, peer group associations, family dynamics, drug use) that that we should target with treatment interventions. The inclusion of both static and dynamic risk factors into single classification tools have strengthened their predictive validity. While we have certainly made great strides in improving our assessment tools over the past several decades, we continue to face challenges with their predictive validity with certain populations, particularly racial and ethnic minorities. Shepherd and Anthony (2017) draw attention to the fact that these tools are often validated on the majority populations and are less accurate with minorities, particularly Indigenous groups. The authors then make suggestions for steps that agencies can take to supplement or amend their classification tools to reflect the needs of all inmates. These recommendations are especially important for jurisdictions that regularly incarcerate Indigenous individuals.

Popping the Cultural Bubble of Violence Risk Assessment Tools

Stephane M. Shepherd and Thalia Anthony

Introduction

Risk indicators inform decisions in an array of justice interventions. They permeate assessments and diagnoses on an individual's prospects of reoffending and seek to control risk elements to prevent future harm. Their future focus is not concerned with historical unmet needs resulting from a systemic lack of support. Their predication on futurity makes them prone to uncertainty (McCulloch, Maher, Fitz-Gibbon, Segrave, & Roffee, 2016). Far from neutral instruments, they are also laden with cultural assumptions and moral and political governance strategies (Maurutto & Hannah-Moffat, 2006; O'Malley, 2004). This article explores the assumptions in risk assessment tools that apply to assessing offenders before and after criminal sentencing. It argues that risk models exclude broader socio-historical factors and culturally specific phenomena, the omission of which could have adverse implications for certain populations (i.e. Indigenous people). Based on studies of generating pre-sentence information for Indigenous people in Canada, a proposal for a culturally integrated assessment framework is advanced. A conventional risk instrument could run alongside a separate reporting mechanism to reflect the free-flowing community narrative in relation to the individual. The model accepts that both are required because the risk assessment is generally inhibited to risk assumptions and therefore limited in its capacity to assess an individual from a holistic culturally appropriate platform.

The Risky Business of Penal Assessment

Violence risk assessment instruments guide evaluations by justice professionals of a client's level of violence risk for risk management and treatment purposes (Douglas, Cox, & Webster,

1999). They are widely used in courtroom and correctional settings as well as holding an influential role in medico-legal decision-making in relation to people at risk of reoffending (McSherry, 2004; Urquhart & Viljoen, 2014; Viljoen, McLachlan, & Vincent, 2010; Vitacco, Kurus, Erickson, & Apple, 2012). Offender and patient management decisions (i.e. parole, probation, prisoner transfer, therapeutic initiatives, community day leave, civil commitment, involuntary commitment, community supervision orders, admission to programs, and indeterminate sentencing), and restrictions accompanying such arrangements, are often informed by evidence drawn from risk instruments. This process can have significant societal and personal ramifications. For example, an overestimation of a client's risk for violence may engender restrictions to their personal liberty (i.e. denial of parole). Conversely, recommending inappropriate sentencing options for a client prone to violence may have implications for public safety. As such, there is a moral and practical obligation to ensure the accuracy of any violence risk assessment used to inform decision-making.

Risk instruments encompass a suite of risk items that can be static or dynamic in nature. Static risk items refer to events that are unchangeable (i.e. age at first arrest) while dynamic factors comprise adjustable phenomena (i.e. peer group delinquency). Risk items are simply calculated (actuarial approaches) or clinically contextualised (structured professional judgment approaches) to help categorise individuals into groupings (i.e. high/low risk) that pertain to their likelihood of re-offense. There is an extensive validation literature attesting to the predictive validity of several widely utilised risk instruments. Adult (i.e. HCR-20; LS/CMI) and youth specific (YLS/CMI; SAVRY) instruments have consistently demonstrated associations with future offending and other problem behaviours (Douglas & Reeves, 2010; Olver, Stockdale, & Wormith, 2009, 2014; Singh, Grann, & Fazel, 2011). Moreover, it is well established that risk instruments are generally more accurate at predicting re-offending than clinical discretion alone

(Grove, Zald, Lebow, Snitz, & Nelson, 2000). Despite these advances in offender risk assessment, much less academic attention has been afforded to the applicability of such measures to non-white populations (Shepherd & Lewis-Fernandez, 2016). It is nonetheless established in penology research that risk instruments as applied to pre-sentence reports do not promote an assessment of the individual's cultural background and culturally relevant relationships and rehabilitation options. Pre-sentence reports tend to lack any substantive information about the individual's identification with a cultural community, as identified in qualitative research in Canada and Australia (Anthony, Marchetti, Behrendt, & Longman, 2017; Hannah-Moffat & Maurutto, 2010). This is because the actuarial risk data they produce relate predominantly to *individual* criminal history and risk, which ignores the individual's *collective* lived experience (Anthony et al., 2017; Hannah-Moffat & Maurutto, 2010). Rather, they exhibit the hallmarks of cultural neutrality that can result in 'implicit racial bias' because in fact they do draw from a set of cultural assumptions relating to European cultures (Anthony et al., 2017; Hannah-Moffat & Maurutto, 2010).

Are Culturally Neutral Risk Assessments Capable of Accounting for Cultural Diversity?

A growing body of literature is challenging the notion that risk instruments are commensurately applicable to all cultural groups in their current iterations (Shepherd, 2016; Shepherd & Lewis-Fernandez, 2016). This critique is multi-faceted and encompasses the following points: (i) the predictive accuracy of risk instruments is often lower for non-white groups compared to white groups (and notwithstanding that white groups may also receive imperfect information flowing from the assessments); (ii) the risk item content predominantly reflects the experiences, understandings and expressions of White North American offenders and patients; and (iii) there have been insufficient attempts to establish if the instruments are measuring risk the same way across culture (Hart, 2016). A further concern relates to the application of the risk assessment that may result in a person with a specific cultural background (generally European) misinterpreting the behaviour of a person from another cultural background.

No existing violence risk instrument explicitly integrates cultural-specific information into its assessment format. Consequently, unique culturally relevant information for some minority populations (i.e. Indigenous peoples) may be neglected during the assessment process resulting in particularly disadvantageous legal/medical outcomes. Shepherd and Lewis-Fernandez (2016) assert that risk assessment methods must be culturally relevant, so that risk profiles are accurate, and the health and legal needs of clients from all cultural backgrounds are equally likely to be identified. This is of particular importance for populations who have endured histories of discrimination by mental health and criminal justice systems and/or are over-represented in custodial environments (Dudgeon, Rickwood, Garvey, & Gridley, 2014; Gillies, 2013; Shepherd & Phillips, 2015; Tonry, 2011).

A further critique of risk assessment is the focus on a specific suite of risk items (i.e. substance use, family dysfunction, low educational attainment, previous contact with the justice system, negative attitudes) which in turn can frame risk in narrow, punitive terms (Hannah-Moffat & Maurutto, 2010; Shepherd & Willis-Esqueda, 2017; Ward & Maruna, 2007). Here, the identification of risk factors is assessed with a view to 'penal managerialism' (Hannah-Moffat & Maurutto, 2010). In other words, harm reduction (to the community or institution) is elevated over client rehabilitation. It pits risks against needs, or otherwise reallocates needs to the category of 'risk elements' (see Hannah-Moffat, 2005). The scope for such an outcome is heightened in light of the expanding use of computerised algorithm-driven approaches to risk that reduce transparency and disproportionately focus on client demographics and criminal history. Research in Canada has shown that

pre-sentence reports, when structured through the prism of actuarial risk assessment, increasingly connect risk factors and recommendations (Hannah-Moffat & Maurutto, 2010). A potential by-product is that less emphasis may be afforded to an individual's holistic circumstances and cultural, collective needs. A cultural peer review of the SAVRY, a widely administered youth violence risk instrument, detailed that Native American youth may be disadvantaged by the instrument due to its environmental de-contextualisation, its absence of cultural norms and experiences and negative labelling potential (Shepherd & Willis-Esqueda, 2017). The non-consideration of cultural context in the assessment of risk gives rise to concerns that risk instruments effectively serve as profiling systems. Risk factors such as unemployment, low educational attainment, previous arrests, and delinquent peers may be characteristic of particular disadvantaged jurisdictions. As such an individual's demographics may be inadvertently criminalised, reinforcing race and/or class disparities. Moreover, the narrow criminogenic framing of risk may disregard any structural imbalances that may underpin community-level or individual-level risk factors. For example, the over-policing of particular neighbourhoods may increase the likelihood of arrest; however, the arrest may not have led to a conviction (often not differentiated on instruments).

Need for Strengths-Based Cultural Information in Risk Assessment

Calls to integrate culturally unique information into risk assessment frameworks have been infrequent and largely inchoate. Previous suggestions include: (i) the creation of a cultural addendum or set of cultural guidelines to accompany the risk instrument/assessment (see Shepherd & Lewis-Fernandez, 2016; Shepherd & Willis-Esqueda, 2017); (ii) amending the operational descriptions of risk items to include culturally relevant definitions; and (iii) developing instruments tailored for specific cultural groups (Messing, Amanor-Boadu, Cavanaugh, Glass, & Campbell, 2013; Shepherd &

Lewis-Fernandez, 2016). To date, testing the utility of additional culturally relevant information to risk assessment frameworks has not occurred (Shepherd, 2014).

What is more, there have been few indications as to what specific cultural information could (or should) be included as part of a risk assessment. A survey of Native American community leaders and justice health workers revealed that historical injustices (i.e. residential schools, dislocation, forced acculturation) and family-level risk factors (i.e. family histories of mental health, grief, substance use, and suicide) should be gauged in tandem with individual-level factors during a risk assessment (Shepherd & Willis-Esqueda, 2017). Logically, it would appear to be a paradox that an instrument focused on assessing an individual's capacity for reoffending should sit alongside systemic issues relating to racism and colonisation, which are embedded in the criminalising system and discourse. The former issues implicate the individual; the latter focus implicates the system and the state. However, even cultural issues—which are often framed as *deficit* factors—can be appropriated for the purpose of individual risk.

In the above survey, community leaders and justice health workers encouraged the inclusion of *strengths* based, culturally specific social norms, relationships, and practices (i.e. parenting styles, kinship systems) that could mitigate against risk and provide appropriate avenues for rehabilitation. Cultural alienation/separation was considered to be a risk factor whilst cultural engagement was viewed as a protective factor (Shepherd & Willis-Esqueda, 2017). This could inform recommendations for community reintegration rather than imprisonment. Prior research has found that cultural engagement/connection is associated with lower rates of both psychological distress and future violence for Indigenous offenders (Shepherd, Delgado, & Paradies, 2017; Shepherd, Delgado, Sherwood, & Paradies, 2017). In light of the limited discussion on cross-cultural approaches to risk assessment, it first appears necessary to demarcate a range of cultural considerations for use in

tandem with (or within) risk assessment frameworks. We tailor this discussion to matters relevant to Indigenous populations in the CANZUS regions.

Alternative Approaches to Client Information in a Comparable Jurisdiction: Indigenous Narrative Reports

In Canada, an alternative pre-sentence report has emerged because of the weaknesses in risk-based reports in telling a story about the collective experience of Indigenous peoples and to fulfil the purposes of the Canadian *Criminal Code* by providing the court with information not normally presented before the court (see Hannah-Moffat & Maurutto, 2010; Kicknosway, 2015). Provision 718.2(e) of the Canadian *Criminal Code* requires courts to take into account the unique circumstances and collective experiences of First Nations individuals when sentencing and to consider alternatives to imprisonment (*Criminal Code*, RSC, 1985; see *R v Gladue*, 1999). The Supreme Court of Canada determined that 'evidence will be required' to provide appropriate sentences for Aboriginal offenders (R *v Gladue*, 1999). A similar position was adopted by the High Court of Australia in *Bugmy* when the majority stated, 'it is necessary to point to material tending to establish background' if it to be relevant in sentencing (*Bugmy v The Queen*, 2013). Therefore, if cultural issues are to be submitted to the court in relation to the Aboriginal person, it requires evidence to support this submission.

In Canada the particular reference was made to the need for evidence of Aboriginal community issues receiving 'special attention in pre-sentence reports' (R *v Gladue*, 1999). Nonetheless, subsequent judicial and legal practitioner observations of pre-sentence reports in Canada have found that there is minimal consideration of these issues, including because Aboriginal people did not feel comfortable discussing cultural issues with people working in community corrections (Kicknosway, 2015). The information about culture in Canadian pre-sentence reports is a secondary or supplementary issue to the central and primary focus on actuarial risk information based on an 'objective' risk assessment (Hannah-Moffat & Maurutto, 2010, p. 265). Indeed, Hannah-Moffat and Maurutto (2010, p. 265) suggest that since *Gladue*, the emphasis on objective factors has increased to the detriment of considerations of culture that historically have been conceived as subjective factors.

In order to give proper attention to the systemic factors that may bring an Aboriginal person before the court and provide information regarding community-based and culturally appropriate rehabilitation options, Aboriginal legal services initiated a separate reporting mechanism, known as *Gladue* Reports. These reports do not rely on a risk assessment tool. Instead, they invoke community perspectives of the First Nations individual to provide a holistic narrative of the individual's circumstances and options. They are accepted by Canadian sentencing courts, which can request a '*Gladue* Report' for a 'First Nations individual', prepared by a caseworker, who is also often of First Nations background him- or herself (April & Magrinelli Orsi, 2013; *R v Gladue*, 1999). The Supreme Court of Canada in *R. v. Ipeelee* (2012) referred to the significance of *Gladue* Reports in the following manner:

> A *Gladue* report is an indispensable sentencing tool to be provided at a sentencing hearing for an Aboriginal offender and it is also indispensable to a judge in fulfilling his duties under s. 718.2(e) of the Criminal Code.
>
> (p. 437)

Gladue Reports comprise information relevant to the client's Aboriginal background including unique community circumstances, systemic factors underpinning offending, and culturally appropriate options for sentencing (see Anthony, Bartels, & Hopkins, 2015; Council of Yukon First Nations, 2015; Farrelly, Rosner, Kienzel, & Shields, 2014). Attention is also afforded to how offending behaviours may

manifest from disadvantage and marginalisation fashioned by past injustices (Anthony et al., 2015; Council of Yukon First Nations, 2015; Farrelly et al., 2014). A non-exhaustive list of the types of information contained in a *Gladue* Report is shown in Table 1.

Table 1 Gladue *Cultural Factors*

Gladue Cultural Factors	
Relationships with family, community	Has attempted suicide
Substance abuse	Has access to culturally relevant healing resources?
Attended residential school/member of stolen generations	Family members were stolen generations/ attended residential school
Childhood disadvantage	Subject was in foster care/child protection
Loss of cultural identity	Placed with non-Indigenous caregivers?
Is substance use common in the community?	Intergenerational trauma
Preventable/early deaths in family/ community?	Lack of educational opportunities/barriers
Experiences of racism/ discrimination	Unresolved issues affecting the local community
Exposed to lateral violence	Suicide among friends/ family
Witnessed violence in family/community?	Lack of employment opportunities
Connection to Aboriginal culture and community	Experienced physical/ sexual/emotional abuse
Serious health problems	Learning disabilities/ cognitive impairment/ FASD
Involved in cultural activities when incarcerated?	Community circumstances at the time of birth
Strengths/personal attributes	History of subject's community
Cultural practices/ activities performed in the community?	What treatment approaches have worked/ not worked in the past?

Many of the *Gladue* items listed in the table are not explicitly referred to in risk assessment models. While some of the specific items are included in some risk models (i.e. suicide attempts, substance use, exposure to violence) emphasis rests on the individual's behaviours and personal choices. This means that some of the unique and/or broader contributing mechanisms to offending or desistance from offending may go undetected. A consideration of culturally relevant environmental and historical phenomena extends beyond the accumulation of individual risk items—it provides a contextual understanding as to why and how certain risk items materialise. For example, a client's substance abuse problems may be induced by elevated levels of psychological distress stemming from experiences distinctive to their particular community (i.e. discrimination, frequent deaths of close friends and family in the community, poverty) (Shepherd, Delgado, Sivasubramaniam, & Paradies, 2017). *Gladue* Reports also accommodate a review of the types of available treatment options (i.e. requirements, eligibility, and limitations) with regard to the client's well-being profile, community circumstances, and cultural obligations (Council of Yukon First Nations, 2015; Farrelly et al., 2014). Presently, *Gladue*-style matters will be arbitrarily considered during a risk assessment and the extent to which this occurs depends heavily on the (i) cross-cultural expertise of the clinician and (ii) the rigidity/expediency of the risk assessment model administered. Either way, cultural considerations during an assessment of risk are unsystematically or perhaps haphazardly applied. The *Gladue* Report, however, designates a way forward for advancing culturally appropriate risk assessment approaches. Specifically, the *Gladue* template (see Table 1) may present a meaningful cultural supplement to generic risk assessments.

Conclusion

Existing risk assessment approaches have been criticised for their mono-cultural and risk-heavy composition. In combination, these two concerns may facilitate erroneous risk evaluations and unreasonable medico-legal consequences for certain non-white populations. Appeals to cultivate culturally appropriate risk assessment tools and models have occurred periodically in the literature. However, the question of how cultural differences will be appraised in a risk assessment framework and which specific cultural factors should be considered remains unaddressed. Provisions under the Canadian *Criminal Code* allow for *Gladue* Reports to be sought by judicial officers prior to sentencing. *Gladue* Reports provide insights into an Indigenous client's unique circumstances that may have led to their offending—information that is equally as useful when assessing an Indigenous client's risk for violence. Further, taking into account the circumstances of Indigenous offenders provides a holistic complement to the risk-centric and often punitive outlook of risk assessment. *Gladue* information offers the forensic assessment discipline a starting point for future empirical investigations.

However, some caution must be taken prior to the integration of risk and cultural materials. The Canadian experience raises some concerns about attempts to incorporate *Gladue* material within existing systems such as pre-sentence reports, even where stipulated by legislation and case law. The limitations exist, first, because of barriers that preclude Aboriginal persons from disclosing community, cultural, or even personal background information to corrections report writers who are part of a system responsible for their criminalisation. Second, the inclusion of cultural information may be misused and simply serve to amplify the risk of the individual. There are strong grounds for including a person's background, including their relationship with a community and culture, in sentencing. This warrants further exploration of the extent to which risk assessment frameworks can accommodate culturally relevant material.

Discussion Questions

1. Discuss the ways that the results of some risk assessment tools generate implicit racial bias.

2. What are some of the ways that professionals can work to make classification tools more appropriate for use with minority groups?

References

Anthony, T., Bartels, L., & Hopkins, A. (2015). Lessons lost in sentencing: Welding individualised justice to Indigenous justice. *Melbourne University Law Review, 39*, 47–76.

Anthony, T., Marchetti, E., Behrendt, L., & Longman, C. (2017). Individualised justice through Indigenous reports in sentencing. *Australasian Journal for the Administration of Justice, 26*(1), 1–20.

April, S., & Magrinelli Orsi, M. (2013). *Gladue practices in the provinces and territories.* Retrieved from www.justice.gc.ca/eng/rp-pr/csj-sjc/ccs-ajc/rr12_11/rr12_11.pdf

Bugmy v The Queen. (2013). 249 CLR 571.

Council of Yukon First Nations. (2015). *Yukon Gladue—Research & Resource Identification Project.* Retrieved from www.lawsocietyyukon.com/pdf/YukonGladueReport2015.pdf

Criminal Code, RSC. (1985). c C-46, 718.2(e).

Douglas, K. S., Cox, D. N., & Webster, C. D. (1999). Violence risk assessment: Science and practice. *Legal and Criminological Psychology, 4*, 149–184. https://doi.org/10.1348/135532599167824

Douglas, K. S., & Reeves, K. (2010). The HCR-20 violence risk assessment scheme: Overview and review of the research. In R. K. Otto & K. S. Douglas (Eds.), *Handbook of violence risk assessment* (pp. 3–19). New York, NY: Routledge/Taylor & Francis Group.

Dudgeon, P., Rickwood, D., Garvey, D., & Gridley, H. (2014). A history of Indigenous psychology. In P. Dudgeon, H. Milroy, & R. Walker (Eds.), *Working together: Aboriginal and Torres Strait Islander mental health and wellbeing principles and practice* (2nd ed., pp. 39–54). Canberra: Australian Government Department of the Prime Minister and Cabinet.

Farrelly, A., Rosner, F., Kienzel, O., & Shields, P. (2014). *What Gladue reports must contain.* British Columbia: Legal Services Society.

Gillies, C. (2013). Establishing the United Nations' declaration on the rights of Indigenous peoples as the minimum standard for all forensic practice with Australian Indigenous peoples. *Australian Psychologist, 48*, 14–27. https://doi.org/10.1111/ap.12003

Grove, W. M., Zald, D. H., Lebow, B. S., Snitz, B. E., & Nelson, C. (2000). Clinical versus mechanical prediction: A meta-analysis. *Psychological Assessment, 12*, 19–30. https://doi.org/10.1037/1040-3590.12.1.19

Hannah-Moffat, K. (2005). Criminogenic needs and the transformative risk subject: Hybridizations of risk/need in penalty. *Punishment & Society, 7*, 29–51. https://doi.org/10.1177/1462474505048132

Hannah-Moffat, K., & Maurutto, P. (2010). Re-contextualizing pre-sentence reports: Risk and race. *Punishment & Society, 12*, 262–286. https://doi.org/10.1177/1462474510369442

Hart, S. D. (2016). Culture and violence risk assessment: The case of Ewert v. Canada. *Journal of Threat Assessment and Management, 3*, 76–96. https://doi.org/10.1037/tam0000068

Kicknosway, C. (2015). *Gladue reports: Not just a sentencing report.* Retrieved from https://blog.legalaid.on.ca/2015/03/13/gladue-reports-not-just-a-sentencing-report/

Maurutto, P., & Hannah-Moffat, K. (2006). Assembling risk and the restructuring of penal control. *British Journal of Criminology, 46*, 438–454. https://doi.org/10.1093/bjc/azi073

McCulloch, J., Maher, J., Fitz-Gibbon, K., Segrave, M., & Roffee, J. (2016). *Review of the family violence risk assessment and risk management framework (CRAF).* Prepared for the Department of Health and Human Services by the School of Social Sciences, Focus Program on Gender and Family Violence: New Frameworks in Prevention, Monash University.

McSherry, B. (2004). *Risk assessment by mental health professionals and the prevention of future violence behavior* (Trends & Issues in Crime and Criminal Justice no. 281). Canberra: Australian Institute of Criminology.

Messing, J. T., Amanor-Boadu, Y., Cavanaugh, C. E., Glass, N. E., & Campbell, J. C. (2013). Culturally competent intimate partner violence risk assessment: Adapting the danger assessment for immigrant women. *Social Work Research, 37*, 263–275. https://doi.org/10.1093/swr/svt019

Olver, M. E., Stockdale, K. C., & Wormith, J. S. (2009). Risk assessment with young offenders: A meta-analysis of three assessment measures. *Criminal Justice and Behavior, 36*, 329–353. https://doi.org/10.1177/0093854809331457

Olver, M. E., Stockdale, K. C., & Wormith, J. S. (2014). Thirty years of research on the level of service scales: A meta-analytic examination of predictive accuracy and sources of variability. *Psychological Assessment, 26*, 156–176. https://doi.org/10.1037/a0035080

O'Malley, P. (2004). *Risk, uncertainty and government.* London: Cavendish Publishing Limited.

R v Gladue. (1999). 1 SCR 688.

R. v. Ipeelee. (2012). 1 S.C.R. 433.

Shepherd, S. M. (2014). Finding color in conformity: A discourse on culturally specific risk factors for violence in Australia. *International Journal of Offender Therapy and Comparative*

Criminology. Advance online publication. https://doi.org/10.1177/0306624X14540492

Shepherd, S. M. (2016). Violence risk instruments may be culturally unsafe for use with Indigenous patients. *Australasian Psychiatry, 24,* 565–567. https://doi.org/10.1177/1039856216665287

Shepherd, S. M., Delgado, R. H., & Paradies, Y. (2017). *The impact of cultural identity on distress, agency, safety and discrimination for Indigenous people in custody.* Manuscript submitted for publication.

Shepherd, S. M., Delgado, R. H., Sherwood, J., & Paradies, Y. (2017). *The impact of Indigenous cultural identity and cultural engagement on violent offending.* Manuscript submitted for publication.

Shepherd, S. M., Delgado, R. H., Sivasubramaniam, D., & Paradies, Y. (2017). *Predictors of distress and the protective impact of cultural engagement for Indigenous prisoners.* Manuscript submitted for publication.

Shepherd, S. M., & Lewis-Fernandez, R. (2016). Forensic risk assessment and cultural diversity—Contemporary challenges and future directions. *Psychology, Public Policy, & Law, 22*(4), 427–438. https://doi.org/10.1037/law0000102

Shepherd, S. M., & Phillips, G. (2015). Cultural "inclusion" or institutional decolonisation? How should prisons address the mental health needs of Indigenous prisoners? *The Australian and New Zealand Journal of Psychiatry, 50,* 307–308.

Shepherd, S. M., & Willis-Esqueda, C. (2017). Indigenous perspectives on violence risk assessment—A thematic analysis. *Punishment & Society, 20*(2).

Singh, J. P., Grann, M., & Fazel, S. (2011). A comparative study of violence risk assessment tools: A systematic review and metaregression analysis of 68 studies involving 25,980 participants. *Clinical Psychology Review, 31,* 499–513. https://doi.org/10.1016/j.cpr.2010.11.009

Tonry, M. (2011). *Punishing race: A continuing American dilemma.* New York, NY: Oxford University Press.

Urquhart, T., & Viljoen, J. (2014). The use of the SAVRY and YLS/CMI in adolescent court proceedings: A case law review. *International Journal of Forensic Mental Health, 13,* 47–61. https://doi.org/10.1080/14999013.2014.885470

Viljoen, J. L., McLachlan, K., & Vincent, G. M. (2010). Assessing violence risk and psychopathy in juvenile and adult offenders: A survey of clinical practices. *Assessment, 17,* 377–395. https://doi.org/10.1177/1073191109359587

Vitacco, M. J., Kurus, S., Erickson, S. K., & Apple, B. N. (2012). The role of the violence risk appraisal guide and historical, clinical, risk-20 in U.S. courts: A case law survey. *Psychology, Public Policy, and Law, 18,* 361–391. https://doi.org/10.1037/a0025834

Ward, T., & Maruna, S. (2007). *Rehabilitation: Beyond the risk paradigm.* New York, NY: Routledge.

Reading 6.4   Fieldwork Protocol as a Safety Inventory Tool in Public Places

Crime Prevention through Environmental Design (CPTED) demonstrates that architects, city planners, law enforcement, and criminologists can work together to promote safety and social cohesion. Part of this effort involves evaluating public spaces to determine if changes are necessary and whether such changes are effective. A typical part of such evaluations is fieldwork observations, often using premade data collection instruments. Ceccato's (2019) article on the use of fieldwork protocol to assess the safety of multiple types of public spaces gives readers examples of how the validity and reliability of data collection methods can vary with the setting. The research also illustrates the benefit of multiple data collection methods as validity and reliability checks. Ceccato used ten years of fieldwork data to consider how observations fared in terms of content validity, criterion validity, reliability, and generalizability. Some locations differed in their uniformity, as the appearance and visibility of public spaces, such as parks, are likely to change with the seasons. Seasonal variations are unlikely to be found in subway stations or shopping centers.

Fieldwork Protocol as a Safety Inventory Tool in Public Places

Vania Ceccato

Introduction

There is no novelty in stating that crime and fear of crime vary over time and space. To tackle problems of safety, researchers have long been developing tools in an attempt to capture the situational conditions that could lead to crime and/or trigger fear of crime. Some researchers have focused on capturing the quantitative character of the urban landscape and how that affects crime levels and/or fear (Ceccato, Haining, & Signoretta, 2002; de Melo, Matias, & Andresen, 2015; Weisburd, Morris, & Groff, 2009). Others have devoted attention to finding ways of qualitatively assessing links between safety and features of the urban landscape (Armitage, 2013; Bamzar, 2019; Cozens, Saville, & Hillier, 2005; Ekblom, 2019; Grönlund, 2012). Among these quantitative and qualitative approaches, fieldwork protocols (FPs) stand out as a popular tool for data collection. Creswell (2013, p. 168) defines FP as 'a predesigned form used to record information collected during an observation or interview.' Despite the vast use of FP in other research fields (e.g. Creswell, 2013) and also in criminology, there is a lack of

studies assessing their potentialities to collect in-depth data.

The aim of this study is to report on experiences using FPs in guiding the inventory of safety conditions in public places based on environmental criminology theories and approaches. By using validity, reliability, and generalizability criteria, we assess how well FPs work for inspecting and collecting data through observation in subway stations, parks, and shopping centers. We submit that a well-designed FP enhances the quality of the data obtained on-site, which is fundamental for further analysis, either qualitative or quantitative. Principles of environmental criminology, such as situational crime prevention and crime prevention through environmental design (CPTED) and routine activity, work as a theoretical reference in the elaboration of these protocols.

The novelty of this article is that the evaluation of FPs done here combines interdisciplinary knowledge of architecture, urban planning, and environmental criminology. The article is also novel because it systematizes robust evidence in a methodological comparison of studies applied to public places of the same municipality (Stockholm, Sweden) and one in a northern European capital city (Vilnius, Lithuania), stretching over a period of more than 10 years.

Theoretical Background

Safety in Public Places

A public place can take a variety of forms and shapes. It can be a *public park*, open for all, a *station*, where many people pass by but may be restricted at certain hours of the day, or a hermetic *shopping center* that is public but not publicly owned, which means that not all parts are accessible by all. Social interactions and their results in these public places, such as being a victim of crime, are affected by differences in accessibility to these environments both temporally and spatially (Brantingham & Brantingham, 1995; Felson, 2002; Rhodes & Conly, 1981). This constitutes a reason for reflecting about the concept of public place. Public place can be defined as a space legally open and accessible to all without permission of anyone else, like a common (Németh, 2012). Most public places are conditionally free because actions allowed in these spaces fall under the laws of the locality in which these spaces are located.

A public place is more than an accessible place. It may bear a morality, which defines which behaviors are welcome, allowed, wanted, or enforced (Ceccato, 2016). Crime is dependent on a place's morality. The moral norms and the efficacy of their enforcement largely 'depend on what kinds of activities take place within them and what kinds of people tend to be present, both of which are likely to vary by time of day, week and/or year' (Wikström & Treiber, 2017, p. 82). The routine activity approach establishes that crime only occurs where and when the 'basic conditions' for crime are present (Cohen & Felson, 1979) and only when a crime-prone person spends enough time in a criminogenic setting (Wikström, Mann, & Hardie, 2018). A public place 'may become criminogenic when their activities and users encourage (or do not discourage) behavioral norms that conflict with the law, and/or they are ineffective at enforcing the law' (Wikström & Treiber, 2017, p. 82). This criminogenic setting depends on how its microenvironments are designed, how it is used through the day by residents and visitors, and how well it is interlinked to the rest of the neighborhood and city.

Urban Environments and Crime Prevention Through Environmental Design

The type of building, its function, and architectural design influence what occurs in the building, including in places surrounding it. According to situational crime theory (Clarke, 1983, 1997), this implies that environments can be planned following principles that reduce the opportunities for crime. Situational crime theory focuses on opportunity-reducing processes that are aimed at particular forms of crime; entail the management, creation, or manipulation of the immediate environment in as organized and permanent manner as possible; and result in crime being more difficult and risky or less rewarding and justifiable (Clarke, 1997). In an environment, this can be done by stimulating surveillance, fostering territoriality, and reducing areas of conflict by controlling access and improving overall perceived safety (Armitage, 2013; Cozens et al., 2005; Ekblom, 2011, 2019; Iqbal & Ceccato, 2016; Jeffery, 1977; Newman, 1972; Saville, 2013). These principles underlie what is called crime prevention through environmental design (CPTED). CPTED is defined by Crowe (2000, p. 46) as 'the proper design and effective use of the built environment which can lead to a reduction in the fear of crime and the incidence of crime, and to an improvement in the quality of life.' The most traditional principles of CPTED are natural surveillance, access control, territorial reinforcement, and space management, but since the 1960s other principles (Jacobs, 1961; Newman, 1972; Reynald & Elffers, 2009) have been incorporated to include the social dimensions of neighborhoods (Armitage, 2013; Cozens et al., 2005; Saville, 2013; Saville & Clear, 2000). The international literature has shown evidence that incorporating some of these principles of CPTED can help to create a safe and secure environment that encourages social interaction, promoting safety (for a review, see Cozens and Love, 2015).

According to Ceccato, Falk, Parsanezhad, and Tarandi (2018), most CPTED interventions have been implemented together with other situational crime prevention techniques (Clarke, 2012) with reference to housing developments and neighborhoods (e.g. Armitage, 2013; Ceccato & Bamzar, 2016; Clarke, 1983; DeKeseredy, Donnermeyer, & Schwartz, 2009), transportation systems (Ceccato & Paz, 2017; Loukaitou-Sideris, 2012), parks (Iqbal & Ceccato, 2016), and commercial properties and shopping centers (Ceccato & Tcacencu, 2018; Ceccato et al., 2018; Lindblom & Kajalo, 2011).

Observers are the ones that collect the information through inspection of the environment. They have a central role implementing CPTED because they 'inspect' a particular environment, its design (internal and external), how it relates to the rest of the area, and how all these aspects affect crime opportunities and/or perceived safety. Although not free from criticism (Armitage, Monchuk, & Rogerson, 2011; Pain, 2000; Shaftoe & Read, 2005; Sutton, Cherney, & White, 2008) and showing contradictory evidence (Cozens et al., 2005), CPTED is valuable. This approach aims at gaining a better understanding of the effect of micro-spaces on individual behavior, either as a potential target or an offender seeking opportunities.

The most widely known CPTED principle relies on the notion of natural surveillance, which can be implemented in many ways. Open lines of sight in parks by guardians, handlers, and park managers can help to enhance natural surveillance (Felson, 1995), as can the implementation of closed-circuit television (CCTV). Another important dimension refers to *territoriality* and indicates how the physical design can develop a sense of ownership in specific areas (Reynald & Elffers, 2009). Saville (2013) states that *sense of ownership* can help to create the idea of shared standards among different user groups (including gender perspective and people with special needs). *Access control* refers to property control using barriers, enclosures, and entry portals as well as pedestrian-friendly urban streetscapes or the installation of safety information signs through wireless network transmissions (audio/video) in smart cities. This can be combined with *activity support* that encourages interactions between residents and other users, thereby discouraging crime. *Target hardening* is about how the design of a space can make it difficult for people to steal or damage private and/or public property. *Image of the place/ maintenance* informs how pleasant esthetics keep potential criminals away because well-kept environments show that people are in control of the area. These principles have been called in the North American literature, the first generation of CPTED. According to Saville (2018), the second-generation CPTED includes principles that attempt to combine a place's physical features with the social dimension of the environment and promote safety as part of sustainable development through social cohesion, connectivity, and community participation. There is also a third-generation CPTED that relies on the potential of technology solutions to improve safety while adopting a green approach (Saville, 2018). In Scandinavia, CPTED principles have been implemented in the last three decades as a mix of first, second, and third generation in both new and existent residential areas much more as synonym of situational crime prevention than linked to the acronym CPTED.

In principle, CPTED can be implemented in FPs to inspect a particular feature of the environment in relation to safety, be that a park, a building, or a whole neighborhood. These protocols allow data to be gathered on-site after visual inspection or counting of items in the environment by the observer. Data are organized in an analog and/or digital form (through templates, structured questionnaires, checklists, diaries, or notes, for example).

Fieldwork Protocols: Validity, Reliability, and Generalizability

Previous research has shown that fieldwork protocols are able to capture what is most important in the environment to explain why crime (or fear) happens at that particular place and time (Ceccato et al., 2018; Iqbal & Ceccato, 2016). What should one expect from a safety inventory tool such as an FP?

First, it is expected that FPs can work effectively in collecting unbiased data (see issues of the validity and reliability criteria, for example). Second, FPs should provide stable measurements across items in the protocol (see issues of internal validity). Third, FPs can be created in a uniform way but can still be flexible and 'be translated' into different types of public places and contexts (see issues of criterion generalizability, for example). In summary, Table 1 offers a list of the basic conditions for protocols expected to be satisfied when designing protocols for data collection and/or on-site analysis for safety inventory.

Validity refers to the extent to which the FPs capture and measure the 'right' (expected) elements that need to be measured (Kelley, 1972). *Content validity* is the extent to which an FP includes all the constructs of interest, while *criterion validity* is the extent to which an observer's responses to variables in the protocol are correlated with other variables that one would expect them to be correlated with (not necessarily from the FPs). Examples of validity in data collection and on-site analysis using FPs are shown in Table 1.

Equally important when designing the FP is to consider the *reliability* of the tool which, according to Leung (2015), refers to exact replicability of the processes and the results coming from the protocols. This assumes that the use of FPs can be repeated (in different points in time or space) and/or that two or more observers can reach similar interpretations of 'a reality' by using the same questions, categories, and procedures. Measurements and observations on-site are expected to be accurate and consistent across places and across observers. In order to ensure that, time must be dedicated to thorough planning of the fieldwork, data-gathering procedures, sampling size of observers, and on-site techniques. Table 1 shows that *reliability* can be assessed in three ways: across time, across items, and across different observers.

Table 1 Basic Conditions of Fieldwork Protocols in Safety Inventory

Fundamental Elements of FPs	Characterization of FPs for Research
Validity—how successfully the fieldwork protocol has actually achieved what it set out to do.	*Content validity* means that if the protocol is created to assess the presence of four CPTED principles (natural surveillance, access control, territorial reinforcement, and space management) in an area, then these principles should be the backbone of the fieldwork protocol.
	Criterion validity is the extent to which records collected using the protocol correlate (at a particular time or in the feature) with other pre-existing records, as initially hypothesized.
Reliability—the consistency of a measure in the fieldwork protocol, over time, internally, and across observers. It depends on how measurable the hypotheses/relationships are.	*Reliability over time* is the extent to which data collected are consistent over time, e.g. data collected at rush hour compared with data recorded at the same time of the day. *Internal consistency* is dependent on the stability of the measurements across items in the protocol, typically a measure based on the correlations between different items on the same test.
	A fieldwork protocol should promote *inter-observer reliability*, i.e. different observers should show a capacity to identify 'the same reality' or similar evidence when assessing CPTED principles in a particular place.
Generalizability—whether the fieldwork protocol (or findings) can be applicable in other research contexts or situations.	Potential causal links between crime and types of environment (obtained by fieldwork protocols) should be tested and, whenever possible, applied to other environments of the same type, to other contexts, and to other types of events in similar environments.

If one is interested in using FPs in other contexts or other situations, then one should be checking the *generalizability* of the data and analysis on-site. In the case of safety inventories, testing *generalizability* is a challenge and, sometimes, not even desirable, because case studies are often bound to a single framework applied to one or more phenomena (e.g. sexual harassment) in a certain public place (e.g. a park), in a particular context (e.g. city center); hence generalizability of qualitative research findings is usually not a required attribute of quality. However, as demand for knowledge synthesis from qualitative research has grown, evaluation of generalizability has lately increased via qualitative meta-synthesis, by summarizing qualitative findings from disparate studies into a single framework, so that the findings can be used more often in practice and policy (Finfgeld-Connett, 2010; Leung, 2015).

Drawing from the current body of knowledge, we submit that the performance of FPs can be compared using case studies as it is going to be reported in this study.

The Current Study

Study Areas

Fieldwork protocols (FPs) are used for data collection in three different types of public place: subway stations, parks, and shopping centers in Sweden's capital, Stockholm, and a park in the capital of Lithuania, Vilnius. The municipality of Stockholm (*Stockholms stad*) has a population of 960,031 inhabitants (2019), spread over 188 square kilometers, the largest in Sweden and in Scandinavia. As a municipality, the City of Stockholm is subdivided into district councils or boroughs, which carry the responsibility for primary schools and social, leisure, and cultural services within their respective areas. The implementation of CPTED principles started voluntarily in the late 1990s in Sweden. It was not until 2005 that the National Housing Board incorporated some CPTED principles in its policies (Grönlund, 2012). However, even today these principles are not mandatory in new housing developments or commercial buildings.

Stockholm's *subway system* is the 20th longest in the world, with a track length of 110 kilometers divided among three lines: green, red, and blue. The Central Station (*T-Centralen* subway station) has the largest number of passengers per day, in a system composed of 100 stations, of which 47 are underground and 53 above ground (Ceccato, 2013). The *shopping center* used here as study area is a mall located adjacent to a metro line on the outskirts of Stockholm, in an area with relatively high crime levels. When built in the late 1970s, and even when later refurbished, the shopping center was not planned with CPTED principles in mind. Finally, evidence from *parks* is based on two case studies, one from Stockholm, Sweden, and the other from Vilnius, Lithuania. For details about the parks, see Ceccato and Lukyte (2011) and Iqbal and Ceccato (2016).

Data and Methods

In this article, we concentrate on reporting activities under step 4. **Step 1** describes the data collection used in study cases. Note that each case study was developed independently over a course of about 10 years. As step 1 illustrates, rather than adopting a single perspective, this research makes use of both qualitative and quantitative perspectives—a mixed method approach—to allow a better understanding of the problems being researched (Clark & Creswell, 2011). This means we combined data from maps, crime, police data, photographs, and observations with FPs described in detail in each study. **Step 2** describes the processes of combining data from different sources and finding common patterns as well as aspects and issues that showed different patterns when these different data sources were put together. In **step 3**, findings were reported in four different studies as described below.

Steps 1, 2, and 3—Data Collection and Analysis

For the case study of the *subway stations*, FPs were composed of checklists, combined with photographs, and later analyzed with secondary data sources using georelational databases, spatial statistical techniques, and geographical information systems (GIS). Although the internal environments of subway stations follow some common standards (e.g. illumination, platform/lobby structures), they are not exactly the same, which can impact on the stations' vulnerability to crime and perception of safety. To capture these environmental differences, a systematic and detailed inspection using FPs was used in all stations of the subway system. The FPs were detailed checklists implemented in spreadsheets divided into five different parts following the station's parts: the platform, the transition area, the lobby, the exits, and the immediate surrounding area (see Appendix). The station *platform* is where the trains arrive and passengers wait. The *transition area* is the area between the platform and the gates/ticket booths and commonly includes stairs and elevators to the platform. The *lobby* is the area between the gates/ticket booths and the exits or tunnels. The *exits* are areas limited to entering the lobby area, either directly from the street or via a tunnel. The surroundings include the *immediate surroundings* around each exit, i.e. the field of view from a station exit.

In each part, different aspects of the station's environment were collected and measured. For instance, visibility, surveillance capacity, crowdedness, and smell in the elevators were assessed using a low-medium-high scale. Visibility was a function of how much one could see from the location, thereby giving an inside-outside perspective, 'you' in relation to others, while surveillance was defined as how well others can see 'you,' providing the outside-inside perspective. For instance, for all stations the visibility and possibility of surveillance were assessed; any dark places or vandalism was noted and registered using the protocols. Likewise, the presence of security cameras and guards, drunken people, overall crowdedness, and area-specific features such as types of entrance gates, cash machines, and types of wall were noted. For instance, crowdedness was classified as low for 0–5 people, medium for 6–10 people, and high for more than 11 people in each section of the station. Unlike pure

quantitative research which deals primarily with numerical data and quantifiable interpretations of reality, this type of data collection and on-site analysis also involves qualitative research dealing with non-numerical information and its phenomenological interpretation, which directly relates to the human senses and subjectivity (Leung, 2015): in other words, the way we use and perceive the environment. Thus, smell was subjectively categorized (as low, medium, or high) by its strength from, for instance, urine. The features that characterize the stations' surroundings (e.g. the presence of shops, bus stops, parking, ATMs, bars, motorways, parks, litter, drunken people) were checked using these FPs, including in which type of immediate surrounding the station was embedded, such as residential, commercial, or mixed. All subway stations were inspected on a weekday, between 10 am and 4 pm, thus avoiding atypical hours (peak hours and busy weekends) in the summertime. Using crime and perceived safety as dependent variables, we used the data collected at the stations in the FPs as covariates in regression models. (For details, see Ceccato & Uittenbogaard, 2014; Ceccato, Uittenbogaard, & Bamzar, 2013)

For the case study of the *shopping center*, on-site data collection was performed using checklists. Results were later compared with secondary data and complemented with questions from a digital safety survey (Google forms) and photographs. Both results were later mapped using a 3-D model implemented in building information modeling (BIM). Drawing on CPTED principles, a conceptual framework for assessing spaces and times that are criminologically relevant to crime and perceived safety was proposed. How much visitors are exposed to crime depends on their location at a particular time in the mall as well as internal and external features such as good lighting; design and position of doors, windows and staircases; and entrances. The analysis was carried out looking at *functional spaces*, those spaces which have a defined function in the shopping mall, such as stores, restaurants, banks, or toilets. *Open public spaces* in a shopping mall have a key role in terms of safety, as they are settings of convergence at all times. Shopping centers also have *transitional areas*, such as corridors, stairs, and paths. Length and width, location, types of materials, enclosure, and design all affect how safe these transitional areas are. The *entrances/exits* carry the identity of the shopping center. They can be of many types, for pedestrians and for cars, giving access to the parking lot, for example. In any case, well-functioning entrances allow the flow of people (or cars), under normal and emergency conditions. The shopping center's *immediate surroundings* are also an important criminogenic factor for what happens inside the mall. Data were collected through fieldwork inspection using protocols in a spreadsheet completed during a series of visits to the shopping center in particular environments most targeted by crime and incidents of public disturbance. Spots showing high crime areas were inspected using FPs. Fieldwork information was later combined with reports of occurrences of crime (secondary data) over a period of 17 months (from January 2015 to May 2016) and a perceived safety survey applied using mobile telephones and photographs of the shopping center (For details, see Kajalo & Lindblom, 2010; Ceccato et al., 2018; Ceccato, 2018). The crime records constituted by police recorded data collected from three sets of coordinates covering the location of the shopping center and cartographic maps were later digitalized using either AutoCad or GIS.

For the case study of the *parks*, FPs were used on a 'safety walk' (Vilnius case) and a park inspection (case studies in Stockholm), allowing the visual inspection of the park through observations. In Vilnius, the safety walk (or audit) is an inventory of the features of an area (or a park) that affect individuals' perceptions of safety. Safety walks help individuals to look at a space that feels unsafe and determine why it feels unsafe, applying CPTED principles, routine activity theory, and situational crime prevention as guidance. Safety walks can be used to demonstrate how daily fears translate into concerns about the physical environment, which is useful information for planners (Ceccato & Hansson, 2013). During the walk, participants decided when and where to stop if they

felt they had something to tell. Twenty-five individuals participated in the safety walk, which took about one and a half hours on a weekday in the spring of 2011.

The protocol (Figure 1)[1] allowed for each participant to indicate where in the park problems occur, descriptions of the problems, and some basic participant information, such as age and gender. In the example of the park by Iqbal and Ceccato (2016), FPs were also used as a safety inventory tool with safety walks in combination with maps of police-recorded data as well as safety questionnaires as alternative sources of information. Observers using FPs in the park varied their observations over time in an effort to collect data that reflect the park at all times (For details, see Ceccato & Hansson, 2013; Iqbal & Ceccato, 2016).

Step 4—Comparative Assessment of FPs and Scores

Step 4 illustrates how FPs were assessed based on how well FPs performed in 'inspecting and collecting data through observation' in terms of validity, reliability, and generalizability. Since different scales of analysis were used in each study, 'the original data' were not appropriate to indicate how well FPs performed as a data collection/inspection tool. In order to be able to compare the data collected from these studies, 'data' were transformed into 'a qualitative assessment' and 'scores' varying from high to medium and low in terms of validity, reliability, and generalizability, as illustrated in the next section. For example, FPs from parks got much more discrepant evaluations from observers than stations did. This means that stations got a higher score in *generalizability*, for example, than FPs applied to parks did, assuming constant potential differences in the profile of inspectors, such as age and gender.

The final comparative assessment (**Step 4**) was systematically performed for all three public places using three subjective scores—*high*, *medium*, and *low*—linked to the criteria of *validity*, *reliability*, and *generalizability* of FPs. This means that the public place that imposed 'less of a challenge' for FPs as a data collection tool

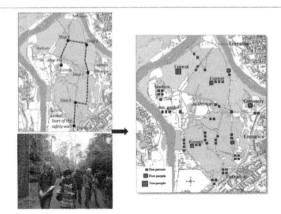

Use of protocols in safety walks

1. Preparation

Invite participants (strive as far as possible to gather people of different backgrounds and interests) that reflect the people who reside and/or work in that particular place. Define time & place for a preparation meeting.

2. Meeting the participants

Explain the aim of the walk. Show how the area to be visited and how they may be split into groups to cover the area. Produce maps of the area where the walk will be held. Show the protocol to be used and how it can be filled in. One aim of the walk is to strengthen the feeling of the area. Discuss with participants the history of the park and changes that have occurred. Encourage participants to bring mobile phones to record the safety walk by taking photographs and recording comments along the way.

3. Introduction to the walk & protocol

Meet at the designated place and time. Propose a route to participants and immediate actions to participants (what to see, what to make notes about, as previously discussed in 2). The leader can plan 1–2 locations as examples and help participants fill in the protocols.

4. Actions along the walk

Ask participants to find places/times that tend to concentrate visitors and whether they can be improved. Ask them to express how it feels (or how they imagine it feels) to be alone at different locations at different times of the day, as well as in different seasons. Stop along the route and keep the conversation open so everyone gets their say. Make sure they keep their eyes open for things that pop up along the way. What does the entrance look like? Is better illumination needed? Are there environmental features that create barriers to access for visitors? Highlight that different groups think of different things when they think of "safety" (be prepared for conflicting views).

5. Actions along the walk

Compile all completed protocols from the participants into a single database. Summarize the experiences and identify problematic locations and any meaningful differences and points of conflict between participants' views. Inform the next steps in the study (using data collected on-site). Provide your contact details to participants so they can get in touch and add information or further thoughts and can get feedback from the fieldwork organizer.

Figure 1 Fieldwork Protocol Used in a Safety Walk through Vingis Park, Vilnius, Lithuania (the route of the safety walk (upper-left corner), participants, and the output map with identification of places described as unsafe)

Source: Based on Ceccato and Hansson (2013)

in terms of *validity*, *reliability*, and *generalizability* earned the highest score (high). Conversely, FPs from parks got much more discrepant evaluations in terms of *validity*, *reliability*, and *generalizability* than FPs applied to stations did, so FPs from parks scored *medium/low* in all assessment criteria. If moderate challenges in the application of an FP were found during the fieldwork in a particular environment, a score of *medium* was associated with the FP. For example, the internal reliability was *medium/low* for parks (because of heterogeneous differences of the park environments, size, and location) but *high* for stations (the standardization of the stations facilitates internal reliability).

Results

Reporting Findings by Type of Public Place

Subway Stations

Findings showed that safety conditions in transport nodes depend on "multi-scale conditions that act at various levels in an urban environment." The analysis involved an evaluation of the relationship between events of crime and environmental attributes of subway stations and surrounding areas collected using FPs, which were later analyzed using regression models and GIS. These conditions are determined by the environmental attributes of the station, the characteristics of the immediate environment, the type of neighborhood in which the station is located, and the relative position of both the station and the neighborhood in the city (Ceccato, 2013). The temporal dimension (peak/off-peak, day of the week, and season) was considered an important dimension of the study.

Shopping Centers

The study showed that violent and property crimes and acts of public disturbance in shopping environments are spatially and temporally clustered in three-dimensional space. In order to assess the environments where crime is most concentrated, a systematic and detailed inspection of the crime locations in the shopping center (including photographic documentation) using FPs was conducted, together with an assessment of the surrounding area of the shopping center.

Results from the visualization combined with the fieldwork inspection provided the basis for making suggestions for improvement of the most targeted settings and/or areas in the shopping center. This analysis was also combined with perception of safety by visitors and published in two publications (Ceccato, 2018; Ceccato et al., 2018) reporting the adequacy and challenges of using FPs when different data sources do not match each other (criterion validity) and when FPs are used in public places that are privately owned.

Parks

The inspection of these two parks brought out a range of issues often found in previous women's safety audits: broken lights, places where it is difficult to get one's bearings (lack of signs), bushes growing in places which would make individuals feel unsafe, graffiti, trash, dogs running around freely, slippery pavement in the winter, prohibited parking areas, and bikers riding on walking paths. These two studies indicate that the most important methodological challenge was to translate CPTED principles into features that could be identified in the parks using FPs to serve as an inventory tool to pinpoint safety problems. Features of territoriality, activity support and target hardening were visible, as was park maintenance. Also, the size of the park made it difficult to control the whole area, and in some places, the design made it permeable for cars. As expected, the problem of poor inter-observer reliability was much more evident in the safety survey in the Vilnius park than in the Stockholm case study. However, FPs were regarded as useful tools of data collection and fieldwork analysis (For details, see Ceccato & Hansson, 2013; Iqbal & Ceccato, 2016). Some of the most important challenges are discussed in detail in the next section.

Assessment of Fieldwork Protocols

Table 2 summarizes how well FPs perform in terms of validity, reliability, and generalizability of the evidence captured by one or more observers in the environment of subway stations, shopping centers, and parks. By comparing the evidence from FPs among themselves as a safety inventory tool (stations, a shopping center, and parks) and with other data sources, one can assess how well this evidence can establish links with these environments. Below we provide a few examples.

Table 2 shows that when using FPs for all three types of public places, it is easier for the observer (the one inspecting the environment) to ensure content validity (how successfully the FP has actually achieved what it set out to do by covering all dimensions under CPTED principles) than criterion validity (e.g. the extent to which observer measures are correlated with other, pre-captured measures). Example: High robbery rates are often validated against measures of poor surveillance or other environmental features of places that promote anonymity (the criterion). Content validity is dependent on the theoretical preparedness and experience of the observer: how well they can transfer their knowledge into the protocol. The observer can ensure that by making sure that all dimensions of the FPs cover the theoretical principles that are being tested. Different types of public place pose challenges to the performance of FPs in terms of validity. They perform better in subway stations (albeit depending on the part of the station) than they do in shopping centers and parks. High validity is found, for instance, in built-up areas of the parks, but low validity in open, forested, or the most remote areas.

Reliability over time is the extent to which data collected are consistent over time, e.g. data collected at rush hour compared with data recorded at the same time of the day. Example: Noise levels in decibels at a subway station's

Table 2 Validity, Reliability, and Generalizability of Evidence from Fieldwork Protocols by Type of Environment

		Environmental Features—Safety Inventory		
		Subway Stations	Shopping Center	Parks
Validity	Content	**High**—depends on the parts of the station, e.g. high validity in the platform but low in transition or surrounding areas. CPTED theory fits well for micro-spaces, but not all elements of it.	**Medium**—depends on the parts and size of the shopping center, e.g. high validity in functional spaces such as stores but low in transition areas and entrances. Theory—as for subways.	**Medium/Low**—not all CPTED principles can be tested in parks (e.g. territoriality). Park size and city location impose limitations to fieldwork protocols. High validity in built-up areas of the park, low in open areas.
	Criterion	**Medium**—factors collected by the protocol do not always automatically indicate causal links with pre-existent measures, e.g. the evidence of presence of CCTVs in a station by the protocol does not automatically validate good levels of surveillance at the station at a particular time and/or in the future.	**Medium**—fieldwork protocols suggest that high levels of luminance in a store (or other functional places) do not automatically validate good levels of illumination or high declared levels of perceived safety, at a particular time or in the future (predictive validity).	**Medium**—as in stations and shopping environments, it is not easy to ascertain the extent to which a measure is related to an outcome using the fieldwork protocol, because causality also depends on pre-existent measures as well as the knowledge and experience of the observer/researcher.

Continued

		Environmental Features—Safety Inventory		
		Subway Stations	Shopping Center	Parks
Reliability	Time	**High/medium**—based on the assumption that the use of fieldwork protocols (with the same questions, categories, and procedures) can be repeated over time. It is crucial to identify beforehand temporal patterns before comparisons are made, e.g. peak and off-peak hours at subway.	**High/medium**—fieldwork protocols produce stable and consistent results as an inventory safety tool. As in stations, knowledge about potential temporal variations of a phenomenon in the shopping center over time is fundamental, such as the number of visitors to the center by hours of the day, days of the week, and season.	**Medium/low**—a park's environment is bound to change with daily, weekly, and seasonal variations (in particular in contexts where winters include cold temperatures), which limits the degree to which fieldwork protocols as an inventory safety tool produce stable and consistent results.
	Internal	**High**—fieldwork protocols used in stations measure whether several items (that propose to measure the same general construct) produce similar scores.	**High**—as in stations, standardized entrance halls facilitate comparisons between different items (e.g. indoor illumination) on the same test using dummy or numerical scales.	**Medium/low**—fieldwork protocols might impose limitations when used for parks because of heterogeneous differences of the park environments, size, and location.
	Observer	**High**—passengers at particular times share commonalities (they are all in transit, going somewhere), which facilitates the use of fieldwork protocols and comparisons within and between groups at particular times.	**Medium**—visitors to a shopping center are far from being homogeneous, looking for different products and/or services. Fieldwork protocols and comparisons within and between groups can be facilitated by grading and Likert scales but also by photographs and notes from different observers.	**Medium**—as in shopping centers, park visitors are far from being homogeneous (passing through to school, sitting on benches, drinking), but they all share a commonality: they are spending time at the park. Fieldwork protocols allow for a variety of different park users in urban planning to increase validity of the tool.
Generalizability		**High/medium**—fieldwork protocols using CPTED principles when applied to stations can easily be generalized throughout the transit system, although differences in contexts (inner city, end stations) impose limitations to the degree of generalization.	**Medium**—potential causal links between crime and types of environments in a shopping center obtained using a fieldwork protocol can be generalizable to other types of shopping centers. However, shopping centers vary highly in size, complexity of services, and location.	**Medium**—as in shopping centers, parks vary highly in size and function (urban forests, neighborhood parks, water parks) as well as location, limiting the generalizability of findings coming from fieldwork protocols, either from inventory of crime location and/or perception of safety.

platform at early rush hour should be similar to noise levels recorded on other days at about the same time. Concerning *reliability* of the measures *over time*, the protocol also scores higher in subway stations than in other environments. Open spaces, such as parks, impose the biggest challenge to the use of FPs, because they vary over time, even more so for a park (unpredicted flow of visitors) than for an indoor shopping mall (predicted flow of visitors).

Internal consistency is dependent on the stability of the measurements across items in the protocol, typically a measure based on the correlations between different items on the same test. In our case studies, we have seen examples when high scores of poorly maintained place correlated with high scores of 'poorly lighted,' broken lamps, and damage illustrating a high score for internal consistency.

It is expected that an FP should promote *inter-observer reliability*, i.e. different observers should show a capacity to identify 'the same reality' or similar evidence when assessing CPTED principles in a particular place. This means that an experienced researcher identifies evidence of territoriality (e.g. detects the presence of a wall between private and public space) in a way similar to how a novice student would, guided by the same FP. This is because the use of FPs assumes that observers share a similar theoretical template to be able to identify similar 'things' in the environment that indicate a problem with safety, or 'environmental weakness' (Ekblom, 2011).

However, it is not always easy to impose this 'common template' from the start, since we may all come together with 'different cognitive templates' regardless how many years of experience as observers we have. This is well illustrated by Ekblom (2011) in his attempt to define 'territoriality' in CPTED. The author points out the difficulty of choosing indicators of territoriality in the field, between the 'real and obvious' hinders and 'the symbolic and subtle' barriers:

> In practical terms (territoriality) is realized often through barriers both symbolic (such as signage or changes in road surface), and real (such as fences defining particular spaces).
>
> (Ekblom, 2011)

The difficulty of keeping a high *inter-observer reliability* can be remediated if observers are always well trained based on the same visual cues before they set off for the fieldwork. From the example above, this means that observers should discuss thoroughly 'the visual cues and boundaries' of CPTED definitions before they go to fieldwork.

A high inter-observer reliability becomes a challenge when CPTED principles are imposed in different country/cultural contexts (Armitage, 2013; Ekblom, 2011). Ekblom (2011) suggests that the concepts and the practical definitions of territoriality—for instance, public, semi-public, and private space as suggested by Newman (1972)—are likely to be individually and culturally determined, particularly with regard to the balance of the individual versus the collective dimensions. The author states that 'territoriality also requires particular roles to be understood: owner, occupier, visitor, intruder and so forth' (Ekblom, 2011, p. 23).

We argue here that poor *inter-observer reliability* promoted by FPs (resulting, say, from observers varying widely on how they assess a particular reality) is not necessarily a limitation of the tool for practical purposes. This is because these differences in perceptions and opinions indicated by observers can be a desirable feature in participatory planning schemes, reflecting perhaps a more interdisciplinary take on a problem.

Overall, when all these criteria were assessed together, FPs scored higher in transit environments than they did in those environments found in shopping centers or parks with regards to generalizability (Tables 2 and 3).

This means that conclusions about a station (drawn from the evidence in these protocols) can more easily be generalized throughout the transit system than can be done for information collected for a shopping center or a park. The standardization of transit systems is the reason for this outcome. While 100 subway stations have some similar elements in their design, structure, and size, shopping centers vary greatly, from a strip mall with a limited number of stores to a large grouping of establishments with a number of eclectic services and functions, including sports, culture, and entertainment. In summary, Table 3 indicates that FPs applied to

Table 3 Overall Assessment of Validity, Reliability and Generalizability of FPs Applied to Subway Stations, Shopping Center, and Parks

	Environmental Features Collected Using FPs*		
	Subway Stations	Shopping Center	Parks
Validity	High	Medium	Medium/Low
	Medium	Medium	Medium
Reliability	High/Medium	High/Medium	Medium/Low
	High	High	Medium/Low
	High	Medium	Medium
Generalizability	High/medium	Medium	Medium
	3 High	**4 Medium**	**3 Medium**
	1 Medium/High	**1 High**	**3 Medium/Low**
	1 Medium	**1 High/Medium**	

* For example, because of differences of the park environments, size, and location, the internal reliability of FPs for parks was classified as *medium/low* while for FPs for stations, where the standardization of the stations facilitates internal reliability, the score assigned was *high*.

subway stations scored 'high' in all three aspects of evaluation (validity, reliability, and generalizability), while parks did not score 'high' in any of them.

Discussion of the Results

Results show that safety inventories in subway stations, a shopping center, and parks indicate the adequacy of FPs as a tool for data collection through observation. Using different methods of analysis, each individual study illustrates that environmental features were captured using FPs. However, FPs as a safety inventory tool for data collection are not free of problems. Some of the challenges relate to validity (content and criterion): in other words, the adequacy of CPTED principles applied to transit environments as well as among the different measures. Others are related to reliability or generalizability.

Overall, FPs are better suited for collecting on-site information for subway stations than for shopping centers or parks. Note, however, that these conclusions are dependent on the following three assumptions.

(1) The observer starts from similar theoretical principles of CPTED/environmental criminology and fear of crime when employing this protocol, which is not always the case. There might be variations in knowledge and experience with the tool or theories that are bound to affect what one sees in reality. On top of that, cultural differences in the way observers approach CPTED are bound to affect the use of FPs (as reference, see the previous discussion about *territoriality*, pointed out by Ekblom (2011)) and how the data collected on-site are interpreted as evidence.

(2) The evidence from the protocols is compared with other data sources, and among types of environment, as done in this study. This ensures a certain degree of validity of the evidence collected in the field.

(3) The relationship between safety and environment captured by the observer is dependent on city-country contexts as well as temporal variations at the time of data collection. Issues of *generalizability* have to be considered for each particular case. As previously discussed, *generalizability* is not always a desirable or relevant feature of research and should not be considered as the 'only' measure of the quality of FPs for data collection. Qualitative meta-synthesis (summarized qualitative findings from disparate studies into a single framework) should be encouraged (Finfgeld-Connett, 2010; Leung, 2015), since the search for *generalizability* from different types of studies and frameworks is fundamental to create a common base for practice and policy.

Conclusions and Recommendations

The aim of this study was to report on the experiences of FPs as a guide for taking inventory of safety conditions in public places. By using validity, reliability, and generalizability criteria, we assessed how well these FPs worked for collecting data in subway stations, parks, and shopping centers. The article summarizes more than 10 years of the research in this field in Sweden and Lithuania, involving different observers using similar FPs. These protocols varied in the way they were employed in the field, from well-structured checklists in subway stations to a loose itinerary template employed in safety walks in parks. Although the inspection of an environment using protocols is not conclusive with regards to whether the environment is the main cause of crime, this article provides some evidence as to how data gathered by these tools can help elucidate the links between crime and environment in a more systematic way. This also applies to the use of protocols to capture the relationship between environment and people's perceived safety.

Future research should devote time to improving *inter-observer reliability* of the data collected using the FPs. This means that different observers should show a capacity to identify (or perceive) similar evidence when assessing CPTED principles in a particular place. Issues of 'minimum agreeable knowledge' of the theoretical concepts among observers before starting the fieldwork would be desirable in future studies, not only related to crime (e.g. CPTED, situational crime prevention, routine activity) but also perceived safety (e.g. basic notions about environmental and personal triggers of fear).

This also involves a discussion of 'a minimum sample of observers' and 'group representativeness' (number of participants by type inspecting an area) taking part in the fieldwork before drawing conclusions about 'types of observer' and 'perceptions of safety' for a particular environment. For detection of problems with both crime and perception of safety, the use of grading and Likert scales as well as photographs and notes can facilitate and guide comparability between measures from different observers. The

internet, mobile phones, and apps of all sorts should be further explored to facilitate data collection. Regardless of the method, pretests such as pilot studies using principles of research validity, reliability, and generalizability are encouraged before applying FPs in full as an inventory tool in a particular study.

This study shows evidence that FPs can be a valuable tool in planning because they can be used by a wide variety of groups of experts and in different circumstances and offer a wide range of benefits to participants from different backgrounds. However, as any other tool, they are not problem-free. Based on current evidence, FPs perform better in subway stations (albeit depending on the part of the station) than they do in shopping centers and parks. FPs, as part of safety walks in particular, have potential as suggested by Dymén and Ceccato (2012) to be a supportive tool for urban planners and safety experts to engage individuals to take action and 'correct' safety problems while contributing to citizens' empowerment.

Discussion Questions

1. What data collection techniques were used at each location of interest? How did the data collection plans address concerns about validity and reliability?
2. Discuss the unique challenges to data collection that the researchers experienced at each site.
3. In what ways did the protocol display problems with reliability?

Note

1   In the edited version for this textbook, the editor renumbered this Figure, as it was labeled Figure 4 in the original article.

References

Armitage, R. (2013). *Crime prevention through housing design: Policy and practice*. Basingstoke: Palgrave Macmillan.

Armitage, R., Monchuk, L., & Rogerson, M. (2011). It looks good, but what is it like to live there? Exploring the impact of innovative housing design on crime. *European Journal on Criminal Policy and Research, 17*, 29–54.

Bamzar, R. (2019). Assessing the quality of the indoor environment of senior housing for a better mobility: A Swedish case study. *Journal of Housing and the Built Environment, 34*(1), 23–60. https://doi.org/10.1007/s10901-018-9623-4.

Brantingham, P., & Brantingham, P. (1995). Criminality of place: Crime generators and crime attractors. *European Journal on Criminal Policy and Research, 3*, 1–26.

Ceccato, V. (2013). *Moving safely: Crime and perceived safety in Stockholm's subway stations*. Plymouth: Lexington.

Ceccato, V. (2016). Public space and the situational conditions of crime and fear. *International Criminal Justice Review, 26*, 69–79.

Ceccato, V., & Bamzar, R. (2016). Elderly victimization and fear of crime in public spaces. *International Criminal Justice Review, 26*, 115–133.

Ceccato, V., Falk, Ö., Parsanezhad, P., & Tarandi, V. (2018). Crime in a Scandinavian shopping centre. In R. Armitage & V. Ceccato (Eds.), *Retail crime: International evidence and prevention* (pp. 179–213). Cham: Palgrave Macmillan.

Ceccato, V., Haining, R., & Signoretta, P. (2002). Exploring crime statistics in Stockholm using spatial analysis tools. *Annals of the Association of American Geographers, 22*, 29–51.

Ceccato, V., & Hansson, M. (2013). Experiences from assessing safety in Vingis park, Vilnius, Lithuania. *Review of European Studies, 5*(5), 1–16.

Ceccato, V., & Lukyte, N. (2011). Safety and sustainability in a city in transition: The case of Vilnius, Lithuania. *Cities, 28*(1), 83–94. https://doi.org/10.1016/j.cities.2010.10.001.

Ceccato, V., & Paz, Y. (2017). Crime in São Paulo's metro system: Sexual crimes against women. *Crime Prevention and Community Safety, 19*, 211–226.

Ceccato, V., & Tcacencu, S. (2018). Perceived safety in a shopping centre: A Swedish case study. In V. Ceccato & R. Armitage (Eds.), *Retail crime* (pp. 215–242). Cham: Palgrave Macmillan.

Ceccato, V., & Uittenbogaard, A. C. (2014). Space-time dynamics of crime in transport nodes. *Annals of the Association of American Geographers, 104*, 131–150.

Ceccato, V., Uittenbogaard, A. C., & Bamzar, R. (2013). Safety in Stockholm's underground stations: The importance of environmental attributes and context. *Security Journal, 26*, 33–59.

Clark, V., & Creswell, J. W. (2011). *Designing and conducting mixed methods research*. Thou-sand Oaks, CA: Sage.

Clarke, R. V. (1983). Situational crime prevention: Its theoretical basis and practical scope. In M. M. Tonry & N. Morris (Eds.), *Crime and justice: An annual review* (pp. 225–256). Chicago: University of Chicago Press.

Clarke, R. V. (1997). *Situational crime prevention: Successful case studies*. New York, NY: Harrow & Heston.

Clarke, R. V. (2012). *The theory of crime prevention through environmental design*. Rutgers University, NJ: CPTED.

Cohen, L. E., & Felson, M. (1979). Social change and crime rate trends: A routine activity approach. *American Sociological Review, 44*, 588–608.

Cozens, P. M., & Love, T. (2015). A review and current status of crime prevention through environmental design (CPTED). *Journal of Planning Literature, 30*, 393–412.

Cozens, P. M., Saville, G., & Hillier, D. (2005). Crime prevention through environmental design (CPTED): A review and modern bibliography. *Property Management, 23*, 328–356.

Creswell, J. W. (2013). *Qualitative inquiry & research design: Choosing among five approaches*. Thousand Oaks, CA: Sage.

Crowe, T. (2000). *Crime prevention through environmental design: Applications of architectural design and space management concepts*. Oxford: Butterworth-Heinemann.

DeKeseredy, W. S., Donnermeyer, J. F., & Schwartz, M. D. (2009). Toward a gendered second generation CPTED for preventing woman abuse in rural communities. *Security Journal, 22*, 178–189.

de Melo, S. N., Matias, L. F., & Andresen, M. A. (2015). Crime concentrations and similarities in spatial crime patterns in a Brazilian context. *Applied Geography, 62*, 314–324.

Dymén, C., & Ceccato, V. (2012). An international perspective of the gender dimension in planning for urban safety. In V. Ceccato (Ed.), *The urban fabric of crime and fear* (pp. 311–339). Netherlands: Springer.

Ekblom, P. (2011). Deconstructing CPTED . . . and reconstructing it for practice, knowledge management and research. *European Journal on Criminal Policy and Research, 17*, 7–28.

Ekblom, P. (2019). Sharpening up CPTED—Towards an ontology based on crime science and ecology. In P. Ekblom & R. Armitage (Eds.), *Rebuilding crime prevention through environmental design: Strengthening the links with crime science* (p. 266). Abingdon, Oxon: Routledge.

Felson, M. (1995). Those who discourage crime. In J. E. Eck & D. Weisburd (Eds.), *Crime and place* (pp. 53–66). Monsey, NY: Criminal Justice Press.

Felson, M. (2002). *Crime and everyday life*. Thousand Oaks, CA: Sage.

Finfgeld-Connett, D. (2010). Generalizability and transferability of meta-synthesis research findings. *Journal of Advanced Nursing, 66*, 246–254.

Grönlund, B. (2012). Is Hammarby Sjöstad a model case? Crime prevention through environmental design in Stockholm, Sweden. In V. Ceccato (Ed.), *The urban fabric of crime and fear* (pp. 283–310). Heidelberg, Netherlands: Springer.

Iqbal, A., & Ceccato, V. (2016). Is CPTED useful to guide the inventory of safety in parks? A study case in Stockholm, Sweden. *International Criminal Justice Review, 26*, 150–168.

Jacobs, J. (1961). *The death and life of great American cities*. New York: Vintage Books.

Jeffery, C. R. (1977). *Crime prevention through environmental design*. Beverly Hills, CA: Sage.

Kajalo, S., & Lindblom, A. (2010). The perceived effectiveness of surveillance in reducing crime at shopping centers in Finland. *Property Management, 28*, 47–59.

Kelley, T. L. (1972). *Interpretation of educational measurements*. New York: Macmillan.

Leung, L. (2015). Validity, reliability, and generalizability in qualitative research. *Journal of Family Medicine and Primary Care, 4*, 324–327.

Lindblom, A., & Kajalo, S. (2011). The use and effectiveness of formal and informal surveillance in reducing shoplifting: A survey in Sweden, Norway and Finland. *The International Review of Retail, Distribution and Consumer Research, 21*, 111–128.

Loukaitou-Sideris, A. (2012). Safe on the move: The importance of the built environment. In V. Ceccato (Ed.), *The urban fabric of crime and fear* (pp. 85–110). Heidelberg, Netherlands: Springer.

Németh, J. (2012). Controlling the commons: How public is public space? *Urban Affairs Review, 48*(6), 811–835

Newman, O. (1972). *Defensible space—Crime prevention through urban design*. New York: Collier Books.

Pain, R. (2000). Place, social relations and the fear of crime: A review. *Progress in Human Geography, 24*, 365–387.

Reynald, D. M., & Elffers, H. (2009). The future of Newman's defensible space theory: Linking defensible space and the routine activities of place. *European Journal of Criminology, 6*, 25–46.

Rhodes, W., & Conly, C. (1981). Crime and mobility: An empirical study. In P. J. Brantingham & P. L. Brantingham (Eds.), *Environmental criminology* (pp. 167–188). Beverly Hills, CA: Sage.

Saville, G. (2013). *Third generation of CPTED*. Retrieved from www.alternation.ca.

Saville, G. (2018). *Safe Growth: Building neighborhoods of safety & livability 230*. Charleston, SC: CreateSpace.

Saville, G., & Clear, T. (2000). Community renaissance with community justice. *The Neighborworks Journal, 18*, 18–24.

Shaftoe, H., & Read, T. (2005). Planning out crime: The appliance of science or an act of faith? In N. Tilley (Ed.), *Handbook of crime prevention and community safety* (pp. 245–265). Devon: Willan Publishing.

Sutton, A., Cherney, A., & White, R. (2008). *Evaluating crime prevention*. Melbourne: Cambridge University Press.

Weisburd, D., Morris, N., & Groff, E. (2009). Hot spots of juvenile crime: A longitudinal study of arrest incidents at street segments in Seattle, Washington. *Journal of Quantitative Criminology, 25*, 443–467.

Wikström, P.-O. H., Mann, R. P., & Hardie, B. (2018). Young people's differential vulnerability to criminogenic exposure: Bridging the gap between people- and place-oriented approaches in the study of crime causation. *European Journal of Criminology, 15*, 10–31.

Wikström, P.-O. H., & Treiber, K. (2017). Beyond risk factors: An analytical approach to crime prevention. In B. Teasdale & M. S. Bradley (Eds.), *Preventing crime and violence* (pp. 73–87). Cham: Springer International Publishing.

7 Measuring Crime

The UCR, NIBRS, and NCVS

There are numerous data-collection initiatives that provide us with valuable information about crime, victimization, criminal case processing, and the corrections system. It is not possible to review all of them in this book, although I do touch on a few in later chapters. For now, I want to cover some of the largest and most commonly used measures of crime in the United States: the Uniform Crime Reports (UCR), the National Incident-Based Reporting System (NIBRS), and the National Crime Victimization Survey (NCVS).

Uniform Crime Reports

The FBI started the **UCR program** in 1930 as an effort to collect aggregate statistics for crime reported to the police. Aggregate, or summary-based, statistics provide us with the number of each type of crime that occurred in a geographic area over a period of time but no details about each individual offense. Over 18,000 federal, state, county, city, tribal, and college/university law enforcement agencies provide yearly data for this voluntary reporting program. While not every agency in the United States participates, most do. As of 2010, agencies with jurisdiction over 300 million people in the United States contributed to the UCR, covering over 97% of the nation's population (Federal Bureau of Investigation, 2010a). States must demonstrate that they have reporting programs in compliance with the UCR program standards and that they maintain quality-control procedures before they are able to participate (Federal Bureau of Investigation, 2010b).

The UCR is divided into two types of crimes—Part I and Part II. Part I crimes are known as index offenses and are serious crimes such as criminal homicide (including murder and non-negligent manslaughter), robbery, aggravated assault, burglary, larceny, motor vehicle theft, and arson. Participating agencies send data regarding the number of Part I offenses known to the police in their jurisdictions to the UCR each month, along with the number of those crimes cleared by arrest or other means. For Part II offenses, jurisdictions only share data for crimes that ended in arrests (Federal Bureau of Investigation, 2011). A full list of Part I and II offenses is available in Figure 7.1.

The UCR produces two sets of statistics—raw numbers of crimes and crime rates. The raw numbers of Part I crimes, for example, tells us how many of each type of crime were reported to the police in a particular area, such as the entire nation, state, county, city, tribal territory, or college or university. The crime rate differs from raw numbers in that rates take into account the size of the population for that jurisdiction. This goes a long way in helping us understand crime in different areas. It is difficult to compare crime in cities and states with different populations. By calculating rates, we can make the numbers much more comparable across both jurisdictions and time. Table 7.1 includes UCR violent crime and homicide data from 2018 for two large cities, New York City, New York and Dallas, Texas. New York City, being much larger, has higher raw numbers of both violent crimes and homicides. If we just looked at those numbers and knew nothing about the two cities, we would assume that New York City is more dangerous. When we calculate the crime rates by taking the number of crimes over the population and then multiply that calculation

Part I	Part II
Criminal homicide	Other assaults (simple)
Forcible rape	Forgery and counterfeiting
Robbery	Fraud
Aggravated assault	Embezzlement
Burglary	Stolen property
Larceny	Vandalism
Motor vehicle theft	Weapons
Arson	Prostitution and commercialized vice
	Sex offenses (except forcible rape, prostitution, and commercialized vice)
	Drug abuse violations
	Gambling
	Offense against the family children
	Driving under the influence
	Liquor laws
	Drunkenness
	Disorderly conduct
	Vagrancy
	All other offenses (except traffic violations)
	Suspicion – arrested for no specific offense and release without formal charges
	Curfew and loitering laws (persons under 18)
	Runaways (persons under 18)

Figure 7.1 UCR Part I and II Offenses

Source: Federal Bureau of Investigation (2010a). *Crime in the United States: About the Uniform Crime Reporting (UCR) Program.* Washington, DC: United States Department of Justice, Federal Bureau of Investigation

Table 7.1 2018 UCR Data for New York City and Dallas, Texas

	Population	Violent Crimes	Violent Crime Rate	Homicides	Homicide Rate
New York, NY	8,523,171	22,436	26.32	156	1.83
Dallas, TX	1,362,465	4,763	34.96	81	5.95

Source: Federal Bureau of Investigations (2019)

by 100,000, we get a much different picture. New York City actually has less violent crimes and fewer homicides per 100,000 residents than Dallas.

In addition to data on Part I and Part II offenses, the UCR also collects data on the age, sex, and race of people arrested; law enforcement officers killed or assaulted; and estimates of reported hate crimes (Federal Bureau of Investigation, 2011). The UCR also includes the Supplemental Homicide Report, which provides detailed information about murders and non-negligent manslaughters.

The UCR has a number of drawbacks as a measure of crime. It is largely a summary-based report, meaning the data are aggregated by jurisdiction. The UCR can provide us with data about crime rates in our own cities, but we cannot then disaggregate the data to focus on more specific locations, such as neighborhoods, streets, or census tracts. With the exception of homicides, the UCR lacks detailed data about each crime incident. Additionally, the UCR instructs jurisdictions to use the hierarchy rule when recording offenses. The rule "requires that when more than one Part I offense is classified, the law enforcement agency must locate the offense that is highest on the hierarchy list and score that offense involved and not the other offense(s) in the multiple-offense situation" (Federal Bureau of Investigation, 2004, p. 10). The result of the hierarchy rule is an undercounting of crimes known to the police. Imagine a scenario in which someone robs a convenience store, murders the clerk, carjacks someone outside, and then eludes the police and resists arrest. Most of those crimes will not be included in the UCR. The exception to the hierarchy rule is an incident that involves multiple crimes including arson. In that case, arson plus the other most serious offense are both counted (Federal Bureau of Investigation, 2004). The UCR also does not include some important categories of offenses, such as white-collar or financial crimes and any computer-based offenses.

Additional weaknesses of the UCR stem from the use of police records. Using police-generated data to measure "**victimless crimes**," such as drug dealing, drug use, prostitution, and gambling, is problematic. Think about how crimes come to the attention of police. The police will occasionally observe crime themselves or even participate in undercover operations to try to catch offenders, but most crime comes to the attention of police through victims and witnesses calling the police for help. For offenses in which both parties were willing participants, it is very unlikely that either will call the police, so these "victimless crimes" are very likely to go underreported whenever police data are the source of information.

Even when we consider crimes for which there are clear victims, there is no certainty that people will report them to the police. Several steps must take place for a crime to wind up in the UCR. An individual must notice that something happened and interpret that incident to be a crime. I might notice my wallet is missing, but I could assume that I was careless and lost it when, in fact, it was stolen. Assuming that the person does recognize that a crime was committed, that individual must deem it worthwhile to contact the police. There are a number of reasons why people would be hesitant or unwilling to do so. One possibility is that people might not think that the harm was worth police involvement, or they may think that calling the police is a waste of time since the offender is unlikely to be caught. For the example of my wallet, if I do think it was stolen, I still might not report it if I have no idea who might have taken it. If I do know who took it, I might not call if I suspect it was a friend or relative, as I might not want to get that person in trouble. Other reasons for not calling the police are distrust of law enforcement, fear of reprisals for "snitching," and the need to keep one's own criminal involvement secret. Additionally, marginalized populations, such as LGBT individuals and undocumented immigrants, might fear interacting with the police (Langton, Planty, & Lynch, 2017). If I do call the police, the dispatcher has to interpret what happened, based on my description, and give it a code. After that, the police have to come, determine whether there is evidence of a crime, and decide whether to file a report. Based on what I just described, you can see how lots of incidents will not be recorded and, therefore, never make it into the UCR. That is why the UCR, and any other police-based reporting systems, must always be viewed with caution as reports to the police miss what is called the **dark figure of crime**, or crimes not known to the police.

The Part I UCR crimes that tend to have the least problems with civilian non-reporting are homicides and motor vehicle theft. The reasons for this are simple. Homicide is the most serious offense, and with offense seriousness comes less discretion exercised among individuals about whether to call the police and among police regarding whether to write a report. Plus, as I always tell my students, if there is a dead body lying around, we are all going to be motivated to call some-one about it. For motor vehicle thefts, auto insurance companies require a police report for anyone to file a claim, making it much more likely that people will file a police report.

One final problem with using police data as a measure of crime is that those statistics are subject to manipulation. There are members of police departments whose jobs or promotions depend on being able to produce good numbers and demonstrate that they are effective at reducing crime. Police who are attempting to convince the mayor or governor's office to provide them with more funding might even be tempted to artificially inflate crime statistics to make it seem as though crime is worse than it actually is. In 2009, an officer with the New York City Police Department revealed that his fellow officers were purposely downgrading felonies, neglecting to fill out reports, and even discouraging victims from filing complaints to give the appearance that crime was decreasing in their jurisdiction (Francescani, 2012). Rape statistics are particularly susceptible to manipulation, and police departments in St. Louis, Philadelphia, New Orleans, and Baltimore were found to have manipulated rape statistics to make it appear as though crime was dropping or that the police were doing an exceptional job of solving crimes (Yung, 2014). Throughout the 1990s, the St. Paul, Min-nesota, Police Department claimed to have a 90 to 100 percent clearance rate for rape cases. By 1999, they were claiming to have "cleared" 108% of the city's rapes, which is obviously impossible (Fazlollah, 2001).

The Philadelphia Police Department submitted very inaccurate crime statistics to the UCR during the 1990s, and these figures were only corrected after a new police commissioner ordered a thorough audit of crime reporting. Commissioner John Timoney was immediately suspicious of Philadelphia's statistics, as they appeared to be too low for such a large city. Upon investiga-tion, it became evident that the police had been doing what they called "going down with crime." For example, following an incident in which a woman with a knife chased an elderly man into his apartment bathroom and stole items from his house, this crime, initially written up as a robbery, was later reclassified as a disturbance. This is important, since robbery is a Part I offense that would have required UCR reporting, so this downgrade essentially made the crime disappear from Philadelphia's UCR records. Police also routinely wrote up burglaries as "lost property" and rapes as "investigate persons," meaning that neither of these types of crimes were making it to the UCR. Several other offenses were downgraded from Part I to Part II (Fazlollah, Matza, & McCoy, 1998).

Commanders of individual precincts and even the police chiefs can feel pressure to lower crime rates and be tempted to help their officers, and their own careers, by tampering with statistics. Unfortunately, the public is often at the mercy of those collecting the data, and we have to rely on them to be honest. Luckily, there are people like the commissioner who questioned the Philadelphia statistics and members of the media who monitor irregularities and expose them when they do occur. Even statisticians and non–law enforcement crime experts can be of assistance. Jan Chaiken, then director of the Bureau of Justice Statistics, noted that he and others who reviewed the Phila-delphia crime data from the 1990s were suspicious partially because of one major irregularity. As I mentioned earlier, homicide data from the UCR are generally reliable because those numbers are too difficult to manipulate. Cities typically report 50 aggravated assaults for every single homicide, yet Philadelphia was reporting only about 15 aggravated assault for every homicide, and that made some crime experts suspicious (Fazlollah et al., 1998).

National Incident-Based Reporting System

NIBRS, introduced by the FBI in the mid-1980s, is a more comprehensive reporting system and expands on the country's crime data collection efforts. The FBI set a goal of moving entirely from UCR to NIBRS by January 1, 2021. Progress on this has been slow, given what a substantial undertaking this is. Like the UCR, NIBRS is a measure of crimes known to the police. As of 2014, 44% of the country's 17,429 agencies were providing NIBRS data to the FBI, and thousands more agencies have committed to being NIBRS compliant by the early 2020s (Federal Bureau of Investigation, 2020).

Unlike the UCR, NIBRS is an incident-based reporting system. As a summary measure, the UCR requires departments to provide numbers of how many crimes occurred each month. The only crimes that are treated as incident based in the UCR are murder and non-negligent manslaughter, since those data appear in the UCR's Supplemental Homicide Report. For homicides, agencies report not only how many murders and non-negligent manslaughters they responded to each month but also victim and offender demographics, murder weapon, victim-offender relationship, and other circumstances surrounding the crime (e.g., gang-related, robbery, argument, etc.) (United States Bureau of Justice Statistics, 2014). For all other offenses, the UCR serves as a simple count of crimes reported for Part I offenses and arrests for Part II offenses.

Not only does NIBRS require more details about each crime, it also includes more crimes than the UCR. Instead of Part I and Part II offenses, NIBRS has Groups A and B. Group A consists of 46 specific crimes lumped into 22 crime categories (see Figure 7.2). Law enforcement agencies are required to provide information about all these crimes that are reported to the police. Group B includes 10 offense categories that are only reported to NIBRS if an arrest is made. The NIBRS also classifies offenses by their type of harm, specifically to society, to other persons, or to property. Crimes against society are what are typically thought of as "victimless" crimes, such as drug offenses, gambling, and prostitution. For each crime, NIBRS collects information about several characteristics of the crime, each of which is referred to as a data element. There are currently 57 different data elements contained in six data segments—administrative, offense, victim, property, offender, and arrest report—that need to be collected for each reported crime (Federal Bureau of Investigation, 2011). Since there are both a wider range of offenses and more detailed data collection requirements for NIBRS than for the UCR, it is easy to see how much more work needs to be put into NIBRS reporting.

Group A offenses		Group B offenses	
Arson	Kidnapping/abduction	Bad checks	
Assaults (aggravated, simple, intimidation)	Larceny/theft	Curfew/loitering/ vagrancy	Liquor law violations
Bribery	Motor vehicle theft	Disorderly conduct	Peeping Tom
Burglary	Pornography/Obscene material	Driving under the influence	Trespass of real property
Counterfeiting/forgery	Prostitution offenses	Drunkenness	All other offenses
Drug/narcotic offenses	Robbery	Family offenses, nonviolent	
Embezzlement	Sex offenses, forcible		
Extortion/blackmail	Sex offenses, nonforcible		
Fraud	Stolen property offenses		
Gambling	Weapons law violations		
Homicide			

Figure 7.2 NIBRS Offenses

Source: Federal Bureau of Investigation (2011). *A guide to understanding NIBRS.* Washington, DC: United States Department of Justice, Federal Bureau of Investigation.

Since NIBRS is incident based, it does not use the hierarchy rule. This means that up to ten offense types can be recorded within one incident. For the example of a convenience store robbery that turned into a murder, followed by a carjacking, eluding the police, and then resisting arrest, all these crimes would be eligible to be counted by NIBRS, unlike with the UCR. Additionally, the NIBRS definitions tend to be more encompassing, so intimidation is now recorded under assaults, and specific forcible and non-forcible sex offenses are included, instead of just rape as in the UCR. NIBRS also makes the distinction between attempted and completed crimes. Victimless crimes, or crimes against society, are included in Group A for NIBRS, meaning that all police reports of those crimes appear in NIBRS reports, whereas they are Part II UCR crimes and would only be reported in the event of an arrest. NIBRS also allows for data collection concerning whether a computer was used in the process of committing a crime, something that the UCR does not do. While NIBRS is a substantial improvement over the UCR, we must remember that it is still subject to all the reporting problems inherent in the use of police data. NIBRS is still largely reliant on people reporting crimes to the police and the police accurately recording each incident. While NIBRS expands what we know about crime, it will still not reveal the dark figure of crimes not reported to the police.

National Crime Victimization Survey

The **NCVS** is a panel study conducted by the US Census Bureau. The research involves a nationally representative sample of households in the United States. Once selected, every member of the household who is at least 12 years old participates in an in-person interview using computer-assisted personal-interview software, followed by six additional interviews spaced six months apart, most of which occur over telephone. After 3.5 years, households are rotated out of the sample and replaced by new ones. In 2018, 151,055 households and 242,928 individuals completed interviews (Morgan & Oudekerk, 2019).

The purpose of the NCVS is to capture data on victimization (threatened, attempted, and completed crimes) against the individuals interviewed or their households. NCVS collects detailed information about each reported victimization, but more so for violent offenses. When an individual reports violent victimization, interviewers seek information about the victim's demographic characteristics, victim-offender relationship, type of crime, whether a weapon was involved, whether the offense was reported to the police, type of injuries, and where the incident occurred. For property crimes against the household, NCVS includes information about the household itself, including house size, household income, region, location of residence, and type of crime.

NCVS serves an important purpose in that it collects data on crimes that both are and are not reported to the police. NCVS provides three different types of victimization measurements—victimization, incidents, and prevalence. For victimizations, researchers calculate the **victimization rate** by dividing the number of victimizations during a time period by the number of persons in that population and multiplying that by 1,000. In the event of a property crime, the denominator for the equation becomes the number of households rather than the number of people. Incidents differ from victimizations in that the former counts the number of specific criminal acts. Since **incidents** can have more than one victim involved, incident estimates are adjusted to account for the possibility of multiple victims reporting one incident. Finally, **prevalence** rates count the number of unique persons or households experiencing at least one victimization during a period of time. Prevalence rates are the number of victims or households experiencing victimization during a given time period over the total number of persons or households, multiplied by 100. In the calculation of incidents, a person being robbed twice during an interview period would count as two incidents but as one victim in the prevalence rate calculation. The prevalence rate gives us an estimate of the percentage of the population that was victimized at least once during a specified period of time (Morgan & Oudekerk, 2019).

NCVS faces a number of challenges, including those related to relying on respondents' memories to correctly recall incidents. One issue that researchers face is telescoping, or people recalling victimizations but placing them in the incorrect time periods. NCVS researchers work to reduce telescoping by **bounding**. They do the initial interview with respondents and then for the subsequent interview ask "since the last interview . . ." to help with their frames of reference. While placing incidents into the wrong time period is one problem, another is completely forgetting about victimizations that occurred. This is one reason why people might underreport. Another reason for underreporting might be that people sometimes frame victimization at the hands of friends and family as something other than criminal behavior. People also might be too ashamed or embarrassed to report some incidents.

Since NCVS began in 1973, researchers have worked and reworked the survey to trigger participants' memories and make them feel comfortable about answering questions. Figure 7.3 includes NCVS questions that are used to inquire about recent victimizations. If respondents answer affirmatively to any of these, researchers complete a crime incident report to obtain more information about each incident. Notice how the questions provide examples of different methods of assault, such as being hit with a fist, choked, or even being hit with a frying pan. These are attempts to help people remember incidents, including those involving domestic violence. For the sexual assault questions, researchers begin by acknowledging that this is a difficult subject to discuss. Then, they specifically ask about incidents not only involving strangers but also with acquaintances and people who were well known to the victims. These prompts aim to encourage people to report a wide range of sexual assaults, including date rape and assaults at the hands of a relative.

Measuring series victimization is always a challenge in victimization surveys. NCVS defines **series victimization** as crimes that are "similar in type to one another but occur with such frequency that a victim is unable to recall each individual event or describe each event in detail" (Morgan & Oudekerk, 2019, p. 22). These types of victimizations accounted for 1.5% of all victimizations recorded by NCVS in 2018. Excluding or counting these as one victimization would undercount the number of victimizations that actually occurred, but that has traditionally been the practice of

---

1. Other than any incidents already mentioned, has anyone attacked or threatened you in any of these ways…

   a. with any weapon, such as a gun or knife?

   b. with anything like a baseball bat, frying pan, scissors, or stick?

   c. by something thrown, such as a rock or bottle?

   d. by grabbing, punching, or choking?

   e. any rape, attempted rape, or other types of sexual attack?

   f. any face-to-face threats?

   g. any attack or threat of use of force by anyone at all? Please mention it even if you are not certain it was a crime?

2. Incidents involving forced or unwanted sexual acts are often difficult to talk about. Other than any incidents already mentioned, have you been forced or coerced to engage in unwanted sexual activity by…

   a. someone you did not know?

   b. a casual acquaintance?

   c. someone you know well?

Figure 7.3 NCVS Victimization Questions

Source: Morgan, R. E. & Oudekerk, B. A. (2019). *Criminal Victimization, 2018.* Washington, DC: United States Department of Justice Bureau of Justice Statistics.

victimization surveys. Series victimizations tend to be problematic as victims have to estimate how many incidents occurred, and they do not always recall details of each incident. During the early stages of the NCVS, formerly called the National Crime Survey (NCS), series victimization was defined as at least three incidents of the same general type of crime, but researchers discovered that victims were better able to remember details of incidents within series that involved at least six criminal incidents. This discovery prompted NCVS to change their series victimization criteria to at least six incidents during the data collection period. NCVS caps the number of incidents in one series at ten as researchers found that reliability of series reporting began to suffer in series with more than ten incidents. If respondents report that the series included at least six victimizations but are unsure of the exact number of incidents, for reliability purposes, those series are coded as including six incidents (Lauritsen, Owens, Planty, Rand, & Truman, 2012).

In the 2010s, the NCVS embarked on a significant redesign. NCVS was initially developed with the goal of comparing NCVS victimization figures to the UCR index crime numbers, so the original NCVS survey largely focused on street crimes. The first major set of changes with this redesign expanded the types of crimes included in the NCVS. Stalking, fraud, and identity theft were recently added. NCVS identity theft data revealed that victims lose more to identity theft than to all other property crimes included in the survey. Additionally, the trauma suffered by victims of identity theft often reaches the level of psychological harm experienced by victims of violent crime. Second, NCVS started to collect more information about all respondents, including disability status, gender identity, and whether they identify as LGBT. These questions are important, given the overrepresentation of these groups in crime victimization. Researchers also began asking about veteran status. The third major addition in this redesign is a set of questions measuring residents' perceptions of the police. Those questions serve two purposes. First, it gives us much-needed information about police-community relations. Second, researchers hope that these additional questions will help reduce attrition of participants over the 3.5 years of data collection. Household members who do not have any victimization to report are more likely than recent crime victims to decline to participate in the NCVS follow-up surveys because they do not believe it is worthwhile to sit for an interview when they have nothing to say. These additional questions will be asked of respondents regardless of whether they were victims of crime over the past six months (Langton et al., 2017).

While NCVS and other victimization surveys are important to our understanding of crime, particularly those not reported to the police, they do have their weaknesses. One is that murder and manslaughter are not included in the victimization statistics for the obvious reason that it is not possible to interview someone who is deceased. Another drawback is the lack of information on victimization of children 11 and under since they are not included in the survey plan. Since the NCVS targets households and asks for information about property crime and personal victimization, many crimes are excluded from measurement. Bank robberies; crimes against businesses such as shoplifting, vandalism, and breaking and entering of an office; and white-collar offenses such as insider trading and embezzlement are currently excluded. The use of households for sampling also excludes crimes committed against nonresident visitors to the country, homeless individuals, and institutionalized populations including jail and prison inmates. These exclusions are problematic, given that these groups tend to be at a higher risk for victimization than people living in households. NCVS also does not include victimizations that occurred outside the United States (Morgan & Oudekerk, 2019). Like the UCR and NIBRS, NCVS is also weak when measuring victimless crimes, referred to as crimes against society in the NCVS, such as prostitution, drug dealing, drug use, and gambling.

As of this writing, NCVS data are aggregated at the national level. We can use data on incidents included in NCVS to do incident-level analysis similar to what is possible with NIBRS data. Unlike the UCR and NIBRS, the NCVS does allow for analysis at the individual and household levels, but when looking at geographic areas, NCVS has not allowed for research on specific jurisdictions. This, however, is changing. In 2016, NCVS adjusted their sampling plan to substantially increase the sample size. The purpose of this is to generate state-level victimization estimates for the 22 most populous states (Morgan & Oudekerk, 2019), allowing for some state-level analysis.

Summary

The UCR/NIBRS and NCVS provide the United States with important crime data, but each offers very different types of information. As a summary measure, the UCR gives us figures for selected serious crimes known to the police. The data are aggregated at the university, tribe, city, state, or national level. The UCR includes rules that limit the data's usefulness, including the hierarchy rule prohibiting more than one offense in a crime incident from being reported. The UCR also only provides information on a very limited number of crimes. NIBRS has been expanding with the eventual plan of replacing the UCR, but progress has been slow in light of the very substantial undertaking that is the NIBRS data collection plan. Unlike the UCR, NIBRS is an incident-based measure, meaning for every recorded crime comes the need to collect information about the victim, offender, crime circumstances, and arrest. NIBRS also collects data on a wider variety of crimes than the UCR. Since both measures are generated from police reports, both the UCR and NIBRS are vulnerable to some of the same limitations. Not all crime comes to the attention of the police. Some offenses, particularly those without a clear victim, are especially difficult for the police to detect, resulting in a substantial proportion of those crimes going unreported in the UCR and NIBRS. Police are often reliant on civilians to report crimes, but there are several reasons why someone would choose not to notify the police. Finally, police data are susceptible to manipulation by individuals whose job performance is being measured by the numbers.

The NCVS approaches crime not through police data, but by sampling households and then interviewing all residents who are at least 12 years old about personal and household victimization. While the NCVS reports more crime than what is known to the police, there are still reasons why people underreport victimizations during the interviews. People might not consider what happened to them to be a crime, especially if the perpetrator was someone they knew. Individuals may have forgotten about relatively minor offenses, and they might be too ashamed or embarrassed to report more serious incidents. The NCVS also misses some important types of crime and crime victims. For example, since this is a household-based survey, crimes against businesses are excluded, as are crime victims who live military barracks or in prisons or are homeless.

Keywords

Uniform Crime Reports (UCR)	Series victimization	Dark figure of crime
National Incident-Based Reporting System (NIBRS)	Victimless crimes	Bounding
	National Crime Victimization Survey (NCVS)	

Discussion Questions

1. From the moment a crime is committed, go over all the ways that the information might fail to wind up being reported in the UCR or NCVS.
2. What types of crime are better measured with the UCR/NIBRS than the NCVS?
3. What types of crime are better measured with the NCVS than the UCR/NIBRS?

References

Fazlollah, M. (2001). City, national rape statistics highly suspect. *We News*. https://womensenews.org/2001/01/city-national-rape-statistics-highly-suspect/

Fazlollah, M., Matza, M., & McCoy, C. R. (1998). How to cut city's crime rate: Don't report it. *Philadelphia Inquirer*, A1.

Federal Bureau of Investigation (2004). *Uniform Crime Reporting Handbook*. Washington, DC: United States Department of Justice, Federal Bureau of Investigation.

Federal Bureau of Investigation (2010a). *Crime in the United States: About the Uniform Crime Reporting (UCR) Program*. Washington, DC: United States Department of Justice, Federal Bureau of Investigation.

Federal Bureau of Investigation (2010b). *Crime in the United States: Methodology*. Washington, DC: United States Department of Justice, Federal Bureau of Investigation.

Federal Bureau of Investigation (2011). *A Guide to Understanding NIBRS*. Washington, DC: United States Department of Justice, Federal Bureau of Investigation.

Federal Bureau of Investigation (2019). *January—June 2019 Crime in the United States*. Washington, DC: United States Department of Justice, Federal Bureau of Investigation.

Federal Bureau of Investigation (2020). *National Incident Based Reporting System*. Washington, DC: United States Department of Justice, Federal Bureau of Investigation.

Francescani, C. (2012). NYPD report confirms manipulation of crime stats. *Reuters*. www.reuters.com/article/us-crime-newyork-statistics/nypd-report-confirms-manipulation-of-crime-stats-idUSBRE82818620120309

Langton, L., Planty, M., & Lynch, J. P. (2017). Second Major Redesign of the National Crime Victimization Survey (NCVS). *Criminology & Public Policy*, 16(1), 1049–1074. https://doi.org/10.1111/1745-9133.12335

Lauritsen, J. T., Owens, J. G., Planty, M., Rand, M. R., & Truman, J. L. (2012). *Methods for counting high-frequency repeat victimizations in the National Crime Victimization Survey*. Washington, DC: United States Department of Justice, Bureau of Justice Statistics.

Morgan, R. E., & Oudekerk, B. A. (2019). *Criminal Victimization, 2018*. Washington, DC: United States Department of Justice Bureau of Justice Statistics.

United States Bureau of Justice Statistics (2014). *The Nation's Two Measures of Homicide*. Washington, DC: United States Department of Justice Bureau of Justice Statistics.

Yung, C. R. (2014). How to lie with rape statistics: America's hidden rape crisis. *Iowa Law Review*, 99(3). https://ilr.law.uiowa.edu/print/volume-99-issue-3/how-to-lie-with-rape-statistics-americas-hidden-rape-crisis/

Reading 7.1   Urban Crime Rates and the Changing Face of Immigration

Crime has been a national campaign issue since presidential candidate Barry Goldwater discussed crime during his failed presidential run, followed by Richard Nixon's emphasis on "law and order" in his 1968 presidential campaign. Part of the crime debate has been the role of immigration in contributing to criminal behavior across the country. In 2015, Donald Trump used claims that other countries were sending crime-prone immigrants to the United States as a campaign tool. It was such an important part of his campaign that his first speech as a presidential candidate was on immigrant-generated crime. Immigration might impact crime directly through immigrants themselves either committing crimes or abstaining from illegal behavior. Another possibility is their indirect impact on crime, with their presence in the job market hurting the employment prospects of native-born racial minorities, who are then driven to criminal behavior to support themselves. Adelman, Reid, Markle, Weiss, and Jaret (2017) used publicly available data to study the potential direct and indirect impacts of immigration on crime in cities across the United States over a 40-year period.

Urban Crime Rates and the Changing Face of Immigration: Evidence Across Four Decades

Robert Adelman, Lesley Williams Reid, Gail Markle, Saskia Weiss, and Charles Jaret

Introduction

> When Mexico sends its people, they're not sending their best. They're not sending you. They're not sending you. They're sending people that have lots of problems, and they're bringing those problems with us. They're bringing drugs. They're bringing crime. They're rapists. And some, I assume, are good people.
>
> —Donald Trump, June 16, 2015

From the beginning of the twentieth century to today in the twenty-first, immigrants' alleged propensity for crime has been a common theme in the political discourse surrounding state and federal immigration law (Carter & Steinberg, 2006; Higgins, Gabbidon, & Martin, 2009; Moehling & Piehl, 2009; Sampson, 2008). This theme, as expressed in Donald Trump's statement above, however, stands in sharp contrast

to the findings of existing research on the topic. Immigration-crime research over the past 20 years has widely corroborated the conclusions of a number of early twentieth-century presidential commissions (Wickersham, 1931) that found no support for the immigration-crime connection. Although there are always individual exceptions to aggregate patterns and trends, immigrants commit fewer crimes, on average, than native-born Americans (Bersani, 2014; Butcher & Piehl, 1998; Feldmeyer, 2009; Hagan & Palloni, 1998; Morenoff & Astor, 2006; Olson, Laurikkala, Huff-Corzine, & Corzine, 2009).

Immigration does not occur at a stable and consistent pace. Rates of immigration in the United States have fluctuated dramatically over time and across geographic spaces (Portes & Rumbaut, 2014). For example, in each decade from 1880 to 1930, well over five million immigrants entered the United States, and the foreign-born comprised over 12% of the total population. But from 1930 to 1960, due to restrictive immigration laws, the Great Depression, and World War II, immigration dropped to an average of 1.3 million per decade, and the foreign-born declined from 12% to 5% of the total population (Portes & Rumbaut, 2014). Currently, the percentage of the total U.S. population that is foreign-born is 13%, and the immigrant population itself is 47% Latino, 26% Asian, 18% white, and 8% black (Cohn, 2015). However, annually since 2009, the percentage of Asian immigrants (36%) has surpassed that of Latino immigrants (31%), leading researchers to project that by 2065, the U.S. immigrant population will be 38% Asian and 31% Latino, with the proportion of whites and blacks unchanged (Taylor et al., 2013). Moreover, immigrants are settling in a wider range of states than in the past, with many going to parts of the United States that previously did not have large immigrant communities (e.g., Georgia, Nevada), and many immigrants now directly settle in suburban areas such as Prince William County, Virginia, and Montgomery County, Maryland (Baird, Adelman, Reid, & Jaret, 2008; Wilson & Singer, 2011). Since immigrants are less likely to be criminal offenders than the native-born, it is possible that immigration, as an aggregate-level phenomenon, can affect the overall rate of crime in different places and at different times. In this study, we explore these possible geo-temporal effects of immigration on crime at the macro level.

There are a variety of macro-level explanations about the relationship between immigration and crime. Some scholars contend that immigration indirectly increases aggregate levels of crime by reducing the economic opportunities of native-born Americans (Beck, 1996; Borjas, 1987; Catanzarite, 2003; Johannsson & Shulman, 2003; Shihadeh & Barranco, 2010; Stewart & Hyclak, 1986; Waldinger, 1996, 1997). Immigrants might, for example, displace native-born workers from jobs, forcing the latter to participate in illegal labor markets (Grogger, 1998). In this scenario, immigrants themselves do not commit crimes but instead change the

opportunity structure of non-immigrant workers, which drives them to offend. Other scholars contend that immigrants improve local labor markets by creating jobs and revitalizing inner-city neighborhoods in ways that improve conditions for both immigrants and native-born workers (Adelman & Jaret, 1999; Grant & Parcel, 1990; Light & Gold, 2000; Lyons, Vélez, & Sontoro, 2013; Stansfield, 2013). As a consequence, immigration reduces aggregate levels of crime as increasing labor market opportunities improve native-born Americans' ability to earn an income in legal labor markets (Feldmeyer & Steffensmeier, 2009; Lee & Martinez, 2009; Lee, Martinez, & Rosenfeld, 2001; Reid, Weiss, Adelman, & Jaret, 2005).

Aside from these possible economic-based links between immigration and crime rates, researchers have debated whether immigration creates changes in urban social organization that affect the crime rate. Work examining pre-1900 immigration and crime has focused on impoverished Irish Catholics in American cities. Researchers describe criminally violent Irish street gangs in New York and Philadelphia, mention increased crime rates in the Irish immigrant neighborhood of South Boston, and contend that Irish immigration contributed to higher homicide rates between 1850 and 1875 (Asbury, 1927; Fallows, 1979; Monkkonen, 1989). Wirth (1938) contended that as cities increased in size, density, and heterogeneity (much of it due to immigration), a weakening of traditional and informal means of social control occurred, and an anomic, competitive, even exploitative way of life arose in which crime was more frequent. Other classic Chicago School urban sociologists found high rates of juvenile delinquency and criminal behavior in poor immigrant neighborhoods. They contended this was produced by poverty, lack of opportunities, and social disorganization manifested in so-called broken families, neighborhood instability, and lack of common community standards or morals (Burgess & Bogue, 1964). This view of disorganized, crime-ridden immigrant neighborhoods was challenged and amended by subsequent research showing them to be highly organized and relatively safe places (Suttles,

1968; Sanchez-Jankowski, 2008). More recently, the debate on immigrants and crime was reopened with Putnam's (2007) assertion that increases in metropolitan areas' social diversity (e.g., more and a wider variety of immigrants) causes a decline in social solidarity, social capital, and interpersonal trust, which leads to higher crime.

We evaluate the relationship between the size of the foreign-born population in U.S. metropolitan areas and crime rates in those areas between 1970 and 2010. Examining these longitudinal data allows us to assess whether the relationship between immigration and crime has changed over time and geographic space in the context of changes in the broader U.S. economy and changes in the size and origination of immigrant flows. As the relationships between other socioeconomic factors and crime are historically and geographically contingent, so too may be the relationship between immigration and crime.

Studying the Immigration-Crime Relationship

Some of the most influential and enduring theories within sociology and criminology developed when the founders of the Chicago School observed the social consequences of rapid immigration during the first half of the twentieth century (Park & Burgess, 1924; Shaw & McKay, 1942; Shaw, Zorbaugh, McKay, & Cottrell, 1929). Even during this period of rapid immigration and pervasive anti-immigrant sentiment, data did not indicate a positive relationship between immigration and crime (Hart, 1896; Hourwich, 1912). During the 1930s, researchers' concern about immigrants as a cause of crime waned, largely due to the precipitous drop in immigration resulting from the restrictive immigration laws passed the previous decade. This concern reappeared after Congress passed the Hart-Celler Immigration Reform Act of 1965. Commonly referred to as the Hart-Celler Act, the Immigration and Nationality Act of 1965 amended previous U.S. immigration policy by abolishing the national origins quota system, in place since 1921, and replacing it with a

preference system focusing on relatives of U.S. citizens and permanent residents, professional and highly skilled workers or unskilled workers in needed occupations, and those seeking refuge from violence, persecution, or national calamities (Bureau of Security and Consular Affairs, 1968; Immigration and Nationality Act of 1965; Keely, 1971). By abolishing the quota system and prioritizing family reunification, the common perception was that this law would increase immigration from Latin American countries (Rumbaut, 1994). Although the direct effects of the Hart-Celler Act have been overstated (Massey, 1996; Rumbaut, 1994), overall increases in immigration, not only from nations similar to the United States but also from Asian and Latin American countries, have greatly increased the diversity of U.S. immigrants (Zhou, 2001) and rekindled public concern about its consequences.

Likewise, recent immigration has renewed researchers' interest in the potential connection between immigration and crime. Over the past 15 years, research has attempted to answer two general questions. The first, posed at the individual, or micro, level, asks whether immigrants have a higher propensity to commit crime than the native-born. The second question, posed at the aggregate, or macro, level, asks whether immigrants affect the crime rate by any means, either directly or indirectly.

The Immigration-Crime Relationship Among Individuals

Sociological theories predicting immigrants to be more criminal are frequently based on the assumption that new arrivals are poor (Clark, 1998; DeJong & Madamba, 2001). Basing their arguments on the characteristics of immigrants in the early twentieth century, researchers often followed Merton's (1938) premise, suggesting that immigrants enter the United States poor and experience discrimination in labor markets and blocked pathways to social and economic mobility (Lee et al., 2001; Waldinger, 1997). They consequently use crime in order to improve their economic standing. Moreover, blocked economic opportunities may engender frustration that could lead to violence (Agnew, 1992; Blau & Blau, 1982; Tonry, 1997). Furthermore, systematic discrimination and barriers to social and economic mobility could also lead to the formation of criminal immigrant subcultures that develop into gangs, especially among the children of immigrants (Bankston, 1998; Short, 1997).

These arguments are clearly countered, however, by empirical results showing that immigrants offend less than the native-born U.S. population (Bersani, 2014; Harris, 1999; Sampson, Morenoff, & Rudenbush, 2005; Sampson, 2008). Extant empirical evidence finds that immigrants are less criminal than the native-born population, although there are exceptions for specific immigrant groups. Investigating the relationship between immigration and different types of crime in San Diego and El Paso, Hagan and Palloni (1999) found that immigrants and the native-born have similar rates of arrest for drug, property, and violent crimes. Martinez and Lee (2000) observed that in Miami rates of criminal offending among Haitian, Jamaican, and Mariel Cuban immigrants were less than those of the native-born. Examining homicide among Mariel Cubans, non-Mariel Latinos, whites, Afro-Caribbeans (Haitians and Jamaicans), and native-born blacks, Martinez, Nielsen, and Lee (2003) showed virtually no effect of immigrant status. The only exception was that Afro-Caribbeans were more likely than native-born blacks to commit drug-related homicides. Olson et al. (2009) found that native-born citizens had the highest rate of arrest for homicide, attempted homicide, robbery, and aggravated assault compared to foreign-born citizens, naturalized citizens, and noncitizens in Orange County, Florida (Orlando), but noncitizens had the highest rate of arrest for sexual assault. Nielsen and Martinez (2011) examined arrests for robbery and aggravated assault among specific immigrant groups in Miami and noted that immigrants from Cuba, Haiti, Honduras, Nicaragua, Dominican Republic, and other countries were less likely to be arrested for robbery than for aggravated assault compared to the native-born.

Although immigrants have offending levels lower than those of the native-born, this does not necessarily hold true for their children. Research indicates the likelihood of committing violence increases with successive generations of immigrants (Bersani, 2014; Morenoff & Astor, 2006; Sampson et al., 2005). In Chicago, the odds of committing violence for children of immigrants were 1.33 times those of immigrants themselves, and the odds of violence for grandchildren of immigrants were twice those of immigrants themselves (Sampson et al., 2005). However, it is important to note that, in spite of these generational increases in offending, children and grandchildren of immigrants approach, but do not exceed, the level of offending of the native-born population. Moreover, evidence suggests that the children of more recent immigrants are less delinquent than children whose parents immigrated in the middle part of the twentieth century (Dinovitzer, Hagan, & Levi, 2009).

The Immigration-Crime Relationship at the Macro Level

A number of studies have found that immigrants challenge the wage and job opportunities of the native-born, especially African Americans (e.g., Aydemir & Borjas, 2007; Borjas, 2003). Rosenfeld and Tienda (1999) contend that blacks and some immigrants (e.g., foreign-born Latino) compete in the secondary labor market where jobs require less human capital and offer low wages and harsh working conditions (see also Catanzarite, 2003; Johannsson & Shulman, 2003). Consequently, many non-white immigrants and blacks compete for the same jobs within a metropolitan area (see also Browne, Tigges, & Press, 2001; Moss & Tilly, 2001; Ong & Valenzuela, 1996; Rosenfeld & Tienda, 1999).

Beck (1996) is particularly concerned because immigrants have lower expectations in terms of wages, and he argues that blacks are moved down the job queue by the existence of immigrants in labor markets. Further, Borjas (2003) argued that when examining matched pairs of immigrant and native-born workers based on education, experience, and skill levels, immigrants challenge native-born wages and job security. And ethnographic research suggests that many employers prefer hiring immigrant workers over African Americans (Beck, 1996; Waldinger, 1996, 1997; Wilson, 1987). They perceive the former as reliable while stereotyping native-born blacks as lazy and unreliable (Neckerman & Kirschenman, 1991). Even if immigrants are not themselves involved in crime, their influx into local labor markets could displace native-born workers who must shift their employment to a legitimate/illegitimate work mix in order to survive (Freeman, 1996).

In contradiction to this argument, Zhou (2001) contended that "[t]he image of the poor, uneducated, and unskilled 'huddled masses,' used to depict the turn-of-the-century European immigrants, does not apply to today's newcomers" (p. 206). Since the passage of the Hart-Celler Act, immigrants in the United States have become increasingly diverse with regard to their countries of origin; their racial, ethnic, and religious backgrounds; and their levels of education. Although some groups of immigrants enter the United States with, on average, very low levels of education (e.g., Mexicans), others arrive with college degrees from their home country with which they are able to successfully compete for highly skilled jobs (Zhou, 2001). Consequently, arguments about displacement may overestimate the danger immigrants pose to the occupational opportunities of U.S. low-skilled workers.

Additionally, recent immigrants may not compete directly with native-born workers because they are often employed in ethnically owned niche businesses (Zhou, 1992). If this is the case, then they do not compete with native-born workers and do not reduce the labor market opportunities of the native-born. Moreover, immigrant businesses may provide native-owned businesses with work. Even if an ethnically owned business fills a niche and does not directly compete in the native-born economy, services and materials they require (e.g., transportation, raw materials, and warehousing) likely still improve labor market opportunities for native-born workers (Kotkin, 2000).

Furthermore, as consumers of goods and services, immigrants may increase the customer-base for native-owned businesses (Kotkin, 2000).

In fact, a body of research suggests that immigrant settlement in inner-city areas, many of which still suffer from the population declines and economic disinvestment of the 1970s (Bluestone & Harrison, 1982), has revitalized some of these places (Alba, Denton, Shu-yin, & Logan, 1995; Winnick, 1990). Consequently, it is possible that immigration reduces aggregate levels of crime by actually increasing the labor market opportunities of native-born workers *and* revitalizing urban neighborhoods (Graif & Sampson, 2009; Lee & Martinez, 2009; Lee et al., 2001; Lyons et al., 2013; Reid et al., 2005; Stansfield, 2013). Lyons et al. (2013) argued that immigrants' potential for neighborhood revitalization lies not only in their positive effect on local economies, but in their tendencies toward two-parent families and strong community relationships that enhance social organization.

Extending Immigration-Crime Research

Our study adds to these bodies of research by carefully considering the geographically and temporally contingent nature of the immigration-crime relationship at the macro level. Our study contributes to the current literature in at least two important ways. First, we investigate the possibility that the immigration-crime relationship is temporally and spatially contingent by examining it across metropolitan areas and over a period during which patterns of immigration in the United States varied greatly. Since most contemporary immigration-crime research has been conducted with data from 1990 or later, when the U.S. economy has been relatively prosperous until very recent years, current results might be missing the potential impact of large economic changes. Moreover, the post-1990s were years of high immigration, prohibiting comparisons with earlier eras of lower immigration. Together, these trends make it necessary to reach further back into the history of the United States to investigate the immigration-crime relationship. Therefore, we investigate the relationship between immigration and crime at four points in time over a 40-year period between 1970 and 2010. Second, we consider a much broader range of criminal offenses. Prior research has focused almost entirely on violent crime, specifically homicide, because it is more accurately measured and more troubling to the population (Mosher, Miethe, & Hart, 2010); however, since homicide is statistically rare, we study a broader range of violent crime as well as property crime. In summary, our goal is to describe the ongoing and changing association between immigration and a broad range of violent and property crimes.

Data and Methods

For this study, we drew a stratified sample of 200 Metropolitan Statistical Areas (MSAs) as defined in the 2010 census. We stratified the sample based on region and population size, and thus the sample is representative of the regional distribution of U.S. metropolitan areas. In our sample, all metropolitan areas with a population of one million or more are included, and we chose smaller ones (population 75,000 to one million) with an equal probability of selection method. We matched MSAs over time, merging or separating county-level data as necessary and where possible to account for changes in MSA geographies over time. Without missing data our sample would consist of 1,000 observations (200 for each year under observation). However, due to missing values on both independent and dependent variables, the number of observations for specific years changes.

Variables

Violent and Property Crimes

The dependent variables for this study represent rates (per 100,000 people) of murder and non-negligent manslaughter, aggravated assault, robbery, burglary, and larceny that were known to police at five points in time (1970, 1980, 1990, 2000, and 2010). We obtained the data from the

uniform crime reporting (UCR) program of the FBI (U.S. Department of Justice, 2002, 2012), although missing data also made it necessary to construct some crime rates for specific MSAs using county-level FBI data (U.S. Department of Justice, 2002, 2012) and files from a UCR data utility created by Maltz and Weiss (2006). In those cases in which the latter data had to be used to construct MSA-level crime rates, we added the reported number of offenses for the individual counties composing the MSA (based on FIPS codes) updated through 2010 and transformed them into rates using the reported population of the counties. In addition to rates for individual crimes, we also developed indices for both violent and property crime. The first index sums the rates of murder and non-negligent manslaughter, aggravated assault, and robbery, while the second index sums the rates of burglary and larceny. The two indices will be referred to as the violent crime index and the property crime index, respectively. UCR data follow the hierarchy rule, which means that, in multiple-offense incidents, only the most serious offense is recorded. While National Incident-Based Reporting System (NIBRS) data corrects for this shortcoming, only about one-third of agencies participate in NIBRS today, and NIBRS data are not publicly available prior to 2011. The impact of the hierarchy rule on underestimating UCR crime rates is modest, however. Comparisons of UCR and NIBRS data report that the difference in crime estimates tends to be small, with NIBRS violent crime rates being about 1% higher than the UCR, and NIBRS property crime rates being 2–3% higher than the UCR (Rantala, 2000; U.S. Department of Justice, 2015).

Immigration

The percentage of the MSA population that was born abroad, our main variable of interest, was obtained from the decennial censuses of 1970, 1980, 1990, 2000, and 2010. For this and other variables, 1990–2010 data come directly from the census summary files for the respective years. Data for 1970 and 1980 come from Census of Population and Housing, 1970:

Extract Data (Adams, 1970) and Census of Population and Housing, 1980: Extract Data (Adams, 1980). Since we are interested in how the immigration-crime relationship has changed over the past 40 years, we use 1970 as the reference year. 1970 serves as a useful baseline start date because it is five years after the passage of the Hart-Celler Act and represents a time when unemployment, immigration, and crime were relatively low.

Economic Variables

The effect of immigration on crime may be contingent on the economic situation of a given metropolitan area. In order to test this, we include a number of variables that operationalize the labor market structures and economic well-being of residents in our sample of MSAs. We include a variable that represents the level of unemployment in MSAs in 1970, 1980, 1990, 2000, and 2010. This variable is operationalized as the percentage of the civilian population aged 16 and over that was unemployed at the time of the census data collection in the respective year. Temporally disaggregated descriptive statistics (for space reasons not provided in this article) show that, compared to 1970 (mean = 4.36, std. dev. = 1.4), unemployment in our sample was more prevalent and demonstrated a greater range in 1980 (mean = 6.38, std. dev. = 1.99) and 1990 (mean = 11.07, std. dev. = 3.19), before showing improvement in 2000 (mean = 5.63, std. dev. = 1.73) but then increases sharply in 2010 (mean = 10.65, std. dev. = 2.54). Our sample is, therefore, adequate in determining the potential effects of this variable on the immigration-crime relationship as it represents both increases and decreases in unemployment throughout the past four decades, as well as large regional differences in unemployment across the country.

Manufacturing jobs, such as those of metal workers, woodworkers, fabricators, or assemblers, are usually considered relatively good jobs for less-educated workers. They pay comparatively well, provide chances for advancement and training, and tend to be relatively stable. However, since the late 1960s and early 1970s,

such jobs have increasingly given way to low-skill service sector jobs, jobs that pay little, are unstable, and provide little chance for advancement (Doeringer & Piore, 1971; Gordon, 1972; Osterman, 1975). This has led to fundamental changes in the structure of labor markets in U.S. metropolitan areas, with low-skill jobs becoming far more prevalent and manufacturing declining rapidly. Since immigrants may reduce native-born Americans' chances of employment, it is important that our analyses contain a measure of the relative sizes of the low-skill service and manufacturing sectors. The two variables measuring labor market structure were obtained from the census of the respective years and represent the percentage of the civilian workforce that was employed in these jobs. Specific occupational categories were combined to create a low-skill service sector employment variable based on prior research on segmented labor markets and categorization schemes within this research (Boston, 1990). Similar categorizations have been used previously within criminology (Crutchfield, 1989; Haynie, Weiss, & Piquero, 2008; Weiss & Reid, 2005).

Finally, we account for the economic distress experienced by residents of the MSAs by creating an economic deprivation index. The scale we created incorporates standardized values of the following variables: the natural log of the median family income, the percentage of families living below poverty, the percentage of African American residents, and the percentage of all households in an MSA that are headed by a female householder with no husband present (Reid et al., 2005).

Control Variable

It is a well-established finding that criminal offending is more prevalent among youth and young adults, and is related to the age structure more generally (Moffitt, 1993; Sampson & Laub, 1993; Sampson & Laub, 2001; Farrell, Laycock, & Tilley, 2015). In order to control for the age structure of the population within our MSAs, we include a variable representing the percentage of the population that is below the age of 25.

Analytic Strategy

To begin, we examine the effect of percentage foreign-born on the dependent variables; we also compare the coefficients using 1970 data to those of subsequent years. We employ fixed effects models in this analysis because, compared to random effects models, the technique makes fewer assumptions about the independence of time-varying independent variables (Ousey & Kubrin, 2009).

Our approach in the following analyses is to investigate the effect of the foreign-born population on rates of violent and property crime indices as well as rates of specific crimes. We suspect that the relationship between immigration and crime is not static; rather, it changes over decades as demographic and economic characteristics of U.S. metropolitan areas change.

Results

Trends in Immigration, Violent Crime, and Property Crime Between 1970 and 2010

Figures 1 and 2 show mean rates of violent and property crime per 100,000 residents for our sample of MSAs. In Figure 1, violent crime rates

increased after 1970, peaked around 1990, and then continued to decrease through 2010. Compared to 1970, the violent crime index rate for 1980 showed an increase of 213 crimes per 100,000 persons in the population. In 1990, the rate of violent crime was, on average, 316 incidences above the rate of 1970 before falling to a rate of 157 above the 1970 levels in 2000 and 74 in 2010.

The results for the violent crime index mask some differences observable when we disaggregate them into individual crime categories. Within the 1970–2010 period under study, and with 1970 serving as the reference point, murder appears to have peaked around 1980, with a rate that was, on average, about 2 offenses higher than in 1970. By 1990, murder rates in U.S. metropolitan areas had decreased again and were no longer different from those in 1970. By 2000 and 2010, rates of murder in U.S. metropolitan areas had further decreased to levels that were significantly lower than they were in 1970 (around 5 murders per 100,000).

Robbery follows a similar trend. It appears to have peaked around 1980 (around 69 robberies per 100,000 more than in 1970) and then began to drop. With reference to the 1980 data, the

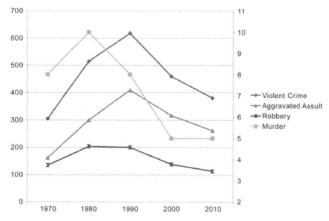

Figure 1 Average Rates of the Violent Crime Index, Murder, Aggravated Assault, and Robbery Across U.S. Metropolitan Areas, 1970–2010 (For scaling reasons, the right axis represents the rate of murder while the left axis represents rates of violent crime, aggravated assault, and robbery)

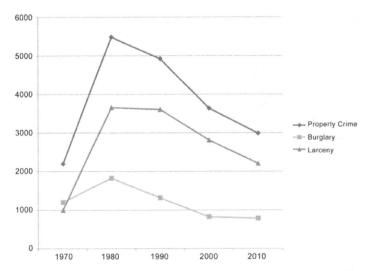

Figure 2 Average Rates of the Property Crime Index, Burglary, and Larceny Across U.S. Metropolitan Areas, 1970–2010

rate of robbery in 1990 had decreased by 3 robberies per 100,000 people. However, even in this year robbery remained 66 crimes per 100,000 people higher than it had been in 1970. By 2000, the rates of robbery had dropped to about the same rate of robbery as in 1970, and in 2010, rates of robbery had decreased again to about 114 robberies per 100,000 people, the lowest level in the robbery data.

The trend for assault is somewhat different from both robbery and murder and is likely the reason for the overall temporal trend in the violence index. Rather than peaking in 1980, as was the case with murder and robbery, rates of aggravated assault increased throughout the 1980s, peaked around 1990, with a rate of aggravated assault that was 247 crimes per 100,000 people higher than in 1970, and declined after that. In 2000, the rate was 154 aggravated assaults higher than in 1970, and even through 2010 the rate was 99 assaults higher. Thus, while murder and robbery occurred most around 1980 and then declined to below 1970 levels in 2010, aggravated assault

peaked ten years later in 1990 and, while it declined somewhat, remained high even by the year 2010 in these metropolitan areas.

Property crime also peaked in 1980 (see Figure 2) and then began to decline. However, as with the case of the violent crime index, the property crime index also masks differences for the two different types of property crime we investigate. Compared to 1970, larcenies increased and peaked around 1980 (3,656 larcenies per 100,000). They then decreased throughout the 1990s and 2000s, when the larceny rate of 2,205 larcenies per 100,000 people for 2010 remained higher than 1970 but was lower than in the three decades before.

The pattern for burglaries is very different. The rates for this crime peaked around 1980 and then began to fall precipitously so that by 1990 the rate was similar to the 1970 rate (about 1,200 versus 1,300 per 100,000 people). By 2000, the rate of burglary had declined to a new low that was 376 burglaries per 100,000 people lower than in 1970, and by 2010 it had dropped even further to 413 burglaries lower, on average, per 100,000 people (at a rate of 786 burglaries per 100,000 people).

Table 1 displays the average crime rates for the 25 MSAs with the largest percentage of foreign-born residents and the 25 MSAs with the smallest percentage of foreign-born residents for each decade between 1970 and 2010. This table shows a linear trend across both sets of MSAs over time. Those MSAs with large foreign-born populations had an average percentage foreign-born of 9.9% in 1970 that grew to 27.3% by 2010. MSAs with small foreign-born populations experienced a similar pattern of growth, beginning with an average percent foreign-born of 1.0% in 1970 and increasing to 2.6% in 2010. These results support the general trend of increasing immigration in the United States as a whole discussed earlier.

Violent crime rates overall began to decline after 1990 in both MSAs with high percentages of foreign-born residents and low percentages of foreign-born residents, following steady increases since 1970. This is consistent with broader trends in violent crime (Parker, 2006).

The violent crime rate is driven primarily by trends in aggravated assault and robbery; looking specifically at homicide reveals some deviations from this overall trend. Homicide rates in MSAs with small foreign-born populations declined across the entire 1970–2010 time period. However, in MSAs with large foreign-born populations, homicide rates peaked in 1980 and then declined through 2010. This decline in homicide rates in MSAs with large foreign-born populations was greater than in MSAs with small foreign-born populations. The result is that, as of 2010, homicide rates are highest in MSAs with small foreign-born populations. By contrast, rates of aggravated assaults and robbery are lowest in those MSAs.

Property crime rates in MSAs with large and small foreign-born populations parallel national trends in property crime (Parker, 2006). Overall property crime rates, as well as rates of burglary and larceny specifically, increased between 1970 and 1980. After 1980, property crime rates began to decline, with the rate of decline increasing after 1990. Moreover, the rate of

Table 1 Average Crime Rates for the 25 MSAs with the Largest Foreign-born Population and the Smallest Foreign-born Population

		2010	2000	1990	1980	1970
Violent crime	Large % foreign born	451.0	557.4	868.3	699.4	360.6
	Small % foreign born	391.5	454.3	551.2	479.0	318.8
Homicide	Large % foreign born	5.2	4.8	10.3	12.0	7.4
	Small % foreign born	6.2	7.3	9.8	10.1	11.3
Aggravated assault	Large % foreign born	291.3	378.0	506.3	363.8	159.6
	Small % foreign born	270.7	308.8	387.0	299.2	196.3
Robbery	Large % foreign born	154.6	174.6	351.7	323.6	193.6
	Small % foreign born	114.5	138.3	154.3	169.7	111.3
Property crime	Large % foreign born	2659.0	3117.8	5139.5	5902.3	2461.8
	Small % foreign born	3370.9	4071.4	4797.5	5176.4	2117.0
Burglary	Large % foreign born	656.6	699.0	1489.8	2121.6	1385.9
	Small % foreign born	963.9	1006.3	1380.2	1725.3	1176.7
Larceny	Large % foreign born	2002.4	2418.9	3649.8	3780.7	1075.9
	Small % foreign born	2407.0	3065.1	3417.3	3451.1	940.3
% foreign born	Large % foreign born	27.3	26.9	21.1	14.1	9.9
	Small % foreign born	2.6	1.9	1.2	1.6	1.0

decline over this time period was more rapid in those MSAs with large foreign-born populations than in those MSAs with small foreign-born populations. Although all property crime rates were higher in MSAs with large foreign-born populations in 1970, by 2010 this pattern had reversed, and MSAs with large foreign-born populations had lower property crime rates than MSAs with small foreign-born populations.

Foreign-Born Group Size as a Predictor of Violent and Property Crime

Most important for the purpose of our research are the postulated relationships between the size of the foreign-born population in U.S. metropolitan areas and rates of crime. In Table 2, we examine a series of models predicting murder, aggravated assault, and robbery in addition to a summary index of the three variables, the violent crime index. In three of the four models, the coefficient for percentage

foreign-born is significant and negative indicating that, as the relative size of the foreign-born population increases, rates of violent crime, murder, and robbery decrease. More specifically, every 1% increase in the foreign-born population decreases the overall violent crime rate by 4.9 crimes. For murder, the decrease is 0.11 crimes (a small but significant effect, especially given the relatively low numbers of murders per 100,000 people) and for robbery, 4.3 crimes per 100,000 population. Percentage foreign-born is not significantly associated with aggravated assault, but we think it is important to note that the direction of the effect is negative.

As a consequence of these results, our findings mirror the larger literature showing either a negative effect of immigration on crime or no significant effect. Following 40 years of increases in immigration in American metropolitan areas, we find no evidence of displacement related to measures of violent crime.

Table 2 Fixed Effects Regression Results for Rates of Violent Crime, Murder, Aggravated Assault, and Robbery on Foreign-born Population

	Violent Crime		Murder		Aggravated Assault		Robbery	
Foreign born (%)	−4.90*	(2.34)	−0.11**	(0.04)	−0.66	(1.71)	−4.27***	(1.00)
Unemployment rate (%)	2.89	(3.63)	0.05	(0.07)	0.24	(2.64)	2.76	(1.70)
Manufacturing (%)	−0.48	(1.56)	−0.08***	(0.03)	−0.52	(1.12)	0.03	(0.72)
Low service sector (%)	−0.42	(2.04)	0.01	(0.04)	−0.79	(1.48)	0.32	(0.96)
Deprivation	−2.04	(4.04)	0.01	(0.07)	−3.15	(2.94)	1.05	(1.90)
Young population (%)	3.72	(4.03)	−0.10	(0.07)	2.08	(2.91)	1.37	(1.89)
Year 1980[†]	218.86***±	(20.29)	1.98***±	(0.38)	140.02***±	(14.70)	74.54***±	(9.48)
Year 1990[†]	357.40***±	(34.62)	1.22±	(0.63)	276.12***±	(25.04)	79.95***±	(16.14)
Year 2000[†]	215.50***	(31.63)	−2.77***±	(0.60)	172.36***±	(22.88)	43.94***	(14.75)
Year 2010[†]	54.08	(78.51)	−1.04±	(3.68)	76.57***	(56.69)	−15.86	(36.55)
N_{obs}	855		857		864		866	
N_{groups}	200		200		200		200	
R^2 overall	0.081		0.134		0.144		0.001	

*$p ≤ 0.05$; **$p ≤ 0.01$; ***$p ≤ 0.001$ (two-tailed)

[†]Coefficients for years represent the average differences in crime compared to 1970 while independent variables are controlled. ± Multiplicative term between percentage foreign-born and dichotomous designator for that year is statistically significant.

Standard errors are in parentheses.

Table 3 Fixed Effects Regression Results for Rates of Property Crime, Burglary, and Larceny on Foreign-born Population

	Property Crime		Burglary		Larceny	
Foreign born (%)	−98.96***	(11.44)	−44.62***	(4.13)	−54.28***	(8.65)
Unemployment rate (%)	43.16*	(17.67)	19.37**	(6.38)	23.64	(13.37)
Manufacturing (%)	6.61	(7.54)	−1.24	(2.72)	7.68	(5.70)
Low service sector (%)	11.54	(9.96)	3.01	(3.60)	8.54	(7.53)
Deprivation	12.59	(19.74)	6.83	(7.13)	5.62	(14.94)
Young population (%)	13.08	(19.53)	1.33	(7.05)	11.92	(14.78)
Year 1980[†]	3,332.46***	(98.59)	646.34***[‡]	(35.61)	2,685.62***	(74.60)
Year 1990[†]	2,765.56***	(167.94)	127.92*	(60.63)	2,639.82***	(127.08)
Year 2000[†]	2,083.14***	(153.37)	−165.78	(55.39)	2,247.57***	(116.06)
Year 2010[†]	1,063.32**	(380.36)	−270.43*	(137.25)	1,327.10***	(287.82)
N_{obs}	865		866		865	
N_{groups}	200		200		200	
$R^2_{overall}$	0.395		0.277		0.499	

*p < 0.05; **p < 0.01; ***p < 0.001 (two-tailed)

[†]Coefficients for years represent the average differences in crime compared to 1970 while independent variables are controlled. [‡]Multiplicative term between percentage foreign-born and dichotomous designator for that year is statistically significant.

Standard errors in parentheses.

An even stronger examination of the relationship between immigration and crime is to study the effect of immigration on property crime because people often commit crimes to acquire economic goods. Our results for property crime in Table 3 show that the size of the foreign-born population is significantly and negatively related to the property crime index, rates of burglary, and rates of larceny. Every 1% increase in the foreign-born population decreases overall property crime by about 99 offenses; it decreases the rate of burglary by 45 crimes and the rate of larceny by around 54 crimes per 100,000 people. This finding is consistent with results of previous research that shows immigrants bring economic improvement by revitalizing formerly deteriorated areas (Reid et al., 2005).

It appears, then, that for the latter part of the twentieth century and early part of the twenty-first, the presence of immigrants consistently helped to decrease violent and property crime in U.S. metropolitan areas. Few other coefficients were significant in the models presented in Tables 2 and 3. The negative effect of manufacturing on murder rates in Table 2 and the positive effect of unemployment on the property crime index and burglary in Table 3 are in directions predicted by the literature. Most of the indicators for year are significant, which means that in these years, crime rates are actually higher or lower (depending on the sign) than they were in 1970, controlling for the independent variables included in the models.

As expected, the explanatory power of our models varies by the crimes under observation. Our economic and demographic variables account for more variation in property crimes than violent offense rates. We explain 40% of the variation in property crime in our data compared to 8% of the variation in violent crime. This is not surprising, since violent crimes are usually based on affect, or emotional processes such as anger. By contrast, property crimes are instrumental in nature and closely tied to economic conditions in both geographic areas and time periods.

Discussion and Conclusion

Despite continuing nativist arguments alleging a causal relationship between immigration and crime, individual-level research based on arrest and offense data of the foreign-born shows that they are overall less likely to offend than native-born Americans. Some argue, however, that regardless of immigrants' relatively low involvement in crime at the individual level, immigration might nevertheless be tied to increases in crime through structural and macro-level mechanisms. In this study, we investigated arguments that suggest immigration displaces native-born residents to such an extent that crime would increase or that immigration in a metropolitan area could help revitalize that area. Thus, we examine how the relationship between immigration and crime varies across four decades during which the United States underwent considerable economic and demographic change, working from the premise that understanding the aggregate-level relationship between immigration and crime requires a longitudinal investigation that includes times of economic stress, as well as times of relative economic well-being.

Our results indicate that, for property crimes, immigration has a consistently negative effect. For violent crimes, immigration has no effect on assault and a negative effect on robbery and murder. This is strong and stable evidence that, at the macro level, immigration does not cause crime to increase in U.S. metropolitan areas, and may even help reduce it. The interpretation of our results gives us pause when considering the current cultural ethos in the United States. The variety of legislation at the state level aimed at immigrants, legal or not, is underscored by popular sentiments about how current immigration is detrimental to the U.S. economically and socially. But at least when it comes to crime—and in fact, on many other counts addressed in the literature—there is no evidence at a metropolitan level of these severe impacts. Our results are clear and overarching that immigration does not lead to increases in crime in American metropolitan areas.

What does lead to increases, or decreases, in crime over time in the United States? One weakness of our article is that we could not include the breadth of variables that have been proposed as possible answers to this question in recent years beyond immigration. We partially capture some, like changes in the size of the youth population that affect the initiation of adolescent offending (Farrell et al., 2015) and shifts in the composition of urban labor markets due to industrial restructuring (Parker, 2008). However, our use of nationally representative longitudinal data at the level of metropolitan areas makes the inclusion of other proposed explanatory factors impossible. Explanatory factors proposed in recent research cover a wide range of phenomena that include such things as changes in gang activity and the militaristic policing of gangs, especially in minority neighborhoods (Costanza & Helms, 2012); increases in cell phone use generating more effective crime prevention through guardianship and increased efficiency in reporting crimes (Orrick & Piquero, 2015); and declines in the uses of cash for financial transactions, including welfare benefits (Wright et al., 2014). It is likely that many factors drove the persistent decline in crime after the early 1990s. Immigration is just one of these.

Clearly, the relationship between immigration and crime is complex, and future research needs to work toward a better understanding of that complexity, including the role of other factors in shaping trends over time. However, the relationship between immigration and our crime measures is robust and consistently negative throughout the four data points we compared to 1970. Since the Hart-Celler Act went into effect only a few years before 1970, this year represents a time period when relatively few new immigrants had entered the country. And, in spite of the varying social conditions in 1970, 1980, 1990, 2000, and 2010, the immigration-property crime relationship remains consistently negative throughout the entire period. Metropolises with higher percentages of foreign-born populations had consistently lower rates of murder, robbery, burglary, and larceny. Thus, our research leads us to conclude that revitalization is most likely the dominant mechanism linking immigration to crime in U.S. metropolitan areas over the past four decades, further solidifying scholarly support for the idea that immigrants, on the whole, have positive impacts on American social and economic life.

Discussion Questions

1. Exactly where did the researchers get their data? Why did they choose one crime database over the other? How might that have impacted the study?

2. What are the other possible factors that might explain some of the changes in crime rates in the selected cities over the 40-year period?

3. How has our occasional reliance on anecdotal information instead of patterns of aggregates impacted the dialog on immigration and crime?

References

Adams, T. K. (1970). *Census of Population and Housing.* United States: Extract Data [computer file]. ICPSR09694-v3. Ann Arbor, MI: Inter-University Consortium for Political and Social Research [distributor], 2007–12–21. https://doi.org/10.3886/ICPSR09694

Adams, T. K. (1980). *Census of Population and Housing.* United States: Extract Data [computer file]. ICPSR09693-v3. Ann Arbor, MI: Inter-University Consortium for Political and Social Research [distributor], 2007–12–21. https://doi.org/10.3886/ICPSR09693

Adelman, R. M., & Jaret, C. (1999). Poverty, race, and U.S. metropolitan social and economic structure. *Journal of Urban Affairs, 21,* 35–56.

Agnew, R. (1992). Foundation for a general strain theory of crime and delinquency. *Criminology, 30,* 47–87.

Akins, S., Rumbaut, R. G., & Stansfield, R. (2009). Immigration, economic disadvantage, and homicide: A community-level analysis of Austin, Texas. *Homicide Studies, 13*(3), 307–314.

Alba, R. D., Denton, N. A., Shu-yin, J. L., & Logan, J. R. (1995). Neighborhood change under conditions of mass immigration. *International Migration Review, 29*(3), 625–656.

Allison, P. D. (2009). *Fixed effects regression models.* Thousand Oaks, CA: Sage Publications.

Asbury, H. (1927). *The gangs of New York: An informal history of the underworld.* New York, NY: Garden City Publishing Co.

Aydemir, A., & Borjas, G. J. (2007). A comparative analysis of the labor market impact of international migration: Canada, Mexico, and the United States. *Journal of the European Economic Association, 5,* 663–708.

Baird, J., Adelman, R. M., Reid, L. W., & Jaret, C. (2008). Immigrant settlement patterns: The role of metropolitan characteristics. *Sociological Inquiry, 78*(3), 310–334.

Bankston III, C. L. (1998). Youth gangs and the new second generation: A review essay. *Aggression and Violent Behavior, 3,* 35–45.

Barranco, R. E. (2013). Latino immigration, interaction, and homicide victimization. *Sociological Spectrum, 33,* 534–553.

Beck, R. (1996). *The case against immigration.* New York, NY: Norton and Company.

Bersani, B. E. (2014). An examination of first and second generation immigrant offending trajectories. *Justice Quarterly, 31*(2), 315–343.

Blau, J. R., & Blau, P. M. (1982). The cost of inequality: Metropolitan structure and violent crime. *American Sociological Review, 47,* 114–129.

Bluestone, B., & Harrison, B. (1982). *The deindustrialization of America: Plant closings, community abandonment and the dismantling of basic industry.* New York, NY: Basic Books.

Borjas, G. J. (1987). Immigrants, minorities, and labor market competition. *Industrial and Labor Relations Review, 40,* 382–392.

Borjas, G. J. (2003). The labor demand curve *is* downward sloping: Reexamining the impact of immigration on the labor market. *Quarterly Journal of Economics, 118,* 1335–1374.

Boston, T. D. (1990). Segmented labor markets: New evidence from a study of four race-gender groups. *Industrial and Labor Relations Review, 44*(1), 99–115.

Browne, I., Tigges, L., & Press, J. (2001). Inequality through labor markets, firms, and families: The intersection of gender and race-ethnicity across three cities. In A. O'Connor, C. Tilly, & L. Bobo (Eds.), *Urban inequality: Evidence from four cities* (pp. 372–406). New York, NY: The Russell Sage Foundation.

Bureau of Security and Consular Affairs. (1968). *Report of the visa office.* Washington, DC: Department of State.

Burgess, E. W., & Bogue, D. J. (1964). The delinquency research of Clifford R. Shaw and Henry D. McCay and associates. In E. W. Burgess & D. J. Bogue (Eds.), *Urban sociology* (pp. 293–317). Chicago, IL: University of Chicago Press.

Butcher, K. F., & Piehl, A. M. (1998). Recent immigrants: Unexpected implications for crime and incarceration. *Industrial and Labor Relations Review, 51,* 654–679.

Carter, B., & Steinberg, J. (2006, March 29). Anchor-advocate on immigration wins viewers. *The New York Times.* Retrieved March 1, 2014 from www.nytimes.com/2006/03/29/politics/29dobbs.html?ex=1301288400&en=d51eba9ff19dd15d&ei=5090%0D%0D&partner=rssuserland&emc=rss&_r=0

Catanzarite, L. (2003). Occupational context and wage competition of new immigrant Latinos with minorities and whites. *Review of Black Political Economy, 31,* 77–94.

Chavez, J. M., & Griffiths, E. (2009). Neighborhood dynamics of urban violence: Understanding the immigration connection. *Homicide Studies, 13*(3), 261–273.

Clark, W. (1998). Mass migration and local outcomes: Is international migration to the United States creating a new urban underclass? *Urban Studies, 35*(3), 371–383.

Cohn, D. (2015). *Future immigration will change the face of America by 2065.* Washington, DC: Pew Research Center. Retrieved from www.pewresearch.org/fact-tank/2015/10/05/future-immigration-will-change-the-face-of-america-by-2065/

Costanza, S. E., & Helms, R. (2012). Street gangs and aggregate homicides: An analysis of effects during the 1990s violent crime peak. *Homicide Studies, 16*(3), 280–307.

Crutchfield, R. D. (1989). Labor stratification and violent crime. *Social Forces, 68*(2), 489–512.

Davies, G., & Fagan, J. (2012). Crime and enforcement in immigrant neighborhoods: Evidence from New York City. *Annals of the American Academy of Political & Social Science, 641*(1), 99–124.

DeJong, G. F., & Madamba, A. B. (2001). A double disadvantage? Minority group, immigrant status, and underemployment in the United States. *Social Science Quarterly, 82*(1), 117–130.

Desmond, S., & Kubrin, C. (2009). The power of place: Immigrant communities and adolescent violence. *The Sociological Quarterly, 50,* 581–607.

Dinovitzer, R., Hagan, J., & Levi, R. (2009). Immigration and youthful illegalities in a global edge city. *Social Forces, 88*(1), 337–372.

Doeringer, P. B., & Piore, M. J. (1971). *Internal labor markets and manpower analysis.* Toronto: D.C. Heath.

Fallows, M. R. (1979). *Irish Americans: Identity and assimilation.* Englewood Cliffs, NJ: Prentice Hall.

Farrell, G., Laycock, G., & Tilley, N. (2015). Debuts and legacies: The crime drop and the role of adolescence-limited and persistent offending. *Crime Science, 4*(16). https://doi.org/10.1186/s40163-015-0028-3

Feldmeyer, B. (2009). Immigration and violence: The offsetting effects of immigrant concentration on Latino violence. *Social Science Research, 38*(3), 717–731.

Feldmeyer, B., & Steffensmeier, D. (2009). Immigration effects on homicide offending for total and race/ethnicity-disaggregated populations (white, black, and Latino). *Homicide Studies, 13*(3), 211–226.

Fitzgerald, M. (2005). Greater convenience but not greater turnout. *American Politics Research, 33*(6), 842–867.

Freeman, R. (1996). The supply of youths to crime. In S. Pozo (Ed.), *Exploring the underground economy* (pp. 81–102). Kalamazoo, MI: W. E. Upjohn Institute for Employment Research.

Gordon, D. M. (1972). *Theories of poverty and unemployment.* Lexington, MA: D.C. Heath.

Graif, C., & Sampson, R. J. (2009). Spatial heterogeneity in the effects of immigration and diversity on neighborhood homicide rates. *Homicide Studies, 13,* 242–260.

Grant, D., & Parcel, T. (1990). Revisiting metropolitan racial inequality: The case for a resource approach. *Social Forces, 68,* 1121–1142.

Grogger, J. T. (1998). Immigration and crime among young black men: Evidence from the national longitudinal survey of youth. In D. S. Hamermesh & F. D. Bean (Eds.), *Help or hinderance? The economic implications of immigration for African Americans* (pp. 322–341). New York, NY: Russell Sage.

Hagan, J., & Palloni, A. (1998). Immigration and crime in the United States. In J. P. Smith & B. Edmonston (Eds.), *The immigration debate: Studies on the economic, demographic, and fiscal effects of immigration* (pp. 367–387). Washington, DC: National Academy Press.

Hagan, J., & Palloni, A. (1999). Sociological criminology and the mythology of Hispanic immigration and crime. *Social Problems, 46,* 617–632.

Harris, C. T., & Feldmeyer, B. (2013). Latino immigration and white, black, and Latino violent crime: A comparison of traditional and nontraditional immigrant destinations. *Social Science Research, 42,* 202–216.

Harris, C. T., Gruenewald, J., & Painter-Davis, N. (2015). Hispanic immigration and black violence at the macro-level: Examining the conditioning effect of victim race/ethnicity. *Sociological Forum, 30,* 62–82.

Harris, K. M. (1999). The health status and risk behaviors of adolescents in immigrant families. In D. J. Hernandez (Ed.), *Children of immigrants: Health, adjustment, and public assistance* (pp. 286–347). Washington, DC: National Academy Press.

Hart, H. H. (1896). Immigration and crime. *American Journal of Sociology, 2,* 369–377.

Haynie, D. L., Weiss, H. E., & Piquero, A. (2008). Race, the economic maturity gap, and criminal offending in young adulthood. *JQ: Justice Quarterly, 25,* 595–622.

Higgins, G. E., Gabbidon, S. L., & Martin, F. (2009). The role of race/ethnicity and race relations on public opinion related to the immigration and crime link. *Journal of Criminal Justice, 38,* 51–56.

Hourwich, I. A. (1912). Immigration and crime. *American Journal of Sociology, 17,* 478–490.

Immigration and Nationality Act of 1965. Pub. L. 89–336; 79 Stat. 99.

Jacobs, D., & Tope, D. (2008). Race, crime, and Republican strength: Minority politics in the post-civil rights era. *Social Science Research, 37,* 1116–1129.

Johannsson, H., & Shulman, S. (2003). Immigration and the employment of African American workers. *The Review of Black Political Economy, 31,* 95–110.

Kail, B. L., Quadagno, J., & Dixon, M. (2009). Can states lead the way to universal coverage? The effect of health-care reform on the uninsured. *Social Science Quarterly, 90,* 1341–1360.

Keely, C. B. (1971). Effects of the immigration act of 1965 on selected population characteristics of immigrants to the United States. *Demography, 8*(2), 157–169.

Kotkin, J. (2000). Movers and shakers. In F. Siegal & J. Rosenberg (Eds.), *Urban society.* Guilford, CT: McGraw Hill/Dushkin.

Kubrin, C. E., & Ishizawa, H. (2012). Why some immigrant neighborhoods are safer than others: Divergent findings from Los Angeles and Chicago. *Annals of the American Academy of Political & Social Science, 641,* 148–173.

Lee, M. T. (2003). *Crime on the border: Immigration and homicide in urban communities.* New York, NY: LFB Scholarly Publishing LLC.

Lee, M. T., & Martinez, R. (2009). Immigration reduces crime: An Emerging scholarly consensus. *Sociology of Crime, Law & Deviance, 13,* 3–16.

Lee, M. T., Martinez, R., & Rosenfeld, R. (2001). Does immigration increase homicide? Negative evidence from three border cities. *Sociological Quarterly, 42,* 559.

Light, I., & Gold, S. (2000). *Ethnic economies.* San Diego, CA: Academic Press.

Lyons, C. J., Vélez, M. B., & Sontoro, W. A. (2013). Neighborhood immigration, violence, and city level immigrant political opportunities. *American Sociological Review, 78,* 604–632.

MacDonald, J. M., Hipp, J. R., & Gill, C. (2013). The effects of immigrant concentration changes in neighborhood crime rates. *Journal of Quantitative Criminology, 29,* 191–215.

Maltz, M. D., & Weiss, H. E. (2006). *Codebook for 'creating a UCR utility'* [Electronic version]. Retrieved from www.ncjrs.gov/pdffiles1/nij/grants/215342.pdf

Martinez, R., Jr., & Lee, M. T. (2000). Comparing the context of immigrant homicides in Miami: Haitians, Jamaicans and Mariels. *International Migration Review, 34,* 794–812.

Martinez, R., Jr., Nielsen, A. L., & Lee, M. T. (2003). Reconsidering the Marielito legacy: Race/ethnicity, nativity, and homicide motives. *Social Science Quarterly, 84,* 397–411.

Martinez, R., Jr., & Stowell, J. I. (2012). Extending immigration and crime studies: National implications and local settings. *Annals of the American Academy of Political & Social Science, 641,* 174–191.

Martinez, R., Jr., Stowell, J. I., & Cancino, J. (2008). A tale of two border cities: Community context, ethnicity, and homicide. *Social Science Quarterly, 89,* 1–16.

Martinez, R., Jr., Stowell, J. I., & Lee, M. T. (2010). Immigration and crime in an era of transformation: A longitudinal analysis of homicides in San Diego neighborhoods, 1980–2000. *Criminology, 48,* 797–829.

Massey, D. S. (1996). The false legacy of the 1965 Immigration Act. *World on the Move, 3,* 2–4.

Merton, R. K. (1938). Social structure and anomie. *American Sociological Review, 3,* 672–682.

Moehling, C., & Piehl, A. M. (2009). Immigration, crime, and incarceration in early twentieth-century America. *Demography, 46,* 739–763.

Moffitt, T. E. (1993). Adolescence-limited and life-course-persistent antisocial behavior: A developmental taxonomy. *Psychological Review, 100,* 674–701.

Monkkonen, E. H. (1989). Diverging homicide rates: England and the United States, 1859–1875. In T. R. Gurr (Ed.), *Violence in America, volume 1: The history of crime* (pp. 80–101). New York, NY: Sage Publications.

Morenoff, J. D., & Astor, A. (2006). Immigrant assimilation and crime: Generational differences in youth violence in Chicago. In R. J. Martinez & A. J. Valenzuela (Eds.), *Immigration and crime: Race, ethnicity, and violence.* New York, NY: New York University Press.

Mosher, C. J., Miethe, T. D., & Hart, T. C. (2010). *The mismeasure of crime.* Thousand Oaks, CA: Sage Publications, Inc.

Moss, P., & Tilly, C. (2001). *Stories employers tell: Race, skill, and hiring in America.* New York, NY: Russell Sage Foundation.

Neckerman, K., & Kirschenman, J. (1991). Hiring strategies, racial bias, and inner-city workers. *Social Problems, 38,* 433–447.

Nielsen, A. L., & Martinez, Jr., R. (2009). The role of immigration for violent deaths. *Homicide Studies, 13*(3), 274–287.

Nielsen, A. L., & Martinez, Jr., R. (2011). Nationality, immigrant groups, and arrest: Examining the diversity of arrestees for urban violent crime. *Journal of Contemporary Criminal Justice, 27*(3), 342–360.

Olson, C. P., Laurikkala, M. K., Huff-Corzine, L., & Corzine, J. (2009). Immigration and violent crime: Citizenship status and social disorganization. *Homicide Studies, 13*(3), 227–241.

Ong, P., & Valenzuela, A. (1996). The labor market: Immigrant effects and racial disparities. In R. Waldinger & M. Bozorgmehr (Eds.), *Ethnic Los Angeles* (pp. 165–191). New York, NY: Russell Sage Foundation.

Orrick, E., & Piquero, A. (2015). Were cell phones associated with lower crime in the 1990s and

2000s? *Journal of Crime and Justice, 38*(2), 222–234.

Osterman, P. (1975). An empirical study of labor market sectoration. *Industrial and Labor Relations Review, 28,* 508–523.

Ousey, G. C., & Kubrin, C. E. (2009). Exploring the connection between immigration and violent crime rates in U.S. cities, 1980–2000. *Social Problems, 56,* 447–473.

Ousey, G. C., & Kubrin, C. E. (2014). Immigration and the changing nature of homicide in U.S. cities, 1980–2010. *Journal of Quantitative Criminology, 30,* 453–483.

Park, R. E., & Burgess, E. W. (1924). *Introduction to the science of sociology.* Chicago, IL: University of Chicago Press.

Parker, K. (2008). *Unequal crime decline: Theorizing race, urban inequality, and criminal violence.* New York, NY: New York University Press.

Portes, A., & Rumbaut, R. (2014). *Immigrant America: A portrait,* 4th edition. Berkeley, CA: University of California Press.

Putnam, R. D. (2007). *E Pluribus Unum:* Diversity and community in the twenty-first century. *Scandinavian Political Studies, 30,* 137–174.

Ramey, D. M. (2013). Immigrant revitalization and neighborhood violent crime in established and new destination cities. *Social Forces, 92,* 597–629.

Rantala, R. R. (2000). *Bureau of justice statistics special report: Effects of NIBRS on crime statistics.* Washington, DC: U.S. Department of Justice, Office of Justice Programs.

Reid, L. W., Weiss, H. E., Adelman, R. M., & Jaret, C. (2005). The immigration-crime relationship: Evidence across U.S. metropolitan areas. *Social Science Research, 34,* 757–780.

Rosenfeld, M., & Tienda, M. (1999). Mexican immigration, occupational niches, and labor market competition: Evidence from Los Angeles, Chicago and Atlanta, 1970–1990. In F. Bean & S. B. Rose (Eds.), *Immigration and opportunity: Race, ethnicity, and employment in the United States* (pp. 64–105). New York, NY: Russell Sage Foundation.

Rumbaut, R. G. (1994). Origins and destinies: Immigration to the United States since World War II. *Sociological Forum, 9,* 583–621.

Sampson, R. J. (2008). Rethinking crime and immigration. *Contexts: Understanding People in Their Social Worlds, 7,* 28–33.

Sampson, R. J., & Laub, J. H. (1993). *Crime in the making.* Cambridge, MA: Harvard University Press.

Sampson, R. J., & Laub, J. H. (2001). Crime and deviance in the life course. In A. Piquero & P. Mazerolle (Eds.), *Life-course criminology* (pp. 21–42). Belmont, CA: Wadsworth.

Sampson, R. J., Morenoff, J. D., & Raudenbush, S. W. (2005). Social anatomy of racial and ethnic disparities in violence. *American Journal of Public Health, 95*(2), 224–232.

Sanchez-Jankowski, M. (2008). *Cracks in the pavement: Social change and resilience in poor neighborhoods.* Berkeley, CA: University of California Press.

Schnapp, P. (2015). Identifying the effects of immigration on homicide rates in U.S. cities: An instrumental variable approach. *Homicide Studies, 19*(2), 103–122.

Shaw, C. R., & McKay, H. D. (1942). *Juvenile delinquency in urban areas.* Chicago, IL: University of Chicago Press.

Shaw, C. R., Zorbaugh, F., McKay, H. D., & Cottrell, L. S. (1929). *Delinquency areas.* Chicago, IL: University of Chicago Press.

Shihadeh, E. S., & Barranco, R. E. (2010). Latino employment and Black violence: The unintended consequence of U.S. immigration policy. *Social Forces, 88,* 1393–1420.

Shihadeh, E. S., & Winters, L. (2010). Church, place, and crime: Latinos and homicide in new destinations. *Sociological Inquiry, 80,* 628–649.

Short, J. F. (1997). *Poverty, ethnicity, and violent crime.* Boulder, CO: Westview Press.

Stansfield, R. (2013). Safer cities: A macro-level analysis of recent immigration, Hispanic-owned businesses, and crime rates in the United States. *Journal of Urban Affairs, 36,* 503–518.

Stansfield, R., Akins, S., Rumbaut, R. G., & Hammer, R. B. (2013). Assessing the effects of recent immigration on serious property crime in Austin, Texas. *Sociological Perspectives, 56,* 647–672.

Stewart, J. B., & Hyclak, T. J. (1986). The effects of immigrants, women, and teenagers on the relative earnings of Black males. *The Review of Black Political Economy, 15,* 93–101.

Stowell, J. I. (2007). *Immigration and crime: The effects of immigration on criminal behavior.* New York, NY: LFB Scholarly Publishing, LLC.

Stowell, J. I., & Martinez, Jr., R. (2007). Displaced, dispossessed, or lawless? Examining the link between ethnicity, immigration, and violence. *Journal of Aggression and Violent Behavior, 12,* 564–581.

Stowell, J. I., & Martinez, Jr., R. (2009). Incorporating ethnic-specific measures of immigration in the study of lethal violence. *Homicide Studies, 13,* 315–324.

Stowell, J. I., Messner, S. F., McGeever, K. F., & Raffalovich, L. E. (2009). Immigration and the recent violent crime drop in the United States: A pooled, cross-sectional time-series analysis of metropolitan areas. *Criminology, 47,* 889–928.

Suttles, G. D. (1968). *The social order of the slum.* Chicago, IL: University of Chicago Press.

Taylor, P. (2013). *The rise of Asian-Americans.* Washington, DC: Pew Research Center. Retrieved from www.pewsocialtrends.org/2012/06/19/the-rise-of-asian-americans/

Tonry, M. (1997). *Ethnicity, crime, and immigration.* Chicago, IL: University of Chicago Press.

U.S. Department of Justice, Federal Bureau of Investigation. (2002). *Uniform Crime Reporting program data [United States]: County-level detailed arrest and offense data, 2000* [Electronic Version].

U.S. Department of Justice, Federal Bureau of Investigation. (2012). *Crime in the United States, 2010* [Electronic Version].

U.S. Department of Justice, Federal Bureau of Investigation. (2015). *Effect of NIBRS on crime statistics.* Washington, DC: U.S. Department of Justice-Federal Bureau of Investigation.

Vélez, M. B. (2009). Contextualizing the immigration and crime effect: An analysis of homicide in Chicago neighborhoods. *Homicide Studies, 13*(3), 325–335.

Wadsworth, T. (2010). Is immigration responsible for the crime drop? An assessment of the influence of immigration on changes in violent crime between 1990 and 2000. *Social Science Quarterly, 91,* 531–553.

Waldinger, R. (1996). *Still the promised city? African-Americans and new immigrants in postindustrial New York.* Cambridge, MA: Harvard University Press.

Waldinger, R. (1997). Black/immigrant competition re-assessed: New evidence from Los Angeles. *Sociological Perspectives, 40,* 365–386.

Weiss, H. E., & Reid, L. W. (2005). Low-quality employment concentration and crime: An examination of metropolitan labor markets. *Sociological Perspectives, 48*(2), 213–232.

Wickersham Commission. (1931). *National commission on law observance and enforcement: Crime and the foreign born.* Washington, DC: U.S. Government Printing Office Report No. 10.

Wilson, J. H., & Singer, A. (2011). *Immigrants in 2010 metropolitan America: A decade of change.* Washington, DC: Brookings Metropolitan Policy Program, State of Metropolitan America.

Wilson, W. J. (1987). *The truly disadvantaged: The inner city, the underclass, and public policy.* Chicago, IL: University of Chicago Press.

Winnick, L. (1990). *New people in old neighborhoods: The role of new immigrants in rejuvenating New York's communities.* New York, NY: Russell Sage.

Wirth, L. (1938). Urbanism as a way of life. *American Journal of Sociology, 44,* 3–24.

Wolff, K. T., Baglivio, M. T., Intravia, J., & Piquero, A. (2015). The protective impact of immigrant concentration on juvenile recidivism: A statewide analysis of youth offenders. *Journal of Criminal Justice, 43,* 522–531.

Wright, R., Tekin, E., Topali, V., McClellan, C., Dickinson, T., & Rosenfeld, R. (2014). *Less cash, less crime: Evidence from the electronic benefit transfer program* (Working Paper No. 19996). Cambridge, MA: National Bureau of Economic Research. Retrieved May 12, 2016.

Zhou, M. (1992). *Chinatown: The socioeconomic potential of an urban enclave.* Philadelphia, PA: Temple University Press.

Zhou, M. (2001). Contemporary immigration and the dynamics of race and ethnicity. In N. J. Smelser, W. J. Wilson, & F. Mitchell (Eds.), *America becoming: Racial trends and their consequences* (pp. 200–242). Washington, DC: National Academy Press.

Reading 7.2   The Consequences of Identity Theft Victimization

Identity theft was not much of a concern when the UCR and NCVS came into existence in 1930 and 1972, respectively. This is now one of the fastest-growing crimes, necessitating the addition of a supplement to the NCVS so we can learn about its frequency and impact on victims. In Chapter 5, I discussed dimensions of concepts. In this article, Golladay and Holtfreter (2017) chose to focus on the nonmonetary loss dimensions of identity theft, specifically negative emotional and physical health symptoms following victimization. For their analysis, Golladay and Holtfreter used multiple NCVS survey items to create indeces, one measuring various types of emotional consequences and one for physical health symptoms. By doing so, they were able to increase their levels of measurement from nominal to ratio and make data analysis much easier. The authors also included several control variables that they suspected were related to the types of emotional and physical consequences that people experienced following identity theft.

The Consequences of Identity Theft Victimization: An Examination of Emotional and Physical Health Outcomes

Katelyn Golladay and Kristy Holtfreter

Introduction

Defined as "the unlawful use of another person's identifying information," identity theft has become one of the most feared and fastest-growing crimes (Piquero, Cohen, & Piquero, 2011, p. 438). There have been considerable legislative efforts to respond to and prevent identity theft, but the crime continues to rise (Holtfreter & Holtfreter, 2006). In the United States, more than 34.2 million people over the age of 16 will be victims of identity theft at one point in their lives. The average loss experienced by identity theft victims was approximately $2,183 in 2012 (Harrell & Langton, 2013). Prior research has addressed the monetary consequences of identity theft victimization (e.g., dollar amount lost). However, little is known about the *nonmonetary* losses experienced by victims (e.g., post-traumatic stress disorder). While monetary losses are important, emotional and physical consequences of victimization also warrant empirical attention, as these symptoms may be presented to victim service providers. If left untreated, such

negative consequences may result in maladaptive coping (e.g., self-medicating via substance abuse) and a host of further problems for victims, including revictimization (Turanovic & Pratt, 2014).

Anecdotal evidence suggests identity theft victimization also contributes to outcomes such as emotional distress (e.g., depression and anxiety), physical consequences (e.g., headaches and high blood pressure), and life disruption (e.g., missed time from work). Nonetheless, these identity theft victimization consequences have rarely been empirically examined. Guided largely by Agnew's (1992, 2001, 2002, 2006) general strain theory (GST), such consequences have been studied in other crime contexts, such as violence. Macmillan (2000) identifies four categories of violent victimization consequences: out-of-pocket expenses; lost wages and productivity; psychological trauma; and pain, suffering, and reduced quality of life. The consequences-of-victimization body of literature shows evidence of negative reactions experienced by victims of "street" crime, but the breadth of the literature is not sufficient and falls short in its examination of identity theft victimization. Greater empirical understanding of the consequences of identity theft will contribute to the literature base, and will also inform victim service providers with evidence-based strategies for developing effective treatments.

Identity Theft Research

Defining Identity Theft

Identity theft has been conceptualized in several different ways, and is often used interchangeably with identity fraud. This mingling of terms confuses the concept, however, which is actually more complicated: *theft* refers to the unlawful taking of information (e.g., personal account numbers or even tangible items such as credit cards or checkbooks) while *fraud* entails actually using the information to the perpetrator's benefit (e.g., to open a new account). While the majority of consumer-based frauds include direct communication between victim and offender as a necessary condition, identity theft is unique in that it typically does not entail any contact or relationship between victim and offender. Along these lines, it is not surprising that a recent panel of fraud victimization experts recommended keeping identity theft outside the realm of consumer fraud to avoid further conceptual confusion (Beals, DiLiema, & Deevy, 2015).

In the United States, knowledge about identity theft has been generated by two entities: government agencies and academic researchers. The former source includes the Bureau of Justice Statistics (BJS) and the Federal Trade Commission (FTC). Both federal agencies rely on similar operational definitions of identity theft. For example, the BJS's definition used in the NCVS defines identity theft as "the unauthorized use or attempted use of an existing account, such as a credit or debit card, checking, savings, telephone, online, or insurance account" (Harrell & Langton, 2013, p. 1). Similarly, the FTC operationalizes an identity theft victim as "anyone whose existing accounts—either credit card accounts or non–credit card accounts, such as bank accounts, utility accounts, or telephone accounts—have been misused" (Anderson, 2005, p. 2). Crime and justice researchers have used similar definitions in studies of identity theft (Anderson, Durbin, & Salinger, 2008; Copes, Kerley, Huff, & Kane, 2010; Piquero et al., 2011; Reyns, 2013; Sharp, Shreve-Neiger, Fremouw, Kane, & Hutton, 2004). While the definitions articulated above include a wide variety of types of identity theft, 85% of identity theft involves the fraudulent use of an existing account (e.g., credit card and bank account) (Harrel & Langton, 2013). In modern society, noncash transactions are becoming more common, further increasing the opportunity for identity theft victimization.

Predictors of Identity Theft

Much of the research on identity theft has focused on demographic characteristics that are associated with increased risk of victimization. For example, the BJS and FTC report that identity theft is most common among individuals between the ages of 25 and 64. After age 64, victimization decreases with age (Anderson, 2006; Harrell & Langton, 2013). Victimization also varies based on race. Those who do not identify as a single race (e.g., African American, Hispanic, Asian, or white) have slightly higher rates of victimization (Anderson, 2005; Harrell & Langton, 2013). These findings, however, should be interpreted cautiously because it is difficult to attribute the results to a single causal factor. For example, those who identify with more than one race often self-select into the "other" category, inflating the number of participants in the modal category (Anderson, 2005). Victimization risk does not significantly differ for men and women (Harrell & Langton, 2013).

More notable differences emerge when looking at marital status, income, location, and number of children. Family structure is important when assessing identity theft victimization risk due to the amount of time and attention available to catch fraudulent activity. Two-person-headed households and families with fewer than three children experience less victimization than single-parent households and households with three or more children. Additionally, those who live in Pacific states experience more victimization (Allison, Schuck, & Lersch, 2005; Anderson, 2005). Victimization also increases with income level: those who make over $75,000 annually experience higher rates of identity theft (Anderson, 2005; Harrell & Langton, 2013). While data from government agencies provides valuable descriptive information on identity theft, a weakness of this source is its lack of theoretical measures.

While not directly focused on identity theft victimization, there have been notable theoretical developments in the area of fraud victimization that can inform the study of identity theft. For example, consumers' routine activities and low self-control have been linked to increased rates of fraud victimization (Holtfreter, Reisig, & Pratt, 2008; Reisig & Holtfreter, 2013). Along these lines, a number of "risky" behaviors, such as responding to unsolicited e-mails, making purchases from nonreputable vendors, using credit cards on unsecured websites, and the like have been found to increase targeting by fraud perpetrators (Pratt, Holtfreter, & Reisig, 2010; Reisig, Pratt, & Holtfreter, 2009). Similar activities reflecting low levels of guardianship, such as media downloading and visiting unsecured online forums, have also been associated with identity-related crimes and other forms of online victimization (Reyns, 2013; Reyns, Henson, & Fisher, 2011; van Wilsem, 2013). Although these studies are an improvement on prior research given their strong theoretical base, they are somewhat limited in terms of generalizability due to a reliance on selective samples (e.g., college students).

Taking the linked theoretical perspective a step further, a recent study found that low self-control increased the likelihood of making a purchase in response to an unsolicited e-mail, and making such a purchase, in turn, significantly increased the probability of identity theft victimization (Holtfreter, Reisig, Pratt, & Holtfreter, 2015). In sum, while the literature has certainly begun to shed some light on the underlying causal mechanisms of identity theft, there have been few attempts to move beyond the offense itself. Put differently, with a few notable exceptions, little research examining the context of fraud and related crimes has considered the aftermath of the victimization event (Holtfreter, Van Slyke, & Blomberg, 2005; Walsh & Schram, 1980). As articulated in more detail below, the consequences of identity theft—much like violent crime—often linger beyond the event itself.

Strain Theory and Victimization

Social scientists have increasingly drawn on Agnew's (1992) general strain theory [GST] (Agnew, 2001, 2002, 2006) in examining the consequences of victimization. While Agnew's (1992) original theory examined the relationship between stressful life events (or strains) and maladaptive coping in the form of offending, subsequent research (Agnew, 2001, 2006) further clarified the role of negative emotions (e.g., anger and depression) as well as coping resources (e.g., social support and self-esteem) as potential mediators between the strain-offending relationship. In other words, strain may lead *directly* to offending (or analogous forms of negative coping, such as alcohol abuse), or it may occur *through* negative emotions. Within this theoretical framework, victimization—regardless of its specific form—can be conceptualized as a strain (Agnew, 2002). Similar to other negative life events, (e.g., loss of a job or partner), the strain of victimization produces negative emotions (e.g., anger, depression, and the like) and subsequently creates pressures for individuals to engage in coping strategies for "corrective action" (Agnew, 2006, p. 13).

To date, several studies have conceptualized victimization as a strain, applying GST in various national samples of adolescents. Researchers have tested the original strain-offending relationship as well as more elaborate models considering potential mediators (e.g., Hay & Evans, 2006). Agnew's (2002) research revealed that several types of victimization—actual, vicarious (i.e., knowledge of close friends being hurt), and even *anticipated* victimization—had strong effects on delinquency. Using data from the National Survey of Adolescents, Carson, Sullivan, Cochran, and Lersch (2008) also found support for GST in that early victimization predicted both the onset and frequency of drug use; the links between victimization and offending were only partially mediated by social bonds and negative emotions. Hay and Evans (2006) reported similar findings in their secondary analysis of two waves of data from the National Survey of Children. Specifically, their results indicated that strain in the form of early victimization predicted subsequent delinquency, even after controlling for prior delinquency. These relationships were partially mediated by anger, and the effects of victimization on delinquency were conditioned by a child's level of self-control. In a recent analysis of the connections between victimization, negative emotions, and offending, Turanovic and Pratt (2013) argued for the linkage of GST and self-control theories as a means of understanding the causal pathways between victimization and offending. Consistent with GST as well as a growing body of literature (Carson et al., 2008; Hay & Evans, 2006; Turanovic & Pratt, 2013), the current study conceptualizes victimization as a strain. In fact, we suggest that identity theft victimization exhibits many of the qualities Agnew (2006) links to strains that are particularly *criminogenic*, i.e., most likely to lead to offending: it is often perceived as being *unjust* ("what did I do to deserve getting my personal information stolen and my credit ruined?" wonders the victim) as well as *high in magnitude* (knowing an offender has possession of something so personal as one's social security number invokes intense anxiety and fear).

Consequences of Victimization

While little is known empirically about the consequences of identity theft, there is a growing body of research addressing the post-victimization outcomes of other types of crime, such as property and violence. Extending this research to the context of identity theft assumes that different forms of victimization share underlying causal mechanisms—a theoretical assumption that has been supported empirically (Pratt, Turanovic, Fox, & Wright, 2014; Turanovic & Pratt, 2013). Victims of violent offenses experience emotional troubles such as depression, shock, insecurity, anger, and fear (Agnew, 2002; Boney-McCoy & Finkelhor, 1995; Langton & Truman, 2014; Macmillan, 2001; Norris & Kaniasty, 1994; Shapland & Hall, 2007). In addition to emotional distress, victims of property crime not only lose their property, but also experience indirect losses, such as loss of wages due to time off work while recovering (Macmillan, 2000; Miller, Cohen, & Wiersema, 1996). Depression that follows the offense can also manifest itself in other negative emotional outcomes, including helplessness, lack of interest in daily activities, worthlessness, and lack of life satisfaction (Hoyl et al., 1999; Rinaldi et al., 2003; Strawbridge, Deleger, Roberts, & Kaplan, 2002). According to GST, similar post-victimization experiences would also extend to the context of identity theft; this remains an open empirical question.

Documented losses resulting from identity theft include financial and legal troubles that stem from restoring one's credit and protecting personal information. Compared to property offenses, identity theft, on average, tends to be more costly to the victim. The mean dollar amount lost for property offenses is $915 while the mean amount lost from identity theft is $2,183 (Harrell & Langton, 2013). Those who are victims of identity theft experience more than twice the amount of losses compared to those who fall victim to property offenses. In 2012, both direct and indirect losses were estimated at about $24.7 billion (Harrell & Langton, 2013). It is important to note, however, that banks and credit card companies are increasingly covering much of the financial loss associated with identity theft victimization (Synovate, 2007). About 14% of victims reported an out-of-pocket loss associated with their identity theft victimization, with a majority reporting a loss of less than $250 (Harrell & Langton, 2013). In addition to financial losses, identity theft can also be time consuming to resolve. On average, victims spend about 15–30 hours, often spread out over several years, resolving financial problems related to identity theft (Copes et al., 2010; Lynch, 2005; Slosarik, 2002). It is no surprise that the extensive post-victimization efforts to restore financial creditability and protect personal information likely take an emotional and physical toll.

Current Focus

Guided in part by Agnew's (1992, 2001, 2006) theoretical framework, this study addresses a gap in current research related to the consequences of identity theft victimization. Specifically, the link between identity theft victimization and emotional and physical symptomology will be addressed. Past studies of identity theft have focused primarily on the financial and time-consuming consequences victims face; however, this does not tell the whole story.

Data and Sample

The NCVS is administered by the BJS to gauge rates of victimization. The NCVS began in 1972 and is considered to be the largest dataset of victimization, impact, and offender characteristics. Historically, the main goal of the NCVS was to gain insight on the prevalence of crime and criminal victimization that might not be reported to police officials. Once selected, households remain in the sample for a span of three years. Surveys are administered semiannually and reflect victimization that occurred during the previous six months. A total of seven surveys are given throughout a household's participation in the NCVS. The first survey is given in person followed by six telephone interviews every six months. The survey inquires about different types of victimization divided into two categories: personal crimes (e.g., rape, assault, and robbery) and household property crimes (e.g., burglary and motor vehicle theft).

Throughout its history, the NCVS has included several supplemental surveys to expand the scope of the types of victimization covered. Three different supplemental surveys have been administered. The School Crime Supplement (SCS) has been administered at five different stages: 1999, 2001, 2009, 2011, and 2013. In 2006 a Supplemental Victimization Survey (SVS) was administered to measure experiences of stalking and unwanted contact. The Identity Theft Supplement (ITS) is a supplemental component of the NCVS. Since identity theft is considered to be one of the fastest-growing crimes (Piquero et al., 2011), gathering information from victims of identity theft is imperative.

The current study uses the 2012 dataset, which is the second installment of the ITS (the previous installment was administered in 2008). This survey supplement is unique and has yet to be used by crime and justice researchers. The ITS survey is measured individually rather than as a household and had a 91.9% response rate. Put differently, in the greater NCVS study, a single respondent answers the survey on behalf of the household; however, the ITS survey is answered by the single respondent reflecting on their own personal experiences. If the individual respondent representing the household was over the age of 16, they were asked to participate in the ITS. The survey inquires about details from the respondent's experience with identity theft over the past 12 months. Of the respondents surveyed, 3,709 reported experiencing some form of identity theft in the past 12 months.[1] Following reports of identity theft victimization, respondents were asked to acknowledge any emotional and/or physical distress that arose as a consequence of their victimization. For example, respondents were asked if they experienced any emotional distress (e.g., anger, depression, anxiety) or any physical consequences (e.g., headaches, trouble sleeping, changes in eating habits) for a month or more following their identity theft victimization. Over 80% of respondents who experienced identity theft victimization reported experiencing emotional consequences. Additionally, over 21% of respondents experienced physical consequences following their identity theft victimization.

Measures

Dependent Variables

Emotional Consequences

The *emotional consequences* variable is a count variable constructed by summing the responses to 8 items. Respondents were asked to identify any emotional consequences they experienced for a month or longer following their most recent identity theft victimization. Respondents were asked to identify emotional consequences that were a direct result of their identity theft victimization. Consequences resulting from other forms of victimization were asked separately. Emotional consequences included feelings of "worry/anxiety," "anger," "depression," "vulnerability," "violation," "like you couldn't trust people," "unsafe," and "confused." These emotional consequences represent the emotional consequences identified by the NCVS and are representative of emotional consequences used in previous studies (Identity Theft Resource Center, 2014; Sharp et al., 2004). The scale ranges from 0 to 8, with higher scores reflecting the experience of more emotional consequences. On average, respondents reported experiencing about 3 of the negative emotions following their victimization (mean = 3.03, SD = 2.13).

Physical Consequences

Similarly, the *physical consequences* variable is a count variable of the responses to 7 items reflecting physical consequences following their identity theft victimization. Respondents were asked whether they had experienced any of the following physical consequences for a month or more after their most recent identity theft experience. These responses did not include physical consequences that may have been a result of other forms of victimization such as violent, property, or personal victimization. These physical consequences included headaches, trouble sleeping, changes in eating habits, upset stomach, fatigue, high blood pressure, and muscle tension or back pain. The physical consequences variable includes an extensive list of physical consequences including items used in previous studies (Identity Theft Resource Center, 2014; Sharp et al., 2004). The physical consequences summary measure ranges from 0 to 7, with higher scores representing a greater number of physical consequences experienced by the respondent (mean = 0.59, SD = 1.53).

Independent Variables

The *number of ID theft victimizations* variable is a combined measure taking into account the different types of identity theft that a respondent may have experienced in the past 12 months. This measure is a sum of yes/no responses to the following types of identity theft: "someone trying to use your checking or savings account," "someone using or attempting to use one of your existing credit cards," "someone misusing one of your existing accounts (e.g., telephone, utilities, PayPal, insurance, etc.)," "someone has used your personal information to open a new account," and "someone has used your personal information for fraudulent purposes (e.g., getting medical care, a job, government benefits, etc.)." A majority of respondents reported experiencing a single account of identity theft victimization over the past 12 months (1 = 87.65%, 2 = 10.84%, 3 = 1.27%, 4 = 0.22%, 5 = 0.03%). The scale ranges from 1 to 5 with higher scores representing a greater number of identity theft victimization experiences. Since this study focuses on the consequences of identity theft victimization, the sample includes only those who experienced some form of identity theft victimization in the past 12 months.

Control Variables

Several known correlates of the consequences of victimization and demographic variables are included in the multivariate analyses to control for potential spuriousness. *Property victimization* is a 3-item scale that reflects whether individuals experienced property victimization during the past six months. Property victimization includes having something stolen, attempted break-in, and motor vehicle theft. Scores were dichotomously coded 1 (yes) and 0 (no). Additionally, violent victimization is controlled for. *Violent victimization* is a 3-item scale that measures violent victimization experiences. Variables included assault by location, assault by type of assault, and being sexually assaulted. Scores are dichotomously coded 1 (yes) and 0 (no). These variables are included to control for harm that may result from being victimized outside of the scope of identity theft. For example, a respondent may be more likely to experience emotional or physical consequences following their identity theft victimization if they also experienced property or violent victimization. *Prior ID theft victimization* was included to control for the respondent's previous experience with identity theft victimization beyond the 12-month period focused on by the ITS. The variable is a count variable with scores ranging from 0 to 4. Finally, several demographic variables are included: *age* (the respondent's age in years), *male* (1 = male, 0 = female), *racial/ethnic minority* (1 = nonwhite, 0 = white, non-Hispanic), *education* (1 = none/kindergarten, 2 = elementary school, 3 = middle/high school, 4 = college, 5 = master's degree, 6 = professional degree, 7 = doctoral degree), *married* (1 = married, 0 = single), and *income²* (1 = < $5,000, 2 = $5,000–7,499, 3 = $7,500–9,999, 4 = $10,000–12,499, 5 = $12,500–14,999, 6 = $15,000–17,499, 7 = $17,500–19,999, 8 = $20,000–24,999, 9 = $25,000–29,999, 10 = $30,000–34,999, 11 = $35,000–39,999, 12 = $40,000–49,999, 13 = $50,000–74,999, 14 = > $75,000). Descriptive statistics are provided in Table 1.

Results

Table 1 provides an assessment of the bivariate correlations between study variables. The independent variables of interest are significantly associated with the key dependent variables in the positive direction. While the zero-order correlations do not exceed the standard cutoff of an absolute value of 0.40, additional diagnostics were conducted to further rule out issues of collinearity. The variance inflation factors (VIF) for the variables ranged from 1.02 to 1.47, which

fall well below the standard threshold of 4.0 (Fox, 1991).

Negative binomial regressions were run to regress emotional consequences onto identity theft victimization and the control variables. Table 2 provides the analysis for the effects of victimization on emotional consequences. Model 1 demonstrates that identity theft victimizations were significant and positive ($p <$ 0.001). The positive coefficient indicates that the more identity theft victimization a respondent experiences, higher levels of emotional consequences are experienced. Several control variables in the model were also significant. Age was significant and positive ($p < 0.001$), the amount lost was significant and positive ($p <$ 0.01), and being nonwhite was also significant and positive ($p < 0.001$). Put differently, being of a minority race, experiencing greater losses related to the identity theft victimization, and being older are associated with greater emotional consequences following identity theft victimization. The findings with regard to amount lost are in the hypothesized direction. However, income ($p < 0.001$) and education ($p < 0.01$) were both significant and negative, suggesting that those who are better off in terms of socioeconomic status suffer less than their counterparts with limited resources. Additionally, marriage ($p < 0.01$) is also significant in the negative direction. To be sure, spouses are often vicariously victimized by identity theft given that they share credit history with the victim. In this regard, emotional symptoms might also be shared between spouses, resulting in the negative relationship observed here. Married victims may also simply have greater support than their single counterparts, an interpretation that is consistent with a larger body of stress-process literature suggesting that family members buffer individuals from harmful effects of trauma (Holtfreter, Reisig, & Turanovic, 2016, 2015; Pearlin, 1999).

Given the positive effect of victimization on emotional consequences, hypothetically we may expect to see a similar effect of *prior* identity theft victimization on the emotional consequences experienced by respondents. Put simply, if respondents experience higher levels of

Table 1 Bivariate Correlation for Study Variables

	Mean	SD	X_1	X_2	X_3	X_4	X_5	X_6	X_7	X_8	X_9	X_{10}	X_{11}	X_{12}	X_{13}
X_1 Emotional consequences	3.03	2.13	–												
X_2 Physical consequences	0.59	1.53	0.48***	–											
X_3 # of ID theft victimizations	1.14	0.40	0.17***	0.12***	–										
X_4 Prior ID theft victimization	1.06	0.49	0.29***	0.12***	0.12***	–									
X_5 Property victimization	0.10	0.33	0.15***	0.29***	0.12***	0.01	–								
X_6 Violent victimization	0.03	0.17	0.08**	0.09***	0.06***	-0.01	0.13***	–							
X_7 Amount lost	0.98	6.84	0.00***	0.04	0.04**	0.11***	-0.00	-0.00	–						
X_8 Age	49.28	15.23	0.86***	-0.02	-0.02	-0.02	-0.04*	-0.02	0.04*	–					
X_9 Male	0.16	–	-0.01	0.03	-0.00	0.01	-0.01	0.02	0.02	-0.16***	–				
X_{10} Minority	0.13	–	0.10***	0.08**	-0.05**	-0.03	0.04*	0.01	0.00	-0.10***	0.02	–			
X_{11} Education	3.03	0.81	-0.09***	-0.07**	0.03	-0.03	-0.03	0.00	0.04*	-0.10***	0.00	0.00	–		
X_{12} Married	0.66	–	-0.09***	-0.11***	-0.03	-0.05	-0.03	-0.05**	-0.00	0.12***	-0.51***	-0.08***	0.01	–	
X_{13} Income	12.45	2.64	-0.18***	-0.18***	-0.05**	-0.02	-0.10***	-0.05**	0.02	0.02	-0.07***	-0.11***	0.19***	0.33***	–

$*p \leq 0.05$; $**p \leq 0.01$; $***p \leq 0.001$ (two-tailed test)

Table 2 Emotional Consequences Regression Models

| | Emotional Consequences[a] | | | | | | | | | | | |
| | Model 1 (n = 1,221) | | | Model 2 (n = 740) | | | Model 3 (n = 887) | | | Model 4 (n = 740) | | |
	b	SE	z-test	b	SE	z-test	b	SE	z-test	b	SE	z-test
# of ID theft victimizations	0.20	0.03	7.04***	0.20	0.03	6.06***	0.20	0.04	5.47***	0.17	0.03	5.12***
Prior ID theft victimization	–	–	–	0.31	0.05	6.45***	–	–	–	0.32	0.05	6.70***
Property victimization	–	–	–	–	–	–	0.17	0.06	3.02**	0.16	0.06	2.73**
Violent victimization	–	–	–	–	–	–	0.20	0.09	2.34*	0.18	0.10	1.87
Amount lost	0.00	0.00	2.90**	0.01	0.00	2.65**	0.01	0.00	2.56**	0.01	0.00	2.85**
Age	0.01	0.00	4.18***	0.01	0.00	3.47***	0.00	0.00	3.18***	0.01	0.00	3.42***
Male	-0.14	0.06	-2.19*	-0.13	0.08	-1.65	-0.12	0.07	-1.76	-0.12	0.08	-1.60
Minority	0.16	0.05	3.22***	0.15	0.06	2.42*	0.12	0.06	2.05*	0.14	0.06	2.26*
Education	-0.06	0.02	-2.52**	-0.03	0.03	-1.04	-0.04	0.03	-1.56	-0.03	0.03	-1.03
Married	-0.12	0.05	-2.57**	-0.09	0.06	-1.57	-0.13	0.05	-2.52**	-0.09	0.06	-1.52
Income	-0.03	0.01	-3.61***	-0.03	0.01	-3.72***	-0.02	0.01	-2.58**	-0.03	0.01	-3.50***
Constant	1.13	0.14	8.33***	0.72	0.18	4.08***	1.04	0.15	6.80***	0.69	0.17	3.99***
	Wald χ^2 = 143.09***			Wald χ^2 = 148.88***			Wald χ^2 = 70.81***			Wald χ^2 = 170.62***		
	McFadden's R^2 = 0.02			McFadden's R^2 = 0.04			McFadden's R^2 = 0.03			McFadden's R^2 = 0.04		
Likelihood-ratio test of alpha	89.77***			36.26***			99.89***			31.84***		

[a] Negative binomial regression model

*$p \leq 0.05$; **$p \leq 0.01$; ***$p \leq 0.001$ (two-tailed test)

emotional consequences following their victimization, we could expect to see prior identity theft victimization exerting a similar effect on the respondent's emotional consequences. Model 2 includes prior victimization into the model predicting emotional consequences. As hypothesized, prior identity theft victimization has a significant positive effect on emotional consequences ($p < 0.001$); however, *recent* identity theft victimization (i.e., in the past 12 months) remains a significant predictor of emotional consequences ($p < 0.001$). Additionally, amount lost ($p < 0.01$), age ($p < 0.001$), and minority status ($p < 0.05$) persist as significant and positive predictors of emotional consequences. Income remains a significant negative predictor of emotional consequences ($p < 0.001$), suggesting that victims who are in a better position financially may be able to cope with the emotional burdens of identity theft better than those in lower income brackets. Put differently, being a victim of identity theft may be more devastating to an individual who is less financially stable than someone with a high amount of income.

Model 3 evaluates the effect of recent identity theft victimization while also controlling for recent property and violent victimization. When controlling for property and violent victimization, levels of identity theft victimization remain a significant predictor of emotional consequences ($p < 0.001$). Property victimization ($p < 0.01$) and violent victimization ($p < 0.05$) also reach statistical significance. Consistent with GST, these findings indicate that victimization of *any* kind results in negative emotional consequences. Several control variables remain significant in Model 3. Amount lost ($p < 0.01$), age ($p < 0.001$), and being nonwhite ($p < 0.05$) are also significant predictors of emotional consequences. Additionally, being married ($p < 0.01$) and income ($p < 0.01$) remain significant and negative. These findings are consistent with previous models.

Predictors of emotional consequences are slightly more conservative when the analysis consists of a more comprehensive model. Model 4 regresses emotional consequences onto levels of identity theft victimization, prior identity theft victimization, property victimization, violent victimization, and control variables. Recent identity theft victimization remains significant ($p < 0.001$). This finding indicates that net of control variables and other victimization, identity theft within the past 12 months is a significant predictor of emotional consequences experienced. Consistent with previous models, prior identity theft victimization ($p < 0.001$) and property victimization ($p < 0.01$) also reach statistical significance. Several control variables remain significant. Amount lost ($p < 0.01$), age ($p < 0.001$), and being nonwhite ($p < 0.05$) are all significant predictors of emotional consequences. Income, however, remains a significant negative predictor of emotional consequences ($p < 0.001$). This persistent finding suggests that those who have the financial capability to recover from identity theft experience fewer emotional consequences.

Similar patterns are revealed when looking at the effects of the variables on physical consequences. Model 1 in Table 3 shows that identity theft victimization has a significant positive effect on physical consequences experienced following victimization ($p < 0.001$). Put simply, as the number of identity theft victimizations increases, so too does the level of physical consequences. Several control variables also emerged as significant. Being married ($p < 0.01$) and income ($p < 0.001$) exerted significant *negative* effects on physical consequences of victimization, parallel to the findings observed for emotional consequences.

Model 2 controls for prior identity theft victimization in predicting physical consequences following identity theft victimization. Consistent with what is presented in Table 2, prior victimization is a significant predictor of experiencing physical consequences after identity theft ($p < 0.001$). Recent identity theft victimization remains a significant predictor of physical consequences ($p < 0.001$). Being of a minority race ($p < 0.05$) is also significant and positive. Consistent with Model 1, being married ($p < 0.01$) and income ($p < 0.001$) are significant and negative. As discussed previously, we suspect that the income measure is tapping into resource availability. Along these

Table 3 Physical Consequences Regression Models

| | Physical Consequences[a] | | | | | | | | | | |
| | Model 1 (n = 1,242) | | | Model 2 (n = 747) | | | Model 3 (n = 906) | | | Model 4 (n = 747) | | |
	b	SE	z-test	b	SE	z-test	b	SE	z-test	b	SE	z-test
# of ID theft victimizations	0.33	0.10	3.30***	0.46	0.14	3.43***	0.44	0.13	3.43***	0.47	0.15	3.08**
Prior ID theft victimization	—	—	—	0.60	0.17	3.43***	—	—	—	0.55	0.15	3.57***
Property victimization	—	—	—	—	—	—	1.69	0.20	8.35***	1.41	0.26	5.39***
Violent victimization	—	—	—	—	—	—	0.77	0.26	2.95**	0.55	0.37	1.49
Amount lost	0.01	0.01	0.99	0.03	0.02	1.24	0.01	0.01	1.39	0.02	0.01	1.24
Age	0.00	0.01	0.66	0.01	0.01	0.67	0.01	0.01	1.45	0.01	0.01	1.58
Male	-0.01	0.22	0.04	-0.22	0.28	-0.76	-0.00	0.25	-0.01	-0.04	0.29	-0.13
Minority	0.20	0.19	1.05	0.51	0.25	2.04*	0.21	0.22	0.97	0.42	0.25	1.71
Education	-0.20	0.10	-1.91	-0.14	0.13	-1.10	-0.19	0.12	-1.64	-0.18	0.13	-1.38
Married	-0.45	0.17	-2.61**	-0.47	0.23	-2.02*	-0.59	0.20	-2.96**	-0.57	0.23	-2.50**
Income	-0.09	0.02	-4.01***	-0.12	0.03	-3.82***	-0.10	0.03	-3.78***	-0.13	0.03	-4.18***
Constant	0.65	0.52	1.26	-0.24	0.73	-0.33	-0.12	0.57	-0.20	-0.67	0.66	-1.01
	Wald χ^2 = 124.53***			Wald χ^2 = 72.94***			Wald χ^2 = 130.76***			Wald χ^2 = 150.55***		
	McFadden's R^2 = 0.02			McFadden's R^2 = 0.04			McFadden's R^2 = 0.05			McFadden's R^2 = 0.07		
Likelihood-ratio test of alpha	1047.35***			487.88***			762.93***			439.40***		

[a] Negative binomial regression model

*$p \leq 0.05$; **$p \leq 0.01$; ***$p \leq 0.001$ (two-tailed test)

lines, an identity theft loss of $250 is not likely to put much of a damper on finances for an individual with an above-average income who has money in the bank. Comparatively, a victim living paycheck to paycheck who experiences the same loss may be hit by added financial burdens (e.g., the inability to pay rent), thus increasing negative consequences. With regard to marriage, a spouse can provide social, emotional, and instrumental support in the aftermath of identity theft, and by doing so, help lessen the impact of victimization on physical symptomology (Arias, Lyons, & Street, 1997; Choenaron, Williams, & Hagerty, 2005; Evans, Steel, Watkins, & DiLillo, 2014; Thoits, 1995).

Model 3 evaluates the influence of property and violent victimization on physical consequences experienced after identity theft victimization. Property victimization ($p < 0.001$) and violent victimization ($p < 0.01$) both serve as significant predictors of physical consequences. Identity theft victimization continues to remain statistically significant ($p < 0.001$). Consistent with the previous two models, being married ($p < 0.01$) and income ($p < 0.001$) remain significant and negative predictors. Similar to what was found for emotional consequences, being married may provide emotional support that reduces physical consequences experienced. Similarly, those who have more capacity to absorb losses may be more financially able to recover from identity theft victimization.

Model 4 provides a comprehensive evaluation of the predictors of physical consequences following identity theft victimization. Consistent with the previous models, recent identity theft victimization ($p < 0.01$) and prior identity theft victimization ($p < 0.001$) are both predictors of physical consequences. Property victimization ($p < 0.001$) is significant, while violent victimization fails to reach statistical significance. Again, consistent with the previous models, being married ($p < 0.01$) and income ($p < 0.001$) remain and are negative. The amount lost, however, is not a significant predictor of physical consequences; this may be due to the fact that much of the financial burden of identity theft is placed on banks and credit card companies as opposed to the victim (Synovate, 2007).

In other words, prompt handling of identity theft cases, such as crediting the victim's account for fraudulent charges, may help reduce the long-term impacts of victimization.

Discussion

Much like what has been reported for other forms of crime, such as bullying and violence, the consequences of identity theft extend beyond financial losses and also include considerable emotional and physical symptoms. The relationships we observed are consistent with anecdotal evidence documenting the distress involved in recovering from identity theft, such as restoring one's credit and protecting personal information from a future attack (Dadisho, 2005). The results also lend some empirical support to GST in that identity theft victimization can be conceived of as a stressor that results in a host of negative emotions such as depression and anxiety (Agnew, 2006). In doing so, this research adds to the body of evidence demonstrating a link between stressful life events and negative emotionality, and also speaks to the importance of considering negative physical consequences as a component of the GST model. Documenting these relationships is but a first step in understanding the complex chain of events that follows victimization.

Coping with strain is also largely influenced by the availability of social support from friends, family, and others in one's social network (Thoits, 1995). In that vein, we found that being married was associated with fewer negative consequences. Future work examining the responses to negative emotional and physical symptomology among identity theft victims would thus benefit from attention not just to measures of the presence of friends and family, but also to the quality of those relationships. Toward that end, efforts to further untangle the processes and mechanisms involved in coping with identity theft would be a welcome addition to the literature. Taken with the results of the current study, such efforts would contribute to theory and could also inform treatment strategies (e.g., promoting prosocial ways of coping) for victim service providers. Our findings demonstrate that the outcomes of identity theft are more than just financial, as reflected by both emotional and physical consequences. Accordingly, criminal justice system officials working with identity theft victims should be aware of these consequences so they can direct victims to programs and services designed to address the emotional and physical aftermath. Due to data limitations, the current study was not able to include any measures of victim treatment (e.g., individual counseling, group therapy, or other resources) that may have been accessed by participants. Future work in this area should examine availability and use of mental and physical health services among identity theft victims, and ultimately the effectiveness of these services in reducing emotional and physical symptomology. Such efforts would help providers determine whether existing, "general" treatment modalities (e.g., cognitive behavioral theory) can be applied to identity theft victims, or whether specialized, crime-specific programs and services are warranted.

In the end, this research highlights the importance of moving beyond the prediction of victimization itself to the broader, nonfinancial indicators of victim harm in the form of emotional and physical symptomology. Although such efforts are common in other victimization contexts (e.g., violence), the current study is just one of a handful of studies addressing the repercussions stemming from identity theft victimization. In doing so, this work contributes to the increasing body of literature on the consequences of victimization. While it is often assumed that fraud-related crimes like identity theft are not "as serious" as violent crimes, the level and types of harm experienced by victims certainly do not suggest that to be the case. While this study has identified some previously unexplored consequences of identity theft, there is still much to learn to better serve its victims.

Discussion Questions

1. What criminological theories were used to explain the reasons why some people might become victims of identity theft and the physical and emotional consequences that they experience?
2. Which of the control variables wound up being associated with negative emotional and physical consequences of identity theft?
3. What type of research design is this? The researchers used NVCS data, but how many waves of data collection did they use?

Notes

1. We are aware that the sample used here is whittled down significantly from those originally included in the household-level NCVS. This raises possible concerns about bias in our estimates—namely, that respondents who completed the ITS are unique from those who completed other portions of the interview or who did not complete the study at all. These concerns are lessened by the knowledge that the original researchers found little or no bias stemming from nonresponse in the ITS estimates (Harrell & Langton, 2013).
2. The NCVS measures *income* as a categorical variable rather than a continuous variable.

References

Agnew, R. (1992). Foundation for a general strain theory of crime and delinquency. *Criminology, 30*, 47–88. https://doi.org/10.1111/crim.1992.30.issue-1

Agnew, R. (2001). Building on the foundation of general strain theory: Specifying the types of strain most likely to lead to crime and delinquency. *Journal of Research in Crime and Delinquency, 38*, 319–361. https://doi.org/10.1177/0022427801038004001

Agnew, R. (2002). Experienced, vicarious, and anticipated strain: An exploratory study on physical victimization and delinquency. *Justice Quarterly, 19*, 603–632. https://doi.org/10.1080/0741882020095371

Agnew, R. (2006). *Pressured into crime: An overview of general strain theory*. Los Angeles, CA: Roxbury.

Allison, S. F. H., Schuck, A. M., & Lersch, K. M. (2005). Exploring the crime of identity theft: Prevalence, clearance rates, and victim/offender characteristics. *Journal of Criminal Justice, 33*, 19–29. https://doi.org/10.1016/j.jcrimjus.2004.10.007

Anderson, K. B. (2005). *Identity theft: Does the risk vary with demographics?* Washington, DC: Bureau of Economics, Federal Trade Commission.

Anderson, K. B. (2006). Who are the victims of identity theft? The effect of demographics. *Journal of Public Policy & Marketing, 25*, 160–171. https://doi.org/10.1509/jppm.25.2.160

Anderson, K. B., Durbin, E., & Salinger, M. A. (2008). Identity theft. *The Journal of Economic Perspectives, 22*, 171–192. https://doi.org/10.1257/jep.22.2.171

Andridge, R. R., & Little, R. J. A. (2010). A review of hot deck imputation for survey nonresponse. *International Statistical Review, 78*, 40–64. https://doi.org/10.1111/j.1751-5823.2010.00103.x

Arias, I., Lyons, C. M., & Street, A. E. (1997). Individual and marital consequences of victimization: Moderating effects of relationship efficacy and spousal support. *Journal of Family Violence, 12*, 193–210. https://doi.org/10.1023/A:1022888728475

Beals, M., DiLiema, M., & Deevy, M. (2015). *Framework for a taxonomy of fraud.* Palo Alto, CA: Stanford University Center on Longevity.

Boney-McCoy, S., & Finkelhor, D. (1995). Observations on the measurement of chance. *Journal of Consulting and Clinical Psychology, 62*, 726–736. https://doi.org/10.1037/0022-006X.63.5.726

Breusch, T. S., & Pagan, A. R. (1979). A simple test for heteroskedasticity and random coefficient variation. *Econometrica, 47*, 1287–1294. https://doi.org/10.2307/1911963

Carson, D. C., Sullivan, C. J., Cochran, J. K., & Lersch, K. M. (2008). General strain theory and the relationship between early victimization and drug use. *Deviant Behavior, 30*, 54–88. https://doi.org/10.1080/01639620802050023

Choenaron, C., Williams, R. A., & Hagerty, B. M. (2005). The role of sense of belonging and social support on stress and depression in individuals with depression. *Archives of Psychiatric Nursing, 19*, 19–29.

Copes, H., Kerley, K. R., Huff, R., & Kane, J. (2010). Differentiating identity theft: An exploratory study of victims using a national victimization survey. *Journal of Criminal Justice, 38*, 1045–1052. https://doi.org/10.1016/j.jcrimjus.2010.07.007

Dadisho, E. (2005). Identity theft and the police response: The problem. *The Police Chief, 72*, 25–29.

Evans, S. E., Steel, A. L., Watkins, L. E., & DiLillo, D. (2014). Childhood exposure to family violence and adult trauma symptoms: The importance of social support from a spouse. *Psychological Trauma: Theory, Research, Practice, and Policy, 6*, 527–536. https://doi.org/10.1037/a0036940

Fox, J. (1991). *Regression diagnostics.* Newbury Park, CA: Sage.

Gmel, G. (2001). Imputation of missing values in the case of a multiple item instrument measuring alcohol consumption. *Statistics in Medicine, 20*,

2369–2381. https://doi.org/10.1002/(ISSN)1097-0258

Harrell, E., & Langton, L. (2013). *Victims of identity theft, 2012* (NCJ 243779). Washington, DC: Bureau of Justice Statistics.

Hay, C., & Evans, M. M. (2006). Violent victimization and involvement in delinquency: Examining predictions from general strain theory. *Journal of Criminal Justice, 34*, 261–274. https://doi.org/10.1016/j.jcrimjus.2006.03.005

Holtfreter, K., Reisig, M. D., & Pratt, T. C. (2008). Low self-control, routine activities, and fraud victimization. *Criminology, 46*, 189–220. https://doi.org/10.1111/j.1745-9125.2008.00101.x

Holtfreter, K., Reisig, M. D., Pratt, T. C., & Holtfreter, R. E. (2015). Risky remote purchasing and identity theft victimization among older Internet users. *Psychology, Crime, & Law, 21*, 681–698. https://doi.org/10.1080/1068316X.2015.1028545

Holtfreter, K., Reisig, M. D., & Turanovic, J. J. (2015). Depression and infrequent participation in social activities among older adults: The moderating role of high quality familial ties. *Aging & Mental Health, 1*–10. Advance online publication. https://doi.org/10.1080/13607863.2015.1099036

Holtfreter, K., Reisig, M. D., & Turanovic, J. J. (2016). Self-rated poor health and loneliness in late adulthood: Testing the moderating role of familial ties. *Advances in Lifecourse Research, 27*, 61–68. http://doi.org/10.1016/j.alcr.2015.11.006

Holtfreter, K., Van Slyke, S., & Blomberg, T. G. (2005). Sociolegal change in consumer fraud: From victim-offender interactions to global networks. *Crime, Law, & Social Change, 44*, 251–275. https://doi.org/10.1007/s10611-006-9006-8

Holtfreter, R. E., & Holtfreter, K. (2006). Gauging the effectiveness of U.S. identity theft legislation. *Journal of Financial Crime, 13*, 56–64. https://doi.org/10.1108/13590790610641215

Hoyl, M. T., Alessi, C. A., Harker, J. O., Josephson, K. O., Pietruszka, F. M., Koelfgen, M., . . . & Rubenstein, L. A. (1999). Development and testing of a five-item version of the geriatric depression scale. *Journal of the American Geriatrics Society, 47*, 873–878. https://doi.org/10.1111/j.1532-5415.1999.tb03848.x

Identity Theft Resource Center. (2014). *Identity theft: The aftermath 2013.* Retrieved from www.idtheftcenter.org/images/surveys_studies/Aftermath2013.pdf

Langton, L., & Truman, J. (2014). *Socio-emotional impact of violent crime* (NCJ 247076). Washington, DC: Bureau of Justice Statistics.

Licht, M. H. (1995). Multiple regression and correlation. In L. G. Grimm & P. R. Yarnold (Eds.), *Reading and understanding multivariate statistics* (pp. 16–64). Washington, DC: American Psychological Association.

Lynch, J. (2005). Identity theft in cyberspace: Crime control methods and their effectiveness in combating phishing attacks. *Berkeley Technology Law Journal*, 20, 259–300.

Macmillan, R. (2000). Adolescent victimization and income deficits in adulthood: Rethinking the costs of criminal violence from a life course perspective. *Criminology*, 38, 553–588. https://doi.org/10.1111/crim.2000.38.issue-2

Macmillan, R. (2001). Violence and the life course: The consequences of victimization for personal and social development. *Annual Review of Sociology*, 27, 1–22. https://doi.org/10.1146/annurev.soc.27.1.1

Miller, T. R., Cohen, M. A., & Wiersema, B. (1996). *Victim costs and consequences: A new look*. Washington, DC: National Institute of Justice.

Norris, F. H., & Kaniasty, K. (1994). Psychological distress following criminal victimization in the general population: Cross-sectional, longitudinal, and prospective analyses. *Journal of Consulting and Clinical Psychology*, 62, 111–123. https://doi.org/10.1037/0022-006X.62.1.111

Pearlin, L. I. (1999). The stress process revisited: Reflections on concepts and their interrelationships. In C. S. Aneshensel (Ed.), *Handbook of the sociology of mental health* (pp. 395–415). New York, NY: Kluwer Academic/Plenum Publishers.

Piquero, N. L., Cohen, M. A., & Piquero, A. R. (2011). How much is the public willing to pay to be protected from identity theft? *Justice Quarterly*, 28, 437–459. https://doi.org/10.1080/07418825.2010.511245

Pratt, T. C., Holtfreter, K., & Reisig, M. D. (2010). Routine online activity and Internet fraud targeting: Extending the generality of routine activity theory. *Journal of Research in Crime and Delinquency*, 47, 267–296. https://doi.org/10.1177/0022427810365903

Pratt, T. C., Turanovic, J. J., Fox, K. A., & Wright, K. A. (2014). Self-control and victimization: A meta-analysis. *Criminology*, 52, 87–116. https://doi.org/10.1111/crim.2014.52.issue-1

Reisig, M. D., & Holtfreter, K. (2013). Shopping fraud victimization among the elderly. *Journal of Financial Crime*, 20, 324–337. https://doi.org/10.1108/JFC-03-2013-0014

Reisig, M. D., Pratt, T. C., & Holtfreter, K. (2009). Perceived risk of Internet theft victimization: Examining the effects of social vulnerability and financial impulsivity. *Criminal Justice & Behavior*, 36, 369–384. https://doi.org/10.1177/0093854808329405

Reyns, B. W. (2013). Online routines and identity theft victimization: Further expanding routine activity theory beyond direct-contact offenses. *Journal of Research in Crime and Delinquency*, 50, 216–238. https://doi.org/10.1177/0022427811425539

Reyns, B. W., Henson, B., & Fisher, B. S. (2011). Being pursued online: Applying cyberlifestyle-routine activities theory to cyberstalking victims. *Criminal Justice and Behavior*, 38, 1149–1169. https://doi.org/10.1177/0093854811421448

Rinaldi, P., Mecocci, P., Benedetti, C., Ercolani, S., Bregnocchi, M., Menculini, G., . . . & Cherubini, A. (2003). Validation of the five-item geriatric depression scale in elderly subjects in three different settings. *Journal of the American Geriatrics Society*, 51, 694–698. https://doi.org/10.1034/j.1600-0579.2003.00216.x

Shapland, J., & Hall, M. (2007). What do we know about the effects of crime on victims? *International Review of Victimology*, 14, 175–217. https://doi.org/10.1177/026975800701400202

Sharp, T., Shreve-Neiger, A., Fremouw, W., Kane, J., & Hutton, S. (2004). Exploring the psychological and somatic impact of identity theft. *Journal of Forensic Science*, 49, 1–6.

Slosarik, K. (2002). Identity theft: An overview of the problem. *Criminal Justice Studies*, 15, 329–343.

Strawbridge, W. J., Deleger, S., Roberts, R. E., & Kaplan, G. A. (2002). Physical activity reduces the risk of subsequent depression for older adults. *American Journal of Epidemiology*, 156, 328–334. https://doi.org/10.1093/aje/kwf047

Synovate. (2007). *Federal trade commission: 2006 identity theft survey report*. Retrieved from www.ftc.gov/reports/federal-trade-commission-2006-identity-theft-survey-report-prepared-commission-synovate

Thoits, P. A. (1995). Stress, coping, and social support processes. Where are we? What next? *Journal of Health & Social Behavior*, 35, 53–79. https://doi.org/10.2307/2626957

Turanovic, J. J., & Pratt, T. C. (2013). The consequences of maladaptive coping. Integrating general strain and self-control theories to specify a causal pathway between victimization and offending. *Journal of Quantitative Criminology*, 29, 321–345. https://doi.org/10.1007/s10940-012-9180-z

Turanovic, J. J., & Pratt, T. C. (2014). "Can't stop, won't stop": Self-control, risky lifestyles, and repeat victimization. *Journal of Quantitative Criminology*, 30, 29–56. https://doi.org/10.1007/s10940-012-9188-4

Turanovic, J. J., Reisig, M. D., & Pratt, T. C. (2015). Risky lifestyles, low self-control, and violent victimization across gendered pathways to crime. *Journal of Quantitative Criminology*, 31, 183–206. https://doi.org/10.1007/s10940-014-9230-9

van Wilsem, J. (2013). "Bought it, but never got it": Assessing risk factors for online consumer fraud victimization. *European Sociological Review*, 29, 168–178. https://doi.org/10.1093/esr/jcr053

Walsh, M. E., & Schram, D. D. (1980). The victim of white-collar crime: Accuser or accused? In G. Geis & E. Stotland (Eds.), *White-collar crime: Theory and research* (pp. 32–51). Thousand Oaks, CA: Sage Publications.

8 Sampling

Polling agencies constantly survey the general public to find out what we think of the latest presidential, senate, and gubernatorial candidates or how favorably we perceive proposed legislation. We will watch a presidential debate one night and have polling results identifying the general public's "winner" that same week. Pretty impressive, given that there are over 200 million people in the United States who are of voting age. How do the polling groups do it? By taking samples that are, hopefully, representative of the voting population.

It is often too expensive and too time consuming to reach the entire population of interest when we do research. In fact, it is so challenging that we only attempt it every ten years when we do the national census. Otherwise, we rely on **samples**. Sampling involves selecting a subunit of the population of interest, with the hopes of then generalizing the results of the research to the entire population.

One of the first steps that we must take when planning research is to determine our unit of analysis. The unit of analysis is who or what the researcher chooses to study. Maxfield and Babbie (2012) identified four different types of units of analysis, including (1) individuals, such as prisoners; (2) groups, including prison gangs; (3) organizations, such as the prisons or jails; and (4) social artifacts, including media content, prison disciplinary records, and police data. The **unit of observation** is frequently, but not always, the same as the unit of analysis. The unit of observation is exactly who is providing us with information about the unit of analysis. Let's go over a few examples to make this clear. When Klein, Bailey, and Sample (2018) were interested in learning about the lives of registered sex offenders, they reached out to the sex offenders themselves. In this case, both the unit of analysis and the unit of observation were the same—individuals. I was once interested in the design and management characteristics of jails that were identified in the National Institute of Corrections directory as podular direct supervision facilities. To learn more about these jails, I sent a mail survey to each facility, and I asked for someone in administration to complete it. All the questions on the survey were aimed at getting information about the jail itself, so my unit of analysis was the organization. Since I needed a representative of that organization to complete it, the unit of observation was the responding jail administrator. We must identify our units of analysis and observation at a very early stage in the research plan. Knowing this will guide not only our sampling plan but also our entire data collection strategy.

We need to identify the unit of analysis for two reasons. First, as I already noted, we need to know who or what we are studying before we actually do the study. If you plan to survey households, then you have to decide who in the household is going to serve as the representative for the inhabitants. The National Crime Victimization Survey surveys every member of the selected household who is at least 12 years old for personal victimization interviews. For those surveys, NCVS had to determine what constitutes a household member. The researchers decided that people who are using the sampled home's address as their usual place of residence at the time of the interview *and* currently lack any other usual places of residence will count as household members. For the section of the NCVS interview that just concerns crimes against the household, such as vandalism and burglary, the interviewers need to identify a reference person who will represent the entire house.

That person is usually the owner or renter, but it does not necessarily have to be. They generally seek the person who is most knowledgeable about the house (Morgan & Oudekerk, 2019).

The second reason the unit of analysis matters is that it impacts the conclusions that we can safely draw from the results. We want to avoid making the mistakes of ecological fallacy and exception fallacy. **Ecological fallacy** means that we came to conclusions about individuals based on research conducted on groups or organizations. This is problematic, because researchers have found examples in which there was a relationship between two variables when comparing groups, but when that same variable was tested with individuals, the relationship disappeared (Schwartz, 1994). Findings from some recent medical marijuana research provides a good illustration of this problem. Each year, more states allow for the use of medical marijuana. Naturally, there is concern that more widespread availability of medical marijuana will result in greater misuse and abuse of the drug. Recent findings that there is an association between state-level medical marijuana laws and increases in drug treatment admissions in those same states has only served to reinforce those worries. Caputi (2020) cautions, however, that we cannot take those state-level findings and draw conclusions about individuals. A state-level association between the legality of medical marijuana and number of individuals checking into drug treatment does not tell us whether the people checking into rehab are the same ones who used medical marijuana. There are a number of possibilities why this state-level association would exist, including a concurrent legalization of medical marijuana and expansion of drug treatment slots in the state. The increase of the number of people entering treatment might be a reflection of the number of beds that are now available. In this example, we should not take a state-level analysis and draw conclusions about the behaviors of individuals. To find out if the increased availability of marijuana is responsible for the uptick in people seeking treatment, we would need to research *individuals* entering rehab to find out what drugs they used and, if marijuana was used, how they obtained it.

Exception or **individualistic fallacy** is another potential problem, but in the opposite way as ecological fallacy. Here, we attempt to draw conclusions about large groups after learning about an exceptional circumstance with one or a few individuals. Earlier in the book, I discussed the problem of using anecdotal evidence to dismiss clear trends found in research. We hear of a particularly upsetting crime, and based on that one case, we will call for policy changes that will affect large groups of people. In 2007, two parolees in Connecticut committed a heinous crime, murdering three members of a family in their home. That same year, one other parolee from Connecticut stole a car at knifepoint. In the wake of those two incidents, the governor suspended parole for every violent offender in the entire state and ordered all other parolees to be returned to prison for the remainder of their terms for even the smallest of violations (Berman & Fox, 2016). In 2020, prisons and jails looked to reduce their incarceration populations to stem the spread of COVID-19 behind bars. Across the country, thousands of inmates were released from prisons and jails. Many counties and states met resistance from politicians who believed this to be a dangerous move. In my home state, a sheriff immediately went to the media to complain when one out of the dozens of inmates released early from his jail was rearrested within a few days of release. The sheriff used the behavior of one person as justification to protest the release of all inmates (Wall, 2020). These are just two of many examples in criminal justice of how the behavior of one or two individuals can be generalized to entire populations.

Sample Bias

As I mentioned earlier, the goal of sampling is to select a subset of the population that closely resembles the population. Failure to handle sampling well may result in sample bias, which is a threat to both the internal and external validity of research. Sample bias can impact the results and, in turn, threaten our ability to generalize the results to the population from which we selected the sample. Sample bias can occur due to purposeful actions by those who are involved in research, or it can be completely unintentional and just a matter of chance. One potential motivation for intentional sample bias is a desire to see a program succeed. People whose jobs rely on the existence of a program, or even people who are just passionate about it succeeding, might, consciously or not, select only participants they believe are most likely to succeed. This is known as **creaming**, since they are selecting only the "cream of the crop" to be in the program. This is why there have been instances of correctional interventions and school programs being populated with lower-risk, higher-achieving individuals. The goal of such selection bias is to include people thought to be most likely to succeed. Even in instances when people with a stake in the program's success lack control over who is admitted to the program, they may attempt to introduce sample bias into the program evaluation to skew the results. Years ago, I was tasked with evaluating a parenting program in a medium-security juvenile facility. While I was conducting observations, the instructor whose employment was contingent on the continued funding of the program repeatedly requested that I conduct interviews with 3 of her former students. The research plan that I agreed to with the facility administration did not involve any interviews, but the instructor kept pushing it, as she felt it was crucial to the program evaluation. I later learned that she had developed a very close relationship with these three and had used her own money to purchase them lots of clothing and other items, and they had remained in the community for some time without recidivating. The instructor was only expressing a desire to contact and arrange meetings for me to interview those 3 individuals, and not the other 42 program participants. So, while this practitioner had been unable to cream the participant list, she was attempting to facilitate the researcher's access to only the most successful participants who would undoubtedly have nothing but good things to say about her.

Sample bias can appear for other reasons, including how the poll or survey is made available to potential participants. With the proliferation of websites and media outlets, people now have the ability to choose to get news (or even conspiracy theories being peddled as news) only from sources that ascribe to particular political leanings. When a site chooses to conduct a poll by posting a survey link on their webpage, those who are most likely to see and respond to it are people who share the political views espoused by that show, publication, or network. It is unlikely that a poll shared in that manner will reach people with diverse opinions. When a conservative radio show or website asks its fans to provide approval ratings of a liberal politician, the results are likely to be very negative. The same goes for opinions about conservative politicians being judged by fans of a liberal talk show. This type of sample bias can impact criminal justice opinion polls and surveys. National Public Radio (NPR) conducted a randomized telephone survey in 2018, asking respondents about their preferred television news network and their opinion regarding "are immigrants an important part of our American identity?" Seventy-eight percent of respondents who preferred CNN responded affirmatively, compared to just 52 percent of those who preferred Fox News. So, if a poll appears on a CNN or Fox News website and invites people to click to vote, there is likely to be a good deal of sample bias built into the design (Rose, 2018). But if studies like this are biased, why should we even trust the results of the NPR survey? We can feel comfortable with it because they conducted a telephone survey of a random sample of households instead of posting a link in a location where only certain people would see it.

Over the next few pages, I will discuss sampling techniques and how they might impact our chances of selecting a representative sample. After that, I will revisit the sample bias issue and review ways to detect bias.

Probability Sampling

The preferred approach to sampling is a design that incorporates the **Equal Probability Selection Method** (EPSM), which includes probability sampling. Probability sampling ensures that every possible participant has an equal chance of being selected, and the hope is that this will prevent sample bias. To do this, researchers randomly select participants, cases, locations, or groups to be involved in the study. Since everyone has an equal chance of being selected by randomization, this also maximizes our chances of selecting a sample that will most closely represent the population. Randomization is also considered the fairest way to separate participants into experimental and control groups. One step typically involved in EPSM sampling is to get access to a **sampling frame**, or a comprehensive list of everyone or everything in the population from which we are about to select our sample. If I wanted to survey students at my university regarding their opinions of the state of parking on campus, I would need to get a list of all students who are registered for at least one class or are on maintenance of matriculation status for this semester. Then, once I have that, I would be able to engage in any of the EPSM sampling methods listed here.

Simple Random Sampling

At some point, you have probably participated in **simple random sampling**. In its most basic form, it involves picking a name out of a hat. All that is required for the process to be fair is for all the possible names be placed in the hat and for the hat to undergo a good shaking. Of course, this is impractical if you are taking a sample from a population of 1,000, as that would require a giant hat. Fortunately, there are random number generators available online that allow us to input our sample size. It will then generate a number (97 for this example). We would select the 97th person, case, or location on the sampling frame and then select again and again until we have the desired sample size.

Polling agencies often use random digit dialing when conducting telephone surveys. If the target population lives in a certain area, the researchers will program phones to dial certain area codes followed by randomized phone numbers. If the researchers are seeking a very specific area, they can use specific area codes and prefixes (the first three digits of a phone number) and then randomize the last four digits. Of course, use of random digit dialing for specific locations is complicated by geographically mobile people keeping their cell phone numbers when they move to a new area.

Systematic Random Sampling

Systematic random sampling techniques are easy for those who have access to a sampling frame. Once the researchers have a list of the population, they will choose every nth (5th, 10th, etc.) participant to obtain the desired sample size. When I was conducting an evaluation at my local county jail, I needed a sample of 500 recently released individuals to serve as a comparison group for a reentry program evaluation. The jail staff identified 5,000 potential comparison group members, so I asked them to select every 10th person on the list. A potential drawback and threat to randomization is if the sampling frame is listed in some sort of order that could generate sample bias if every certain number of cases or people are selected. It is recommended that researchers select a random start point on the sampling frame and then proceed with picking every nth case.

Stratified Random Sampling

Stratified random sampling requires that researchers are a bit more knowledgeable about the characteristics of the sampling frame from which the sample is being selected. That is because stratified random sampling involves dividing the population into different strata, often based on demographics such as sex, race, age, or socio-economic status, depending on how important adequate representation of these groups is for the study (Hagan, 2007). From there, researchers select random samples of participants from each stratum. This sampling plan is appropriate anytime it is particularly important for certain segments of the population to be adequately represented. Randomization maximizes, but does not guarantee, a representative sample. Stratification safeguards researchers against accidentally randomly selecting mostly whites for a study when it is essential to hear from various racial groups.

Stratified sampling techniques can be proportionate or disproportionate. **Proportionate stratified samples** include selection of enough cases or individuals to ensure that each stratified group has the same ratio of representation in the sample as they have in the population. It might be desirable to select a sample that has proportions of representation that do not match the population, and that is when it is appropriate to conduct **disproportionate stratified sampling**. For disproportionate stratified sampling, we would oversample some groups and undersample others. Researchers who are looking to study the impact of racial discrimination on the lives of residents of a particular county or state would likely want to oversample racial minorities.

Multistage Cluster Sampling

As I noted, stratified sampling requires some knowledge about the individuals or cases that are being stratified, as their memberships in certain groups needs to be apparent to the researchers in the early stages of sampling. **Multistage cluster sampling** involves division of census tracts, blocks, other areas, or even population units and then taking a probability sample from each cluster (Hagan, 2007; Maxfield & Babbie, 2012). This can be particularly useful when a sampling frame is not available. When studying the impact of police intervention on possible crime displacement, Weisburd et al. (2006) identified both intervention areas and nearby catchment areas that might be impacted by spatial displacement. Data collection involved random selection of street segments within those clusters for social observations and random selection of households in the same clusters for victimization surveys.

The National Crime Victimization Survey utilizes a stratified, multistage cluster sample to select households for their panel study of victimization. The first step of their sampling plan is to stratify by primary sampling units (PSUs), including counties, groups of counties, and large metropolitan areas. All the large PSUs are automatically included in the sample, but the smaller ones are grouped by geographic and demographic characteristics derived from the US census. After randomly selecting some of the smaller PSUs, the researchers divide all the PSU areas into types of housing (such as group quarters, individual houses, etc.) and select clusters of units from those housing types (United States Bureau of Justice Statistics, n.d.).

Nonprobability Sampling

It is not always possible to conduct random sampling for a variety of reasons. For one, placement into the criminal justice system does not occur at random. Judges do not randomly assign people to either probation or incarceration. Even within those specific populations, such as incarcerated individuals, it might not be possible to obtain a random sample for research purposes. Wardens of only some of the prisons might have granted researchers access, and the correctional administration might only be providing the new treatment program that is the target of your evaluation on certain cell blocks. Inmates are not placed in prisons or particular units at random, as their security/custody level and treatment needs dictate where they will live. When studying therapeutic interventions, there are also likely to be ethical issues that will prevent the use of random assignment. There are a number of scenarios in criminal justice in which it is not going to be possible to conduct any of the previously reviewed sampling procedures. Instead, you will likely have to do **nonprobability sampling**, which encompasses any sampling plan that does not abide by the Equal Probability

Selection Method. Non-probability, or non-random, selection plans vary in their ease of implementation and their quality.

Convenience or Accidental Sampling

Convenience or **accidental sampling** is simply a sampling plan designed to be convenient for the researcher. Examples include research that professors conduct by handing out surveys to their own students (Hartley, 2011) or the "man on the street" interviews in which local news reporters and camera crews step outside their studios and ask two or three people walking down the street what they think of an issue (Hagan, 2007). If you wanted to get students' opinions about your university's newest academic policies and you set up a table outside one of the school dining halls on a Tuesday, that would be a convenience sample. You might have chosen a Tuesday afternoon because that is the only day you are free during lunch. While you will get responses, you are going to miss everyone who does not have class on Tuesday, does not eat in that dining hall, or only comes to school at night. Earlier, I discussed posting surveys on websites for news organizations. Special interest groups and even sports teams might post links to surveys this same way. These are all very easy and convenient ways for the researchers to collect responses, but these techniques are very unlikely to produce samples that are representative of the population.

Purposive Sampling

Purposive sampling plans are based on the researchers' needs but also involves the researchers' judgment about how to obtain an appropriate sample. A colleague and I became curious about students' motivations for selecting criminal justice as a major. For sampling, we perceived two challenges. First, we knew that we needed to reach a variety of criminal justice students, ideally from different colleges in multiple states, for generalizability purposes. Second, we realized that, even within majors, some students would be attracted to certain classes while avoiding others based on their academic and career interests. Unfortunately, we were not in possession of the names and email addresses of every criminal justice college student in the nation, nor did we have extensive connections at every school in the United States, so we had to get creative. We addressed our first concern by contacting colleagues at universities in multiple states and requesting their assistance with survey dissemination. Next, we decided to target specific classes. We wanted to avoid electives, as students are likely to self-select into different electives based on their career goals. We decided to target two mandatory core courses—Introduction to Law Enforcement and Research Methods—to ensure that we reached a good cross-section of majors at each university (Krimmel & Tartaro, 1999; Tartaro & Krimmel, 2003). While we were not able to arrange for a random sample of college criminal justice students across the nation, our purposive sampling plan likely produced a more representative group of students than if we had just surveyed students in our own classes at the two colleges where we worked or surveyed students in elective courses.

A common use for purposive sampling is the construction of **focus groups**, or small groups of people (usually 8 to 15) brought together at one time for moderated group interviews. Ideally, the participants should be unfamiliar with each other, and they are typically selected because they all have certain common characteristics (e.g., they are all shoppers at a type of store, all registered voters in a state, all employees of a university, etc.) (Marczak & Sewell, n.d.). Focus groups are used often in marketing research and political polling. In the social sciences, focus groups can be particularly helpful in the early stages of research when the research team is working constructing surveys. Focus group members can help the researchers consider aspects of the topic that they had not thought of previously. For practitioners, these interviews allow service providers to hear directly from consumers about their needs.

Quota Sampling

Quota sampling is similar to stratified random sampling, but it does not involve randomization. As with stratified sampling, the goal of quota sampling is to guarantee that certain groups are represented in the sample. Lee et al. (2014) were interested in recognition of and reaction to elder mistreatment among elderly individuals and how culture might impact their responses. They were particularly interested in Korean culture, so Lee and colleagues used a quota sampling strategy to obtain one sample of elderly Korean Americans living in Los Angeles and another sample of elderly individuals living in Korea. Since the researchers suspected that sex and age would be associated with likelihood of recognizing elder mistreatment and responding to it, they selected their samples in a way to recruit an even balance of both sexes and different age groups. This was a wise decision, given that their results revealed that sex was a factor in seeking help, with females being more likely than males to take that step.

Snowball Sampling

Snowball sampling is a non-probability technique that can help researchers access very hard-to-reach populations. The goal here is to find at least one member of the population of interest and then have that person refer others. Those referrals will, hopefully, introduce the researchers to more potential participants and so on until the small sample increases in size, just like a snowball being rolled through the snow. Perhaps the most well-known example of snowball sampling in criminal justice research is Wright, Decker, Redfern, and Smith's (1992) research on active residential burglars. Active offenders are an especially tough-to-find group. Researchers cannot exactly put an ad in the newspaper asking for active criminals to please call a number or send an email to be part of a study. This is a very suspicious group, and for good reason. Admitting to illegal behavior carries with it the possibility of arrest and prosecution. The most common way that researchers get access to offenders is through police, courts, and corrections departments. The drawback, of course, is that everyone known to the criminal justice system has been caught and, to a certain extent, can be seen as someone who failed at being a good criminal at least once. For that reason, Wright and associates wanted to obtain a sample of active burglars in a way other than going through criminal justice system records. Instead, they hired a well-regarded individual in the neighborhood who used to be an offender but was paralyzed in a shooting. This individual acted as a **gatekeeper** who helped vouch for the credibility of the researchers and made the active offenders comfortable about discussing their criminal activity. Through these introductions, Wright and colleagues did some initial interviews and then encouraged the offenders to introduce them to their associates. The researchers found that their sample of active offenders did, indeed, differ from the sample they would have obtained by going through the corrections system. Forty-two percent of Wright and colleagues' sample had never been arrested for burglary, while 33 percent had been arrested for, but never convicted of, burglary. Those who had never been arrested reported breaking into nearly twice as many homes as the respondents who had been arrested for burglary.

Snowball sampling is an important tool for researchers as it allows us to reach groups that would otherwise be impossible to locate, but it does come with a substantial drawback, and that is the very strong possibility of sample bias. I am sure you have heard the saying "birds of a feather flock together." There is truth to that. If you are doing gang research and start a snowball sample with one or two members of one gang, you are likely to finish your study with a sample consisting of members of that gang and maybe some people in allied gangs. It is very unlikely that the people you meet and interview will introduce you to members of rival gangs. In other words, if you start with Bloods, you are going to get lots of Bloods and probably no Crips. One way to mitigate, but not eliminate, the sample bias inherent in snowball sampling is to use **respondent-driven sampling**. This is a type of snowball sample that seeks to reduce the influence of the initial informant or informants by (1) using as many initial informants as possible and (2) limiting the number of referrals from each initial informant. The goal here is reduce the influence of the small number of initial informants and then to draw a more diverse sample (Weisheit, 2015).

Revisiting Sample Bias

Checking Your Data—Confidence Intervals and Confidence Levels

When we take a sample, how do we know whether it is a good representation of the population? There are ways that we can check this. I do want to caution you that even the best researchers will always find at least a little difference between the sample and the population, as it is inevitable. That difference is called **sampling error**, and it is simply part of research life. As I have discussed throughout this chapter, there are ways to increase one's chances of selecting a representative sample, thereby reducing sampling error. One way includes the use of random selection. The other is selecting a large enough sample size. I will get to appropriate sample size in a little bit. Before I do that, I want to discuss how to compare your sample to the population from which it was selected.

The first way to compare your sample to the population is the easiest, and that is to just look at the **sample statistics** and **population parameters** (Maxfield & Babbie, 2012). A sample statistic provides a summary description of a variable in the sample, whereas the population parameter gives the same information about a variable in the population. Whenever population parameters are known, we can get an idea of how representative our sample is by comparing the numbers to our sample statistics. If I took a random sample of residents in a particular state, I could then look at my sample statistics for resident demographics, such as race and sex, and compare those numbers to the state's published census results.

When we do not have the population statistics available, we can use some very basic statistical techniques to determine confidence intervals and confidence levels. **Confidence intervals** are a range of values in which the true population parameter is likely to be. For example, let's take a sample of jails across the country and ask them to indicate the percent capacity at which they were operating on June 30 that year. We get a range of responses on our surveys and calculate the mean facility capacity of our sample to be at 84 percent. We can figure out the size of the confidence interval in which the population capacity mean lies by determining our **confidence level**, or the probability that our population value falls within a particular confidence interval. So we have our sample mean of 84 percent capacity for the jails. We now need a few other statistics, including the standard deviation, which is a measure of the average deviation from the mean for each of our sample statistics. We also need to know the size of the sample we selected. Once we have those figures, we can calculate a confidence interval. We can then adjust the size of confidence interval, depending on how confident we wanted to be that we had captured the true population value. The drawback here is that the higher our confidence *level* is, the less precise our confidence *interval* will be.

Let me share an example I often use with my students to illustrate the trade-off between the confidence level and the size of the confidence interval. I'll ask someone what time of day they were born. Let's say the student answers 2:15 p.m. Then, I ask if they are really sure, and the student says, "Well, sometime between 1:30 and 2:45." Next, I tell the student that they will get an automatic F in the class if I find out that they are wrong, and they respond, "Sometime between 1 p.m. and 3p.m." I do this with my students all the time, and the higher I make the stakes for being wrong, the less precise they get because they want to be confident that their time interval captures the actual time that they are born. So we could use our available sample mean, standard deviation, and sample size to calculate the amount of sampling error. That would give us an idea of how closely our sample resembles the population. The smaller the calculated sampling error, the better our sample matches the population.

Going back to my hypothetical jails example, my mean occupancy rate was 84 percent. I could then use this information and the other statistics that I already mentioned and calculate a confidence interval. If I wanted to be just 50 percent sure that I knew what the actual population mean was, I might use the sample mean, sample size, and standard deviation to calculate a confidence interval that would probably be pretty small given that we are sacrificing confidence for precision here. In this hypothetical example, we come up with a mean of 84 percent and an interval of + or −3 percent, meaning that I am 50 percent sure that the nationwide jail occupancy rate is somewhere between 81 percent and 87 percent. People rarely only want to be 50 percent sure though. We are much more likely to want to be 95 percent or 99 percent confident in our results. If I were to calculate the confidence interval with a 95 percent confidence level, that would produce a larger confidence interval, perhaps 84 percent + or −7 percent, or anywhere from 77 percent to 91 percent occupancy rate.

I began this chapter discussing political polls. Have you ever noticed that poll results are always accompanied by a margin of error, usually 1 to 5 percent? That is because the poll is based on a sample, not the whole voting population, and the margin of error is the confidence interval. If there is an upcoming election and Politician A has 51 percent support while Politician B has 48 percent, why is it that the reporters say that they are in a "statistical dead heat" when one is 3 percent ahead in the polls? That is because there is likely at least a 3 percent margin of error associated with this sample, so the true population level of support for Politician A is actually anywhere from 48 percent to 54 percent, and for Politician B, the confidence interval is 45 percent to 51 percent. So, based on this sample, we cannot completely rule out the possibility that Politician B is actually ahead in the polls.

Sample Bias and Random Assignments to Groups

Propensity Score Matching

If we are doing a quasi-experimental design, that means that we were unable to randomly assign research participants to either the experimental or comparison groups. This could result in a problem with sample bias, as our groups might differ on some key characteristics. We might be able to address this by matching individuals in the experimental group with similar people in the comparison group. This can be done manually, but another approach is to engage in **propensity score matching** (PSM). PSM allows researchers to match individuals or cases from different groups to each other based on theoretically relevant variables. Jennings, Fridell, Lynch, Jetelina, and Reingle Gonzalez (2017) utilized propensity score matching when they were unable to randomly assign police officers to either wear body-worn cameras or serve as a control group member without a camera. Instead, they had 60 officers who were wearing the cameras and used propensity score matching to find 60 officers in the same jurisdiction who were not wearing cameras who also matched the experimental group officers on sex, race/ethnicity, age, years of law enforcement experience, and number of physical-response-to-resistance incidents in the previous 12 months. The PSM procedure made the two groups much more comparable, and while there is still the possibility of sample bias due to other variables that were not considered, this matching technique substantially enhanced the validity and generalizability of the results.

A Note About Randomization into Groups for Experimental Designs

Random assignment is important as it can help increase our chances of selecting groups that are equal in many important respects. Taking this step, however, is not a guarantee against sample bias if the pool of potential participants is somehow different from the general population. In Chapter 3, I discussed the Zimbardo Stanford Prison Experiment that had to be discontinued after just six days due to the aggressive behavior of the young men who were randomly selected to act as corrections officers. As I noted in Chapter 3, one reason to be concerned about the validity and generalizability of these results is that there is evidence that Zimbardo encouraged the same aggressive behavior that he later found so noteworthy. Another problem with the study was his sample selection.

To find participants, Zimbardo put an ad in a local newspaper calling for "volunteers for a study of the psychological effects of prison life." Once he gathered a pool of volunteers, the research team conducted "diagnostic interviews and personality tests to eliminate candidates with psychological problems, medical disabilities, or a history of crime or drug abuse," giving Zimbardo a sample of "an average group of healthy, intelligent, middle-class males" (Zimbardo, 2020). What Zimbardo either did not consider or did not discuss in his research findings was the strong possibility of sample bias resulting from his recruitment approach. Carnahan and McFarland (2007) wanted to test this idea, so they replicated Zimbardo's recruitment plan and then compared it to another recruitment effort for a generic psychological test. Carnahan and McFarland sent out two different ads to recruit research participants. The first had the same wording as Zimbardo's solicitation, just with a higher offer of pay to account for inflation. The second ad also called for paid participants for a "psychological study" but left out any further details. The researchers administered personality tests to the volunteers for each of the advertised studies, and they found that the people who expressed interest in the prison study differed from those who volunteered for the generic psychological study. Specifically, those interested in the prison study had higher scores indicating greater degrees of aggressiveness, authoritarianism, narcissism, social dominance, and Machiavellianism. It appears that people who are attracted to research in which they could role-play being part of the prison system have some personality characteristics that make them not necessarily representative of the typical college-age male population. While Zimbardo did randomly assign students to the prisoner condition and the correctional officer condition, the manner in which he acquired the volunteers prior to that randomization introduced sample bias. I note this because I noticed that my students tend to see the word "randomization" and immediately conclude that there cannot be any problems with the sample, and that is not always the case. We must consider how the participant pool being randomized was selected.

Finding the Right Sample Size—Statistical Power

As I noted in Chapter 4, statistical conclusion validity may be a problem when we test our hypotheses, as it could affect our ability to correctly discern whether the independent and dependent variables are related. During the sampling phase of research, we might be able to be proactive and take steps to prevent this from being a problem for data analysis. To review, smaller sample sizes might leave our statistical tests lacking sufficient power. Power impacts the probability of correctly rejecting a null hypothesis when it is appropriate to reject it. As we set up our data collection protocol, it might be possible to increase our sample size. I say "might" because, as someone who frequently engages in small program evaluations for individual criminal justice agencies, there are times when I have no say in the number of program participants.

If researchers have the freedom to determine the sample size, it would be wise to conduct a power analysis, which is a quick mathematical test that will inform you how large your sample size must be for you to be confident that you have enough statistical power. There are free and easy-to-use power calculators available on the internet. Generally, increasing the sample size increases our chances of preventing "flukes" such as accidentally picking a small sample that tends to be unlike the rest of the population. Think of coin flips. If you flip a coin ten times, you might actually wind up getting tails eight out of ten times. If you were betting on getting tails, this probably made you happy and led you to believe you were on a hot streak. If you kept flipping a thousand times, the heads/tails ratio would likely be even or extremely close to it. That is because, as you increased your sample size, you would have encountered a few streaks in which you continually got heads, too, canceling out the influence of your tails streak. Large sample sizes are much less susceptible to these flukes, which is why they are more likely to represent the population.

Summary

We do not always have the time or money to observe or survey an entire population, so sampling is a common component of most research designs. The goal of sampling is to select one that is representative of the population from which it was selected. The only exception to this rule is when it is necessary to oversample a group to ensure adequate representation of certain individuals in the sample. The fairest, least biased way of selecting a sample is through random selection, in which every potential participant has an equal chance of being selected. There are several different approaches to random sampling.

Random sampling is not always possible for a number of reasons, so researchers may have to resort to using a non-probability sampling method. These techniques vary in quality, and researchers must be mindful of how the selected sample might differ from the population. Sample bias is a threat to both the internal and external validity of a study, so researchers must consider how representative their sample appears to be before generalizing the results to the population. There are ways to check for similarities and differences between samples and populations, and if the research involves splitting the sample into treatment and non-equivalent comparison groups, matching techniques can help reduce the group differences. It is important to remember that even random sampling does not guarantee a representative sample. The larger a sample size gets, the more likely it is to be representative of the population.

Keywords

Sample
Exception or individualistic fallacy
Sampling frame
Stratified random sampling
Multistage cluster sampling
Purposive sampling
Snowball sampling
Sampling error
Confidence interval
Unit of observation

Creaming
Simple random sampling
Proportionate stratified sampling
Nonprobability sampling
Focus groups
Gatekeeper
Sample statistic
Confidence level
Ecological fallacy
Equal Probability Selection Method (EPSM)

Systematic random sampling
Disproportionate stratified sampling
Convenience/accidental sampling
Quota sampling
Respondent-driven sampling
Population parameter
Propensity score matching

Discussion Questions

1. Discuss steps that we can take to try to avoid sample bias.
2. Why is using EPSM no guarantee that you will produce a representative sample? Discuss steps that you can take to check to see if your sample appears to be representative of the population.
3. Identify the pros and cons of snowball sampling.

References

Berman, G., & Fox, A. (2016). *Trial and error in criminal justice reform: Learning from failure* (revised ed.). Washington, DC: The Urban Institute Press.

Caputi, T. L. (2020). Medical marijuana laws, substance use, treatment admissions, and the ecological fallacy. *Addiction, 115*(1), 188.

Carnahan, T., & McFarland, S. (2007). Revisiting the Stanford Prison Experiment: Could participant self-selection have led to the cruelty? *Personality and Social Psychology Bulletin, 33*(5), 603–614. https://doi.org/10.1177/0146167206292689

Hagan, F. (2007). *Essentials of research methods in criminal justice and criminology* (2nd ed.). Boston, MA: Pearson.

Hartley, R. D. (Ed.). (2011). *Snapshots of research*. Thousand Oaks, CA: Sage Publications.

Jennings, W. G., Fridell, L. A., Lynch, M., Jetelina, K. K., & Reingle Gonzalez, J. M. (2017). A quasi-experimental evaluation of the effects of police body-worn cameras (BWCs) on response-to-resistance in a large metropolitan police department. *Deviant Behavior, 38*(11), 1332–1339. https://doi.org/10.1108/PIJPSM-03-2017-0032

Klein, J. L., Bailey, D. J. S., & Sample, L. L. (2018). Researching the registered: Challenges and suggestions for researchers studying sex offender populations. *Criminal Justice Studies, 31*(2), 192–211. https://doi.org/10.1080/1478601X.2018.1430033

Krimmel, J. T., & Tartaro, C. (1999). Career choices and characteristics of criminal justice undergraduate students. *Journal of Criminal Justice Education, 10*(2), 277–290. https://doi.org/10.1080/10511259900084591

Lee, H. Y., Yoon, H. S., Yoon, J. Y., Kwon, J. H., Park, E. S., Nam, R., . . . & Park, K. H. (2014). Perception and help-seeking intention of intimate partner violence in later life: An international perspective. *Journal of Aggression, Maltreatment, & Trauma, 23*, 45–66. https://doi.org/10.1080/10926771.2014.864744

Marczak, M., & Sewell, M. (n.d.). Using focus groups for evaluation. *CYFERnet—Evaluation*. Tucson, AZ: University of Arizona. Retrieved from https://cals.arizona.edu/sfcs/cyfernet/cyfar/focus.htm

Maxfield, M. G., & Babbie, E. (2012). *Basics of research methods for criminal justice and criminology* (3rd ed.). Belmont, CA: Thomson Wadsworth.

Morgan, R. E., & Oudekerk, B. A. (2019). *Criminal victimization, 2018*. Washington, DC: United States Department of Justice Bureau of Justice Statistics.

Rose, J. (2018). Poll: Where you watch TV news predicts your feelings on immigration. *National Public Radio*. Retrieved from www.npr.org/2018/07/16/629320653/poll-where-you-watch-tv-news-predicts-your-feelings-on-immigration

Schwartz, S. (1994). The fallacy of ecological fallacy: The potential misuse of a concept and the consequences. *American Journal of Public Health, 84*(5), 819–824.

Tartaro, C., & Krimmel, J. T. (2003). The effect of race on criminal justice students' career choices. *American Journal of Criminal Justice, 28*(1), 109–124.

United States Bureau of Justice Statistics. (n.d.). *National crime victimization survey methodology*. Washington, DC: United States Department of Justice Bureau of Justice Statistics.

Wall, J. (2020). Sheriff Golden says concerns validated as one of Governor Murphy's released prisoners is quickly rearrested. *Tap into Middletown*. Retrieved from www.tapinto.net/towns/middletown/articles/sheriff-golden-says-concerns-validated-as-one-of-governor-murphy-s-released-prisoners-is-quickly-rearrested

Weisburd, D., Wyckoff, L. A., Ready, J., Eck, J. J., Hinkle, J. C., & Gajewski, F. (2006). Does crime just move around the corner? A controlled study of spatial displacement and diffusion of crime control benefits. *Criminology, 44*(3), 549–592. https://doi.org/10.1111/j.1745-9125.2006.00057.x

Weisheit, R. A. (2015). Researching drug crime using qualitative methods. In H. J. Copes & M. Miller (Eds.), *The Routledge handbook of qualitative criminology* (pp. 191–203). London: Routledge.

Wright, R., Decker, S. H., Redfern, A. K., & Smith, D. L. (1992). A snowball's chance in hell: Doing fieldwork with active residential burglars. *Journal of Research in Crime and Delinquency, 29*, 148–161. https://doi.org/10.1177/0022427892029002003

Zimbardo, P. G. (2020). *The Stanford Prison Experiment*. Retrieved from www.prisonexp.org/setting-up

Reading 8.1   Methodology Matters

Jury research is an important yet difficult type of inquiry. Since jury deliberations and decisions are made in private, researchers are often left to try to mimic the process through use of vignettes with pools of eligible jurors. Given researchers' easy access to college students, they are frequent research targets, but is that a wise move? College students do not represent a cross-section of society, and as such, their opinions may differ from the population of jury pool members. The internet provides researchers access to a willing pool of participants—for a small fee. This is an intriguing alternative to using students for research, but there are also questions about how representative this sample is of the population of jury pool members. Maeder, Yamamoto, and McManus (2018) sought to explore how college students and paid online survey participants might differ from a sample of adults from the community when asked about jury decision-making. The authors were also cognizant of the fact that survey distribution modality could produce biased results, so they chose to test for differences in responses among those who took the survey in person and those who completed it online. While online surveys offer more privacy and less risk of having answers influenced by social desirability concerns, a potential drawback is inattention to the survey items as people rush to complete them. The researchers discussed the potential benefits of attention/manipulation checks while also cautioning that they are not always an effective proxy for data quality.

Methodology Matters: Comparing Sample Types and Data Collection Methods in a Juror Decision-Making Study on the Influence of Defendant Race

Evelyn M. Maeder, Susan Yamamoto, and Laura A. McManus

Like many (if not all) social scientists, jury researchers often face a crossroad between internal and external validity. Limited resources understandably call for cheaper, more efficient recruitment alternatives, and consequently, many turn to student samples or online crowd-sourcing platforms. Some also argue that people are more honest when they have discussions online (Joinson, 1999; Suler, 2004a). Moreover, these techniques can accelerate productivity and provide data from otherwise inaccessible populations (e.g. from other countries); however, they carry the risk of selection bias and lower data quality. A substantial proportion of researchers nonetheless deem such samples acceptable. For instance, an overwhelming 85.9% of surveyed jury researchers did not perceive a college sample to be sufficiently artificial to prohibit publication (Lieberman, Krauss, Heen, & Sakiyama, 2016). Lieberman et al.

(2016) also found that 36.4% of respondents preferred internal over ecological validity, and 33.3% rated them of equal importance. Incidentally, the guidelines for admissible expert testimony in court (*Daubert v. Merrell Dow Pharmaceuticals*, 1993; *Frye v. United States*, 1923) hold that witnesses must rely on methods that are generally accepted in the field (Bornstein, 1999; Lieberman et al., 2016). Yet failure to meet largely variable standards of ecological validity can lead not only to journal article rejections, but also to the court's rejection of important findings (Bornstein, 1999; Lieberman et al., 2016; McCabe, Krauss, & Lieberman, 2010).

While many researchers consider online and student samples acceptable, there are lingering doubts over participant representativeness, inattention, and non-naïveté. As Lieberman et al. (2016) indicated, even meta-analyses examining methodological differences can be limited by research laboratory idiosyncrasies (e.g. the trial stimulus). Further, because people may be more comfortable expressing some opinions online rather than in person (e.g. Suler, 2004b), these methodological questions become even more important in studies involving race.

As such, we sought to determine whether 'methodology matters' by testing a jury paradigm involving race in four different samples. We compared student to community samples, and online to in-person data collection methods, in a mock jury paradigm involving a criminal trial with a White, Black, or Aboriginal Canadian defendant. Following Lieberman et al.'s (2016) findings, we employed a general methodology that is reasonably considered 'standard' in the field: a written trial stimulus featuring jury instructions. Lack of substantive differences between samples might suggest that dismissal of research based on participant type obscures legitimate information. In any case, partialing out the differences arising from sample and data collection methods across the same context might arm researchers with better guidelines on generalizability.

Student vs. Community Samples

Juror selection is much like an experiment; a jury should be made up of a randomly selected sample of citizens, representative of the relevant population. Indeed, representativeness is one of researchers' main concerns about student samples. Not only are these participants unlikely to serve on juries, having less experience as venirepersons (Bray & Kerr, 1982), but they may constitute a selection bias in terms of demographics as well as thought-processing (Sears, 1986). Hosch, Culhane, Tubb, and Granillo (2011) found that their community sample was significantly older and more highly educated (which had greater variance), but had a similar gender breakdown, as compared to a student sample. Research on the effects of education on bias is mixed. Some argue that among White people, a high level of education results in rejection of racial stereotypes, but others argue that education simply provides more cognitive tools

to justify one's own prejudice (Wodtke, 2012). Notably, research has generally shown a weak relationship between demographic variables and verdict decisions (Bornstein, 1999; McCabe et al., 2010). However, the effect of demographics depends largely on the study context. For instance, jurors who are women tend to be harsher in rape cases than jurors who are men (Bornstein, 1999; Ugwuegbu, 1979). More recently, Devine and Caughlin (2014) conducted a meta-analysis to investigate the extent to which individual characteristics impact on mock juror decisions. They observed negligible effects of education level and prior jury service. They did observe a weak effect of juror gender, such that women had a slightly higher preference for conviction.

Studies directly comparing student and community juror decision-making have yielded mixed findings. An early review (Bornstein, 1999) found trivial differences between them. More recently, Keller and Wiener (2011) demonstrated that community members were more punitive in assigning guilt in mock homicide trials than were students. Conversely, Hosch et al. (2011) found no differences between student and community samples in verdicts in a mock criminal trial, but did observe that students were overall more punitive in sentencing than were community members. McCabe and colleagues (2010) examined potential differences between students and community members in the context of cognitive processing style. Their main conclusion was that students have a greater proclivity to engage in effortful cognitions (i.e., need for cognition) than do community members, which was significantly associated with their verdict decisions. The community sample also evinced greater gender differences and was more punitive. Devine and Caughlin (2014) did not observe any consistent differences in effect size magnitude for several variables when comparing student, community, venireperson, and mixed samples.

In brief, differences among community and student samples appear to be dependent on specific features of the study, such as the outcome of interest and case type. Accordingly, Diamond (1997) concluded that jury researchers should abide by a two-step method: conduct the initial study using a student sample and then replicate it with a more representative one. Nevertheless, there are yet other significant recruitment decisions to consider. Among student subject pools, for instance, competition for research participants may be heavy in part due to the appeal of online studies. The prospect of online data from other sources can also help jury researchers reach a potentially more representative subject pool but carries other threats to reliability and validity.

Online vs. In-Person Samples

Online data collection is in general less labor-intensive. It can also cast a wider recruitment net, providing access to a larger pool of participants across different geographic locations. However, the paucity of research on specific platforms has left researchers suspicious of online techniques. Some have argued that there are few significant differences between these modes of data collection and that these differences may be due to chance rather than systematic variations in data collection methods (O'Neil & Penrod, 2001). Still others suggest that crowdsourcing platforms can be a valuable resource for forensic psychology researchers (Baker, Fox, & Wingrove, 2016). However, different online collection platforms produce unique issues.

Quality Controls

A concern that all online methods face is that lack of control over the study environment can lead to participant carelessness and, hence, to lower-quality data. Without direct researcher intervention, participants can choose their own time constraints, complete the task non-independently, or may simply feel less pressure to pay attention. For these reasons, researchers sometimes integrate 'attention checks' that test whether the participant has read the questions carefully. For instance, Paolacci, Chandler, and Ipierotis (2010) asked participants to indicate whether they ever had a 'fatal heart attack'. Other researchers disguise attention checks as questionnaire items; we might include a question such as: 'It is important to verify that you are paying attention; please select five'. Jury studies, regardless of data collection method, tend to feature 'manipulation check' items asking participants to remember details of the trial (e.g., the race of the defendant). While these techniques are prima facie useful, some online crowdsourcing platforms still challenge their effectiveness.

Mechanical Turk

Amazon's Mechanical Turk (MTurk) is a popular crowdsourcing platform that connects 'requesters' (i.e., researchers) with 'workers' (i.e., participants) who complete set tasks for modest monetary compensation. As Mason and Suri (2012) noted, MTurk has the advantages of a large, diverse subject pool that can facilitate a cost-effective and more efficient experimental cycle. Nonetheless, MTurk workers, like students, are somewhat distinct in terms of demographics. Paolacci et al. (2010) surveyed 1,000 MTurk workers, the majority of whom were women, and found that they have higher than average education levels, but lower than average salaries. Mason and Suri (2012) reported an average income of US $30,000 among workers.

MTurk gives the researcher considerable agency over the recruitment process, such as which characteristics participants need and how much to pay them. These decisions potentially have unintended consequences. However, conventional decisions can also work in researchers' favor. Because it is common to base payment on completion of attention checks, Hauser and Schwarz (2016) reasoned that MTurk workers are more attentive to instructions than undergraduate subject pool participants. Hauser and Schwarz (2016) compared undergraduate and MTurk participants' performance on instructional manipulation checks; for example, a long set of instructions included a prompt to write 'I read the instructions' in lieu of filling out a questionnaire. Across three studies, Hauser and Schwarz (2016) reported that MTurk workers tended to outperform undergraduates on instructional manipulation checks. This greater performance undermines the notion that traditional participants are more attentive than MTurk workers. Granted, it is possible that in practice workers are actively searching for attention checks while disregarding other items. Another means of quality control involves worker qualifications. Specifically, MTurk allows recruiters to restrict participation to workers with certain approval ratings (e.g., requesters have approved at least 95% of their work). Peer, Vosgerau, and Acquisti (2014) showed evidence that using only workers with a high approval rating (greater than 95%) yields higher quality data.

Buhrmester, Kwang, and Gosling (2011) assessed the reliabilities of six personality measures at three different compensation amounts (2, 10, and 50 cents), and found no notable differences other than data collection speed. They did show that participation rates were lower for a 30-minute survey relative to 5- and 10-minute tasks. Rouse (2015) found that scores on a personality measure were significantly less reliable (using coefficient alpha) for an MTurk sample compared to the reliability reported for a sample of adult community members (who received the questionnaire in the mail) from the original study (Goldberg, 1999). Importantly, elimination of those who had failed attention checks did not improve reliability. However, participants who had been asked to consider whether they had paid sufficient attention yielded significantly higher reliability compared to those who did not see this question. There is indeed some evidence of MTurk workers' divided attention during tasks. Chandler, Mueller, and Paolacci's (2014) survey showed that although most workers reported completing tasks alone (73%), a sizeable proportion (38%) reported doing other activities at the same time. Nevertheless, replication studies of classic psychology experiments (e.g., the Prisoner's Dilemma; Horton, Rand, & Zeckhauser, 2011) on MTurk have yielded promising parallel results. Bates and Lanza (2013) reported differences in some study contexts (i.e., regional patterns of religious attitudes), but have generally echoed other researchers in finding MTurk sufficiently reliable (Cokely, Galesic, Schulz,

Ghazal, & Garcia-Retamero, 2012; Gardner, Brown, & Boice, 2012; Paolacci et al., 2010).

A final consideration surrounds the potential non-naïveté of MTurk workers, given that they may be highly practiced at psychological surveys. For instance, Chandler et al. (2014) found that 56% of their respondents had previously taken part in the well-known Prisoner's Dilemma paradigm. Chandler et al. (2014) also reminded us that some MTurk workers will continue to participate in new experiments for a longer period than would undergraduates, thus constituting a lower turnover rate than student samples. They did note that practice effects can apply to virtually any sample, and as such are a general recruitment caution. Still, it is likely that MTurk workers are particularly well-versed in completing attention checks. Participants may not only be well-practiced, but also may sometimes communicate aspects of a study to other workers.

Chandler et al. (2013) therefore warned researchers to be aware of information sharing over online communities such as Reddit, which they found can influence task traffic. As with student samples, the effect of online data collection seems to depend upon the specific topic of interest. In fact, it might even be that for some studies online data collection methods produce experimental benefits, such as mitigating social desirability.

Race and Juror Decision-Making

Researchers have identified two main routes by which jurors might process trial information: systematic and heuristic (Chaiken, 1980; Levett & Kovera, 2009). Systematic processing is characterized by methodical evaluation of relevant information, whereas heuristic processing is more automatic and less effortful. Juror decision-making can be mentally taxing and is thus susceptible to the dangers of heuristic processing. Hence, jury researchers require a clear picture of participants' attention to a trial stimulus to accurately interpret results. If a participant's attention is divided, that could influence the likelihood of phenomena like racial bias.

Because modern racial bias tends to manifest in circumstances of ambiguity and fewer social desirability pressures (Dovidio & Gaertner, 1991, 2004; Gaertner & Dovidio, 1986; Sommers & Ellsworth, 2001), studies featuring student and online participants might vary considerably from more traditional samples. It is possible that racial attitudes naturally differ between student and community mock jury populations (as suggested by Schuller, Kazoleas, & Kawakami, 2009). Students' potential higher propensity toward rational processing (i.e., analytic thinking; McCabe et al., 2010) might better protect against biased decision-making, which tends to manifest when jurors rely on mental shortcuts rather than direct information (Levett & Kovera, 2009). In a meta-analysis, Mitchell, Haw, Pfeifer, and Meissner (2005) found that community participants expressed more racial bias in sentencing, but not verdict, decisions. However, the number of studies included in this comparison was quite small due to a lack of studies using community samples.

Further, there is potential for participants in online studies to feel more comfortable expressing racial bias. The phenomenon responsible is known as the 'online disinhibition effect', in which people feel less constricted by social desirability (Joinson, 1999; Suler, 2004b). Joinson (1999) found that online student participants showed lower social desirability and social anxiety for an online survey compared to a pen and paper one. Suler (2004a) argued that, in general, students tend to express various opinions in online discussion boards that they would not otherwise in the classroom. Suler (2004b) posited that the invisibility, lack of real-time and face-to-face communication, and minimization of authority contribute to this disinhibition. Online studies may also more effectively avoid unintended experimenter influences. However, if MTurk workers are non-naïve to racial bias studies, then the social desirability of appearing unprejudiced might motivate them to conceal their biases. Indeed, making mock jurors aware of their own proclivity for bias is among the most effective techniques for combatting it (Sommers & Ellsworth, 2001, 2009). To our knowledge, there are no existing studies comparing in-person to online samples in the context of a jury decision-making study involving race. At this juncture, it is necessary to test empirically what, if any, benefits or detriments arise from different combinations of student/community and online/in-lab data.

The Current Study

Researchers and the courts alike have expressed concerns that use of student and online samples in juror decision-making studies significantly decrements the trustworthiness of results. Both student samples and online data collection methods risk low representativeness, data quality, and practice effects, and these issues may manifest differently in studies testing racial bias. The purpose of this study was to test whether relying on student and online samples might yield unique demographics, differential attentiveness to the trial stimulus, and ultimately, disparate verdict decisions. Participants read a fabricated robbery trial transcript—in which we manipulated the defendant's race (White, Black, Aboriginal Canadian)—then made verdict decisions and completed manipulation/attention checks. We administered this study to four different Canadian samples: non-student community members online (i.e., MTurk workers), non-student community members who came to the lab, a group of students online, and a group of students who came to the lab.

Hypothesis 1

In line with the literature demonstrating greater harshness against minority defendants (Devine & Caughlin, 2014; Mitchell et al., 2005), research has also demonstrated harsher decisions against Aboriginal Canadian defendants, potentially relating to historical mistreatment of Indigenous Peoples in Canada (Maeder, Yamamoto, & Saliba, 2015; Mitchell et al., 2005). Therefore, we expected a main effect of race across all samples, such that the Aboriginal Canadian defendant would yield the greatest proportion of guilty verdicts, followed by the Black defendant, with the White defendant yielding the lowest proportion of guilty verdicts.

Hypothesis 2

We predicted an interaction between defendant race and sample type, such that the effect of race would be stronger in the community samples compared to the student samples (McCabe et al., 2010; Mitchell et al., 2005; Schuller et al., 2009). We also expected an interaction between defendant race and data collection method, such that it would be stronger in the online samples than the in-person samples (Joinson, 1999; Suler, 2004b).

Hypothesis 3

We expected a higher attention check failure rate among online participants relative to in-lab participants. However, because MTurk workers are familiar with attention checks, an interaction effect was possible, in that we might expect online community participants to outperform online student participants.

Method

Participants

A total of 319 (79 men, 192 women, 1 trans individual, and 47 who did not specify gender) students participated online (mean age = 20.96, SD = 5.71). One-hundred eighty-seven (61 men, 113 women, 2 trans individuals, and 11 who did not specify gender) students participated in-lab (mean age = 20.02, SD = 3.84). Two-hundred forty-four (83 men, 70 women, 1 trans individual, and 90 who did not specify gender) community members participated online (mean age = 30.31, SD = 8.94). Finally, 197 (95 men, 90 women, 1 trans individual, and 11 who did not specify gender) community members participated in-lab (mean age = 28.45, SD = 11.61).

Materials and Procedure

Upon initial recruitment, participants answered a brief demographics survey to ensure juror eligibility (i.e., Canadian citizens, 18 years of age or older, with no prior convictions of indictable offenses and a strong comprehension of the English language). Participants in the online community sample were recruited through Amazon's Mechanical Turk, while the in-lab community sample was recruited by placing ads in local papers and online advertising sites. Online and in-lab student participants were recruited using the Carleton University Psychology Department's electronic recruitment database. These participants were all enrolled in a first-year introductory psychology class. Students were only permitted to participate in either the online or in-person study, which we ensured by setting automatic exclusion criteria within the system.

All participants were directed to complete the study using Qualtrics, an online survey software. The survey took approximately 30 minutes. Those who participated in-person completed the study on computers in the lab; those who completed the study online could participate in the location of their choosing. Informed consent was obtained from all participants, who were then randomly assigned to read a six-page transcript of a robbery trial involving a White, Black, or Aboriginal Canadian male defendant. Qualtrics software was set to randomly present one condition each time a survey was initiated. The race of the defendant was manipulated using stereotypical surnames, as well as photographs, which were pilot tested to match on perceived likeability, attractiveness, and age. The six-page transcript detailed the facts in evidence, such that the victim was walking to his vehicle when he was physically assaulted by a man who demanded his watch and wallet. The trial featured testimony/cross-examination from the victim and the accused, as well as a witness and the arresting officer. The arresting officer testified that the police discovered muddy footprints, which were matched to the defendant's shoe size. He also testified that a pair of muddy shoes along with the victim's camera were discovered at the defendant's apartment. To help inform mock juror judgments, participants were provided with the Canadian Criminal Code criteria for the charge, as well as instructions regarding the burden of proof and reasonable doubt.

Participants were then asked to render a verdict using a dichotomous guilty/not guilty measure. On a separate page following the trial questionnaire, participants were asked to identify the race of the defendant, to ensure that they were attentive to the case. Finally, participants provided demographic information such as their gender, race, and age before being debriefed and thanked for their participation. Community participants were compensated with cash—those who participated in the lab received $15 (this included compensation for parking/transit), and those who completed the study on MTurk received $5[1]—while all students received course credit as compensation. Notably, per MTurk research conventions, workers were informed that their payment would be based on attention checks. However, participants who incorrectly identified the race of the defendant still received payment. We also restricted participation to Canadian workers having approval ratings greater than 95%.

Analytic Strategy

We tested our hypotheses regarding verdict and manipulation checks using hierarchical loglinear analysis (HILOG). Hierarchical loglinear analysis is used to test for relationships among categorical variables, and is preferred over the use of Chi-squared analyses for investigations of multiple categorical variables in that it allows for examinations of 3-way or higher interactions (Green, 1988). In a HILOG, effects of categorical independent variables on a categorical dependent variable are tested via investigations of their interactions. Sample differences were tested using HILOG and analyses of variance (ANOVA)/t-tests where applicable.

Results

Demographic Comparisons

Gender

To examine whether gender composition differed by sample type and data collection method (or their interaction), we conducted a 2 (sample

type: community, student) $\times$ 2 (data collection method: online, in-lab) $\times$ 2 (gender: man, woman[2]) hierarchical loglinear analysis (HILOG). This analysis revealed a significant sample type $\times$ gender interaction, $\chi^2(1, N = 797) = 28.44, p < .001, v = .19$. The student sample included a lower percentage of men (33%) than did the community sample (52%). No other interactions were significant.

Race

To determine whether sample type and data collection method were related to racial composition, we conducted a 2 (sample type: community, student) $\times$ 2 (data collection method: online, in-lab) $\times$ 2 (participant race: White, minority[3]) HILOG. This revealed a significant sample type $\times$ participant race interaction, $\chi^2(1, N = 803) = 4.94, p = .03, v = .08$. The student sample included a lower percentage of White participants (63%) than did the community sample (70%). The analysis also revealed a significant data collection method $\times$ participant race interaction, $\chi^2(1, N = 803) = 10.72, p = .001, v = .12$. The in-lab sample included a lower percentage of White participants (60%) than did the online sample (71%). The interaction between sample type, data collection method, and participant race was not significant.

Age

To examine whether sample type, data collection method, or their interaction was related to participant age, we conducted a 2 (sample type: community, student) $\times$ 2 (data collection method: online, in-lab) Analysis of Variance (ANOVA) with participant age as the dependent variable. Levene's test revealed that the variance between the two sample types was significantly different, $F = 182.91, p < .001$. In other words, our student sample was more homogenous with respect to age than our community sample. Relying on Welch's statistic, this analysis revealed a significant main effect of sample type, $F (1, 433.41) = 213.96, p < .001$. Unsurprisingly, our student sample was significantly younger (M = 20.50, SD = 4.83) than was our community sample (M = 29.53, SD = 10.34). No other main effects or interactions were significant.

Education

Given the nature of our student sample, all participants in this group held some college education. To determine whether community sample education differed by data collection method, we conducted an independent groups *t*-test with collection method as the grouping variable and education level as the dependent variable. This analysis revealed a significant difference as a function of data collection method, *t* (637) = –4.29, *p* < .001, such that the in-lab participants (M = 4.74, SD = 1.79) had a higher level of education than the online participants (M = 4.14, SD = 1.72).

Manipulation Check

In order to determine whether sample type and data collection method were related to the likelihood of passing our manipulation check, we conducted a 2 (sample type: community, student) × 2 (data collection method: online, in-lab) × 3 (defendant race: White, Black, Aboriginal Canadian) × 2 (manipulation check result: pass, fail) HILOG. This analysis revealed a significant interaction among sample type, defendant race, and manipulation check result. There were no differences in failure rates for White and Black defendant conditions (all failure rates at or below 20.8%), but in the Aboriginal Canadian defendant condition, students (57%) were more likely to fail[4] the manipulation check than were community members (39%), $\chi^2(1, N = 401) = 13.75, p < .001, v = .19$. Notably, manipulation check result was not related to data collection method. Those who failed the manipulation check were eliminated from subsequent analyses, leaving us with 137 in-lab students, 191 online students, 159 in-lab community members, and 165 online community members.

Verdict

To determine whether sample type and data collection method were related to verdict decisions as a function of defendant race, we conducted a 2 (sample type: community, student) × 2 (data collection method: online, in-lab) × 3 (defendant race: White, Black, Aboriginal Canadian) × 2 (verdict: guilty, not guilty) HILOG. This analysis revealed a significant relationship between sample type and verdict, $\chi^2(1, N = 650) = 6.33, p = .012, v = .10$. Regardless of data collection method or defendant race, students were more likely to convict (46%) than were community members (36%).

This analysis also revealed a significant interaction among data collection method, defendant race, and verdict, $\chi^2(2, N = 650) = 8.61, p = .013$. Examining this effect in terms of data collection method revealed that while there was no effect of defendant race on verdict among those who participated online, defendant race significantly affected verdict decisions for those who participated in-lab, $\chi^2(1, N = 296) = 8.44, p = .015, v = .10$. Specifically, in-lab participants were most likely to convict White defendants (52%), followed by Aboriginal Canadian defendants (43%), with Black defendants (32%) receiving the lowest conviction rates. Looking at this interaction in another way, data collection method yielded different patterns on verdict as a function of defendant race. Notably, online participants were more lenient towards White defendants than were in-lab participants, $\chi^2(1, N = 214) = 4.40, p = .04, v = .14$; no differences were observed for Black or Aboriginal Canadian defendants.

Discussion

Jury decision-making researchers have long faced questions regarding methodology and ecological validity. Both researchers and the courts have questioned the representativeness and quality of student as well as online samples. The purpose of this study was to test for differences between four different sample types (i.e., comparing student/community and online/in-lab participants) in a mock jury paradigm involving a criminal trial with a White, Black, or Aboriginal Canadian defendant. Following research arguing that people may be more comfortable expressing bias online (Joinson, 1999; Suler, 2004b) and that students might express less racial bias than community members (Mitchell et al., 2005; Schuller et al., 2009), we predicted that the online and community samples would yield a greater proportion of guilty verdicts for Aboriginal Canadian and Black defendants (Maeder et al., 2015; Mitchell et al., 2005). We also expected a higher manipulation check failure rate for the online samples owing to the lack of control over the study environment. Results did not support these predictions, but do lead to some interesting conclusions.

With respect to demographic differences, we found that the student sample had a greater proportion of women compared to the community sample. Interestingly, both online samples were more likely to abstain from providing demographic information than were in-person participants. In line with previous findings (Hosch et al., 2011), the student sample was significantly younger and the ages less varied compared to the community sample.

Unsurprisingly, the community sample was more diverse in terms of education level than was the student sample. Both the student and online samples were more ethnically diverse than their counterparts. Contrary to our prediction that the online sample would show a higher manipulation check failure rate, students were more likely to fail the manipulation check in Aboriginal Canadian defendant conditions than were community members, requiring additional data collection to fill these cells. Whether this speaks to attentiveness or a lack of exposure to Aboriginal Canadians among our student samples is unknown; future researchers may wish to study racial identification accuracy among various groups. Addressing one of the common criticisms of online samples, those who participated online were no more likely to fail than those who completed the study in-person.

Arguably our most interesting finding comes from the interaction among data collection method, defendant race, and verdict. Participants who completed the study online were more lenient towards White defendants compared to in-lab participants, suggesting that the mere presence of a research assistant (and/or other participants) in the room while participants completed the study had an effect on the expression of racial bias. This finding supports the notion that people may be more disinhibited online than in person (Joinson, 1999; Suler, 2004a, 2004b). Future researchers may wish to test for effects of race salience as a function of completing a study in the presence of members of a racial minority. Previous jury decision-making research suggests that individual verdicts show evidence of race salience effects (i.e., White mock jurors showing equivalent conviction rates for Black and White defendants, rather than harsher verdicts toward Black defendants) in situations wherein mock jurors are told they will be *deliberating* in diverse (rather than all-White) groups (Keii, Hymes, Anderson, & Weathers, 1995; Sommers, 2006). As such, the mere presence (or even hypothetical future presence) of minority jurors can suppress racial bias. It is possible that this effect extends to the presence of fellow participants in a study with no stated deliberation component—future research should test this systematically, as we are unable to make causal claims with our current findings.

Limitations

Given that this study represents a comparison of samples from only one lab, the findings warrant caution in generalizability. The area in which this study took place has a low proportion of Black (4.9%) and Aboriginal Canadians (2%; Statistics Canada, 2008). Hence, our results regarding racial bias and race-based manipulation questions may represent our participants' exposure (or lack thereof) to specific minority groups. These findings might differ not only from other Canadian regions, but also compared to U.S.-based samples. Some Canadian findings on race and juror decision-making have diverged from U.S. research (e.g. Maeder, Yamamoto, & McManus, 2015; Maeder, Yamamoto, McManus, & Capaldi, 2016). Moreover, our online sample was from a highly specific online recruitment platform (Canadians on Mechanical Turk), and so we cannot speak to effects of other crowdsourcing platforms such as Qualtrics Panels.

Further, because of the relative scarcity of Canadian MTurk workers, we relied on a comparatively high pay rate ($5.00). While some research suggests few differences between smaller pay increments (Buhrmester et al., 2011), it is possible that lower pay rates would produce lower quality work after a certain monetary threshold. We also do not know how these findings might apply to a study involving experimental attempts to reduce bias, such as making race a salient issue at trial (Sommers & Ellsworth, 2001, 2009). Additionally, while it is important for researchers to know the extent of participant attentiveness, we do not have data about jurors' attentiveness during real trials, which might be long and complex. It may be that techniques for bolstering participant attention decrease the ecological validity of the findings. Research shows that lack of attentional resources or motivation can lead to heuristic processing (Levett & Kovera, 2009), in which jurors rely on mental shortcuts rather than directly processing evidence. Hence, greater attention might attenuate bias.

Relatedly, there are limitations to using attention/manipulation checks as a proxy for data quality. MTurk workers—especially those with high approval ratings—are likely well versed in correctly answering these questions. It is possible that workers look for attention-related items specifically and are less vigilant with other questionnaire items. Examining only workers with high approval ratings might also result in a selection bias. However, recruiting those without such qualifications arguably presents greater challenges. Such workers, after all, are either new to MTurk or have a demonstrable history of work rejection. Moreover, we wished to test this sample under the conditions likely to be applied in practice, and studies of MTurk tend to recommend this qualification (see Peer et al., 2014).

Peer et al. (2014) also suggested that workers might see attention checks as an indirect accusation of non-attention. Although workers are explicitly told that they can withdraw from the study without penalty, some may view doing so as sunk cost and feel hostile at the idea of returning a task. The online community participants were the only ones in the current study for whom compensation had specific (forewarned) criteria, and therefore their experience was distinct. However, again this is conventional, and one could argue that highly qualified workers likely believe their tasks will be evaluated in this way even without warning. Clearly, MTurk has a unique culture surrounding beliefs about fair practices. There is an active online community featuring discussion forums and task review systems (e.g., Turkopticon, a website where workers can rate requesters on fairness, communication, and pay). This study was intended to test for overall differences between each sample type, while underscoring idiosyncrasies that researchers may find relevant. Future researchers might consider surveying workers for their impressions about jury studies and general procedures.

Conclusion

This project lends data to the question of whether researchers should rely on student and online samples. Our findings are encouraging in terms of some common criticisms, such as higher manipulation check failure rates, for which there were minor differences between groups. We have also shown some limitations of certain samples, including clear demographic differences (specifically gender and race breakdown). Results even seem to indicate that online samples might be preferred over in-lab ones when measuring phenomena strongly affected by social desirability, given that our in-lab samples showed some bias over-correction (although it is important to keep in mind that with regards to juror decision-making, a real trial is necessarily an in-person affair). In any case, we encourage researchers to pay adequate mind to potential differences, for example by asking participants which region they live in or about their exposure to certain groups. Overall, our findings echo previous researchers (Baker et al., 2016; Bornstein, 1999; O'Neil & Penrod,

2001) in suggesting that student/online samples are likely no more threatening to ecological validity in this context than are traditional samples.

Notes

1. Although this may seem like a high compensation rate for MTurk, Canadians on MTurk are exceedingly rare, and this rate was necessary to attract participants who met our eligibility criteria. Data collection took a few months to complete, suggesting that this rate did not elicit selection bias.
2. Cell sizes for individuals identifying as another gender were too small to include as a separate category. Additionally, a number of participants did not provide information regarding their gender and were therefore excluded from this analysis.
3. Cell sizes for individuals identifying as a race other than White were too small to include as separate categories. Additionally, many participants did not respond to our race question and were therefore excluded from this analysis.
4. Students tended to indicate that the Aboriginal Canadian defendant was Hispanic/Latino or Asian, suggesting that most perceived him to be a racial minority.

Disclosure Statement

No potential conflict of interest was reported by the authors.

Funding

This work was supported by a Social Sciences and Humanities Research Council of Canada Insight Development Grant awarded to the first author.

Discussion Questions

1. How did the results for surveys completed in person differ from those completed online? What are the possible explanations for the differences?
2. Discuss the advantages and disadvantages of using students and paid online survey takers for research.
3. How did social desirability potentially play a role in the findings?

References

Baker, M. A., Fox, P., & Wingrove, T. (2016). Crowdsourcing as a forensic psychology research tool. *American Journal of Forensic Psychology*, 34(1), 37–50.

Bates, J. A., & Lanza, B. A. (2013). Conducting psychology student research via Mechanical Turk crowdsourcing service. *North American Journal of Psychology*, 15(2), 385–394.

Bornstein, B. H. (1999). The ecological validity of jury simulations: Is the jury still out? *Law and Human Behavior*, 23, 75–91.

Bray, R. M., & Kerr, N. L. (1982). Methodological considerations in the study of the psychology of the courtroom. In N. L. Kerr & R. M. Bray (Eds.), *The psychology of the courtroom* (pp. 287–323). San Diego, CA: Academic Press, Inc.

Buhrmester, M. D., Kwang, T., & Gosling, S. D. (2011). Amazon's Mechanical Turk: A new source of inexpensive, yet high quality data. *Perspectives on Psychological Science*, 6(1), 3–5.

Chaiken, S. (1980). Heuristic versus systematic information processing and the use of source versus message cues in persuasion. *Journal of Personality and Social Psychology*, 39, 752–766. https://doi.org/10.1037/0022-3514.39.5.752

Chandler, J., Mueller, P., & Paolacci, G. (2014). Nonnaïveté among Amazon Mechanical Turk workers: Consequences and solutions for behavioral researchers. *Behavior Research Methods*, 46(1), 112–130. https://doi.org/10.3758/s13428-013-0365-7

Cokely, E. T., Galesic, M., Schulz, E., Ghazal, S., & Garcia-Retamero, R. (2012). Measuring risk literacy: The Berlin Numeracy Test. *Judgment and Decision Making*, 7(1), 25–47.

Daubert v. Merrell Dow Pharmaceuticals. (1993). 509 U.S. 579.

Devine, D. J., & Caughlin, D. E. (2014). Do they matter? A meta-analytic investigation of individual characteristics and guilt judgments. *Psychology, Public Policy, and Law*, 20, 109–134. https://doi.org/10.1037/law0000006

Diamond, S. S. (1997). Illuminations and shadows from jury simulations. *Law and Human Behavior*, 21, 561–571.

Dovidio, J. F., & Gaertner, S. L. (1991). Changes in the expression and assessment of racial prejudice. In H. J. Knopke, R. J. Norrell, & R. W. Rogers (Eds.), *Opening doors: Perspectives on race relations in contemporary America* (pp. 119–148). Tuscaloosa, AL: The University of Alabama Press.

Dovidio, J. F., & Gaertner, S. L. (2004). Aversive racism. In M. P. Zanna (Ed.), *Advances in experimental social psychology* (Vol. 36, pp. 1–51). San Diego, CA: Academic.

Frye v. United States. 292 F. 1013 (D.C. Cir. 1923).

Gaertner, S. L., & Dovidio, J. F. (1986). The aversive form of racism. In J. Dovidio & S. Gaertner (Eds.), *Prejudice, discrimination and racism* (pp. 61–89). Toronto: Academic Press.

Gardner, R. M., Brown, D. L., & Boice, R. (2012). Using Amazon's Mechanical Turk website to measure accuracy of body size estimation and body dissatisfaction. *Body Image, 9*(4), 532–534.

Goldberg, L. R. (1999). A broad-bandwidth, public-domain, personality inventory measuring the lower-level facets of several five-factor models. In I. Mervielde, I. Deary, F. De Fruyt, & F. Ostendorf (Eds.), *Personality psychology in Europe* (Vol. 7, pp. 7–28). Tilburg, The Netherlands: Tilburg University Press.

Green, J. A. (1988). Loglinear analysis of cross-classified ordinal data: Applications in developmental research. *Child Development, 59*(1), 1–25.

Hauser, D. J., & Schwarz, N. (2016). Attentive Turkers: MTurk participants perform better on online attention checks than do subject pool participants. *Behavior Research Methods, 48*(1), 400–407. Retrieved from http://doi.org.proxy.library.carleton.ca/10.3758/s13428-015-0578-z

Horton, J. J., Rand, D. G., & Zeckhauser, R. J. (2011). The online laboratory: Conducting experiments in a real labor market. *Experimental Economics, 14*(3), 399–425.

Hosch, H. M., Culhane, S. E., Tubb, V. A., & Granillo, E. A. (2011). Town vs. Gown: A direct comparison of community residents and student mock jurors. *Behavioral Sciences and the Law, 29,* 452–466.

Joinson, A. (1999). Social desirability, anonymity, and internet-based questionnaires. *Behavioral Research Methods, Instruments and Computers, 31*(3), 433–438.

Keller, S. R., & Wiener, R. L. (2011). What are we studying? Student jurors, community jurors, and construct validity. *Behavioral Sciences and the Law, 29,* 376–394.

Kerr, N. L., Hymes, R. W., Anderson, A. B., & Weathers, J. E. (1995). Defendant-juror similarity and mock juror judgments. *Law and Human Behavior, 19*(6), 545–567.

Levett, L. M., & Kovera, M. B. (2009). Psychological mediators of the effects of opposing expert testimony on juror decisions. *Psychology, Public Policy, and Law, 15*(2), 124–148.

Lieberman, J. D., Krauss, D. A., Heen, M., & Sakiyama, M. (2016). The good, the bad, and the ugly: Professional perceptions of jury decision-making research practices. *Behavioral Sciences and the Law, 34,* 495–514.

Maeder, E. M., Yamamoto, S., & McManus, L. A. (2015). Race salience in Canada: Testing multiple manipulations and target races. *Psychology,*

Public Policy, and Law, 21(4), 442–451. https://doi.org/10.1037/law0000057

Maeder, E. M., Yamamoto, S., McManus, L. A., & Capaldi, C. (2016). Race-crime congruency in the Canadian context. *Canadian Journal of Behavioural Science/Revue Canadienne des Sciences du Comportement, 48*(2), 162–170. https://doi.org/10.1037/cbs0000045

Maeder, E. M., Yamamoto, S., & Saliba, P. (2015). The influence of defendant race and victim physical attractiveness on juror decision making in a sexual assault trial. *Psychology, Crime & Law, 21,* 62–79. https://doi.org/10.1080/1068316X.2014.915325

Mason, W., & Suri, S. (2012). Conducting behavioral research on Amazon's Mechanical Turk. *Behavior Research Methods, 44,* 1–23. https://doi.org/10.3758/s13428-011-0124-6

McCabe, J. G., Krauss, D. A., & Lieberman, J. D. (2010). Reality check: A comparison of college students and a community sample of mock jurors in a simulated sexual violent predator civil commitment. *Behavioural Sciences and the Law, 28,* 730–750.

Mitchell, T. L., Haw, R. M., Pfeifer, J. E., & Meissner, C. A. (2005). Racial bias in mock juror decision-making: A meta-analytic review of defendant treatment. *Law and Human Behavior, 29,* 621–637. https://doi.org/10.1007/s10979-005-8122-9

O'Neil, K. M., & Penrod, S. D. (2001). Methodological variables in Web-based research that may affect results: Sample type, monetary incentives, and personal information. *Behavior Research Methods, Instruments, & Computers, 33*(2), 226–233.

Paolacci, G., Chandler, J., & Ipierotis, P. (2010). Running experiments on Amazon Mechanical Turk. *Judgment and Decision Making, 5*(5), 411–419.

Peer, E., Vosgerau, J., & Acquisti, A. (2014). Reputation as a sufficient condition for data quality on Amazon Mechanical Turk. *Behavior Research Methods, 46*(4), 1023–1031. http://doi.org.proxy.library.carleton.ca/10.3758/s13428-013-0434-y

Rouse, S. V. (2015). A reliability analysis of Mechanical Turk data. *Computers in Human Behavior, 43,* 304–307.

Schuller, R. A., Kazoleas, V., & Kawakami, K. (2009). The impact of prejudice screening procedures on racial bias in the courtroom. *Law and Human Behavior, 33,* 320–328. https://doi.org/10.1007/s10979-008-9153-9

Sears, D. O. (1986). College sophomores in the laboratory: Influences of a narrow database on social psychology's view of human nature. *Journal of Personality and Social Psychology, 51,* 515–530. https://doi.org/10.1037/0022-3514.51.3.515

Sommers, S. R. (2006). On racial diversity and group decision making: Identifying multiple effects of racial composition on jury deliberations. *Journal of Personality and Social Psychology, 90,* 597–612. https://doi.org/10.1037/0022-3514.90.4.597

Sommers, S. R., & Ellsworth, P. C. (2001). White juror bias: An investigation of prejudice against Black defendants in the American courtroom. *Psychology, Public Policy, and Law, 7,* 201–229. https://doi.org/10.1037/1076-8971.7.1.201

Sommers, S. R., & Ellsworth, P. C. (2009). "Race salience" in juror decision-making: Misconceptions, clarifications, and unanswered questions. *Behavioral Sciences & the Law, 27,* 599–609. https://doi.org/10.1002/bsl.877

Statistics Canada. (2008). *Ethnocultural portrait of Canada highlight tables, 2006 census.* Government of Canada.

Suler, J. (2004a). In class and online: Using discussion boards in teaching. *Cyber Psychology and Behavior, 7*(4), 395–401.

Suler, J. (2004b). The online disinhibition effect. *Cyber Psychology and Behavior, 7*(3), 321–326.

Ugwuegbu, D. C. E. (1979). Racial and evidential factors in juror attribution of legal responsibility. *Journal of Experimental Social Psychology, 15,* 133–146.

Wodtke, G. T. (2012). The impact of education on intergroup attitudes: A multiracial analysis. *Social Psychology Quarterly, 75*(1), 80–106.

Reading 8.2 The Effect of Community-Level Alarm Ownership on Burglary Rates

One of the earliest decisions that researchers must make when formulating the data collection process is what the unit of analysis will be. We need to decide exactly who or what we are studying before designing sampling plans, writing surveys, etc. Roth, Lee, and Joo (2018) begin their article on burglary prevention by noting the impact that use of different units of analysis can have on our ability to understand the relationship between alarm ownership and crime. Households are the most frequent units of analysis in burglary research, and that is helpful when we want to learn about individual residents' work to protect their homes. Household-level research, however, cannot tell us about possible impact of aggregate-level target hardening in the form of alarm ownership. With the goal of examining neighborhood context while studying burglar alarm ownership and crime, Roth and associates used secondary data of census tracts within one city in the United States.

The Effect of Community-Level Alarm Ownership on Burglary Rates

Jeffrey Roth, Seungmug Lee, and Jae-jin Joo

Researchers have examined the predictors of burglary at a variety of levels, including individual households, neighborhoods, and cities (e.g., Nobles, Ward, & Tillyer, 2016; Pollock, Joo, & Lawton, 2010; Roth, 2016; Tilley, Thompson, Farrell, Grove, & Tseloni, 2015). Each of these approaches offers unique advantages. Household-level studies may provide useful information about how residents can protect their homes, but do not account for the influence of the residential context. Alternatively, city-level comparisons can assess the influence of the larger context, but do not account for within-city variations in the burglary rate and its predictors. For example, a jurisdiction may have low burglary overall, but high rates in a few areas of the city. Analyzing within-city variation in burglary rates requires neighborhood-level (or multilevel) research (Rountree & Land, 2000; Smith & Jarjoura, 1989; Tseloni, 2006). Studies taking this approach have illuminated the influence of neighborhood context on burglary, and their findings are summarized in the literature review. However, the effect of burglar alarms, which is typically examined in household-level studies or research with burglars, has been neglected in neighborhood-level research despite evidence that aggregate target hardening enhances the effectiveness of household security measures (Wilcox, Madensen, & Tillyer, 2007). Thus, the present study undertook an examination of the relationship between aggregate alarm ownership and neighborhood-level burglary rates that controlled for sociodemographic contextual factors.

Literature Review

Target Hardening and Alarms

Overall, the literature clearly establishes relationships between burglary rates and community traits (e.g., Martin, 2002; Nobles et al., 2016; Tseloni, 2006). However, these neighborhood-level studies have almost never considered the effects of aggregate target hardening on burglary. Inattention to aggregate target hardening is problematic in light of the possibility that burglars make generalizations about possible targets within an area (Groff & LaVigne, 2001; Wilcox et al., 2007). For example, they may assume that most homes within a particular neighborhood are well protected and thus select targets from other areas. One study which has considered the effects of aggregate target hardening is the multilevel analysis by Wilcox and colleagues (2007), which was based on interviews with several thousand Seattle residents. In that work, aggregate target hardening was measured as the average number of security measures used by households in each neighborhood. This variable interacted with household-level target hardening, such that "the negative effect of individual target hardening became stronger (more negative) as neighborhood-level target hardening increased" (Wilcox et al., 2007, p. 789). This finding was an important step in establishing the influence of aggregate target hardening. However, the target-hardening variable included multiple prevention measures and so could not illuminate the neighborhood-level effects of specific measures such as alarms. This distinction may be important, since burglars are not equally deterred by all target hardening measures (Cromwell & Olson, 2004; Wright & Decker, 1994).

Other forms of research support that alarm use should be related to burglary rates, but are not in agreement about the direction of that association. Research with burglars suggests that alarm ownership should be associated with lower burglary risk. Although burglars will sometimes claim to disable alarms or quickly complete offenses before police respond, the majority are deterred by alarms (Cromwell & Olson, 2004; Wright & Decker, 1994). Other studies using photographs to simulate target choices with incarcerated or active burglars are concordant with the ethnographic work (Roth & Roberts, 2015; Wright, Logie, & Decker, 1995). However, evidence from household-level victimization data is less consistent. Several analyses using victimization surveys have found that alarm systems were associated with a reduced risk of burglary (Buck, Hakim, & Rengert, 1993; Hakim, Rengert, & Shachmurove, 2001; Miethe & Meier, 1990). However, recent analyses of British victimization data found that alarms had no effect or actually increased burglary risk, depending on the other security measures in place at the home (Tilley et al., 2015; Tseloni, Thompson, Grove, Tilley, & Farrell, 2014). Potential explanations for the surprising possibility of a positive association between alarm systems and burglary are explored in the discussion section, but clearly additional research regarding alarm ownership is needed to more fully understand its effects (Tilley et al., 2015).

Demographics

Prior studies have established that neighborhood demographics are another type of contextual variable that can affect burglary rates. For example, young people collectively commit more offenses than older ones, and so a large youth population may increase burglary rates in a community (Martin, 2002; Osborn & Tseloni, 1998; Smith & Jarjoura, 1989). Evidence also indicates that the ethnic composition of a community can affect burglary rates. Studies using data from the United Kingdom have found that racial diversity has negative or insignificant effects on property crime (Osborn & Tseloni, 1998; Tseloni, 2006). However, community-level ethnic heterogeneity was positively associated with burglary risk in The Hague, the Netherlands (Bernasco & Luykx, 2003). In the United States, several studies have found higher burglary rates among neighborhoods with more racial or ethnic heterogeneity (Nobles et al., 2016; Smith & Jarjoura, 1989). One explanation for these findings is that areas with more minorities have more burglary because they are economically disadvantaged. However, the plausibility of this explanation is reduced by the fact that these studies also controlled for economic factors (Nobles et al., 2016; Smith & Jarjoura, 1989). Another possibility is that ethnic heterogeneity decreases interaction among residents (Bellair, 1997), thereby reducing the likelihood that neighbors know each other's routines sufficiently to recognize and report burglars at each other's homes. This possibility is supported by evidence that neighborhoods with more social integration and community involvement experience fewer burglaries (Martin, 2002; Smith & Jarjoura, 1989).

Residential Stability

Burglary rates may also be influenced by residential stability, as communities with many long-term residents presumably have stronger relationships among neighbors. This may increase residents' ability and willingness to report suspicious activity, which can affect police response time and thus the chances that burglars are caught in the act (Cihan, Zhang, & Hoover, 2012; Coupe & Girling, 2001). Studies in the Netherlands, Canada, and the United States have found that lower levels of neighborhood-level residential stability are associated with increased burglary risk for residents (Bernasco & Luykx, 2003; Malczewski & Poetz, 2005; Smith & Jarjoura, 1989). Conversely, Martin (2002) found that communities with more stability tended to experience more burglaries. This might be viewed as evidence that such areas (which may also be more affluent) are more appealing for burglars. Alternatively, Martin (2002) noted that this finding could also be due to higher rates of crime reporting by residents in these areas.

Economic Disadvantage

Studies also commonly examine the role of economic variables in shaping burglary rates. In the United States, data from the National Crime Victimization Survey (NCVS) indicate that burglary rates are higher among low-income residents (Walters, Moor, Berzofsky, & Langton, 2013). Variables such as neighborhood-level poverty, unemployment, and the portion of residents without high school diplomas all exhibit positive associations with burglary (Malczewski & Poetz, 2005; Martin, 2002; Nobles et al., 2016; Smith & Jarjoura, 1989; Wilcox et al., 2007). There are conflicting findings, however, when economic disadvantage is measured using aggregate real estate values (Bernasco & Luykx, 2003; Malczewski & Poetz, 2005). It is important to note that the effect of aggregate disadvantage appears to be distinct from the impact of household-level economic status (Smith & Jarjoura, 1989). That is, a household's risk of burglary is shaped not only by its own financial situation, but also by the collective economic status of the neighborhood.

Overall, neighborhood context provides "an important 'backcloth'" in which home security measures operate (Wilcox et al., 2007, p. 794).

Variables such as aggregate poverty, residential instability, and demographics are likely to influence the occurrence of burglary in a community (Bernasco & Luykx, 2003; Malczewski & Poetz, 2005; Nobles et al., 2016; Smith & Jarjoura, 1989). Similarly, aggregate target hardening (the typical amount of burglary prevention in an area) can shape homes' risk of burglary (Wilcox et al., 2007). That finding, combined with ethnographic and household-level research indicating the importance of security systems, provides reason to explore the association between aggregate alarm ownership and burglary rates. As this topic has been insufficiently explored, we undertook a tract-level study of the relationships among burglary, alarm ownership, and sociodemographic factors.

Methods

The sample for this study consisted of the 90 census tracts within a city in the Northeastern United States with a population of about 275,000. This number of tracts approximates Soper's (2016) recommendation of $N = 91$ for regression analyses using five predictors to detect moderate effects ($f^2 = 0.15$) with a power of .80 and $p = .05$. Socioeconomic data about the tracts were obtained from the 2000 U.S. Census. City residents were primarily non-White (73.69%), and the portion of households in poverty (28.8%) was notably higher than the national average of 9.2% (see Table 1). Additionally, alarm permit records were provided by the city government, and reported burglaries for the years 2001–2005 were obtained from the police department.

Following examination of the descriptive statistics, several regression models were produced (see Table 2). The dependent variable was the tract-level burglary rate per 1,000 households for the year 2001. Several demographic and economic variables were included as predictors in these regression models. Although homes in poorer areas may have fewer valuable goods within them, poverty may also increase the number of financially motivated offenders in the area and limit the ability of residents to bolster their home security (Tilley, Tseloni, & Farrell,

Table 1 Descriptive Statistics

	U.S.	Mean	Median	Std. Dev.	Min.	Max.
Burglary rate	7.28	31.91	25.87	25.98	8.32	177.46
Non-White	30.90	77.43	90.45	25.71	13.80	100.00
Poverty	9.20	30.24	28.00	11.67	13.80	63.40
Age 15–24	13.90	16.79	16.25	4.84	8.20	43.50
Renter occupied	33.80	75.74	74.65	14.00	12.60	100.00
Alarm use	N/A	1.79	1.20	1.80	0.00	9.30

Table 2 Ordinary Least Squares (OLS) Regression of Predictor Variables on Burglary Rates

	Model 1			Model 2			Model 3		
	b	S.E.	Beta	b	S.E.	Beta	b	S.E.	Beta
Constant	18.445	23.267		9.878	22.824		16.398	22.766	
Non-White	.043	.121	.042	−.033	.121	−.032	.081	.134	.080
Poverty	.742*	.367	.334	.757*	.356	.340	.772*	.351	.347
Age 15–24	.984	.566	.183	.890	.550	.166	.785	.545	.146
Renter occupied	−.380	.283	−.205	−.267	.279	−.144	−.403	.284	−.217
Alarm use				3.871*	1.537	.268	2.071	1.797	.143
Alarm poverty							.299	.160	.234
r^2	.115			.177			.210		

*$p < .05$

2011). Poverty was thus included in the models as the percentage of households with an income under the poverty level. Similarly, because many offenders are young, areas with larger populations of young people may experience more crime (Pollock et al., 2010; Roth, 2016). Thus, the percentage of residents aged 15 through 24 was included as a predictor. Residential instability was a third independent variable. Previous studies have employed a variety of measures of this concept; in the present work, we measured it as the portion of renter-occupied homes (LaGrange, 1999). The literature also suggests a need to control for racial heterogeneity, and so the portion of non-White residents was also included in the models (Pollock et al., 2010). The final independent variable was tract-level alarm usage, measured as the percentage of homes with an alarm system as indicated by city

alarm permit records. This variable is thus unique from prior work that has combined several items into an aggregate target-hardening measure (Wilcox et al., 2007) or examined alarm ownership at the household level (Tilley et al., 2015).

Analysis

Prior to conducting the regression analyses, descriptive statistics for the variables were examined (Table 1). There was one extreme outlier on the dependent variable; one tract had a burglary rate of 435.90 per 1,000 households while the next highest rate was 123.46. So that this outlier did not unduly influence the models, it was constrained to three standard deviations from the mean (177.46) for these analyses. When compared to national averages, the descriptive statistics reveal that the city had a larger minority population, more households in poverty, more renter-occupied housing, slightly more young people, and a notably higher burglary rate.

The initial ordinary least squares (OLS) regression model (Model 1) contained only the demographic and economic variables. Examination of correlations, tolerances, and variance inflation factors suggested that collinearity was not a problem among these predictors. In this model, each percentage point increase in poverty was associated with a statistically significant .742 increase in the burglary rate. The effect of larger portions of young people (p < .10) also neared conventional significance standards, but only in this first model. Overall, the r^2 value indicates that these demographic variables collectively explained 11.5% of the variation in tract-level burglary rates.

A second model was then analyzed, which included the portion of alarmed homes as a predictor (Model 2). In this model, the association between poverty and burglary rates remained significant and positive; tracts with greater poverty had more burglary. Aggregate alarm ownership was also significantly associated with burglary rates, but not in the expected negative direction. Specifically, each percentage point increase in aggregate alarm ownership was associated with about four more burglaries per 1,000 households. Overall, the inclusion of alarm ownership improved model performance, as the r^2 value rose to .177. The increase in the r^2 values from the first to second model indicates that aggregate alarm ownership accounted for 6.2% of the variation in burglary rates across the tracts.

One explanation for the positive association between burglary rates and alarm ownership is that burglaries in wealthier areas are likely to be reported regardless of whether the home is alarmed, while in poorer areas burglaries of alarmed homes are more likely to come to the attention of police than those of unalarmed homes (Martin, 2002). To explore this possibility, we examined a third model containing an interaction between poverty and alarm ownership (Model 3). Although this variable was not

statistically significant, its p value (.066) approached conventional standards, and so we plotted this interaction for exploratory purposes. The effect of alarm ownership was similar between tracts whose poverty rate fell in the top three quartiles. Yet among wealthier tracts (i.e., those with a poverty rate in the bottom quartile), the positive association between alarm ownership and burglary rates was much weaker. The implications of this finding are further examined in the discussion section.

The OLS models indicated that alarm ownership was associated with higher tract-level burglary rates. A further question, then, was whether that association was stable from year to year. Burglary and alarm ownership data were obtained for the years 2001 through 2005, but tract-level demographic information for that period was not available. We were thus unable to examine the effects of aggregate alarm ownership from year to year while controlling for the other variables. However, the data included tract-level burglary rates for alarmed and unalarmed homes. That is, for each of the 90 tracts, we obtained the portion of alarmed homes that were burglarized, and the same figure for unalarmed homes. Because these two figures within each tract cannot be considered independent of one another, we analyzed them using paired samples t-tests. The results of these tests (Table 3) place the OLS results for 2001 in a larger context. For 2001 and 2002, aggregate burglary rates were higher among alarmed homes, which is consistent with the results of the regression analyses. The eta squared statistic for effect size indicates that for 2001, alarm ownership accounted for 7.7% of the variation in tract-level burglary rates. This figure is comparable to the 6.2 percentage point increase in the r^2 values associated with the inclusion of the alarm ownership variable. For 2002, the eta squared value nearly doubled to 14.7%. However, in each of the subsequent three years (2003–2005), the difference in the rates among alarmed and unalarmed homes was not significant. The eta squared values indicate that aggregate alarm ownership accounted for less than 2% of the variation in tract-level burglary rates in each of those years.

Discussion

These findings should be viewed in light of several limitations. One is that the analyzed census tracts were located within a single large city. It is thus not clear that the results are applicable in cities with different population demographics or to other settings such as small towns, suburban communities, and rural areas. Additional research is necessary to clarify this issue and establish the generalizability of the findings. A second limitation is that, because household-level data were not available, the models included only tract-level variables. While aggregate predictors are clearly relevant to considerations of burglary rates (Messner & Blau, 1987; Pollock et al., 2010), there is also evidence that they may interact with household-level factors to affect the likelihood of burglary (Wilcox et al., 2007), and the present work could not account for that possibility. Finally, the burglary rates used as the outcome measures in this study were based upon incidents known to the police. NCVS data suggest that about 40% of burglaries go unreported (Walters et al., 2013). Thus, the results could be influenced by patterns in the non-reporting of burglary.

The positive association between aggregate alarm ownership and burglary rates across census tracts was the most notable finding of this study. This was contrary to the expected effect, as prior research has found that alarm systems strongly deter most burglars (e.g., Buck et al., 1993; Cromwell & Olson, 2004; Roth & Roberts, 2015; Wright & Decker, 1994). However, the present work is not the only study to find a positive association between alarm ownership

and burglary (Miethe & Meier, 1990; Tilley et al., 2015; Tseloni, Wittebrood, Farrell, & Pease, 2004; Tseloni et al., 2014). Notably, in this study it appeared that this positive relationship was far weaker in wealthier tracts.

There are several explanations for the association between burglary and alarm ownership. One possibility is that within poorer areas, households with alarms are more likely to report burglaries to the police. This explanation would account for the weaker relationship between burglary and alarm ownership in wealthier areas by suggesting that residents in those communities are likely to report burglary regardless of whether there is an alarm present. However, there is mixed evidence about whether poorer residents are less likely to report crime (Goudriaan, Wittebrood, & Nieuwbeerta, 2006; Schaible & Hughes, 2012; Tarling & Morris, 2012). A second option is an alternative causal order in which alarms were installed in response to, rather than prior to, a burglary incident (Evans, 2001; Tilley et al., 2015; Tseloni et al., 2004; Tseloni et al., 2014). In the present study, the interaction effect implied that the association between alarms and burglary may be stronger in poor and middle-class tracts. This may be because wealthier residents are more likely to use alarms as a standard precaution (Tilley et al., 2011), while poor and middle-class residents install them in response to existing burglary problems. It is difficult to assess the likelihood of this explanation in the present study, as we did not have access to data regarding the timing of alarm installation. However, its plausibility is diminished by recent analyses that account for

Table 3 Paired Samples T-tests of Tract-Level Mean Burglary Rates per 1,000 Homes

	Unalarmed	Alarmed	Difference	Std. Dev.	t	d.f.	Eta Sq.
2001	34.5	75.5	−41.0**	1.43	−2.718	89	.077
2002	32.9	91.1	−58.2**	1.41	−3.916	89	.147
2003	29.8	36.2	−6.4	0.72	−0.844	89	.008
2004	32.2	23.4	7.8	0.65	−1.134	89	.014
2005	20.2	21.3	−1.1	0.41	−0.253	89	.001

**$p < .01$

the security actually in place at the time of the burglary, which still found that alarms had positive or insignificant effects on burglary risk (Tilley et al., 2015; Tseloni et al., 2014). Another possibility is that alarms denote the presence of goods worth protecting (and thus worth stealing), and so serve as rewards cues to potential burglars (Tilley et al., 2015; Tseloni et al., 2014). However, NCVS data indicate that wealthier households (which presumably own more valuable items) are at lower risk for burglary (Walters et al., 2013). A similar relationship was present in this study, where tracts with greater poverty had elevated burglary rates.

Additional research is certainly needed regarding these competing explanations for the positive association between alarm ownership and burglary. For example, scholars might study the predictors of burglary reporting to establish whether certain groups of residents are more likely to report their victimizations to the police. Future research might also follow the lead of Evans (2001) by examining the self-protective responses of burglary victims after the crime.

The other notable finding concerns the apparent variation in the effect of alarms from year to year. In two years, there were large differences in the burglary rates for alarmed and unalarmed homes at the tract level. In the subsequent three years, there were no significant differences between the two, largely because of a significant drop in the burglary rate among alarmed homes. This finding illustrates the value of longitudinal research regarding the impact of home security measures. There are limited longitudinal analyses of burglary (e.g., Jang, Hoover, & Lawton, 2008; Pollock et al., 2010), and fewer that include the impact of alarms (e.g., Tilley et al., 2015). Thus, future longitudinal studies are necessary to consider yearly variation in the alarms-burglary relationship, and should ideally include other relevant predictors such as those used in the regression models of this study. It would be interesting to explore, for example, whether the association between burglary and tract-level poverty also experiences such large annual variations.

In addition to highlighting areas in need of additional research, the present study also has implications for the prevention of burglary. The observed association between poverty and burglary rates is troubling considering that poorer residents may be unable to afford the cost of improving their home security. For example, both Evans (2001) and Tilley and colleagues (2011) noted that wealthier residents were more able to implement prevention measures at their homes. One solution is some form of income-restricted governmental aid to poor residents who desire to increase their home security (Evans, 2001). One possibility for this aid is financial support or reimbursement for the purchase of home security measures, as described by Mawby (2004) and Hirschfield, Newton, and Rogerson (2010). Alternatively, depending on the security measures in question, it may be more cost efficient for the agency to purchase those items (e.g., deadbolt locks) directly and in bulk and then provide them to qualifying residents.

Even if governmental aid is politically or financially infeasible, agencies can use educational efforts to help residents improve home security. These endeavors can take many forms (e.g., home visits, agency websites, letters to victims or new residents, articles in local media, brochures), and so can be tailored to the resources of the agency and needs of the community (Gelders, Peeraer, & Goossens, 2007). Hope and Lab (2001) advise that agency efforts to increase crime prevention among residents "should consider differentiating their crime prevention messages according to the perceived security needs of different groups of people" (p. 19; also Gelders et al., 2007). The results of Symons, Deklerck, Gelders, and Pleysier (2010) suggest that residents are receptive to such advice and are willing to implement suggestions for improving security.

In sum, burglar alarms are a common target-hardening measure in the situational crime prevention approach (Clarke, 1997). It is not surprising, then, that the deterrent value of alarms has been examined with a variety of methods (Buck et al., 1993; Cromwell & Olson, 2004; Roth & Roberts, 2015; Tilley et al., 2015; Tseloni et al., 2014; Wright et al., 1995). Although Wilcox and colleagues (2007) considered the effects of aggregate target hardening, the present study is unique in specifically examining the effects of aggregate alarm ownership. The unexpected positive association between burglary and alarm ownership, as well as the large annual variations in the differences between the mean burglary rates of alarmed and unalarmed homes, reveal a need for additional research in this vein.

Discussion Questions

1. How does poverty seem to interact with alarm ownership and burglaries?
2. How did the use of official records to measure burglary possibly impact the results of the study?
3. How else could the researchers have studied this in order to address the causal order problem?

References

Bellair, P. E. (1997). Social interaction and community crime: Examining the importance of neighbor networks. *Criminology*, 35(4), 677–703. https://doi.org/10.1111/j.1745-9125.1997.tb01235.x

Bernasco, W., & Luykx, W. (2003). Effects of attractiveness, opportunity and accessibility to burglars on residential burglary rates of urban neighborhoods. *Criminology*, 41(3), 981–1001. https://doi.org/10.1111/j.1745-9125.2003.tb01011.x

Buck, A. J., Hakim, S., & Rengert, G. F. (1993). Burglar alarms and the choice behavior of burglars: A suburban phenomenon. *Journal of Criminal Justice*, 21(5), 497–507. https://doi.org/10.1016/0047-2352(93)90034-K

Cihan, A., Zhang, Y., & Hoover, L. (2012). Police response time to in-progress burglary: A multilevel analysis. *Police Quarterly*, 15(3), 308–327. https://doi.org/10.1177/1098611112447753

Clarke, R. V. (1997). *Situational crime prevention: Successful case studies* (2nd ed.). Albany, NY: Harrow and Heston.

Coupe, R. T., & Girling, A. J. (2001). Modelling police success in catching burglars in the act. *Omega: The International Journal of Management Science*, 29(1), 19–27. https://doi.org/10.1016/S0305-0483(00)00030-X

Cromwell, P., & Olson, J. N. (2004). *Breaking and entering: Burglars on burglary*. Belmont, CA: Wadsworth/Thomson Learning.

Evans, D. J. (2001). Levels of possession of security measures against residential burglary. *Security Journal*, 14(4), 29–41. https://doi.org/10.1057/palgrave.sj.8340096

Gelders, D., Peeraer, H., & Goossens, J. (2007). Public communication about home burglary prevention in Belgium: Strengths and weaknesses tested by content analysis and focus group interviews. *Policing: An International Journal of Police Strategies & Management*, 30(4), 567–586. https://doi.org/10.1108/13639510710833875

Goudriaan, H., Wittebrood, K., & Nieuwbeerta, P. (2006). Neighborhood characteristics and reporting crime: Effects of social cohesion, confidence in police effectiveness, and socio-economic disadvantage. *British Journal of Criminology*, 46(4), 719–742. https://doi.org/10.1093/bjc/azi096

Groff, E. R., & La Vigne, N. G. (2001). Mapping an opportunity surface of residential burglary. *Journal of Research in Crime and Delinquency*, 38(3), 257–278. https://doi.org/10.1177/0022427801038003003

Hakim, S., Rengert, G. F., & Shachmurove, Y. (2001). Target search of burglars: A revised economic model. *Papers in Regional Science*, 80(2), 121–137. https://doi.org/10.1007/PL00013617

Hirschfield, A., Newton, A., & Rogerson, M. (2010). Linking burglary and target hardening at the property level: New insights into victimization and burglary protection. *Criminal Justice Policy Review*, 21(3), 319–337. https://doi.org/10.1177/0887403409356965

Hope, T., & Lab, S. P. (2001). Variation in crime prevention participation: Evidence from the British crime survey. *Crime Prevention and Community Safety*, 3(1), 7–22. https://doi.org/10.1057/palgrave.cpcs.8140078

Jang, H., Hoover, L. T., & Lawton, B. A. (2008). Effect of broken windows enforcement on clearance rates. *Journal of Criminal Justice*, 36(6), 526–538. https://doi.org/10.1016/j.jcrimjus.2008.09.003

LaGrange, T. C. (1999). The impact of neighborhoods, schools, and malls on the spatial distribution of property damage. *Journal of Research in Crime and Delinquency*, 36(4), 393–422. https://doi.org/10.1177/0022427899036004003

Malczewski, J., & Poetz, A. (2005). Residential burglaries and neighborhood socioeconomic context in London, Ontario: Global and local regression analysis. *The Professional Geographer*, 57(4), 516–529. https://doi.org/10.1111/j.1467-9272.2005.00496.x

Martin, D. (2002). Spatial patterns in residential burglary. *Journal of Contemporary Criminal Justice*, 18(2), 132–146. https://doi.org/10.1177/1043986202018002002

Mawby, R. (2004). Reducing burglary and fear among older people: An evaluation of a help the aged and homesafe initiative in Plymouth. *Social Policy and Administration*, 38(1), 1–20. https://doi.org/10.1111/j.1467-9515.2004.00373.x

Messner, S. F., & Blau, J. R. (1987). Routine leisure activities and rates of crime: A macro-level analysis. *Social Forces*, 65(4), 1035–1052. https://doi.org/10.1093/sf/65.4.1035

Miethe, T. D., & Meier, R. F. (1990). Opportunity, choice, and criminal victimization: A test of a theoretical model. *Journal of Research in Crime and Delinquency*, 27(3), 243–266. https://doi.org/10.1177/0022427890027003003

Nobles, M. R., Ward, J. T., & Tillyer, R. (2016). The impact of neighborhood context on spatiotemporal patterns of burglary. *Journal of Research in Crime and Delinquency*, 53(5), 711–740. https://doi.org/10.1177/0022427816647991

Osborn, D. R., & Tseloni, A. (1998). The distribution of household property crimes. *Journal of Quantitative Criminology*, 14(3), 307–330. https://doi.org/10.1023/A:1023086530548

Pollock, W., Joo, H. J., & Lawton, B. (2010). Juvenile arrest rates for burglary: A routine activities approach. *Journal of Criminal Justice*, 38(4), 572–579. https://doi.org/10.1016/j.jcrimjus.2010.04.028

Roth, J. J. (2016). Gender differences in acquisitive delinquency: A macro-level routine activities analysis. *American Journal of Criminal Justice*, 41(4), 796–813. https://doi.org/10.1007/s12103-016-9335-9

Roth, J. J., & Roberts, J. J. (2015). Now, later, or not at all: Personal and situational factors impacting burglars' target choices. *Journal of Crime and Justice*. Advance online publication. https://doi.org/10.1080/0735648X.2015.1078253

Rountree, P. W., & Land, K. C. (2000). The generalizability of multilevel models of burglary victimization: A cross-city comparison. *Social Science Research*, 29(2), 284–305. https://doi.org/10.1006/ssre.2000.0670

Schaible, L. M., & Hughes, L. A. (2012). Neighborhood disadvantage and reliance on the police. *Crime and Delinquency*, 58(2), 245–274. https://doi.org/10.1177/0011128708322531

Smith, D. A., & Jarjoura, G. R. (1989). Household characteristics, neighborhood composition and victimization risk. *Social Forces*, 68(2), 621–640. https://doi.org/10.1093/sf/68.2.621

Soper, D. (2016). *A-priori sample size calculator for multiple regression* [Software]. Retrieved from www.danielsoper.com/statcalc

Symons, L., Deklerck, J., Gelders, D., & Pleysier, S. (2010). Burglary prevention advice: Determinants of satisfaction and implementation by the public—The Belgian case. *Crime Prevention and Community Safety*, 12(1), 58–73. https://doi.org/10.1057/cpcs.2009.21

Tarling, R., & Morris, K. (2012). Reporting crime to the police. *British Journal of Criminology*, 50(3), 474–490. https://doi.org/10.1093/bjc/azq011

Tilley, N., Thompson, R., Farrell, G., Grove, L., & Tseloni, A. (2015). Do burglar alarms increase burglary risk? A counter-intuitive finding and possible explanations. *Crime Prevention and Community Safety*, 17(1), 1–19. https://doi.org/10.1057/cpcs.2014.17

Tilley, N., Tseloni, A., & Farrell, G. (2011). Income disparities of burglary risk. *British Journal of Criminology*, 51(2), 296–313. https://doi.org/10.1093/bjc/azr010

Tseloni, A. (2006). Multilevel modelling of the number of property crimes: Household and area effects. *Journal of the Royal Statistical Society: Series A (Statistics in Society)*, 169(2), 205–233. https://doi.org/10.1111/j.1467-985X.2005.00388.x

Tseloni, A., Thompson, R., Grove, L., Tilley, N., & Farrell, G. (2014). The effectiveness of burglary security devices. *Security Journal*. Advance online publication. https://doi.org/10.1057/sj.2014.30

Tseloni, A., Wittebrood, K., Farrell, G., & Pease, K. (2004). Burglary victimization in England and Wales, the United States and the Netherlands. *British Journal of Criminology*, 44(1), 66–91. https://doi.org/10.1093/bjc/44.1.66

Walters, J. H., Moor, A., Berzofsky, M., & Langton, L. (2013). *Household burglary, 1994–2011*. Washington, DC: United States Department of Justice, Bureau of Justice Statistics.

Wilcox, P., Madensen, T. D., & Tillyer, M. S. (2007). Guardianship in context: Implications for burglary victimization risk and prevention. *Criminology*, 45(4), 771–803. https://doi.org/10.1111/j.1745-9125.2007.00094.x

Wright, R. T., & Decker, S. H. (1994). *Burglars on the job*. Boston, MA: Northeastern University Press.

Wright, R. T., Logie, R. H., & Decker, S. H. (1995). Criminal expertise and offender decision making: An experimental study of the target selection process in residential burglary. *Journal of Research in Crime and Delinquency*, 32(1), 39–53. https://doi.org/10.1177/0022427895032001002

Reading 8.3   Ayúdame! Who Can Help Me?

Victims of intimate partner violence may be reluctant to seek formal help involving contact with law enforcement, medical professionals, attorneys, and counselors for a variety of reasons. When those victims are undocumented immigrants, there are potentially additional risks to involving the authorities, as coming to the government's attention could lead to deportation of the victim and/or perpetrator. Mowder, Lutze, and Namung (2018) recruited a sample of immigrant and non-immigrant Latino women who experienced intimate partner violence to learn about their informal and formal help-seeking experiences. Since they sought undocumented immigrants, finding and recruiting participants was challenging.

Ayúdame! Who Can Help Me?: The Help-Seeking Decisions of Battered Undocumented Latinas

Denise Mowder, Faith Lutze, and Hyon Namgung

Introduction

Intimate partner violence is responsible for one-fifth of all violent crime within the United States and translates into the victimization of one-third of American women by their intimate partners (Black et al., 2011; Dobash, 2003). Intimate partner violence (IPV) occurs within every class, race, and ethnic group in the United States, with recent estimates of IPV incidences within Latino/a families more than one-third (37.1%) (Black et al., 2011; Cummings, Gonzalez-Guarda, & Sandoval, 2013; Gonzalez-Guarda, Vermeesch, Florom-Smith, McCabe, & Peragallo, 2013; Tjaden & Thoennes, 2000). Within the Latino/a population, IPV can be particularly destructive because of issues that are unique to Latino/a victims involving culture and immigration status (Bauer, Rodriguez, Quiroga, & Flores-Ortiz, 2000). As a result, studies have searched for associations between IPV and Latino/a cultural and/or structural factors that interfere with a victim's access to relevant social services (Aldarondo, Kantor, & Jasinski, 2002; Bauer et al., 2000; Moracco, Hilton, Hodges, & Frasier, 2005), especially when these services were originally developed primarily for white, middle-class women (Macy, Giattina, Parish, & Crosby, 2010).

As victimization by intimate partners becomes more visible in every arena of the criminal justice system, police agencies and victim advocates need more information to understand the help-seeking behaviors of victims and, in particular, how ethnicity plays a role in a victim's decision to ask for help. Numerous studies have investigated the help-seeking efforts of IPV victims generally (Belknap, Melton, Denney, Fleury-Steiner, & Sullivan, 2009; Ansara & Hindin, 2010; Dutton, Orloff, & Hass, 2000); however, less is known about the differences between ethnicity and culture concerning these types of decisions. In particular, previous research has not delineated between immigrants and U.S.-born Latinas when it comes to help-seeking (Reina, Lohman, & Maldonado, 2014). Research shows that immigrant Latinas experience higher rates of IPV than nonimmigrant women (Caetano, Field, Ramisetty-Mikler, & McGrath, 2005; Kyriakakis, 2014), along with unique barriers that may hinder their ability to access help, including language barriers, lack of familiarity with services, social isolation, negative experiences with law enforcement in their home country, and fears of deportation (Bauer et al., 2000; Grossman & Lundy, 2007; Kyriakakis, 2014; McFarlane, Wiist, & Soeken, 1999). The purpose of this study is to build upon prior research by exploring the effects of immigration status on the help-seeking activities of the battered Latina.

The Help-Seeking Abilities of the Immigrant Battered Latina

Ethnic and cultural differences influence the help-seeking behaviors of IPV victims. A victim's cultural values can define a woman's decision to put family over her own safety (Liang, Goodman, Tummala-Narra, & Weintraub, 2005), her distrust of the criminal justice community (Gondolf, 1999), and whether culturally competent services even exist (Raj, Silverman, Wingood, & DiClemente, 1999). Ethnic and cultural differences can also reflect socioeconomic class differences that make getting help much more problematic. Problems accessing services often include transportation, language, childcare, and the ability to miss work (Flicker et al., 2011).

For immigrant victims, sociocultural norms such as class and immigration status will affect when and how a victim decides to seek help. This finding documents a propensity for Latinas to be less willing to seek out help in order to stop the violence than their non-Latina counterparts. The consequences of their inability to access services result in a higher exposure to IPV for the immigrant woman (Dutton et al., 2000; Ingram, 2007). Therefore, it is important to know the specific factors that exist in Latino/a communities that keep immigrant IPV victims from accessing services.

Formal or Informal Help-Seeking Decisions

Many IPV survivors employ numerous strategies to actively engage in help-seeking behaviors (Macy, Nurius, Kernic, Holt, & Holt, 2005). Victims will often employ private strategies that include placating the violent partner followed by more public-type efforts (Cattaneo, Stuewig, Goodman, Kaltman, & Dutton, 2007). Potential support for battered women falls into two main areas: informal and formal

help-seeking groups. Informal groups are networks of people who the victim believes care and value them, such as family, relatives, coworkers, and neighbors. On their own, battered women will often reach out to an informal group, for instance talking to their mother or best friend. Formal support, in contrast, comes from societal or governmental institutions and is often a result of an outside agency coming to the victim. For instance, police response to a neighbor's call will bring law enforcement and perhaps the district attorney's office into the victim's life. The formal help-seeking group includes medical personnel, law enforcement, attorneys, and counselors (Belknap et al., 2009). In a study of Canadian IPV victims, Ansara and Hindin (2010) found victims who experienced severe violence were more likely to contact formal sources while those who experienced less physical aggression were likely to seek informal sources. The formal sources commonly contacted in the Ansara and Hindin (2010) study were both medical professionals and police, while family and friends became the most common informal sources.

For immigrant victims, sociocultural norms such as class and immigration status will affect a victim's decision to seek help. The result is that Latinas are less willing to seek out help in order to stop the violence than their non-Latina counterparts (Dutton et al., 2000; Ingram, 2007; Choi, Elkins, & Disney, 2016). Further, there is limited literature explaining when and how Mexican immigrant women seek help in IPV circumstances. A handful of studies highlight how Latina IPV victims have more barriers to deal with than just physical injury when it comes to help-seeking. Problems accessing services often include lack of knowledge about existing resources, language (Choi et al., 2016), immigration status, childcare, and the inability to miss work (Flicker et al., 2011). Additionally, fear of deportation of oneself and the entire family becomes a serious help-seeking barrier resulting in a higher exposure to IPV. Therefore, it is important to know the specific factors that exist that keep immigrant IPV victims from getting services (Dutton et al., 2000; Ingram, 2007, Choi et al., 2016).

Battered Latinas employ the same types of informal and formal strategies as other IPV victims. Like many victims, battered Latinas will often first turn to informal sources, such as friends and family, concerning the abuse (Dutton et al., 2000; West, Kantor, & Jasinski, 1998).

However, the literature shows the types of help sought and the resulting effectiveness tend to differ drastically compared to non-Latinas (Kyriakakis, 2014). Research suggests that compared to other IPV victims, battered Latinas are less likely to initiate contact with both informal and formal sources of support (Brabeck & Guzman, 2008; Dutton et al., 2000; Ingram, 2007). This wariness is intensified for victims with undocumented status, with social isolation, language barriers, fears of deportation, and past experiences with police in their country of origin being the biggest worries (Ammar, Orloff, Dutton, & Aguilar-Hass, 2005; Kyriakakis, 2014). Attempts to remove or minimize these worries are often unsuccessful and stem from a lack of cultural competence within society. However, advocacy can be used to identify and educate within these areas in order to assist victims (Ammar et al., 2005; Ingram, 2007; Reina et al., 2014).

For the battered immigrant Latina, attempts to access formal channels to obtain help are hindered by their immigration status. Without documented status, there is limited access to community resources, educational opportunities, and gainful employment. Undocumented immigrants are not eligible for most social service benefits that could result in financial independence from the abuser (Dutton et al., 2000). Further, undocumented immigration status deters the battered Latina from contacting any governmental agency because of a belief that the contact would lead to deportation. Reina and Lohman (2015) found that lack of immigration status gave the batterer increased power and control over victims. Latina IPV victims often believe that if authorities are called about the abuse, the end result would be deportation. Additionally, the abuser will exploit this fear by telling the victim that the children will remain with him in the United States while she is deported. Lack of information regarding how

the criminal justice system responds to domestic violence within immigrant communities creates a cumulative effect in which these particular battered women are left with limited personal resources for accessing advocacy services (Ingram et al., 2010; Vidales, 2010). Another twist to this complicated situation is the immigration status of the abuser. If law enforcement is notified and the abuser is arrested, he may be deported as well. At this point, the victim is left without any source of income, hardship on the children, and no standing in the community. Victims often see themselves in a worse financial position than if the abuse was allowed to continue. The result is a vulnerability to further abuse by the abuser and allows the abuser to exercise greater control over the victim (Espenoza, 1999; Raj & Silverman, 2002; Wood, 2004; Salcido & Adelman, 2004; Grossman & Lundy, 2007).

The culture of the Latino/a family also affects the victim's decision to find help. Within the Latino culture, the value of "la familia" pertains to immediate and extended family and is above any one person's needs. Separating themselves from the family, regardless of the reason, could result in being ostracized from the family unit (Choi et al., 2016). The foundation for this value system begins within the family and results in many IPV victims unwilling to leave a violent home for fear of tearing the family unit apart and losing familial and cultural support. This ideology still exists in many Mexican American and immigrant Mexican families today and serves to perpetuate the belief that family violence is entirely a private affair (Choi et al., 2016; Davis & Erez, 1998; Espenoza, 1999; Kelly, 1998; Malley-Morrison & Hines, 2004). Through interviews with immigrant Latinas, Edelson, Hokoda, and Ramos-Lira (2007) reported that victims viewed their abuse as shameful and private. The phrase "La ropa sucia se lava en casa" ("The dirty laundry is washed at home") was used to explain why going outside for help is not a consideration (Edelson et al., 2007, p. 2). Further, immigrant battered Latinas know that police officers in their country also subscribe to this belief system and do not expect the police to be a source of help. The expectation is that the police would treat the abuse as a private problem and not the business of law enforcement. Even after migrating to the United States, many immigrant Latinas expect this same attitude and treatment by U.S. law enforcement (Bauer et al., 2000).

A combination of deportation fears and negative experiences with law enforcement along with language barriers and social isolation creates an impossible situation for the undocumented immigrant battered Latina. Consequently, the victim is forced to either remain with the abuser or turn to officials she was taught to mistrust. Thus, the current study examines the undocumented immigrant battered Latina and seeks to answer the following two questions:

1. Is there a difference in help-seeking decisions based on a battered Latina's immigration status?
2. Is there a relationship between a victim's immigration status and her experiences with police response?

In other words, does having an undocumented status trump all other concerns a battered woman considers before she will ask for help? In addition, when the police respond, do undocumented women's experiences with law enforcement differ from her documented counterparts? Few studies exist that consider the pressure of being undocumented and an IPV victim. Further, studies rarely focus on whether immigration status plays a role in a victim's decision to access services, legal or otherwise (Grossman & Lundy, 2007). It is this gap in the empirical literature that this research seeks to fill.

Methodology

The study was conducted in South-Central Washington State during the summer of 2009 and spring of 2010. This area of Washington State has a large population of migrant workers from Mexico who are employed in the local agricultural, landscaping, and construction industries. Participants were recruited from

Benton and Franklin Counties of Washington State, along with the Sunnyside area of Yakima County, Washington. A large number of potential interviewees temporarily, semi-permanently, or permanently reside in this area of Washington. At the time of the study, the estimated population in Benton County was 175,171, with 18.7% being of Hispanic ethnicity, and for Franklin County the population was 78,163, with 51.2% being of Hispanic ethnicity. The percentage of the population living below the federal government's poverty level was 10.9% and 38.1%, respectively. As of 2016, the population demographics for both counties remained similar, with a slight increase in the overall population. Benton County's population has increased to 193,686, with 21.4% being of Hispanic ethnicity, and the estimated population of Franklin County is 90,160, with 53.0% being of Hispanic ethnicity (U.S. Census Bureau, 2010–2016).

Research Sample

Participants were recruited from battered women's shelters that serve Spanish-speaking clients, the domestic violence coordinator for the police department's victim assistance program, and other agencies that serve the greater Latino/a community in each county. More specifically, this study used convenience and snowball sampling procedures and recruited the 173 participants from two rural communities and three urban communities over an 18-month time period. The 173 recruited participants identified themselves with a Latino/a ethnicity and had a history of IPV victimization. Of these, 119 were undocumented residents, and 54 were U.S. citizens. The majority of participants were referred and screened by advocates from women's shelters, police department advocate offices, and Head Start offices. In addition, some participants were referred through word-of-mouth and made personal contact with either the researcher or agency advocates expressing a desire to participate. Methods of recruitment included solicitation of agency staff referrals, distribution of flyers, and group presentations.

Even with the cooperation and assistance of these agencies, finding participants for this study proved to be a challenge because of women's immigration status and their distrust of government and community agencies. In addition, they experienced the typical fears associated with IPV victims. Distrust and fear appeared to be the biggest issue for potential participants—fear of telling someone about the abuse, and distrust that the research was a ploy by immigration to find undocumented immigrants. In general, stories circulated within the Latino/a community about how Immigration Customs and Enforcement (ICE) would falsely advertise for workers who would respond only to be arrested and deported. Further, an issue regarding safety arose because many women work in the same area as their husbands, and speaking with researchers created too much of a risk.

Research Procedure

Prior to data collection, detailed information about the study was presented in English and Spanish, and written informed consent was obtained. Study participants were given an opportunity to ask questions. The participant's safety, both emotional and physical, was a primary concern throughout this research, along with the need to maintain strict confidentiality. Participant safety was addressed through advocate training concerning intimate personal violence. To ensure participant safety, a domestic violence advocate was present and available to each participant in the event of any emotional distress. Physical safety concerns of the participant were addressed by allowing the participant to choose the time and place to take part in the survey or participate in a follow-up interview. Advocate and researcher safety concerns were addressed by agreeing to meet in pairs in either public places (restaurants, libraries, or schools) or at law enforcement agencies or at the local women's shelter.

Measures

The survey instrument employed in the study was adapted from the National Violence Against Women (NVAW) Survey (Tjaden & Thoennes,

1999). The survey included a set of 82 questions featuring dichotomous, ordinal, and Likert-type scale answers, and the survey instrument was prepared in both English and Spanish. The survey instrument sought information regarding the participant's victimization, the nature of their help-seeking behavior, the results of their seeking help, the nature of their interaction with police, and demographic characteristics.

Dependent Variables

Study participants were asked to identify the personal and community resources accessed after the initial incident of abuse occurred. These resources ranged from support of family or friends to counseling to legal services. In order to measure what resources were sought, study participants answered the survey question, "*Have you used any of the following services as a result of domestic violence?*" These variables are also dichotomous measures and are coded 0 for "no" and 1 for "yes" for each type of resource. A factor analysis was conducted on all 12 variables in order to reduce the data into measures that are interrelated. The *formal sources of help* measures include responses for those types of contacts made by the victims to official agencies such as the police or prosecutor's office. The *formal sources* scale includes six variables with a strong coefficient alpha of 0.788. The second category, *informal sources of help*, includes responses for those types of contacts made by the victims to unofficial groups such as family and friends, clergy, Head Start, and the Migrant Council. The *informal sources* scale includes six variables with a moderate coefficient alpha of 0.655. Participants were also asked if within the past 12 months they were worried about being deported (no = 0; yes = 1).

Police response was measured by a six-item Likert scale concerning responding officers' attitudes toward the victim. The statements are a mixture of negative and positive statements, ranging from "*officers showed concern*" to "*officers were hostile or nasty toward me.*" The statements were written to represent "Strongly Agree" as a 1 and "Strongly Disagree" as a 6. Some items were reversed coded with a lower score representing negative experiences and higher scores positive experiences of police response.

Independent and Control Variables

The key independent variable is immigration status, which the participants self-reported and was coded 0 for "documented" and 1 for "undocumented." To explore the effect of immigration status on dependent variables net of other factors, several control variables are included: current age (categorical), education level, employment, household annual income, marital status, and cohabitants.

Measures for IPV were developed based on the *Power and Control Wheel* created by the Domestic Abuse Intervention Project derived from the Duluth Model of domestic violence victimization. Study participants were asked to answer 18 statements concerning what type of abuse they endured. These statements are dichotomous measures and are coded 0 for "no" and 1 for "yes." Factor analysis produced two major types of violence. The *emotional abuse* measure includes responses for name calling, receiving angry stares, and putting down family or friends. These questions identify emotional abuse along with abuse through intimidation and isolation. The *physical abuse* category includes responses for threats of violence and destruction of property, along with focusing on an increased level of physical harm including driving a car recklessly, rape, and physical injury. The *emotional abuse scale* includes 7 variable items and has a very high coefficient alpha of 0.855, and the *physical abuse scale* includes 11 variable items and has a very high coefficient alpha of 0.906.

Findings

Descriptive Differences by Immigration/ Citizenship Status

Significant differences were found between documented and undocumented Latinas in the areas of education, number of children, and employment (see Table 1). However, both documented and undocumented participants had a mean age of 34 with the majority being between the ages of 18 and 39 (77%). Differences in education existed between those with less than a 12th-grade education (84.9% of undocumented and 33.4% documented). While the majority reported being employed outside the home (65%), there was a difference between documented (78%) and undocumented participants (59%) who worked. Both groups showed a ten-point difference in the sole wage earner category (58% documented vs. 69% undocumented) with an average household income for both groups below $10,000 (74%) per year. A difference existed between those participants who remained living with the abuser (50% documented vs. 28% undocumented) but a similarity concerning the number of children in the household (an average of three). Similarities existed concerning which participants told the police of their abuse (51% documented vs. 43% undocumented), but a large difference existed concerning deportation worries (4% documented vs. 53% undocumented).

Concerning their experiences with IPV, as a whole, the study participants experienced one or more incidences of emotional abuse (98%) and/or physical abuse (94%). Based on immigration status, there were no significant differences in the type of abuse, with both documented and undocumented women reporting similar amounts of physical and emotional abuse (see Table 1).

Immigration Status and Types of Help-Seeking Behavior

To examine the impact of immigration status and worry about deportation on informal help-seeking, formal help-seeking, and police responsiveness, we employed several linear regression models. In each of the multivariate analyses, Model 1 includes the variable "status" to determine whether documented and undocumented Latinas differ in their help-seeking behavior. In each of the analyses, Model 2 includes only undocumented Latinas and adds the variable "worry about deportation" to determine whether one's worries about the potential of being deported influence each type of help-seeking behavior. In

Table 1 Description of the Sample

	Documented n = 54% (n)	Undocumented n = 119% (n)	Total Sample N = 173% (n)	X^2/t -test	Sig.
Immigration Status	31.2 (54)	68.8 (119)	100.0 (173)		
Age (n = 173)					
Mean =33.63	34.72 (54)	33.13 (119)	33.63 (173)	1.013	0.312
Range = 18–61					
# of Children: (n = 173)					
0	16.7 (9)	3.4 (4)	7.5 (13)	20.212	0.005
1	20.4 (11)	11.8 (14)	14.5 (25)		
2	9.3 (5)	16.8 (20)	14.5 (25)		
3	37.0 (20)	30.3 (36)	31.2 (54)		
4	7.4 (4)	17.6 (21)	14.5 (25)		
5	7.4 (4)	10.1 (12)	9.2 (16)		
> 6	1.9 (1)	10.1 (12)	7.5 (13)		
Mean = 2.89	2.28	3.18	2.89		
Education (n = 165)					
< 6th grade	7.4 (4)	26.9 (32)	20.8 (36)	49.567	0.000
7th–8th grade	9.3 (5)	10.9 (13)	10.4 (18)		
9th, 10th, 11th grade	16.7 (9)	47.1 (56)	37.6 (65)		
Graduated HS	51.9 (28)	13.4 (16)	25.4 (44)		
Post HS	14.8 (8)	1.7 (2)	5.8 (10)		
Household Annual Inc.					
Less than $4,000	25.0 (13)	31.9 (38)	29.8 (51)	9.405	0.225
$4,000–6,999	36.5 (19)	30.3 (36)	32.2 (55)		
$7,000–9,999	15.4 (8)	11.8 (14)	11.9 (22)		
$10,000–14,999	9.6 (5)	12.6 (15)	11.7 (20)		
$15,000–19,999	1.9 (1)	7.6 (9)	5.8 (10)		
$20,000–24,999	7.7 (4)	1.7 (2)	3.5 (6)		
$25,000–29,999	3.8 (2)	1.7 (2)	2.3 (4)		
$30,000 +	0.0 (0)	2.5 (3)	1.8 (3)		
Employed					
Yes	77.8 (42)	58.8 (70)	64.7 (112)	5.846	0.016
No	22.2 (12)	41.2 (49)	35.3 (61)		
Sole Wage Earner					
Yes	57.5 (31)	68.9 (82)	65.3 (113)	2.437	0.296
No	42.6 (23)	31.1 (37)	34.7 (60)		
Lives with Abuser					
Yes	50.0 (27)	27.7 (33)	34.7 (60)	8.131	0.004
No	50.0 (27)	72.3 (86)	65.3 (113)		
Worry about Deportation					
Yes	3.7 (2)	52.9 (63)	37.6 (65)	38.392	0.000
No	96.3 (52)	47.1 (56)	62.4 (108)		
Tell the police					

Continued

	Documented n = 54% (n)	Undocumented n = 119% (n)	Total Sample N = 173% (n)	X²/t -test	Sig.
Yes	50.9 (27)	42.9 (51)	45% (78)	0.967	0.325
No	49.1 (26)	57.1 (68)	55% (94)		
Emotional Abuse					
Mean (Range: 0–7)	6.15	5.66		1.612	0.109
Physical Abuse					
Mean (Range: 0–12)	8.57	7.98		1.057	0.292
Help Seeking Informal					
Mean (Range:0–6)	2.28	2.86		−2.193	0.030
Help Seeking Formal					
Mean (Range: 0–6)	2.70	2.53		0.527	0.599
Police Response					
Mean (Range: 0–30)	24.793	22.650		3.341	0.001

each of the models, demographic characteristics are controlled for in the multivariate analyses.

Bivariate analyses were conducted to determine if baseline differences existed between undocumented and documented Latinas and their help-seeking behavior. The results of the independent t-tests (see Table 1) show that undocumented Latinas were significantly more willing to make informal help-seeking contacts ($M = 2.86$, $SD = 1.729$; $t(173) = -2.193$, $p = 0.030$) than documented Latinas ($M = 2.28$, $SD = 1.309$). There were no significant differences between undocumented and documented Latinas ($t(173) = 0.527$, $p = 0.599$) concerning the choice to seek help from formal sources. Multivariate linear regression analyses were conducted to confirm these findings when controlling for demographic characteristics.

Informal Help-Seeking

Table 2 shows the results for a Latina's likelihood to seek informal forms of support within their immigration status, controlling for *education, number of children, age, sole wage earner*, and *physical abuse*. Model 1 shows an overall significant model ($R^2 = 0.145$; $p = 0.000$) and indicates that immigration status is significantly related to informal help-seeking behavior when other relevant variables are held constant.

Undocumented women are more likely than documented women to seek help from informal sources. In addition, Model 1 shows that Latinas who are *sole wage earners* and those experiencing greater levels of *physical abuse* are also more likely to seek help from informal sources.

Model 2 includes only undocumented participants and the variable *worry about deportation*. Model 2 shows an overall significant model ($R^2 = 0.153$; $p = 0.004$) and indicates that Latinas' *worry about deportation* is not significantly related to informal help-seeking behavior when other relevant variables are held constant. Model 2 also shows that being the *sole wage earner* and increasing levels of *physical abuse* are significant predictors of informal help-seeking.

Formal Help-Seeking

Table 3 shows the results for a Latina's likelihood to seek formal types of support within their immigration status, controlling for *education, number of children, age, sole wage earner*, and *physical abuse*. Model 1 shows an overall significant model ($R^2 = 0.164$; $p = 0.000$) and indicates that immigration status is not related to formal help-seeking behavior when other relevant variables are held constant. Similar to informal help-seeking, being the sole wage

Table 2 Linear Regression: Informal Help-seeking

Independent Variable	MODEL 1					MODEL 2				
	B	SE	Beta	T	Sig.	B	SE	Beta	t	Sig.
Constant	0.334	0.664		0.503	0.616	0.756	0.748		1.010	0.314
Status	0.684	0.287	0.195	2.382	0.018	–	–	–	–	–
Education	0.093	0.115	0.068	0.810	0.419	0.014	0.149	0.009	0.094	0.925
Children	0.041	0.043	0.074	0.968	0.335	0.044	0.058	0.067	0.745	0.458
Age	0.006	0.013	0.035	0.449	0.654	0.007	0.017	0.036	0.384	0.702
Sole wage earner	0.530	0.261	0.152	2.029	0.044	0.833	0.342	0.219	2.435	0.016
Physical abuse	0.120	0.037	0.252	3.254	0.001	0.126	0.045	0.254	2.759	0.007
Deportation worry	–	–		–	–	0.222	0.303	0.064	0.733	0.465
Model statistics	$R^2 = 0.145$, $df = 6$, $n = 173$, $p = .000$					$R^2 = 0.153$, $df = 6$, $n = 119$, $p = 0.004$				

Table 3 Linear Regression: Formal Help-seeking

Independent Variable	MODEL 1					MODEL 2				
	B	SE	Beta	t	Sig.	B	SE	Beta	t	Sig.
Constant	0.137	0.811		0.169	0.866	0.160	0.828		0.194	0.847
Status	0.049	0.351	0.011	0.139	0.889	–	–	–	–	–
Education	0.214	0.140	0.126	1.525	0.129	0.092	0.165	0.051	0.560	0.576
Children	0.047	0.052	0.067	0.891	0.374	0.056	0.065	0.077	0.869	0.386
Age	−0.006	0.016	−0.030	−0.389	0.698	0.001	0.019	0.004	0.044	0.965
Sole wage earner	0.804	0.319	0.186	2.520	0.013	0.861	0.379	0.202	2.275	0.025
Physical abuse	0.186	0.045	0.316	4.126	0.000	0.181	0.050	0.329	3.624	0.000
Deportation worry	–	–		–	–	−.133	.335	−.034	.397	.692
Model statistics	$R^2 = 0.164$, $df = 6$, $n = 173$, $p = 0.000$					$R^2 = 0.177$, $df = 6$, $n = 119$, $p = 0.001$				

earner and experiencing greater levels of physical abuse were significantly related to formal help-seeking.

Model 2 includes only undocumented participants and the variable *worry about deportation*. The overall model is significant ($R^2 = 0.177; p = 0.001$) and indicates that *worry about deportation* status is not significantly related to formal help-seeking behavior when other relevant variables are held constant. In this model, the two variables *sole wage earner* and *physical abuse* are significant predictors of formal help-seeking.

Immigration Status and Experiences With Police Response

The bivariate analyses show significant differences in perceptions of police responses based on a battered Latina's immigration status. The results of the independent t-tests (see Table 1) show that documented Latinas experienced significantly more positive police responses ($M = 24.793$, $SD = 3.8476$; $t(173) = 3.341$, $p = 0.001$) than undocumented Latinas ($M = 22.650$, $SD = 3.967$). No significant differences were found concerning Latinas' worry about deportation and perceptions of the police.

Multivariate linear regression analyses were conducted to confirm these findings controlling for group differences.

Two separate linear regression models are used to determine whether these bivariate relationships remain between *immigration status* and *police response* when controlling for group differences (see Table 4). Model 1 includes every participant regardless of immigration status or police contact. This model controls for the demographic differences of *education, number of children, age, sole wage earner,* and *physical abuse.* Model 1 is significant ($R^2 = 0.142$; $p = 0.002$) and indicates that that undocumented battered Latinas have significantly more negative experiences with police responses than their documented counterparts. In addition, as the number of children increases, so do more positive perceptions of the police, regardless of status.

Model 2 includes only undocumented participants and only those who had contact with the police to determine whether *worry about deportation* is related to perceptions of police response. The overall model ($R^2 = 0.088$; $p = 0.212$) was not significant and indicates that *worry about deportation* is not related to perceptions of police when other relevant variables are held constant.

Discussion

This study contributes to a growing body of research concerning immigrant battered women and their help-seeking decisions. Prior research shows that battered Latinas, like many IPV victims, will often turn first to sources like friends and family before accessing formal agencies (Dutton et al., 2000; Kyriakakis, 2014; West et al., 1998). For immigrant Latinas, though, seeking help differs from nonimmigrant victims and often takes on different types of strategies to contact informal sources before accessing any formal resources (Dutton et al., 2000; Kyriakakis, 2014). The current study shows that immigration status matters in a victim's decision to seek informal help. Undocumented victims, sole wage earners, and those enduring increased levels of physical abuse were more likely to seek informal sources of help. Conversely, when it came to formal help-seeking, a victim's immigration status was not a deciding factor. Victims are more likely to seek formal help when they are the sole wage earners and experiencing greater levels of physical abuse. As in the case of any other battered woman, however, our study found that for victims experiencing increasing levels of physical harm, outside factors like immigration status did not stop the victim from seeking help. This conclusion corresponds to the work completed by Ansara and Hindin (2010), who reported that victims who experienced severe violence were more likely to access formal sources while those with less severe abuse contacted friends or family.

Table 4 Linear Regression: Police Responsiveness

Independent Variable	MODEL 1					MODEL 2				
	B	SE	Beta	T	Sig.	B	SE	Beta	t	Sig.
Constant	24.724	2.187		11.304	0.000	22.971	2.269		10.122	0.000
Status	−3.352	0.903	−0.343	−3.712	0.000	−	−	−	−	−
Education	−0.324	.0372	−0.084	−0.872	0.385	−0.946	0.455	−0.231	−2.080	0.040
Children	0.298	0.137	0.191	2.175	0.031	0.239	0.177	0.147	1.349	0.181
Age	−0.039	0.041	−0.085	−0.963	0.337	−0.020	0.049	−0.045	−0.401	0.689
Sole wage earner	0.709	0.828	0.071	0.856	0.394	0.416	1.044	0.043	0.398	0.692
Physical abuse	0.126	0.119	0.091	1.058	0.292	0.042	0.136	0.033	0.311	0.756
Deportation	−	−		−	−	−0.181	0.900	−0.021	−201	0.841
Model Statistic	$R^2 = 0.142$, $df = 6$, $n = 138$, $p = 0.002$					$R^2 = 0.088$, $df = 6$, $n = 96$, $p = 0.212$				

Interestingly, in the current study, worrying about being deported was not significantly related to whether the undocumented participant chose informal or formal help-seeking. Previous research by Dutton et al. (2000) found 27% of their sample noted fear of deportation as the primary reason to remain in the abusive relationship, and 21% remained because they feared being reported to immigration authorities. Dutton argued that fear of being deported rated as the first or second reason victims remained with their abusers. The current study, however, found that although worry about deportation was reported by 38% of the research participants, it was not significantly related to seeking help. In addition, worrying about being deported did not show a significant relationship to a victim's perception of the police.

Similar to prior research, the current study also shows that the relationship between undocumented Latinas and the police can be tenuous. Ammar et al. (2005) and Kyriakakis (2014) found that undocumented victims are extremely wary of making contact with police based on their own past experiences in their country of origin. In our study, we found that immigration status did influence a battered Latina's perceptions of law enforcement. Those victims who were undocumented were more likely to have a negative perception of police than documented victims. Interestingly, regardless of immigration status, women with children were more likely to find the police to be responsive to their needs.

Limitations of the Study

Although this study adds to our knowledge about how battered Latinas seek help and perceive the police, there were limitations. Undocumented battered Latinas are a difficult population to access, and the methods used were modified as the study went on. Posting flyers in laundromats, local markets, childcare facilities, and churches seemed like a viable possibility. However, this approach did not produce many participants, and the study turned to those women working as fieldworkers. This approach was frayed with safety concerns for the women, and finally, the study settled to accessing women in shelters, IPV support groups, and through the district attorney victim advocate offices. This final method posed sampling limitations that need to be considered when interpreting the current findings as well as when planning future research.

First, accessing battered Latinas through local victim advocacy agencies and through victim advocates housed in prosecutor's offices brought participants already semi-familiar with the justice system. Additionally, we feared a lack of trust between Latinas and the research team because they were generally unknown to the Latino population, and most contact was made through the advocates in shelters and district attorneys' (DAs') offices. Many of the participants in our study had already sought help from friends and family or had come to the attention of formal agencies via police agencies. This sampling left out those victims who have never told anyone about their abuse, were uncertain whether they should tell anyone, or may not have felt safe enough to contact the researchers to tell their story.

Second, at the time this study was conducted, the Latino community appeared to have a relatively open relationship with local law enforcement, who resisted working with federal agencies to identify undocumented Latinos living and working in the community. Since this study was conducted, tensions between the police and the Latino community in Central Washington have intensified due to national political immigration reform and the local shooting of an unarmed Latino (Helsel, 2015). For example, this study began in 2010, before much of the current political rhetoric concerning undocumented immigration. Further, this study was placed in Washington State, which is considered a sanctuary state—meaning local law enforcement did not enforce federal immigration regulations. Thus, it was not shocking that undocumented battered Latinas in Washington State in 2010 would choose to go to the police. However, if this same study were done in the current political climate within a state that locally enforced federal regulations, the result could be different.

Conclusion

The current study builds upon prior research in two ways. First, we found that a battered undocumented Latina is going to seek help informally; however, when immigration status is not an issue, formal help-seeking will be used by those victims with severe physical abuse and who are the sole wage earner. Second, we sought to understand the role of immigration status and how victims perceived their police response. We found that immigration status does play a significant role and, undocumented women viewed the police response negatively whereas victims with children viewed police contact in a more positive light.

Overall, the findings of the current study show that undocumented Latinas are most likely to seek help from informal sources. Seeking help from both informal and formal sources appears to be dependent on the increasing severity of the physical abuse and the likelihood of having some financial independence by being the sole wage earner. These findings are important because knowing what sources battered Latinas are likely to reach out to for consultation and help can inform where criminal justice and victim advocacy groups target resources. Providing knowledge and resources about the types of formal help available to battered women may help informal sources such as friends and family to better inform victims and be positioned to provide the help they need. Knowing that Latinas, similar to other women, are most likely to seek help as the levels of physical violence increase should be recognized by police and other formal sources of support as a key indicator of the seriousness of the situation and the potential for future harm to the victim. In addition, knowing that Latinas, regardless of documentation status or worry about deportation, were more likely to seek help from all types of sources as the physical violence increased is important to informing harm reduction approaches likely to reduce serious injury and lethality in IPV cases.

It is clear that communities need to offer immigrant-friendly services for non–English speaking victims, specifically services focusing on understanding IPV, its causes, and the availability of local community resources. Communities need to have availability within medical clinics, food stamp offices, Head Start facilities, and immigration legal services. Further, to overcome the negative perceptions of police response by undocumented victims, police services need to be advertised and disseminated to the immigrant community, including more access to bilingual officers and the hiring of more 911 operators. Within the immigrant community, information concerning resources for English classes, legal services, food banks, housing, childcare, and employment need to be available. The goal of the criminal justice system has always been to protect, serve, and keep the community safe. Undocumented immigrants, especially women who are battered, need to feel confident that the police and other agencies will help them. It is time for society to bring these hidden victims into the folds of our communities.

Discussion Questions

1. What kind of precautions did the researchers take to maintain the safety of everyone involved in the research?
2. How did the sample selection process likely impact the findings of this study?
3. How did the time (years) and location that the study took place likely impact the results? How might the results differ if the researchers replicated this study at another time or place?

References

Aldarondo, E., Kantor, G. K., & Jasinski, J. L. (2002). A risk marker analysis of wife assault in Latino families. *Violence against Women*, 8(4), 429–454. https://doi.org/10.1177/10778012200800403

Allison, P. (1999). *Multiple regression: A primer*. Thousand Oaks, CA: Pine Forge Press.

Ammar, N. H., Orloff, L. E., Dutton, M. A., & Aguilar-Hass, G. (2005). Calls to police and police response: A case study of Latina immigrant women in the USA. *International Journal of Police Science & Management*, 7(4), 230–244. https://doi.org/10.1350/ijps.2005.7.4.230

Ansara, D. L., & Hindin, M. J. (2010). Formal and informal help-seeking associated with women's and men's experiences of intimate partner violence in Canada. *Social Science & Medicine*, 70(7), 1011–1018.

Bauer, H. M., Rodriguez, M. A., Quiroga, S. S., & Flores-Ortiz, Y. G. (2000). Barriers to health care for abused Latina and Asian immigrant women. *Journal of Health Care for the Poor and Underserved*, 11(1), 33–44. https://doi.org/10.1177/1557085109344942

Belknap, J., Melton, H. C., Denney, J. T., Fleury-Steiner, R. E., & Sullivan, C. M. (2009). The levels and roles of social and institutional support reported by survivors of intimate partner abuse. *Feminist Criminology*, 4(4), 377–402. https://doi.org/10.1177/1557085109344942

Bernardi, R. A. (1994). Validating research results when Cronbach's alpha is below 70: A methodological procedure. *Educational and Psychological Measurement*, 54(3), 766–775. https://doi.org/10.1177/0013164494054003023

Black, M. C., Basile, K. C., Breiding, M. J., Smith, S. G., Walters, M. J., Merrick, M. T., . . . & Stevens, M. R. (2011). *The national intimate partner and sexual violence survey (NISVS): 2010 Summary Report*. Atlanta, GA: National Center for Injury Prevention and Control, Centers for Disease Control and Prevention.

Brabeck, K. M., & Guzman, M. R. (2008). Frequency and perceived effectiveness of strategies to survive abuse employed by battered Mexican-origin women. *Violence against Women*, 14(11), 1274–1294. https://doi.org/10.1177/1077801208325087

Caetano, R., Field, C. A., Ramisetty-Mikler, S., & McGrath, C. (2005). The 5-year course of intimate partner violence among White, Black, and Hispanic couples in the United States. *Journal of Interpersonal Violence*, 20(9), 1039–1057. https://doi.org/10.1177/0886260505277783

Cattaneo, L. B., Stuewig, J., Goodman, L. A., Kaltman, S., & Dutton, M. A. (2007). Longitudinal help-seeking patterns among victims of intimate partner violence: The relationship between legal and extralegal services. *The American Journal of Orthopsychiatry*, 77(3), 447–467. https://doi.org/10.1037/0002-9432.77.3.467

Choi, Y. J., Elkins, J., & Disney, L. (2016). A literature review of intimate partner violence among immigrant populations: Engaging the faith community. *Aggression and Violent Behavior*, 29, 1–9. https://doi.org/10.1016/j.avb.2016.05.004

Cortina, J. M. (1993). What is coefficient alpha? An examination of theory and applications. *Journal of Applied Psychology*, 78(1), 98–104. http://doi.org/10.1037/0021-9010.78.1.98

Cummings, A. M., Gonzalez-Guarda, R. M., & Sandoval, M. F. (2013). Intimate partner violence among Hispanics: A review of the literature. *Journal of Family Violence*, 28(2), 153–171. https://doi.org/10.1007/s10896-012-9478-5

Davis, R. C., & Erez, E. (1998). *Immigrant populations as victims: Toward a multicultural criminal justice system*. Washington, DC: U.S. Department of Justice, NCJ. 167571. Retrieved from www.ncjrs.gov/App/Publications/abstract.aspx?ID=167571

Dobash, R. E. (2003). Domestic violence: Arrest, prosecution, and reducing violence. *Criminology Public Policy*, 2(2), 313. https://doi.org/10.1111/j.1745-9133.2003.tb00127.x

Dutton, M. A., Orloff, L. E., & Hass, G. A. (2000). Characteristics of help-seeking behaviors, resources and service needs of battered immigrant Latinas: Legal and policy implications. *Georgetown Journal on Poverty Law & Policy*, 7(2), 245–305.

Edelson, M. G., Hokoda, A., & Ramos-Lira, L. (2007). Differences in effects of domestic violence between Latina and non-Latina women. *Journal of Family Violence*, 22(1), 1–10. https://doi.org/10.1007/s10896-006-9051-1

Espenoza, C. M. (1999). No relief for the weary: VAWA relief denied for battered immigrants lost in the intersections. *Marquette Law Review*, 83, 163–220.

Flicker, S. M., Cerulli, C., Zhao, X., Tang, W., Watts, A., Xia, Y., & Talbot, N. L. (2011). Concomitant forms of abuse and help-seeking behavior among White, African American, and Latina women who experience intimate partner violence. *Violence against Women*, 17(8), 1067–2011. https://doi.org/10.1177/1077801211414846

Gondolf, E. W. (1999). A comparison of four batterer intervention systems. *Journal of Interpersonal Violence*, 14(1), 41–61. https://doi.org/10.1177/088626099014001003

Gonzalez-Guarda, R. M., Vermeesch, A. L., Florom-Smith, A. L., McCabe, B. E., & Peragallo, N. P. (2013). Birthplace, culture, self-esteem, and intimate partner violence among community-dwelling Hispanic women. *Violence against Women*, 19(1), 6–23. https://doi.org/10.1177/1077801212475336

Grossman, S. F., & Lundy, M. (2007). Domestic violence across race and ethnicity. *Violence against Women*, 13(10), 1029–1052. https://doi.org/10.1177/1077801207306018

Helsel, P. (2015, September 9). No charges for Pasco police officers who killed Antonio Zambrano-Montes. *NBC News*. Retrieved April 4, 2018, from www.nbcnews.com/news/us-news/no-charges-pasco-police-officers-who-killed-antonio-zambrano-montes-n424571

Hogeland, C., & Rosen, K. (1990). *Dreams lost, dreams found: Undocumented women in the land of opportunity* [Scholarly project]. Retrieved from http://library.niwap.org/wp-content/uploads/2015/IMM-Rsch-DreamsLostDreamsFound.pdf

Ingram, E. M. (2007). A comparison of help-seeking between Latino and non-Latino victims of intimate partner violence. *Violence Against Women, 13*(2), 159–171. https://doi.org/10.1177/1077801206296981

Ingram, E. M., McClelland, D. J., Martin, J., Montserrat, F. C., Mayorga, M. T., & Gillespie, K. (2010). Experiences of immigrant women who self-petition under the Violence Against Women Act. *Violence Against Women, 16*(8), 858–880.

Kelly, L. (1998). Stories from the front: Seeking refuge for battered immigrants in the Violence Against Women Act. *Northwestern University Law Review, 92*(2), 665–705.

Kyriakakis, S. (2014). Mexican immigrant women reaching out. *Violence Against Women, 20*(9), 1097–1116. https://doi.org/10.1177/1077801214549640

Lance, E., Butts, M. M., & Michels, L. C. (2006). The sources of four commonly reported cutoff criteria: What did they really say? *Organizational Research Methods, 9*(2), 202–220. https://doi.org/10.1177/1094428105284919

Liang, B., Goodman, L., Tummala-Narra, P., & Weintraub, S. (2005). A theoretical framework for understanding help-seeking processes among survivors of intimate partner violence. *American Journal of Community Psychology, 36*(1–2), 71–84. https://doi.org/10.1007/s10464-005-6233-6

Macy, R. J., Giattina, M. C., Parish, S. L., & Crosby, C. (2010). Domestic violence and sexual assault services: Historical concerns and contemporary challenges. *Journal of Interpersonal Violence, 25*(1), 3–32. https://doi.org/10.1177/0886260508329128

Macy, R. J., Nurius, P. S., Kernic, M. A., & Holt, V. L. (2005). Battered women's profiles associated with service help-seeking efforts: Illuminating opportunities for intervention. *Social Work Research, 29*(3), 137–150. https://doi.org/10.1093/swr/29.3.137

Malley-Morrison, K., & Hines, D. A. (2004). *Family violence in a cultural perspective: Defining, understanding, and combating abuse.* Thousand Oaks, CA: Sage Publications.

McFarlane, J., Wiist, W., & Soeken, K. (1999). Use of counseling by abused pregnant Hispanic women. *Journal of Women's Health & Gender-Based Medicine, 8*(4), 541–546.

Moracco, K. E., Hilton, A., Hodges, K. G., & Frasier, P. Y. (2005). Knowledge and attitudes about intimate partner violence among immigrant Latinos in rural North Carolina. *Violence Against Women, 11*(3), 337–351. https://doi.org/10.1177/1077801204273296

Raj, A., & Silverman, J. G. (2002). The roles of culture, context, and legal immigrant status on Intimate Partner Violence. *Violence Against Women, 8*(3), 367–398.

Raj, A., Silverman, J. G., Wingood, G. M., & DiClemente, R. J. (1999). Prevalence and correlates of relationship abuse among a community-based sample of low income African American women. *Violence Against Women, 5*(3), 272–291. https://doi.org/10.1177/10778019922181220

Reina, A. S., & Lohman, B. J. (2015). Barriers preventing Latina immigrants from seeking advocacy services for domestic violence victims: A qualitative analysis. *Journal of Family Violence, 30*(4), 479–488.

Reina, A. S., Lohman, B. J., & Maldonado, M. M. (2014). "He said they'd deport me": Factors influencing domestic violence help-seeking practices among Latina immigrants. *Journal of Interpersonal Violence, 29*(4), 593–615. https://doi.org/10.1177/0886260513505214

Salcido, O., & Adelman, M. (2004). "He has me tied with the blessed and damned papers": Undocumented-immigrant battered women in Phoenix, Arizona. *Human Organization, 63*(2), 162–172.

Tjaden, P., & Thoennes, N. (1999). *Violence and threats of violence against women and men in the United States, 1994–1996* [Computer file]. ICPSR 2566. Denver, CO: Center for Policy Research [producer], 1998. Ann Arbor, MI: Inter-university Consortium for Political and Social Research [distributor], 1999.

Tjaden, P., & Thoennes, N. (2000). *Extent, nature, and consequences of intimate partner violence: Findings from the National Violence Against Women Survey.* Washington, DC: U.S. Department of Justice, National Institute of Justice, NCF 181867. Retrieved from www.ncjrs.gov/pdffiles1/nij/181867.pdf

U.S. Census Bureau. (2010–2016). *Quick facts.* Retrieved from http://quickfacts.census.gov/qfd/states/53/53077.html

Vidales, G. T. (2010). Arrested justice: The multifaceted plight of immigrant Latinas who faced domestic violence. *Journal of Family Violence, 25*(6), 533–544. https://doi.org/10.1007/s10896-010-9309-5

West, C. M., Kantor, G. K., & Jasinski, J. L. (1998). Sociodemographic predictors and cultural barriers to help-seeking behavior by Latina and Anglo American battered women. *Violence and Victims, 13*(4), 361–375.

Wood, S. M. (2004). VAWA's unfinished business: The immigrant women who fall through the cracks. *Duke Journal of Gender Law & Policy, 11*, 141–156.

9 Surveys and Interviews

Surveys and interviews are essential to criminal justice research because they allow us to learn about things that are difficult or impossible to observe. We can only learn about residents' fear of crime in their neighborhoods by asking them about it, as we obviously cannot observe feelings. We cannot follow large groups of people every day for years to record the number of times they are victimized or are perpetrators of illegal activity. The mere presence of the researcher on the street looking to witness a burglary or robbery is likely to deter any would-be offender at that place and time. Researchers have been very innovative in finding ways to observe crime, but even when they are able to conceal themselves enough, they run into another problem: crime is (thankfully) a rare occurrence. What we can do is send people surveys or meet with them to conduct interviews on their thoughts and reported behaviors. It is much easier to sample a large number of individuals, households, or businesses and ask about victimization experiences or to survey individuals and ask about offending patterns. Collecting data this way allows us to obtain a large enough sample size for quantitative data analysis.

In this chapter, I will review the elements of survey construction. Just as I warned readers in Chapter 6 that writing survey questions might initially seem like an easy task, I want to remind you that it is not. There is so much more to this process than most people realize, and I think that will be very clear by the end of this chapter. When we consider how to collect data, we need to decide whether to conduct interviews, either in person, via video chat, or over the phone, or to distribute surveys for respondents to complete on their own. Each method has advantages and disadvantages in terms its impact on of response rates, participant privacy, and the impact of social desirability on answers. Finally, we will consider specific types of surveys, such as focus groups and self-report questionnaires.

Survey Construction

As I noted in Chapter 6, the process of turning vague concepts into measurable variables is difficult, but it is important to get this right. You will only have one shot at getting someone to respond to your survey. While this project might mean a lot to you and your future, it is often seen as a burden to the respondent. Believe me, you will not get away with having people complete a survey and then asking them to complete it again because you just realized that some of your wording is vague or the way you ordered the questions is problematic.

As you prepare to make a survey, the first step is to make a list of all of the variables that you need to remember to include in the survey. If you are putting together a very short document, this probably isn't necessary, but if it is going to be a long survey with lots of variables, you should check your list against the final draft of the survey to make sure you have everything that you need in there. Next, think about your goal, as this will help you determine the appropriate survey format. If you are interested in hypothesis testing, you might want to use close-ended survey items, in which respondents choose from a set of available answer options. These are very helpful when it comes to doing data analysis since there is no additional coding. Surveys with just close-ended questions are known as **structured surveys**. If you think that you might not be able to imagine every possible answer that respondents will give or you really want the respondents to describe things in their own words, then open-ended questions would be better. These avoid the problem of you failing to present exhaustive answer options. While you might get more complete answers using **unstructured surveys**, you will later have to code the answers into categories yourself if the responses are going to be included in quantitative analysis. Open-ended items and less structured surveys are particularly helpful in introducing the researchers to ideas that they had not previously considered. Decker and Rosenfeld (1995) assumed that they knew all the methods that people use to avoid HIV-transmission, including using condoms, practicing monogamy, regular testing, and celibacy. They used open-ended questions when surveying arrestees and were surprised at the answers they received. People responded that they would have their partners drink orange juice and ask them if it burned when they urinated because they thought this served as an at-home HIV test. (It does not.) Others reported washing their genitals with gasoline in order to kill infection. (It does not.) These are ideas that the researchers never would have thought to include as answer options on a structured survey. Another possibility is to have a combination of close-ended and open-ended questions in a **semi-structured survey**. A final option is to not have an actual written survey and to just have a few key words available to guide interviewers as they conduct depth interviews. **Depth interviews** are long conversations, some of which take hours, in which the respondents are able to fully explain their circumstances, and the researcher is free to think of and ask additional questions as topics arise. Less structured surveys and depth interviews are advantageous when researchers are working on theory and hypothesis development or when they are looking to get ideas for what to include in a structured survey.

If you decide against the depth interview and will need a survey, pause before diving into survey construction. There are currently hundreds, if not thousands, of surveys that have already been written, some of which have been tested for validity and reliability. Rather than trying to create your own measures, it might be better to use or even adapt an existing survey for use in your research. As you work on learning about your topic, you should do an extensive review of the existing literature. While doing so, pay attention to how others measured the variables that currently interest you. Are there instruments that have already been tested for their reliability and validity? Someone looking to research depression and suicidal ideation may want to choose from forms that have been validated several times. For example, the Beck Depression Inventory-II (DBI-II) (Beck, Steer, & Brown, 1996), the Beck Hopelessness Scale (Beck, 1988; Beck & Steer, 1988), and the Suicide Probability Scale (Cull & Gill, 1998) are good tools for measuring suicidal ideation. There are even suicide screening tools designed specifically for use with offenders housed in prisons and jails, such as the Brief Jail Mental Health Screen (BJMHS) (Steadman, Scott, Osher, Agnese, & Robbins, 2005; Veysey, Steadman, Morrissey, Johnson, & Beckstead, 1998), the Suicide Risk Assessment Scale (SRAS) (Wichmann, Serin, & Motiuk, 2000), and the Suicide Concerns for Offenders in Prison Environment (SCOPE) (Perry & Olason, 2009).

Before using an existing survey, you need to first consider whether it is permissible. Some surveys are free for others to use and reproduce, provided that adequate credit is given to the survey creators. Others may only be used for a fee. You should look into that and, when in doubt, reach out to the people who developed the survey to ask permission. Provided that you have permission, your second step is to see if the existing survey captures all the variables that you need for your study. If it does not, you may have to add additional items. Third, think about whether it is appropriate for your study population. Going back to the suicide questionnaire example, the reason there are tools specific to the offender population is because some community-level depression and suicide screening surveys lack validity when used to evaluate individuals in custody. For example, the Beck Depression Inventory-II is a valid measure of depression in the community, but it includes statements such as "I feel particularly guilty," and "I feel I am being punished." Those items are intended to measure feelings of depression, but when offenders reflect on those items, they might answer while thinking about how guilty they feel about their crimes and whether they feel that being in jail for that is punishment (Perry, Marandos, Coulton, & Johnson, 2010). In other words, for offenders, those statements might wind up measuring something other than depression. Another question to consider as you think about the appropriateness of an existing survey for your own research is whether it is composed at a suitable reading and comprehension level for your respondents. Fourth, if this is an assignment for a course or some other graded project, always check with your instructor to confirm that you are permitted to adopt a survey from another source. Your instructor may want you to create your own for the learning experience.

Assuming you do need to make your own survey, here are issues to consider:

1. Think about who is supposed to complete the survey. If your unit of analysis is an organization, what is your unit of observation? Do you want it to be the chief/warden/executive director of an organization, or can it be a lower-level employee? Ask yourself the same question if your unit of analysis is the household. Do you want the unit of observation to be anyone over the age of 18 living in the house, the oldest person in the home, the person who does most of the household shopping, or the person whose birthday is coming up next? Figuring out who is going to be completing the survey will help you with some of the next decisions.

2. Make sure the survey is written in a way that is geared toward the people who will be completing it. If I am surveying judges, I will write for a highly educated population and use legal terminology. If I am surveying prison inmates, I will make sure everything is written at a fourth-grade reading level.

3. If you are using close-ended questions, make sure your response options are mutually exclusive and exhaustive. To review, mutually exclusive means that respondents will only be able to select one, and only one, answer option. Exhaustive means that there will be an answer option available for every respondent taking the survey.

4. Do not ask leading questions. I recently received a "survey" in the mail asking me how I felt about a certain political party's "partisan witch hunt" against a specific politician. Is it any wonder how the writers of that survey hoped I would respond? Has anyone ever thought, "I really do enjoy a good partisan witch hunt"? To be fair, a few weeks later, I received a survey from a group at the other end of the political spectrum asking me how concerned I was about "the government's harsh immigration policies that trample on the due process rights . . ." What decent person would be in favor of trampling on people's rights? If I respond that I am *not* concerned, what kind of person am I? Of course, most surveys are much more subtle than these two examples, but they can still wind up accidentally introducing bias into the questions. Choose your wording carefully as some words can be leading. For example, anytime anyone wants an industry to look bad, they add the word "big" before its name. We have had "big tobacco," "big oil," and "big pharma" in media reports over the past few decades. Labeling these industries as "big" communicates that these companies are so overwhelmingly powerful that they can, and will, barrel over the public good for the sake of their own interests. Whether that is true is a debate for another time. The items on a survey are not supposed to lead people to think any particular way about a topic since we want to get respondents' opinions, not their opinions after we slip ideas into their heads.

5. Be clear and concise. The wordier questions are, the more likely people are to get confused and the more likely tired respondents are to skip parts of the question.

6. Avoid vague wording. I distributed a survey to jail administrators years ago with a question asking, "How many sworn staff members work at your facility?" It was a mail survey, and I included my phone number on the cover letter in case people had questions. Within a week of the mailing, I knew I had a problem. I received several phone calls about that one item. It seems that people were interpreting it one of three ways. Some respondents thought I meant "How many sworn staff members are working this shift?" Others thought I meant

"How many sworn staff members are working today?" while a third group of people thought it was "How many sworn staff members total work here?" About a dozen people called for clarification, but the other nearly 200 respondents did not and, instead, just interpreted it in one of the three aforementioned ways and wrote down a number. I was too vague with my wording, and it ruined the question.

7. Make sure you ask only one question at a time. Do not ask double-barreled questions, such as "Did you bring your lunch or get something to eat at the cafeteria today?" If someone answers "yes," what do you actually know about what they did for lunch?

8. Hagan (2007) suggests that researchers avoid "response set" patterns by using reversal questions. In other words, if there are a number of questions in which, on a rating of 1 to 5, 5 means that the person is a good student, people who are good students might get bored and start circling 5. To keep people paying attention, switch things up a bit so an answer of 1 would mean good student for a few of the questions.

9. Consider using an attention check. This is an item to make sure that people are paying attention. The attention check could be something as simple as "This item is to confirm that you are paying attention. If so, circle 3." Another option is to ask a question quizzing the respondents about something that was in an earlier part of the survey. Surveys that involve vignettes, or stories/scenarios, might involve an attention check in which respondents are quizzed about a part of the story.

Flow and Appearance of Survey

The order in which items appear on the questionnaire can impact both the probability of participants completing it and the types of answers they provide. For most surveys, the demographic questions are almost always placed at the very end. Demographic questions are boring and certainly do not capture the respondents' interest. They can also be off-putting to some. It is wise to save them for the end after the respondents have made a bit of a time investment in the project. Surveys should begin with questions that are interesting but not too sensitive or controversial. It is prudent to build up to those more difficult questions after people have warmed up a bit to the survey. For face-to-face administration, researchers can take the time to build a rapport before getting to the delicate questions.

The order in which survey items appear could influence how people answer questions later in the questionnaire, introducing bias into the responses. Picture a survey including lots of items about the opioid epidemic and its impact on public health and neighborhood safety. Toward the end of the survey, the researcher asks people to write what they believe to be the top five greatest threats to our communities. In this case, the opioid epidemic will likely be one of the top five issues that respondents raise, even if it was not something that they considered a particularly serious problem before starting the survey. By focusing respondents' attention on a specific problem for several minutes before asking them to come up with a list of community challenges, the survey structure likely helped to plant that idea in the heads of at least some people. In this scenario, the question about the greatest threats to the community should have come first, before respondents were exposed to any questions that would give them ideas.

Surveys should be as short as possible to encourage people to complete them. Researchers are often tempted to cram as many questions as possible into a small number of pages to give the appearance of brevity. (And perhaps to save money on copies and postage as I did with my own dissertation mail survey!) While you want to make it appear as short as possible, be very careful. Do not reduce the font to the point where it will be hard to read as that will irritate people and make it more difficult to complete. Cramming items anywhere they will fit on the page will increase the chances that people will accidentally skip items. The survey's appearance should serve to improve the chances that all items will be seen and answered. If there are unstructured questions, remember to leave room for people to write their responses.

Using the following scale, please rate your agreement on the following statements. As you read the questions, <u>keep in mind the communities you police</u>, not other communities or American social trends as a whole.

	Strongly Disagree				Strongly Agree
As a police officer, I can get what I need from the community I currently police.	1	2	3	4	5
Members of the community I police help me fulfill my needs as a police officer.	1	2	3	4	5
As a police officer, I feel like a member of the community I police.	1	2	3	4	5
As a police officer, I belong in the community I police.	1	2	3	4	5
As a police officer, I have a say about what goes on in the community I police.	1	2	3	4	5
As a police officer, I feel connected to the community I police.	1	2	3	4	5
As a police officer, I have a good bond with others in the community I police.	1	2	3	4	5
People in the community I police are good at influencing each other.	1	2	3	4	5

Figure 9.1 Matrix Example

Sources: Peterson, N.A., Speer, P.W., & McMillan, D.W. (2007). Validation of a brief sense of community scale: confirmation of the principle theory of sense of community. *Journal of Community Psychology*, 36(1), 61–73. https://doi.org/10.1002/jcop.20217 and Tartaro, C., Bonnan-White, J. Mastrangelo, A., & Mulvihill, R. (2019). *Police and community perceptions of mental illness stigma: a comparison*. American Society of Criminology. San Francisco, CA

One way to facilitate the flow of the survey is to use matrices, meaning that there will be a set of questions or statements that all have the same answer options. The **matrix** in Figure 9.1 was adapted from Peterson, Speer, and McMillan (2007) and used by Tartaro, Bonnan-White, Mastrangelo, and Mulvihill (2019) when surveying police officers in New Jersey. One drawback to matrices is that they could lull participants into response sets, meaning they fall into a pattern of circling one number. The Figure 9.1 example contains just a few items, so it is unlikely that participants will grow tired and start answering them without reading. If the matrix was larger, it would be wise to reverse some items in the middle of the matrix to have a high score mean that the police do *not* feel supported by their communities.

Another tool to assist with survey organization is the inclusion of **contingency questions**. It might not be necessary for every participant to complete every question and section of the survey. For a victimization survey, for example, respondents who have not been burglarized in the past year should be able to skip the questions about what was stolen, whether they were home when it happened, and whether they reported the incident to the police. So, when they answer "no" to "has your house or apartment been burglarized in the past 12 months," self-administered paper/pencil surveys should include directions for the respondent to skip ahead to the next section. Computer or internet-based surveys can be programmed with **skip logic** to move respondents to the next appropriate question contingent on how they respond to previous items. Perhaps you might have been asked to participate in an online survey, but then after answering one or two questions, you were thanked for your time, and the survey closed. That means that you answered a contingency question in a way that excluded you from further participation. This type of survey organization allows researchers to gather the data they need without needlessly taking up respondents' time.

Pretesting

As I noted earlier, researchers have one chance to get the survey right. The contingency questions have to work properly to direct people to the next part of the survey, all questions must be worded clearly and lack biased language, and the format must make every question clearly visible.

Researchers should spend a lot of time constructing, reviewing, and then re-reviewing the instrument. Individuals can only look at things for so long, however, and we are likely to inadvertently overlook things after multiple reviews of the same document. In order to mitigate making mistakes, you should do two things. First, put the survey down, let it sit for a few days, and then take another look with a fresher set of eyes. You are much more likely to find errors once you are refreshed. Second, pretest it with respondents who have a lot in common with your target population. If you plan to survey a sample of police captains, seek out some retired high-level police personnel or some police captains who are not in your intended sample and ask them to take the survey with an eye for anything that might be confusing or inaccurate. My colleagues and I were recently reminded of the value of pretesting when we asked some police officers to give us their opinions about our new survey. We included what we considered an unambiguous question about whether they had discharged their firearm while on duty in the past 12 months. The officers suggested that we reword the question because there was something we failed to consider. While we were attempting to measure their involvement in life-threatening situations, we did not realize that officers in rural jurisdictions regularly use their firearms to put down wildlife hit by cars or injured by hunters. Given their advice, we reworded the question to ask about discharge of firearms over the past year, excluding incidents involving putting down a wild animal. Had we proceeded with distributing the survey to our sample without the pretest, we would have likely wound up with some very confusing results that would make it appear that officers in some relatively low-crime areas had to routinely resort to deadly force.

Ways of Distributing Surveys

In-Person Surveys

Sharing the same space with research participants has numerous advantages. One benefit is that it presents several survey construction and distribution possibilities. When in person, we have flexibility in the types of questions we can ask, the length of time spent interacting with participants, and the extent of contact that we want to have with them. When we are in person, we can use any type of survey format, from depth interviews to completely structured surveys with close-ended questions. Face-to-face is really the best option when considering doing a depth interview or anything that is going to take at least 30 minutes. Two people are more likely to sit and talk for hours when they are together, having coffee. They are less likely to make such a time commitment to talk on the phone, fill out a mail survey, or complete an online survey.

Face-to-face interviews and in-person surveys are also desirable because they tend to elicit a greater response rate. It is so easy to delete an email asking for survey participation, toss a paper survey in the recycle bin, ignore a pop-up survey link while online, or neglect to answer the phone when caller ID indicates it is a research firm or an "unknown number." It is much more difficult to say no to another human who is present. Nix, Pickett, Baek, and Alpert (2019) studied hundreds of policing articles and found that surveys involving any type of in-person administration, whether through an interview or even just in-person distribution of forms, had a 24% higher response rate than surveys circulated via telephone, mail, or online. Also, whereas survey response rates overall have been diminishing over the years, response rates for in-person surveys have remained steady.

When in the presence of respondents, researchers can use multi-media presentations, use audio or video recording devices (provided consent is given), and be available to answer any questions that may arise. If the data collection involves an interview, researchers can not only note the individuals' verbal responses but also observe their body language. If the interview is being conducted in a home setting, observation of the home itself might also add some important context. For example, if you are interviewing a parent about their parenting skills and sense of responsibility and that person is giving all the answers that would indicate that they are a model parent but then stops and screams at a child for no apparent reason, that action is more telling than their survey answers.

When the researchers are on site, they can clear up any misunderstandings or answer questions having to do with the research, something that is not possible with mail or internet surveys. Researchers administering surveys can even probe for more information. Probing is a gentle, neutral prompt from the researchers to encourage the respondents to elaborate on their answers. Researchers can probe with a few different techniques. One is silence. If someone asks you a question, you answer it, and the person just stares at you in silence, the silence is likely to make you uncomfortable and prompt you to talk more. It is a non-verbal way of communicating that the first answer really was not enough. Another probe is to repeat the question. Other options are to say things such as "like what?" or "how?" to elicit more of a response.

Finally, on-site researchers can provide assistance to people who are unable to complete a self-administered survey due to language or literacy barriers. If the survey is going to be administered in a language other than the one in which it was originally written, it should first be completely translated by qualified individuals. Failure to do so could impact the validity and reliability of the survey, as each translator may word questions differently if left on their own to interpret the surveys.

Interacting With the Respondents

The presence of a researcher has a multitude of advantages, but researcher/respondent interaction must be handled very carefully. Just as researchers can read the body language of respondents, the opposite is also true. Researchers can unknowingly introduce bias into the interview if they fail to carefully regulate their own behavior. Researchers' unscripted comments can be particularly problematic during an interview. If the goal is to do a depth interview, the researcher will lack a script and will have to use his or her own skills to generate conversation in a way that is non-judgmental and refrains from leading the discussion in a way that would produce biased results. For example, if I am interviewing someone about victimization in a neighborhood, and upon hearing a response, I remark, "Oh, how awful, that must have been terrifying," I am leading the conversation in a specific direction. Through my comments, I am expressing my opinion that I believe that there are frightening incidents taking place in the area, and this might prompt the respondent to elaborate on the dangers more than would have happened had I just said, "I am sorry to hear that," or "Oh really, can you tell me more about that?" For scripted, more structured surveys, interviewers should be trained to stay on the precise script that is provided, with the exception of acting human and making neutral remarks from time to time.

Verbal responses are not the only way for researchers to influence the respondents' answers. A sigh, gasp, or eye roll can be just as powerful as a comment. People generally dislike being judged, and if it is in a situation in which they are completing a survey for which the results really don't matter to them, what's the use in putting up with the judgment when they can just provide more socially acceptable answers, feel less shame, and just finish the interview? If I am interviewing someone about drinking habits and my face gives away my anger when the person recalls driving while under the influence, the person is likely to be reluctant to continue to divulge sensitive, unflattering information. Criminal justice researchers hear a lot of bad things. It is imperative that researchers withhold their personal opinions and judgments while performing their jobs as researchers.

For in-person work, researchers must give consideration to what they wear to the meetings with respondents. If the research team will be entering office space and interviewing judges or administrators, business attire is appropriate. Instances when the interviews will take place in booking areas of jails or inside jail visitation rooms are different, however, and I have always found it helpful to dress casually to avoid making it seem like I was someone in a position of authority who might be considered a threat to them. The general rule for choosing attire is to dress in a way that is similar to the level of dress of respondents.

Drawbacks to In-Person Surveys

In addition to the risk of biasing the survey through researcher-participant interaction, three further potential drawbacks to in-person survey distribution in criminal justice are time, money, and safety. Researchers must often travel to the respondents for in-person research. In criminal justice, we often work with people who lack financial resources and/or transportation, and in some cases, people are not free to travel on account of incarceration or conditions of community supervision. Researchers can work to arrange or pay for participants to travel to interview locations, but there's concern in our field that this might introduce some artificiality to the work by interviewing people outside their usual environments. That is why, in most cases, researchers travel to the participants. Logan, Walker, Shannon, and Cole (2008) researched domestic violence among families in Appalachia, requiring approximately four hours of driving each day, plus any interview time. Researchers must find funding for the gas, tolls, and time it takes to do this work or face having to pay for them themselves. Since we are often interviewing offenders or people whose lives have been impacted by crime, we frequently visit neighborhoods, housing projects, and correctional facilities that pose safety risks. It is important to have safety protocols in place, such as requiring researchers to stay together, in some fieldwork settings.

Computer Assistance With Survey Administration

If there is a possibility that social desirability might impact participants' survey answers, it might be best to allow them to respond to the survey privately with **computer-assisted interviewing** (CAI) or **computer-assisted survey instruments** (CASI). The CASIs can be placed on laptops and tablets, have the benefit of being able to use skip logic to seamlessly move people from one contingency question to the next appropriate section, and allow for either the respondent to take the whole survey online or the interviewer to read the question while the respondent keys in the answer. Regardless of whether the interviewer is reading the questions or the participant is reading and answering on the tablet, the interviewer will never see the respondents' answers. When taking an in-person survey, CASIs may afford people more privacy than a paper/pencil option. When people are taking long paper/pencil surveys, others in the room can see how long someone is taking on a particular page or section. They can also detect when someone answers a contingency question in a way that results in a skip to another section several pages later, as the paper flipping will be visible. An additional potential advantage to using the CAI or CASI technology includes time and cost saving due to not having to hire data entry staff to log responses from paper surveys. While researchers doing face-to-face surveys without CASI can only promise confidentiality, CASI provides the extra benefit of anonymity. This is an important distinction. With confidentiality, researchers promise participants that they will never divulge their specific responses to anyone, but the researchers still know how participants answered. With anonymity, even the research team is unable to match the respondents with the completed surveys. Anonymity provides the participants with greater privacy, and it frees them from having to worry about being judged by the researcher for giving socially undesirable responses to questions. It is also a much safer way for respondents to self-report illegal activities.

Spark and associates (2015) surveyed adults about their sexual behavior, which is clearly a sensitive topic. They administered nearly 4,500 surveys, half through paper/pencil and half using a CASI. The participants who entered their data with CASI were less likely to skip questions pertaining to their sexual behavior and were more likely to report having a greater number of sexual partners in the past 12 months compared to those who took the paper/pencil survey. The researchers found that, for this study, administration using CASI was cheaper than paper/pencil administration after accounting for copies, postage, and having to pay staff for data entry.

Potential drawbacks to using CASI are front-end costs to purchase the equipment and set up the programs. Anytime technology is involved, there is the possibility that something will go wrong, and data will be lost. Additionally, if one is reliant on internet access for the software to work, lack of available Wi-Fi can be a problem.

Telephone Surveys

Like in-person survey administration, telephone surveys do allow for a degree of interaction between the survey administrator and respondents. Researchers have the benefit of being able to provide clarification if anything is unclear, probe for longer answers when necessary, and note any significant changes in the respondents' tone as the interview progresses. Of course, whenever we can hear the respondents, they can hear us, so it is imperative that the telephone interviewers are properly trained to avoid biasing the interview. As with in-person surveys, it is possible to use technology, with **computer-assisted telephone interviewing** (CATI). CATI lets the researcher read questions from a computer and then immediately input the answers into a database, cutting down on time and money needed for subsequent data entry. CATI does not, however, give participants the anonymity and privacy associated with CASI.

Telephone interviews are beneficial in that calls are very cheap, so the costs for this type of work are substantially lower than for in-person research. It can also be much faster, as the time between phone calls can be seconds, whereas travel between locations for on-site work could take minutes, hours, or days. The safety risks to research staff are also eliminated, as they will remain in a call center instead of being in potentially dangerous environments. Another advantage to phone work is the ease of supervision of workers. One supervisor can be in a room listening to several interviewers at once. This makes it much easier to check for interviewer bias. If the sample is ethnically heterogeneous, there might be a need for bilingual interviewers, and using telephone interviewers in call centers makes it possible to quickly engage staff members who speak the appropriate language. Such quick switching out of interviewers is less likely to be an option when researchers have to fan out through neighborhoods on foot while doing in-person work.

Drawbacks to Telephone Surveys

There are, of course, disadvantages to phone surveys. While it is possible to do long in-person interviews, people are generally very hesitant to stay on the telephone with strangers for long. In graduate school, I was involved in a phone survey project, and if respondents had personally been victimized in a few different ways, the survey could take up to 35 minutes to complete. It was very difficult to convince people to stay on the phone that long, as they tended to lose interest around 20 minutes into the call. Another drawback to this modality is the proliferation of caller ID. Now that it is possible to see who is calling, some people avoid researchers' calls. Telephone survey response rates have decreased from 36% in 1997 to just 9% in 2016 (Keeter, Hatley, Kennedy, & Lau, 2017).

Another, more recent development is the decline in landlines in favor of cell phones. By 2003, over 95% of American homes had landlines, but that percentage began decreasing immediately thereafter (Kempf & Remington, 2007). The National Center for Health Statistics reported that, by June 2018, 55% of households in the United States contained only cell phones. The decision to substitute landlines with cell phones is not random, as over three-quarters of adults 25 to 34 only own cell phones compared to 29% of people 65 and over. Adults living in or near poverty and those living in rented homes are also more likely to have cell phones and no landlines (Blumberg & Luke, 2018). This presents researchers with numerous challenges, as there are substantial differences between people who own only landlines and only cell phones. According to researchers from a multistate public health phone survey project, cell phone only households differed in that they were more likely to be younger, single, Hispanic, or house people who are unemployed or are students (Link, Battaglia, Frankel, Osborn, & Mokdad, 2007). These differences are relevant to criminal justice research, as demographics are associated with crime involvement and victimization.

The popularity of cell phones at the expense of landlines also presents difficulty with identifying the unit of analysis for the study. Landlines generally belong to the entire household, whereas an individual cell phone belongs to a person (Kempf & Remington, 2007). Landlines are easier to work with for survey purposes, as it is possible to identify which exchanges belong to businesses, but that is not the case with cell phones. The growth of the prepaid cell phone business has also generated phones that are regularly activated and then deactivated. Landlines also lack portability, so people who move from one area code to another with a landline have had to change their phone numbers. Cell phone owners keep their numbers regardless of where they move. This makes it difficult to sample a geographic region using random digit dialing of area codes and the first three digits of phone numbers (Kempf & Remington, 2007). A final concern about the involvement of cell phones in surveys is that, when we call landlines, we know that people are in their homes and not behind the wheel of a car. We also know that they are in at least a semi-private location rather than in a grocery store or office. There are concerns that people on cell phones will be more likely to be multitasking while on the phone. In addition to this possibly being dangerous, it could impact their responses. People may give more socially desirable responses when they lack privacy or may be more rushed and give answers that they think will end the interview sooner (Kempf & Remington, 2007; Link et al., 2007). Even if multitasking cell phone users are trying to concentrate on the survey, they may still lack a degree of cognitive engagement (Link et al., 2007).

One final issue that I want to note about telephone surveys is that the quality largely rests on how well the staff are trained and supervised. Have you ever gotten a call from a researcher who you could hear reading the survey to you? I have and, as a researcher, it bothers me a great deal. The staff should have the greeting statement/paragraph memorized and practiced to the point where it can be recited as if the researcher is having a friendly conversation with another individual. As for the rest of the survey, it is not necessary for staff to memorize it, but they must be comfortable enough to be able to go through it while *not* sounding as if they are reading the questions. If the staff is using a paper/pencil survey, they must know where the contingency questions are and be prepared to move to the next section without delay. Researchers are often inconveniencing respondents by taking up their time, and it is our responsibility to show respondents respect by being well-prepared for the job.

Self-Administered Surveys

Traditional Mail or Paper/Pencil

A popular choice for disseminating surveys is through the mail, as this is fast and very inexpensive. Mail surveys have the benefit of allowing researchers to reach a wide geographic region, even globally, with very little cost. Mail surveys are also possible without a research team. My dissertation was based on a mail survey of approximately 1,700 jails, and I handled the mailing myself, with the assistance of a few relatives who were willing to stuff envelopes.

Surveys that participants can complete independently have less of a potential to be impacted by social desirability. One good example of that could be found in the work of Patterson, Hogan, and Cox (2019), who compared three different ways to measure drinking habits among college students. Respondents tended to provide more conservative estimates of their drinking when data were collected through face-to-face interaction with research staff versus completing a drinking diary at home.

Unlike in-person or telephone interviews, surveys that are mailed or otherwise distributed with return instructions can be completed at a time convenient for the respondent, and this could encourage the person to put more consideration into answers. It can also give participants the needed time to look up answers. This is particularly helpful when we are asking criminal justice practitioners information about the populations their agencies serve, as they are unlikely to have that information committed to memory. Finally, the lack of researcher presence eliminates the possibility of interviewer bias.

Online/Email

The fastest, cheapest, and most convenient way to distribute surveys is through websites and email. Online survey distribution is especially useful when you already have a sampling frame containing the email addresses, and you are targeting a population that regularly uses technology. Online surveys are particularly helpful if your instrument relies on a number of contingency questions, as existing survey tools can use skip logic to automatically move people to the next appropriate section of the survey. In contrast, paper surveys must be printed and mailed in full, and then respondents must be relied on to properly follow the skip logic.

Drawbacks to Self-Administered Surveys

Of course, there are disadvantages to these types of surveys. Just as the researchers' absence is an advantage in that it eliminates interviewer bias, it also removes all the benefits of having interviewers present. It will not be possible to collect data about respondent body language or the neighborhood where the respondent lives. The researcher will also not be present to clarify anything or probe for more information. Researchers also lack control over when, if ever, people will complete the surveys and return them.

Another concern with using self-administered surveys instead of interviews is that interviewers can tell if respondents are paying attention. With self-administered surveys, particularly with close-ended questions or statements that involve circling or checking answers, a very valid concern is whether people got bored and started answering at random or fell into a pattern of providing a particular response set. Researchers can check for this using attention checks. Flippin, Reisig, and Trinkner (2019) surveyed college students on their likely responses to hypothetical 911 calls in which the dispatcher was either respectful and professional or rude and confrontational. One survey item was completely unrelated to their hypothesis testing as it asked participants to indicate why the 911 call was being made after they finished reading the vignette. (The correct answer was either a bicycle accident or a burglary.) Less than 3% of respondents failed the attention check, and their surveys were removed from the analysis.

Perhaps the biggest drawback to mail and internet surveys is the response rate. In-person interviews have the best response rates, followed by telephone interviews (although those rates have been declining with the growth of caller ID and reliance on cell phones). With in-person and telephone interviews, there is some social desirability pressure to agree to participate so as not to disappoint the person on the phone or at the front door. Since people toss out junk mail every day, there is little guilt associated with throwing out a letter from a researcher or polling organization.

Online surveys tend to have an even lower response rate than mail surveys. Sax, Gilmartin, and Bryant (2003) studied differences in survey completion when students were given four options:

paper only, paper with internet option, internet only with response incentive, and internet only without response incentive. The total response rate across all four types was 21.5%, with the online options having the lowest rates. The researchers speculated that this could be a product of students not checking their college email regularly as well as possible concerns about privacy. British Columbia Health Survey researchers distributed surveys through a combination of mail and online requests but were more likely to receive responses through traditional mail (Guo, Kopec, Cibere, Li, & Goldsmith, 2016).

There are a few possible reasons for the lower response rates for online and email-generated surveys. First, the proliferation of spam had resulted in inboxes being flooded with unwanted email, and while we also get unwanted paper mail, there is a greater risk involved with opening an email or clicking on a link that might contain a virus. Second, not everyone uses email and the internet, with the elderly and people living in poverty being less likely to be online. Third, of all the survey options to ignore, emails with survey links and online links to surveys are the easiest.

Since mail and internet surveys often have poor response rates, it is frequently necessary to conduct follow-ups. If the survey is being distributed by mail, this will increase how much money it takes to complete the project. While postage is cheap, researchers must pay for postage and self-addressed stamped return envelopes to make it easy for respondents to return the surveys. Never make participants have to go through the trouble of finding their own envelope and paying for their own postage. Project costs multiply with each additional mailing, but it will likely be necessary. When is the right time to send out follow-ups? Track the number of responses you are getting each day. They will eventually peak, and as they start to diminish, that would be a good time to get the next batch ready.

Anyone who does a mail or internet survey is going to need to give serious consideration to how they can work to maximize response rates. As I already noted, one way to do this is to send out reminders with additional copies of the survey. The timing for sending out the initial survey and subsequent reminders is also very important. The holidays, particularly between Thanksgiving and New Year's Day, for example, are not good times to send surveys. It is helpful to think about your target population and their lives. If you are considering surveying accountants about people's tax evasion habits, do not send them during tax season when accountants are especially busy.

One way to encourage people to fill out a survey is to get an endorsement or sponsorship from a well-regarded individual or organization. Approval from a professional association can lend legitimacy to a survey, especially when practitioners might not understand how the work could help the discipline. In Chapter 2, I noted how I asked for and received assistance from a high-ranking member of the American Jail Association when I was planning to send surveys to hundreds of jail administrators. After my initial mailing and two follow-ups, I had a 50% response rate, which is very good for a mail survey. The American Jail Association endorsement was important, as jail administrators who opened the envelope immediately saw a cover letter with the AJA logo.

Regardless of whether you can get someone or some influential group to write the cover letter for you, the letter or introductory email/message itself is very important, and you should take great care writing it. You will not personally be there to plead your case why your research is important and why it is worthy of anyone's time. The letter is your one chance to do it. At minimum, you should identify yourself and your affiliation (likely a college or university right now) and explain what you are studying and how the results of the study could be beneficial to individuals, groups, agencies, or society in general. Don't overstate this, though, or you will lose credibility. Give respondents the opportunity to let you know if they would like to see a copy of the results once you are finished with data collection and analysis. When you explain the purpose of the study, keep in mind that you might need to be a bit vague in order to prevent introducing bias into the results. If you find that you need to be vague and omit any information in the cover letter, you could include a debriefing statement at the end of the survey. The cover letter also usually has the contact information of the person who can answer any questions that the participants might have. For surveys, cover letters may also serve as informed consent documents, so please review Chapter 3 for a refresher on that.

Prior to sending the full survey, it might be advisable to do a prenotification (Jennings & Reingle Gonzalez, 2019). A prenotification is a letter or some other form of communication stating that the respondent has been chosen for survey participation and that the survey will be arriving shortly. If the sample size is relatively small, phone calls are also effective for prenotifications. Mail prenotifications also give researchers the chance to confirm that the mailing address is correct and remains functional.

Hagan (2007) provided additional suggestions for attempting to boost response rates, including renumeration, appeals to altruism, using an attractive survey format, personalization, and a shortened format. Researchers with the British Columbia Health Survey (BCHS) tested types of data collection methods to see if they had an impact on response rates. Renumeration served as a good incentive for survey completion. Surveys sent with an instant lottery ticket were 35% more likely to be returned than those that were not. The researchers found that providing instant financial compensation was more persuasive to people than a promise of sending compensation upon completion of the survey. The BCHS researchers also found that people were more likely to complete and return a 10-minute version of the survey than they were the 30-minute version (Guo et al., 2016), but others have not found survey length to be associated with differences in response rates (Stolzmann et al., 2019).

Specific Types of Surveys

Focus Group

Focus groups are a type of in-person interview popular with market research firms as, they are a quick and easy way to get feedback about a product. They consist of small groups, usually 8 to 15 people, who participate in a guided discussion with a facilitator. Focus groups are usually constructed through purposive sampling, with the goal of bringing together certain groups of individuals, such as household members responsible for weekly grocery shopping or registered voters from a specific community. Companies that are nearing the release of a product might gather a sample of shoppers to get their opinions about the taste, texture, and even the bottle shape of a new type of salad dressing. News networks frequently put together focus groups of potential voters to watch political candidates debate and then engage in guided discussions about each politician's performance.

Focus groups can be useful as researchers prepare to write structured surveys but have not yet decided what to ask and what answer options to use. Data obtained from focus groups can also be used to supplement survey data in order to better understand the nature of the problem at hand. Dyson (2005) distributed structured questionnaires to young offenders housed in Scottish correctional facilities but also hosted 11 small focus groups with an average of four to seven juveniles. The groups revealed factors impacting bullying that the researcher had not included in the survey, specifically how bullying might differ by officer shift. With regard to validity and reliability, juveniles' descriptions of bullying did differ between what was said in the focus groups and what juveniles reported on the anonymous surveys. In the surveys, juveniles disclosed being bullied by both staff and other juveniles but would only discuss staff bullying in the group setting. It appears that the juveniles did not want to "rat" out their peers or admit to being victims of peer bullying when they were speaking in front of other juveniles.

It is generally desirable to select focus group members who do not already know each other, as familiarity might mean that already-established social dynamics will influence who gets to speak the most during the sessions. In the bullying example mentioned earlier, Dyson (2005) was unable to arrange for the focus groups to consist of strangers, as all the young men were incarcerated together. As a result, the facilitator noticed that sessions tended to be dominated by one or two offenders while the rest usually quietly agreed with the points made by the vocal individuals.

Self-Report

Self-report surveys serve an important purpose in our discipline, as they give us the opportunity to ask people directly about their behavior. Researchers have employed self-report surveys on various scales, ranging from interviews with a single person to large, nationally representative data collection endeavors such as the **National Youth Survey** (NYS), Monitoring the Future (MTF), and the **Arrestee Drug Abuse Monitoring** (ADAM) Program. The NYS started in 1976 with a national sample of males and females, 11 to 17 years old, living in the United States. The NYS is a longitudinal design that included numerous waves of data collection with the goal of studying delinquent behavior (Brauer, 2009; Pogarsky, Kim, & Paternoster, 2005). NYS results have been used in a several publications and are considered valid and reliable data. The Monitoring the Future survey began in 1975 and serves as a measure of adolescent attitudes and drug behavior. MTF releases yearly reports and most recently surveyed over 42,000 students from nearly 400 public and private schools (National Institute on Drug Abuse, 2020). MTF helps researchers and policymakers understand trends in drug use, including newer developments such as vaping. The Arrestee Drug Abuse Monitoring Program, originally called the Drug Use Forecasting Program, was discontinued in 2003 due to budget cuts. It was reinstated as ADAM II in 2007. ADAM researchers interview newly arrested individuals and ask them to self-report drug use and provide a urine sample to enhance validity and reliability (Office of National Drug Control Policy, n.d.).

With self-reports, we are usually asking people to admit to behavior that might not make them look very good. The behavior in question, if it were to become publicly available, could bring embarrassment, impact one's employment or student status, and even lead to arrest. That means there are reasons people would be tempted to be less than forthcoming. Fortunately, research indicates that self-reports generally have good validity and reliability. Connell and Farrington (1997) studied the reliability and validity of self-reported bullying and victimizations in correctional facilities, and Sekol and Farrington (2013) did a follow-up several years later. The results of both studies support the use of self-reports as reliable indicators of bullying in institutions. Sutton, Bellair, Kowalski, Light, and Hutcherson (2011) surveyed prisoners and asked them to self-report criminal behavior. The researchers conducted a follow-up survey three months later to check for reliability, and their test-retest strategy provided evidence of good reliability.

There are steps that researchers can take to help to enhance the accuracy and stability of self-reports. As with any survey asking for information over time, telescoping, or placing an incident into an incorrect time period, could be a problem here. For example, if I am filling out a survey and am asked if I got a traffic ticket anytime over the last year, I might accidentally say yes when my most recent ticket was actually 18 months ago. To combat this, researchers doing longitudinal self-report surveys could employ bounding, or do an initial interview as part of a panel study and then use that first interview as a time boundary (Hagan, 2007). After the initial interview, researchers may ask, "Since our last interview . . .," to hopefully help respondents place incidents in the correct time frame. If researchers are not implementing a panel design, another suggestion would be to try to use memorable moments as a reference point. So, for students, asking them about incidents that occurred during specific times in their lives, such as "since the start of the semester" or "during summer break" might help prevent telescoping.

We can increase our confidence in self-report data by conducting reliability checks. As noted earlier, the ADAM data collection project involves the use of multiple data collection methods.

Not only do participants answer questions about their drug use, but they also provide a urine sample. Researchers asking students about their delinquent activity might include some questions that can then be verified using other records. For example, schools have records of suspensions, so researchers can ask students to self-report the number of suspensions they received this year and check this against school records later. Reliability checks, including using test-retest and measures of internal consistency (see Chapter 6 for a review) are also valuable tools to monitor respondents' consistency.

An obviously difficult aspect of some self-report surveys is broaching sensitive subjects with people who are complete strangers. There are some things that we have not even admitted to our own friends and families, and yet we might find ourselves sitting across from a researcher or staring at a computer screen and being asked to disclose this information. There are a few ways for researchers to approach asking about sensitive information. One is the **randomized response technique** (RRT) designed by Warner (1965). A research participant would flip a coin or use some other randomization technique to select one of two available statements—"I cheated on my taxes at least once," or "I have never cheated on my taxes"—and then answer that question. Only the respondent will know which question was actually asked, shielding them from the embarrassment of having to give a socially undesirable answer to the researcher. A drawback to RRT is that it is a rather complicated scheme to understand, and people will only shed their social desirability concerns if they both understand the process and trust that their anonymity is being protected (Jann, Jerke, & Krumpal, 2012). Yan and Cantor (2019) also suggest either using a "forgiving introduction" or asking questions presupposing the behavior. **Forgiving introductions** aim to lessen the impact of social desirability by prefacing the questions with a brief statement about how commonly some things occur, such as taking office supplies or being stopped by the police. Yan and Cantor describe questions that presuppose the behavior as types of "loaded" questions that assume that people committed a particular behavior at least once. Instead of asking if a person ever took home office supplies, one might ask, "How many times in the past six months did you take home office supplies?"

Is a Survey the Right Tool for My Study?

Surveys are obviously very powerful tools in our data collection arsenal. They allow us to get information about thoughts and feelings as well as incidents that are too difficult to observe. Without surveys, we would have little information on crimes not reported to the police. Maxfield and Babbie (2012) observed that surveys generally perform well on reliability but may lack validity. With surveys, we are not observing what people actually did, but, instead, we are asking what they did or what they *would* do in certain situations. Due to social desirability, recall error, dishonesty, or an unrealistic view of oneself, the answers might not reflect people's true behavior. Additionally, the way we construct the survey might inhibit our full understanding of an issue. Structured surveys are quick and can be very reliable, but if we forgot to ask some questions or include a full range of answer options, we could emerge from the project with a limited understanding of the topic.

When conducting surveys, we must remember that our sample may not be truly representative of the population. The US Census Bureau (2019) has identified four categories of hard-to-count (HTC) populations—hard to locate, hard to contact, hard to persuade, and hard to interview. Among these groups are very marginalized segments of our society, including people who are homeless, transient, or incarcerated; have language barriers; or have disabilities. This is especially concerning, given that these groups' lives tend to be disproportionately impacted by crime, whether as offenders or as victims. Projects with large budgets and staff members can put resources into working to identify and locate HTC individuals, work with community organizations to gain trust, and attempt to have these groups represented in data collection. This is obviously much more difficult, if not impossible, for studies involving fewer resources. The result is sample bias. The NCVS, which surveys households, does work to collect data from residents living in dormitories, rooming houses, and religious group dwellings, but they do not survey people who are in military barracks or institutions (including correctional facilities) (United States Bureau of Justice Statistics, n.d.). While a survey might ultimately be the best option for what you are looking to study, it is important to keep in mind that there are difficult-to-reach populations that you will likely miss, and their exclusion will result in sample bias.

Is a self-report appropriate for what you are looking to study? Self-reports can be very helpful when we are trying to collect data on criminal behavior and victimization, particularly when we are looking to capture information on crimes not known to the police. If you are looking to find out about the age of onset for individuals' criminal offending, Moffitt, Caspi, Rutter, and Silva (2001) found that self-report data will likely yield different information than official records. Specifically, self-reports tend to reveal offending commencing about three to five years before people start to develop arrest histories that would be found by searching official records. While that's a strength of self-reports relative to official records, self-reports have also been found to be less precise than official records on account of memory and honesty issues with respondents. Farrington and associates (2003) note that, while self-reports might be less precise on dates, they can provide us with information that may not be available in official records, particularly the UCR, such as specifics regarding the offense, motives, and levels of planning involved.

Summary

Since we cannot always observe the activities that we wish to study, we frequently rely on surveys in criminal justice to understand thoughts and behaviors. How we choose to construct the survey will likely impact the quality of the data we collect. We must decide whether we want to provide answer options, or we want respondents to answer using their own words. While the former will be easier to use during data analysis, it also comes with the risk that we will fail to consider and include every possible answer option that respondents would want to choose. As we work to construct surveys, we have to think about our sample and their reading and verbal comprehension levels because the survey language must be written in a way that they can understand. Questions and statements on the surveys must be completely unambiguous to reduce problems with validity and reliability. The physical layout of the survey can impact the chances of participants seeing and responding to every item. Researchers must be very careful when they construct surveys, and they have to spend a tremendous amount of time writing, reviewing, editing, and re-reviewing the instruments. Pretesting with a few people who are similar to the target population is a valuable experience that can prevent distribution of a survey before it is ready.

The various methods of survey distribution—in-person, telephone, mail, email/web—each have strengths and weaknesses. In-person distribution tends to produce the highest response rates. Face-to-face survey administration can provide us not only with survey data but also with information about the respondents' surroundings, their body language, and possibly their interactions with family and friends. While this is very helpful, we must be mindful of the potentially costly drawbacks to this type of data collection. Work that requires researchers to travel will cost more time and money, and in criminal justice, it might also require data collectors to risk their personal safety. Telephone surveys present an opportunity for very fast data collection while still allowing for some researcher-respondent interaction. Any time the researchers will be speaking to respondents, they need to be properly trained to administer the survey so that they avoid biasing the interview. Telephone surveys have become more of a challenge over the past few decades with the proliferation of caller ID and the reduction of landlines in favor of cell phones. Mail and email/web surveys are also inexpensive alternatives that give respondents a good amount of privacy and plenty of time to complete the survey, but low response rates are common. Of the types of survey administration, mail and email/web surveys are the easiest for people to discard.

Self-report surveys give researchers the opportunity to learn about behaviors that we are probably unlikely to witness. In criminal justice, these surveys often address sensitive topics, including asking people to recall victimization experiences and their offending histories. Given the risks associated with disclosing such information, it is natural to wonder how forthcoming and truthful respondents will be. If possible, reliability checks should be conducted to inform researchers about how confident they should be in the results. Any time researchers ask individuals to share personal information, it is the research team's duty to follow ethical rules to safeguard the data and prevent respondents from being harmed by their willingness to participate in the study.

Keywords

Structured survey	Unstructured survey	Contingency question
Depth interview	Matrix	Computer-assisted survey
Skip logic	Computer-assisted	instruments (CASI)
Computer-assisted telephone	interviewing (CAI)	Arrestee Drug Abuse
interviewing (CATI)	National Youth Survey (NYS)	Monitoring (ADAM)
Randomized response	Forgiving introduction	
technique (RRT)	Semi-structured survey	

Discussion Questions

1. Discuss each type of survey administration and how they fare with getting good response rates. What kind of steps can researchers take to improve their response rates?
2. What are the advantages and disadvantages to using structured or unstructured surveys?
3. What are the pros and cons to using computer-assisted survey instruments (CASI)?
4. Discuss the different ways that our wording on surveys could serve to confuse respondents or introduce bias.
5. How can the appearance of a survey instrument encourage or discourage full and accurate completion of the survey?

References

Beck, A. T. (1988). *BHS, Beck Hopelessness Scale*. San Antonio, TX: Psychological Corporation.

Beck, A. T., & Steer, R. A. (1988). *Manual for the Beck Hopelessness Scale*. San Antonio, TX: Psychological Corp.

Beck, A. T., Steer, R. A., & Brown, G. K. (1996). *BDI-II, Beck Depression Inventory*. San Antonio, TX: Psychological Corporation.

Blumberg, S. J., & Luke, J. V. (2018). *Wireless substitution: Early release of estimates from the National Health Interview Survey, January—June 2018*. Hayattsville, MD: National Center for Health Statistics.

Brauer, J. (2009). Testing social learning theory using reinforcement's residue: A multilevel analysis of self-reported theft and marijuana use in the National Youth Survey. *Criminology, 47*(3), 929–970. https://doi.org/10.1111/j.1745-9125.2009.00164.x

Connell, A., & Farrington, D. P. (1997). The reliability and validity of resident, staff, and peer reports of bullying in young offender institutions. *Psychology, Crime, and Law, 3*(4), 287–300. https://doi.org/10.1080/10683169708410824

Cull, J. G., & Gill, W. S. (1998). *Suicide Probability Scale (SPS) manual*. Los Angeles, CA: Western Psychological Services.

Decker, S. H., & Rosenfeld, R. (1995). "My wife is married and so is my girlfriend:" Adaptations to the threat of AIDS in an arrestee population. *Crime & Delinquency, 41*(1), 37–53.

Dyson, G. (2005) Examining bullying among institutionalized young offenders: Triangulation of questionnaires and focus groups. In J. L. Ireland (Ed.), *Bullying among prisoners* (pp. 84–108). Devon, UK: Willan Publishing.

Farrington, D. P., Jolliffe, D., Hawkins, J. D., Catalano, R. F., Hill, K. G., & Kosterman, R. (2003). Comparing delinquency careers in court records and self-reports. *Criminology, 41*(3), 933–958. https://doi.org/10.1111/j.1745-9125.2003.tb01009.x

Flippin, M., Reisig, M. D., & Trinkner, R. (2019). The effect of procedural injustice during emergency 911 calls: A factorial vignette-based study. *Journal of Experimental Criminology, 15*, 651–660. https://doi.org/10.1007/s11292-019-09369-y

Guo, Y., Kopec, J. A., Cibere, J., Li, L. C., & Goldsmith, C. H. (2016). Population survey features and response rates: A randomized experiment. *American Journal of Public Health Methods, 106*(8), 1422–1426. https://doi.org/10.2105/AJPH.2016.303198

Hagan, F. (2007). *Essentials of research methods in criminal justice and criminology* (2nd ed.). Boston, MA: Pearson.

Jann, B., Jerke, J., & Krumpal, I. (2012). Asking sensitive questions using the crosswise model. *Public Opinion Quarterly, 76*(10), 32–49. https://doi.org/10.2307/41345966

Jennings, W. G., & Reingle Gonzalez, J. M. (2019). *Criminological and criminal justice research methods.* New York, NY: Wolters Kluwer.

Keeter, S., Hatley, N., Kennedy, C., & Lau, A. (2017). *What low response rates mean for telephone surveys.* Pew Research Center. Retrieved from https://assets.pewresearch.org/wp-content/uploads/sites/12/2017/05/12154630/RDD-Non-response-Full-Report.pdf

Kempf, A. M., & Remington, P. L. (2007). New challenges for telephone survey research in the twenty-first century. *Annual Review of Public Health, 28*(1), 113–126. http://doi.org/10.1146/annurev.publhealth.28.021406.144059

Link, M. W., Battaglia, M. P., Frankel, M. R., Osborn, L., & Mokdad, A. H. (2007). The U.S. cell phone generation: Comparison of cell phone survey results with an ongoing landline telephone survey. *Public Opinion Quarterly, 71*(5), 814–839. https://doi.org/10.1093/poq/nfm051

Logan, T. K., Walker, R., Shannon, L., & Cole, J. (2008). Combining ethical considerations with recruitment and follow-up strategies for partner violence victimization research. *Violence Against Women, 14*(11), 1226–1251. https://doi.org/10.1177/1077801208323976

Maxfield, M. G., & Babbie, E. (2012). *Basics of research methods for criminal justice and criminology* (3rd ed.). Belmont, CA: Thomson Wadsworth.

Moffitt, T., Caspi, A., Rutter, M., & Silva, P. A. (2001). *Sex differences in antisocial behavior.* Cambridge: Cambridge University Press.

National Institute on Drug Abuse. (2020). *Monitoring the future.* Retrieved from www.drugabuse.gov/related-topics/trends-statistics/monitoring-future

Nix, J., Pickett, J., Baek, H., & Alpert, G. P. (2019). Police research, officer surveys, and response rates. *Policing and Society, 29*(5), 530–550. https://doi.org/10.1080/10439463.2017.1394300

Office of National Drug Control Policy. (n.d.). *Arrestee drug abuse monitoring program.* Washington, DC: Office of National Drug Control Policy. Retrieved from https://obamawhitehouse.archives.gov/ondcp/arrestee-drug-abuse-monitoring-program

Patterson, C., Hogan, L., & Cox, M. (2019). A comparison between two retrospective alcohol consumption measures and the daily drinking diary method with university students. *The American Journal of Drug and Alcohol Abuse, 45*(3), 248–253. https://doi.org/10.1080/00952990.2018.1514617

Perry, A. E., Marandos, R., Coulton, S., & Johnson, M. (2010). Screening tools assessing risk of suicide and self-harm in adult offenders: A systematic review. *International Journal of Offender Therapy & Comparative Criminology, 54*(3), 803–828. https://doi.org/10.1177/0306624X09359757

Perry, A. E., & Olason, D. T. (2009). A new psychometric instrument assessing vulnerability to risk of suicide and self-harm behaviour in offenders. *International Journal of Offender Therapy & Comparative Criminology, 53*(4), 385–400. https://doi.org/10.1177/0306624X08319418

Peterson, N. A., Speer, P. W., & McMillan, D. W. (2007). Validation of a brief sense of community scale: Confirmation of the principle theory of sense of community. *Journal of Community Psychology, 36*(1), 61–73. https://doi.org/10.1002/jcop.20217

Pogarsky, G., Kim, K., & Paternoster, R. (2005). Perceptual change in the National Youth Survey: Lessons for deterrence theory and offender decision-making. *Justice Quarterly, 22*(1), 1–29. https://doi.org/10.1080/07418820420003333627

Sax, L. J., Gilmartin, S. K., & Bryant, A. N. (2003). Assessing response rates and nonresponse bias in web and paper surveys. *Research in Higher Education, 44*(4), 409–432.

Sekol, I., & Farrington, D. P. (2013). The reliability and validity of self, peer and staff reports of bullying and victimization in correctional and care institutions. *Psychology, Crime & Law, 19*(4), 329–344. https://doi.org/10.1080/1068316X.2011.631541

Spark, S., Lewis, D., Vaisey, A., Smyth, E., Wood, A., Temple-Smith, M., . . . & Hocking, J. (2015). Using computer-assisted survey instruments instead of paper and pencil increased completeness of self-administered sexual behavior questionnaires. *Journal of Clinical Epidemiology, 68*, 94–101. https://doi.org/10.1080/1068316X.2011.631541

Steadman H. J., Scott, J. E., Osher, F., Agnese, T., K., & Robbins, P. C. (2005). Validation of The Brief Jail Mental Health Screen. *Psychiatric Services, 56*(7), 816–822. https://doi.org/10.1176/appi.ps.56.7.816

Stolzmann, K., Meterko, M., Mller, C. J., Belanger, L., Seibert, M. N., & Bauer, M. S. (2019). Survey response rate and quality in a mental health clinic population: Results from a randomized survey comparison. *Journal of Behavioral Health Services & Research, 46*(3), 521–532. https://doi.org/10.1007/s11414-018-9617-8

Sutton, J. E., Bellair, P. E., Kowalski, B. R., Light, R., & Hutcherson, D. T. (2011). Reliability and validity of prisoner self-reports gathered using the life event calendar method. *Journal of Quantitative Criminology, 27*, 151–171. https://doi.org/10.1007/s10940-010-9101-y

Tartaro, C., Bonnan-White, J., Mastrangelo, A., & Mulvihill, R. (2019). *Police and community perceptions of mental illness stigma: A comparison.* San Francisco, CA: American Society of Criminology.

United States Bureau of Justice Statistics. (n.d.). *National crime victimization survey methodology.* Washington, DC: United States Department of Justice Bureau of Justice Statistics. Retrieved from www.bjs.gov/developer/ncvs/methodology.cfm

United States Census Bureau. (2019). *Counting the hard to count in a census.* Washington, DC: U.S. Census Bureau. Retrieved from www.census.gov/content/dam/Census/library/working-papers/2019/demo/Hard-to-Count-Populations-Brief.pdf

Veysey, B. M., Steadman, H. J., Morrissey, J. P., Johnsen, M., & Beckstead, J. W. (1998). Using the referral decision scale to screen mentally ill jail detainees: Validity and implementation issues. *Law & Human Behavior, 22*(2), 205–215. https://doi.org/10.1023/a:1025794104048

Warner, S. L. (1965). Randomized response: A survey technique for eliminating evasive answer bias. *Journal of The American Statistical Association, 60*, 63–69. https://doi.org/10.1080/01621459.1965.10480775

Wichmann, C., Serin, R. C., & Motiuk, L. (2000). *Predicting suicide attempts among male offenders in federal penitentiaries.* Ottawa, Canada: Correctional Service of Canada.

Yan, T., & Cantor, D. (2019). Asking survey questions about criminal justice involvement. *Public Health Reports, 134*(1), 46s–56s. https://doi.org/10.1177/0033354919826566

Reading 9.1　The Malleability of Attitudes Toward the Police

Cell phone cameras have changed so much about how we disseminate information, and this is certainly true about how we learn about specific parts of the criminal justice system. It is now rare for a month to go by without videos of some type of police action going viral. How much of an impact do these videos have on individuals' opinions about the police? Boivin, Gendron, Faubert, and Poulin (2017) decided to test this using college students. The researchers discuss some interesting research methods issues, such as the potential impact that survey question order might have on the answers respondents select. They also start off by collecting data with one level of measurement but then recode and collapse some of the answer options to turn ordinal variables into nominal.

The Malleability of Attitudes Toward the Police: Immediate Effects of the Viewing of Police Use of Force Videos

Rémi Boivin, Annie Gendron, Camille Faubert, and Bruno Poulin

Introduction

Images of controversial police interventions regularly 'go viral,' circulating rapidly and widely across various media. Videos are distributed from person to person across social networking sites, blogs, and emails, with the most striking videos and stories often shown or commented on in news media, reaching an even larger audience (Broxton, Interian, Vaver, & Wattenhofer, 2013). This form of emotional contagion (Guadagno, Rempala, Murphy, & Okdie, 2013) leads to a rapid increase in the number of people aware of—and commenting on—a given intervention (Brown, 2016; Goldsmith, 2010). Although research throughout the more economically developed world has shown that the police use force infrequently (Hall, Votova, & Wood, 2013; Kuhns & Knutsson, 2010) and in very specific circumstances (Adams, 2005), many individuals are aware of images of disturbing but uncommon police interventions (Butler & Hall, 2008). Academics have investigated how such negative representations of the police affect the perceptions of non-involved individuals (Chermak, McGarrell, & Gruenewald, 2006; Jefferis, Kaminski, Holmes, & Hanley, 1997; Kaminski & Jefferis, 1998; Lasley, 1994), but it remains unknown if the opinions reported represent an individual's personal understanding and evaluation of a situation or simply a repetition of the content conveyed by the media.

This paper examines how videos of controversial police interventions shape opinions of the police and, consequently, if attitudes toward use of force are malleable in the short term. After a brief review of the literature on attitudes and the effects of media exposure, the results of an experiment are presented. All research participants were asked to report their general opinion of police legitimacy, trustworthiness, and tendency to use force against citizens. One group of research participants was shown short fictional videos of interventions involving the use of force by police before responding to a questionnaire; the other group of participants was not. The analysis investigates how these videos affected responses. We conclude with a discussion of the potential implications of the results in a time when 'unedited' images of police interventions are increasingly available.

Attitudes Toward Use of Force and the Effect of Media Exposure

There are a number of empirical and theoretical studies of correlates of attitudes toward the police (for reviews, see Brown and Reed

Benedict (2002) and Wu, Sun, and Triplett (2009)). Researchers consistently find that various individual characteristics (e.g. age, gender, race, socioeconomic status), personal experiences (victimization, police-initiated contact), and neighborhood conditions (disadvantaged, violent crime rates) are predictors of attitudes. Several theoretical models have been used to explain these findings, including a sense-of-injustice model that posits that public attitudes toward criminal justice agencies are heavily influenced by the belief that police treatment has been unjust, whether experience with the police is personal or vicarious (Wu et al., 2009). Recent history has shown that video recordings of police interventions, widely broadcasted by the media, often provoke strong public reactions, including feelings that the individuals involved have been treated unfairly

Engel (2005) has shown that the media play an important role in the development of the beliefs and expectations regarding the police. However, the media depict the police in both positive and negative ways (Surette, 2011). Researchers have found that reality police shows, crime dramas, and broadcasted news exaggerate the proportion of arrests and the frequency of proactive police activity, thus contributing to create the image of an efficient and effective force (see Dowler and Zawilski (2007) for a review). Studies of media consumption in general have consistently found that watching reality police shows increased citizens' confidence in the ability of the police to do their job (Callanan & Rosenberger, 2011; Eschholz, Blackwell, Gertz, & Chiricos, 2002). However, recent studies have also found that repeated media exposure to images of police abuse led to increased belief in the frequency of police misconduct (Dowler & Zawilski, 2007; Weitzer & Tuch, 2004). In other words, media exposure appears to inflate positive opinions about the police but also leads respondents to overestimate the level of misconduct and, presumably, the use of force. Several researchers explain these contradictory results as a consequence of the fact that most citizens have limited direct experience with law enforcement (Frank, Smith, & Novak, 2005;

Surette, 2011). Furthermore, any direct experience they do have is largely positive, in the sense that police intervention was required by the respondent (e.g. emergency call) (Callanan & Rosenberger, 2011; Eschholz et al., 2002; Frank et al., 2005) or consisted of brief interactions, such as receiving a traffic ticket (Surette, 2011).

However 'many people, particularly those who do not frequently interact with law enforcement, may vicariously experience police-citizen interactions through media consumption' (Eschholz et al., 2002, p. 328; see Callanan and Rosenberger (2011) for a similar discussion). Rosenbaum, Schuck, Costello, Hawkins, and Ring's (2005) study of vicarious experiences of police activity found that both positive and negative vicarious experiences were associated with corresponding changes in attitudes. News media in particular often report on cases of police use of force and/or misconduct, while continual news networks, such as CNN, often show the same images of controversial interventions repeatedly. The rise of video-sharing sites such as YouTube and Dailymotion make it possible for users to watch videos whenever they want and to share them with whomever they want. Regular viewers of network news, who see more images of police use and abuse of force, are more likely to believe that these practices occur frequently (Dowler & Zawilski, 2007). Recognizing this, other researchers have investigated the impact of publicized cases of police misconduct on attitudes. In his pioneer study, Lasley (1994) found that the infamous Rodney King incident, during which LAPD officers were filmed beating an African American citizen, had strong and immediate negative effects on citizen attitudes toward police. After the incident, respondents reported significantly lower perceptions of police fairness. Also, Jefferis et al. (1997) found that a highly publicized and controversial videotaped arrest had a negative impact on citizens' perceptions of force used by police during arrest situations, and Weitzer (2002) suggests that a series of incidents of misconduct in New York and Los Angeles negatively influenced citizen satisfaction and evaluation of job performance of police in these cities.

Images of Police Interventions: General and Specific Effects

There are thus both theoretical and empirical reasons to expect that images of police interventions made available by the media—whether traditional or 'social'—will influence attitudes toward the police. However, it remains unclear whether these effects are diffuse—that is, affect general and long-established attitudes toward the police—or specific to an issue. Evidence suggests that most of the effects are specific: for example, Kaminski and Jefferis (1998) found that a televised violent arrest influenced perceptions of violence by police officers but did not significantly affect general support for the Cincinnati Police Department. Likewise, Chermak et al. (2006) found that citizens who read more about a publicized case of police violent misconduct—the 'Indianapolis Downtown Brawl'—were more likely to think the officers involved were guilty, but no significant impact on general attitudes toward the police and police services was found. These results are in line with a large literature that consistently finds that citizens are generally satisfied with police services and regard the police as legitimate, at least in Western countries (see Brown and Reed Benedict (2002) and Weitzer and Tuch (2005) for reviews).

Many researchers note that media information is not received in the same way by all viewers. Individuals with specific personal circumstances and experiences may interpret media messages differently, while individuals who share certain characteristics may form 'interpretive communities' (Eschholz et al., 2002) or hold 'group positions' (Weitzer & Tuch, 2004). Such varying responses have been found in studies of attitudes toward the police, especially those involving issues of racial profiling. For example, researchers found that the effects of incidents of racial profiling on attitudes were greater among non-Caucasians, perhaps because respondents feel more closely related to the victim (Callanan & Rosenberger, 2011; Eschholz et al., 2002; Graziano, Schuck, & Martin, 2010; Rosenbaum et al., 2005; Weitzer & Tuch, 2004). Consistently, Callanan

and Rosenberger (2011) found that the media had no significant influence on attitudes reported by respondents with prior arrests. Also, police officers and their families have direct experience of police work and thus might form a community that is less influenced by spectacular cases of use of force (Lester, 1995; Paoline & Terrill, 2011). Images of controversial police interventions can thus be expected to have significant effects on public attitudes toward the police, but these effects will be most noticeable in certain groups (individuals with little direct experience of police contact and individuals who share characteristics with the subject of the intervention).

Current Study

This paper examines how videos of controversial police interventions shape opinions of the police and, consequently, if attitudes toward use of force are malleable in the short term. While other researchers have investigated the issue, the current study complements previous research in various ways. First, it makes it possible to test the null hypothesis that videos of police interventions have no impact on the general public's attitudes toward the police. Callanan and Rosenberger (2011) point out that it is impossible for researchers to compare participants who have and have not been exposed to traditional or social media, because individuals in the latter group are almost non-existent. The experimental design used for this study allows for such a comparison while also reducing the selection bias generated by the fact that media consumption is usually not random—viewers choose media that reflect their political and ideological affinities (Iyengar & Hahn, 2009). Whereas previous studies have measured the intensity of exposure (more or less exposed), the current study tests the immediate effect of exposure versus non-exposure in order to evaluate the strength of effects among respondents. Such information is particularly important for any organization hoping to anticipate the effect of releasing controversial images.

Second, as mentioned above, controversial police interventions are quickly commented on by many different people. Previous studies have assumed that individuals who consume more media (or see more images of controversial interventions) are better informed and thus that their opinions have a stronger basis. It is, however, difficult to know if viewers create their own understanding of a situation or if they simply circulate content and comments found in the media. Participants in our studies were shown videos of fictional situations only and were asked to provide their own opinion of the situation without having previously discussed it. It is therefore reasonable to assume that reported opinions in this study indicate respondents' positions, uncontaminated by the opinions of others.

Third, most previous studies have focused on situations involving obvious misconduct. For example, the *Washington Post* conducted a poll in 1992 and concluded that the 'overwhelming majority' of Americans believed that the four Los Angeles police officers accused of beating Rodney King should have been found guilty (Morin & Warden, 1992); in other words, any individual questioned about the incident was likely to report a negative opinion of the LAPD or these particular officers. In these circumstances, it is unsurprising that researchers found that this incident affected attitudes toward the police. However, relatively few incidents generate such a unanimous response from the public— most interventions give rise to debates as to whether or not officer(s) acted properly. The situations presented in the videos in our research were deliberately unclear as to their appropriateness; respondents who viewed the videos could—and did—report opinions ranging from 'the intervention was excellent' to 'officers should be subject to criminal prosecution.'

Methodology

Context

This study was conducted as part of an ongoing research on attitudes toward police use-of-force. The procedure consisted of a self-administered survey where respondents had to 1) answer general questions about the police

and 2) watch four videos and answer specific questions about each intervention immediately after watching them. All videos lasted between 45 and 90 seconds and depicted fictional interventions in which some level of force was used against a citizen. Two videos showed takedowns without apparent injury to the subject, and two involved the use of a firearm with suggested serious injury. (The subject falls to the ground and stops responding to officers.) The videos were scripted by police instructors to enhance their realistic nature. Respondents were informed that the videos were scripted situations inspired by actual interventions but played by actors. The questionnaire included 11 general questions and 6 specific questions for each video, for a total of 35 questions. Respondents had to choose between three or four possible answers, usually on a Likert-type scale (strongly agree, somewhat agree, somewhat disagree, strongly disagree). The data collection process took about 25 minutes, including watching the videos.

While planning the main data collection, we considered putting general questions about the police at the end of the questionnaire (after specific questions related to the videos) to allow participants to respond at their own pace— respondents would hand over their questionnaire whenever they finished. However, the research team raised a concern, based on the literature reviewed above, that watching videos of police interventions could influence responses. The current paper reports the results of the experiment that was put in place to test that proposition.

Experiment

The study sample consisted of undergraduate students in criminology from the Université de Montréal (n = 248 respondents) recruited in their classrooms by the research team and invited to participate immediately during class time. Two non-redundant groups were selected from introductory classes; both groups were equivalent in terms of demographics and background. Response rate was 100%, as all students agreed to participate. Groups were randomly allocated to one of two tasks: group A (n = 109) was asked general questions only, while group B (n = 139) watched the four videos and had to answer specific questions first, followed by general questions. Videos were broadcasted on big screens at the front of the classroom. Students were asked to answer questions individually; at least two research team members as well as the class professor were present to enforce this instruction and, hence, minimize contamination between respondents. For the purpose of this study, only general questions are analyzed, meaning that group A is the control group, and group B is the experimental group, having watched the videos before they completed the survey.

The following analysis focuses on 6 of the 11 general questions asked about use of force and police performance. Respondents reported their feelings about the frequency of police brutality and indicated their level of agreement or disagreement with five statements. The following questions were asked:

- Do you think police brutality is [more, less, or as] frequent as in the past?
- The police use force too often against citizens.
- Police officers who injure citizens while performing their duty should automatically be prosecuted.
- In general, police officers in Québec [the province where the study took place] are aggressive.
- In Québec, the work of the police is adequate.
- The criminal justice system is too lenient toward police officers involved in acts of misconduct.

We first compared the answers of both groups using bivariate statistical analyses, assuming that significant differences could be explained by the experimental condition—one group had seen the videos; the other had not. The second part of the analysis compared individual responses of similar respondents. An analysis based on propensity scores was conducted to match a respondent from group B with the most similar respondent from group A (the 'nearest neighbor'). Eight variables were used to match respondents: age, gender, ethnicity, education, officer in the family, work, experience as a security agent, and experience of police use of force as a subject. It was assumed that the main difference between an individual and his match was that the latter had not watched the videos before responding to the general survey.

Results

Table 1 displays opinions about the police. Column C reports bivariate statistical tests comparing the answers of both groups on the original measurement scale, meaning that both groups were compared on the four possible answers they could opt for in the survey: 'strongly agree,' 'somewhat agree,' 'somewhat disagree,' and 'strongly disagree.' Column D reports bivariate tests for the same questions on a recoded scale, meaning that the four possible answers were dichotomized into whether the respondent agreed or disagreed with the statement. Significant results in column C indicate that respondents from one group reported more nuanced answers to the survey than those in the other group (e.g. 'somewhat disagree' instead of 'strongly disagree'); in column D, a significant result indicates that the proportion of respondents who agreed with a statement was significantly different in both groups. Non-significant results at $p < 0.05$ are identified by 'n.s.'. It should be noted that multivariate tests (ordinal and binomial regressions) confirmed all results but are not reported in Table 1 for the sake of simplicity.

The group of respondents who had seen the videos before completing the general survey (group B) reported opinions that are significantly less favorable to the police. The proportion of respondents who thought police brutality was more frequent than in the past is about twice that of the control group (29.7% vs. 14.7%). Similarly, the proportion of respondents who reported that police brutality is less frequent than in the past is about half for the group who had seen the videos prior to the general survey (18.1% vs. 35.8%).

Table 1 Reported Opinions of Experimental and Control Groups

Question	Answers	A Did Not Watch Videos	B Watched Videos Before Completing Survey	C More Nuanced	D Agree vs. Disagree
Number of cases		109	139		
Police brutality is:	More frequent than before	14.7%	29.7%	V = 0.233**	-
	As frequent	49.5%	52.2%		
	Less frequent than before	35.8%	18.1%		
Officers use force too often	Strongly disagree	13.9%	4.9%	V = 0.342**	Phi = 0.332**
	Somewhat disagree	65.3%	41.8%		
	Somewhat agree	18.8%	45.9%		
	Strongly agree	2.0%	7.4%		
Automatic prosecutions when injury	Strongly disagree	21.0%	27.1%	V = 0.218**	Phi = 0.215**
	Somewhat disagree	42.9%	55.6%		
	Somewhat agree	29.5%	15.0%		
	Strongly agree	6.7%	2.3%		
Officers are aggressive	Strongly disagree	41.7%	20.7%	V = 0.241**	n.s.
	Somewhat disagree	46.6%	63.1%		
	Somewhat agree	11.7%	14.4%		
	Strongly agree	0.0%	1.8%		
Police do a good job	Strongly disagree	1.0%	2.4%	n.s.	n.s.
	Somewhat disagree	9.6%	12.8%		
	Somewhat agree	77.9%	79.2%		
	Strongly agree	11.5%	5.6%		
Justice system is lenient toward police	Strongly disagree	3.1%	3.3%	n.s.	n.s.
	Somewhat disagree	37.5%	26.4%		
	Somewhat agree	35.4%	42.1%		
	Strongly agree	24.0%	28.1%		

**$p < 0.01$

Respondents in group B were also more likely to agree that officers use force too often. Furthermore, while most respondents in both groups disagree with the statement that officers are aggressive, the experimental group provided more nuanced answers: in both cases, more than 85% of respondents disagree with the statement, but the majority of respondents who had seen the videos 'somewhat disagree', while a comparable proportion of the group A 'somewhat' and 'strongly disagree'.

As mentioned above, it was expected that respondents would be consistent with themselves (respondents who thought police brutality is more frequent than before were expected to agree that officers use force too often). Consequently, the finding that respondents from the group who had seen the videos before were less likely to support automatic prosecution when individuals are injured during police intervention was therefore surprising. Respondents from group B were proportionally more likely to 'somewhat disagree' (55.6% vs. 42.9%) or 'strongly disagree' (27.1% vs. 21.0%) with that proposition and therefore to disagree overall (82.7% vs. 63.9%). This result could be explained by the fact that none of the videos showed completely gratuitous police violence but situations in which individuals displayed some level of resistance toward the police. The videos may have acted as a reminder that such situations are often complex.

There were no significant differences between groups in their responses to the other two statements, which were more general claims about the police and the criminal justice system's reaction to police misconduct, suggesting that the videos mainly affected opinions directly related to the use of force rather than to overall assessment of the work of the police and the criminal justice system.

Propensity Score Matching

While there were significant differences in opinions between group B, who had seen the videos prior to responding to general questions, and group A, who had not, the extent of this effect remains unknown. Furthermore, groups were balanced in terms of characteristics that have been found in the literature to be associated with attitudes toward use of force (e.g. Phillips, 2015), but differences between individuals were expected and observed. We therefore looked at whether the occurrence of more nuanced opinions and/or opposite opinions varied at the individual level, i.e. among matched respondents from both groups. Table 2 shows statistics for all six items. Column A reports the proportion of respondents from group A whose answer is in the same direction (agree or disagree) as their match in group B but 'somewhat' rather than 'strongly'. Column B reports the proportion of respondents from group A who provided an opinion opposite to their match (agree vs. disagree). Column C reports the proportion of respondents from group A who provided the same answer to the element.

The proportion of respondents from group B who reported the same opinion as their 'match' from group A varies between 28.8% and 68.0%. When a different opinion was reported, it was more likely to be a complete opposite rather than a more nuanced opinion for all items except 'automatic prosecutions'. In other words, many respondents had opposite opinions about the police than their match, suggesting that attitudes can completely change after watching videos of controversial police interventions. Overall, 80.6% of respondents who watched the videos provided at least one opinion opposite that reported by their match, suggesting that opinions about police use of force

Table 2 Responses from Group B and Nearest Match in Group A

Question	Number of Cases	More Nuanced (%)	Opposite Opinion	Same Opinion (%)
Frequency of police brutality	135	57.8	-	42.2
Officers use force too often	119	5.0	52.1	42.9
Automatic prosecution when injury	130	30.7	28.5	40.8
Officers are aggressive	108	22.2	24.1	53.7
Police do a good job	122	7.4	24.6	68.0
Justice system is lenient toward police	118	25.4	45.8	28.8

are highly sensitive to anecdotal incidents, at least in the short term.

Discussion

The results of this study strongly suggest that controversial videos of police interventions have effects on reported opinions about use of force, at least in the short term. First, respondents in group B (who watched the videos before answering general questions) reported that police use of force was more frequent than those in group A (who answered the questions before seeing the videos). The fact that they had just seen (fictional) interventions seems to have influenced group B respondents to overestimate the true occurrence of police use of force. Group B respondents were also more likely to agree with the statement that the police too often use force against individuals. These results are consistent with the voluminous research on the availability heuristic—a mental shortcut that occurs when people make judgments about the probability of events based on the ease with which examples come to mind (Tversky & Kahneman, 1973)—and on the effect of recency on beliefs and attitudes (Zdep & Wilson, 1968). The results raise questions in line with previous work on media consumption and attitudes toward police (Dowler & Zawilski, 2007; Weitzer & Tuch, 2004) that suggest that individuals who are more exposed to videos of police intervention are more likely to overestimate the frequency of use of force and their own risk of being subjected to force during an encounter with the police. These results are particularly relevant at a time when police organizations and the media have started releasing images of police interventions (e.g. caught by cell phones or body-worn cameras) with the intention of getting the public to see 'their' point of view (White, 2014). The results presented here show that such images are likely to have adverse effects on public attitudes.

Second, respondents who had seen the videos were less likely to support automatic prosecutions when citizens are injured during police interventions. While this result was unexpected, it may relate to the difference between direct and indirect experience (Rosenbaum et al., 2005). Most respondents (237/248, or 95.6%) had never been involved in a situation in which a police officer used force against them and thus had to rely on indirect experience to form their opinions (Surette, 2011). The videos showed situations in which the subject's behavior—whether resistance or aggression—led to the use of force by officers and to potential injuries to the subjects, suggesting that the subjects were in part responsible for the use of force. This echoes a diverse literature that shows that situations where the victim can be considered to be, at least in part, responsible for the police action are treated differently by the police and the court (e.g. Saunders & Size, 1986; Sleath & Bull, 2012) but also by the public (e.g. Gracia & Tomas, 2014; Weller, Hope, & Sheridan, 2013). This result is also consistent with the insistence of police organizations that most use of force situations are not in black or white but in infinite shades of grey, meaning that the outcome (the use of force) is the result of complex interactions between officers and subjects. The videos might have illustrated this idea for respondents, who, consequently, were then not in favor of such a drastic measure as automatic prosecution.

Third, the videos had little impact on general attitudes toward the police. Respondents in both groups reported similar opinions about police aggressiveness, police efficiency, and the perceived harshness of the criminal justice system toward police officers who commit acts of misconduct. These results are consistent with Chermak et al. (2006), who found that a publicized police misconduct trial had no significant effect on general attitudes toward police and police services but did affect citizens' assessment of the specific case.

Future research should investigate the persistence of opinions and attitudes toward the police. Comparing diversified groups assumes that all respondents were equally sensitive to videos, and does not make it possible to determine if there are specific characteristics that distinguish those immediately responsive to the video. However, consistent with previous studies (e.g. Rosenbaum et al., 2005), exploratory analyses suggest that some respondents were more responsive to the videos than others, but the number of respondents per specific categories was too small to provide definitive results. Among other results, respondents who had a police officer in their family were significantly less likely to report opinions opposite to those of their match in their assessment of police aggressiveness in Québec (aggressive officers) and the importance of automatic charges in case of injuries (automatic prosecution following injury). These results support the idea that opinions about the police held by respondents with a police officer in their family are better established than those of other respondents.

Conclusion

It raises concerns that we were able to significantly affect attitudes toward police use of force simply by showing videos of controversial—but fictional—police interventions. More than 80% of those who watched the videos prior to answering the questionnaire provided at least one opinion (out of six) that was opposite to that of their match, who had not seen the videos. This supports the idea that footage of actual interventions—including appropriate ones—might have unexpected negative impacts on public attitudes toward the police. Anecdotal situations have repeatedly been found to have considerable impact on decision-makers and, by extension, on the public (Christen & Gunther, 2003). The current study investigated whether videos of specific interventions influence attitudes toward police use of force—and results were consistent.

Like any study, the present one has some limitations; two deserve specific mention. First, while all data collection involving survey respondents is subject to measurement bias, our research team was particularly concerned about social desirability, i.e. the tendency to give answers that respondents feel are socially desirable or that will please the researcher/interviewer rather than to reveal their true opinions (Groves et al., 2004). The study was developed in collaboration with the École nationale de police du Québec (Québec's police academy); the Academy is the official reference for matters of policing in Québec, and their involvement might have suggested that interventions followed their standards. To avoid that respondents believe the questionnaire was a test with 'correct' and 'incorrect' answers, the role of the Academy was not explicitly stated but could have been noticed by attentive respondents (filming locations, uniforms, credits). It remains a possibility that some respondents were influenced by social desirability. Another limitation is well known by social scientists: the respondents were all undergraduate students in criminology, and there are historical concerns about inappropriate reliance on undergraduate research participants (see, for example, Endler and Speer (1998)). Many studies have found that undergraduates are not representative of the population and report opinions that are significantly different. This should not be a major problem for this study since the objective was to measure the effect of an 'experience' rather than to capture general public opinion. Reliance on this type of research participants would be an issue only if undergraduates reacted differently to videos they were shown and there is no empirical evidence supporting or negating this argument.

This study shows that exposure to video images of controversial police intervention could have short-term effects on attitudes toward use of force. Police organizations must account for these potential negative effects in their communication strategy before they release videos of controversial interventions.

Discussion Questions

1. How could the use of different research designs have impacted the findings? Specifically, what might pretests have told us?
2. What was the researchers' sampling procedure? How might that have impacted the results?
3. What kind of impact, if any, did watching the videos have on student opinions of the police?

References

Adams, K. (2005). What we know about police use of force. In R. G. Dunham & G. P. Alpert (Eds.), *Critical issues in policing* (5th ed., pp. 532–546). Long Grove, IL: Waveland Press.

Brown, B., & Reed Benedict, W. R. (2002). Perceptions of the police. *Policing: An International Journal of Police Strategies and Management, 25,* 543–580.

Brown, G. R. (2016). The blue line on thin ice: Police use of force modifications in the era of cameraphones and YouTube. *The British Journal of Criminology, 56,* 293–312.

Broxton, T., Interian, Y., Vaver, J., & Wattenhofer, M. (2013). Catching a viral video. *Journal of Intelligent Information Systems, 40,* 241–259.

Butler, C., & Hall, C. (2008). Police/public interaction: Arrests, use of force by police, and resulting injuries to subjects and officers—A description of risk in one major Canadian city. *Law Enforcement Executive Forum, 8,* 141–157.

Callanan, V. J., & Rosenberger, J. S. (2011). Media and public perceptions of the police: Examining the impact of race and personal experience. *Policing & Society, 21,* 167–189.

Chermak, S., McGarrell, E., & Gruenewald, J. (2006). Media coverage of police misconduct and attitudes toward police. *Policing: An International Journal of Police Strategies & Management, 29,* 261–281.

Christen, C. T., & Gunther, A. C. (2003). The influence of mass media and other culprits on the projection of personal opinion. *Communication Research, 30,* 414–431.

Dowler, K., & Zawilski, V. (2007). Public perceptions of police misconduct and discrimination: Examining the impact of media consumption. *Journal of Criminal Justice, 35,* 193–203.

Endler, N. S., & Speer, R. L. (1998). Personality psychology: Research trends for 1993–1995. *Journal of Personality, 66,* 621–669.

Engel, R. S. (2005). Citizens' perceptions of distributive and procedural injustice during traffic stops with police. *Journal of Research in Crime & Delinquency, 42,* 445–481.

Eschholz, S., Blackwell, B. S., Gertz, M., & Chiricos, T. (2002). Race and attitudes toward the police. *Journal of Criminal Justice, 30,* 327–341.

Frank, J., Smith, B. W., & Novak, K. J. (2005). Exploring the basis of citizens' attitudes toward the police. *Police Quarterly, 8,* 206–228.

Goldsmith, A. J. (2010). Policing's new visibility. *British Journal of Criminology, 50,* 914–934.

Gracia, E., & Tomas, J. M. (2014). Correlates of victim-blaming attitudes regarding partner violence against women among the Spanish general population. *Violence Against Women, 20,* 26–41.

Graziano, L., Schuck, A., & Martin, C. (2010). Police misconduct, media coverage, and public perceptions of racial profiling: An experiment. *Justice Quarterly, 27,* 52–76.

Groves, R. M., Fowler, F. J. Jr., Couper, M. P., Lepkowski, J. M., Singer, E., & Tourangeau, R. (2004). *Survey methodology.* Hoboken, NJ: Wiley-Interscience.

Guadagno, R. E., Rempala, D. M., Murphy, S., & Okdie, B. M. (2013). What makes a video go viral? An analysis of emotional contagion and Internet memes. *Computers in Human Behavior, 29,* 2312–2319.

Hall, C., Votova, K., & Wood, D. (2013). *Prospective analysis of police use of force in four Canadian cities: Nature of events and their outcome.* Ottawa, Ontario, Canada: National Defence R & D–Centre for Security Science.

Iyengar, S., & Hahn, K. S. (2009). Red media, blue media: Evidence of ideological selectivity in media use. *Journal of Communication, 59,* 19–39.

Jefferis, E. S., Kaminski, R. J., Holmes, S., & Hanley, D. E. (1997). The effect of a videotaped arrest on public perceptions of police use of force. *Journal of Criminal Justice, 25,* 381–395.

Kaminski, R. J., & Jefferis, E. S. (1998). The effect of a violent televised arrest on public perceptions of the police. *Policing: An International Journal of Police Strategies & Management, 21,* 683–706.

Kuhns, J. B., & Knutsson, J. (Eds.). (2010). *Police use of force: A global perspective.* Santa Barbara, CA: Praeger.

Lasley, J. R. (1994). The impact of the Rodney King incident on citizen attitudes toward police. *Policing and Society, 3,* 245–255.

Lester, D. (1995). Officer attitudes toward police use of force. In W. A. Geller & H. Toch (Eds.), *And justice for all: Understanding and controlling police abuse of force* (pp. 177–186). Washington, DC: Police Executive Research Forum.

Morin, R., & Warden, S. (1992, May 3). Views on the King verdict. *The Washington Post,* p. A26.

Paoline, E. A., & Terrill, W. (2011). Listen to me! Police officers' views of appropriate use of force. *Journal of Crime and Justice, 34,* 178–189.

Phillips, S. W. (2015). Police recruit attitudes toward the use of unnecessary force. *Police Practice and Research, 16,* 51–64.

Rosenbaum, D. P., Schuck, A. M., Costello, S. K., Hawkins, D. F., & Ring, M. K. (2005). Attitudes toward the police: The effects of direct and vicarious experience. *Police Quarterly, 8,* 343–365.

Saunders, D. G., & Size, P. B. (1986). Attitudes about woman abuse among police officers, victims, and victim advocates. *Journal of Interpersonal Violence, 1,* 25–42.

Sleath, E., & Bull, R. (2012). Comparing rape victim and perpetrator blaming in a police officer sample: Differences between police officers with and without special training. *Criminal Justice and Behavior, 39,* 646–665.

Surette, R. (2011). *Media, crime, and criminal justice: Images, realities, and policies* (4th ed.). Belmont, CA: Wadsworth Publishing Co.

Tversky, A., & Kahneman, D. (1973). Availability: A heuristic for judging frequency and probability. *Cognitive Psychology, 5*, 207–232.

Weitzer, R. (2002). Incidents of police misconduct and public opinion. *Journal of Criminal Justice, 30*, 397–408.

Weitzer, R., & Tuch, S. A. (2004). Race and perceptions of police misconduct. *Social Problems, 51*, 305–325.

Weitzer, R., & Tuch, S. A. (2005). Determinants of public satisfaction with the police. *Police Quarterly, 8, 279–297.*

Weller, M., Hope, L., & Sheridan, L. (2013). Police and public perceptions of stalking: The role of prior victim-offender relationship. *Journal of Interpersonal Violence, 28*, 320–339.

White, M. D. (2014). *Police officer body-worn cameras: Assessing the evidence.* Washington, DC: Office of Community Oriented Policing Services.

Wu, Y., Sun, I. Y., & Triplett, R. A. (2009). Race, class or neighborhood context: Which matters more in measuring satisfaction with police? *Justice Quarterly, 26*, 125–156.

Zdep, S., & Wilson, W. (1968). Recency effects in opinion formation. *Psychological Reports, 23*, 195–200.

Reading 9.2   "Well, There's a More Scientific Way to Do It!"

In Chapter 1, I discussed the criminal justice field's movement toward evidence-based practice (EBP). Incorporating EBP into policing will allow us to best utilize taxpayer money while we implement only programs and practices that have been found to be effective. As Kalyal (2019) notes, criminal justice has been relatively slow to adopt EBP. The purpose of this article was to explore why high-level police personnel in Canada do eventually choose to adopt EBP. For data collection, Kalyal conducted 30-to-45-minute telephone interviews with sworn and civilian personnel. In Chapter 9, I cautioned against attempting long telephone interviews, but that was assuming that a researcher would be calling a stranger at home to participate in a survey that the person was unlikely to find interesting. In this study, the author initially contacted everyone via email to ask permission for a telephone interview, so only people who were interested in this topic and willing to make the commitment to complete it participated. Additionally, respondents were given the chance to select a time that was convenient for them to receive the phone call.

"Well, There's a More Scientific Way to Do It!": Factors Influencing Receptivity to Evidence-Based Practices in Police Organizations

Hina Kalyal

Introduction

Organizational changes occur due to myriad factors that may be internal or external to the organization such as change of leadership, financial constraints, or pressure from external stakeholders (Cochran, Bromley, & Swando, 2002). In the last two decades, the public sector has faced intense pressure to innovate for the enhancement of organizational performance and productivity (Lewis, Ricard, & Klijn, 2018). For organizations such as police, rising operational costs have prompted the need for more effective utilization of public funds. In this context, researchers and policymakers have recommended the use of scientific evidence in police operations to ensure enhanced organizational efficiency and effectiveness (Griffiths, 2014; Public Safety Canada, 2013). The adoption of evidence-based policing (EBP) therefore represents a viable solution for achieving these goals.

EBP is a decision-making perspective based on the premise that police practices should be supported by rigorous research evidence (Lum, Telep, Koper, & Grieco, 2012) or 'what works best' (Sherman, 1998, p. 2). A more comprehensive definition of the concept has been provided by Lum and Koper (2017, p. 1):

> Evidence-based policing means that research, evaluation, analysis and scientific processes should have "seat at the table" in law enforcement decision-making about tactics, strategies and policies. Further, we define evidence-based policing as not just about the process or products of evaluating police practices, but also about translation of that knowledge into digestible and usable forms and the institutionalization of that knowledge into practice and policing systems.

Since police strategies based on credible research are likely to be more justifiable and effective in reducing crime than decisions based on hunches and guesswork (Lum, 2009), institutionalization of the same is imperative. Proactive strategies such as COMPSTAT, problem-oriented policing, intelligence-led policing (Ratcliffe, 2008), and hot-spots policing (Sherman & Weisburd, 1995) have been found to be more advantageous compared to random and reactive models. However, the uptake of EBP by police organizations has been rather slow despite their noted benefits (Lum et al., 2012). Policing literature suggests that there is a dearth of studies that examine the role of personal and organizational factors influencing police use of research (Tseng, 2010). As police organizations are considered militaristic, conservative, and change-averse (Lum & Koper, 2017), it would be useful to determine the factors which help initiate change, as little empirical research is available on the topic.

The current study is based on 38 detailed interviews of police executives and senior civilian employees of police across Canada, using thematic analysis (Braun & Clarke, 2006) for data analysis. The study fills several gaps in receptivity to EBP literature. Firstly, it is interdisciplinary in nature and draws upon literature in policing, organizational change, and diffusion of innovation to identify contextual factors which impact police openness toward the use of research evidence. Contextual studies are highly recommended on topics such as the adoption of evidence-based practices, to specifically identify factors leading to openness toward such changes (Stetler, Ritchie, Rycroft-Malone, Schultz, & Charns, 2009; Watson et al., 2018). Secondly, it is an addition to the few existing qualitative studies available on EBP, which are in demand by both academics and practitioners to better understand the factors affecting the phenomenon (Lumsden, 2016; Veltri, Lim, & Miller, 2014). Finally, the results of the present study would enable police practitioners and decision-makers to develop more effective policies for EBP adoption, as they focus specifically on the initial phase of the innovation process, which ensures acceptance and subsequent implementation of the initiative.

Literature Review

Evidence-based policing has been described as an innovation in policing literature (Weisburd & Braga, 2006). Innovation is defined as any new product, service, or process adopted by an organization (Damanpour, 1991) for the purpose of improving organizational performance (Damanpour & Schneider, 2006). EBP strongly supports the use of research evidence in making decisions at the strategic, tactical, and operational levels of policing and the translation of research into practice (Lum & Koper, 2017). However, there are only a few prior studies available that specifically address organizational receptivity and openness toward EBP.

In the UK, researchers have found that mid- and upper-level police (Hunter, Wigzell, May, & McSweeney, 2015) reading government publications (Palmer, 2011) and studies utilizing simple qualitative methods (Koehle, Six, & Hanrahan, 2010) were more receptive to EBP. Wilkinson et al. (2017) used the Action Research approach to introduce and embed EBP within the Devon and Cornwall Police (DCP) Service in the UK. Training workshops were developed collaboratively by researchers and police officers to enhance knowledge and skills to utilize research-based practices to inform organizational decision-making. Based on the feedback obtained after the workshops, the training sessions were deemed successful not only in familiarizing police officers with EBP but also in ensuring that the strategy was utilized effectively within the organization.

For police organizations in the US, a receptivity survey developed by Telep and Lum (2014) revealed that higher levels of officer education lead to openness toward research-based practices. However, Telep and Winegar (2016) found support for but lack of clear understanding of EBP-related concepts among senior officers. Jenkins (2016) has argued that police officers are more receptive to strategies they believe to be highly innovative, such as community policing and crime mapping. Steinheider, Wuestewald, Boyatzis, and Kroutter (2012) argue that although police practitioners and researchers hold widely different views regarding research partnerships, knowledge integration and building a climate of trust could lead to more effective collaboration between the two groups. On the other hand, the results of a study by Rojek, Alpert, and Smith (2012) show that although police leaders claim to make evidence-based decisions, the extent to which research evidence is actually used in the decision-making process and the resulting operations could not be determined.

In the Canadian perspective, EBP research is fairly new. A replication of Telep and Lum's (2014) receptivity survey by Blaskovits et al. (2018) has shown that Canadian police officers are more receptive to EBP compared to those in the US. Huey, Blaskovits, Bennell, Kalyal, and Walker (2017) have identified a lack of confidence in top management to be the reason behind the lack of receptivity toward evidence-based practices. To further promote the adoption of EBP, it is important to determine how organizational receptivity toward an innovation such as EBP develops and to enable police and civilian officers to recognize and understand the importance of research in their decision making activities (Lum & Koper, 2017).

In organizational change literature, the phases involved in the adoption of innovation can be categorized generally as initiation, adoption, and implementation (Rogers, 1995). It is at the first or initiation stage that organizational members recognize the need for change, search for suitable solutions, share the appropriate choices with colleagues, and propose measures for its adoption (Meyer & Goes, 1988; Rogers, 1995). Openness to change is therefore the first essential step in the planned change process to reflect support for and confidence in the benefits of change (Miller, Johnson, & Grau, 1994). This stage reflects the motivation to proceed with a change initiative and is affected by external organizational environment as well as internal organizational characteristics such as mission, structure, and level of bureaucracy (Damanpour, 1991; Damanpour & Schneider, 2006).

Given the importance of the initial phase of change and paucity of literature related to EBP adoption by police organizations, the present study explores the factors that lead to receptivity and openness toward these initiatives. In other words, what drives EBP adoption in police organizations? To answer this question, the present research is based on Aarons, Hurlburt, and Horwitz's (2011) conceptual model of evidence-based practice implementation in the public services sector. The four different phases of the model are exploration, adoption, implementation, and sustainment. However, the present paper will focus only on the exploration phase as it is the initial stage of change during which organizations become aware of an issue requiring an innovative solution (Grol, Bosch, Hulscher, Eccles, & Wensing, 2007). Factors influencing the exploration phase are explained in the following sections:

The Outer Context

Several factors in the outer context are believed to impact the exploration phase or an organization's openness to innovation in the public sector. These factors may be socio-political in nature and can include governmental policies promoting innovation, the availability or tightening of government funding, improved performance demands by advocacy groups, and interaction with other agencies employing evidence-based practices (Davies & Nutley, 2008; Frambach & Schillewaert, 2002; Greenhalgh, Robert, Macfarlane, Bate, & Kyriakidou, 2004).

The Inner Context

The inner context includes organizational and individual characteristics that are expected to affect the exploration phase.

Organizational Characteristics

Aarons et al. (2011) identify three organizational characteristics that have an impact on the exploration stage. The first is an organization's absorptive capacity or the existing skills and knowledge possessed by an organization to identify and implement new initiatives (Greenhalgh et al., 2004; Grol et al., 2007). The second factor is readiness for change, which is linked to an organization's self-perceived ability to undertake change. Organizational context is the third factor, which includes organizational culture (shared values), organizational climate (employee   perception   of   the   work environment), and strong leadership committed to encouraging change.

Individual Adopter Characteristics

Aarons et al. (2011) also focus on the individuals in the organization and how their values, social networks, and perceived need for change influence receptivity to EBP. Those interested in new ideas usually keep themselves updated on new academic and professional developments in their field (Berwick, 2003). They try to engage with others outside the organization to share and gain new knowledge and perceive themselves as being capable of undertaking new challenges.

The present paper is part of a larger study exploring factors that facilitate or inhibit receptivity to EBP practices in Canada. Given the dearth of academic research explaining the factors affecting organizational and officer receptivity toward EBP, this study adopts a contextual approach in highlighting factors which might shape responses toward EBP.

Methods

Recruitment

The population of interest for the present study is executive-level police officers (Inspectors and above) and senior civilian staff across English-speaking provinces in Canada. The organizations contacted are listed as members on the Canadian Society of Evidence-[Based] Policing (CAN-SEBP) website. The Canadian Society of Evidence-Based Policing (CAN-SEBP) was formed in April 2015 (CAN-SEBP, 2019). It provides a platform to police practitioners, academic researchers, public policymakers, and others to create and disseminate quality research related to EBP. CAN-SEBP members are able to access the latest research tools and new developments from the website, undertake research projects, and actively interact with fellow EBP researchers and practitioners through this forum. Organizational membership in the CAN-SEBP was therefore considered an indicator of leadership's support for evidence-based policing

practices. CAN-SEBP member organizations actively utilize EBP strategies in their decision-making processes as indicated in the Results section.

Data were collected based on in-depth interviews with the participants. The purpose of these interviews was to gain insight into the reasons behind the adoption of EBP by these organizations. Research approval was obtained from Western University's research ethics board prior to conducting the interviews. The author emailed the top leadership of all 24 partner organizations listed as members on the CAN-SEBP website (April 2017). A total of 16 police organizations responded, resulting in a total sample of 38 officers and civilian staff members consenting to be interviewed.

The interviews were conducted via telephone at the convenience of the participants. Each interview lasted approximately 30–45 minutes, and the questions were based on a semi-structured guide. The interviews were audio recorded, and written consent was obtained from all participants prior to the interview. The present paper is based on two questions: (1) What were the reasons behind your agency joining the CAN-SEBP? (2) What were the motivating factors behind your agency's adoption of EBP?

Analysis

The present paper employs Braun and Clarke's (2006) thematic analysis approach to data analysis. Analysis involved several stages of coding beginning with initial coding conducted by the author and another independent researcher as they read and reread the interview transcripts. The results of the initial round of coding revealed key themes that were very similar to the exploration phase of Aarons et al.'s (2011) model. Open codes were then developed and organized into broader categories or themes. At this stage, we coded the data using elements of Aarons et al.'s (2011) model as coding criteria. The author and the independent reviewer inspected the themes for accuracy and reanalyzed the data till a clear pattern emerged. The results were compared to establish inter-rater reliability, and the final themes were retained after discussion.

Sample Characteristics

Our respondents included officers (n = 33) and civilian employees (n = 5) (see Table 1). Most respondents were male (n = 34) with four (n = 4) female participants (see Table 2). A total of 16 (n = 16) police organizations across seven (n = 7) different provinces (see Table 3).

Results

The study participants described the EBP initiatives undertaken by their organizations, which mostly included community policing, problem-oriented policing, Compstat, intelligence-led policing, and hot-spots policing. Two main themes emerged during data analysis which align with the outer and inner organizational contexts of the exploration phase of Aarons et al.'s (2011) framework. However, the framework is partially represented by the current results as the participants focused mainly on organizational characteristics but did not discuss individual characteristics included in the framework. The following section presents the results of the study.

Outer Context

Three sub-themes represent the external environment affecting openness to EBP or the external drivers of change:

Monitoring and Review

Several participants (n = 11) believed that the decision to adopt EBP was prompted by the need to justify organizational decisions to external stakeholders. One interviewee, an Inspector, mentioned how anecdotal reporting is no longer acceptable to oversight bodies, stating, 'we're in the environment now where any sort of decision-making, reporting to the public, or to our oversightees, these really have to be evidence-based.' Others agreed that the oversight bodies had become more involved in policing issues

Table 1 Sample Characteristics—Police Officer or Civilian

Police officers	33
Civilian employees	5
Total	38

Table 2 Sample Characteristics—Gender

Male	35
Female	3
Total	38

Table 3 Sample Characteristics: Police Organizations by Province

Alberta	2
British Columbia	5
Manitoba	1
Newfoundland and Labrador	2
Nova Scotia	1
Ontario	4
Saskatchewan	1
Total	16

over the years and were acutely aware of the importance of evidence-based practices. Commenting on this, a Deputy Chief reflected:

> I've noticed in my twenty years in policing, whether we're dealing with community groups or councils or even police boards, twenty years ago if the police said, "hey we have this problem and we propose the solution is this," most people would say "humph, that sounds good, they're the experts, let's do that." Rarely do I go to a high-level meeting now and we suggest something, and they go, "what makes you think that's a good idea?" so you know to be able to say, "this is why."

A Deputy Commissioner attributed the adoption of EBP to public expectations in relation to performance and high expectations of accountability especially in relation to decision-making, noting that 'evidence-based decision-making helps in sort of that accountability model.' At least two officers pointed out the importance of adopting EBP to successfully measure program outputs and objectives. A Superintendent considered such measures important in justifying organizational decisions so that he was in a position to 'attribute facts to that program if it were to come under attack or a bunch of pressures.' Similar views were echoed by a Chief of Police who supported the adoption of EBP in his agency for more accurate evaluation of programs and 'to be able to actually demonstrate returning value.' However, not all interviewees seemed convinced of the benefits of externally imposed EBP initiatives. As one Superintendent recalled:

> When I reference my time starting in my unit, back in 2006, I mean, those are the times when Compstat out of New York was really starting to take hold and our city here tried to adopt that program. It certainly created more accountability for just visual matters.

Funding

Some of the participants (n = 7) highlighted competition for public funds as a driver of EBP adoption. With limited availability of funds and a growing demand for improved organizational efficiency and effectiveness, police organizations are focusing on improving the quality of decision-making to satisfy the funders. In the words of a civilian officer, 'we're being held more accountable or are spending our dollars wisely, and we have to show that by making good tactical decisions.' A Chief also acknowledged the growing pressure and scrutiny from the councils especially to justify increases to police budgets in times of fiscal restraint. He commented, 'it's incumbent upon police leaders to look at evidence-based research and to find and demonstrate that the tax payers are getting the best value for the money they're putting.' An Inspector recalled how his agency had to justify hiring two additional staff members to the oversight bodies:

> With that came a requirement from city council that we're able to produce neutral metrics for them to be able to see the utility and the efficacy

of having police officers embedded within the team. And so that has caused us now to approach the University of XYZ (name of university) and now we've asked them to do a study for us and the faculty of Psychology has agreed to do that.

Inter-Organizational Networks

Direct Networking

Some participants (n = 8) noted the benefits of networking with academics outside the organization to gain a better perspective regarding EBP. They admitted that police agencies sometimes require objective and expert opinion for the improvement of organizational performance, or in the words of a Superintendent, 'to readjust your program, fine-tune it.' The same officer explained the importance of external research support:

> That's [research] probably one of the missing links when we first started doing this about ten years ago. It was kind of, you know, "I'm not sure the profit within," all that kind of stuff. We really bought into it back then. But now, with the objective, outside research-based academics looking at this and evaluating it for us, really should benefit the program, and again, provide the needed support.

Another Inspector shared similar views and asserted that police agencies should benefit from academic expertise to get a better understanding of the EBP philosophy: 'We're the police but there's a lot of people out there with an interest and the expertise that we just simply don't have, right?' Commenting on a research project his agency had conducted with the help of external academics, the same officer noted: 'We would've lacked the expertise internally to do that correctly without screwing it up.' A Superintendent from another agency explained how an unusually high number of homicides in their region made them realize the importance of research: 'So we ended up bringing in Dr. ABC [name of academic] and she did that for us. And then we were able to target those high-risk areas that were resulting in those sorts of crimes.'

Indirect Networking

One of the interview questions asked the participants their motivation for joining the CAN-SEBP. Most of the responses (n = 23) pointed toward the importance of a platform providing networking opportunities with other policies agencies and research organizations to learn about the current evidence-based practices. A Chief of Police viewed CAN-SEBP membership as an opportunity to 'be able to advocate provincially and nationally of the need for more evidence-based decision-making, and more collaboration nationally and provincially around our profession.' A civilian officer stressed the need to maintain a community of practice given the interdisciplinary nature of police work. Similar views were expressed by a Deputy Chief who also believed in the benefits of becoming a part of the EBP community 'to move ourselves one step closer to a more evidence-based driven organization.' The participants were also convinced that networking through EBP would enable them to learn from other agencies and tailor programs to their individual needs. As one Chief explained: 'If there is work that is been done in a particular area that we are looking at then we want to be able to tap into that information and use it to our advantage to avoid duplication of resources.'

A Staff Sergeant expressed similar views regarding the conservation of resources by making use of research by other agencies. He suggested reviewing 'what research has been done to support one direction or another and incorporating all that into the recommendation and decision-making process.' Another Chief stressed the need to avoid 'reinventing the wheel,' reflecting that: 'We're holding off on a strategy until we see that it's working elsewhere and that there's sound policy that isn't going to erode public trust.'

Inner Context

Absorptive Capacity (Knowledge/Skills)

Openness to new ideas depends on the level of existing skills and knowledge base of the employees. Some of the participants of the present study (n = 9) suggested the importance of having a dedicated and diverse group of researchers within the organization for exploring and facilitating EBP. According to a civilian employee, it is the presence of research-minded individuals and subject-matter experts within the organization which encourages exploration of new strategies like EBP. He credited these individuals with bringing about the realization that 'we're already working hard; we just need to work smarter.' An Inspector considered higher education to be instrumental in the adoption of EBP by talking about his own experience: 'My education in university, talking and learning about evidence-based practices and how the evidence-based practices out there can make us more efficient, more effective, as long as we start to link academia with policing.'

Diversity of educational backgrounds and skillsets was also supported by one civilian officer who had several highly qualified researchers working under his supervision: 'So, the common denominator is diverse. I'm not saying that we're doing anything ground breaking, but it is almost second nature.' A Superintendent lauded his agency's efforts in mostly hiring individuals with undergraduate degrees. As a result, the agency has gradually developed an evidence-based focus. According to the officer:

> Pretty much every policy, project involves some form of evidence. I can say in our research and audit section, everything involves that. We've got fulltime researchers where a large segment of their work is exclusively researching academic papers, documents, subject matter experts, scan of organizational data, that sort of thing. That happens all the time. There isn't a piece of policy that doesn't include that.

A Deputy Chief highlighted the importance of aligning the operational and administrative functions to create an environment that supports EBP. He explained his agency's efforts toward ensuring that a significant component of their priorities is data-driven or analysis-based. On the administrative side, hiring external consultants to assist in assessing their service delivery can enhance organizational efficiency and effectiveness. A civilian officer commented on the role of top leadership in adopting and encouraging evidence-based practices in his organization by noting that:

> they're [management] not going to make a decision on flimsy information. They're going to ask, "Well, how did you get that information?" "What makes you so confident?" "Did you think of this?" "Did you think of that?" So, the decisions on how police resources are deployed and whether a program is effective or not, you definitely have to be very mindful of the evidence that you're collecting and what you're basing your findings on.

Culture

A number of officers (n = 14) believed that organizational culture that is open to change and calculated risk taking is an important factor affecting receptivity to EBP. An Inspector explained how his organization arrived at the decision to adopt EBP through trial-and-error, subsequently adopting a model that suited their needs. The Chief of the same agency believed that there was a gradual shift in police culture to embrace research-based practices as many earlier practices can no longer be justified. A Superintendent explained how members of his agency made a conscious effort to adopt EBP:

> It goes back to the whole idea of more proactive, preventive, intervention-based policing tactics, rather than the traditional, you know, reactive call for service and pinball policing, and really trying to change the culture of policing, certainly in our organization.

A civilian employee appreciated his organization's efforts in aligning organizational culture and EBP strategies through 'a relatively extensive consultation process' with members of the organization. Another Deputy Chief also talked about the importance of involving and consulting with employees at various organizational levels to ensure a culture-strategy fit for EBP adoption. A Chief of Police explained his organization's transition from simply working on

hunches to establishing focused strategic plans. He expressed the hope that in the future, documents and reporting processes would be even more finely tuned to ensure that for new programs they would 'rely on [their] research staff here to do the homework before a program gets launched.' Officers also indicated the importance of inculcating innovation as a core cultural value. As one Sergeant commented:

> I think looking at innovative ideas is important to maintain that core value and then to also be a steward and consolidator of it as well. So, you have to be able to walk the talk in that regard.

Another civilian employee recalled her agency's efforts to incorporate EBP in the past. She believed that the focus on EBP has even affected their hiring strategies, noting that 'when we're hiring our business strategists, we have people with doctorates in research, and I don't remember a time when that wasn't in existence in the organization since I've been here.' A Chief highlighted the efforts by his department to develop a research culture across the organization by providing adequate resources and research material:

> So, we're trying to build that expectation within the organization and as we start getting things that aren't supported by back-up documents, we're sending them back to encourage staff to do more research, and at the same time, making those tools available to them. We're trying to expose this to everybody in the organization, so it becomes a new way of thinking for everybody, not just decision-makers.

Climate

Organizational climate is based on how employees perceive organizational expectations of employee behavior. It plays a significant role in creating openness to EBP as evidenced by responses from a majority of participants (n = 19). A Deputy Chief acknowledged that sometimes articles in practitioner journals encourage them to explore new strategies with the expectation that it would improve the quality of decisions. A civilian employee believed that police organizations are accustomed to emulating agencies that have a demonstrated record of program effectiveness. He considered it a 'recognition that we need to change how we do business and that these groups look to offer an opportunity to either expose ourselves to things we don't know or help us shape things within the organization.' A Superintendent explained his agency's efforts in observing effective EBP strategies locally and internationally since: 'crime changes, resourcing funding changes and we have to shift our direction and focus and what's working out there and how can we incorporate it here.' The pressure to undertake evidence-based research despite limited resources was described by an Inspector in the following way:

> We simply lack the resources to be able to do our own research. We try to and individuals who are extremely busy, we try to do it off the corner of our desks, often times we may not be experts in certain fields but just because of where you're currently working you've been asked to research it and come up with the information to inform or to guide policy for the police department.

A Deputy Commissioner considered EBP to be driven by some issue or what he described as a 'quasi-crisis.' The officer believed that in such a scenario 'there's a need to rationalize a service, figure out ways to do the same thing for less money, or do better things for the same money, or worst-case scenario, do better things with less money.' Similar views were expressed by two other participants. A Deputy Chief identified specific issues such as gang violence and fentanyl overdoses that led his organization to explore an evidence-based approach to decision-making. An Inspector described how a specific type of gang violence related to a particular minority group prompted them to adopt more research-based solutions to the problem: 'So we're trying to figure out, outside of traditional investigations and trying to put people in jail, what can we do to try and curve this, bearing in mind that there is a cultural aspect to it.'

Leadership

The officers (n = 10) highlighted the efforts of top leadership in creating openness to EBP practices. One inspector stated: 'essentially, it comes right from our chief and one of his key guiding principles is everything has to be evidence-based.' The results also indicate that once initiated, EBP practices are generally embraced by the successive leadership. A Chief of Police credited one of his predecessors for setting a strategic direction for the agency based on research, ingraining it in the organizational culture. The Chief further added that EBP was a natural fit for his organization as they were accustomed to such practices, observing that 'when a lot of services are talking about all these really cool things, we're kind of like, "Yeah, we did that," or "Yeah, we do that."'

The participants believed that top management's level of education and exposure to research are key to EBP adoption. As one inspector commented:

> Yeah, so our chief and one of our former deputies . . . they read a lot of literature and then brought studies to the table. Our chief, he's always challenging us to try new things. So, a lot of it comes from within, to look and see if there is research in other areas.

Another Inspector from a different agency appreciated his senior leadership, the Chief, and the Deputy for having good academic backgrounds and the open-mindedness to embrace new ideas like EBP. One of the Chiefs explained how a quest for improved accountability and introduction to international practices became his motivation to explore evidence-based practices:

> What sort of got me down that road is the economics discussion and trying to make sure that we have the kind of accountability to say that the programs we're running are the most high value. I had the opportunity to go out with the director from the Police College in the UK to look at a program. It's a good opportunity for our service to start looking for how we're going to start assigning better metrics, better evidence to the work we do.

Discussion

The application of externally sourced evidence-based knowledge is considered important for organizations, not only because it can lead to the enhancement of their knowledge base but also because it can ensure organizational effectiveness and economic performance (Bierly, Damanpour, & Santoro, 2009; Nonaka & Takeuchi, 1995). In view of these benefits, the present study serves as an attempt to identify factors that help to develop receptivity toward evidence-based practices in a particularly change-averse segment of the public sector, namely, police organizations.

The results, based on in-depth interviews with senior police management across Canada, partially support a model of receptivity to EBP advanced by Aarons et al. (2011). The author was interested in the first stage of the model that is delineated as the exploration stage, as organizations are believed to become receptive to new ideas at this juncture. Interview responses highlighted factors present in the external and internal organizational environment that tend to impact a police agency's receptivity or openness to change. In terms of the internal environmental context, while the participants highlighted the organizational characteristics that created openness to change, they did not discuss the individual adopter characteristics as identified by Aarons et al. (2011).

The impact of outer organizational context on EBP was supported by four sub-themes. The first two sub-themes in the outer organizational context related to monitoring and review of police agencies by external stakeholders for ensuring accountability under growing fiscal pressures. The participants considered EBP adoption essential for justifying performance and funding needs. This finding aligns with previous literature, which suggests that by increasing oversight, the governing bodies in Canada aim to secure public interest and trust by ensuring optimal utilization of public funds by police organizations (Sheard, 2016).

The focus on accountability has encouraged Canadian police agencies to adopt research-based strategies, thus enabling them to provide more scientific performance measures to police boards. Since police organizations perform value work involving public safety (Crank, 2003; Mastrofski, 1988), it requires them to adopt goals and strategies favored by influence groups to maintain legitimacy through enhanced organizational performance and continued funding (Willis, Mastrofski, & Weisburd, 2007). With continuously shrinking budgets, police agencies must try their best to demonstrate the effectiveness of new strategies such as EBP while competing for public funds. However, police boards in Canada insist on assessing agencies mainly on the basis of efficacious utilization of funds while ignoring the myriad factors affecting performance, which is a source of concern for police organizations (Perrin, 2011). Besides accountability, the rising cost of policing in Canada has prompted the government to push for the adoption of EBP to enhance organizational effectiveness (Mazowita & Greenland, 2016; Public Safety Canada, 2013).

Directly networking with researchers outside the organization for research consulting also emerged as one of the factors that is believed to be pivotal to enhancing openness and receptivity to EBP. This finding aligns with previous research on utilization of research knowledge which highlights the importance of 'relational capital' (Chagnon, Pouliot, Malo, Gervais, & Pigeon, 2010, p. 10) or the trust that develops between researchers and practitioners through continued interaction. This trust is one of the key factors contributing to receptivity to research and highlights the importance of social linkage between the two groups (Amara, Ouimet, & Landry, 2004; Chagnon et al., 2010; Landry, Amara, & Lamari, 2001).

Since organizational membership with CAN-SEBP was one of the inclusion criteria in the study, participants were asked their thoughts on why their agency had joined the platform. A majority of responses identified indirect networking as a sub-theme and considered idea sharing a major reason for joining such a network. This result aligns with previous findings which suggest that practitioners tend to rely more on their professional peers and opinion leaders for information rather than academic sources (Ferlie & Shortell, 2001; Lum et al., 2012; Palmer, 2011; Weiss & Bucuvalas, 1980). Weiss (1998) encouraged the creation of forums where practitioners, researchers, and experts could benefit from current developments in their field and tailor the knowledge to their own circumstances. As a response, several societies of evidence-based policing have been established across the globe to ensure that the best evidence and practices are available to police agencies thereby also ensuring the uptake of evidence-based practices (Rousseau & Gunia, 2016).

Besides the importance of factors in the outer organizational context, the respondents also indicated how the inner context affects receptivity to EBP. Four main sub-themes based on organizational characteristics emerged during analysis. The first sub-theme suggested the importance of absorptive capacity or the ability to utilize externally obtained knowledge for creating an organizational advantage (Cohen & Levinthal, 1990). Some of the participants considered the level and diversity of education and skill along with specialized positions helpful in supporting the uptake and dissemination of research within the agency. Previous research suggests that having an in-house EBP mentor and connections with EBP supporters outside the organization is believed to lead to openness to new ideas as organizational members begin to recognize the benefits of the initiatives (Aarons, 2006; Melnyk, Fineout-Overholt, Gallagher-Ford, & Kaplan, 2012; Rousseau & Gunia, 2016).

Organizational culture was the next sub-theme believed to affect openness toward EBP identified by the participants, which aligns with previous studies on research utilization. The evolution of organizational culture depends on knowledge acquisition by an organization. Differences in organizational cultures therefore determine the manner in which knowledge is adopted and incorporated, thereby leading to varied absorptive capacity by different agencies (Belkhodja, Amara, Landry, & Ouimet, 2007). This difference in absorptive capacities is also one of the reasons why EBP adoption varies between agencies (Cabell et al., 2013).

Organizational changes that are internally driven and are not in direct conflict with organizational culture and identity are more easily adopted than ones that are unfamiliar (Jacobs, Witteloostuijn, & Christe-Zeyse, 2013). Rousseau and Gunia (2016) consider organizational changes such as EBP implementation to be a time-consuming, adaptive process as cultural norms may take a generation to be modified (Rogers, 1995). Such changes therefore require constant support by organizational leaders and peers to be successful.

Another theme related to organizational culture was the influence of organizational climate on receptivity to EBP. An organization's climate is based on the perceptions of individuals regarding work expectations (Burke & Litwin, 1992). Therefore, managerial focus on knowledge acquisition and application through incentives and rewards can create openness toward EBP amongst employees (Aarons et al., 2011; Hemsley-Brown & Sharp, 2003). Damanpour and Schneider (2006) also argue that specifically rewarding change-related behavior can create an organizational climate that is perceived as being receptive to new ideas and innovation, thus facilitating change in the organization.

Leadership support also emerged as an important theme supporting openness to EBP. Prior literature highlights the importance of leadership's role in enhancing innovation capacity through the introduction and support of change initiatives (Lewis et al., 2018; Piening, 2011). Rousseau and Gunia (2016) describe leadership support as a countervailing force which helps offset any threats to professional identities, thus creating openness and acceptance toward evidence-based practices. Since the adoption of new ideas requires expertise and knowledge to deal with potential challenges, leaders with higher levels of education are expected to deal with such situations more effectively (Damanpour & Schneider, 2006). Educated leaders are able to scan the environment for new ideas and facilitate the adoption of innovation by building employee confidence and abilities to support such changes (Mumford et al., 2000; Rogers, 1995).

Limitations

The present study was an attempt to gain insight into police organizations' receptivity to evidence-based practices. Due to the exploratory nature of the study, the associated limitations warrant a discussion as they pose a challenge to the generalizability of findings. Firstly, the sample size was limited since data were collected only from organizations that are CAN-SEBP members. A second limitation is agency location as the sample consisted mainly of urban police agencies across English-speaking provinces in Canada. Lastly, the sample consisted mainly of top management, which is again a limitation of the present study as the views of officers at other hierarchical levels have not been taken into account.

Conclusion

For the past two decades, scholars in policing have supported the idea of EBP adoption for the enhancement of organizational efficiency and effectiveness (Lum et al., 2012; Mastrofski, 1999; Sherman, 1998). However, openness to EBP, which is the very first step toward its adoption, has generally been overlooked by researchers. The present study utilized the exploration phase of the EBP adoption framework by Aarons et al. (2011) to identify factors in both the external and internal organizational environments which affect police organizations' receptivity to EBP. For police organizations, oversight bodies responsible for performance monitoring and allocation of funds can influence the adoption of innovations such as EBP. However, to avoid conflicts of interest which create the perception of EBP being forcefully imposed, police agencies should clearly communicate and justify their funding requirements and operational realities to oversight bodies. Furthermore, building close partnerships with the academic community and other agencies can be mutually beneficial in introducing police organizations to the benefits of EBP.

In terms of internal environmental factors, the level of officer education can be instrumental in ensuring openness to new ideas such as EBP. Officers exposed to research and knowledge of the latest innovations in policing and believed to be convinced of the benefits are likely to be more supportive of such ideas (Kalyal, Peladeau, & Huey, 2017). Besides a strong skill base, other factors such as leadership support as well as organizational culture and climate also affect openness to EBP. It is the responsibility of top leadership to ensure an organizational climate conducive to EBP adoption. Although it is more challenging to attempt cultural change, especially in police organizations that are set in their ways, it is not entirely impossible to do so. Aarons et al. (2011) recommend proceeding gradually by adopting strategies to improve organizational climate. These range from investing in training and development exercises to maintaining open channels of communication within and outside the organization to ensure openness to evidence-based practices.

Discussion Questions

1. Why does it seem that police have been slow to adopt evidence-based practice?
2. How did the researcher select the sample? How might the sample selection have impacted the findings?
3. How do interacting with other organizations and hiring a diverse set of employees seem to impact receptivity to EBP?

References

Aarons, G. A. (2006). Transformational and transactional leadership: Association with attitudes toward evidence-based practice. *Psychiatric Services*, 57(8), 1162–1169.

Aarons, G. A., Hurlburt, M., & Horwitz, S. M. (2011). Advancing a conceptual model of evidence-based practice implementation in public service sectors. *Administration & Policy in Mental Health & Mental Health Services Research*, 38, 4–23.

Amara, N., Ouimet, M., & Landry, R. (2004). New evidence on instrumental, conceptual, and symbolic utilization of university research in government agencies. *Science Communication*, 26(1), 75–106.

Belkhodja, O., Amara, N., Landry, R., & Ouimet, M. (2007). The extent and organizational determinants of research utilization in Canadian health services organizations. *Science Communication*, 28(3), 377–417.

Berwick, D. M. (2003). Disseminating innovations in health care. *JAMA*, 289(15), 1969–1975.

Bierly, P. E., Damanpour, F., & Santoro, M. D. (2009). The application of external knowledge: Organizational conditions for exploration and exploitation. *Journal of Management Studies*, 46(3), 481–509.

Blaskovits, B., Bennell, C., Huey, L., Kalyal, H., Walker, T., & Javala, S. (2018). A Canadian replication of Telep and Lum's (2014) examination of police officers' receptivity to empirical research'. *Policing and Society*, 1–19. https://doi.org/10.1080/10439463.2018.1522315

Braun, V., & Clarke, V. (2006). Using thematic analysis in psychology. *Qualitative Research in Psychology*, 3, 77–101.

Burke, W. W., & Litwin, G. H. (1992). A causal model of organization performance and change. *Journal of Management*, 18(3), 523–545.

Cabell, A., Casteel, C., Chronister, T., Nocera, M., Vladutlu, C. J., & Peek-Asa, C. (2013). Factors influencing law enforcement decisions to adopt an evidence-based robbery prevention program. *Health Education Research*, 28(6), 1105–1115.

CAN-SEBP. (2019). *The Canadian Society of Evidence-Based Policing*. Retrieved from www.can-sebp.net/

Chagnon, F., Pouliot, L., Malo, C., Gervais, M.-J., & Pigeon, M.-E. (2010). Comparison of determinants of research knowledge utilization by practitioners and administrators in the field of child and family social services. *Implementation Science*, 5, 41. Retrieved from www.implementationscience.com/content/5/1/41

Cochran, J. K., Bromley, M. L., & Swando, M. J. (2002). Sheriff's deputies' receptivity to organizational change. *Policing: An International Journal of Police Strategies & Management*, 25(3), 507–529.

Cohen, W. M., & Levinthal, D. A. (1990). Absorptive capacity: A new perspective on learning and innovation. *Administrative Science Quarterly*, 35, 128–152.

Crank, J. P. (2003). Institutional theory of police: A review of the state of the art. *Policing: An International Journal of Police Strategies & Management*, 26(2), 186–207.

Damanpour, F. (1991). Organizational innovation: A meta-analysis of effects of determinants and moderators. *Academy of Management Journal*, 34, 555–590.

Damanpour, F., & Schneider, M. (2006). Phases of the adoption of innovation in organizations: Effects of environment, organization, and top managers. *British Journal of Management*, 17, 215–236.

Davies, H. T. O., & Nutley, S. M. (2008). *Learning more about how research-based knowledge gets used:*

Guidance in the development of new empirical research. New York, NY: William T. Grant Foundation.

Ferlie, E. B., & Shortell, S. M. (2001). Improving the quality of health care in the United Kingdom and the United States: A framework for change. *Milbank Quarterly*, 79(2), 281–315.

Frambach, R. T., & Schillewaert, N. (2002). Organizational innovation adoption: A multi-level framework of determinants and opportunities for future research. *Journal of Business Research. Special Issue: Marketing Theory in the Next Millennium*, 55(2), 163–176.

Greenhalgh, T., Robert, G., Macfarlane, F., Bate, P., & Kyriakidou, O. (2004). Diffusion of innovations in service organizations: Systematic review and recommendations. *Milbank Quarterly*, 82(4), 581–629.

Griffiths, C. (2014). Economics of policing: Baseline for policing research in Canada. *Report Commissioned by Public Safety Canada*. Retrieved from www.publicsafety.gc.ca/cnt/rsrcs/pblctns/bsln-plcng-rsrch/index-eng.aspx

Grol, R., Bosch, M. C., Hulscher, M. E. J. L., Eccles, M. P., & Wensing, M. (2007). Planning and studying improvement in patient care: The use of theoretical perspectives. *The Milbank Quarterly*, 85(1), 93–138.

Hemsley-Brown, J., & Sharp, C. (2003). The use of research to improve professional practice: A systematic review of the literature. *Oxford Review of Education*, 29(4), 449–471.

Huey, L., Blaskovits, B., Bennell, C., Kalyal, H. J., & Walker, T. (2017). To what extent do Canadian police professionals believe that their agencies are 'targeting, testing, and tracking' new policing strategies and programs? *Police Practice and Research*, 18, 544–555.

Hunter, G., Wigzell, A., May, T., & McSweeney, T. (2015). *An evaluation of the "what works centre for crime reduction" year 1: Baseline*. London: Institute for Criminal Policy Research.

Jacobs, G., Witteloostuijn, A. V., & Christe-Zeyse, J. (2013). A theoretical framework of organizational change. *Journal of Organizational Change Management*, 26(5), 772–792.

Jenkins, M. J. (2016). Police support for community problem-solving and broken windows policing. *American Journal of Criminal Justice*, 41, 220–235.

Kalyal, H., Peladeau, H., & Huey, L. (2017). Senior officer and recruiter views on "big topics" in policing for new recruits. *Journal of Community Safety and Well-Being*, 2(3), 112–115.

Koehle, G., Six, T., & Hanrahan, K. (2010). Citizen concerns and approval of police performance. *Professional Issues in Criminal Justice*, 5, 9–24.

Landry, R., Amara, N., & Lamari, M. (2001). Utilization of social science research knowledge in Canada. *Research Policy*, 30, 333–349.

Lewis, J. M., Ricard, L. M., & Klijn, E. H. (2018). How innovation drivers, networking and leadership shape public sector innovation capacity. *International Review of Administrative Sciences*, 84(2), 288–307.

Lum, C. (2009). *Translating police research into practice*. Ideas in American Policing. Washington, DC: Police Foundation.

Lum, C., & Koper, C. (2017). *Evidence-based policing: Translating research into practice*. Oxford: Oxford University Press.

Lum, C., Telep, C. W., Koper, C. S., & Grieco, J. (2012). Receptivity to research in policing. *Justice Research and Policy*, 14, 61–95.

Lumsden, K. (2016). Police officer and civilian staff receptivity to research and evidence-based policing in the UK: Providing a contextual understanding through qualitative interviews. *Policing: A Journal of Policy and Practice*, 11, 157–167.

Mastrofski, S. D. (1988). Community policing as reform: A cautionary tale. In J. R. Greene & S. D. Mastrofski (Eds.), *Community policing: Rhetoric or reality* (pp. 47–67). New York: Praeger.

Mastrofski, S. D. (1999). *Policing for people*. Ideas in American Policing, Series No. 3. Washington, DC: Police Foundation.

Mazowita, B., & Greenland, J. (2016). Police resources in Canada, 2015. *Juristat*, 1–22. Retrieved from www.statcan.gc.ca/pub/85-002-x/2016001/article/14323-eng.htm

Melnyk, B. M., Fineout-Overholt, E., Gallagher-Ford, L., & Kaplan, L. (2012). The state of evidence-based practice in US nurses: Critical implications for nurse leaders and educators. *The Journal of Nursing Administration*, 42(9), 410–417.

Meyer, A. D., & Goes, J. B. (1988). Organizational assimilation of innovation: A multilevel contextual analysis. *Academy of Management Journal*, 31, 897–923.

Miller, V. D., Johnson, J. R., & Grau, J. (1994). Antecedents to willingness to participate in a planned organizational change. *Journal of Applied Communication Research*, 22, 59–80.

Mumford, M. D., Zaccaro, S. J., Johnson, J. F., Diana, M., Gilbert, J. A., & Threlfall, K. V. (2000). Patterns of leader characteristics: Implications for performance and development. *Leadership Quarterly*, 11, 115–133.

Nonaka, I., & Takeuchi, H. (1995). *The knowledge creating company*. New York: Oxford University Press.

Palmer, I. (2011). *Is the United Kingdom police service receptive to evidence-based policing? Testing attitudes towards experimentation*. Master's thesis submitted to University of Cambridge, Cambridge.

Perrin, B. (2011). *What is a results/performance based delivery system?* Invited presentation: European Parliament Committee on Regional Development Public Hearing: Moving towards a more results/performance-based delivery system in Cohesion Policy, 26 May 2011, Brussels [Online]. Retrieved from www.europarl.europa.eu/document/activities/cont/201112/20111214ATT34149/20111214AT T34149EN.pdf

Piening, E. P. (2011). Insights into the process dynamics of innovation implementation. *Public Management Review*, 13(1), 127–157.

Public Safety Canada. (2013). *Summit on the economics of policing: Strengthening Canada's policing advantage*. Ottawa: Government of Canada.

Ratcliffe, J. H. (2008). *Intelligence led policing*. Cullompton, Devon: Willan Publishing.

Rogers, E. M. (1995). *Diffusion of innovations*. New York, NY: Free Press.

Rojek, J., Alpert, G., & Smith, H. (2012). The utilization of research by the police. *Police Practice & Research: An International Journal*, 13(4), 329–341.

Rousseau, D. M., & Gunia, B. C. (2016). Evidence-based practice: The psychology of EBP implementation. *Annual Review of Psychology*, 67, 667–692.

Sheard, M. (2016). *Police governance in Canada: A parallax perspective*. Unpublished PhD thesis. London Metropolitan University.

Sherman, L. W. (1998). *Ideas in American policing: Evidence-based policing*. Washington, DC: Police Foundation.

Sherman, L. W., & Weisburd, D. (1995). General deterrent effects of police patrol in crime "hot spots": A randomized, controlled trial. *Justice Quarterly*, 12(4), 625–648.

Steinheider, B., Wuestewald, T., Boyatzis, R. E., & Kroutter, P. (2012). In search of a methodology of collaboration: Understanding researcher-practitioner philosophical differences in policing. *Police Practice & Research: An International Journal*, 13(4), 357–374.

Stetler, C. B., Ritchie, J. A., Rycroft-Malone, J., Schultz, A. A., & Charns, M. P. (2009). Institutionalizing evidence-based practice: An organizational case study using a model of strategic change. *Implementation Science*, 4, 78.

Telep, C. W., & Lum, C. (2014). The receptivity of officers to empirical research and evidence-based policing: An examination of survey data from three agencies. *Police Quarterly*, 17(4), 359–385.

Telep, C. W., & Winegar, S. (2016). Police executive receptivity to research: A survey of chiefs and sheriffs in Oregon. *Policing*, 10(3), 241–249.

Tseng, V. (2010). Learning about the use of research to inform evidence-based policy and practice: Early lessons and future directions. *William T. Grant Foundation 2009 Annual Report*. New York, NY: William T. Grant Foundation.

Veltri, G. A., Lim, J., & Miller, R. (2014). More than meets the eye: The contribution of qualitative research to evidence-based policy-making. *Innovation: The European Journal of Social Science Research, 27*(1), 1–4.

Watson, D. P., Adams, E. L., Shue, S., Coates, H., McGuire, A., Chesher, J., . . . & Omenka, O. I. (2018). Defining the external implementation context: An integrative systematic literature review. *BMC Health Services Research, 18*, 209.

Weisburd, D., & Braga, A. A. (2006). *Police innovation: Contrasting perspectives.* New York, NY: Cambridge University Press.

Weiss, C. (1998). Have we learned anything new about the use of evaluation? *American Journal of Evaluation, 19*, 21–33.

Weiss, C., & Bucuvalas, M. J. (1980). *Social science research and decision-making.* New York, NY: Columbia University Press.

Wilkinson, K., Boyd, K., Pearson, M., Farrimond, H., Lang, I. A., Fleischer, D., . . . & Rappert, B. (2017). Making sense of evidence: Using research training to promote organisational change. *Police Practice and Research: An International Journal,* 1–19. https://doi.org/10.1080/15614263.2017.1405266

Willis, J. J., Mastrofski, S. D., & Weisburd, D. (2007). Making sense of COMPSTAT: A theory-based analysis of organizational change in three police departments. *Law & Society Review, 41*(1), 147–188.

10 Field Research

One of the criticisms of survey research is that it can be weak on validity since we are asking people about what they did in the past or what they would do in a hypothetical situation. Numerous factors impact the accuracy of the answers we will receive, including honesty, quality of one's memory, and concerns about social desirability. Trust in the researcher may be another consideration, as we often ask people in criminal justice to self-report sensitive matters, some of which even involve illegal behavior. We might be able to get a better, more complete understanding of individuals' circumstances and their behavior though field research. Not only is field research beneficial when we want to learn about people and group behavior, but it can also help us learn about the environment. Going out into the field allows us to see the layout of neighborhoods and streets and learn about how physical characteristics of spaces can make them more or less attractive to potential offenders.

This chapter covers field research, which addresses a wide range of data collection activities. Field research includes no-contact activities in which researchers are making note of buildings, traffic patterns, and landscaping, as well as observations of people who are unaware they are being monitored. At the other end of the spectrum, fieldwork can involve some of the most extensive contact between researchers and participants, with researchers spending weeks, months, and even years immersing themselves in a group's culture. In between these two extremes are depth interviews, focus groups, and in-person survey dissemination, topics that were addressed in previous chapters. In this chapter, I will focus on two types of field research—participant observation and structured field observations.

Roles for Field Researchers

Gold (1958) discussed four different roles for researchers operating in the field (Figure 10.1). The extent of researcher interactions with informants varies a great deal in each of these. First, there is the **complete observer** who has no contact at all with research participants, and participants might not even notice that they are being observed. A complete observer might sit on a park bench near a picnic area and take note of the number of people who use the available trash cans to dispose of their trash, how many pack up and take their waste away with them, and how many leave their litter in the park. The next type of field researcher is the **observer as participant**. Gold noted that this group does one-visit interviews with participants. The work of Wright, Decker, Redfern, and Smith (1992), interviewing active residential burglars, would be considered observer as participant work. While informants are clearly aware of the researchers' presence, neither party has extensive

Complete observer ----- Observer as participant ----- Participant as observer ----- Complete participant

Figure 10.1 Roles for Field Researchers, by Level of Interaction with Informants

exposure to the other. Complete observers and observers as participants can serve various roles in the field, and as a result, some might be there to collect quantitative data, including the percentage of park-goers who litter, or qualitative data coming from interviews.

The next two groups spend considerable amounts of time interacting with and participating in the lives of research participants and primarily collect qualitative data. **Participants as observers** reveal their identity and purpose to their informants but then participate in the daily lives of the group they are looking to study. A classic example of this is Bill Whyte's (1943) *Street Corner Society*. Whyte was a researcher at Harvard University who spent four years living and doing research in a low-income Italian American neighborhood in Boston. The individuals in the neighborhood with whom he had the most frequent contact were aware of his identity and purpose. Given Whyte's constant presence in the neighborhood and his skill at making individuals feel comfortable around him, he was able to gain a thorough understanding of the neighborhood's culture, to the point where informants were discussing criminal behavior and even recruiting Whyte to engage in some illegal activities. Finally, **complete participants** keep their true identity secret from informants (Gold, 1958). As you would expect, complete participation introduces a number of ethical concerns and should only be used if there is no other way to collect the data, and the work is being carefully monitored by an Institutional Review Board. I will get into a more detailed discussion of ethical concerns in fieldwork later in this chapter. These last two roles, participant as observer and complete participant, are types of ethnographic fieldwork. Hammersly and Atkinson (1995) define ethnography as the researcher "participating, overtly or covertly, in people's daily lives for an extended period of time, watching what happens, listening to what is said, asking questions—in fact, collecting whatever data are available to throw light on the issues that are the focus of the research" (p. 1). Ethnography is an approach to research that is very common in anthropology and sociology.

Qualitative Field Research

In Chapter 1, I briefly discussed the differences between qualitative and quantitative research. Whereas quantitative research designs require large sample sizes and work to draw generalizations from samples after conducting statistical analysis, qualitative work largely relies on interviews and observations of much smaller groups. Quantitative research gives us information about broad patterns and trends, but as Weisheit (2015) observed, "what it gains in breadth it loses in depth" (p. 191). Weisheit correctly noted that quantitative researchers who study drugs may amass an entire body of scholarship without ever actually having a conversation with someone who uses drugs. Rather than considering numbers and generalizing results to populations, qualitative research focuses more on learning as much as possible about small groups and even a few individuals. In these studies, which are smaller in scope but often take much more time to complete, the goal is to develop a deep understanding. Max Weber (Weber & Shils, 1949) referred to this as verstehen, which means "understanding" in German. Ferrell (1998) defined **verstehen** as

> a process of subjective interpretation on the part of the social researcher, a degree of sympathetic understanding between social researcher and subjects of study, whereby the researcher comes to share, in part, the situated meanings and experiences of those under scrutiny.
>
> (p. 27)

Quantitative research rarely, if ever, involves a level of contact between researchers and participants in which the researcher shares experiences to this extent. This level of understanding comes from extensive periods of time in the field, interacting with, and even participating in the activities of, the individuals being studied. Most recently, qualitative research has been used in criminal justice primarily to study gangs, drug dealing and use, property crimes, and transmission of crimi-nogenic values (Miller & Miller, 2015).

Qualitative research often begins by approaching research differently than projects with a quan-titative orientation. As you know from earlier chapters, quantitative work is firmly situated in the deductive approach. Research using quantitative methods begins with the researcher developing a strong familiarity with the existing theory and literature, and from there, one proceeds to generate hypotheses based on that previous knowledge. After that, data collection or observations take place. Inductive reasoning has a different starting point, with observations being the first step in the research process. This methodological shift is especially appropriate when the research goal is to learn about a new topic and/or generate new theories. Some researchers might even purposely avoid exposure to relevant literature or theories so they can consider their observations without any preconceived ideas. Thomas Vander Ven (1998) wanted to study crime in a city he referred to as "Chronictown," which had a reputation for being high in crime. He described his experience of going into the field as frightening, not only because of the neighborhood's reputation, but also because he struggled to make sense of what he was seeing. He initially had hopes of explaining his observations by using social disorganization theory, a popular criminological theory that explains why some neighborhoods have high crime rates while others do not. Eventually, he stopped trying to force the explanations of his observations with that one theory and just simply observed. Once he allowed himself to do that, he realized that his observations were better explained by a different perspective called labeling theory.

Glaser and Strauss (1967), in their classic work on theory in sociological research, warned of the same problem that Vander Ven experienced years before he entered "Chronictown." Glaser and Strauss identified two problems that can arise when social scientists take a deductive approach to research. First, they might continue to force a fit between a theory and observations when it is time to write up the results. Second, once they decide on a theory to test, researchers might prac-tice "exampling," whereby they actually work to find field examples to support the theory. The latter was precisely what Vander Ven found himself doing when he went into the field with the plan of using social disorganization as the basis of his research. Instead of using the deductive approach and starting with theory, Glaser and Strauss recommended that researchers take the inductive approach and generate their theories with data rather than collecting data and trying to make the findings fit existing theories. This is called grounded theory because theory is gener-ated right there on the ground through observations. Qualitative research that includes observa-tions and listening to informants explain phenomena in their own words is well suited for such theory generation.

Gaining Access for Research

Participant observation requires a tremendous commitment on the part of the researcher, but it also requires individuals, groups, and organizations to grant the researcher access. Imagine if, sud-denly, someone wanted to spend long periods of time following you around at work or hanging around and observing you and your friends all the time. It can be inconvenient at best and invasive at worst. If you and your friends are involved in illegal behavior, having a stranger observing what you are doing all the time can also be frightening as you might suspect that the researcher is under-cover law enforcement. Even if you are confident that the person is, in fact, a researcher, you and your friends would be justified in worrying whether they will share information with the police.

The stakes may not be quite as high for people who work for organizations, such as courts, police, or corrections departments, but a researcher's presence is not always welcome. Staff and adminis-trators may not want to have to deal with the inconvenience of having an outsider observing and asking questions. The larger concern is likely to be what will come of this research? Will it reveal that the agency is ineffective in achieving its goals? Will it shed light on unethical or even illegal behavior among staff members? Worry about illegal behavior is uncommon, as most agencies and their employees are law abiding. The concern about an unflattering portrayal of the staff and the agency as a whole, however, is likely to be more widespread and even justified. Some people have had unpleasant experiences with researchers in the past, while others are just a bit paranoid about what might happen, especially if they have reason to distrust the researcher.

When thinking about gaining access, we need to take different approaches depending on the type of group we want to study. Obviously, we would want to approach a formal organization differently than we would a gang or a group of people who hang out in front of the local liquor store.

Organizations

Getting in touch with someone who can arrange for you to have access to a criminal justice or social service agency can be very challenging. Let's face it: no one is sitting around and hoping to get a call or a letter from a researcher. They have other things on their minds and a long list of things to do. So how do you make your case for gaining access?

Maxfield and Babbie (2012) suggest finding a sponsor, and if it is at all possible for you to do this, this is definitely the preferred way to approach an agency. A **sponsor** is someone who is known and respected by the agency contact, likely the director or administrator of the organization. The sponsor can give you valuable insight about which agencies to contact or avoid and which individuals within those agencies might be willing to assist you. Personally, I have two outstanding colleagues who have served this role for me several times. Both are retired criminal justice practitioners who were born and raised in this area. (I moved here several years ago for the job, so my roots in the community are not as deep.) Between their personal and professional connections, they have been able to help my students and I gain access to agencies for various class projects and research activities. They always know which police department or which judge might be amenable to working with me or my students. Perhaps of equal value is that they have steered me away from agencies and individuals that I should avoid. If you do not personally know people who can help, it is quite possible that your professor does, so ask.

If you are very lucky, your professor or another well-connected contact will serve as a gatekeeper and contact the agency to vouch for you. It is more likely, though, that you will need to do the legwork yourself. You should reach out first in writing, through either a letter or an email. Be professional! I cannot stress enough how you should never, ever communicate with a professional contact or your professors the same way you do with your friends. It is a guaranteed way to ensure that you will never gain access to that agency. Your written communication should serve to introduce yourself, briefly explain the purpose of your research, and then explain what you would like from the agency. Maxfield and Babbie (2012) suggest ending it with a date and time when you will call them, along with a request that they let you know if they would prefer a different time. When you talk over the phone, you can elaborate a bit more on what you are hoping to do and, hopefully, schedule a date and time to start. If you are looking to do a one-shot interview with the administrator and/ or get some data from the agency, you will not need the cooperation of too many people. If your work with the agency requires you get the cooperation of multiple staff members, you could be in for a challenge. Just because the director or administrator has agreed to work with you, there is no guarantee that the cooperation is going to extend to the entire agency. I have personally experienced several instances when the upper administration has invited me into their agency to do research, yet I have run into resistance, and even a certain degree of sabotage, from civilian and sworn staff. You must handle this very carefully. First, consider how much of an obstacle that problematic behavior is to your work. If it is not a big deal, I would suggest just ignoring it. Also keep in mind whether you requested agency access or if they invited you to work with them. If the latter, you can be more forthcoming with supervisors about the resistance you are experiencing. Your professor is an excellent resource, so I suggest scheduling a meeting with him/her to get advice.

Subcultures

Gaining access to a subculture is quite different and can be more difficult. How do you get a group of people, including those who are involved in criminal activity, to trust you? There are a few ways that people have succeeded. One is to find a gatekeeper. A **gatekeeper** is a person who is a well-known, respected, and trusted member of that subculture. In the sampling chapter, I briefly discussed the work of Wright and colleagues (1992), who sought to interview active residential burglars but without using the police or corrections agency records as a sampling frame. Since few of us happen to have the contact information of active residential burglars saved in our phones, Wright et al. faced the dual hurdles of finding people and gaining their trust. They hired an ex-offender as a gatekeeper. This individual used to be involved in criminal activity in that area but had retired from that life after being shot and paralyzed. Now in a wheelchair, he was still well-known and a respected member of the community. The gatekeeper identified some local people who were still "hustling" and some streetwise law-abiding individuals who knew lots of contacts. Once it was time to make contact with the potential research participants, the gatekeeper vouched for the researchers, made assurances that they were not affiliated with law enforcement, and promised that their interviews would remain confidential.

Phillippe Bourgois (2002) did not have a gatekeeper when he moved to Spanish Harlem, New York, in the hopes of doing qualitative research. Once he decided that he would focus on the lives of crack dealers, he had to find a way to introduce himself and become accepted among a group of dealers. Gaining access to a group was not easy. He has fair skin, so the neighborhood residents initially thought he was either an undercover police officer or just another white drug addict who traveled to a non-white neighborhood in search of drugs. For the first three months, he worked to make himself visible around town and became friendly with some of his neighbors. He then asked a neighbor who was addicted to crack to introduce him to Primo, the man who owned the crack houses in the neighborhood. (Primo was not his real name. Bourgois gave all of his informants **pseudonyms** to protect their identity.) Primo initially dismissed Bourgois as an undercover police officer, but after two more weeks of seeing Bourgois every day in the neighborhood, he invited him over for a drink. Bourgois was up front from the beginning that he was a professor looking to write a book about the neighborhood. Primo and Bourgois wound up spending years together, as the drug dealer later admitted that he always wanted to "conversate" with someone from "drug free" white America.

Many field researchers lack contacts in the field and have to find ways to get a foothold on their own. Polsky (1967) suggested that, when starting from scratch, the best way to approach individuals would be to connect with them at "play" instead of at "work." Polsky grew up playing pool, so his favorite place to go to meet active offenders was the pool halls. He suggested that researchers play to their own strengths and knowledge, so if, for example, they like to play cards, finding out where there are some card games happening might be a good approach. People who can hold their liquor might try bars. Polsky cautioned that, while the researcher may initially pose as just another bar patron or pool player, they should quickly explain who they are before they have too many conversations and develop connections. That serves to prevent potential informants from feeling betrayed. Additionally, Polsky suspected that most potential informants are likely to guess that the researcher is somehow different anyway, so the researcher might as well be forthcoming.

Bill Whyte (1943) was a pioneer in urban anthropology, and he spent three years living in a low-income Italian American neighborhood in Boston while conducting participant observation. He struggled to gain access, as he and his mentors lacked connections in the neighborhood that he selected for his study. Whyte made multiple attempts to gain access to the locals' social circles. First, he asked a housing agency for their sponsorship in exchange for him sharing the research results. They agreed, so he started knocking on doors and asking residents questions about their living arrangements. Whyte eventually realized that this approach was rather invasive and was not helping him build the relationships that he needed for an ethnographic study. His second attempt was quite comical. Whyte walked into a bar, walked up to three people who were sitting together, and asked to join them. The male in the group promptly offered to toss Whyte down a flight of stairs. His third, successful attempt involved going to a settlement house and meeting with the social workers. Whyte explained his research objectives, and a helpful social worker offered to arrange a meeting with one of the locals, whom Whyte referred to as "Doc" in his book. Doc was amenable to working with Whyte and offered to take him around the neighborhood. This gave Whyte the "in" he needed.

Sandberg and Copes (2012) interviewed 15 ethnographers who studied drug use and dealing and found that most gained access by going to where dealers and users congregate and hanging out with the hopes of being seen and becoming a familiar face in the area. Jacobs (1998) introduced himself to drug dealers this way. He walked up and down the street in a particular area every day. Dealers initially assumed he was a police officer and would yell warnings to fellow dealers that they should disperse. What eventually helped him, ironically, was several incidents in which the police stopped, questioned, and searched him on the streets. Witnessing that made the drug dealers feel confident that he was not actually working for law enforcement. Sandberg and Copes (2012) found that gaining access always took longer than researchers anticipated, with one person working for eight months before making the proper connections.

Issues Specific to Ethnographic Research

Sampling

Random sampling is not typically used for studies involving ethnographic work. Weisheit (2015) identified convenience sampling (also called availability sampling) and snowball sampling as two of the most frequently used methods for qualitative work. Researchers may utilize convenience sampling to select individuals or groups already known to them or to recruit participants via posters or ads. An additional way to find participants is to work with probation and parole officers and treatment centers to identify potential people. As discussed in Chapter 8, snowball sampling involves respondents identifying other possible research participants, so the sample grows similar to a snowball being rolled on the ground. This is sometimes the only possible option, especially when subcultures and offenders are the subjects of research.

During her participant observation study of drug-using club-goers, Perrone (2010) used a combination of convenience and snowball sampling. When she started the project, she selected her first club to observe because she had an acquaintance who went there and knew some of the other club-goers. When she arrived, she ran into an old acquaintance who, upon learning about her research plans, offered to take her to additional clubs and introduce her to more informants.

Mowder, Lutze, and Namgung (2018) were interested in learning about how undocumented women seek help after being involved in intimate partner violence. Undocumented individuals have an incentive to maintain a low profile, and they might hesitate to respond to a flyer or other advertisement recruiting them, as some government agencies have set up fake schools and other programs to conduct immigration stings. Mowder et al initially recruited participants from battered women's shelters that specifically serve Spanish-speaking individuals and received referrals from victim assistance coordinators. After that, they continued to build their sample through word of mouth. Of course, selection bias is a problem inherent in snowball sampling, so we always must be mindful of the fact that we are unlikely to produce a representative sample this way. Ethnographic research, however, tends to be less concerned with finding a representative sample as, the goal is to fully appreciate and understand one specific subculture or group of individuals and not necessarily generalize findings to a larger population.

The Work's Impact on the Researcher

Working on research is bound to have an impact on researchers' lives, with some projects requiring more of a commitment and sacrifice than others. The two more involved types of participant observation—participant as observer and complete participant—take a level of commitment that is often well beyond what is required for most quantitative projects. This commitment can be thought of in four parts: time/money, personal cost, danger, and ethical dilemmas.

Time/Money

Bill Whyte (1943) was able to move into a low-income section of Boston and live among the residents for years because he had a fellowship at Harvard University that paid for him to do so. Whyte is far from being the only researcher to consider it necessary to live among those he was studying. Bourgois (2002) made the same decision and moved his family to Spanish Harlem for the duration of his data collection on neighborhood crack dealers. Quantitative work generally does not involve such a dramatic commitment as moving to a location with a lower quality of life than the middle-class environment where college faculty usually live. The time commitment is also much more intense for this type of work. Ethnographers spend large portions of their time in the field. Even when they are at home or in their offices, they are often faced with hours of note taking, trying to catalog everything that they saw and heard while in the field. Over the course of my career, I have done more quantitative work than qualitative. I took a qualitative research methods class in graduate school and loved it, but the time commitment and patience that is required proved to be too much for me. While the time commitment is difficult, what might be even more of a hurdle is finding funding to allow one to spend so much time observing and interviewing instead of earning money by teaching or working on other projects.

Personal Cost

I already noted that some of these researchers felt the need to uproot their entire lives, give up their middle-class lifestyles, and spend extraordinary amounts of time observing, interviewing, and taking notes. What might be just as difficult is the mental challenge of having to be two different people at the same time. Gold (1958) discussed constantly reminding oneself that the role is to observe and to make sure that one doesn't become too invested in the participant aspect of what is happening. Whyte (1943) recalled having to find a way to navigate the two different worlds in which he operated—life at Harvard as a research fellow and life on the streets of Cornerville. He eventually chose to keep the two worlds separate as he worried that the Harvard associates would unintentionally say things that would complicate his relationships with the Cornerville residents.

Ted Conover (2000), a reporter for the *New York Times*, entered a corrections officer academy and spent a full year working as an officer while not telling anyone that he was actually there to write a story about his experience. As he spent months working in a maximum-security prison, he found himself growing bored at dinner parties with his intellectual friends. Conover began to resent their discussions of topics that he now considered trivial because he believed he had bigger problems facing him at work. He also noticed that his relationships with his family changed, and he even put his hands on his child in anger, something he had never done before. Conover realized that his role of being an officer was starting to consume him to the point that it was changing both his thoughts and behavior while on and off duty.

What happened to Conover and what at times happened to Whyte (1943) is that they both started to "go native," meaning that they started to identify with the people they were studying. As was evident with Conover, **going native** can cause a multitude of problems in one's personal life, but it can also have a negative impact on the research. Hammersly and Atkinson (1995) define going native as abandoning the task of analysis in "favor of the joys of participation" and bias arising from "over-rapport." This is problematic for a few reasons. From a professional standpoint, this interferes with the researcher's ability to notice what is happening, resulting in a failure to analyze events. Whyte (1943) discussed struggling with this after spending a long time living in the field. He wrote

> I had to balance familiarity with detachment, or else no insights would have come. There were fallow periods when I seemed to just be marking time. Whenever life flowed so smoothly that I was taking it for granted, I had to try to get outside of my participating self and struggle again to explain the things that seemed obvious.
>
> (p. 357)

When we hang out in our own social circles, we rarely question why things are the way they are. We don't think to question why we might go to the same restaurant every Sunday for lunch, that large gatherings only occur at one person's house, or that spouses are only invited to certain events. We don't sit back and analyze whether the person who hosts the big events is the leader of the group or if she is using those parties to somehow enhance her reputation among the circle of friends. (Maybe some of us overthinkers contemplate these things, but we can't be objective about our own social groups.) Most of us, overthinkers excluded, just go with the flow and don't analyze these things. Approaching a qualitative study by going with the flow and failing to analyze would be pointless, so one must always maintain some sense of detachment from the group being observed and their activities. Otherwise, as Whyte noted, the researcher will lose the ability to have insight. This is why experts on qualitative research strongly discourage people from researching groups with which they are close or of which they are already a member. It is difficult enough to spend months or years with other groups and still maintain a certain level of detachment. It is just about impossible to do if one is already a member of the group that is subject to study.

The second problem with going native in the social sciences is that it can turn us into law breakers and prompt engagement in very dangerous activities. Whyte (1943) got caught up in the excitement of a local election and illegally voted several times to try to help the candidate favored by the group he was studying. Lyng (1998) worked as a skydiving company pilot while in graduate school and became interested in the extreme risk-taking behavior of skydivers who did drugs in the plane before jumping. Since his observations had to end at the point when they jumped out of the plane and he was left to land it, he quit his job and decided to spend more time with the group both in the air and on the ground. One characteristic of extreme risk taking is that this group would intentionally do things to make an already-dangerous activity even more treacherous. Skydiving had to be done in conjunction with drug use. Riding a motorcycle was too boring, so they would ride at high speeds while under the influence of drugs or alcohol. Doing so is illegal in every state. After taking a curve at 120 miles per hour while under the influence, Lyng lost control, crashed his bike, and nearly killed himself. After having some time to reflect, Whyte regretted his ballot stuffing, realizing that he got caught up in the moment. Lyng certainly regretted becoming so involved in the culture of risk takers that he stopped seeing the danger to himself and others.

Danger

Even if a researcher maintains a sense of detachment and avoids going native, the nature of ethnographic research in criminal justice presents risks to one's personal safety and legal status. Being an ethnographer can be like being a police officer in that significant amounts of time are filled with boredom, but then there are moments that are extremely frightening. Jacobs (1998) was robbed at gunpoint and then repeatedly harassed by a drug-dealing informant who felt that the researcher disrespected him. During their burglary study, Wright and colleagues' (1992) research staff were giving an informant a ride when he started to yell that he was going to shoot the person walking on the street. The informant repeatedly yelled at the driver to stop the car so he could show them how a drive-by happens. Instead, the driver increased speed to prevent the shooting. Bourgois's (2002) decision to move himself and his family to Spanish Harlem for his research came at a price, as they witnessed several major crimes. These incidents included a deadly shotgun shooting and a bombing and machine-gunning of rival gang members, both of which Bourgios witnessed from his apartment window. He was also mugged while living in that neighborhood.

Ferrell (1998) and Inciardi (Inciardi, Lockwood, & Pottieger, 1993) were arrested while doing fieldwork on graffiti artists and crack users, respectively. Bourgeois (2002) and Jacobs (1998) were repeatedly stopped, searched, and berated by the police. These incidents actually helped strengthen the fieldworkers' reputations among the people they were attempting to study, as they reinforced the fact that they were not working with law enforcement. While the police interaction helped them gain credibility with people in the neighborhood, legal trouble does come with significant costs, including legal fees paid to lawyers and the risk of developing a criminal record.

Perrone (2010) was frequently faced with unwanted sexual advances during her club-drug research. She often had to tell men that she was not interested in having sex, tell them to stop touching her, and remove their hands from her. Her concern about being sexually assaulted impacted her decisions about which events to attend.

Ethical Dilemmas

One particularly difficult aspect of qualitative research is anticipating and responding to ethical dilemmas. Researchers who are not in the field are in a better position to respond to ethical problems since we are more likely to have the time to consult with colleagues, mentors, and ethics boards. When researchers in the field are confronted with ethical dilemmas, they are often forced to respond immediately without the benefit of time to reflect or the ability to seek advice. Polsky (1967) recommended that researchers try to limit their exposure to such problems by being up front with informants immediately about what they are and are not willing to witness and hear. Polsky was also resigned to the belief that, if the fieldwork involved active criminals, the field researcher was going to wind up also breaking the law at some point during the project.

> He need not be a "participant" observer and commit the criminal acts under study, yet he has to witness such acts or be taken into confidence about them and not blow the whistle. That is, the investigator has to decide that when necessary he will "obstruct justice" or have "guilty knowledge" or be an "accessory" before or after the fact, in the full legal sense of those terms. He will not be enabled to discern some vital aspects of criminal lifestyles and subcultures unless he (1) makes such a moral decision, (2) makes the criminals believe him, and (3) convinces them of his ability to act in accord with his decision.
>
> (p. 124)

Even when researchers work to establish specific boundaries, they might not always be respected. Polsky (1967) said that his request to be shielded from certain crimes and discussions of them was respected most of the time, but not always. Toward the end of his fieldwork, Bourgois (2002) started being pressured by one of the most powerful drug dealers in the community to launder money. Luckily, his quick thinking helped him talk his way out of doing it without putting himself or his work in danger.

Should researchers engage in illegal behavior for the sake of research? I will first note my bias here. I am not a qualitative researcher, and most of the work that I've done throughout my career has started with a call to a police station or correctional agency to get their cooperation because I generally do evaluation research. My point is that it is difficult for me to personally relate to this type of dilemma, so my immediate response would be that researchers should not break the law. I am sympathetic, however, to the fact that some minor law breaking could go a very long way to gaining trust. Researchers must understand and then be willing to accept the consequences of that. Personally, I would not be willing to get a criminal record for the sake of participant observation, but that is also because my clean record is something that I need to gain access to criminal justice agencies for my evaluation work.

Of course, there are ethnographers who do not depend on a clean criminal record as I do and either participated in some illegal behaviors as recreation even before their study or felt that the benefits of committing minor crimes for the sake of research outweighed the costs. Ethnographers studying drug use and drug dealers reported to Sandberg and Copes (2012) that their own drug use helped signal to the potential research participants that they were not police or social workers. Adler (1993) only met her key informant for her drug dealing study because she used recreational drugs herself. Adler, her husband, and "Dave" were neighbors, started socializing, and spent many nights using marijuana and cocaine together. It was through those experiences that Dave began to trust her and eventually revealed that he was a dealer. Researchers who witnessed and/or participated in illegal activities, such as Polsky (1967), Ferrell (1998), and Adler (1993), argue that, from a methodological standpoint, obeying the law could act as a barrier to understanding the subculture. Ferrell (1998) suggests "criminological verstehen" can be best achieved in some instances by being there in the criminal moment but urges that criminologists do this "as best they can within limits of patronal responsibility and professional identity" (p. 28). Both Ferrell (1998), with his graffiti research, and Lyng (1998), with extreme risk taking, noted that it was only after their informants witnessed their participation in these activities that they began to open up and explicitly discuss their own involvement.

What about witnessing criminal behavior? It is inevitable that, when one studies drug dealers or users, one will witness lots of drug dealing and using. When deciding what you can observe without notifying authorities, you should give this lots of thought and anticipate as many scenarios as possible before entering the field. Work with an experienced fieldworker or someone who is familiar with that setting. As Polsky (1967) suggests, you should then be clear about what you are and are not willing to witness while maintaining confidentiality. For example, if you are observing gang members, you should tell them that you do not want to hear about plans for assaulting or murdering anyone, nor do you want to be around for any of that. Sandberg and Copes (2012) surveyed ethnographers about the dilemmas they have faced with reporting issues to the police. Like Polsky, these researchers asked their informants to avoid talking about specific persons, using real names of individuals, or discussing future crimes. The researchers who did hear information about serious crimes, such as murders that had already occurred, did not report the information to the police because what they heard was so general that it would not have aided in any investigation. The general rule adopted by these ethnographers was that they would go to the police if they learned of any serious crimes that were in the planning stages or if children or other innocent "third parties" were at risk. Weisheit (2015) noted that, depending on the researchers' occupation and where they live, they may be mandated reporters. For example, as a college professor in New Jersey, I am a mandated reporter. If I witness or hear a credible report of child abuse or neglect, I am legally obligated to report it to the authorities, regardless of any promise of confidentiality that I made as part of my research. Of course, as a responsible researcher, I would want to anticipate this and warn the people I was about to interview if I thought that this subject might arise in our conversations.

What if the police approach you and ask for information? You likely promised confidentiality to all your participants. Priests and attorneys are legally shielded from having to give up information on their parishioners and clients, respectively. Most researchers have no such protections. I say most because there are federal certificates of confidentiality, but these are rare. They are available for certain federal grants, such as those provided by the National Institutes of Health and the Department of Health and Human Services. Researchers who are doing work without federal funds can apply for such a certificate, but granting it is at the discretion of the federal agencies (National Institute of Health, 2019). Weisheit (2015) recommends that researchers who lack these certificates give much thought in advance of their fieldwork about what they are willing to do if police or prosecutors request fieldnotes or testimony. Adler (1993) purposely avoided all publicity and held back on publishing her ethnographic work on drug dealing until after she moved away from the area so she would not come to the attention of the authorities while she was still doing data collection. Speaking of publishing findings, how do we avoid harming our participants by publishing stories about their criminal behavior? Researchers handle this by being vague about where they collected their data. This is why Vander Ven (2001) identified his research site as "Chronictown" and Whyte (1943) called his location "Cornerville." Additionally, for fieldnotes, interview notes, and the actual publications of their work, researchers use pseudonyms rather than people's real names.

Another set of ethical issues arise when researchers choose to engage as complete participants, otherwise called covert participants. People who do research in a complete observer role may conceal their identities from those they are studying, but they also refrain from actually interacting with them, making deception unnecessary (Miller & Miller, 2015). Miller and Miller listed a number of potential ethical problems associated with **covert participation**, including invasion of privacy, lack of informed consent, and potential exposure of unwitting research participants to danger. Is it advisable to do this? Polsky (1967), who studied hustlers at pool halls, argued against it. He wrote:

> In doing field research on criminals you damned well better not pretend to be "one of them," because they will test this claim out and one of two things will happen: either you will, as Sutherland and Cressy [famous criminological theorists] indicate, get sucked into "participant" observation of the sort you would rather not undertake, or you will be exposed, with still greater negative consequences. You must let the criminals know who you are; and if it is done properly, it does not sabotage the research.
>
> (p. 110)

Other researchers argue that, in certain circumstances, covert work is simply the only way to research some very important topics. Goode (2015) recalled the backlash that Laud Humphreys (1970) received after doing complete observation of men having secret, anonymous sex with other men. His university tried to revoke his degree and called his publisher to urge them not to publish the book. Despite that, *Tearoom Trade* won a prestigious research award. Goode noted that this and other classic sociological studies conducted would now be considered unethical. Goode also used a modern-day example of Scientology, a group that has developed a reputation for fiercely attacking anyone who criticizes them. He argued that anyone wishing to do ethnographic research on Scientology would have to do it covertly as they would put themselves at too great of a risk otherwise. When thinking about whether covert activities are necessary, this decision should be made on a case-by-case basis (Miller & Miller, 2015), and Goode (2015) noted the necessity of demonstrating that the benefits of covert research outweigh the risks. If there is any way that the work can be done without using covert tactics, researchers should explore that option. Adler (1993) was covert with some participants but honest with others about her identity and purpose. When she met people, she initially remained quiet about her intentions. She would then work to gain their trust by offering favors, such as loaning out her car and lending people her telephone. As she gained people's trust, she would either have those who already knew her identity approach them and vouch for her trustworthiness, or if she felt comfortable enough, she would have that conversation with the new potential participants herself.

If you recall the discussion of Institutional Review Boards (IRBs) from Chapter 3, you are probably wondering right now how some of these research practices would be received by ethics boards. Ever since the passage of the National Research Act in 1974, ethnographers have been concerned about restraints on their ability to collect data. Miller and Miller (2015) noted that IRBs' reluctance to approve research that proposes extensive contact with participants, and perhaps some deception, has impacted researchers' ability to conduct research. Europe's ethical guidelines for research vary from location to location, and Sandberg and Copes (2012) found that many of the European ethnographers who did drug research did their work without clearing it with ethics boards. In the United States, drug researchers engaging in participant or complete observation recalled having difficulty convincing the IRBs that requesting signed consent forms would have a chilling effect on participant recruitment. There are numerous people encountered during field research whom the researcher never interviews and maybe never speaks with, so providing informed consent to each would be impractical (Goode, 2015; Sandberg & Copes, 2012). American IRBs have been criticized for serving more as a vehicle to prevent universities and members of the IRB themselves from being sued than understanding the difficulty of field research and weighing the risks and benefits of the work. The lack of flexibility has prompted some fieldworkers to be intentionally vague and leave out important details about their planned work in their IRB applications for the sake of getting approval while others have skipped IRB approval entirely, forgoing the legal protection that they would otherwise receive from their universities (Sandberg & Copes, 2012). As was discussed in Chapter 3, failure to obtain IRB approval for research involving human subjects can lead to serious legal and career-threatening trouble for the researcher.

Goode (2015) recommended that, instead of attempting to apply rigid guidelines, many of which were written with medical research in mind, IRBs and investigators work together to develop protocols with the following principles in mind: no physical harm to participants, no coercion to participate in research, no sexual harassment, no acts that would constitute exploitation of participants, no serious felonious behavior by researchers, no behavior that that will "spoil" the research site/population for future investigators, and make every effort to conceal the identity of the research participants.

Note Taking for Qualitative Research

Another difficult aspect of participant and complete observation is recording what is happening. You are not really participating in the activities of the group if you have a notepad or your cell phone in your hands, jotting down notes about what is taking place. Time spent in the field can last hours at a time, and it is very hard to keep track of everything. Whyte (1943) used to make trips to the men's room to write a few notes before returning to the group. He would also work to make mental maps of rooms and try to remember which groups of people interacted with each other. As soon as he returned home, he would immediately draw the map and then finish taking his notes. While in the field, some researchers use mnemonics to try to remember events that took place. **Mnemonic devices** are rhymes or other verbal tools used to help us remember things. When we were in grade school learning the colors of the rainbow, we were told to memorize ROYGBIV (red, orange, yellow, green, blue, indigo, violet) (Hagan, 2007; Miller, 1995). One of the reasons qualitative research is so time consuming is that those who do it spend hours and hours in the field, but when they get home, they are not even close to being finished with the day's work. Whatever short notes with a few keywords that they jotted down must now be expanded into detailed notes about what people said and did.

When it comes to conducting interviews, field researchers have mixed opinions about using recording devices (Sandberg & Copes, 2012). Some worry that audio or videotaping interviews will scare respondents, particularly those who are involved in illegal behavior. Polsky (1967) was of the belief that researchers should not seek to record interviews with active criminals. Adler (1993) did tape all her depth interviews with informants who discussed how they entered and then progressed in the field of drug dealing. In addition to concerns about the comfort of respondents, researcher also identified some practical barriers to recording interviews, including the setting where the interview is being conducted. Some settings, such as bars and even parks, might be too noisy to make effective use of recording devices (Sandberg & Copes, 2012).

Structured Field Observations

This section addresses fieldwork that does not include participant or complete observation. Previous chapters of this book, such as Chapter 9, have provided information about the work of observers as participants, who enter the field for the purpose of interviewing or otherwise survey-ing participants. Here, I would like to discuss the work of people who are complete observers. Through this type of work, we can conduct social as well as physical observations. For social observations, the act of researchers witnessing behavior addresses an important threat to validity found in survey research. With surveys, people can incorrectly recall or lie about how they handled a situation in the past, and for hypothetical questions about how they would handle something in the future, they may give us an inaccurate account of what they would do. (Think of anyone in your life who talks tough but does not act that way in practice.) Field research largely eliminates that problem by allowing us to observe human behavior as it happens. I wrote "largely eliminates" because there is still the possibility of reactivity, or people changing their behavior because they become aware that they are being observed. When we are seeking to learn about the characteristics of places, we can get some of what we need through surveys (e.g., rates of household burglar alarm ownership, presence of CCTV cameras in convenience stores), but there are other features of the environment that would best be measured by trained researchers to ensure reliability.

Field observation can provide us with data that would be otherwise impossible to collect. We can do telephone interviews with crime victims about recent auto thefts or household burglaries or send mail surveys to business owners to find out how many times in the past year their business has been robbed. Unfortunately, those surveys will not tell us much about the environment where the crime occurred. Knowing about a home's visibility from the road, the physical layout of the parking lot where the car was parked, or the design of the business that was robbed can tell us a lot about the crime and the chances of revictimization. A parking garage might have more thefts and inci-dences of vandalism than others in the same town because of a design flaw that would be evident upon observation. For example, a review of one parking garage with high rates of vandalism revealed that the side walls were easy to climb, providing convenient access to juveniles who were entering and exiting the garage without being seen by security (Poyner, 1997). Through interviews with offenders, researchers know what makes certain homes and businesses attractive targets for crime. For example, convenience stores that lack visibility from the street are considered more attractive locations to target as there is less of a chance of the robbery being detected while in progress (Hunter & Jeffrey, 1997). Researchers who are studying convenience store robberies would likely want to visit the stores to assess the visibility of the cashiers from the street to measure the target's attractiveness for robbery.

A colleague and I did field research to study locations in Atlantic City, New Jersey, that had repeat reports of auto theft either in 2004–2005 or 2006–2007. The local police department shared with us the dates of the reported thefts and the locations where the cars were parked. We did site visits of the 2004–2005 locations in the summer of 2006 and visited the 2006–2007 locations in the summer of 2008. At each location, we used a structured data collection form to collect information about the WALLS: watchers (people present to serve as informal social control), activity nodes (locations that draw heavy use for legal and illegal activities), location (landscaping and design features), lighting, and security indexes (Levy & Tartaro, 2010). We visited each location both during the day and after sunset. While one researcher completed the data collection form, the other took photographs with a GPS camera. Data from the GPS camera were used to help map the theft locations. While we could have taken the addresses of the theft locations from the police data and mapped that information without going out into the field, there really was no other way to collect the data for the physical characteristics of each street. In this study, we used three different types of data collection—unpublished agency records, structured observation forms, and photographs—two of which required our presence in the field.

One common criticism of crime prevention techniques is that they might displace crimes to another time or location. To measure that, Weisburd and colleagues (2006) worked with the Jersey City, New Jersey, police department to observe neighborhoods targeted for police interventions as well as areas adjacent to the targeted neighborhoods. The research team measured crime and victimization several different ways over nine months, including over 6,000 20-minute social observations conducted by researchers. Researchers went to each randomly selected street segment and sat in their cars, or stood on the sidewalk if they did not have cars, for 20 minutes. Using a structured observation form, they noted any instances of drug activity, prostitution activity, public intoxication, fights, police presence, and loud music. Researchers also conducted physical observations of those same street segments during each wave of the project.

For structured observations, training is essential. If there are multiple field researchers collecting data, lack of rigorous training will likely produce problems with inter-rater reliability. I was one of the student field researchers on the Weisburd et al. (2006) project who conducted social and physical observations. For the physical observations, my coworkers and I went into the neighborhoods and took note of the conditions before, during, and after the police interventions. This took a lot of preparation and continued reliability checks as we all had to come to an agreement about what was "a little" bit of litter versus "a lot." Not only did we all undergo initial training, but we also did reliability checks every day that we conducted observations. If observers were seeing things differently, we discussed it until we came to an agreement. Even if there is only one person conducting field observations, it is important that the individual rate items consistently each day.

Validity and Reliability of Field Research

How does field research compare to other types of inquiry with regard to validity and reliability? As I just noted, structured field observations, if handled properly, are generally high in reliability. They are also generally high in validity, but there is one issue that might have a detrimental effect on validity—reactivity. If you were about to attempt to break into a car, my guess would be that the first thing you would do is look around to see if anyone was watching. A researcher standing on the sidewalk or sitting in a car could prompt the would-be thief to either skip stealing that day or go somewhere a little more private to do it. Somewhat surprisingly, a researcher's presence does not always inhibit criminal behavior. As Weisburd et al. (2006) explained, the field researchers in their study spent so much time on the streets that the locals, including those involved in drug dealing and prostitution, grew accustomed to the field staff and learned that we were not calling the police to report what we observed each day. While we likely influenced some people's behavior through our presence, we were still able to capture numerous instances of illegal acts. Researchers did make every effort to blend in and act as though they were not actively watching people. While conducting a social observation from my car, a fight broke out about two feet away from the driver's-side window. I tried to act casual and uninterested. I had an old newspaper, so I picked it up and pretended to be reading it while two men yelled and even came to blows right next to me.

A strength of ethnographic work is its high degree of validity. Researchers are able to witness actions, including offending, rather than relying exclusively on offenders' recollections and interpretation of past attempts. By being in the field, researchers can get a very accurate picture of the actions and motivations of individuals. They can personally witness group dynamics and understand the context in offender decision-making. James Marquart (1986) did research on the culture of corrections officers and their legal and illegal activities on the job while working as a corrections officer. Marquart personally witnessed 30 incidents of officers physically punishing inmates. It is very unlikely that he would have learned about a fraction of what he was eventually able to report had he mailed officers surveys or even sat down and interviewed them, given the culture of silence found among corrections and police officers. Field researchers also have the advantage of observing and speaking to people in their natural setting, where they are most comfortable and most likely to act naturally.

Research that focuses on small samples, specific groups, and individual locations tends to be weak on generalizability. What Bill Whyte (1943) learned while observing men and women in one small Italian American neighborhood in Boston is unlikely to be applicable to another neighborhood, even within the same city. As Maxfield and Babbie (2012) note, "Because field researchers get a full and in-depth view of their subject matter, they can reach an unusually comprehensive understanding. By its very comprehensiveness, however, this understanding is less generalizable than results based on rigorous sampling and standardized measurements" (p. 213). Marquart's (1986) observations of officer culture at a specific prison at one point in time in Texas has some lessons that are certainly applicable to other corrections settings, but we must also understand that prisons are closed institutions that can easily develop their own culture and practices that might not even be transferrable to other prisons within that state department of corrections. We could possibly generalize some findings regarding officer solidarity and willingness to protect each other. But we would also have to look at the Texas Department of Corrections at that particular time, understand its peculiarities (they had a now-illegal building tender system, in which some of the most violent inmates were chosen to serve as quasi-guards and a first line of defense for the officers), and appreciate the impact that their unique security and discipline processes had on officer reactions to inmates.

Reliability tends to be questionable with ethnographic research. Unlike research involving structured data collection tools, observations and unstructured/depth interviews inherent in qualitative work are subject to interpretation by researchers. Each researcher's life experiences, and even the criminological theories that they use to interpret what they see, will likely color their interpretations. We also must realize that people in the field may react to us one way and to other researchers differently based on our own backgrounds. Pawson and Kelly (2014) conducted participant observations of jam band and hip-hop concerts with the goal of understanding the role of marijuana consumption in the experience. In their limitations, they cautioned that the fact that they are white made it much easier for them to blend in at the jam band events and more difficult at hip-hop concerts. In other words, two African American researchers who conducted this same project may have had different experiences in the field and, therefore, generated different results.

Summary

In this chapter, I used Gold's (1958) four roles for field researchers—complete observer, observer as participant, participant as observer, and complete participant. Chapter 9 largely addressed observer as participant, so the focus of this chapter was the three remaining roles.

Participant as observer and complete participant are characterized by extensive field presence and the researchers' involvement in the lives of the group under observation. Unlike quantitative research, which almost always approaches topics with a deductive approach to problems, qualitative research with participant observation or complete observer roles is more likely to approach issues using inductive reasoning. This type of research is more conducive to generating theories. Ethnographic work can also let us observe a group for so long and in such detail that we can gain a greater understating of a specific phenomenon than is possible with quantitative research.

One significant challenge to fieldwork is gaining access to the group or organization that we want to study. Ideally, we would be able to use our contacts to put us in touch with people and maybe even help set up a meeting. If we do not have such resources, then we have to work to gain access ourselves by sending an introductory letter or email and requesting a meeting. Subcultures may be much more difficult to access, given individuals' rightful suspicion that outsiders might be undercover law enforcement. Negotiating access to an organization or subculture is only one of several challenges faced by ethnographers. This work generally takes longer than quantitative studies, might require sacrifices such as spending long hours in dangerous areas and exposing oneself to victimization, and can pose ethical challenges that must be addressed without benefit of being able to seek advice from colleagues or supervisors. Covert participation, in which the researcher is engaging in complete participation without revealing his/her true identity, presents additional ethical and safety dilemmas and should only be done if the work cannot be conducted otherwise and the benefits of going covert outweigh the risks and costs.

A very different type of field research that includes little to no contact with human research participants is complete observer work. There is great value in researchers going out to communities to personally see the environment and gauge its impact on contributing to or preventing crime. Researchers can bring field observation sheets with them, and they can also use still and video cameras to document characteristics, such as visibility, cleanliness, amount of foot and vehicle traffic, and security or law enforcement presence. This information can be used alone or in combination with other types of data to contribute to our understanding of crime and crime prevention.

Keywords

Complete observer	Observer as participant	Participant as observer
Complete participant	Verstehen	Sponsor
Pseudonym	Going native	Covert participation
Mnemonic device		

Discussion Questions

1. What are the four roles of researchers, according to Gold (1958), and how do they differ from each other?
2. Generally, how well does field research fare with generating valid, reliable, and generalizable results?
3. What are the ethical concerns associated with covert research participation?
4. Why is going native problematic? What steps can researchers take to prevent that from occurring?
5. What types of sampling procedures are common in ethnographic research?

References

Adler, P. A. (1993). *Wheeling & dealing: An ethnography of upper-level drug dealing and smuggling community* (2nd ed.). New York, NY: Columbia University Press.

Bourgois, P. (2002). *In search of respect: Selling crack in El Barrio*. Cambridge, UK: Cambridge University Press.

Conover, T. (2000). *New Jack: Guarding Sing Sing*. New York, NY: Random House.

Ferrell, J. (1998). Criminological verstehen. In. J. Ferrell & M. S. Hamm (Eds.), *Ethnography at the edge* (pp. 28–42). Boston, MA: Northeastern University Press.

Glaser, B. G., & Strauss, A. (1967). *The discovery of grounded theory: Strategies for qualitative research*. Chicago, IL: Aldine Publishing Co.

Gold., R. L. (1958). Roles in sociological field observations. *Social Forces, 36*, 217–223.

Goode, E. (2015). Ethical issues in the qualitative study of deviance and crime. In H. J. Copes & M. Miller (Eds.), *The Routledge handbook of qualitative criminology* (pp. 49–59). London, UK: Routledge.

Hagan, F. (2007). *Essentials of research methods in criminal justice and criminology* (2nd ed.). Boston, MA: Pearson.

Hammersly, M., & Atkinson, P. (1995). *Ethnography*. London, UK: ITP.

Humphreys, L. (1970). *Tearoom trade: Interpersonal sex in public places*. Hawthorne, NY: Aldine Publishing Company.

Hunter, R. D., & Jeffrey, C. R. (1997). Preventing convenience store robbery through environmental design. In R. V. Clarke (Ed.), *Situational crime prevention* (2nd ed., pp. 191–199). Albany, NY: Harrow and Heston.

Inciardi, J. A., Lockwood, D., & Pottieger, A. E. (1993). *Women and crack cocaine*. New York, NY: Macmillan.

Jacobs, B. (1998). Researching crack dealers: Dilemmas and contradictions. In J. Ferrell & M. S. Hamm (Eds.), *Ethnography at the edge* (pp. 160–177). Boston, MA: Northeastern University Press.

Levy, M. P., & Tartaro, C. (2010). Repeat victimization: A study of auto theft in Atlantic City using the W.A.L.L.S. variables to measure environmental indicators. *Criminal Justice Policy Review, 21*(3), 296–318. https://doi.org/10.1177/0887403409350190

Lyng, S. (1998). Dangerous methods: Risk taking and the research process. In J. Ferrell & M. S. Hamm (Eds.), *Ethnography at the edge* (pp. 221–251). Boston, MA: Northeastern University Press.

Marquart, J. W. (1986). Prison guards and the use of physical coercion as a mechanism of prisoner control. *Criminology, 24*(2), 347–365.

Maxfield, M. G., & Babbie, E. (2012). *Basics of research methods for criminal justice and criminology* (3rd ed.). Belmont, CA: Thomson Wadsworth.

Miller, J. M., & Miller, H. V. (2015). Edge ethnography and naturalistic inquiry in criminology. In H. J. Copes & M. Miller (Eds.), *The Routledge handbook of qualitative criminology* (pp. 88–102). London, UK: Routledge.

Miller, M. (1995). Covert participant observation: Reconsidering the least used method. *Journal of Contemporary Criminal Justice, 11*(2), 97–105.

Mowder, D., Lutze, F., & Namgung, H. (2018). Ayúdame! Who can help me? the help-seeking decisions of battered undocumented Latinas. *Journal of Ethnicity in Criminal Justice, 16*(3), 205–224. https://doi.org/10.1080/15377938.2018.1498818

National Institute of Health (2019). *Certificates of Confidentiality* (CoC). Bethesda, MD: National Institutes of Health. https://grants.nih.gov/policy/humansubjects/coc.htm

Pawson, M., & Kelly, B. C. (2014). Consumption and community: The subcultural contexts of disparate marijuana practices in jam band and hip-hop scenes. *Deviant Behavior, 35*, 347–363.

Perrone, D. (2010). Gender and sexuality in the field: A female ethnographer's experience researching drug use in dance clubs. *Substance Use & Misuse, 45*, 717–735. https://doi.org/10.3109/10826081003595127

Polsky, N. (1967). *Hustlers, beats, and others*. Garden City, NY: Anchor Books.

Poyner, B. (1997). Situational crime prevention in two parking facilities. In R. V. Clarke (Ed.), *Situational crime prevention* (2nd ed., pp. 157–166). Guilderland, NY: Harrow & Heston.

Sandberg, S., & Copes, H. (2012). Speaking with ethnographers: The challenges of researching drug dealers and offenders. *Journal of Drug Issues, 43*, 176–197. https://doi.org/10.1177/0022042612465275

Vander Ven, T. M. (1998). Fear of victimization and the interactional construction of harassment in a Latino neighborhood. *Journal of Contemporary Ethnography, 27*(3), 374 – 398. doi:10.1177/089124198027003004

Weber, M., & Shils, E. (1949). *Max Weber on the methodology of the social sciences*. Glencoe, IL: Free Press.

Weisburd, D., Wyckoff, L. A., Ready, J., Eck, J. J., Hinkle, J. C., & Gajewski, F. (2006). Does crime just move around the corner? A controlled study of spatial displacement and diffusion of crime control benefits. *Criminology, 44*(3), 549–592. https://doi.org/10.1111/j.1745-9125.2006.00057.x

Weisheit, R. A. (2015). Researching drug crime using qualitative methods. In H. J. Copes & M. Miller (Eds.), *The Routledge handbook of qualitative criminology* (pp. 191–203). London, UK: Routledge.

Whyte, W. F. (1943). *Street corner society*. Chicago, IL: University of Chicago Press.

Wright, R., Decker, S. H., Redfern, A. K., & Smith, D. L. (1992). A snowball's chance in hell: Doing fieldwork with active residential burglars. *Journal of Research in Crime and Delinquency, 29*, 148–161. https://doi.org/10.1177/0022427892029002003

Reading 10.1   Consumption and Community

Public attitudes toward marijuana consumption have changed dramatically since the 1980s and early 1990s, with multiple states legalizing or decriminalizing recreational use while others expand the availability of medical marijuana. Since drug use, particularly marijuana consumption, is a component of some subcultural identities, Pawson and Kelly (2014) planned to compare and contrast the role of marijuana consumption in two New York City nightlife scenes—jam band and hip-hop. The two researchers went into the field to conduct observations and interviews so they could better understand the two subcultures and the role that marijuana plays in participants' enjoyment of concerts.

Consumption and Community: The Subcultural Contexts of Disparate Marijuana Practices in Jam Band and Hip-Hop Scenes

Mark Pawson and Brian C. Kelly

Introduction

Marijuana remains the most commonly used illicit drug in the United States, particularly among young people. A majority of Americans ages 18 to 25 have used marijuana during their lifetimes, and almost one-third have done so within the past year (SAMHSA 2010). Several studies report how young people perceive marijuana as having relatively few health and social risks (Parker et al. 2002). This, no doubt, plays a role in its widespread prevalence. In this regard, marijuana use has become a normalized behavior among American youth.

Marijuana has been incorporated into the lifestyles of a wide range of individuals (Hathaway 1997). The normalization of marijuana use within American society has become especially apparent through various media outlets. Increasingly, movies and television shows are depicting marijuana use in more neutral and sometimes even positive ways (Hathaway et al. 2011). Research by Howard Parker claims that scenarios making light of recreational marijuana use would have previously received widespread criticism, but now go relatively unnoticed. He indicates that this is evidence of a general shift in the way that the public perceives marijuana use (Parker et al. 2002). Furthermore, the recent trend of decriminalizing possession of the drug in certain states as well as the proliferation of the medical marijuana industry in states such as

Colorado and California have also been cited as signifying shifts in the public's perception of the drug and willingness to normalize its use (Hathaway et al. 2011; O'Brien 2013).

As marijuana use became an increasingly normalized behavior, researchers began to focus on the rituals and norms surrounding its use amongst young adults (Dunlap et al. 2006; Golub et al. 2006; Kelly 2006; Zimmerman and Wieder 1977). Some studies have noted that different marijuana smoking practices require different smoking etiquette (Kelly 2006). Meanwhile, others have shown how specific social settings can influence the ways in which, as well as how much of, the drug is consumed (Dunlap et al. 2006). In this regard, social contexts shape not only the consumption of drugs but also the way these consumption practices unfold.

This article builds on previous examinations of marijuana use as a cultural practice by highlighting how different subcultural contexts influence interaction rituals surrounding marijuana consumption. Drawing upon the tradition of symbolic interactionism, the present research is based on 12 months of ethnographic fieldwork on marijuana consumption routines within two distinct nightlife scenes in New York City, the hip-hop scene and the jam band scene. Throughout the article, we assess the ways in which subcultural norms and attitudes influence distinct marijuana consumption practices within each of these two youth subcultures. We not only delve into the implications that these subcultural practices have for producing varied levels of marijuana intoxication, but also discuss how these patterns shape different experiences of solidarity and community for the two scenes' respective participants and, in doing so, reinforce the norms and values of that subcultural system.

Subcultural Norms and Drug Use

The use of marijuana has been linked to both hip-hop and rock subcultures for decades (Davis and Munoz 1968; Golub et al. 2006; Hunt 2008; 2010; 2012; Timberlake 2009; Zimmerman and Wieder 1977). More recently, the use of blunts—slang for marijuana rolled in cigar paper—has been specifically associated with participation in hip-hop culture, especially among young men (Golub et al. 2006; Timberlake 2009). Several studies on the jam band scene have highlighted the central role and cultural importance of marijuana consumption within this context (Davis and Munoz 1968; Hunt 2012; Zimmerman and Wieder 1977). In this regard, marijuana is deeply embedded in both of these subcultural scenes.

Youth subcultures have been the focus of many studies on drug use since illicit substance use remains a prominent element in the formation of subcultural identities for some young people (Duff 2003; Pilkington 2007). Subcultures contain particular sets of beliefs, values, symbols, language, norms, customs, and activities that render them as distinct groups that exist within a larger culture (Jensen 2006). As such, subcultures inherently shape the behaviors of the people who participate within them (Thornton 1995). The complex process of conforming to subcultural norms can have significant impacts on a wide array of consumption patterns, especially with regard to drug use (Bennett 1999; Mulder et al. 2007).

Consumption patterns remain a prominent means by which people seek to formalize aspects of their identities (Gottdiener 2000). By dressing in a particular manner or ingesting specific drugs in a certain way, individuals are both consuming and projecting the symbol that the product represents to others within a particular group (Best

1989). Objects consumed within the subcultural sphere have particular symbolic value within that context. In this regard, the consumption practices of young adults are particularly informative when observed within the context of participation within a particular subculture.

Youth subcultures can function to homogenize their participants' consumption patterns as members seek to dress, act, and interact in concert with others within that particular subcultural scene. By adhering to what is—as well as what is not—considered to be of good taste within a particular subculture, a participant's behavior becomes a public display that validates one's status as a member (Thornton 1995). Displays of group-validated behavior can also translate themselves to patterns of drug consumption. Various studies have noted how certain subcultures are associated with particular drug trends, including the use of blunts (Golub et al. 2006), amphetamines (Hebdige 1979), and ecstasy (Kavanaugh and Anderson 2008; Perrone 2009).

Many youth subcultures place symbolic value on particular forms of drug use. In doing so, these contexts contribute to their participants' conceptions of the traits and meanings associated with drug behavior (Becker 1953). The maintenance of subcultural norms and values within the subcultural context provides expectations about how a particular drug should be used. Moreover, drug use within some youth subcultures provides opportunities for subcultural participants to share together in ritualistic activities that can create a sense of solidarity and community within the scene (Dunlap et al. 2006; Kavanaugh and Anderson 2008). In this manner, consuming certain drugs in specific ways can shape social bonds within that scene and influence social status.

The Hip-Hop Scene

Hip-hop emerged in the late 70s in the South Bronx as deejays began to sample, mix, and scratch records to create extended breakbeats for people to dance to at parties (Fricke and Ahearn 2002). Emceeing soon followed as party promoters and hosts began to talk or rap over the records being played as well as utilizing call-and-response chants to keep the audience involved in the music (Chang 2007). As emcees evolved from being hosts of parties to lyricists and song writers, hip-hop became much more than just a new form of music, but also developed into its own subculture as participants within the scene adopted particular forms of dress like wearing oversize jewelry, and constructed unique language, attitudes, and activities like breakdancing and graffiti art (Blair 1993; Chang 2007; Fricke and Ahearn 2002).

As hip-hop music continued to flourish throughout the 1990s, an inner city cultural backlash to the heroin epidemic of the 1970s and crack epidemic of the 1980s led to the decline of hard drug use (Golub et al. 2006). During this time, blunts—marijuana rolled up in cigar shells—became an exceedingly popular and trendy way for participants within the hip-hop subculture to get high (Golub et al. 2006; Timberlake 2009). Blunts subsequently became integrated within the broader social repertoire of those involved in hip-hop subcultures.

The denigration of hard drug use by inner city youth played a prominent role in the entrenchment of marijuana, particularly in the form of blunts, as the drug of choice among members of the hip-hop scene (Allen 1996; Golub et al. 2006). Subsequently, using marijuana in the form of smoking blunts became a practice distinctly associated with the hip-hop subculture (Sifaneck et al. 2006). The blunt's overtly larger size in comparison with joints is commonly referenced as being in conjunction with hip-hop's core subcultural values, particularly that of living a "large" lifestyle (Allen 1996; Sifaneck et al. 2006). Moreover, the ubiquitous presence of blunt smoking within hip-hop media such as music videos, magazines, and movies reinforces the notion that the consumption of marijuana in this form is embraced as a unique aspect of the hip-hop subculture (Sifaneck et al. 2006).

The Jam Band Scene

The jam band subculture arose out of the "Deadhead" subculture. Throughout the 1990s, the subculture grew from a few bands, the most prominent being Phish, to hundreds of bands playing music within the scene. A core aspect of the scene became live performances involving extended musical improvisations. The subculture now consists of music fans from a few different genres, unified by their enjoyment of live improvisational music performances. Similar to the performances of the Grateful Dead, some jam band shows also feature extravagant light shows that promote and complement the usage of psychedelic drugs.

Ritualistically occurring every summer is a series of festivals that feature various jam bands. These festivals, similar in style to that of Woodstock, span several days in a row and in many ways function as the heart of the jam band subculture. Many young adults involved in the scene may "tour" several different festivals during the course of the summer (Hunt 2008). The festivals often involve outdoor camping and are infused with "hippie" values, such as encouraging a connection with the earth and others.

Drug use is prevalent at festivals with particular focus on taking psychedelic drugs for spiritual purposes, to enhance the enjoyment of the improvisational music, or as a means of establishing a sense of community or connection with others (Hunt 2012; Millman and Beeder 1994). Although jam band shows and festivals are often places to use psychedelic drugs, the scene's most pervasively used drug is marijuana, which is often cited as being the drug staple of the subculture (Davis and Munoz 1968; Hunt 2008; 2010; 2012; Zimmerman and Wieder 1977). Moreover, some members of the jam band subculture believe that the sale and use of psychoactive substances should be legalized to varying degrees (Hunt 2012). In this regard, drug use in general, and marijuana use specifically, have become an entrenched aspect of this subculture.

Current Study

Despite the commonality of marijuana use, the specific routines and practices of marijuana consumption differ markedly between these scenes. The ways that members participating in the two scenes expected the drug to be consumed can be considered a result of the drastic differences in the subcultures' symbolic systems that inform normative behaviors and value systems within these scenes. As described below, the adherence to subcultural norms and values translated into marijuana being consumed primarily in the form of blunts within the hip-hop scene and via bowls and joints within the jam band scene. Furthermore, as a result of participants conforming to subcultural norms and values, the ways in which marijuana was used among participants within the hip-hop scene differed greatly from the way in which marijuana was shared among participants within the jam band scene. These differing marijuana routines, in turn, reinforced the symbolic system of each scene. In this regard, these core drug use practices reinforce the structure and function of the subcultural "community" within each scene.

Methods

The present research was part of a larger study designed to examine contextual factors of drug use among young adults within nightlife scenes. The first phase centered on ethnographic fieldwork involving participant observation and informal interviewing. The data presented in the current article are derived from this phase, a one-year ethnographic study of several youth subcultural scenes in New York. Specifically, this article focuses on the fieldwork conducted over the course of 12 months, from March 2010 to March 2011, within New York City's jam band and hip-hop scenes.

Participant observation was a critical component of this ethnography. Through this method, ethnographers directly observed and participated in the activities of the two subcultures by attending concerts and events associated with the two scenes and engaging in conversations with subcultural members at various shows. Participant observation has long been documented as an effective means for watching, listening, and gaining knowledge about a particular group and has been utilized to study drug patterns amongst various other nightlife scenes (Perrone 2009; Thornton 1995). When feasible, individuals with whom we were in extended contact were informed about the study, but it was not possible

to extensively discuss this with each person who was observed or spoken to during fieldwork.

On multiple nights each week, we attended clubs, concerts, open mic nights, and other venues housing these subcultural scenes. The focus of our fieldwork at these venues centered on how the broader aspects of the two subcultures influenced the varied patterns of drug use found within them. Specifically, attention toward the culturally situated context in which drug-related rituals and practices were performed was upheld throughout the fieldwork process. Throughout the one year of ethnographic fieldwork, we met regularly to assess and reassess strategies for immersing ourselves within various youth subcultural scenes in New York City.

Additionally, our extensive presence within these scenes allowed for access to key informant interviews with select subcultural scene members. Some of these key informant interviews were recorded, transcribed, coded, and analyzed to add clarification to our experiences out in the field. Others occurred in the field and were reconstructed in fieldnotes and analyzed within the contexts established by these notes. The details gathered through our ethnographic fieldnotes and key informant interviews were crucial in allowing us to recreate our experiences in ways that made locating patterns of behavior, and more importantly deciphering their meanings, possible.

All fieldwork conducted resulted in full documentation in ethnographic fieldnotes. Fieldnotes contained descriptions of observations and informal interviews within the two subcultures. Over the course of the 12 months of fieldwork, the ethnographers spent more than 120 hours immersed within these two subcultures, which produced over 500 pages of single-spaced fieldnotes. Our extended presence within these subcultures enabled thick descriptions of the norms, values, and behaviors adopted by the various subcultural participants.

Analysis

The authors regularly met to review and discuss fieldnotes throughout the course of the 12 months of fieldwork. In this regard, the data acquired during participant observation were analyzed continuously so as to direct and redirect our approach (Strauss and Corbin 1998). After the completion of the data collection, we analyzed the fieldnote data through an iterative process. Fieldnote analyses presented particular patterns of participants' behaviors while key informant interview analysis provided an additional contextual understanding of those experiences. Through this process, we identified the routines and behaviors surrounding marijuana use, including when, where, and how the drug was used in addition to the ritual interactions related to the drug within each respective subculture. All fieldnote data reported in the results highlight key aspects found within these two youth subcultural scenes, not isolated phenomena.

Results

The Jam Band Scene

Participants within the jam band subculture consisted mostly of white males who were motivated to participate in the scene due to their appreciation for live improvisational music, desire to connect with the scene's cultural norms and values, and to form relationships with others who share similar tastes. Participants within the scene all tended to be very friendly with others in attendance, including ethnographers. Most interactions revolved around conversations about previous shows, musical interests, and experiences at various jam band festivals.

Throughout our time attending jam band shows, the ethnography revealed patterns in how scene members presented themselves and interacted with one another. For instance, members of the jam band subculture were seen to regularly exhibit behaviors that value kindness, generosity, sharing, and reciprocity. The subculture's ethos of tolerance and kindness found within the jam band scene translates well with the adoption of communal-type behaviors. Examples of these behaviors can be seen in how scene participants openly and freely share a variety of things with other scene members such

as drinks—be they water or alcohol—cigarettes, lighters, marijuana, and other drugs. These practices also take shape in the form of easy interactions with other scene members, an affinity for sharing preferences for particular bands, retelling tales from previous festivals or shows, or sharing information about upcoming shows with others.

Also articulated within our fieldwork was how accommodating jam band participants were of one another. This became explicitly apparent when considering circumstances of scene members tolerating others bumping into them due to being too intoxicated or due to their desire to dance to the music in cramped spaces. The following fieldnote excerpt details such an occurrence and also illustrates how others within the scene would tolerate such behaviors that might not be acceptable in other nightlife scenes:

The first band played about a 40-minute set. During this time, I watched the guy with the dreadlocks dance around, bumping into all the people around him, myself included, and also hitting people with his dreads as he flailed about. Interestingly enough, this guy bumping into people didn't seem to cause any problems. I assume that getting bothered, upset, or confrontational at the show from something as minor as being bumped into or smacked in the face with a dreadlock would be seen as an overreaction. But I can honestly state that if that were to happen in a bar or club, it would not be so easily excused. I attribute this to the overall relaxed vibe of the scene and frame of mind that respects other people's freedom to express themselves while the music is being played, even if that expression ends up compromising someone else's personal space (MP022610).

The extremely high level of acceptance that jam band participants exhibit toward each other is indicative of how members seek to get along with one another and enjoy the scene's music in a shared sense of solidarity and community.

As previously stated, marijuana is seen as the drug staple of the jam band subculture, and its use within the scene was extraordinarily common. Jam band scene participants smoke mostly joints and sometimes utilize pipes or "bowls" to smoke marijuana. Interestingly, we never observed scene participants smoking blunts at jam band shows. As a result of the jam band subculture's core values of kindness and generosity, ethnographers often received invitations to partake in using the drug with other scene members. The following fieldnotes describe such occurrences:

> As the lights began to dim, the crowd cheered, and a group of three young guys slid on by and took the empty table in front of me. They immediately lit up a joint and began to pass it around. The guy closest to me leaned in and asked if I wanted a hit.
>
> (MP032610)

> As I made my way through the crowd I noticed two young guys standing next to each other smoking pot out of a pipe that looked like a cigarette. I positioned myself next to them and I was amazed to see that one of the guys, a complete and total stranger, said in a low tone, "Hey, here, man, you want a hit?" while gesturing to me in a way that he was reaching out to hand the pipe off to me.
>
> (MP031910)

Such casual offerings by strangers happened frequently during our time immersed within the jam band scene and highlighted scene participants' desire to connect with other participants by openly partaking in the valorized ritual of smoking marijuana. In this context of drug sharing, it would be an egregious breach of etiquette for someone in the scene to smoke a joint all to himself and not pass it to other co-participants. This again is due to the scene's subcultural ethos of generosity and anti-hoarding, which can at times elevate marijuana to the status of being a pseudo communal commodity. An excerpt from a key informant interview highlights this sentiment: "The minute you walk in, it's just like hey what's going on? You want to hit this [joint]? It's just like love, love to the max" (MP111110).

Again, we can see how the subcultural norms of generosity and kindness in the jam band scene are reflected in participants' interactions

with one another and how the smoking of marijuana can act as a way to share in a sense of community with those in attendance.

Another important aspect of the jam band scene was how participants appeared to utilize shows as opportunities to develop new friendships with others who share similar values, attitudes, and tastes. An interesting pattern that emerged was the recognition that sharing marijuana with other scene members was a common "ice breaker" or way to establish a conversation and meet new people at shows:

> I grabbed a beer and approached a table where a girl and guy with big dreads and a blue and red tie-dye Dead shirt sat. I asked if the empty seat was taken and they told me it was free and that I should "have a seat." I sat down and the guy immediately handed me a big glass "bowl." Again, I was shocked at how kind and generous people at this show were to offer a complete and total stranger some of their marijuana. I laughed and gestured to him that I wasn't interested. He nodded signaling that he understood. The girl then leaned in and asked if I was writing about the show.
>
> (MP032610)

The scene above highlights how an ethnographer was welcomed into sitting at a table by two strangers with the generous offer of smoking some of their marijuana. Many situations where ethnographers were able to establish personal ties with scene members began with an initial offering of a joint or a bowl. Even despite the refusal of the ethnographer to partake in smoking the offered marijuana, conversations grew out of these encounters, and relationships were established. This pattern of behaviors not only indicates scene members' tolerance of others who do not consume the scene's most popular psychoactive substance, but it also illustrates how scene members utilize sharing marijuana with strangers as a way to forge new relationships with others in the scene.

Given the central symbolic value of the drug, scene members use it as a form of social currency in the establishment and maintenance of social ties. In this manner, offers of marijuana within the jam band scene can also be made as expressions of esteem or gratitude. Its value as a social currency makes it useful for expressions of appreciation:

> The angry looking usher came storming back up the aisle. She funneled those dancing in the aisle back up toward the rear of the venue. As she approached with another usher in tow, I grabbed two teenagers, Will and Darren, by the backs of their tie-dyed t-shirts and pulled them into the row with me. Wide smiles burst onto their faces as they turned to me realizing that they had been saved from an escort back to their seats in the rear. Will, standing next to me, gave me a pat on the back. Shortly thereafter, Darren turned to me and extended a lit joint in his hand, a gesture of appreciation. "Thanks man, I'm good though," I said declining his offer. Darren smiled and nodded his head heartily as he took a drag from his joint before passing it to Will.
>
> (BK100810)

Such gestures of appreciation are made with marijuana specifically because of its wide use as a social artifact. The social currency the drug holds within the scene, as a key symbolic object, makes it a sincere gesture from those embedded in the subculture.

Overall, the subcultural norms present in the jam band scene encouraged participants to be sociable and generous with one another. These factors made possible an atmosphere where freely sharing marijuana with others in the scene was a frequent occurrence and a common courtesy. Moreover, we experienced scene members sharing the drug as a means to establish a social connection and enable conversation with others in the community. In this regard, marijuana played a key role in forging and maintaining community within the scene.

The Hip-Hop Scene

While the sharing of marijuana was a common way to forge new relationships within the jam band scene, drugs were hardly ever shared in the hip-hop scene. When members of the hip-hop scene shared marijuana, it was only among close friends. Its dissemination was much more tightly contained, and this was influenced by the broader subcultural ethos of the scene and in turn served to reinforce this ethos publicly.

Throughout our time immersed within New York City's hip-hop subculture, we found the use of marijuana to be widespread and normalized. Consumption of the drug was primarily in the form of blunts: cigar shells filled with marijuana. This particular form of smoking marijuana has long been associated with hip-hop music through its frequent reference in lyrics and its ubiquitous presence in photo shoots in hip-hop magazines, music videos, and movies. Moreover, blunts have been identified as being as much of a part of hip-hop culture as graffiti art (Sifaneck et al. 2005). This is mainly because the use of blunts, which are oversize in comparison with joints, corresponds with other hip-hop cultural expressions of "living large" like consuming "forties" (40-ounce bottles of beer or malt liquor) or wearing oversize jewelry commonly referred to as "bling." Interestingly, scene members were never publicly observed smoking marijuana out of bowls or pipes, likely due to the symbolic status accorded to blunts within the scene.

Participants' desires to connect with hip-hop culture led to the display of two distinct subcultural norms that ultimately influenced the ways in which blunts were consumed within the scene. Foremost, displays of hypermasculinity greatly diminished the sociability of participants at hip-hop shows. The norms of hypermasculinity led participants to dismiss sharing behavior as a sign of weakness and encouraged users to consume marijuana in a way that publicly embraced hoarding practices. Also, the culture of conspicuous consumption was identified as having a significant impact on the behavioral patterns of participants as they sought out different ways to conspicuously consume many of the commodified aspects of the hip-hop subculture, of which the consumption of marijuana through smoking blunts was one of the most common and prominently displayed activities.

Within the hip-hop subculture, most members were intent on performing a self that was tough, stoic, and potentially dangerous to others. As a result, there was typically a profound lack of sociability at hip-hop shows as participants rarely spoke with others outside their immediate group. A passage from a key informant interview highlights this phenomenon:

R: It's like you go to hip-hop shows and most cats are like on some like, you know, whatever okay you quiet you stay silent.
I: Why do you think that is?
R: Because, you know what it is, I think that hip-hop presents more of an attitude and there's something there and I think that people bring that with them and there's this tension, this attitude.

This "attitude" and "tension" cultivated through the portrayal of hypermasculine posturing create an atmosphere that discourages many forms of social interaction within the hip-hop scene. As noted above, it was uncommon for men to socialize with other men outside of their inner circle. In such a context, interactions often became problematic and were opportunities for a presentation of self in accordance with the valued traits of hypermasculinity. Mistakenly bumping into somebody, which is rather common at crowded venues, can be met with open hostility and threats of violence. The following excerpt describes how members of the hip-hop community didn't tolerate others infringing upon their personal space while at a show:

> People were being bumped and knocked into, drinks were being spilled, and one guy, who could barely walk straight, got shoved into me by another guy. The crowd of people laughed as he hit the floor and I tried to use this distraction to push my way through the crowd and head towards the door. Unfortunately, this was met with a lot vulgar responses and dirty looks. It felt like a fight was going to break out at any moment.
>
> (MP033110)

This display of violence and verbal insults was a common exhibit of hypermasculinity as subcultural participants demonstrated to others that

they would defend their own personal space from being intruded on by others in the scene. The tense atmosphere engendered by hypermasculinity disables many common forms of interaction present within the jam band scene and limits the acceptable means by which hip-hop's subcultural participants can share in a sense of community with other members.

Although at times there were some brief observable moments of community within the hip-hop scene, the most prominent example being when members of the crowd collectively wave their hands back and forth at the stage or participate in call and response chants, the values of hypermasculinity by and large hamper members' abilities to connect with other members in more personal ways. For instance, unlike subcultural participants' experiences within the jam band scene, hip-hop scene members did not share in public conversations with others about their tastes in hip-hop music or invite others in the scene to share in valued subcultural ritualistic activities like partaking in a round of shots or a blunt session. In other words, meeting new people and forging new friendships and relationships were not valued aspects of scene participation. Within the context of hypermasculinity, being seen as friendly and generous—two characteristics heavily valued within the jam band subculture—has connotations of weakness within the hip-hop subculture. Only sharing marijuana with personal friends is condoned within this symbolic order, unless other activities mitigate the marijuana sharing.

On the few occasions where a blunt was shared between scene members who were not close friends, the interaction was very different from that observed within the jam band scene as the marijuana being smoked was not shared freely. Instead, men worked out barter arrangements on the spot. For instance, a person might ask to be included in a round of blunt-smoking in exchange for contributing other drugs or buying drinks:

> As Teddy and Tall Paul were smoking, this short bearded white guy came up to them and asked if he could hit the blunt. Tall Paul told him that if he bought the birthday boy a shot of Hennessey

that he could take a couple of pulls. The guy agreed and hit the L twice before going off to buy the shot. I was amazed that this guy just paid $10 to take two hits off of a blunt. After a couple of songs, the guy came back with not one, but two shots of Hennessey, one for Teddy and one for Paul. Tall Paul then asked his girlfriend to spark up the blunt clip so that the guy could hit it again.

(MP042011)

This exchange highlights an important fact concerning marijuana consumption in this scene. Freely sharing blunts contradicts the culture of conspicuous consumption as sharing limits the amount each participant consumes. Furthermore, freely sharing within this scene can be perceived as a sign of weakness. This leads scene participants to barter other prized commodities with one another in order to share in a culturally acceptable manner. The overwhelming presence of hypermasculine values and desire to connect with the culture of conspicuous consumption create an atmosphere in which marijuana will only be smoked by those who are in possession of the drug or those who are willing to barter to gain access to a blunt session.

Hypermasculinity also comes into play with the monopolization of substances, rather than sharing. Being seen as one who overindulges and tests one's limits by consuming large quantities of alcohol or marijuana has connotations of showing stamina and success. In this regard, monopolizing marijuana enables the presentation of a masculine self:

Once the blunts were rolled, the one guy immediately sparked his; the guy smoked his blunt the same way he did the last time, smoking most of it for himself and only occasionally passing it to a friend.

(MP042011)

The above scene presents a scenario where an entire blunt of marijuana is used primarily by one person and rarely shared, even with one or two others in connection with that person. The participants' reliance on presenting hypermasculine traits discourages them from sharing the blunt with others and encourages their overindulgence of the drug as they project the willingness and ability to consume most of the blunt by themselves.

Just as displays of hypermasculinity diminished sociability amongst participants and discouraged sharing practices, the culture of conspicuous consumption negatively impacted the sharing of culturally relevant products, such as blunts. Throughout the course of our fieldwork, we found that almost every type of consumption practice possible in the club environment was incorporated into a culture of conspicuous consumption. Binge drinking in the form of taking shots of expensive liquor in highly visible fashion was rampant, which may have been aided by advertisements present in the club containing hip-hop icons who promoted specific brands of alcohol. Furthermore, the purchase of bottle service, which is when an entire bottle of liquor is sold to customers at a considerable markup, encouraged participants to consume entire bottles of liquor. Even space within the club became a commodified product as some scene members paid extra for VIP membership, which provided a form of elevated spatial exclusion and a status distinct from others in the club.

The same pattern of conspicuous consumption extended to the use of marijuana. In no other scene studied was the consumption of marijuana so consistently public and thick with messages intended for onlookers. Unlike the jam band scene, where participants chose to discretely consume the drug and freely share it with fellow scene members in close proximity, participants in the hip-hop scene not only often picked a highly conspicuous way to consume the drug by rolling and smoking blunts, but scene participants at times also chose to smoke an entire blunt to themselves. The following passage where two people decided to roll up two separate blunts instead of sharing one between the two of them is a good illustration of this:

The two guys rolled the pot up and instantly lit them. The two guys then basically smoked the blunts to themselves, occasionally passing them to the girl who helped break up the weed. Watching the group smoke the two blunts I found it interesting that there were all these people standing around this group all eagerly watching with a look of desire on their faces and the two guys chose to ignore that people around them definitely wanted to smoke some of their pot.

(MP042011)

Contrasting subcultural participants' experiences within the jam band scene, the hip-hop scene did not present its members many opportunities to establish connections with others within the scene. By and large, scene members participated in the hip-hop subculture in order to see live hip-hop music and decidedly not to socialize with other scene members. The extent of subcultural participation within the scene was notable only through adherence to the scene's core values of conspicuous consumption and hypermasculinity. This was especially evident through scene members' consumption of blunts as, instead of smoking blunts with others in the scene to establish a bonding ritual, blunts were hoarded and used in excess to flaunt one's stamina, toughness, and masculinity.

Discussion

Studying youth subcultures is important to understand the contexts of some youth behaviors, including drug use. Participation within youth subcultures allows individuals to define themselves by aligning with a meaningful symbolic system that informs ways of dress, types of music to listen to, and appropriate ways to interact with others in the scene (Perrone 2009; Thornton 1995). These symbolic systems also shape drug consumption practices. The ethnography of the jam band and hip-hop subcultures described above revealed drastic differences in the behavioral patterns of marijuana consumption among participants within each scene, despite the fact that they were engaged in the consumption of the same substance. These are notable for considering various aspects of the ways youth cultures, as subcultural systems, influence drug consumption and related social practices.

Social interactions within each of the subcultures were shaped by the normative values embraced by that community. For instance, the values and normative behaviors most characteristic of the jam band scene led to high levels of social interaction amongst participants, including complete strangers, as they sought out ways to gain new friendships and experiences while attending shows. Conversely, members participating within the hip-hop scene proved to be far less sociable as interactions with others within the scene were largely discouraged by various forms of hypermasculine posturing and the more insular network dynamics of that scene. These values were played out through the practices by which these young adults engaged in marijuana consumption. In this regard, the interaction processes related to drug use were highly structured by the broader symbolic system in which these youth operate.

Beyond their derivation from the symbolic system of the subcultural domain, these marijuana consumption routines also serve to maintain that very symbolic order by serving as public reinforcers of those norms and values. The public nature of these practices and their role in the interaction processes within the scene allow participants to publicly enact the underlying tenets of the scene. In this manner, marijuana consumption routines enable the maintenance of the norms and values of that scene within the public domain. While also serving as a vehicle for the accumulation of subcultural capital and status for the individuals who play out these routines (Thornton 1995), these publicly practiced routines enable the reproduction of essential cultural mechanisms of that subculture.

These differences in values and interaction norms have particularly powerful impacts on sociality and the ways in which participants within each subculture consume marijuana. Although marijuana is the drug staple of both the hip-hop and jam band subcultures, we identified differences in consumption patterns by contrasting how the subcultural norms and values espoused within each scene impact the nuances of drug using practices and related interactions. For instance, the normative patterns of interaction and the values present within the jam band scene, such as generosity and kindness, encouraged the sharing of marijuana with others, even complete strangers. Furthermore, as participants within the jam band subculture utilized events to develop new friendships with others in attendance, the practice of sharing marijuana with others was also found to function as a means to initiate interactions with other participants within the subculture. By contrast, the value systems endorsed by the hip-hop subculture led to a significant lack of marijuana being shared among scene participants as socializing outside of one's immediate social circle was limited by the presence of hypermasculine behavioral norms. Sharing the drug with others in the scene also conflicted with scene members' desires to indulge in the conspicuous consumption of the drug.

The work of Howard Becker identified how the values that subcultures place on marijuana provide the context that can inform their participants' consumption patterns and behavior (Becker 1953). These considerations remain salient to this day. The differences in ritualistic activities surrounding marijuana consumption within these two subcultures culminated in creating disparities in the marijuana consumption routines. The highly visible nature of solitary blunt smoking in these nightlife settings led to the potential for overindulgence. Yet, these tendencies within the hip-hop nightlife scene contrast with research on blunt smoking rituals in other settings. Dunlap et al. (2006) observed that blunt smoking rituals and group expectations encouraged moderate rather than excessive consumption practices. This was evident in their observation of how blunt smokers abided to a puff-puff-pass routine and were sanctioned when participants deviated from such a ritual. This notion of moderating the consumption of marijuana contradicts the hip-hop subcultural values of exhibiting hypermasculine traits and engaging in conspicuous consumption in nightlife scenes as members sought to show off their ability to endure consuming large quantities of marijuana as they smoke an entire blunt to themselves. Previous studies on blunt smoking rituals contrast this trend as they indicate that a majority of blunt smokers preferred to smoke

blunts in groups as smoking a blunt alone was seen as being too large a quantity to consume while also being seen as a waste of money (Dunlap et al. 2006).

These drastic differences in blunt smoking rituals may be a function of the context in which this form of marijuana consumption takes place. Put simply, there is more at stake with regard to sending symbolic messages within these nightlife scenes than in their ordinary, everyday routines among friends. Interestingly, the very same reasons provided against smoking a blunt by oneself were, in the cultural context of the hip-hop scene, deemed valued traits. As a result, the scene's cultural normative values encouraged hoarding practices and thus discouraged the sharing of blunts with other scene participants. Symbolically communicating masculinity may be less imperative within one's own neighborhood, where one is known, in comparison to the city's nightlife scene. This highlights the importance of nightlife scenes as a public stage for the performance of subcultural norms and values.

Finally, the interaction rituals observed within the hip-hop and jam band scenes provided unique insight into how these subcultures function as sites of community. Kavanaugh and Anderson (2008) note how collective participation in rituals within the rave scene provides its participants with experiences of solidarity with others within the scene. These experiences frequently extend themselves to drug use and can engender a deep sense of community and spiritual connection with others within the scene (Kavanaugh and Anderson 2008). Similarly, the jam band scene provides its members with a sense of belonging and community that is augmented through marijuana consumption routines. This is evident in participants' inclinations to utilize the subculture as a means to meet and form new relationships with others who share similar values, tastes, and interests. Jam band participants were also very tolerant of other members' behavior as they sought to get along with each other and enjoy the scene's music in a shared sense of solidarity. Scene members' communal behaviors like sharing marijuana with one another function as key rituals in establishing the deep sense of community that is present within the scene.

Meanwhile, the hip-hop scene provides limited opportunities for scene members to encounter these experiences. The lack of sociability engendered by hypermasculine posturing prevents most forms of interaction and socializing with other scene members in attendance. Also, scene members' desire to uphold the cultural dynamic of conspicuous consumption limits the opportunities that drug sharing rituals can offer in establishing members' sense of solidarity and community within the scene. In fact, the lack of a sense of community observed within the hip-hop subculture was seen as a result of how hip-hop clubs function solely as sites of consumption for the individual. Various examples are indicative of this as scene members attended clubs to consume live hip-hop music without socializing with others and consume alcohol and marijuana in large quantities, but instead of using it with others to establish a bonding ritual, it is used to depict to others one's capacity for overconsumption.

Limitation

Although this research presents an ethnographic analysis of the ways in which the marijuana consumption routines are differentially shaped by the norms and values of that subculture and in turn reinforce that subculture's symbolic system, some limitations must be considered. First, the sheer volume of venues that offered opportunities to enjoy hip-hop music led us to narrow our scope to those venues deemed most viable for studying the scene's core. As a result, certain venues were focused on to the exclusion of others in order to gain a greater in-depth presence within the venues that embodied the scene's cultural center. Specifically, we focused primarily on live hip-hop performances. Additionally, within the hip-hop subculture, the ethnographers' Caucasian racial status was at times observed as being a marker of being a subcultural outsider in some venues and could create additional barriers to navigating the community's already difficult social scene. Lastly, the time spent at various venues that showcased jam bands, although fruitful in establishing conversations, relationships, and insights into the scene's subcultural

norms and values, was recognized as lacking particular aspects of the subculture that are only found in the festival scene that takes place in rural areas during the summertime. Despite these limitations, this ethnographic work provides an important comparative framework for the consideration of specific practices across different youth cultures.

Discussion Questions

1. What kind of fieldwork role did the respondents adopt? What kind of data did they collect, and how did they handle note taking?
2. What kind of roles did marijuana play in both subcultures?
3. What challenges to reliability and generalizability are present here?

References

Allen, Ernest. 1996. "Making the Strong Survive: The Contours and Contradictions of Message Rap." Pp. 159–191 in *Droppin Science: Critical Essays on Rap Music and Hip Hop Culture*, edited by William Eric Perkins. Philadelphia: Temple University Press.

Becker, Howard S. 1953. "Becoming a Marihuana User." *American Journal of Sociology* 59:235–242.

Bennett, Andy. 1999. "Subcultures or Neo-Tribes? Rethinking the Relationship between Youth, Style and Musical Taste." *Sociology* 33:599–617.

Best, Steven. 1989. "The Commodification of Reality and the Reality of Commodification: Jean Baudrillard and Post-Modernism." *Current Perspectives in Social Theory* 9:23–51.

Blair, M. Elizabeth. 1993. "Commercialization of the Rap Music Youth Subculture." *The Journal of Popular Culture* 27:21–33.

Chang, Jeff. 2007. *Can't Stop Won't Stop: A History of the Hip-Hop Generation*. New York: Macmillan.

Davis, Fred and Laura Munoz. 1968. "Heads and Freaks: Patterns and Meanings of Drug Use among Hippies." *Journal of Health and Social Behavior* 9:156–164.

Duff, Cameron. 2003. "The Importance of Culture and Context: Rethinking Risk and Risk Management in Young Drug Using Populations." *Health, Risk & Society* 5:285–299.

Dunlap, Eloise, Bruce D. Johnson, Ellen Benoit, and Stephen J. Sifaneck. 2006. "Sessions, Cyphers, and Parties: Settings for Informal Social Controls of Blunt Smoking." *Journal of Ethnicity in Substance Abuse* 4:43–80.

Fricke, Jim and Charlie Ahearn. 2002. *Yes Yes Y'all: The Experience Music Project: Oral History of Hip-hop's First Decade.* Cambridge, MA: Da Capo Press.

Golub, Andrew, Bruce D. Johnson, and Eloise Dunlap. 2006. "The Growth in Marijuana Use among American Youths during the 1990s and the Extent of Blunt Smoking." *Journal of Ethnicity in Substance Abuse* 4:1–21.

Gottdiener, Mark. 2000. *New Forms of Consumption: Consumers, Culture and Commodification.* Lanham, MD: Rowman & Littlefield.

Hathaway, Andrew D. 1997. "Marijuana and Lifestyle: Exploring Tolerable Deviance." *Deviant Behavior* 18:213–232.

Hathaway, Andrew D., Natalie C. Comeau, and Patricia G. Erickson. 2011. "Cannabis Normalization and Stigma: Contemporary Practices of Moral Regulation." *Criminology and Criminal Justice* 11:451–469.

Hebdige, Dick. 1979. *Subculture: The Meaning of Style.* London: Routledge.

Hunt, Pamela M. 2008. "From Festies to Tourrats: Examining the Relationship between Jamband Subculture Involvement and Role Meanings." *Social Psychology Quarterly* 71:356–378.

———. 2010. "Are You Kynd? Conformity and Deviance Within the Jamband Subculture." *Deviant Behavior* 31:521–551.

———. 2012. "Examining the Affective Meanings of Interaction Settings in the Jamband Music Subculture." *The Journal of Public and Professional Sociology* 4:5–25.

Jensen, Sune Qvotrup. 2006. "Rethinking Subcultural Capital." *Young* 14:257–276.

Kavanaugh, Philip R. and Tammy L. Anderson. 2008. "Solidarity and Drug Use in the Electronic Dance Music Scene." *The Sociological Quarterly* 49:181–208.

Kelly, Brian C. 2006. "Bongs and Blunts: Notes from a Suburban Marijuana Subculture." *Journal of Ethnicity in Substance Abuse* 4:81–97.

Millman, Robert B. and Ann Bordwine Beeder. 1994. "The New Psychedelic Culture: LSD, Ecstasy, "Rave" Parties and the Grateful Dead." *Psychiatric Annals* 24:148–150.

Mulder, Juul, Tom Ter Bogt, Quinten Raaijmakers, and Wilma Vollebergh. 2007. "Music Taste Groups and Problem Behavior." *Journal of Youth and Adolescence* 36:313–324.

O'Brien, Patrick K. 2013. "Medical Marijuana and Social Control: Escaping Criminalization and Embracing Medicalization." *Deviant Behavior* 34:423–443.

Parker, Howard, Lisa Williams, and Judith Aldridge. 2002. "The Normalization of 'Sensible' Recreational Drug Use Further Evidence from the North West England Longitudinal Study." *Sociology* 36:941–964.

Perrone, Dina. 2009. *The High Life: Club Kids, Harm and Drug Policy.* Boulder, CO: Lynne Rienner.

Pilkington, Hilary. 2007. "Beyond 'peer pressure': Rethinking Drug Use and 'Youth Culture.'" *International Journal of Drug Policy* 18:213–224.

SAMHSA. 2010. "Results from the 2009 National Survey on Drug Use and Health: Volume I. Summary of National Findings." *NSDUH Series H-38A.* Rockville, MD: Substance Abuse and Mental Health Services Administration Office of Applied Studies.

Sifaneck, Stephen J., Bruce D. Johnson, and Eloise Dunlap. 2006. "Cigars-for-Blunts: Choice of Tobacco Products by Blunt Smokers." *Journal of Ethnicity in Substance Abuse* 4:23–42.

Strauss, Anselm and Juliet Corbin. 1998. *Basics of Qualitative Research. 1998.* Thousand Oaks, CA: Sage.

Thornton, Sarah. 1995. *Club Cultures: Music, Media and Subcultural Capital.* London: Routledge.

Timberlake, David S. 2009. "A Comparison of Drug Use and Dependence between Blunt Smokers and Other Cannabis Users." *Substance Use & Misuse* 44:401–415.

Winders, James A. 1983. "Reggae, Rastafarians and Revolution: Rock Music in the Third World." *The Journal of Popular Culture* 17:61–73.

Zimmerman, Don H. and D. Lawrence Wieder. 1977. "You Can't Help but Get Stoned: Notes on the Social Organization of Marijuana Smoking." *Social Problems* 25:198–207.

▌▌ Less Obtrusive Methods

Chapter 10 described work that involves time spent in the field and some of the most extensive contact between data collectors and participants found in any type of research. This chapter is going to cover research that is just the opposite. The purpose of this chapter is to review a number of unobtrusive, or at least less obtrusive, methods, meaning research that we can conduct with little to no contact with research participants. There are a number of different techniques that we can use, including content analysis, gathering agency records, obtaining another researcher's dataset for secondary data analysis, conducting simulations, crime mapping, or doing systematic or meta-analyses.

Content Analysis

Kassarjian (1977) defined **content analysis** as the "scientific, objective, systematic, quantitative, and generalizable description of communications content" (p. 10). When performing content analysis, we examine communication or some type of social artifact and attempt to analyze its meaning. One of the earliest content analyses was in World War II, when the United States government funded research to analyze the content of enemy propaganda. Since then, content analysis has been used widely in the fields of social science and mass communications (Prasad, 2008). This type of research can help us understand types of communication and how the creators of that work seek to shape narratives. For example, how "true" are "true crime" books? These books might provide accurate depictions of a specific incident, but do the books give readers an understanding of what is typical of crime in the United States? As I mentioned in Chapter 2, researchers studied true crime books, as some members of the lay public use these books and documentaries to formulate their understanding of crime and the criminal justice system. Are these books helpful in educating the public? Durham, Elrod, and Kinkade (1995) conducted a content analysis of true crime books and compared the books' content to national crime statistics. What they discovered is that these books largely describe atypical crimes, victims, and perpetrators. Whereas the typical murder in the United States involves an African American male perpetrator shooting an African American male victim, true crime books almost always described white offenders killing white victims, often with something other than a firearm.

Conducting a content analysis consists of long hours reading publications, viewing advertisements, and watching television shows. You should not think that this research is the same as sitting down and flipping through your favorite websites or magazines, nor is it similar to a relaxing TV marathon with friends. Like the other research methods discussed throughout this book, content analysis follows the rules outlined in the scientific method. Specifically, Prasad (2008) identified three elements of content analysis. The first is objectivity. When doing this type of work, researchers develop and then follow explicit rules for selecting and reviewing materials. This will allow multiple researchers to obtain the same results from the same sets of documents or audio or video messages. Second is the systematic nature of content analysis. Before the start of data collection, we establish a strict set of inclusion and exclusion criteria for the materials eligible for analysis.

The third element is generalizability as the results found here should be applicable to similar types of content. Adherence to these elements will greatly enhance the validity and reliability of the research.

Prasad (2016) identified six steps involved in content analysis. First, as with any study, we need to formulate a research question. Second, we identify a type of content to be the focus of our research. Once we do that, we can see how much content is available. It may be necessary at this point to develop a sampling procedure if there is too much material for us to review. Third, we operationalize our variables and put the definitions in writing to ensure consistency once data collection begins. Fourth is finalization of units of measurement. In this step, we have to get more specific about the type of content we are analyzing. We might have already decided on television commercials in step two, but what, exactly, about those commercials interests us? We might want to be so specific that we are looking for the presence of a specific word, phrase, or symbol, or we can look for themes of commercials. Other options would be looking at specific characteristics of news stories (e.g., where did it appear in the newspaper, what was the size or word count of the article), entire articles (e.g., inclusion of terrorism research papers in criminal justice journals before and after 9/11), characters in stories, or a symbol. Prasad (2008) referred to this specific information as recording units or context units. Other, more common vocabulary for these are **manifest content** and **latent content**. Examples of recording units and manifest content are obvious, clearly measurable items. Manifest analysis "describes what the informants actually say, stays very close to the text, uses the words themselves, and describes the visible and obvious in the text" (Bengtsson, 2016, p. 10). In a manifest analysis, a researcher might view military recruiting commercials and then record the number of commercials that used the word "honor" or the number of commercials that show the American flag. Context units or latent content is more subtle and requires an analysis of the underlying meaning of the content (Bengtsson, 2016). For latent analysis, we might watch those same military recruitment commercials, and, rather than counting the number of times a word is used, we might analyze how the commercials appeal to viewers' sense of patriotism. For the fifth step of content analysis, develop a coding instrument, pilot test it, and if there are multiple coders, check for inter-rater reliability. If reliability is poor, consider making definitions more specific and providing additional training before proceeding with the full sample. The sixth and final step is data analysis. If the primary focus was on manifest content, the analysis will be quantitative while analysis of latent content will be qualitative.

Examples of Content Analysis

Ross and Sneed (2017) searched Google and YouTube for commercials involving inmates, prisons, jails, and corrections officers. They created a list of 11 sets of keywords for their online commercial search and found 33 commercials airing between 1970 and 2015 that could be viewed on the web, were in English, and targeted audiences in the United States. The researchers used coding sheets to measure the length of the commercials, including what was being advertised, demographic characteristics of the actors portraying prison officials and inmates, type of correctional activity that was occurring in the commercial, type of humor depicted, and portrayal of the prison officials and inmates. The researchers found that the commercials portrayed the inmate population as being disproportionately white, which is contrary to the reality of the actual correctional population of the United States. Ross and Sneed suggested possible reasons for this inaccurate portrayal of prisoners, including advertisers targeting whites as potential customers or the marketing firms' desire to be politically correct or race sensitive.

Wood (2017) utilized multiple methods for a study of law enforcement screening standards. In addition to obtaining a dataset from the Bureau of Justice Statistics, Wood conducted a content analysis of the country's ten largest local police departments and several federal law enforcement websites. Through her search, Wood was able to give readers an overview of current hiring require-ments and disqualifying factors for these occupations. Common requirements were polygraph tests, intensive background checks, and psychological evaluations. Less common, but still frequently used, were drug screens. The most frequently listed disqualifying factor was felony convictions, followed by domestic violence convictions, misdemeanor convictions, and histories of DUIs or prior illegal drug use.

Secondary Data Analysis and Official Records

Secondary analysis is the "reanalysis of data that were originally gathered or compiled for other purposes" (Hagan, 2007, p. 254). There are three broad categories of data used for secondary analy-sis, including raw data collected by others, publicly available official/agency reports, and non-public agency records. Raw data are referred to as **primary data sources** while data that have already been analyzed and reported are called **secondary data sources** (Hagan, 2007).

Secondary (Published) Agency Records and Primary (Raw) Data

One of the most frequently used sources of secondary data in criminal justice is the **Inter-university Consortium for Political and Social Research** (ICPSR). ICPSR is a collection of over 750 aca-demic institutions and research organizations and maintains a data archive of over 250,000 files pertaining to social and behavioral sciences. Specifically, ICPSR maintains 21 collections of data, including datasets in criminal justice, terrorism, and substance abuse collected by the Bureau of Justice Assistance, Bureau of Justice Statistics, National Institute of Justice, and National Institute of Drug Abuse, among several other agencies (ICPSR, 2020). You should also keep in mind that there are data offered by agencies outside criminal justice that can still be very relevant to what we study. The US Census Bureau, for example, shares data on births, deaths, marriages, divorces, health information, and demographic characteristics of individuals by location. One of my research interests is suicide, and the Census Bureau offers yearly data on suicides among people living in the community. For suicides in prisons and jails, the Bureau of Justice Statistics publishes yearly figures for deaths in custody. One could construct a dataset to study suicides inside and outside prison and jail just by visiting both agency websites.

Throughout this book, I have discussed several major criminal justice surveys, including the National Crime Victimization Survey, Monitoring the Future, the Arrestee Drug Use Monitoring Program, and the National Youth Survey. All make their data available to people who wish to analyze it or combine their figures with other data sources to make new datasets.

Just about every criminal justice and social service agency collects and maintains primary or raw data as part of their regular duties. In earlier chapters, I noted how the majority of law enforcement agencies in the United States participate in the UCR or NIBRS data collection efforts. Law enforce-ment, courts, and corrections agencies often also produce a number of publicly available reports that are displayed on their webpages. Departments of corrections, for example, typically make available reports about the census of each facility, the racial and age breakdown of the prisoners, security classifications, programming, and sometimes even recidivism rates.

Unpublished Agency Records

While organizations write reports and make some of them available to the public, that information typically represents a very small fraction of what they actually collect each year. Every agency has to collect data for various reasons. Since I used to work for a state department of corrections, I will use corrections as an example. Anyone who has ever watched a prison documentary or movie knows that one vital corrections officer duty is counting inmates. When it is time to count, all other activities stop because the count is fundamental to the security of the institution and the surrounding communities. Officers report each cell block's count to supervisors who add the numbers to confirm that the facility has accounted for all its residents. The counts are then sent to the central office to confirm that everyone in state custody is where they belong. In addition to the counts, staff make daily notes of every admission, release, transfer, trip to the hospital, furlough, and death. The same procedures apply to the halfway houses. Halfway houses and work release staff must account for everyone at the facility, confirm that they arrived at their jobs, and then make sure that they returned to the facility at the end of their shifts. Then there are all the classification forms and risk assessments that are administered. Those data have to be properly input and shared with the department's central office. What I just mentioned is the tip of the proverbial iceberg when it comes to data collection for a state department of corrections. Most of these data are never published or otherwise shared with the general public.

Non-published agency data are only available for research by agency staffers or outside researchers who are able to negotiate access to an agency and its files. If it is possible to get that access, the researcher must then either work with a staff member to retrieve the necessary data or be trained and get the proper access credentials to use the databases independently. A word of warning—you might be surprised at the condition of the files and/or the programs used to store them. Files going back a few decades might be in paper form. The more recent cases will be stored in databases, but some of the government-run systems are quite antiquated and are not at all user friendly.

Maxfield and Babbie (2012) urge caution when using agency records, as they might better serve as measures of the organization's priorities than actual trends in criminal behavior. Let's consider recidivism data on parolees. There are two ways that people on parole return to prison. The first is that they commit a new crime while on parole. The second is that they commit a technical violation, which is an act that is not actually a crime but is a violation of one's parole conditions. Examples of technical violations include violating curfew, hanging out with other people with criminal records, drinking alcohol, or even having alcohol in one's house. If a state reports that fewer parolees are being sent back to prison for technical violations, that can mean one of two things. The first option is that parolees have changed their behavior and are abiding by their parole conditions. The second possibility is that the department has modified their supervision practices or adjusted their definition of what constitutes a violation worthy of reincarceration (Berman & Fox, 2016). When the California government was ordered by the Supreme Court to reduce its prison population in 2011, one target of change was the parole system that sent 70 percent of parolees back to prison within three years of release. California instituted an automated decision-making instrument to guide parole officers in making risk-based decisions (Berman & Fox, 2016). This means that reductions in parole violations leading to incarcerations after the introduction of this new system might have been more a product of changes to parole officers' decision-making than a reflection of actual parolee behavior. Sticking with California, the state has witnessed an overall reduction of recidivism, not only for technical violations but also for rearrests. While this is welcome news, and some of it might be attributable to the impact of more available rehabilitation programs, researchers have suggested that at least some of the decline can be traced to the reclassification of crimes. In 2014, California voters approved Proposition 47, which reclassified a number of nonviolent crimes, previously considered felonies, to misdemeanors. This change means that, even when offenders do commit new crimes, they are less likely to be sent to back to prison for offenses that are now misdemeanors (Bird, Goss, & Nguyen, 2019). In other words, the state's decision to reclassify crimes likely explains at least some of California's reduced number of prisoners, reincarceration rates, and even UCR Index crime statistics. While some of the reductions might be a due to less crime, we also must consider the role that the state's change of priorities and reclassification of offenses had on the states' crime and offending statistics.

What about using official records to measure offender behavior rather than using self-reports? Official records, such as arrest, conviction, incarceration, or juvenile adjudication, are helpful in that they provide exact dates when each part of criminal case processing occurred. With agency records, there is no worry about having to rely on someone's memory to recall age of first arrest or incarceration (Huizinga & Elliott, 1986). It is important to remember, though, that a good amount of offending occurs without the perpetrators being caught, and without an apprehension, there are simply no official records of the incident. Moffitt, Caspi, Rutter, and Silva (2001) studied age of onset of criminal offending and compared research using official records to self-reports. Self-report research generally revealed that the onset of individuals' offending began three to five years prior to age of onset recorded in official records. Not only are official records devoid of information on crimes not known to the police, but Huizinga and Elliott also note that available police data might lack some important details. There are details about offending that are not available through agency records, such as motive, level of planning, and co-offenders.

Examples of Studies Using Secondary Data

Green (2016) used a combination of census and UCR data to test the "Trump hypothesis." This hypothesis is drawn from the speech Donald Trump gave when he announced he was running for president in 2015. In that speech, Trump accused Mexico of sending rapists and other criminals to the United States. Since Trump subsequently labeled other ethnic groups entering the United States as being disproportionately crime prone, Green hypothesized that the presence of immigrant populations would have a positive effect on crime rates in the United States. Green defined the independent variable, immigrant populations, four ways: all immigrants, Mexican nationals, all undocumented immigrants, and all undocumented Mexican nationals. For dependent variables, Green examined various types of violent crime and drug-related arrests. He obtained the population data from the Census Bureau's American Community Survey data from 2012 to 2014 and the crime data from the 2012–2014 Uniform Crime Reports. This type of research, with an examination of crime rates across the nation, is only possible through the use of secondary data sources.

Advantages and Disadvantages of Using Secondary Data

There are several advantages of using secondary data, one of which is convenience. I have a very fond memory of the first time I logged into ICPSR and downloaded a dataset. I wanted to study sentencing, and the Bureau of Justice Statistics had a dataset consisting of hundreds of cases and dozens of variables. Just two years earlier, I had spent a lot of time doing field research, including going into noisy, smelly jails; standing outside in below-freezing temperatures; and staying out on the streets until 2 a.m., all for the sake of collecting data. Because of that, I was particularly excited to sit in my climate-controlled office and download a sizable dataset that required no effort on my part to collect. What made it even more exciting was that, since my university is a member of the ICPSR consortium, the download was free.

An additional advantage is secondary data gives us access to so many possibilities for research, and it often allows us to use data collected by very talented, sophisticated researchers. If the data were collected with individuals as the unit of analysis, the information is always de-identified, so there is no concern about needing to take precautions to protect human subjects. Another important advantage is that secondary data made available for public use has already been cleaned. That means that someone, or multiple people, already went through the dataset and checked for data entry errors. **Cleaning** a dataset is a very time-consuming, mind-numbing task, so being able to do research while skipping that step is a real time-saver.

One significant drawback is that, since the data were collected for another purpose, what is there might not match your research needs. Data might not be at the appropriate unit of analysis. UCR data are collected at the city level, but you might be looking to do research on crime in neighborhoods or even on individual streets. Data on your topic might be available, but not for the location you are wishing to study. Since you played no role in the planning or collection of the data, there may be variables that are necessary for your work that are not included in the available data or datasets. If all the desired variables are available, they may not have been operationalized the way you would have preferred.

Another issue to consider is that, while you had no contact with any of the research participants, that may not be the case for the research team that actually did the data collection. Some of the publicly available datasets are based on observations and surveys, meaning that there might have been contact between the research staff and the participants. That means that participants may have changed their behavior in reaction to being observed or modified their survey responses out of concern for social desirability desire or privacy. In other words, secondary data are not always unobtrusive.

When using existing datasets or agency records, you lack any control over the quality of data collection and handling. Most of the available data are good, but keep in mind that mistakes and manipulation do occur from time to time. Remember the examples that I provided in Chapter 7 of police manipulating UCR statistics to place their jurisdictions in a favorable light. Anyone who consulted UCR reports in the 1990s and then used crime index data from Philadelphia before the data manipulation was exposed used invalid data.

A final disadvantage applies only to unpublished agency records. The data that you obtain from an agency, such as police reports, may not be clean. There may be numerous errors that require you to spend hours, days, or even weeks sifting through to fix. It is not uncommon for researchers to get data from an agency that include dates of prison admission that predate the person's date of birth, misspelled names, and misnumbered prison or jail ID numbers. The latter two are problematic when it is necessary to access databases using inmates' names or identification numbers to collect additional information for the project.

Simulations

Surveys only allow us to ask people what they did in the past or would do in a hypothetical situation, but the responses we receive might not reflect respondents' actual behavior. We can attempt to address that drawback by observing actual behavior through fieldwork. Of course, there are two problems with that. First, the fieldworker's presence may alter the behavior of those being observed. The fieldworker sitting in a car or on a bench nearby might make the potential burglar think twice about breaking into a home at that time and place. One way around this is that we can tail a burglar who is willing to take us on a job, but the moral, legal, and ethical problems with that plan make it an absolute "no." While criminologists struggle with the fact that we want to study lots of illegal behavior that we cannot see in progress, there are also legal activities that happen out of our view. One that immediately comes to mind is jury decision-making. No one besides jury members is allowed in the deliberation room for any reason.

One way to witness the aforementioned behaviors safely is to use **simulations** that mimic situations that we cannot necessarily observe ourselves. Simulations are not new to the social sciences. Two famous studies are the **Obedience to Authority Study** and the Stanford Prison Experiment, although both were criticized for their ethical treatment of participants. For a recap of the Stanford Prison Experiment, see Chapter Three. Following the Nazi atrocities in World War II, Stanley Milgram (1974) designed the Obedience to Authority Study as he was interested the common defense of "I was just following orders" that Nazis used to justify torturing and murdering millions of people. He wanted to see how far people would be willing to go when someone in authority ordered them to harm another person. Of course, Milgram could not physically harm anyone, so he made research participants think that they were administering electric shocks to someone else. The research participant would be a "teacher" who would ask the "learner" to memorize and recite a series of words. If the learner was incorrect or failed to answer, the teacher would administer shocks of increasing intensity. Eventually, the learner would scream, beg for help, and then eventually he would silent, suggesting that he had passed out or even died. The research participants were unaware that the learner was acting and was not actually being harmed in any way. What Milgram did succeed in doing was getting a firsthand view of how far people would go when ordered to harm a stranger. It is unlikely that the findings would have been the same had he attempted to study this through a survey. Milgram was criticized for the psychological distress he caused the research participants, who thought they might be seriously harming another individual, and it would be difficult to persuade a modern-day IRB to allow a complete replication of this project to proceed today.

Modern simulation techniques give us the ability to observe human behavior while taking fewer ethical risks. What if we could re-create Milgram's study but with participants being informed that they will be working with a computerized "person" who would receive the shocks for poor performance? The immediate concern here has to be validity. If people know that they are interacting with a computer, will they react the same way as people who participated in the original Milgram study? Slater and colleagues (2006) sought to measure individuals' reactions when participating in Milgram's study, but with a computer "learner," who would get the shocks? Instead of being a real person, the computerized learner would either communicate with the research participant via text (no sight or sound) or appear on a computer screen in earshot and within view of the research participant. The participants who only had contact with the learner through text did not seem to be as emotionally or physically impacted by stress. They were less likely to withdraw from the study, less likely to report afterward that they were tempted to quit and were less likely to delay providing the shock after receiving an incorrect answer or no response. The researchers also tested skin conductance levels and skin conductance responses of the two groups and found significant differences, suggesting higher levels of stress among those who could see and hear the learner. These results suggest that such simulations can mimic realistic scenarios and have high validity.

There have been studies in which researchers have asked offenders about their decision-making, including how they choose houses or businesses to target and how they actually conduct burglaries and robberies. We, of courses, cannot actually watch them commit crimes. Nee et al. (2015) developed a method to allow for observation in a legal and ethical way. They used a computer program to simulate household burglaries. To test this, they compared a sample of people who have burglarized homes in the past to a few university students with no such criminal history. The program started with the "offender" standing in front of the home. They had to decide how they wanted to enter, and then once inside, they were given just a few minutes to "grab" whatever they wanted. The participants would simulate taking items by clicking on them with the computer mouse. Researchers were able to record the order in which the burglars went to each room and the time spent in each part of the house. Not surprisingly, the former offenders and the university students displayed different burglary tactics, with the people with offending experience spending more time in the rooms with high-value items.

Van Gelder, Otte, and Luciano (2014) argue that virtual reality and other computer simulations hold great promise as they allow for levels of interactivity and immersion that are just not possible with surveys and vignettes. They do caution that there are potential validity issues, in that these simulations are artificial. The extent to which simulations are successful at mimicking real life depends on people's willingness to suspend disbelief and imagine being in the situation that is the subject of the simulation. Based on Slater et al.'s (2006) results mimicking Milgram's study, it does appear that simulations are promising in that they can generate some of the stress and realism similar to simulations previously conducted with humans.

The aforementioned examples certainly include at least a little researcher-participant interaction. In that sense, these are not entirely unobtrusive measures. The interaction here is different, in that there are no ethical concerns about researchers condoning and witnessing burglaries, nor are they putting people in a position to harm (or think they are harming) others.

Crime Mapping

Crime mapping studies may require researchers to venture out into the field, but it may not be necessary for every study. This technique is just as it sounds: we map locations of crimes or other items of interest with the intent of finding patterns. Crime mapping has been around for almost 200 years, with the earliest example involving the use of maps to assess the relationship between residents' education level and crime in France (Hunt, 2019). Of course, we have modernized since then and now use sophisticated software to generate and mark maps. Some modern theories of crime emphasize the importance of target location and offender site selection. The routine activities perspective suggests that crime is likely to occur if there is a convergence of a suitable target, a motivated offender, and a lack of a capable guardian in time and space (Cohen & Felson, 1979). The Brantinghams discussed environmental criminology and argued that people generally travel to and from home, work, and play, and that offenders are likely to find criminal opportunities in those areas or en route to them (Brantingham & Brantingman, 1981).

Crime mapping can help us learn a lot about offending patterns. In the previous chapter, I discussed some fieldwork that I did with a colleague. After obtaining police reports on automobile thefts from the Atlantic City, New Jersey, police department, we visited each site to measure several environmental characteristics with the hope of learning which types of factors were common in areas with multiple thefts (Levy & Tartaro, 2010). Figure 11.1 includes a map from our analysis.

Today, many police departments use tactics that involve consideration of spatial distribution of crime, including problem-oriented policing, hot spots policing, and Compstat (Hunt, 2019).

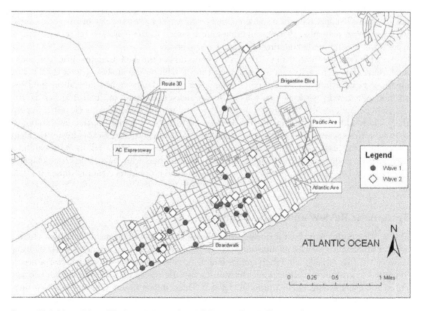

Figure 11.1 Map of Auto Thefts in Atlantic City, NJ, During Two Different Waves of Data Collection

Predictive policing is a relatively new term, but it is a combination of existing police practices, including problem-oriented and intelligence-led policing, along with crime mapping to help police be more proactive in preventing crime. The National Institute of Justice defines **predictive policing** as "taking data from disparate sources, analyzing them and then using results to anticipate, prevent and respond more effectively to future crime" (Pearsall, 2010, p. 16). The goal is to anticipate crime spikes in local areas and then establish prevention plans. For example, Richmond, Virginia, traditionally had a problem with random gunfire on New Year's Eve. In the early 2000s, the police department mapped gunshot incidents from previous years so they could anticipate the time and location of gunfire for the upcoming holiday. By using these data to focus enforcement on New Year's Eve 2003, they helped to reduce random gunfire by 50 percent.

While police were the first branch of the criminal justice system to embrace crime mapping, the judiciary and corrections systems have also adopted mapping to both prevent crimes and better allocate resources. Specifically, corrections departments and probation and parole offices are using mapping to identify violence hot spots inside institutions, direct probationers and parolees to services available near their homes and jobs, and assign officers by geographic location (Karuppannan, 2005).

Crime mapping can be a very powerful tool and help us gain a better understanding of how various blocks and neighborhoods are viewed by potential offenders. Of course, the process of conducting crime mapping is not always smooth, and there are a number of issues that can make the work more difficult and possibly less reliable. The mapping will only be as good as our data. To generate maps, analysts often rely on agency records, such as police calls for service or crime reports. By now, you should be well acquainted with the pitfalls of using police records. To quickly review, crime reports are a better indicator of law enforcement priorities than actual incidents of crime in a particular jurisdiction. Police calls for service data are better in that they involve calls from residents and bystanders and lack the filtering that comes with police discretion at the scene or any other reclassifications of the incident that might occur. Boba (2001) cautioned that policy or law changes can result in what appears to be a sudden uptick or decrease of a certain type of crime. Of course, we must always remember that not all crimes are reported to the police, so reliance on official records will result in undercounting of several types of crime.

An additional potential data problem is the condition of the data. Criminal justice agencies might have data in formats that are not easily transferrable to the analysts (Boba, 2001). As I mentioned earlier in this chapter, some of the government databases are quite antiquated and are not user friendly, so it may be difficult for agencies to capture and then transfer data to researchers. Additionally, the data might be "dirty" and require a good deal of cleaning. Reports that include addresses must have the full addresses, with proper spelling, for that information to be input into software for mapping. If researchers get police reports that lack addresses (as many do) and instead just include landmarks or intersections, the researchers will have to search for each address to input into the mapping software. Researchers who plan to do crime mapping using agency data would be well advised to build in a good bit of "data cleaning" time into their research plans.

Systematic Review and Meta-Analysis

One very frustrating part about reviewing available research is that there might be multiple studies, some of which find a positive relationship between X and Y, some reporting a negative relationship between the two variables, and then studies finding no relationship between X and Y. For people interested in institutional corrections, this was the case for research on the association between prison and jail crowding and institutional violence. The common assumption has been that there is a positive relationship between the two, meaning that increased crowding is associated with increased violence. But with different researchers reporting so many different findings, it was very difficult for corrections administrators and policymakers to make much sense of the existing litera-ture. This is the problem that systematic and meta-analyses are designed to address. Researchers who conduct systematic and meta-analyses seek to learn, overall, what a large body of scholarship tells us about a particular topic. The two approaches differ in the extent of the statistical analysis that they conduct. **Systematic reviews** involve collection and summarization of empirical evidence that meets pre-specified inclusion criteria, whereas a **meta-analysis** includes the work of a systematic review but applies statistical techniques to summarize the research findings (Centre for Cognitive Ageing and Cognitive Epidemiology, n.d.). Systematic reviews differ from literature reviews or reviews of research that you have probably already conducted for papers in other classes. What sets systematic reviews apart is the rigor and systematic approach to searching for and review-ing existing literature (Joanna Briggs Institute, 2001).

If done properly, systematic reviews, and especially meta-analyses, can be very helpful in advancing our knowledge of criminal justice. Figure 11.2 is a hierarchy of evidence pyramid that helps us understand how research designs are generally ranked. As you can see, systematic reviews and meta-analyses are at the top of the pyramid. These types of analysis are currently being used to educate researchers, practitioners, and policymakers on what works and what does not in criminal justice.

There are several steps involved in systematic reviews and meta-analyses. As with all studies, the first step is to identify a research question. Second, researchers must decide on their inclusion and exclusion criteria that they will use to select studies for analysis. One criteria decision that needs to be made has to do with quality of the research design. As we have learned already, not all designs are created equal. A possible useful tool to consider during this step is the **Maryland Sci-entific Methods Scale** (SMS), which is a 5-point scale, introduced by Farrington, Gottfredson,

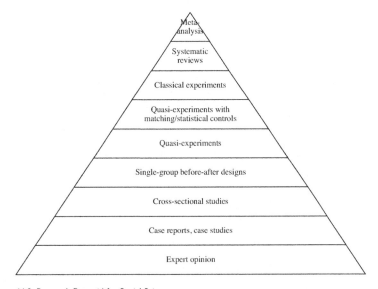

Figure 11.2 Research Pyramid for Social Sciences

Sherman, and Welsh (2002), that measures the quality of research methodologies. Level 1 includes cross-sectional designs that might establish a correlation between a crime prevention program and crime reduction. It, however, fails to address the question of time order between X and Y and rule out many possible threats to internal validity. Level 2 includes studies that do establish time order between X and Y by measuring crime before and after the introduction of some sort of intervention. One-group before-after designs fall into this category, but they still leave open the possibility of several threats to internal validity. Level 3 studies are considered by many researchers, including the developers of the SMS, to be the minimum level that is adequate for drawing conclusions. These are studies that include both a before-after design and an experimental and comparison group. In other words, they are quasi-experiments. Since there is no random selection into the two groups, there is still the possibility of some threats to validity, such as regression to the mean and selection effects. Level 4 studies include quasi-experiments that also control for factors that could influence variation in the dependent variable. Finally, level 5 studies are classical experiments with a sufficiently large sample size of participants randomly assigned to experimental and control groups. As an example of how this can work, Bahr, Masters, and Taylor (2012) did a systematic review of substance abuse treatment programs offered in the custodial setting. They restricted inclusion of studies to only those classified as 3, 4, or 5 on the SMS scale. Other considerations for inclusion/exclusion might be unit of analysis, type of statistical analysis, definitions of independent and dependent variables, setting (prison, jail, offenders under community supervision, etc.), and publication year.

The third step in in this type of research is to conduct an exhaustive literature search and to document all the steps taken in that search. Before you start, you should decide on a series of keywords and databases that you will use. Once you start the search and identify some studies for potential inclusion, you might also want to review the bibliographies of those studies to find more research for consideration. Fourth, once you have gathered an initial sample of studies, the next step is to do a preliminary review and read the abstracts of each article. Just reading the title and abstract will allow you to quickly disqualify a substantial number of articles. Fifth, once the sample size is smaller, now is the time to read all the studies carefully, coding the data that you will need for your analysis and inputting that into a spreadsheet or statistical software package. Sixth, you are ready to do whatever type of analysis you plan to do. If it is a systematic review, the analysis might simply be tallying results of studies.

Madson, Villarosa-Hurlcoker, Schumacher, Williams, and Gauthier (2019) conducted a systematic review of motivational interview training for substance abuse treatment professionals. They provided readers with summaries of the research, including the percentage of studies that were randomized control trials, the components of the treatment programs, and the percentages of each study that included various components (e.g., description of training methods, coaching, and evaluation of motivational interviewing skills of participants).

I previously discussed correctional crowding research and mentioned confusion about the role crowding plays in contributing to correctional violence. Franklin, Franklin, and Pratt (2006) did a meta-analysis to find out, overall, what the research revealed about this topic. After searching three databases and the bibliographies of articles that they found, the authors identified 16 studies that met their inclusion criteria. To be eligible for inclusion, studies had to be (1) quantitative with an empirical evaluation of the relationship between crowding and some type of inmate misconduct, (2) the unit of analysis had to be the institution, (3) crowding had to be measured objectively (number of inmates compared to the facility's design capacity) rather than based on inmates' perceptions, (4) the studies had to be published in a peer-reviewed journal, and (5) each needed to have published adequate statistical analysis for the researchers to derive the necessary data. Their findings were very interesting: crowding does not appear to have a substantial impact on inmate misconduct. Instead, it is the concentration of young inmates in correctional facilities that appears to be a significant predictor of inmate behavioral problems. The findings were contrary to what many believed to be true about crowding and violence.

Of course, systematic reviews and meta-analyses are only as good as the studies that they include. The extent to which studies are screened for methodological rigor is important as it could impact the validity and reliability of the results. A potential weakness of meta-analyses could result from overreliance on published studies. It should be of no surprise that published studies are the easiest to find. The problem is that there is the potential for publication bias. **Publication bias** is the tendency for studies finding support for the research hypothesis, or positive findings, to have a greater chance of being accepted for publication than studies finding no support (Joanna Briggs Institute, 2001).

Mitchell, Wilson, and MacKenzie (2012), for example, found that published studies of incarceration-based drug treatment programs included evaluations of programs that were more effective than those appearing in unpublished studies. Researchers should be aware of the potential for publication bias and try to include unpublished studies in their analysis. One way to find such work is to contact the authors who frequently publish on the topic of interest to ask for their assistance in identifying unpublished studies (Braga, Welsh, & Schnell, 2015). Another technique is to search grey literature databases (Wong, Bouchard, Lee, & Gushue, 2019). **Grey literature** consists of work that has not been formally published in sources such as books or journals. Some university libraries maintain grey literature databases. The Rutgers University Don Gottfredson Library of Criminal Justice is one of them. Their grey literature database includes working papers, conference proceedings, technical reports, online dissertations, and government and agency reports (Rutgers University, n.d.). There are also statistical techniques that researchers can use to determine whether publication bias is impacting their results (Pirelli, Gottdiener, & Zapf, 2011).

Summary

In this chapter, I introduced several unobtrusive, or at least less obtrusive, measures that we can use to study crime. Content analysis gives us an opportunity to study how crime is portrayed in various types of media content, such as "true crime" documentaries, fictionalized crime shows, and newspapers. There is no human interaction necessary as steps involved in this research are to set up rules for a systematic identification of sources; collect data through reading, listening, or watching; and then evaluate the material through a pre-identified analysis plan. Secondary data analysis saves the researcher from collecting his or her own data. Instead, researchers obtain datasets created by others, use publicly available figures from government or private agencies, or access non-public agency records. Secondary analysis gives individual researchers access to data that they might not otherwise have the time or money to collect themselves. While datasets available for download from groups such as ICPSR are generally the product of high-quality work and are already cleaned, agency records might not be as user friendly and might contain errors and, in rare instances, outright manipulation.

There are some activities that are difficult for us to observe due to their infrequency, the private nature of the actions, or ethical limitations of what researchers are permitted to do and witness. Simulations give us a way to make observations by creating scenarios in a safe laboratory setting. Researchers can simulate household burglaries, potentially fight-inducing scenarios in bars and restaurants, and jury deliberations. Validity is a potential problem if participants lack full engagement and do not buy into the scenario.

Crime mapping has been a recognized tool for studying crime, public health problems, environmental disasters, and many other problems for over a century. Police were the first branch of the criminal justice system to appreciate and utilize mapping to investigate crime patterns and apprehend offenders, but mapping is now being used in all branches of the system to track offenders and allocate resources.

Systematic reviews and meta-analyses are helping us learn about what works in criminal justice. These studies help us sift through the large bodies of research currently available and inform us about the trends in research on that topic. An important aspect of this research is that it takes into consideration the methodological rigor of each of the individual studies included in their reviews.

Keywords

Content analysis	Publication bias	Latent content
Secondary data analysis	Manifest content	Secondary data sources
Inter-university Consortium	Primary data sources	Simulation
for Political and Social	Cleaning	Predictive policing
Research (ICPSR)	Crime mapping	Maryland Scientific Methods
Obedience to Authority Study	Meta-analysis	Scale (SMS)
Systematic review	Grey literature	

Discussion Questions

1. What are the advantages and disadvantages of conducting secondary data analysis?
2. What are the similarities and differences between systematic reviews and meta-analysis?
3. Why are simulations susceptible to threats to validity?

References

Bahr, S. J., Masters, A. L., & Taylor, B. M. (2012). What works in substance abuse treatment programs for offenders? *The Prison Journal, 92*(2), 155–174.

Bengtsson, M. (2016). How to plan and perform a qualitative study using content analysis. *NursingPlus Open, 2*, 8–14.

Berman, G., & Fox, A. (2016). *Trial and error in criminal justice reform: Learning from failure* (revised ed.). Washington, DC: The Urban Institute Press.

Bird, M., Goss, J., & Nguyen, V. (2019). *Recidivism of felony offenders in California.* Sacramento, CA: Public Policy Institute of California.

Boba, R. (2001). *Introductory guide to crime analysis and mapping.* Washington, DC: Office of Community Oriented Policing Services.

Braga, A. A., Welsh, B. C., & Schnell, C. (2015). Can policing disorder reduce crime? A systematic review and meta-analysis. *Journal of Research in Crime and Delinquency, 52*(4), 567–588. https://doi.org/10.1177/0022427815576576

Brantingham, P. J., & Brantingham, P. L. (1981). *Environmental criminology.* Beverly Hills, CA: Sage Publications.

Centre for Cognitive Ageing and Cognitive Epidemiology. (n.d.). *Systematic reviews and meta- analyses: A guide.* Edinburgh, UK: University of Edinburgh Centre for Cognitive Ageing and Cognitive Epidemiology.

Cohen, L. E., & Felson, M. (1979). Social change and crime rate trends: A routine activity approach. *American Sociological Review, 44*(4), 588–608. https://doi.org/10.2307/2094589

Durham, A. M., Elrod, H. P., & Kinkade, P. T. (1995). Images of crime and justice: Murder and the "true crime" genre. *Journal of Criminal Justice, 23*(2), 143–152.

Farrington, D. P., Gottfredson, D. C., Sherman, L. W., & Welsh, B. C. (2002). The Maryland Scientific Methods Scale. In L. W. Sherman, D. P. Farrington, B. C. Welsh & D. L. MacKenzie (Eds.), *Evidence-based crime prevention* (pp. 13–22). New York, NY: Routledge.

Franklin, T. W., Franklin, C. A., & Pratt, T. C. (2006). Examining the empirical relationship between prison crowding and inmate misconduct: A meta-analysis of conflicting research results. *Journal of Criminal Justice, 34*(4), 401–412. https://doi.org/10.1016/j.jcrimjus.2006.05.006

Green, D. (2016). The Trump Hypothesis: Testing immigrant populations as a determinant of violent and drug-related crime in the United States. *Social Science Quarterly.* https://doi.org/10.1111/ssqu/12300

Hagan, F. (2007). *Essentials of research methods in criminal justice and criminology* (2nd ed.). Boston, MA: Pearson.

Huizinga, D., & Elliott, D. S. (1986). Reassessing the reliability and validity of self-report delinquency measures. *Journal of Quantitative Criminology*, 2(4), 293–327.

Hunt, J. (2019). *From crime mapping to crime forecasting: The evaluation of place-based policing*. Washington, DC: National Institute of Justice.

Inter-university Consortium for Political and Social Research. (2020). *About ICPSR*. Ann Arbor, MI: Regents of the University of Michigan.

Joanna Briggs Institute for Evidence Based Nursing and Midwifery. (2001). *Changing practice: Evidence based practice information sheets for health professionals* (Supplement 1). South Australia: Joanna Briggs Institute.

Karuppannan, J. (2005). Mapping and corrections management of offenders with geographic information systems. *Corrections Compendium*, 30(1), 1–10.

Kassarjian, H. H. (1977). Content analysis in consumer research. *Journal of Consumer Research*, 4, 8–17.

Levy, M. P., & Tartaro, C. (2010). Repeat victimization: A study of auto theft in Atlantic City using the W.A.L.L.S. variables to measure environmental indicators. *Criminal Justice Policy Review*, 21(3), 296–318. https://doi.org/10.1177/0887403409350190

Madson, M. B., Villarosa-Hurlcoker, M. C., Schumacher, J. A., Williams, D. C., & Gauthier, J. M. (2019). Motivational interviewing training of substance use treatment professionals: A systematic review. *Substance Abuse*, 40(1), 43–51. https://doi.org/10.1080/08897077.2018.1475319

Maxfield, M. G., & Babbie, E. (2012). *Basics of research methods for criminal justice and criminology* (3rd ed.). Belmont, CA: Thomson Wadsworth.

Milgram, S. (1974). *Obedience to authority: An experimental view*. New York, NY: Harper.

Mitchell, O., Wilson, D. B., & MacKenzie, D. L. (2012). The effectiveness of incarceration-based drug treatment on criminal behavior: A systematic review. *Campbell Systematic Reviews*, 18. https://doi.org/10.4073/csr.2012.18

Moffitt, T., Caspi, A., Rutter, M., & Silva, P. A. (2001). *Sex differences in antisocial behavior*. Cambridge, UK: Cambridge University Press.

Nee, C., White, M., Woolford, K., Pascu, T., Barker, L., & Wainwright, L. (2015). New methods for examining expertise in burglars in natural and simulated environments: Preliminary findings. *Psychology, Crime, & Law*, 21(5), 507–513.

Pearsall, B. (2010). Predictive policing: The future of law enforcement? *NIJ Journal*, 266, 16–19.

Pirelli, G., Gottdiener, W. H., & Zapf (2011). A meta-analytic review of competency to stand trial research. *Psychology, Public Policy, and Law*, 17(1), 1–53.

Prasad, B. D. (2008). Content analysis: A method in social science research. In D. K. Lal Das & V. Bhaskaran (Eds.), *Research methods for social work* (pp. 173–193). New Delhi, India: Rawat Publications.

Ross, J. I., & Sneed, V. (2017). How American-based televised commercials portray convicts, correctional officials, carceral institutions, and the prison experience. *Corrections: Policy, Practice, and Research*, 3(2), 72–91. https://doi.org/10.1080/23774657.2017.1318318

Rutgers University. (n.d.). *Criminal justice library*. Newark, NJ: Rutgers University. http://library.law.rutgers.edu/criminal-justice-library

Slater, M., Antley, A., Davison, A., Swapp, D., Guger, C., Barker, C., Pistrang, N., & Sanchez-Vive, M. V. (2006). A virtual reprise of the Stanley Milgram obedience experiments. *PLoS One*, 8(1), e52–66. https://doi.org/10.1371/journal.pone.0052766

Van Gelder, J., Otte, M., & Luciano, E. C. (2014). Using virtual reality in criminological research. *Crime Science*, 3, 10–22. https://doi.org/10.1186/s40163-014-0010-5

Wong, J. S., Bouchard, J., Lee, C., & Gushue, K. (2019). Examining the effects of day reporting centers on recidivism: A meta-analysis. *Journal of Offender Rehabilitation*, 58(3), 240–260.

Wood, M. (2017). Making and breaking careers: Reviewing law enforcement hiring requirements and disqualifiers. *Journal of Criminal Justice Education*, 28(4), 580–597. https://doi.org/10.1080/10511253.2017.1283429

Reading 11.1   "I Hate These Little Turds!"

In the first two chapters of this book, I discussed the challenge of getting people to understand the value of research. I also noted that laypeople sometimes consider themselves more knowledgeable than the experts in our field. This article is a good illustration of ignoring research because a program seems to be a common sense approach to crime prevention. *Scared Straight* has made for decades of entertaining television. It appeals both to people who want to see juveniles humiliated and to those who are truly optimistic that the experience will lead to meaningful change. *Scared Straight* originated in a New Jersey prison in the late 1970s, but we have had evaluation results as early as 1982 to show us that the program is ineffective and possibly harmful. That did not stop the show's creators or its fans from continuing to champion what is widely considered among criminal justice experts to be a failed program. Maahs and Pratt (2017) conducted a content analysis to learn the reasons members of the public either like or dislike *Scared Straight*.

"I Hate These Little Turds!": Science, Entertainment, and the Enduring Popularity of *Scared Straight* Programs

Jeff Maahs and Travis C. Pratt

Americans have an uneasy relationship with scientific methods and scientific findings (Gauchat 2008, 2011). They generally think highly of science when it comes to how new discoveries and technologies might make their lives better (National Science Foundation 2014). The problem, however, is that the public is much less enthusiastic and literate when it comes to basic scientific knowledge. For example, one out of every four citizens is unaware that Earth orbits the sun (Poladian 2014), three in ten think that sound travels faster than light (NSF 2014), and one in five do not know what kind of radiation sunscreen is supposed to protect them from (Pew Research Center 2013).

These figures could be dismissed as humorous were it not for the negative social consequences that stem from the public's lack of scientific knowledge. Measles outbreaks occur when parents fail to immunize their children because they mistakenly think it will cause autism (Axelrod 2015); public school curricula get changed when a critical mass of citizens cling to the idea that Earth is 6,000 years old (Beckwith 2003; Sarfati 1999); and environmental legislation gets blocked when people become skeptical of global warming because

snow still happens (Smith and Leiserowitz 2012).

Crime control policy is no different. And while there is no shortage of examples of a mismatch between the public's knowledge and the scientific consensus, and of media portrayals that depart from scientific reality (Fennell and Boyd 2014; Griffin et al. 2013), one that is particularly illustrative is *Scared Straight* programs. The original *Scared Straight* documentary was based on Juvenile Awareness Project Help (JAPH), a program developed in New Jersey's Rahway prison in 1975 as an intervention for high-risk delinquent youth (Finckenauer 1982). The idea was to take a group of delinquents—most of whom would be drawn from communities plagued by structural disadvantage—into prison for a day to have a bunch of adult inmates yell at them and tell them in graphic detail all of the horrific things that await them should they ever be sentenced there (Feinstein 2005; Sellers 2015). Then, based on an almost religious faith in the deterrent power of threats, the kids could be put back on a bus to go home, cured of their deviant proclivities.

This turned out to be a seductive idea for policymakers because it presented a simple view of the cause of criminal and delinquent behavior (Cullen et al. 2002; Pratt, Gau, and Franklin 2011)—one that the public seemed to have already bought in to. Thus, no longer would policymakers be on the hook to address the criminogenic effects of complex problems like structural inequality or weakened social institutions in urban environments. Crime and delinquency could instead be eradicated by dropping kids off at prison for a day of being browbeaten by inmates serving life sentences (see Cavender 1981; May, Osmond, and Billick 2014). Problem solved. Of course, it helped that this simplistic view of criminal and delinquent behavior resonated well with the generation of citizens who would later support slogans like "just say no to drugs" and "I know what causes crime: Criminals! Criminals! Criminals!"

It should come as no surprise, then, that these programs spread quickly (Finckenauer et al. 1999; see also Heeren and Shichor 1984). Driven in part by the popularity of the 1978 *Scared Straight* film (starring TV's Columbo, Peter Falk, no less), by the end of 1979 alone, more than 13,000 juvenile offenders had participated in the program at Rahway (Lundman 2001). Over the years, similar programs have popped up all over the United States and around the world (Hutchinson and Richards 2013). There was even a *Scared Straight* redux that was shown on MTV in 1999, which contained the same script of inmate taunts of sexual violation and demands that the kids take off their shoes and throw them into a big pile in the middle of the room (along with the same looks of confusion on the youths' faces as to what lesson this was supposed to convey). At the same time, the original *Scared Straight*, now with a 20-year follow-up of the kids and convicts, was rebroadcast on UPN. *Lethal Weapon*'s Detective Murtaugh (Danny Glover) took over the narration reins from Colombo.

While all of this was going on, scholars were working hard to evaluate the effect of *Scared Straight* programs on juvenile offending. In the process, a lengthy roster of studies emerged that showed pretty similar results: the effects of *Scared Straight* programs on recidivism were either null or negative (i.e., they made things worse for youth) (see Petrosino, Turpin-Petrosino, and Buehler 2003; Welsh and Rocque 2014 for reviews and meta-analysis). Yet none of these results did much to curb *Scared Straight's* popularity or to educate people about what is, and is not, scientific research. Indeed, the Arts and Entertainment (A&E) Network's most highly rated weekly series is the latest flare-up of the *Scared Straight* franchise: *Beyond Scared Straight* (2011). The show's producer, Arnold Shapiro, who was also responsible for the original *Scared Straight* documentary, actually claims that his show *is* science. In dismissing the large body of empirical evidence demonstrating the ineffectiveness of *Scared Straight* programs as "irrelevant," he stated that "The only accurate studies that are actually being done on 21st-century programs are mine—are my shows." Shapiro boldly proclaims that "academic studies don't work," while characterizing *Scared Straight: 20 Years Later* as "the longest study ever done" (Denhart 2011).

And therein lies the problem. The line separating scientific reality (the empirical research demonstrating that *Scared Straight* does not work) from "reality" television (and the wishful thinking of those who *really* want it to work) has been blurred. This happens because when people watch *Scared Straight*, the idea that it can be an effective tool for crime control seems plausible given the veneer of legitimacy provided to it by how it is portrayed on television. Indeed, the format of the program (pre-interview, intervention, follow-up interview) roughly mimics a scientific study. Of course, critical differences make this show decidedly non-scientific. There is no comparison group, recidivism data is collected on camera, and footage is heavily edited. Nowhere is this more apparent than in the 20-year follow-up interviews of the original *Scared Straight* youth.

In the interviews, there is no explicit definition for what counts as success. In fact, many of the adults considered "straight" readily admit on camera to committing crime after the *Scared Straight* intervention. Presumably, they are classified as law abiding because they eventually desisted from crime. With no comparison group, however, there is no scientific way to know whether desistence resulted from *Scared Straight* or from extraneous factors. Indeed, scientifically verified (see, e.g., Laub and Sampson 2003; Sampson and Laub 1993) influences on desistence—military service, marriage, and employment—are featured prominently in the interviews. Ironically, though, such factors are portrayed as the result of a successful *Scared Straight* intervention. Thus, with soft music playing and video footage of their children playing basketball and cheerleading in the background, the now "law-abiding adults" proclaim (some after a bit of prompting from the producer) that *Scared Straight* changed their lives.

That *Scared Straight* was given new life on A&E illustrates how stubbornly persistent "correctional quackery" can be—particularly when it is endowed with the entertainment value provided by the spectacle of punishment (Latessa, Cullen, and Gendreau 2002). Accordingly, in an effort to understand why entertainment seems to trump science in this context, in the present study we conduct a qualitative analysis of the user comments from Netflix regarding A&E's *Beyond Scared Straight* program. Our analysis of 141 user comments is intended to provide some insight into public opinion and knowledge about *Scared Straight* programs and their consequences. Qualitative approaches like this, which were once a staple in criminological research (Shaw 1930; Short and Strodtbeck 1965), are experiencing a resurgence in contemporary criminology (Copes, Hochstetler, and Forsyth 2013; Lindegaard, Miller, and Reynald, 2013; Miller, 2008). Qualitative methods are particularly useful when studying complex phenomena that cannot be easily captured by a limited set of survey items from large, publicly available datasets (Copes 2014). This approach allows us to begin with the assumption that public attitudes toward punishment are complex (see, e.g., Applegate et al. 2000; Sundt et al. 2015), and to explore—rather than stifle or otherwise mask—that complexity.

In particular, given that *Scared Straight* programs seem to be both loved and loathed (depending on who you are talking to), our analysis is focused on one primary question:

What are the reasons behind users' positive or negative assessments of *Beyond Scared Straight*? To foreshadow our results a bit, it is important to note that the title of our article is not intended to be gratuitous. It is instead an actual Netflix user comment that captures perfectly a key sentiment found in the data: many viewers simply see these kids as snotty little jerks and find it to be good fun to watch them get their comeuppance. And in the joy of watching it all happen, thoughts about whether or not getting verbally abused by inmates to the point of crying will actually help these children are often pushed aside. Our broader purpose, then, is to shed light on whether and how the public blurs the lines between information and entertainment when it comes to intervening in the lives of some of our most vulnerable youth.

Methods

The data for this study were obtained from all available Netflix "member reviews" of the *Beyond Scared Straight* series. Netflix originated in the late 1990s as an alternative to traditional video stores. Consumers could find movies on the Netflix website and have the DVD delivered via mail. Over the past decade, Netflix has become the industry leader in providing on-demand internet streaming media to viewers in North America (Kerr 2013). Part of the appeal of Netflix is undoubtedly their system of extensive, personalized video recommendations. As opposed to browsing "staff's picks" at a local video store, consumers are offered movie recommendations based on their particular tastes. Much like an online dating service, Netflix uses a complex algorithm to match consumers with specific media. For this system to work, a subscriber must rate movies or other media programs on a scale of one ("hated it") to five ("loved it") stars.

In addition to rating through the star system, many subscribers provide anonymous narrative reviews. Netflix requires that each review be at least 80 characters long. This serves to limit trivial or uninformative reviews. Although Netflix does moderate reviews and reserves the right to delete certain submissions (e.g., those with foul language or criticisms of Netflix service), the company does not examine the content of member-submitted reviews on a regular basis, which means that the content of the comments we examine here are less likely to have been subjected to heavy filtering or editing (Netflix Help Center 2015).

Netflix has provided on-demand streaming access to the *Beyond Scared Straight* series (the particular seasons available have changed) for the past several years. Currently, for example, subscribers can stream seasons four and five. As of February 2015, over 230,000 Netflix members have rated *Beyond Scared Straight*. The subscriber ratings are largely positive, with an average of four out of five stars. On the Netflix scale, four stars means "really liked it." Additionally, there are 141 narrative reviews. As this information is available to any Netflix member or visitor, we were able to retrieve the narrative reviews, the number of stars given by each reviewer, and the number of other members who found the review "helpful." These narrative reviews constitute the data for our analysis. While this approach is somewhat novel, it is not without precedent. Indeed, social scientists have recently used internet-submitted comments or reviews to understand the intersection of media and perceptions generally (Ballantine, Lin, and Veer 2015; Collins and Nerlich 2015; Ksiazek, Peer, and Lessard 2014), and specifically the crime-media nexus (Gosselt, Van Hoof, Gent, and Fox 2015).

We recognize, of course, that we cannot treat this sample of responses as though they would be representative of the opinions shared by the broader American public. This problem of representation is likely compounded by the fact that those who actually take the time and effort to provide written comments likely feel more strongly about the subject, in one way or another, relative to the viewers who did not feel the need to provide such comments. Yet in qualitative research, the representativeness of the sample is typically forfeited in favor of the richness of the qualitative data—richness that may be enhanced when responses tap into emotional content (Creswell 2013). Thus, our purpose is to use this qualitative data to uncover

the complexity in what drives people's opinions of *Scared Straight* in ways that, for example, a large-scale survey with limited items cannot (see, e.g., Cullen, Fisher, and Applegate 2000).

To do so, we employ a form of narrative analysis to uncover patterns in Netflix reviewers' online comments (Holt 2010; Sandberg, Tutenges, and Copes 2015). Both authors examined and analyzed the narrative reviews and independently coded them as positive or negative. Positive reviews recommended the show to others and/or otherwise described the program using positive (e.g., "great show") language, whereas negative reviews used terms such as "horrible program." Reviews that were mixed or ambiguous ("it was OK") were coded as such. A mixed review, for example, might portray the show as emotionally appealing but also caution that the *Scared Straight*-type programs are ineffective. As noted earlier, the reviewers also indicated their level of support using a star system. Table 1 illustrates support levels using both of these dimensions. Classification based on the tone of the review closely corresponded with the number of stars given. Positive reviews (mean = 4.7 stars), for example, generated more stars than ambiguous (3.0) or negative (1.2) reviews. After systematically identifying the tone of the review, researchers relied on thematic content analyses to identify salient themes within the narrative reviews (Loftland and Loftland 1995).

Table 1 Frequency Distributions Indicating the Tone of the Review

Nature of Review	n	%
Coded tone of review		
Negative	37	26
Positive	96	68
Mixed/Ambiguous	8	6
Number of stars (Netflix label)		
One (hated it)	27	20
Two (didn't like it)	10	7
Three (liked it)	12	9
Four (really liked it)	11	8
Five (loved it)	78	57

Results

Although the member-submitted reviews were more positive (68%) than either negative (26%) or ambiguous (6%), there was substantial variation in their tone. Several themes emerged that appear to explain this variability. These themes include the extent to which the reviewer: (1) indicated that *Scared Straight*-type programs reduced crime, (2) commented on the brutality exhibited in the show, (3) portrayed the program as inspirational or emotional, and (4) described the show as either "real" or "scripted." Although we explore these themes individually, it is clear that they are often interrelated in that they are not mutually exclusive. Reviewers could, for example, comment in either positive or negative ways for several of the reasons we specify here (i.e., they could express positive sentiments about the program's emotional content while at the same time praising the program's effectiveness in reducing recidivism).

Program Effectiveness

As noted above, the scientific literature on *Scared Straight*-type programs is unambiguous. Randomized experiments consistently show that at best, these programs have no effect on juveniles' criminal behavior. Some of these experiments, including the Rahway prison program that was the subject of the original 1978 documentary, yield slight to moderate criminogenic effects (Petrosino et al., 2003). When *Beyond Scared Straight* emerged in 2011, representatives of the Office of Justice Programs and the Office of Juvenile Justice and Delinquency Prevention authored an op-ed for the *Baltimore Sun* that denounced the programs as ineffective and potentially harmful (Robinson and Slowikowski 2011). In contrast, and consistent with past *Scared Straight* films, many of the youth filmed for the television series are portrayed as repentant/changed in the "follow-up" segment of the show.

The vast majority of positive reviewers clearly believed that *Scared Straight*-type programs reduced crime. Often, such reviews made specific reference to the post-intervention television interview of the juvenile:

> the concept is great, and many young lives were changed throughout the series. I guess that's all that really matters, isn't it?
>
> *Beyond Scared Straight* is performing a real public service. That is the 1st time I have ever even thought that about any TV show or movie. It offers a public service because it gives every parent of a troubled teen a chance to sit that teen in front of the screen & see for themselves what the teens in the show went through in their jailhouse experience & how it apparently turned many of them around.

Positive reviewers often made connections between the show and their personal life experience. They stated that they: "wished there was a program like this when I was a teen," that this program "would've scared the hell out of me," or that it "makes me realize I wouldn't last 5 minutes in prison."

The following excerpts exemplify this point:

> I wish there was a program like this back in the day (90s) when I was a troubled teen, it would of changed me real quick. I was arrested at 17, fraud and burglary. . . . These teens remind me of how I was as a teen, young and dumb. I thought i was a bad B* when I was that age and in my 20s.
>
> I was just like these girls: attitude for days, stole, did drugs had major anger problems, disrespectful, the works. Was in the system for 2 years but by a miracle I managed to straighten up and be a productive law abiding citizen. These prisoners put there heart and soul in this program. . . . If a teen doesnt get affected by this show then you deserve to be locked up period! These kids need to understand once your locked up there is: no good food, no clean toilets, no video games, no phone, no text, no facebook, no privacy NOTHING. YOU GET NOTHING IN JAIL!

Members who authored positive reviews were not persuaded to be skeptical even when the television follow-ups portrayed kids as unrepentant and unchanged. One member stated: "I still can't believe some people don't change that sad for them. I guess they need to go through the program again until it gets through their heads." Another reviewer said that: "I watch the program to see the kids breakdown and turn their lifes around. If it works 20% of the time or more it's well worth it."

Several commentators fell victim to the illogical but oft-repeated mantra that if a program "saves one child" it is worthwhile. Logically, if a program harms more children than it saves, few people would call it worthwhile. Nevertheless, reviewers noted that: "Even if only one teen gets to avoid going to that horrid place, then the programs have worked," and "Its good to see when these programs work even if just for one child because one is more than 'just' in my book."

It was clear that many who wrote positive reviews were not persuaded by research or other reviewers' reference to scientific studies. One member stated: "I've read that studies have shown that there is really no major impact or change overall among troubled teens who go through this program, but even if the ones who truly change are a minority, it's still wonderful!" In some reviews, there was an explicit attempt to balance the media construction of *Beyond Scared Straight* as effective with the science that suggests otherwise. In this narrative, media clearly trumped science: "This is a fascinating and eye-opening show. . . . *Scared Straight*-ish programs really do seem to make a difference, even though I've read studies that seem to suggest otherwise." Another commentator offered a more blunt assessment of science and government agencies: "A previous reviewer noted that the US Dpt of Justice denounced *Scared Straight* programs as being ineffective. Big deal!!! That doesn't impress me . . . what do they know???"

By comparison, in many of the negative reviews, the lack of effectiveness of *Scared Straight* was a central theme. Authors of negative reviews often referenced terms such as "science," "research," and "evidence." A handful of the reviews cited specific research and provided a web link to this reference. Most, however, referenced research in a more general way. One member noted:

> A lot of research has shown "scared straight" programs do not work. In fact, some research shows it makes kids worse. Consequently, many DOC systems have stopped doing them. After seeing this, I can understand why. The reasons a lot of these kids are troubled in the 1st place are due to complex societal, familial, and other environmental issues. Traumatizing and re-traumatizing them is NOT going to help anything. . . . These programs need to consult mental health experts and criminologists before implementing this kind of treatment to children because no well-educated person would endorse them.

Other negative reviewers were skeptical of the effectiveness of the program not because of their familiarity with the empirical research, but rather because of how they felt about the premise and content of what they were seeing on television. One member noted: "This is just horrific. A bunch of awful parents sending their awful children into an awful program that is completely corny and ridiculous. It is painful to watch." Some negative reviewers rejected the premise that scare tactics would work:

> This is not the way to rehabilitate people, especially minors. This treatment I imagine only brews more anger and rebellion. . . . IMO, rehabilitation is not through yelling, intimidation, and threats, but should be through positive discussion, teaching of ethics, and calm dialogue.

Although it was clear that most people who discussed the issue of effectiveness in their reviews had strong feelings on one side or the other, a few of the reviews were more ambiguous. They balanced knowledge or suspicion that the program did not work with hope that it might work for some. The following "four star" (positive) review exemplifies this more nuanced view:

> I think another reviewer (or more) commented on how the tactics of these programs may not actually help kids. I agree. In many ways I view

the show as simultaneously showing troubled youth get "help" while also showing the tragedy of our society's obsession with punishment. The show strangely sheds light on the problems of both sides. Some of these kids need therapy more than the fear of jail. It's painfully evident in this show. I hope others also see this. If you're uncomfortable with what you see then take a stand against our overbearing criminal justice system. However some of these kids maybe do need a reality check and for those who do, I hope these scared straight programs help.

This reviewer tempered their skepticism about program effectiveness with a perceived value—exposing the brutality of the corrections system—of the show. Indeed, the brutality (or lack thereof) of the inmate-juvenile confrontations emerged as a theme in many reviews.

Brutality

Public enjoyment of the "spectacle of punishment" is not a recent development (Foucault 1977). Dating back to the Roman Coliseum, history is replete with examples of the "carnival of punishment" (Presdee 2000). The infotainment industry is well positioned to meet the public appetite for the shame and humiliation of others. For example, tabloid magazine shows such as TMZ thrive on embarrassing or humiliating videos of celebrities. The A&E Network has also made a spectacle out of other "sick" people on television with their shows like *Hoarders* (2011) and *Intervention* (2005). Similarly, in *Dateline NBC*'s "To Catch a Predator" would-be pedophiles that show up at a bait house are grilled by host Chris Hanson. This confrontation is mixed in with explicit chat logs and close-up shots of condoms, lubricant, and any other sexual items that were discovered on their person or in their vehicle (Kohm 2009).

Unsurprisingly, then, many of the positive reviews of *Beyond Scared Straight* noted the enjoyment of watching "punk" juveniles get their comeuppance from inmates. "I hate these little turds!" exclaimed one reviewer. Another stated that: "I like when 'no good punks' get a once over from folks with experience. I enjoy

that aspect of this series." These comments suggest that the commercial success of this program is at least partially rooted in the public's thirst for the verbal abuse and degradation of others. Reviewers appear to find humor and emotional enjoyment in the "smack-down" of juveniles:

> I love how all these kids think that they are so tough and all end up crying for their mama's when the inmates get in their faces. Just goes to show no matter how bad you think you are, in the end you just want your mama.
>
> The show is funny . . . last episode inmates make kids comb an inmate's chest hair. 10/10 would LOL again.

Some reviewers appear to live vicariously through the inmates' tactics. For example:

> As a middle school teacher, this show is like a mini vacation, where the adults say what I want to say to the kids! I love this show!!!! I used to work in an inner city school, but now I am out in the suburbs where I do not have kids with this lifestyle, yet the overall attitude is the same. It is pervasive and non-stop. At 20 minutes into the first episode, when the cop finally just yells at the stupid kid to "SHUT UP!" I found myself applauding and laughing out loud. . . . I feel really guilty when I take pleasure in the little punk ass boys sobbing so hard they are going to hyperventilate—especially when the demands on their sorry little bottoms are so few and far between in our society.

Many reviews made clear that they thought the program would be more effective if there was more physical brutality. They lamented the fact that kids knew that the inmates could not really follow through with their threats, and had suggestions for how to up the ante:

> I'd like to see more water in the face, more screaming, and MAKE these punks SLEEP overnight in the prison. Have the prisoners rough them up a bit more, within reason, of course. But make it as real as you possibly can for these kids, because some of them are sociopaths, they need to be broken or they will never

snap outta it. A sociopath can be prevented, but only with the toughest intervention.

It seems that each episode the prisoners get softer and softer. The kids know that they cant really do anything to them so it doesnt really have much of an impact. . . . This show is more drama than anything. Would be better if the prisoners were able to slap the hell out the kids once in a while.

As might be expected, many of those who had a negative opinion of the show did not share the thrill of the spectacle of violence. Instead, they framed the inmate threats and intimidation techniques as a form of "child abuse," and pointed out the hypocrisy of using threats of violence in an attempt to reduce violence:

> This is a HORRIBLE show. It's full of adults bullying, verbally abusing, and threatening children. Prisoners threaten to rape the girls on this show. Guards threaten to beat the children up. It is so horrible.

> I wonder why people seem to think this is so great, when all it really highlights is how badly we treat our prisoners. . . . It's sad how all the people who think this show is great don't see the hypocrisy of threatening to hurt minor children, threatening to lock minor children in an adult jail overnight-things that are not just illegal, but a great deal more harmful than many things that the convicted criminals are there for—to teach them to follow the law. It's pathetic.

As the preceding quote illustrates, some reviewers felt that the threats of rape and other violence within prison revealed the inadequacy of American correctional system:

> I am not naive in thinking that this violence does not occur on a daily—if not hourly—basis in these types of institutions; but that does not make it ok. . . . We must re-think the way we are running our prisons. The way we are filling them with non violent offenders, domestic violence victims, black men and boys who were in the "wrong place" at the "wrong time." . . . These kids. These kids. They are not bad kids. They

are not bad people. They do not need to be yelled at, scared, forced into uncomfortable positions and made to eat gross food. They need to be loved. Cared for. . . . It's not hard. I'm rating this 5 stars because it made me reflect.

> This series reminds me of why I back prison reform. The evident prisoner-on-prisoner human rights violations, managed by the institution, shouldnt be used to justify its existence.

Inspirational/Emotional

While some Netflix viewers took guilty pleasure in the shame and humiliation of kids, others described the show as "inspirational," "emotional," and "touching." Many reviews mentioned crying in reaction to the series. The emotional reactions, which were nearly universally found in positive reviews, revolved around two different aspects of the program. First, some people reacted to the transition between the "pre-prison" and "post-prison" segments in which juveniles are first shown in their environment (and interviewed along with parents) and are then given a chance at "redemption." For example, a reviewer stated that the series was: "emotionally gripping when you get to the issues about why these kids are acting the way they are." Another reviewer stated:

> It's a great series to watch, something about it is just so interesting to watch! Also really tugs on your heart strings. First from hearing these stories and all the bad things that they do, and secondly, how most all of them turn their lives around!! Love the show!

Reviewers also got caught up in the drama and uncertainty of how the juveniles would react to the program. The following narrative captures this sentiment:

> I watched every episode in less than 2 days and each one of them ended in tears. At the end of each episode I found myself with my fingers crossed praying that the kids had gotten the message and was so happy with how much impact these programs have.

The second emotional aspect of the series concerned how the reviewers felt about the positive portrayal of inmates. Indeed, one rationale for continuing *Scared Straight*-type programs is that it is "good for the inmates" (Petrosino et al. 2003). Clearly, many who wrote reviews were inspired by inmates attempting to help juveniles. One reviewer noted that: "It is really great that even the most hardened criminals care about what our children do. I cried, on all 7 shows, I cried." Other responses included:

> The inmates deserve all the credit in the world, some of them won't see the light of day for the rest of their life but still choose to focus their life on helping their kids and there is nothing more honorable than that.
>
> This show brought me to tears several times as I witnessed the selfless love and compassion of the prisoners trying to reach these kids so they could avoid the pain they were experiencing because of their mistakes in life. WONDERFUL show!!!

Those who were moved emotionally almost always wrote positive reviews, and many also indicated that they thought the program was effective. Even some of those who were skeptical of the program, however, were still drawn in by the framing of inmates as caring and constructive. One reviewer stated: "Scared straight is known to be a failed program for the kids who go through it. I do like seeing how much concern the convicts show though."

While most of the narratives that mentioned inmates did so in a positive manner, negative comments were certainly still present. For example, a few reviewers pointed out the irony of using prison inmates as role models for juveniles. One commentator stated that: "It's pretty laughable how people that are murderers demand respect from kids that are just there for mild drug use (which could be solved by legalization and making it tougher to obtain), petty theft, and fighting." Another had the following appraisal:

> I also found the way that the inmates (most convicted of MURDER) expected to be

"respected" and called sir or ma'am was a little ridiculous. . . . I don't care how "reformed" they want to claim they are, especially when in the next breath, they want to say "you would be my ***** if you were in here."

Reality

Popular network programs—particularly those within the "reality television" genre—are viewed as especially insidious by those who study the nexus of crime and media because the "stew" of live footage mixed with dramatic music and cinematography blurs the line between news and entertainment. As Surette (2015:19) notes, "The feel with infotainment is that you are learning the real facts about the world; the reality is that you are getting a highly stylized rendition of a narrow, edited slice of the world." This is especially relevant to criminal justice programming, as the vast majority of the public has little direct experience with prison and inmates.

What did Netflix viewers have to say about the reality of *Beyond Scared Straight*? Many comments directly affirmed the "realness" of the series. This was most apparent in the positive reviews. Illustrating the concern of media critics, one Netflix member stated that: "Teens would benefit from this [*Scared Straight*] so much more than reality shows, or music videos." Thus, according to this reviewer, the series was so real that it was not even included in the domain of "reality shows." Another reviewer offered this rebuke to those who questioned the authenticity of the program:

> Just for everyone thinking this show is a bunch of staged crap, it's not. Someone I went to high school with was on this show and it is very real. These scared straight programs are not fake. They treat all of the kids that come through the same way, whether they're being filmed or not. The whole point is to scare them. You think the inmates shoot out empty threats? They won't be so empty when the kid ends up in jail right next to them.

In contrast to the true believers, skeptics of the program—those who provided more negative comments—often saw the program as "fake" and "scripted." One reviewer wrote: "I feel like a lot of this show is staged (like the inmates yelling and screaming at the teens. I'm sure production told them to do so, though I don't doubt that some of them would have done it on their own)." Another narrative focused on the "after" segment:

> And the things they tell their parents afterward! Good God! It sounds so scripted, every time, like it was being repeated by some young actor just starting in acting school. They say things like: I'm going to do better, I'll stop lying, I'll stop fighting, I'll stop stealing. How fake can you get its not a documentary its reality tv, dont be stupid and think its real, its just a bunch of actors.

These comments concerning the authenticity (or lack thereof) of the Scared Straight program point to an interesting contradiction in reviewer preferences: while some viewers applaud the program for its brutality and/or inspirational content, others scorn the program because the brutality and inspiration do not come off as genuine.

Conclusion

In recent years there has been an increased call for "evidence-based" criminal justice policy making (Sherman 2013). This sure sounds good, and success stories certainly exist (Lum, Koper, and Telep 2011), but the reality of the situation is that scientific evidence typically occupies but one chair at the policy-making table (Welsh, Rocque, and Greenwood 2014). And when it comes to Scared Straight, social science research is sitting at the kids' table. Indeed, on the one hand, our analyses reveal that the evidence demonstrating the ineffectiveness of Scared Straight programs has a voice in public conversation. Yet on the other hand, that voice is generally drowned out by those belonging to entertainment, emotion, and the joy that people take in the misfortune of others. The purpose of the present study was to understand these voices and to organize what they tell us about

how people view the tactics employed by Scared Straight. And based on our analyses, three issues warrant particular attention.

First, our analysis sheds light on how viewers make judgments about the effectives of the programs featured in Beyond Scared Straight. In particular, we are encouraged that at least some research is leaking through to the public. Although a small minority, some reviewers were clearly exposed to and persuaded by the science that undermines Scared Straight-type programs. Comments that made explicit reference to "doing some research" on the web after seeing the program are particularly heartening. Unfortunately, the analysis also revealed that many Netflix reviewers saw Beyond Scared Straight as "real," and judged the program effective based on the television "follow-up." Even more problematic are those who rejected science outright, or mobilized an "If it saves one child" defense. Perhaps most disturbing was evidence that some reviewers weighed scientific evidence against the media presentation and went with the entertainment version of truth. Put simply, with respect to reviewers' level of scientific literacy concerning the effectiveness of Scared Straight, many are still reading well below grade level.

Second, and relatedly, it is also apparent that a good part of the attraction to Beyond Scared Straight has little to do with whether the program "works." What often matters instead is how viewers respond to the brutality on display with the program, the extent to which the stories elicit an emotional response, and the extent to which viewers feel as though what they are watching is "real." Indeed, the Scared Straight franchise is built around a narrative that appeals to many: smug, cocky delinquents go to prison and get taught a lesson by "real" criminals. Viewers get satisfaction in watching inmates wipe the smirks off the faces of these young "turds," and they take pleasure in the spectacle of confrontation.

Such realities suggest that criminologists are facing a challenging task if they wish to tame public support for Scared Straight programs. It is also apparent that the Scared Straight franchise will not fold their tent because social scientists tell them to stop. A more realistic approach may be to tailor our "science-based" message toward correctional decision-makers in addition to the public at large—something that corrections scholars have gotten much more adept at in recent years (see, e.g., Latessa 2004; Latessa et al. 2002; Lipsey 2014). Ironically, Mr. Shapiro, the producer of *Scared Straight*, makes this argument (although indirectly) when he asked, "If these programs weren't working and were hurting kids, why would judges, and police officers, and teachers, and school counselors, why would they keep sending kids to these programs month after month after month, and year after year, if they were not seeing positive results?" (Denhart 2011).

Third, our study illustrates how qualitative work can be useful in the area of public opinion about crime and justice. Qualitative studies are becoming more popular in criminology and criminal justice in general (Brezina and Topalli 2012; Giordano 2010; Wright and Bouffard 2014), and in research on corrections in particular (Leban et al. 2015; Miller, Tillyer, and Miller 2012; Turanovic, Rodriguez, and Pratt 2012). This approach allows scholars to get at the complexity of citizens' attitudes in ways that large-scale surveys cannot (Creswell 2013). Employing qualitative methods, including narrative analysis, may prove useful in the future as criminologists continue to assess the dimensions of public support for programs that intervene in the lives of offenders.

In the end, with respect to correctional interventions for high-risk youth, we know that a number of approaches are better than *Scared Straight* (Cullen 2013). The key will be for scholars to do a better job of disseminating that knowledge in a wider and more accessible way. Part of that, according to Pratt (2008:46), requires that scholars "relearn how to talk like a real person again." This means that we need to communicate our work—even if it is complex—using language that is not. It also means that, as scholars, we are permitted to have an opinion. But we need to do more than merely call negative attention to the programs that we dislike. Complaining in the absence of providing alternatives comes off as whining,

not as problem-solving. And *Scared Straight* is a problem. We have a long list of solutions, so let's get to it.

Discussion Questions

1. The show's producer claims that the show itself constitutes research. What are the flaws in the "research" conducted by this show?
2. How might the sampling plan have impacted the findings?
3. Discuss the types of manifest and latent content that they analyzed.

References

Applegate, Brandon K., Francis T. Cullen, Bonnie S. Fisher, and Thomas Vander Ven. 2000. "Forgiveness and Fundamentalism: Reconsidering the Relationship Between Correctional Attitudes and Religion." *Criminology* 38:719–754.

Axelrod, Jim. 2015. "Doctor Blames Discredited Autism Research for Measles Outbreak." *CBS News*, February 10. Retrieved March 10, 2015 (www.cbsnews.com/news/doctor-blames-discredited-autism-vaccine-link-research-for-measles-outbreak).

Ballantine, Paul. W., Yongjia Lin, and Ekant Veer. 2015. "The Influence of User Comments on Perceptions of Facebook Relationship Updates." *Computers in Human Behavior* 49:50–55.

Beckwith, Francis J. 2003. *Law, Darwinism, and Public Education: The Establishment Clause and the Challenge of Intelligent Design*. Lanham, MD: Rowman and Littlefield.

Brezina, Timothy and Volkan Topalli. 2012. "Criminal Self-Efficacy: Exploring the Correlates and Consequences of a 'Successful Criminal' Identity." *Criminal Justice and Behavior* 39:1042–1062.

Cavender, Gray. 1981. "'Scared Straight': Ideology and the Media." *Journal of Criminal Justice* 9:431–439.

Collins, Luke and Brigitte Nerlich. 2015. "Examining User Comments for Deliberative Democracy: A Corpus-Driven Analysis of the Climate Change Debate Online." *Environmental Communication* 9:189–207.

Copes, Heith. 2014. *Advancing Qualitative Methods in Criminology and Criminal Justice*. London: Routledge.

Copes, Heith, Andy Hochstetler, and Craig J. Forsyth. 2013. "Peaceful Warriors: Codes for Violence Among Adult Male Bar Fighters." *Criminology* 51:761–794.

Creswell, John W. 2013. *Research Design: Qualitative, Quantitative, and Mixed Methods Approaches*. 3rd Edition. Thousand Oaks, CA: Sage.

Cullen, Francis T. 2013. "Rehabilitation: Beyond Nothing Works." *Crime and Justice: A Review of Research* 42:299–376.

Cullen, Francis T., Bonnie S. Fisher, and Brandon K. Applegate. 2000. "Public Opinion About Punishment and Corrections." *Crime and Justice: A Review of Research* 27:1–79.

Cullen, Francis T., Travis C. Pratt, Sharon Levrant, and Melissa Moon. 2002. "Dangerous Liaison: Rational Choice Theory as the Basis for Correctional Intervention." Pp. 279–298 in *Rational Choice and Criminal Behavior: Recent Research and Future Challenges*, edited by Alex R. Piquero and Stephen G. Tibbetts. New York: Routledge.

Denhart, Andy. 2011. "Beyond Scared Straight's Real-Life Controversy." *The Daily Beast*, February 23. Retrieved January 6, 2015 (www.thedaily beast.com/articles/2011/02/23/beyond-scared-straights-real-life-controversy.html).

Feinstein, Sheryl. 2005. "Another Look at Scared Straight." *Journal of Correctional Education* 56:40–44.

Fennell, Dana and Michael Boyd. 2014. "Obsessive-Compulsive Disorder in the Media." *Deviant Behavior* 35:669–686.

Finckenauer, James O. 1982. *Scared Straight and the Panacea Phenomenon*. Englewood Cliffs, NJ: Prentice Hall.

Finckenauer, James O., Patricia W. Gavin, Arild Hovland, and Elisabet Storvoll. 1999. *Scared Straight: The Panacea Phenomenon Revisited*. Long Grove, IL: Waveland Press.

Foucault, Michel. 1977. *Discipline and Punish: The Birth of the Prison*. New York: Random House.

Gauchat, Gordon William. 2008. "A Test of Three Theories of Anti-Science Attitudes." *Sociological Focus* 41:337–357.

Gauchat, Gordon. 2011. "The Cultural Authority of Science: Public Trust and Acceptance of Organized Science." *Public Understanding of Science* 20:751–770.

Giordano, Peggy. 2010. *Legacies of Crime: A Follow-up of the Children of Highly Delinquent Girls and Boys*. New York: Cambridge University Press.

Gosselt, Jordy F., Joris J. Van Hoof, Bastiaan S. Gent, and Jean-Paul Fox. 2015. "Violent Frames: Analyzing Internet Movie Database Reviewers' Text Descriptions of Media Violence and Gender Differences from 39 Years of U.S. Action, Thriller, Crime, and Adventure Movies." *International Journal of Communication* 9:547–567.

Griffin, O. Hayden, Alexis Lynn Fritsch, Vanessa H. Woodward, and Richard S. Mohn. 2013. "Sifting Through the Hyperbole: One Hundred Years of Marijuana Coverage in the New York Times." *Deviant Behavior* 34:767–781.

Heeren, John and David Shichor. 1984. "Mass Media and Delinquency Prevention: The Case of 'Scared Straight'." *Deviant Behavior* 5:375–386.

Holt, Thomas J. 2010. "Exploring Strategies for Qualitative Criminological and Criminal Justice Inquiry Using On-Line Data." *Journal of Criminal Justice Education* 21:466–487.

Hutchinson, Terry C. and Kelly Richards. 2013. "Scared Straight: Boot Camps for Queensland." *Alternative Law Journal* 38:229–233.

Kerr, Dara. 2013. "Video Streaming Is on the Rise With Netflix Dominating." *CNET*. Retrieved March 10, 2015 (www.cnet.com/news/video-streaming-is-on-the-rise-with-netflix-dominating).

Kohm, Steven A. 2009. "Naming, Shaming, and Criminal Justice: Mass-Mediated Humiliation as Entertainment and Punishment." *Crime Media Culture* 5:188–205.

Ksiazek, Thomas B., Limor Peer, and Kevin Lessard. 2014. "User Engagement with Online News: Conceptualizing Interactivity and Exploring the Relationship Between Online News Videos and User Comments." *New Media and Society* (https://doi.org/10.1177/1461444814545073).

Latessa, Edward J. 2004. "The Challenge of Change: Correctional Programs and Evidence-Based Practices." *Criminology and Public Policy* 3:547–560.

Latessa, Edward J., Francis T. Cullen, and Paul Gendreau. 2002. "Beyond Correctional Quackery: Professionalism and the Possibility of Effective Treatment." *Federal Probation* 66:43–49.

Laub, John H. and Robert J. Sampson. 2003. *Shared Beginnings, Divergent Lives: Delinquent Boys to Age 70*. Cambridge, MA: Harvard University Press.

Leban, Lindsay, Stephanie M. Cardwell, Heith Copes, and Timothy Brezina. 2015. "Adapting to Prison Life: A Qualitative Examination of the Coping Process Among Incarcerated Offenders." *Justice Quarterly* (https://doi.org/10.1080/074188 25.2015.1012096).

Lindegaard, Marie Rosenkrantz, Jody Miller, and Danielle M. Reynald. 2013. "Transitory Mobility, Cultural Heterogeneity, and Victimization Risk Among Young Men of Color: Insights from an Ethnographic Study in Cape Town, South Africa." *Criminology* 51:967–1008.

Lipsey, Mark W. 2014. "Interventions for Juvenile Offenders: A Serendipitous Journey." *Criminology and Public Policy* 13:1–14.

Loftland, John and Lyn H. Loftland. 1995. *Analyzing Social Settings: A Guide to Qualitative Observation and Analysis*. 3rd Edition. Belmont, CA: Wadsworth.

Lum, Cynthia, Christopher Koper, and Cody W. Telep. 2011. "The Evidence-Based Policing Matrix." *Journal of Experimental Criminology* 7:3–26.

Lundman, Richard J. 2001. *Prevention and Control of Juvenile Delinquency*. 3rd Edition. New York: Oxford University Press.

May, Jessica, Kristina Osmond, and Stephen Billick. 2014. "Juvenile Delinquency Treatment and Prevention: A Literature Review." *Psychiatric Quarterly* 84:295–301.

Miller, Holly V., Rob Tillyer, and J. Mitchell Miller. 2012. "Recognizing the Need for Prisoner Input in Correctional Research: Observations from an In-Prison Driving While Intoxicated Reduction Program Evaluation." *The Prison Journal* 92:274–289.

Miller, Jody. 2008. *Getting Played: African American Girls, Urban Inequality, and Gendered Violence*. New York: New York University Press.

National Science Foundation. 2014. *Science and Engineering Indicators 2014*. Arlington, VA: National Center for Science and Engineering Statistics.

Netflix Help Center. 2015. "Questions about Reviews." Retrieved February 18, 2015 (https://help.netflix.com/en/node/9977).

Petrosino, Anthony, Carolyn Turpin-Petrosino, and John Buehler. 2003. "Scared Straight and Other Juvenile Awareness Programs for Preventing Juvenile Delinquency: A Systematic Review of the Randomized Experimental Evidence." *The Annals of the American Academy of Political and Science* 589:41–62.

Pew Research Center. 2013. *Public's Knowledge of Science and Technology*. Washington, DC: Pew Charitable Trusts.

Poladian, Charles. 2014. "1 out of 4 Americans do not Know the Earth Orbits the Sun, but What do Those Figures Really Mean?" *International Business Times*, February 15. Retrieved April 20, 2015 (www.ibtimes.com/1-out-4-americans-do-not-know-earth-orbits-sun-what-do-those-figures-really-mean-1555810).

Pratt, Travis C. 2008. "Rational Choice Theory, Crime Control Policy, and Criminological Relevance." *Criminology and Public Policy* 7:43–52.

Pratt, Travis C. 2009. *Addicted to Incarceration: Corrections Policy and the Politics of Misinformation in the United States*. Thousand Oaks, CA: Sage.

Pratt, Travis C., Jacinta M. Gau, and Travis W. Franklin. 2011. *Key Ideas in Criminology and Criminal Justice*. Thousand Oaks, CA: Sage.

Presdee, Mike. 2000. *Cultural Criminology and the Carnival of Crime*. London: Routledge.

Robinson, Laurie O. and Jeff Slowikowski. 2011. "Scary—and Ineffective. Traumatizing At-Risk Kids is Not the Way to Lead Them Away from Crime and Drugs." *Baltimore Sun*, January 31. Retrieved February 15, 2015 (http://articles.baltimoresun.com/2011-01-31/news/bs-ed-scared-straight-20110131_1_straight-type-programs-straight-program-youths).

Sampson, Robert J. and John H. Laub. 1993. *Crime in the Making: Pathways and Turning Points through Life*. Cambridge, MA: Harvard University Press.

Sandberg, Sveinung, Sebastien Tutenges, and Heith Copes. 2015. "Stories of Violence: A Narrative Criminological Study of Ambiguity." *British Journal of Criminology* 55:1168–1186.

Sarfati, Jonathan D. 1999. *Refuting Evolution: A Handbook for Students, Parents, and Teachers Countering the Latest Arguments for Evolution*. Brisbane, Australia: Answers in Genesis.

Sellers, Brian G. 2015. "Community-Based Recovery and Youth Justice." *Criminal Justice and Behavior* 42:58–69.

Shaw, Clifford R. 1930. *The Jack-Roller: A Delinquent Boy's Own Story*. Chicago: University of Chicago Press.

Sherman, Lawrence W. 2013. "The Rise of Evidence-based Policing: Targeting, Testing, and Tracking." *Crime and Justice: A Review of Research* 42:377–451.

Short, James F. and Fred L. Strodtbeck. 1965. *Group Process and Gang Delinquency*. Chicago: University of Chicago Press.

Smith, Nicholas and Anthony Leiserowitz. 2012. "The Rise of Global Warming Skepticism: Exploring Affective Image Associations in the United States Over Time." *Risk Analysis* 32:1021–1032.

Sundt, Jody, Francis T. Cullen, Angela J. Thielo, and Cheryl Lero Jonson. 2015. "Public Willingness to Downsize Prisons: Implications from Oregon." *Violence and Victims* 10:365–378.

Surette, Ray. 2015. *Media, Crime and Justice: Images, Realities, and Policies*. 5th Edition. Stamford, CT: Cengage Learning.

Turanovic, Jillian J., Nancy Rodriguez, and Travis C. Pratt. 2012. "The Collateral Consequences of Incarceration Revisited: A Qualitative Analysis of the Effects on Caregivers of Children of Incarcerated Parents." *Criminology* 50:913–959.

Welsh, Brandon C. and Michael Rocque. 2014. "When Crime Prevention Harms: A Review of Systematic Reviews." *Journal of Experimental Criminology* 10:245–266.

Welsh, Brandon C., Michael Rocque, and Peter Greenwood. 2014. "Translating Research into Evidence-Based Practice in Juvenile Justice: Brand-Name Programs, Meta-analysis, and Key Issues." *Journal of Experimental Criminology* 10:207–225.

Wright, Kevin A. and Leanna A. Bouffard. 2014. "Capturing Crime: The Qualitative Analysis of Individual Cases for Advancing Criminological Knowledge." *International Journal of Offender Therapy and Comparative Criminology* (https://doi.org/10.1177/0306624X14549308).

Reading 11.2   A Quasi-Experimental Evaluation of the Effects of Police Body-Worn Cameras (BWCs) on Response-to-Resistance in a Large Metropolitan Police Department

Police departments have adopted body-worn cameras (BWCs) to both foster officer accountability and provide officers protection against false or exaggerated claims of brutality. Jennings, Fridell, Lynch, Jetelina, and Reingle Gonzalez (2017) studied whether officers from the Tampa, Florida, police department who used BWCs would differ from other officers in the same city in their frequency of engaging in physical response-to-resistance. A classical experiment was not possible since officers were given the opportunity to volunteer to wear BWCs. Had the researchers compared the BWC volunteers to a random sample of officers who did not volunteer, there would be a question of whether any differences found between the two groups was a product of the BWCs or due to fundamental differences in the temperament and job performances of the officers. To compensate for the lack of randomization, the authors used propensity scores to pair the BWC officers with a matched group of police not wearing cameras during the same time period. As you will see, the results of this study would have been quite different had the researchers not accounted for the differences between the two groups with a matching procedure.

A Quasi-Experimental Evaluation of the Effects of Police Body-Worn Cameras (BWCs) on Response-to-Resistance in a Large Metropolitan Police Department

Wesley G. Jennings, Lorie A. Fridell, Mathew Lynch, Katelyn K. Jetelina, and Jennifer M. Reingle Gonzalez

Introduction

Given the recent and growing number of tragic incidents such as Michael Brown in Ferguson, Missouri; Eric Garner in New York; Alton Sterling in Baton Rouge, Louisiana; and Philando Castile in St. Paul, Minnesota, where minority individuals are being victims of violence perpetrated by the police, as well as the recent shooting and killing of five police officers in Dallas, Texas, it is clearly a time when people are searching for answers and explanations and justice system reform and prevention strategies. Coinciding with these events, and often in response to these events, public and police interest in police body-worn cameras (BWCs) is emerging. In fact, Lum and colleagues (2015) recently identified 12 existing BWC empirical studies (Ariel, Farrar, and Sutherland 2015; Ellis, Jenkins, and Smith 2015; Goodall 2007; Grossmith et al. 2015; Jennings, Fridell, and Lynch 2014; Jennings, Lynch, and Fridell 2015; Katz et al. 2015; ODS Consulting 2011; Owens, Mann, and Mckenna 2014; Ready and Young 2015; Roy 2014; Young and Ready 2015) and another 30 ongoing empirical studies (for review of the ongoing BWC studies, see Lum et al. 2015).

Relatedly, a number of recent studies have shown that officers are generally supportive of BWCs, and that while their initial perceptions may be less optimistic about the benefits of their use, their favorability ratings toward BWCs generally improves once they become more acquainted with and accustomed to the technology (Jennings et al. 2014, 2015; Katz et al. 2015). For example, Young and Ready (2015) reported that Mesa, Arizona, officers who wore BWCs were more likely to rate BWCs as being helpful in their day-to-day activities, and Grossmith et al.'s (2015) analysis of officers in London revealed that the officers reported BWCs to be useful in handling complaints more effectively, particularly in cases where evidence would have been lacking in the absence of BWCs. Katz et al. (2015) also indicated that the majority of surveyed officers perceived BWCs as a tool to provide a more accurate depiction of events, that the BWC video increases the quality of the evidence that can be obtained, and that nearly 60% of the officers felt that BWCs were comfortable to wear, but were also hoping for some technological improvements for added comfort as well. In addition, emerging research has provided some preliminary evidence that public attitudes generally favor the use of BWCs in police departments and perceive that BWCs will increase the quality of police-citizen interactions. However, some citizens have also noted their concerns about victim and witness cooperation (Sousa, Miethe, and Sakiyama 2015).

Turning toward BWC outcome evaluations specifically, Young and Ready (2015) relied on quasi-experimental field data from Mesa, Arizona, where 50 officers were assigned BWCs and 50 officers represented a matched comparison group who did not wear BWCs. Their results indicated that the BWC officers performed significantly fewer stop and frisks, issued significantly more citations, initiated significantly more contacts with citizens, and rated the BWCs as being particularly helpful in their encounters with citizens. Ariel, Farrar, and Sutherland (2015) conducted a randomized controlled trial of BWCs in Rialto, California, where 54 Rialto police officers (the entire police department) were randomly assigned to shifts where they either wore or did not wear BWCs. Their results suggested that response-to-resistance was twice as likely during shifts where the BWC was not worn relative to the shifts where the BWC was worn. In contrast, Jennings et al. (2015) performed a randomized controlled trial where officers (not shifts) were randomized in Orlando, Florida. The results from this study revealed that the 46 officers who were randomly assigned to wear BWCs had significantly fewer incidents of response-to-resistance in the 12 months post–BWC implementation compared with the 46 officers who were randomly assigned to not wear BWCs, and that wearing BWCs led to a 53.4% reduction in the response-to-resistance for officers who were wearing the BWCs when comparing their response-to-resistance in the 12 months pre–BWC implementation to their response-to-resistance in the 12 months post–BWC implementation.

The Current Study

In recognition of the growing but small amount of existing evaluation research surrounding BWCs, the current study offers an examination of the impact of BWCs on police response-to-resistance. Specifically, relying on data from 60 BWC officers from the Tampa Police Department in Tampa, Florida, and using a propensity score matching (PSM) technique to identify a statistically comparable matched sample of 60 non-BWC officers, this study evaluates the effect of BWCs on the frequency of response-to-resistance in the 12 months post–BWC implementation and compares this frequency with the frequency of response-to-resistance in the 12 months prior to BWC implementation.

Methods

Site and Sample

Tampa, Florida, is a mid-to-large-size metropolitan city with greater than 350,000 residents, and the city is fairly diverse, with roughly 40% of the population being minorities (African American or Hispanic). The sample for the current study includes 761 Tampa Police

Department (TPD) officers that were working for the TPD during the 24-month study period.

Dependent Variable

The dependent variable is a frequency (count) of the number of incidents of physical response-to-resistance that the officers were involved in during the 12 months pre–BWC implementation (March 2014–February 2015) and in the 12 months post–BWC implementation (March 2015–February 2016). Specifically, physical response-to-resistance incidents included behaviors such as empty hand "soft" control techniques (i.e., grabs, holds, and joint locks), empty hand "hard" control techniques (i.e., punches, kicks, countermeasures), less-than-lethal weapons (i.e., batons, projectiles, chemical sprays, conducted energy devices), and firearms.

Independent Variable

Sixty BWCs were purchased by TPD according to a normal bidding process with a host of vendors, and volunteers were recruited from the three police districts in Tampa (e.g., approximately 20 officers per district) to wear the BWCs. As such, the officers were separated into two groups of interest: BWC officers and non-BWC officers.

Covariates

There are a series of officer demographics included as covariates in the analysis, including officer gender (male = 1; female = 0), officer race/ethnicity (White Officer, African American Officer, Hispanic Officer), officer age (measured continuously in years), and officer years of law enforcement experience at TPD (measured continuously in years based on the number of years between TPD hire date and study end date). In addition, the frequency (count) of the number of incidents of physical response-to-resistance that the officers were involved in during the 12 months pre–BWC implementation is included as a covariate in certain analyses as well.

Analytic Procedure

This analysis proceeds in a series of stages. In the first stage, we present descriptive summary statistics for the officers. Next, we employ PSM techniques to approximate a quasi-experimental research design in order to be better positioned to derive more precise estimates between statistically matched samples (see Jennings et al. 2013; Richards et al. 2014; Rosenbaum and Rubin 1983). Specifically, the utilization of PSM permits the ability to remove any observable and systematic differences that may exist between the officers who were wearing a BWC relative to the officers that were not wearing a BWC. In this vein, relying on an R program (Ho et al. 2007, 2011) and statistical convention in the propensity score matching literature including the use of a strict .10 caliper and nearest neighbor matching methods (Austin 2009; Rosenbaum 2002), we derive our propensity score estimates from a logistic regression model where wearing a BWC is considered the "experimental condition," and not wearing a BWC is considered the "control condition" (for further discussion on PSM, see Ho et al. 2011; Pearl 2009; Rosenbaum 2002). This specified propensity score algorithm is also based on the inclusion of a series of officer demographic factors (gender, race/ethnicity, age, and years of experience) and the frequency of response-to-resistance incidents that the officers were involved in during the 12 months pre–BWC implementation. Following the estimation of PSM, we make statistical comparisons via t-tests to compare the demographic factors and the frequency of response-to-resistance pre–BWC implementation between the BWC officers and the non-BWC officers prior to and post–PSM. In the final stage of analysis, we perform statistical comparisons between the BWC officers and the matched sample of non-BWC officers via a t-test for the frequency of response-to-resistance in the 12 months post–BWC implementation and through an examination of percentage changes in the frequency of response-to-resistance pre– to post–BWC implementation for the BWC officers and the matched sample of non-BWC officers.

Results

Summary statistics are presented in Table 1. As illustrated, the majority of officers were male (83.8%), and 71.8% were White, 12.8% were African American, and 15.4% were Hispanic. On average, the officers were 40.11 years of age (SD = 7.83; range = 23–63 years of age), and had been working as police officers at TPD for 11.81 years, on average (SD = 6.62; range = 2–31 years). Overall, the officers were involved in an average of 3.05 incidents where physical force was used during the 12 months pre–BWC implementation, and in an average of 2.73 incidents where physical force was used during the 12 months post–BWC implementation.

Table 2 provides the bivariate comparisons for the covariates (officer gender, officer race/ethnicity, officer age, years of experience, and the frequency of incidents where physical force was used during the 12 months pre–BWC implementation) before and after applying PSM techniques. As can be seen in columns 1 and 2, prior

to matching, most of the covariates significantly differed when comparing the 60 BWC officers with the 701 non-BWC officers. Specifically, a significantly lower percentage of BWC officers were White and a significantly greater percentage of the BWC officers were Hispanic compared with their non-BWC counterparts. Also, the non-BWC officers, on average, were significantly older and had a greater number of years of law enforcement experience at TPD relative to the BWC officers. Finally, the BWC officers had been involved in a significantly greater mean number of incidents where physical response-to-resistance was used in the 12 months pre–BWC implementation compared to the non-BWC officers. Turning toward columns 3 and 4, the results demonstrated that after applying PSM and generating a statistically comparable sample of 60 non-BWC officers in terms of officer demographics and the frequency of physical response-to-resistance pre–BWC implementation that none of the pre-existing significant differences between the two groups remained.

Table 1 Summary Statistics (n = 761)

	M/%	SD	Minimum	Maximum
Officer gender				
Male	83.8	–	–	–
Female	16.2			
Office race/ethnicity				
White	71.8	–	–	–
African American	12.8			
Hispanic	15.4			
Officer age	40.11	7.83	23.00	63.00
Number of years as a TPD officer	11.81	6.62	2.00	31.00
Response-to-resistance frequency: Pre–BWC implementation	3.05	3.69	0.00	29.00
Response-to-resistance frequency: Post–BWC implementation	2.73	3.78	0.00	30.00

Table 2 Bivariate Comparisons of Officer Demographics and Response-to-Resistance Frequency Before and After Matching

	Before Matching		After Matching	
	n = 60	n= 701	n =60	n =60
Variables	BWC officer	Non-BWC officer	BWC officer	Non-BWC officer
Male officer	.80	.84	.80	.74
White officer	**.57**	*.73*	.57	.53
African American officer	.18	.12	.18	.15
Hispanic officer	**.25**	*.15*	.25	.31
Officer age	*38.37*	*40.26*	39.23	38.37
Number of years as a TPD officer	*10.13*	*11.95*	10.13	11.70
Response-to-resistance frequency: Pre–BWC implementation	*3.72*	*2.99*	3.72	4.31

Note: Significant mean differences (*p* < .10) in bold *italics*.

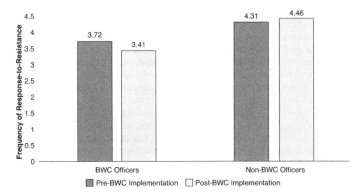

Figure 1 Pre– and Post–BWC Implementation Comparisons in the Frequency of Response-to-Resistance for Matched Experimental and Control Groups (N = 120)

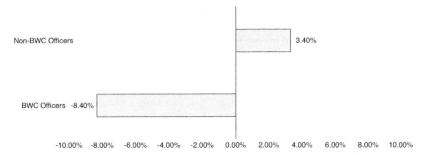

Figure 2 Percentage Change in the Frequency of Response-to-Resistance from Pre– to Post–BWC Implementation for Matched Experimental and Control Groups (N = 120)

Or in other words, prior to matching, the comparisons between BWC officers and non-BWC officers were in effect apples to oranges comparisons, and, after matching, the comparisons were now apples to apples comparisons.

Figure 1 graphically displays the average number of physical response-to-resistance incidents that the 60 BWC officers and the 60 non-BWC matched officers were involved in during the 12 months pre–BWC implementation and in the 12 months post–BWC implementation. As illustrated, the BWC officers were involved in an average of 3.72 physical response-to-resistance incidents in the 12 months prior to BWC implementation, and this involvement declined to an average of

3.41 physical response-to-resistance incidents in the 12 months post–BWC implementation. Comparatively, the non-BWC matched officers were involved in 4.31 physical response-to-resistance incidents pre–BWC implementation and 4.46 physical response-to-resistance incidents post–BWC implementation. Statistical results from a t-test comparison revealed that the post-BWC physical response-to-resistance incidents significantly differed and were significantly less for the BWC officers relative to the non-BWC matched officers. Finally, the percentage changes in the mean frequency of physical response-to-resistance incidents from pre–BWC implementation to post–BWC implementation are displayed in Figure 2. This graph demonstrates that there was an 8.4% decrease in the average number of physical response-to-resistance incidents pre- to post–BWC implementation for the 60 BWC officers compared with a 3.4% increase in the average number of physical response-to-resistance incidents pre- to post–BWC implementation for the matched sample of 60 non-BWC officers.

Discussion

The current study set out to provide an evaluation of the impact of BWCs on police response-to-resistance. Relying on 24 months of response-to-resistance data (12 months pre–BWC implementation and 12 months post–BWC implementation) and PSM techniques, a number of key findings emerged that are highlighted below.

For example, the initial comparisons revealed that the 60 BWC officers significantly differed from the 701 non-BWC officers not only in the extremely unequal sample sizes but also in the, more importantly, on a host of officer demographics and in their average number of physical response-to-resistance incidents pre–BWC implementation. As a result, propensity score matching techniques were applied in an effort to generate a matched sample of 60 non-BWC officers that were statistically similar to the 60 BWC officers in terms of their gender, race/ethnicity, age, years of law enforcement experience at TPD, and their average number of physical response-to-resistance incidents pre–BWC implementation. Once this PSM algorithm and analysis were performed, the results demonstrated that the 60 BWC officers were involved in a significantly fewer number of physical response-to-resistance incidents post–BWC implementation, on average, compared to the matched sample of 60 non-BWC officers. And the BWC officers exhibited an 8.4% decrease in their mean number of physical response-to-resistance incidents when comparing their behavior in the 12 months pre–BWC implementation to their behavior in the 12 months post–BWC implementation. In contrast, the mean number of physical response-to-resistance incidents increased by 3.4% for the matched sample of non-BWC officers when

comparing their pre–BWC implementation frequency to their post–BWC implementation frequency. Although only speculative, if this 8.4% reduction in the mean number of physical response-to-resistance incidents (a reduction of approximately 20 physical response-to-resistance incidents) observed among these 60 BWC officers in the 12 months post–BWC implementation was scaled up to the entire sample of 761 TPD officers, then this would translate to slightly more than a reduction of 250 physical response-to-resistance incidents per year for the department.

These findings notwithstanding, it is important to note several limitations of the current study. First, this study is based on results from one large metropolitan police department in one city, and a city that is a mid- to large-size city with a diverse demographic population. The degree to which these findings would be observed in smaller, less diverse, and more rural police departments and cities may be limited. Second, although a rigorous statistical procedure (i.e., propensity score matching) was used to derive a statistically comparable matched sample of non-BWC officers, these results were not generated from a randomized controlled trial such as those found elsewhere in the literature (see Jennings et al. 2014, 2015). As such, caution should be taken when making comparisons to these studies and in the interpretation of this study's results as the influence of unobserved and unmeasured differences between the BWC officers and the matched sample of non-BWC officers is unknown. Third, this study (similar to other studies in the literature) did not have information from the incidents where response-to-resistance was used regarding suspect demeanor, suspect race, suspect gender, and so on. As these variables are also potentially relevant factors for influencing an officer's decision to use force, it is recommended that future research incorporate these data when available.

Ultimately, the results from this study contribute to the growing body of evidence in support of the utility of police body-worn cameras to reduce police response-to-resistance (Ariel et al. 2015; Grossmith et al. 2015; Jennings et al. 2015). However, it is important to acknowledge that BWCs are not a panacea. In light of the growing number of tragic incidents that are occurring in the United States where minority individuals and police officers are being targeted for violence, it is necessary that police departments consider a range of prevention strategies for reducing officer response-to-resistance and increasing officer safety such as the adoption of BWCs and an increase in police officer training in general and implicit bias training specifically, along with other recognizable and successful practices to improve police—community relations such as community policing and other related strategies (Chappell and Piquero 2010; Zavala and Kurtz 2016). Without this constellation of efforts, the effectiveness of any one strategy may prove relatively futile. In this same vein, society and the police cannot simply expect that putting a BWC on every officer, in and of itself, will provide an immediate cure for the problem of racially biased policing practices, police excessive response-to-resistance, and police officers being targeted for being police officers, but it is perhaps a step in the right direction.

Discussion Questions

1. What were the variables that the authors used to match the BWC officers with police who were not using cameras? Can you think of any additional variables that might have been helpful?

2. What kind of impact did the matching procedure have on the results?

3. For this study, the researchers obtained agency records for their data. Can you think of any other types of data that they could have used to do this study?

References

Ariel, Barak, William A. Farrar, and Alex Sutherland. 2015. "The Effect of Police Body-Worn Cameras on Use of Force and Citizens' Complaints Against the Police: A Randomized Controlled Trial." *Journal of Quantitative Criminology* 31:509–535.

Austin, Peter C. 2009. "Some Methods of Propensity-Score Matching had Superior Performance to Others: Results of an Empirical Investigation and Monte Carlo Simulations." *Biomedical Journal* 51:171–184.

Chappell, Allison T. and Alex R. Piquero. 2010. "Applying Social Learning Theory to Police Misconduct." *Deviant Behavior* 25:89–108.

Ellis, Tom, Craig Jenkins, and Paul Smith. 2015. *Evaluation of the Introduction of Personal Issue Body Worn Video Cameras (Operation Hyperion) on the Isle of Wight: Final Report to Hampshire Constabulary.* Portsmouth, UK: University of Portsmouth: Institute of Criminal Justice Studies.

Goodall, Martin. 2007. *Guidance for the Police Use of Body-Worn Video Devices.* London: Home Office. Retrieved July 1, 2016 (http://library.college. police.uk/docs/homeoffice/guidance-body-worn-devices.pdf).

Grossmith, Lynne, Catherine Owens, Will Finn, David Mann, Tom Davies, and Laura Baika. 2015. *Police, Camera, Evidence: London's Cluster Randomised Controlled Trial of Body Worn Video.* London, UK: College of Policing and the Mayor's Office for Policing and Crime (MOPAC).

Ho, Daniel E., Kosuke Imai, Gary King, and Elizabeth A. Stuart. 2007. "Matching as Nonparametric Preprocessing for Reducing Model Dependence in Parametric Causal Inference." *Political Analysis* 15:199–236.

Ho, Daniel E., Kosuke Imai, Gary King, and Elizabeth A. Stuart. 2011. "Matchit: Nonparametric Preprocessing for Parametric Causal Inference." *Journal of Statistical Software* 8:1–28.

Jennings, Wesley G., Lorie A. Fridell, and Mathew D. Lynch. 2014. "Cops and Cameras: Officer Perceptions of the Use of Body-Worn Cameras in Law Enforcement." *Journal of Criminal Justice* 42:549–556.

Jennings, Wesley G., Mathew D. Lynch, and Lorie A. Fridell. 2015. "Evaluating the Impact of Police Officer Body-Worn Cameras (BWCs) on Response-to-Resistance and Serious External Complaints: Evidence from the Orlando Police Department (OPD) Experience Utilizing a Randomized Controlled Experiment." *Journal of Criminal Justice* 43:480–486.

Jennings, Wesley G., Tara Richards, Elizabeth Tomsich, Angela Gover, and Ráchael Powers. 2013. "A Critical Examination of the Causal Link between Child Abuse and Adult Dating Violence Perpetration and Victimization from a Propensity-Score Matching Approach." *Women and Criminal Justice* 23:167–184.

Katz, Charles M., Mike Kurtenbach, David E. Choate, and Michael D. White. 2015. *Phoenix, Arizona, Smart Policing Initiative: Evaluating the Impact of*

Police Officer Body-Worn Cameras. Washington, DC: U.S. Department of Justice, Bureau of Justice Assistance.

Lum, Cynthia, Christopher Koper, Linda Merola, Amber Scherer, and Amanda Reioux. 2015. *Existing and Ongoing Body Worn Camera Research: Knowledge Gaps and Opportunities.* Fairfax, VA: George Mason University: Center for Evidence-Based Crime Policy.

ODS Consulting. 2011. *Body Worn Video Projects in Paisley and Aberdeen, Self Evaluation.* Glasgow: ODS Consulting.

Owens, Catherine, David Mann, and Roy Mckenna. 2014. *The Essex BWV Trial: The Impact of BWV on Criminal Justice Outcomes of Domestic Abuse Incidents.* London, UK: College of Policing.

Pearl, Judea. 2009. *Causality: Models, Reasoning, and Inference.* 2nd ed. New York: Cambridge University Press.

Ready, Justin T. and Jacob T. Young. 2015. "The Impact of On-Officer Video Cameras on Police-Citizen Contacts: Findings from a Controlled Experiment in Mesa, AZ." *Journal of Experimental Criminology* 11:445–458.

Richards, Tara, M. Dwayne Smith, Wesley G. Jennings, Beth Bjerregaard, and Sondra Fogel. 2014. "An Examination of the Sex Disparity in Capital Sentencing: A Propensity Score Matching Approach." *American Journal of Criminal Justice* 39:681–697.

Rosenbaum, Paul R. 2002. *Observational Studies.* 2nd ed. New York: Springer-Verlag.

Rosenbaum, Paul R. and Donald B. Rubin. 1983. "The Central Role of the Propensity Score in Observational Studies for Causal Effects." *Biometrics* 70:41–55.

Roy, Allyson. 2014. *On Officer Video Cameras: Examining the Effects of Police Department Policy and Assignment on Camera Use and Activation.* (Unpublished master's thesis). Arizona State University, Phoenix, AZ.

Sousa, William H., Terance D. Miethe, and Mari Sakiyama. 2015. *Body Worn Cameras on Police: Results from a National Survey of Public Attitudes.* Las Vegas: Center for Crime and Justice Policy, University of Nevada, Las Vegas.

Young, Jacob T. and Justin T. Ready. 2015. "Diffusion of Ideas and Technology: The Role of Networks in Influencing the Endorsement and Use of On-Officer Video Cameras." *Journal of Contemporary Criminal Justice* 31:243–261.

Zavala, Egbert and Don L. Kurtz. 2016. "Applying Differential Coercion and Social Support Theory to Police Officers' Misconduct." *Deviant Behavior* 37:877–892.

Reading 11.3   Psychometric Properties of the UNCOPE

Risk assessment tools are valuable assets for treatment providers as they work to identify appropriate correctional programs. These instruments are of varying effectiveness, however, since they need to be validated with the population for which they are going to be used. Proctor, Kopak, and Hoffmann (2017) tested the validity and reliability of the Unintended use, Neglect of responsibilities, desire/attempts to Cut down, Objection by others, Preoccupation, and Emotional distress (UNCOPE) screening instrument when used with justice-involved juveniles. UNCOPE is a very short, six-item tool intended to identify substance use disorders in respondents. To test this, the authors collected data on UNCOPE scores for a sample of juveniles who also participated in the Practical Adolescent Dual Diagnostic Interview (PADDI), which provides treatment staff much more information than the UNCOPE but also takes much longer to administer. The researchers obtained their data with the cooperation of a state juvenile justice agency. This article serves as a good example of a test of validity and reliability, but the authors also raise some other very important topics for us to consider when we think about administering screening tools.

Psychometric Properties of the UNCOPE: Screening for DSM-5 Substance Use Disorder Among a State Juvenile Justice Population

Steven L. Proctor, Albert M. Kopak, and Norman G. Hoffmann

Substance use and substance use disorders (SUDs) are prevalent among adolescents involved in the juvenile justice system. Although prevalence estimates of SUDs among juvenile justice populations are variable and largely influenced by the specific settings sampled, previous research has demonstrated considerably higher rates of SUDs across various juvenile justice settings relative to the general adolescent population (Johnson et al., 2004; Karnik et al., 2009; Substance Abuse and Mental Health Services Administration (SAMHSA), 2015; Teplin, Abram, McClelland, Dulcan, & Mericle, 2002). Problematic drug and alcohol use has also consistently been identified as a risk factor for recidivism among juvenile offenders (for review, see Cottle, Lee, & Heilbrun, 2001).

The *Diagnostic and Statistical Manual of Mental Disorders, Fourth Edition* (DSM-IV) (American Psychiatric Association [APA], 1994) classified SUDs into two mutually exclusive categories: substance abuse and substance dependence. According to the DSM-IV, substance abuse is defined by a maladaptive pattern of substance use manifested by recurrent negative consequences related to use and requires the presence of at least one of the four stated criteria (i.e., failure to fulfill major role obligations at work, home, or school; use in physically hazardous situations; substance-related legal problems; and social or interpersonal problems caused or exacerbated by use). Substance dependence, on the other hand, requires a minimum of three of seven criteria and is characterized by impaired control over use, desire or attempts to restrict use, continued use despite harm, tolerance, withdrawal, spending excessive time related to use, and sacrificing activities to use. Another important issue associated with the DSM-IV division between abuse and dependence is that of "diagnostic orphans." The term diagnostic orphans refers to those individuals who meet one or two of the diagnostic criteria for substance dependence yet fail to report indications of substance abuse, thus warranting a no diagnosis classification (Hasin & Paykin, 1998). Previous research suggests that diagnostic orphans are at increased risk for developing subsequent SUDs and use-related problems relative to individuals reporting no positive diagnostic findings at baseline (Degenhardt, Coffey, Carlin, Swift, & Patton, 2008; Harford, Yi, & Grant, 2010; McBride & Adamson, 2010).

The DSM-5, which was released by the APA in 2013, introduced several changes to SUD classification, including, most notably, a shift from the traditional categorical approach to a dimensional approach. Specific changes to SUD diagnostic criteria included the removal of the recurrent legal problems criterion (DSM-IV abuse criterion), addition of a criterion representing craving, and collapsing the DSM-IV abuse and dependence criteria into a single unified SUD category of graded clinical severity. The DSM-5 requires the presence of a minimum of 2 positive criteria in order to assign a SUD diagnosis. The DSM-5 includes 11 total SUD criteria and features three severity specifiers based on the total number of positive criteria: mild (2–3 criteria), moderate (4–5 criteria), and severe (6+ criteria).

Despite the high rates of SUDs among juveniles involved in the criminal justice system, a report from the Office of Juvenile Justice and Delinquency Prevention revealed that only 61% of juvenile justice system facilities reported screening all juveniles for substance use problems (Snyder & Sickmund, 2006). This problem is further compounded by the limited financial and clinical staffing resources typical of most juvenile justice settings, which often preclude thorough and comprehensive substance use assessments of all newly admitted juveniles. Therefore, the need for a reliable and valid screening procedure as a means to rapidly and efficiently identify juveniles in need of further assessment and treatment services is of paramount importance. The selection of an appropriate screening instrument requires careful consideration of several variables, including its accuracy, length, cost, window of detection, and the complexity of its scoring procedure

(SAMHSA, 2005). Similarly, it is essential to consider the target diagnosis, and whether or not the screen can be self-administered. Finally, another important consideration is if the instrument requires extensive and continued staff training.

There are a number of screening instruments that may be used in the context of routine screening for substance use problems among adolescent populations (Knight et al., 1999; Martino, Grilo, & Fehon, 2000; Mayer & Filstead, 1979; Miller, 1990; Miller & Lazowski, 2001; Tarter, 1990; White & Labouvie, 1989), many of which have adequate psychometric properties (Bauman, Merta, & Steiner, 1999; Ginzler, Garrett, Baer, & Peterson, 2007; Knight, Sherritt, Shrier, Harris, & Chang, 2002; Moberg, 1983; Rogers, Cashel, Johansen, Sewell, & Gonzalez, 1997; Stein et al., 2005; Sweet & Saules, 2003; Tarter & Kirisci, 2001). With the exception of the Substance Abuse Subtle Screening Inventory-Adolescent Version (SASSI-A; Miller, 1990), however, perhaps the most noteworthy limitation of most screens is the lack of validation studies with juvenile justice populations. Additional limitations include their restrictiveness (i.e., tendency to assess for alcohol problems only or generic problematic drug use only), inability to identify a specific diagnosis, excessive length, and the financial costs associated with the use of some screens. Extant psychometric support for existing screens has also largely been derived from studies using previous versions of the diagnostic criteria for SUDs (DSM-IV, etc.). This limitation is particularly salient given that with the advent of the DSM-5, it is unclear whether the various screens can discriminate among the severe SUD diagnosis as defined by the DSM-5 and the less clinically severe diagnoses.

One potential screening option that addresses the aforementioned limitations of other commonly used screening instruments is the UNCOPE (Hoffmann, Hunt, Rhodes, & Riley, 2003), which is named for the various constructs of problematic substance use it purports to assess (Unintended use, Neglect of responsibilities, desire/attempts to Cut down, Objection by others, Preoccupation, and Emotional distress).

The UNCOPE was originally developed for screening recent arrestees in the Arrestee Drug Abuse Monitoring (ADAM) system, subsequently funded by the Office of National Drug Control Policy (ONDCP). The UNCOPE has been validated on juvenile offenders (Urofsky, Seiber, & Hoffmann, 2007), state prison inmates (Campbell, Hoffmann, Hoffmann, & Gillaspy, 2005; Proctor & Hoffmann, 2016), and county jail inmates (Proctor, Hoffmann, & Corwin, 2011), and has been shown to have relatively good accuracy in identifying SUDs compared to a comprehensive assessment. The UNCOPE has also demonstrated "good" to "excellent" internal consistency among adult populations with Cronbach's alphas ranging from .85 to .94 (Hoffmann et al., 2003; Proctor & Hoffmann, 2016). The UNCOPE consists of six items (Figure 1). The first five items are compatible with five different DSM-5 SUD diagnostic criteria (i.e., unintended use, failure to fulfill major role obligations, unsuccessful efforts to cut down or control use, recurrent social or interpersonal problems related to use, craving or compulsion to use), and the last item, while not part of the diagnostic criteria, assesses use to alleviate emotional distress consistent with the self-medication hypothesis (Khantzian, 1985).

The UNCOPE can be used as a generic screen to assess for any SUD or specifically for alcohol or other drug-specific use disorders (cannabis, cocaine, etc.), which is a clear advantage relative to other available substance use screening instruments. Additional strengths pertain to its cost, length, window of detection, and the simplicity of its scoring procedure. That is, given that the UNCOPE items are public domain, it represents an inexpensive option. The estimated administration time associated with the UNCOPE is minimal due to its brevity, and it also includes a straightforward scoring procedure (i.e., sum all positive responses). The UNCOPE can be self- or interviewer-administered, and requires limited staff training. Thus, routine screening of SUD using the UNCOPE may prove to be both economical and practical. The UNCOPE items are also in reference to the prior 12-month period, which is consistent with the diagnostic criteria for a current diagnosis. Although the UNCOPE has been found to be effective in the identification of DSM-IV (APA, 1994) substance dependence among juvenile offenders (Urofsky et al., 2007), there remains no research to date evaluating its utility in identifying juveniles at general risk for a DSM-5 SUD diagnosis.

In light of the substantive changes to the SUD diagnostic criteria from the DSM-IV to the current DSM-5, additional research is warranted to determine whether the UNCOPE is effective in the identification of risk for DSM-5 SUD. The present report sought to fill this apparent gap in the research literature by

---

1. **U** – In the past 12 months have you ever spent more time drinking or using drugs than you intended?

2. **N** – Have you ever neglected some of your usual responsibilities because of drinking alcohol or using drugs?

3. **C** – In the past 12 months, have you felt you wanted or needed to cut down on your drinking or drug use?

4. **O** – Has anyone objected to your drinking or drug use?

5. **P** – In the past 12 months, have you found yourself thinking a lot about drinking or using drugs?

6. **E** – Have you ever used alcohol or drugs to relieve emotional discomfort such as sadness, anger, or boredom?

Figure 1 UNCOPE Items

evaluating the psychometric properties of the UNCOPE using data from a large juvenile justice population and determining its: (a) diagnostic accuracy relative to a structured clinical interview, and (b) internal consistency as evidenced by Cronbach's alpha.

Method

Data derived from routine clinical evaluations of consecutive male admissions to juvenile detention facilities and diversion courts in a New England state between the period of February 2002 and April 2005 were used for the present study. The facilities and courts from which the study data were drawn handle all the juvenile cases in the state, so the data accurately represent the population of adolescents coming to the attention of the juvenile justice system in the state. Given that female admissions to the state system were relatively rare during the study period, they were excluded from analyses because there were too few female cases to ensure stable results. All juveniles were administered a structured diagnostic clinical interview by licensed/ credentialed professionals to assess for SUD indications and common co-occurring mental health conditions subsequent to involvement in the state system. Clinical interview information was used by the system to identify potential treatment needs. One of the study authors originally used the data for purposes of review and feedback on the administration of the clinical interview used for routine evaluations and statistical analysis to identify the prevalence of mental health conditions among juveniles entering the state system. The state system approved the release of an anonymous dataset for secondary data analysis, and an appropriate institutional review board granted the study authors permission to use the existing de-identified dataset.

Participants

The total sample comprised 503 male adolescents between the ages of 13 and 18 years (M = 16.35); however, the majority (69.0%) of juveniles were between the ages of 16 and 17 years. The 18-year-old offenders (9.7% of the sample),

although technically adults, were continued in the juvenile system due to prior involvement in the system. The vast majority (88.1%) were White, reflecting the largely rural nature of the state. American Indians were the largest racial-minority group (4.6%) with other racial groups making up the remainder. In terms of educational status, although over half (55.3%) reported that they were currently enrolled in school, 17.9% indicated that they were either suspended, expelled, or had dropped out. Of the total sample, 6.4% were currently working toward their GED, 5.4% had graduated from high school, and 12.1% listed their educational status as "incarcerated." Only 33.2% had passed the 10th grade or higher. Almost one fifth (19.5%) reported experiencing a current reading difficulty, which had caused them to fall behind the rest of the class. A third of the sample (33.6%) reported that they had taken some type of prescribed medication during the previous two weeks, and an additional 27.6% reported a history of medication use. Over four fifths (82.9%) of the sample met DSM-5 criteria for any SUD (i.e., mild, moderate, or severe) with 63.6% receiving a severe SUD diagnosis.

Measures

The Practical Adolescent Dual Diagnostic Interview (PADDI) (Estroff & Hoffmann, 2001) was used as the diagnostic criterion measure to determine the presence of DMS-5 SUD. The PADDI is a structured diagnostic interview designed to identify prevalent SUD and additional mental health conditions likely to co-occur with SUD. The PADDI covers frequency and recent use of alcohol, cannabis, cocaine, amphetamines, opioids, sedatives, hallucinogens, and inhalants. The PADDI has been used with a number of juvenile justice involved and clinical treatment populations, and has evidenced adequate psychometric properties (Abrantes, Hoffmann, Anton, & Estroff, 2004; Hoffmann, Bride, MacMasters, Abrantes, & Estroff, 2004; Proctor & Hoffmann, 2012). The UNCOPE items are contained in the PADDI and were extracted for the analyses. The PADDI is compatible with DSM-IV criteria and includes multiple items for most of the individual criteria. Although based largely on the DSM-IV, the PADDI includes a number of additional criteria items (e.g., craving or compulsive use) that allowed for the consideration of the DSM-5 SUD diagnosis. The PADDI has also since been updated to the PADDI-5 (Hoffmann & Estroff, 2013) following data collection for the present study.

Data Analyses

DSM-5 SUD diagnostic determinations were made from algorithms corresponding to the diagnostic criteria based on the PADDI findings. Algorithms were created in which items assessing each of the 11 DSM-5 criteria were used to determine positive findings for each criterion. The number of positive findings were then divided into categories where zero or one criterion was identified as no diagnosis, two to three were designated as mild, four to five positive criteria defined moderate, and six or more positive criteria constituted a severe SUD diagnosis. The criterion for craving or compulsion to use comprised the preoccupation and compulsion items. Given that the DSM-5 codes a moderate diagnosis the same as a severe diagnosis for billing purposes (i.e., codes are embedded in parentheses within the diagnostic criteria box for each SUD (APA, 2013)), cross tabulations were examined to determine the performance of various recommended UNCOPE cut-scores in identifying juvenile offenders with: (a) moderate to severe, and (b) severe only DSM-5 diagnoses. The six items comprising the UNCOPE were analyzed for internal consistency as indicated by Cronbach's alpha.

Results

As can be seen in Table 1, a cut-score of 3+ positive UNCOPE responses resulted in roughly nine in ten juvenile offenders being correctly classified as having either a moderate or severe DSM-5 SUD, with very high specificity. The diagnostic accuracy of the UNCOPE was improved with respect to identifying offenders with only a severe SUD such that 94.4% of juvenile offenders were

Table 1 Diagnostic Accuracy for DSM-5 Diagnoses by UNCOPE Cut-scores

Cut-score	DSM-5 Severe SUD		
	Sensitivity		Specificity
2+	99.7%		65.0%
3+	94.4%		86.9%
		DSM-5 Moderate/ Severe SUD[0]	
2+	96.7%		78.3%
3+	87.1%		94.2%

Note: DSM-5 = Diagnostic and Statistical Manual of Mental Disorders (5th ed.); SUD = substance use disorder. Composite category consisting of either a moderate or severe diagnosis given both diagnoses receive the same code for billing and reimbursement purposes per DSM-5 guidelines.

correctly classified with a cut-score of 3+ positive responses while specificity remained high. When the threshold was lowered to 2+ positive findings to identify a severe diagnosis only, the findings were similar to those using 3+ positive findings in terms of a high level of sensitivity, but specificity was reduced. With respect to identifying offenders with either a moderate or severe SUD diagnosis using a cut-score of 2+, 96.7% were correctly classified, with specificity remaining adequate, but dropping to 78.3%. The six UNCOPE items yielded a Cronbach's alpha of .915, indicative of a high level of internal consistency (Nunnally, 1978). The internal consistency analysis among the 11 DSM-5 SUD diagnostic criteria revealed a Cronbach's alpha of .920, suggesting that the diagnostic criteria constitute a relatively robust syndrome.

Discussion

If juvenile justice agencies aspire to an objective screening and referral protocol as a means of identifying offenders with a DSM-5 SUD diagnosis in need of further assessment and treatment placement, a valid and reliable screening instrument is a requisite for this effort. To this end, the observed findings suggest that the

UNCOPE is a potentially valid and reliable screen for use in the identification of a DSM-5 SUD among male juvenile justice populations.

In addition, the UNCOPE includes a number of advantages relative to existing screening instruments. Of particular interest, the UNCOPE can be used as a generic screening instrument covering both alcohol and other drugs, thereby avoiding the need for separate screens. Given its brevity and ease of scoring, the UNCOPE can be incorporated into existing evaluation procedures at juvenile detention centers or diversion court programs.

Based on the observed findings, it appears that a cut-score of 3+ positive responses represents a reasonable balance of the UNCOPE's sensitivity and specificity in the identification of juvenile offenders with a likely severe DSM-5 SUD or a moderate to severe SUD. However, in practice, the selection of an appropriate screening threshold (i.e., cut-score) will be influenced by a number of factors, including the setting, context, and intended purpose or goal of screening. It is also noteworthy to mention that while reducing the threshold might allow an agency to effectively identify more juveniles who likely meet DSM-5 criteria for a SUD, the false positive rate will also increase. Previous research with adult offenders suggests that screening conducted by uniformed officers is likely to result in substantial suppression of positive UNCOPE findings (Proctor et al., 2011). Therefore, it is recommended that screening be conducted by someone not viewed as an officer or authority figure, such as medical or behavioral health staff. In settings in which this may not be possible and screening is completed by a uniformed officer, agencies may consider reducing the threshold from 3 to 2+ positive responses. A cut-score of 2+ is recommended in this instance in order to account for the potential underreporting of substance use issues when screening is conducted by uniformed officers, and may result in more accurate findings.

There are additional factors necessitating a careful consideration of the benefits relative to the costs of a cut-score of 2 versus 3+ positive responses on the UNCOPE. The first is the stage at which the screening is conducted. That is, if screening is completed upon first coming to the attention of a state juvenile justice system, then a cut-score of 2+ may be indicated in order to ensure that juveniles with a SUD are not missed, and they subsequently receive more extensive assessment and appropriate treatment services. Second, it is important to consider whether the agency has the capacity in terms of available staff and resources to accommodate the needs of a high number of juveniles who potentially screen positive. If an agency has limited staff and personnel, they likely will be interested in only the "most severe" cases. Thus, a cut-score of 3+ might be warranted in such a situation. A cut-score of 3+ would also ensure that those who screen positive would most likely meet criteria for a mild SUD at the very least given that five of the six UNCOPE items are compatible with the DSM-5 SUD criteria, and only two positive SUD criteria are required for a DSM-5 mild SUD diagnosis. This strategy is a viable option for those agencies hoping to fully utilize their limited resources and not expend effort on cases with a high probability of failing to receive any SUD diagnosis.

The findings should be considered in light of several limitations, which suggest the need for additional work in this area. First, the sample comprised primarily White juvenile offenders. Although representative of the state from which the data were drawn, the underrepresentation of racial minorities warrants caution in generalizing the findings to other juvenile justice systems serving more racially diverse populations. Second, the exclusively male sample warrants further investigation with female juvenile offenders. Third, the UNCOPE items used in the present study's analyses were not administered at a time prior to the clinical assessment, and instead were extracted from the full clinical interview. As a result, this method may have inflated some of the observed sensitivity and specificity estimates. However, it is important to note that study findings were consistent when the UNCOPE items were removed from the diagnostic algorithms in that they remained largely unaffected. That is, findings were similar regardless of whether or not the six UNCOPE items were included among the PADDI items used to assign SUD diagnoses. Finally, as with other clinical interview data, the PADDI relies largely on self-report. The diagnostic determinations were also derived from a single structured clinical interview and did not include verification of the reported problems from additional or collateral sources. Given juvenile arrestees and detainees have been shown to significantly underreport substance use problems (Wislar & Fendrich, 2000), the use of bioassay or other objective methods to substantiate diagnostic determinations is warranted.

Despite the aforementioned study limitations, the findings demonstrate relatively strong support for the clinical utility of the UNCOPE as an effective brief screen for identifying juvenile offenders at risk for a current moderate or severe DSM-5 SUD, which is consistent with previous research evaluating its psychometric performance in identifying DSM-IV SUD diagnoses.

Discussion Questions

1. How has the transition from the DSM-IV to the DSM-V impacted the way we define substance abuse and dependence and identify people who needs treatment?
2. What are the research and practical implications of adjusting the UNCOPE cut score from 3+ to 2+?
3. How might the criminal justice agency's selection of an employee to administer the UNCOPE impact the results of the screening?

References

Abrantes, A. M., Hoffman, N. G., Anton, R. P., & Estroff, T. W. (2004). Identifying co-occurring disorders in juvenile justice populations. *Youth Violence and Juvenile Justice, 2*, 329–341. https://doi.org/10.1177/1541204004267781

American Psychiatric Association. (1994). *Diagnostic and statistical manual of mental disorders* (4th ed.). Washington, DC: Author.

American Psychiatric Association. (2013). *Diagnostic and statistical manual of mental disorders* (5th ed.). Washington, DC: Author.

Bauman, S., Merta, R., & Steiner, R. (1999). Further validation of the adolescent form of the SASSI. *Journal of Child and Adolescent Substance Abuse, 9*, 51–71. https://doi.org/10.1300/J029v09n01_03

Campbell, T. C., Hoffmann, N. G., Hoffmann, T. D., & Gillaspy, J. A. (2005). UNCOPE: A screen for substance dependence among state prison inmates. *Prison Journal, 85*, 7–17. https://doi.org/10.1177/0032885504274287

Cottle, C. C., Lee, R. J., & Heilbrun, K. (2001). The prediction of criminal recidivism in juveniles: A meta-analysis. *Criminal Justice and Behavior, 28*, 367–394. https://doi.org/10.1177/0093854801028003005

Degenhardt, L., Coffey, C., Carlin, J. B., Swift, W., & Patton, G. C. (2008). Are diagnostic orphans at risk of developing cannabis abuse or dependence? Four-year followup of young adult cannabis users not meeting diagnostic criteria. *Drug and Alcohol Dependence, 92*, 86–90. https://doi.org/10.1016/j.drugalcdep.2007.07.003

Estroff, T. W., & Hoffmann, N. G. (2001). *PADDI: Practical adolescent dual diagnosis interview.* Smithfield, RI: Evince Clinical Assessments.

Ginzler, J. A., Garrett, S. B., Baer, J. S., & Peterson, P. L. (2007). Measurement of negative consequences of substance use in street youth: An expanded use of the Rutgers Alcohol Problem Index. *Addictive Behaviors, 32*, 1519–1525. https://doi.org/10.1016/j.addbeh.2006.11.004

Harford, T. C., Yi, H., & Grant, B. F. (2010). The five-year diagnostic utility of 'diagnostic orphans' for alcohol use disorders in a national sample of young adults. *Journal of Studies on Alcohol and Drugs, 71*, 410–417. https://doi.org/10.15288/jsad.2010.71.410

Hasin, D. S., & Paykin, A. (1998). Dependence symptoms but no diagnosis: Diagnostic "orphans" in a community sample. *Drug and Alcohol Dependence, 50*, 19–26. https://doi.org/10.1016/s0376-8716(98)00007-6

Hoffmann, N. G., Bride, B. E., MacMasters, S. A., Abrantes, A.M., & Estroff, T.W. (2004). Identifying co-occurring disorders in adolescent populations. *Journal of Addictive Diseases, 23*, 41–53. https://doi.org/10.1300/J069v23n04_04

Hoffmann, N. G., & Estroff, T. D. (2013). *PADDI-5 manual: Practical adolescent dual diagnostic interview-5.* Carson City, NV: The Change Companies.

Hoffmann, N. G., Hunt, D. E., Rhodes, W. M., & Riley, K. J. (2003). UNCOPE: A brief substance dependence screen for use with arrestees. *Journal of Drug Issues, 33*, 29–44. https://doi.org/10.1177/002204260303300102

Johnson, T. P., Cho, Y. I., Fendrich, M., Graf, I., Kelly-Wilson, L., & Pickup, L. (2004). Treatment need and utilization among youth entering the juvenile corrections system. *Journal of Substance Abuse Treatment, 26*, 117–128. https://doi.org/10.1016/S0740-5472(03)00164-8

Karnik, N. S., Soller, M., Redlich, A., Silverman, M., Kraemer, H. C., Haapanen, R., & Steiner, H. (2009). Prevalence of and gender differences in psychiatric disorders among juvenile delinquents incarcerated for nine months. *Psychiatric Services, 60*, 838–841. https://doi.org/10.1176/appi.ps.60.6.838

Khantzian, E. J. (1985). The self-medication hypothesis of addictive disorders: Focus on heroin and cocaine dependence. *American Journal of Psychiatry, 142,* 1259–1264. https://doi.org/10.1176/ajp.142.11.1259

Knight, J. R., Sherritt, L., Shrier, L. A., Harris, S. K., & Chang, G. (2002). Validity of the CRAFFT substance abuse screening test among adolescent clinic patients. *Archives of Pediatrics and Adolescent Medicine, 156,* 607–614. https://doi.org/10.1001/archpedi.156.6.607

Knight, J. R., Shrier, L. A., Bravender, T. D., Farrell, M., Vander Bilt, J., & Shaffer, H. J. (1999). A new brief screen for adolescent substance abuse. *Archives of Pediatrics and Adolescent Medicine, 153,* 591–596. https://doi.org/10.1001/archpedi.153.6.591

Martino, S., Grilo, C., & Fehon, D. (2000). Development of the drug abuse screening test for adolescents (DAST-A). *Addictive Behaviors, 25,* 57–70. https://doi.org/10.1016/s0306-4603(99)00030-1

Mayer, J., & Filstead, W. J. (1979). The adolescent alcohol involvement scale: An instrument for measuring adolescent use and misuse of alcohol. *Journal of Studies on Alcohol, 40,* 291–300. https://doi.org/10.15288/jsa.1979.40.291

McBride, O., & Adamson, G. (2010). Are subthreshold alcohol dependence symptoms a risk factor for developing DSM-IV alcohol use disorders? A three-year prospective study of 'diagnostic orphans' in a national sample. *Addictive Behaviors, 35,* 586–592. https://doi.org/10.1016/j.addbeh.2010.01.014

Miller, G. A. (1990). *The SASSI—Adolescent manual.* Bloomington, IN: SASSI Institute.

Miller, G. A., & Lazowski, L. E. (2001). *Adolescent SASSI-A2 manual.* Springville, IN: SASSI Institute.

Moberg, D. P. (1983). Identifying adolescents with alcohol problems: A field test of the adolescent alcohol involvement scale. *Journal of Studies on Alcohol, 44,* 701–721. https://doi.org/10.15288/jsa.1983.44.701

Nunnally, J. C. (1978). *Psychometric theory* (2nd ed.). New York, NY: McGraw-Hill.

Proctor, S. L., & Hoffmann, N. G. (2012). Pragmatic determination and correlates of victimization among female adolescents presenting for residential addictions treatment. *Child Welfare, 91,* 85–107.

Proctor, S. L., & Hoffmann, N. G. (2016). The UNCOPE: An effective brief screen for DSM-5 substance use disorders in correctional settings. *Psychology of Addictive Behaviors, 30,* 613–618. https://doi.org/10.1037/adb0000170

Proctor, S. L., Hoffmann, N. G., & Corwin, C. J. (2011). Response bias in screening county jail inmates for addictions. *Journal of Drug Issues, 41,* 117–134. https://doi.org/10.1177/002204261104100106

Rogers, R., Cashel, M. L., Johansen, J., Sewell, K. W., & Gonzalez, C. (1997). Evaluation of adolescent offenders with substance abuse: Validation of the SASSI with conduct-disordered youth. *Criminal Justice & Behavior, 24,* 114–128. https://doi.org/10.1177/0093854897024001007

Snyder, H. N., & Sickmund, M. (2006). *Juvenile offenders and victims: 2006 national report.* Washington, DC: US Department of Justice, Office of Justice Programs, Office of Juvenile Justice and Delinquency Prevention.

Stein, L. A. R., Lebeau-Craven, R., Martin, R., Colby, S. M., Barnett, N. P., Golembeske, C., Jr., & Penn, J. V. (2005). Use of the adolescent SASSI in a juvenile correctional setting. *Assessment, 12,* 384–394. https://doi.org/10.1177/1073191110527 9433

Substance Abuse & Mental Health Services Administration. (2005). *Substance abuse treatment for adults in the criminal justice system* (Treatment Improvement Protocol (TIP) Series, No. 44). Rockville, MD: Substance Abuse and Mental Health Services Administration.

Substance Abuse & Mental Health Services Administration. (2015). *Behavioral health trends in the United States: Results from the 2014 national survey on drug use and health* (HHS Publication No. SMA 15-4927, NSDUH Series H-50). Rockville, MD: Center for Behavioral Health Statistics and Quality.

Sweet, R. I., & Saules, K. K. (2003). Validity of the substance abuse subtle screening inventory-adolescent version (SASSI-A). *Journal of Substance Abuse Treatment, 24,* 331–340. https://doi.org/10.1016/s0740-5472(03)00049-7

Tarter, R. (1990). Evaluation and treatment of adolescent substance abuse: A decision tree method. *American Journal of Drug and Alcohol Abuse, 16,* 1–46. https://doi.org/10.3109/00952999009001570

Tarter, R. E., & Kirisci, L. (2001). Validity of the drug use screening inventory for predicting DSM-III-R substance use disorder. *Journal of Child and Adolescent Substance Abuse, 10,* 45–53. https://doi.org/10.1300/J029v10n04_05

Teplin, L. A., Abram, K. M., McClelland, G. M., Dulcan, M. K., & Mericle, A. A. (2002). Psychiatric disorders in youth in juvenile detention. *Archives of General Psychiatry, 59,* 1133–1143. https://doi.org/10.1001/archpsyc.59.12.1133

Urofsky, R. I., Seiber, E., & Hoffmann, N. G. (2007). UNCOPE: Evaluation of a brief screen for detecting substance dependence among juvenile justice populations. *Journal of School Counseling, 5,* 17.

White, H. R., & Labouvie, E. W. (1989). Toward the assessment of adolescent problem drinking. *Journal of Studies on Alcohol, 50,* 30–37.

Wislar, J. S., & Fendrich, M. (2000). Can self-reported drug use data be used to assess sex risk behavior in adolescents? *Archives of Sexual Behavior, 29,* 77–89.

Reading 11.4 Looking Inside the Black Box of Drug Courts

Drug court originated in Florida in 1989, found some support in the 1990s, and then rapidly expanded across the United States in the first two decades of the 2000s. Drug courts offer an attractive alternative to incarceration by diverting drug users from the corrections system, placing them into judicially monitored community programs. There have been numerous evaluations of drug courts, and the results have been encouraging. As Shaffer (2011) notes, however, a problem with existing evaluations is that the lack of a standardized drug court model has resulted in a lack of uniformity in court philosophy and function. The heterogeneity of programs makes cross-program comparisons difficult and presents a challenge to any researcher who might attempt a meta-analysis. Shaffer chose to measure drug court characteristics and their relative impact on outcomes as a way to look into the "black box." In other words, it is not enough to know whether drug courts in general are effective; we also need to know what characteristics of drug courts are associated with effectiveness. To conduct such a meta-analysis, Shaffer had to take one additional step, and that was calling the drug courts that previous researchers evaluated to try to collect more information about the characteristics of those courts. This allowed her to produce a great deal of information regarding the impact that specific dimensions of drug court have on outcomes.

Looking Inside the Black Box of Drug Courts: A Meta-Analytic Review

Deborah Koetzle Shaffer

Introduction

Drug courts have grown rapidly since their inception in 1989. Today, there are over 2,000 adult drug courts and nearly 500 juvenile drug courts operating across the country and another 267 in the planning stages (Office of Justice Programs Drug Court Clearinghouse and Technical Assistance Project, 2009). Estimates suggest that over 70,000 offenders are receiving drug court services at any given time (Huddleston, Marlowe, & Casebolt, 2008) and that less than a third of these will recidivate two years post-graduation (Roman, Townsend, & Bhati, 2003). The seeming success of the drug court model has spawned an industry of problem-solving courts including mental health courts, domestic violence courts, reentry courts, and, more recently, veterans' courts.

Research surrounding the drug court model has generally been aimed at determining whether the model reduced recidivism and drug-related behaviors. Drug court participants have been found to have lower rates of recidivism compared with non-participants across a variety of settings (Banks & Gottfredson, 2004; Brewster, 2001; Goldkamp & Weiland, 1993; Gottfredson, Kearley, Najaka, & Rocha, 2005; Listwan, Sundt, Holsinger, & Latessa, 2003; Peters & Murrin, 2000; Spohn, Piper, Martin, & Frenzel, 2001; Vito & Tewksbury, 1998; Wolfe, Guydish, & Termondt, 2002). While some studies have failed to find reductions in recidivism (Deschenes & Greenwood, 1994; Granfield, Eby, & Brewster, 1998; Miethe, Lu, & Reese, 2000), meta-analyses have consistently found evidence of a treatment effect (Lowenkamp, Holsinger, & Latessa, 2005; Wilson, Mitchell, & MacKenzie, 2006).

Although drug courts enjoy empirical support, the fact remains that some drug courts "work" better than others. Wilson et al. (2006) estimated a mean odds ratio = 1.66 in their systematic review and reported a range of odds ratios from 0.60 to 25.00. Similarly, Lowenkamp et al. (2005) found a mean logged odds ratio = 0.29 with a range of -0.63 to 1.71. The variability in effect sizes points to the need to explore the characteristics of effective drug courts. Recent studies have focused on drug court effectiveness across offender types (Bouffard & Richardson, 2007; Dannerbeck, Harris, Sundet, & Lloyd, 2006; Gray & Saum, 2005; Hartman, Listwan, & Shaffer, 2007; Listwan, Shaffer, & Hartman, 2009; Shaffer, Hartman, & Listwan, 2009; Shaffer, Listwan, Latessa, & Lowenkamp, 2008), but relatively few efforts have been aimed at examining the impact of programmatic aspects of the drug court model on recidivism (see Festinger, Marlowe, Lee, Kirby, Bovasso, & McLellan, 2002; Goldkamp, White, & Robinson, 2001; Marlowe, Festinger, & Lee, 2004; Marlowe, Festinger, Lee, Dugosh, & Benasutti, 2006; Marlowe et al., 2003).

One challenge in assessing the characteristics of effective drug courts is the lack of a theoretical framework for their initial design and implementation. The first drug court emerged in Florida in 1989 in an effort to manage the growing number of drug offenders processed through the criminal justice system as a result of the war on drugs (see Finn & Newlyn, 1997; Listwan et al., 2003). The early success of the Miami Drug Court, coupled with financial and political support, led to its rapid expansion to jurisdictions throughout the country (Listwan et al., 2003). However, it took nearly a decade before the key components of the model were defined (Drug Courts Program Office [DCPO], 1997) and there was an attempt at providing a theoretical explanation (Hora, Schma, & Rosenthal, 1999) for its success. The lack of a theoretical model during the model's infancy, coupled with a lack of guidance on how to implement the key components, resulted in considerable inconsistency in the structure of the model across jurisdictions (see Goldkamp, 1999). For example, though treatment is considered a key component, some drug courts utilize external providers while others utilize internal providers, and the nature of treatment services differs across drug courts (Bouffard & Taxman, 2004; Taxman & Bouffard, 2002).

Though there have been a sizable number of evaluations, the variation in the implementation of the model makes it difficult to draw conclusions beyond the notion that drug courts reduce recidivism. Prior meta-analyses have attempted to address this by assessing moderators of drug court effectiveness but have been constrained by a general lack of data reported in technical reports and journal articles. The current study overcomes this limitation by supplementing a traditional meta-analytic approach with a survey of drug courts. After merging the two sources of data, moderators of drug court effectiveness are explored.

Theoretical Perspective

Therapeutic Jurisprudence

The main theoretical perspective applied to drug courts is therapeutic jurisprudence (TJ), which focuses on the therapeutic and anti-therapeutic consequences of the law (Wexler, 2000). Conceived as a legal theory, TJ contends that the law should be applied in a manner that maximizes therapeutic benefits within the context of other recognized legal safeguards such as due process (see Wexler, 2000). In practice, this means that the (1) interactions between judges, defendants, and other legal actors; (2) organization of the court and court proceedings; and (3) legal rules and policies all have the potential to be conducted or implemented in a manner that encourages health and positive growth (Rottman & Casey, 1999).

Though developed independently of drug courts, legal scholars have noted that the drug court model is a natural application of TJ (see Hora et al., 1999; Winick & Wexler, 2003). For example, the collaborative approach of the drug court model, the nature of interactions between the drug court judge and participants, the voluntary nature of the drug court, and the provision of treatment services is consistent with a TJ approach to jurisprudence (Hora, 2002). In one of the few empirical tests using TJ within the drug court setting, Senjo and Leip (2001) examined the relationship of court monitoring, treatment, court procedures, and offender characteristics to clean drug tests. Consistent with a TJ perspective, they found that positive comments and court-supported treatment were related to increased clean drug tests, while adversarial comments had a negative relationship with clean drug tests. None of the court procedure measures were related to behavioral change. Their findings provide some support for the TJ model; however, a dearth of research in this area limits the ability to draw definitive conclusions regarding TJ and drug court effectiveness.

Although TJ provides a framework for exploring the drug court model, it is not necessarily comprehensive in its framework. While Senjo and Leip (2001) found that court-supported treatment is related to behavioral change, TJ fails to specify the type of treatment that should be provided to offenders outside the courtroom setting. One of the tenets of TJ is that the law should draw on social science research to inform policies and procedures within the courtroom (Wexler, 2000). For example, Wexler (2000) suggests that judges should consider drawing on cognitive-behavioral techniques in their interactions with offenders. Consistent with this perspective, it would seem that a more comprehensive explanation of the drug court model should also consider the principles of effective interventions (EI) (see Andrews & Bonta, 2006; Gendreau, 1996).

Principles of Effective Intervention

On the basis of narrative and meta-analytic reviews of the literature, the principles of EI identify characteristics associated with the most effective correctional interventions. Specifically, the principles contend that: (1) services should be intensive and behavioral in nature; (2) programs should target the criminogenic needs of high-risk offenders; (3) characteristics of offenders, therapists, and programs should be matched; (4) program contingencies and behavioral strategies should be enforced in a firm but fair manner; (5) therapists should relate to offenders in interpersonally sensitive and constructive ways and should be trained and supervised appropriately; (6) program structure and activities should be designed to disrupt the delinquency network; (7) relapse prevention strategies should be provided; and (8) high levels of advo-

cacy and brokerage should be attempted (Gendreau, 1996, pp. 120–125; see also Andrews & Bonta, 2006).

In sum, the principles provide correctional treatment programs with guidance on the types of offenders that should be targeted for service, the types of behaviors that should be targeted, and the manner in which services should be delivered. Past research has been supportive of the risk principle (i.e., high-risk offenders should receive intensive services) (Andrews & Dowden, 2006; Lowenkamp, Latessa, & Holsinger, 2006; Marlowe et al., 2006; Pratt, Holsinger, & Latessa, 2000), the use of cognitive and cognitive-behavioral strategies (Bourgon & Armstrong, 2005; French & Gendreau, 2006; Pearson & Lipton, 1999; Pearson, Lipton, Cleland, & Yee, 2002), and the importance of staff characteristics (Dowden & Andrews, 2004). Meta-analyses have found that correctional treatment programs in alignment with these principles enjoy the greatest reductions in recidivism (Dowden & Andrews, 1999, 2000).

As with TJ, drug courts were not designed with these principles in mind, though the degree to which they align with them may help to explain the variation in their effectiveness. For example, there is evidence to suggest that the risk principle has relevance within the drug court setting. For instance, Lowenkamp et al. (2005) concluded that drug courts serving higher-risk participants were more effective than programs serving lower-risk participants. In a more direct test of the risk principle, Marlowe et al. (2006) found that high-risk drug court participants who received intensive services were less likely to have positive drug tests and more likely to graduate than high-risk participants who did not receive intensive services.

In sum, TJ provides a framework for understanding the legal aspect of drug courts, while EI offers guidance for understanding the treatment aspect of the model. Taken together, both TJ and EI also provide some context for exploring variation in drug court effectiveness. While neither perspective provides a complete explanation, elements of both can be found in the various frameworks previously proposed for exploring the drug court model.

Previous Frameworks for Exploring Drug Courts

The lack of a clear definition of drug courts at the outset resulted in a great deal of diversity in the model across jurisdictions. At their core, drug courts can be described as using a non-adversarial approach to treatment, court monitoring, and probation supervision (see DCPO, 1997). In an attempt to more fully describe variation in the drug court model, Goldkamp (1999) identified seven dimensions of drug courts including target problem, target population, processing, identification, screening, and evaluation of potential participants, treatment characteristics, client accountability, and system-wide support (pp. 173–174). While stopping short of describing drug courts along these dimensions, he proposed they would be useful for creating a drug court typology.

Sloan and Smykla (2003) used Goldkamp's framework to characterize 36 juvenile drug courts. Using secondary data, they described juvenile drug courts in terms of the courts' primary goals, types of charges juveniles needed to be eligible for the court, and the type and number of agencies that provided services and the types of services provided. They also examined the use of pretrial assessments and drug testing, phase requirements, graduation criteria, and length of program. Finally, they described the types of incentives and sanctions used to encourage participation and compliance. They concluded that while drug courts varied across the domains, there were some similarities in terms of their use of external agencies, sanctions and incentives, and clearly articulated target populations.

Although Goldkamp's dimensions have been useful for describing drug court variability, they have been criticized for being difficult to test (Longshore et al., 2001). Drawing on a TJ perspective, the ten key components, and the existing research, Longshore et al. (2001) proposed a conceptual framework designed to engender direct tests of their dimensions and related hypotheses. Their framework consisted of two structural dimensions and three process dimensions. The structural dimensions included *leverage* and *population severity*. They defined leverage as the possible consequences of failure and hypothesized that drug courts will have better outcomes when leverage is high. In contrast, outcomes are expected to have an inverse relationship with population severity, which refers to the characteristics of program participants.

While the first two dimensions focused on drug court structure, the remaining three dimensions emphasized process. These included *program intensity*, *predictability*, and *rehabilitation emphasis*. Program intensity, hypothesized to be positively related to effectiveness, refers to the requirements for successful program completion including drug testing, review hearings, and treatment requirements. Predictability refers to the extent to which participants can predict the court's response to compliant and non-compliant behaviors. In contrast to Goldkamp (1999), who emphasized the types of sanctions and rewards, Longshore et al. (2001) focused on the certainty and consistency of responses and hypothesized that effectiveness will increase with predictability. The final dimension, rehabilitation emphasis, is most directly tied to TJ and weighs the program's emphasis on rehabilitation versus case processing and punishment. As with the other process measures, Longshore et al. predicted a positive relationship with outcomes. In addition to articulating a number of main effects, they also hypothesized that interaction effects would exist between the domains. For example, they speculated that the impact of program intensity would vary by population severity. Although this framework is the most fully developed model for exploring drug courts, it has yet to be directly tested.

It is likely that other factors, beyond those identified by Longshore et al. (2001), should also be considered. For example, Belenko (2002) recommended that research should consider the role of status review hearings, coercive elements relating to compliance, drug testing and sanctions, the type and length of treatment provided to participants, and the ability of drug courts to address risk and need factors beyond substance abuse in assessing effectiveness. Finally, the level of integration between treatment and the criminal justice system, a key component of drug courts (see DCPO, 1997) should also be considered. Through an examination of structural issues focusing on assessment, treatment, supervision, and program completion, Taxman and Bouffard (2002) identified a continuum of service delivery ranging from a *brokerage model* (participants are referred to existing treatment services in the community) to an *in-house model* (participants receive services provided by the drug court itself).

Current Study

Building on Longshore et al.'s framework, the current study incorporates elements of both TJ and EI to identify characteristics of effective drug courts. Specifically, meta-analytic techniques are used to explore the relationship between six structural (target population, leverage, service delivery, staff, funding, and quality assurance) and five process (assessment, philosophy, treatment, predictability, and intensity) dimensions and drug court effectiveness. Previous meta-analyses have been limited in their ability to analyze moderating factors (Lowenkamp et al., 2005; Wilson et al., 2006). The current study overcomes this limitation by merging survey data with existing primary study data to determine the relative influence of each dimension.

Methods

Sample of Studies

Multiple sources were searched to locate both published and unpublished studies related to drug court effectiveness through January 2006. First, searches of social scientific databases were conducted using the keyword *drug court*. Databases included: Academic Press, Criminal Justice Abstracts, *Criminology: a Sage* publication, Criminal Justice Periodicals Index, Dissertation Abstracts Online, Government Publications Office Monthly, NCJRS, PapersFirst, PsychINFO, Social Sciences Citation Index, and Sociological Abstracts. These results were then compared to previously conducted meta-analyses on drug courts in an effort to identify further studies. Efforts to identify unpublished studies included searches of the American Society of Criminology and the Academy of Criminal Justice Sciences annual conference programs, the *National Drug Court Institute's Publication Guide*, 4th ed., and an online search using the Google search engine.

Inclusion Criteria

The above search process yielded over 300 articles, which included 198 evaluations. To be included in the meta-analysis, studies had to have evaluated a drug court program using an experimental or quasi-experimental design, included a distinct comparison group, and used at least one measure of criminal behavior as an outcome measure with a minimum six-month follow-up period. Finally, the drug court had to be based in the USA and must have been identifiable either within the study itself or via contact with the study authors. Applying these criteria resulted in 115 eligible studies. However, in several cases, multiple publications reported on the same drug court. Only a single study for each drug court was included to maintain independence between the effect sizes. Where multiple manuscripts had been collected, the most recent evaluation was used, and the study with the longest follow-up period was selected when there were overlapping evaluation periods. This process resulted in the identification of 60 outcome evaluations. Six of these studies reported on multiple drug courts that were unable to be disaggregated. The remaining studies reported on 76 distinct drug courts. Of the 60 studies, 18 were included in Lowenkamp et al.'s (2005) meta-analysis, and 30 were included in Wilson et al.'s (2006) study.

Survey

Although meta-analysts traditionally contact authors of primary studies to collect "missing" data (see Dowden & Tellier, 2004; Kelley, Kelley, & Tran, 2004), it was not expected that evaluators would have details on drug court policies and procedures, the primary focus of the current study. Consequently, a telephone survey of drug court personnel was conducted to gain additional details about the drug courts' activities at the time of the evaluation. Telephone interviews were selected in an effort to increase response rates and because they allowed the opportunity to clarify information and ask follow-up questions as needed.

A sample of drug court coordinators was created to reflect the 76 unique drug courts in the study. In instances where potential respondents reported not having knowledge of the drug court at the time of the evaluation, they were asked to identify other drug court staff (current or former) who may have had more direct knowledge of the drug court's operations at the time of its evaluation. Interviews were conducted using a semistructured interview guide (available upon request) and typically lasted 30–45 minutes.

While telephone interviews were selected for their ability to clarify information, some potential respondents were concerned about the potential length of time of the interviews and were given the option of completing a self-administered questionnaire sent via email. Follow-up emails and phone calls were made in this event to clarify information as necessary. The use of telephone interviews, in conjunction with self-administered surveys when necessary, resulted in the completion of 63 surveys. Of these surveys, 47 were completed by telephone (74.6%), and 16 were completed through self-administered questionnaires (25.4%). The overall response rate was 83%. The appendix contains a list of all studies included in the meta-analysis; those matched to a survey are indicated by an asterisk.

Measures

The studies were coded along five categories including

(1) study characteristics (e.g., affiliation of authors, type of publication, and publication year),
(2) sample characteristics (e.g., race, gender, age, and criminal history),
(3) general program characteristics (e.g., program length, setting, adult/juvenile, year implemented, and graduation rate),

(4) methodological characteristics (e.g., study design, sample size, attrition rate, outcomes, length of follow-up, and statistical power), and
(5) outcome characteristics (e.g., type of outcome and calculated effect size).

In addition, the data were collected across 11 dimensions that were hypothesized to be related to drug court effectiveness. These included

(1) target population (e.g., type of charge, type of offender, and motivation),
(2) assessment (e.g., areas assessed and method of assessment),
(3) leverage (e.g., drug court model, consequences of failure, and benefits of graduation),
(4) philosophy (e.g., view toward substance abuse, primary role of judge, and flexibility of policies regarding rewards and sanctions),
(5) treatment characteristics (e.g., length of treatment, graduation rate, type of treatment, treatment targets, and adolescents' participation in Alcoholics Anonymous and Narcotics Anonymous [AA/NA]),
(6) predictability (e.g., system of rewards and punishers and immediacy of response to infractions),
(7) intensity (e.g., average number of contacts and standard conditions and requirements),
(8) service delivery (e.g., single provider, internal provider, and dedicated caseloads),
(9) staff characteristics (e.g., initial training, conference attendance, and team meetings),
(10) funding (e.g., adequate funding and federal funding), and
(11) quality assurance (e.g., internal and external QA and advisory board).

Attempts to use the studies to code the above variables were largely unsuccessful with over 50% of the studies failing to report data on 9 of the 11 dimensions. As a result, these data were based on the surveys. To help minimize threats to validity introduced by this approach, survey respondents were asked about the impact the evaluation had on the program, changes to the program since the evaluation, and whether any changes had been made as a result of the evaluation. Answers to these questions were considered against the answers provided throughout the interview; any inconsistencies were clarified at that point.

A methodological quality index (MQI) was created to control for differences in methodological rigor across studies. The index comprised nine indicators related to the sample, follow-up period, and statistical power. Each indicator was worth one point, and studies received points for using a matched comparison group; describing both the treatment and the comparison group in terms of age, gender, and race; reporting on treatment activities of the comparison group; and experiencing less than 20% attrition. Evaluations that used multiple outcomes, had at least a 12-month follow-up period, had similar follow-up periods for both the treatment and the comparison group, and used a post-program follow-up period were also rated more favorably. Finally, post hoc power analyses were conducted, and studies received a point if they had statistical power at 0.80 or above. After summing these indicators, the MQI had a range of 2–8 and a mean of 5.6. Studies scoring above the mean were considered to be "above average" quality.

Inter-Rater Reliability

The author of the study coded all of the evaluations. A second rater, with substantial experience in meta-analysis, coded a random subsample of studies and variables to assess reliability. The total number of agreements divided by the total number of agreements and disagreements (Yeaton & Wartmon, 1993) resulted in an agreement rating of 93%.

Results

Study Characteristics

The search procedures described above resulted in the identification of 60 eligible studies reporting on 76 distinct drug courts and six "aggregated" drug courts. Table 1 provides descriptives for the included studies. As illustrated, the

Table 1 Sample Characteristics

Characteristic	N	%
Publication type		
Journal/book chapter	16	26.7
Thesis/dissertation	3	5.0
Unpublished report	41	68.3
Publication year		
Prior to 1998	2	3.6
1998–1999	8	14.3
2000–2001	19	33.9
2002–2003	13	23.2
2004–2005	13	23.2
2006	1	1.8
Affiliation of authors		
Academic	36	62.1
Government	10	17.2
Research firm/ consultant	12	20.7
Age of drug court		
Less than one year	3	3.9
1–2 years	19	24.7
3–4 years	36	46.8
5–6 years	14	18.2
7 years	5	6.5
Setting		
Outpatient	69	85.2
Outpatient and residential	11	13.4
Capacity		
0–49	13	21.0
50–99	14	22.6
100–199	15	24.2
200–999	17	27.4
1,000+	3	4.8
Mean	231	
Respondent worked with drug court at time of evaluation		
Yes	48	71.6
No	19	28.4
Years working with drug court		
0–2	9	13.4
3–5	17	25.5

Continued

Characteristic	N	%
6–8	23	34.3
9–11	13	19.4
12+	5	7.5
Position		
Case manager	2	3.0
Coordinator	28	41.8
Director/administrator	7	10.4
Judge	2	3.0
Probation officer	4	6.0
Program manager/ supervisor	18	26.9
Treatment provider	2	3.0

Table 2 Drug Court Characteristics

Characteristic	N	%	$\bar{X}$
Target population			
Felony charges required	15	23.8	
Prior felonies accepted	51	81.0	
Prior non-compliance accepted	48	76.2	
Drug dealers accepted	19	30.2	
Violent offenders accepted	10	15.9	
Substance abuse required	57	90.5	
Motivation required	40	63.5	
Assessment practices			
Assessed at screening	32	51.6	
Mean assessment score[1]	–	–	3.94
Leverage			
Pre-adjudication model	19	30.2	
Post-adjudication model	31	49.2	
Defer sentence to secure facility	22	34.9	
Charges dismissed/expunged	39	61.9	
Failures incarcerated	37	58.7	
Philosophy[2]			
View S/A as a disease	55	88.7	
Judicial role primarily therapeutic	25	39.7	
Minor response to first positive U/A	37	58.3	
Prior failures denied reentry	32	50.8	
Mean flexibility regarding sanctions	–	–	3.78
Mean flexibility regarding rewards	–	–	3.56
Mean flexibility regarding phases	–	–	2.90
Mean rehabilitative orientation	–	–	2.70
Predictability			
Immediate response to minor infraction	29	49.1	
Major infractions responded to within one day	32	54.2	
Formal system of punishers	32	50.8	
Formal system of rewards	18	29.8	
Treatment			
Uses evidence-based approach	17	31.5	
Targets additional criminogenic needs	32	50.8	
Provides relapse prevention	55	90.2	

majority of the studies collected were technical reports (68.3%) with just over 25% published in scholarly journals or as book chapters. One criticism of meta-analyses is the over-reliance on published articles (Wolf, 1986). The sizable number of unpublished evaluations included in this study should help minimize any type of publication bias often associated with meta-analyses.[1] All but 10 of the collected studies were published during or after the year 2000, and the majority of authors were affiliated with universities (62.1%).

Many of the drug courts were evaluated relatively early in their programmatic life. Nearly half of the programs were evaluated during years three or four of their implementation, and approximately 29% were evaluated in the first or second year. Given that drug courts were designed to keep offenders in the community while providing treatment, it is not surprising that 85% of the drug courts were outpatient programs. Programs ranged in terms of capacity with the smaller drug courts serving fewer than 25 clients per year, and the larger courts serving well over 1,000 clients per year.

Drug Court Characteristics

Table 2 reports the characteristics of the drug courts. As indicated, the majority of drug courts accepted offenders with a history of felony

Characteristic	N	%	$\bar{X}$
Provides aftercare services	32	55.5	
Provides family services	10	16.4	
Requires AA/NA	44	69.8	
Graduation rate between 45% and 75%	22	39.3	
Mean length of S/A treatment (months)	–	–	11.50
Intensity			
Requires restitution	11	17.7	
Requires fines	13	20.6	
Requires community service	19	30.2	
Requires employment	48	76.2	
Requires education	38	60.3	
Other requirements	16	25.4	
Requires payment for services	46	74.2	
Mean total contacts	–	–	106.00
Service delivery			
Single provider	23	36.5	
Internal provider	10	16.1	
Mean % drug court team devoted	–	–	0.41
Staff			
Trained on model	44	75.9	
Attend national conferences	43	69.4	
100% of treatment staff D/A certified	36	66.7	
100% of team participates in regular meetings	32	54.2	
Average 4+ meetings per month	32	52.5	
Funding			
Relied on federal funds	25	40.3	
Mean adequacy of funding[3]	–	–	6.70
Quality assurance			
Formal external QA	42	68.9	
Formal internal QA	40	64.5	
Advisory board	34	58.6	

[1]Scores ranged from 0 to 9; alpha = 0.68.

[2]Each of the rated items in this dimension ranged from 1 to 5 with 5 representing the greatest amount of flexibility and the greatest orientation toward rehabilitation.

[3]Respondents were asked to rate the adequacy of funding at the time of the evaluation on a scale of 1–10 with 10 = very adequate.

charges and non-compliance. Most of the programs required that offenders have a substance abuse problem and required some level of motivation on the part of potential participants. Roughly half of the programs reported conducting assessments during the screening process, and the majority of the programs reported using actuarial-based substance abuse assessments and clinical risk/needs assessments. A 12-item scale was created to reflect assessment practices. The scale contained three items each (assessment conducted, actuarial assessment used, and reassessment conducted) for risk, needs, responsivity, and substance abuse. Scores ranged from 0 to 9 with a mean score of 4.

Drug courts were mixed in terms of leverage and philosophy. Nearly half of the drug courts were post-adjudication with less than a third operating as pre-adjudication drug courts. For most, charges were dismissed upon graduation, and the majority of failures were incarcerated following termination. In general, drug courts viewed substance abuse as a disease and viewed the role of the judge as a mix between legalistic, punitive, and therapeutic roles. Most issued an informal sanction to the first positive drug test and reported some flexibility regarding the use of sanctions and rewards.

The types of services provided also varied across the programs. The average length of substance abuse treatment was 12 months, and most drug courts reported providing both relapse prevention and aftercare services. Most also indicated that AA/NA was a required component of the program. The programs also differed in terms of their predictability. On average, drug courts waited a week before issuing a response to a minor infraction, but the majority issued responses to major infractions within a day. Only half of the drug courts had a formal system of punishers, and fewer than a third had a formal system of rewards. In an effort to assess the intensity of drug court services, courts were asked to report the average number of contacts (drug tests, status review hearings, supervision contacts, and treatment hours) per phase. On average, drug courts required a total of 106 contacts across four phases. Most drug courts also required employment, education (as needed), and imposed some fees for service.

Most of the drug courts utilized external providers and had a selection of providers to choose from. In most cases, drug court team members worked with offenders other than drug court participants. On average, 40% of the drug court team was assigned only to the drug court. In general, team members received training when first assigned to the drug court and attended national conferences annually. Over half of the drug courts reported that all treatment staff were drug/alcohol certified, and about half reported that all of the team members participate in regular meetings. Forty percent of the drug courts were solely reliant on federal funds at implementation while a third received funding from multiple sources. On average, respondents rated funding, at the time of the evaluation, as 6.7 on a scale of 10 (10 = very adequate). Finally, over half of the drug courts reported having some type of quality assurance mechanism in place.

Effect Size Analysis

A total of 82 effect sizes were calculated across the studies. Consistent with prior meta-analyses (Lowenkamp et al., 2005; Wilson et al., 2006), Table 3 reveals that drug courts significantly reduce recidivism. Specifically, drug courts have a mean effect size of 0.09 with a confidence interval (CI) of 0.08–0.10. While the effect sizes ranged from -0.33 to 0.35, the majority of studies revealed that drug courts reduced recidivism (78.0%). Using Rosenthal's (1991) BESD, the

mean effect size reveals the drug court group would have a 45.5% recidivism rate while the comparison group would have a 54.5% recidivism rate.

Moderators of Drug Court Effectiveness

The four dimensions explaining the greatest amount of variance are target population, leverage, staff characteristics, and intensity. Three of the four major dimensions were related to structural characteristics of the drug court including target population, leverage, and staff characteristics, with intensity the lone process dimension identified in this category. This suggests that the people involved in the drug court, whether as employees or as participants, have a great deal of influence on its overall effectiveness. In addition to staff and participant characteristics, the basic design of the drug court and its requirements also help explain variation in effectiveness.

The analyses also revealed significant predictors within these four dimensions. Histories of non-compliance and prior violence both were negatively related to effect size within *target population* ($R^2 = 0.19$), indicating drug courts that exclude individuals with a history of noncompliance or violent offenders are more successful than those that accept these types of offenders. These findings may be related to the limited ability of the drug courts to target criminogenic needs associated with violence or noncompliance and suggest the need for drug courts to increase the scope and intensity of services for this population. Drug courts were intended

Table 3 Drug Court Mean Effect Size

Characteristic	k	N	Z+	CI	Z	Q
Overall	82	24,322	0.09	0.08 to 0.10	14.29*	366.06*
Methodological quality						
High	45	15,077	0.07	0.06 to 0.10	11.50*	221.46*
Low	37	9,232	0.12	0.10 to 0.14	11.50*	132.84*

Note: The significant Q indicates a heterogeneous sample; the removal of outliers did not change the results.

*p < 0.001

to serve as an alternative to incarceration; those that fail to provide intensive services to higher-risk populations may be undermining their effectiveness. In terms of *leverage* ($R^2 = 0.17$), pre-adjudication drug courts are more effective than post-adjudication drug courts while both deferring a sentence to a secure facility (at entry) and terminating supervision upon graduation were associated with reduced effect sizes. Together, these findings seem to suggest that drug courts are more effective when the consequence of failure is the imposition of charges rather than the imposition of a sentence. Viewed from a benefit perspective, drug courts are more effective when the benefit of graduation is avoiding a conviction rather than avoiding a proscribed sanction.

Within *staff characteristics* ($R^2 = 0.17$), both regular attendance at national conferences and weekly team meetings were predictive of increased effectiveness. In contrast, formal training on the model at hiring, estimates that all treatment staff are drug and alcohol certified, and 100% attendance at team meetings was associated with reduced effect sizes. This is not to suggest that training, certification, and meetings do not matter. Rather, it may be an indication that the quality of these activities is in need of improvement. For instance, state requirements for drug and alcohol certification differ across states and may not guarantee providers that utilize cognitive-behavioral interventions. In a review of drug court treatment, Bouffard and Taxman (2004) found that drug courts tend to provide eclectic treatment services and draw on 12-step modalities, which may attenuate any benefit gained from having certified drug and alcohol counselors.

A number of predictors were also significant in the *intensity* ($R^2 = 0.14$) analysis. Although some program requirements (restitution, education, and "other" requirements) were positively associated with effectiveness, other requirements (community service, fines, employment, and number of minimum contacts) had a negative relationship. Intensity is likely to interact with target population (see Longshore et al., 2001), and although this finding suggests that imposing additional requirements is

appropriate, drug courts should take care to match requirements to the needs of the offenders they serve.

Two structural dimensions (service delivery and funding) and two process dimensions (treatment and philosophy) were among the more moderate predictors of effectiveness. Despite the importance of treatment in reducing recidivism in the general literature, the *treatment* dimension only explained a moderate level of variance ($R^2 = 0.11$) relative to the other dimensions. The analysis revealed drug courts that keep participants in substance abuse treatment for longer periods of time are more effective than those with shorter treatment periods. Consistent with prior research, the analysis also revealed that required AA/NA participation was negatively associated with effectiveness (see Wells-Parker & Bangert-Drowns, 1995).

Within *philosophy* ($R^2 = 0.11$), the significant predictors were the response to an initial positive drug test and whether program failures were readmitted. Specifically, drug courts that provide a formal response to the first positive drug test are more effective than are those drug courts that bar failures from further participation in the drug court. The finding regarding program failures is expected from a statistical standpoint; previous failures are likely to fail again, which may deflate the effect size. However, it is not clear how many program failures were included in the various treatment samples or how often failures are readmitted to these programs. Interpreting this finding from a programmatic standpoint is less clear. Drug courts that allow previous failures to be readmitted may be construed as having a greater rehabilitative emphasis, which is hypothesized to be positively associated with effectiveness. At the same time, programs that readmit failures may have less leverage over participants, also hypothesized to be positively associated with effectiveness. Further exploration of treatment of program failures is warranted to better assess how it influences effectiveness.

Both predictors within the *funding* ($R^2 = 0.11$) dimension were significant, though in the opposite direction of one another. Relying on federal funds at implementation increased effectiveness whereas programs that identified their funding as more adequate than others had lower effect sizes. It may be that this rating is especially susceptible to recall bias and that respondents rated past funding relative to current funding and services. This finding, therefore, should be viewed with caution. The final cluster within the moderate category was *service delivery* ($R^2 = 0.09$), which examined the relationships and responsibilities among the drug court team members and treatment providers. Both significant predictors within this cluster involved the treatment provider. Drug courts that utilized multiple providers were more effective than those that utilized single providers, while drug courts with internal providers were more effective than those with external providers. Collectively, it may be that these measures are actually an indication of the need for drug courts to have some direct control over their treatment providers. Programs utilizing multiple providers may gain an advantage in two ways. First, they may be able to match participants to specific providers on the basis of need. Second, having a choice of providers may allow programs to systematically refer participants to those agencies perceived as providing better quality services. In contrast, drug courts with a single provider may have to rely on a "one size fits all" treatment approach, often inconsistent with the research on EI.

Finally, *predictability* ($R^2 = 0.06$), *assessment* ($R^2 = 0.05$), both process dimensions, and *quality assurance* ($R^2 = 0.03$), a structural dimension, were all minor predictors of effectiveness. Responding to major infractions immediately and having a formal system of punishers both were positively related to effectiveness while having a formal system of rewards was negatively related. These findings suggest that predictability is important for curbing undesirable behaviors as hypothesized by Longshore et al. (2001). At the same time, a formal system of rewards may actually curtail the courts' ability to provide individualized, meaningful rewards, which may be more relevant than the ability to predict the application of rewards. Finally, as expected, drug courts that have better assessment practices are more effective than those

that do not. This finding is consistent with previous literature on EI and highlights the importance of offender assessment (Gendreau, 1996). It is somewhat surprising that the R-square for this cluster is so low given the saliency of assessment in regard to EI. However, the import of assessment may be less related to whether assessments are completed and more a function of how assessment data are used.

Discussion

Consistent with the previous research, the current study provides support for the drug court model. In general, drug courts reduce recidivism, but only moderately so. While previous meta-analyses explored the impact of basic differences in the drug court model, the focus of the current study was on the impact of drug courts' policies and procedures on effectiveness. The findings suggest that variation in drug court effectiveness can be explained, at least in part, by elements of both TJ and EI.

The dimensions with the greatest explanatory power suggest that the success of drug courts depends on the type of offenders it targets, the leverage it holds over them, the expectations placed upon them, and the quality of their staff. Specifically, the findings suggest that drug courts are more effective when violent and non-compliant offenders are excluded from participation. It also appears that the legal status of participants is important as indicated by the finding that pre-plea drug courts are more effective. The results regarding program intensity may be taken to suggest that drug courts must make sure that the expectations and requirements of participants are appropriate for the population they are serving. The finding regarding the importance of staff characteristics is supportive of both the TJ and EI perspectives. Having well-qualified, competent staff not only increases the likelihood of positive interactions with participants, but also helps ensure that the program is designed as delivered.

While treatment appears to be only moderately related to effectiveness, it is important to recall that the measures of treatment did not assess the *quality* of the treatment services provided. Some may argue the findings provide evidence that the success of the drug court model is more closely tied to TJ rather than treatment in and of itself. That is, while treatment is important, this finding may point to the importance of the broader model for bringing about reductions in recidivism. A more likely explanation is that the quality of treatment is lacking. Few of the drug courts reported using services that are consistent with the literature. It is possible that measures of treatment integrity would be able to explain greater variance in the distribution than those simply measuring the provision of services (Lowenkamp, Latessa, & Smith, 2006).

The philosophy of the drug court also explains some of the variance within the distribution. Specifically, it appears that it is important for drug courts to hold clients accountable within the rehabilitative model while those courts that are perhaps too "warm and fuzzy" are less effective. From a TJ perspective, this is consistent with using court proceedings in a supportive manner to promote behavioral change. Similarly, this finding is in alignment with the research on EI, which speaks to the importance of holding offenders accountable and using a system of rewards and sanctions to promote positive change while extinguishing antisocial behaviors.

In addition to these process measures, the findings suggest that other structural dimensions are also important for explaining variability. In terms of funding, it would seem that the guidelines and regulations implicit in the receipt of federal funds have had their intended impact as programs implemented under federal dollars are more effective than others. Finally, the service delivery model also appears to be moderately predictive of drug court effectiveness. Drug courts that have some amount of control over the treatment provider, either by making choices among multiple providers, or by providing service themselves, are more effective than those programs that are reliant on a single provider.

Less predictive moderators of drug court effectiveness include predictability, assessment, and quality assurance. The findings suggest that the ability to predict the courts' response to behaviors is more important for sanctions than rewards. The limited ability of assessment practices to predict effectiveness is somewhat surprising. It may be that the application of eligibility and exclusionary criteria identified within the target population may act as a quasi-assessment process. Despite its limited ability to explain variance in this study, research on program effectiveness and assessment in general suggests that formalized assessment processes are an important part of EI (Andrews, Bonta, & Wormith, 2006). Similar to treatment, the findings may be an indictment of the manner with which drug courts use assessment results rather than the types of assessments used. As with many correctional programs, drug courts should continue to work to improve their assessment practices (e.g., Listwan, Cullen, & Latessa, 2006).

Although none of the quality assurance measures were predictive, the importance of quality assurance should not be dismissed. In some ways, the drug court model has a number of quality assurance measures built into it. For instance, the use of regular status review hearings and drug testing provide formal measures of offender progress. Regular team meetings provide formal outlets for staff input and discussion of cases. Formal screening processes and the use of eligibility and exclusionary criteria all work together to increase the likelihood that drug courts are receiving appropriate clients. Moreover, all of the drug courts included in this study have undergone an outcome evaluation, providing yet another measure of quality assurance. Thus, while quality assurance, as a dimension, was the least important, it is likely that the various mechanisms built into the drug court model are having the intended effect.

While the current findings provide some insight into the characteristics of effective drug courts, there are some limitations that should be considered. First, many of the drug courts included in the meta-analysis were evaluated several years prior to the current study, and the survey data may be subject to recall bias. However, efforts were made to increase validity through the use of pre-notification cards and prompts throughout the interview intended to focus respondents on the proper time frame. Second, as noted, data related to treatment services emphasized the type of treatment provided rather than the quality of treatment. Future research should explore the relationship between treatment quality and drug court effectiveness. Third, the small sample limited the type of analyses that could be completed. It is likely that many of the dimensions interact with one another, yet the limited number of cases did not allow testing interaction effects. Similarly, splicing the sample into subgroups rendered the groups too small to be able to analyze moderating effects for the different types of drug courts (i.e., pre-adjudication versus post-adjudication, adult versus juvenile). Finally, while the R-square for each dimension provides an indication of their influence relative to one another, it would be preferable to analyze all of the dimensions in a single model.

Despite these limitations, the current study is an important first step in systematically explaining the variability of drug court effectiveness. While the findings provide some support for TJ, the importance of the principles of EI should not be overlooked. Though the contributions are relatively modest in this study, there is ample research documenting the relationship between adhering to these principles and improved outcomes (e.g., Andrews & Dowden, 2006; Bourgon & Armstrong, 2005; Dowden & Andrews, 1999, 2000; French & Gendreau, 2006; Lowenkamp et al., 2006; Pearson et al., 2002). The findings suggest many of the drug courts included in this study may not have fully considered the principles when designing their respective programs. For example, only 32% of the drug courts reported utilizing evidence-based practices, and nearly half of the programs failed to target criminogenic needs beyond substance abuse. Moreover, although half of the drug courts had formal policies regarding the use of sanctions, less than a third had policies in place governing the use of rewards. Policymakers would be well served to draw on the existing literature on EI to develop formal policies governing target populations, assessment, cognitive-behavioral interventions, and the use of rewards and sanctions.

Discussion Questions

1. What steps did Shaffer take to include only methodologically rigorous studies in the meta-analysis?
2. What do the results of this study tell us about the role of staff characteristics in producing successful drug court programs?
3. What were the inclusion and exclusion criteria for studies? Where did the author search for the articles?

Note

1. A fail-safe estimate was calculated using Orwin's formula (1983) as presented by Lipsey and Wilson (2001): $k_0 = k[(\overline{ES}_k/\overline{ES}_c) - 1]$ where k_0 equals the number of studies needed to reduce the mean effect size to the ES_c or the alternative mean effect size. Using this formula, k is the number of studies included in the calculation of the weighted mean effect size and ES_k is the estimated weighted mean effect size. The alternative effect size, ES_c, was set to $(ES_k/2)$. The number of studies necessary to reduce the mean effect size in half was 82.

References

Andrews, D. A., & Bonta, J. (2006). *The psychology of criminal conduct* (4th ed.). Cincinnati, OH: Anderson.

Andrews, D. A., Bonta, J., & Wormith, J. S. (2006). The recent past and near future of risk and/or need assessment. *Crime & Delinquency, 52,* 7–27.

Andrews, D. A., & Dowden, C. (2006). Risk principle of case classification in correctional treatment. *International Journal of Offender Therapy and Comparative Criminology, 50,* 88–100.

Banks, D., & Gottfredson, D. C. (2004). Participation in drug treatment court and time to rearrest. *Justice Quarterly, 21,* 637–658.

Belenko, S. (2002). The challenges of conducting research in drug treatment court settings. *Substance Use & Misuse, 37,* 1635–1664.

Bonta, J., Law, M., & Hanson, K. (1998). The prediction of criminal and violent recidivism among mentally disordered offenders: A meta-analysis. *Psychological Bulletin, 123,* 123–142.

Bouffard, J. A., & Richardson, K. A. (2007). The effectiveness of drug court programming for specific types of offenders: Methamphetamine and DWI offenders versus other drug-involved offenders. *Criminal Justice Policy Review, 18,* 274–294.

Bouffard, J. A., & Taxman, F. (2004). Looking inside the "black box" of drug court treatment services using direct observations. *Journal of Drug Issues, 34,* 195–218.

Bourgon, G., & Armstrong, B. (2005). Transferring the principles of effective treatment into a "real world" prison setting. *Criminal Justice and Behavior, 32,* 3–25.

Brewster, M. P. (2001). An evaluation of the Chester County (PA) drug court program. *Journal of Drug Issues, 31,* 177–206.

Bureau of Justice Assistance Drug Court Clearinghouse Project. (2009). *Summary of drug court activity by state and county.* Washington, DC: Bureau of Justice Assistance Drug Court Clearinghouse Project. Retrieved from http://www1.spa.american.edu/justice/documents/2150.pdf

Dannerbeck, A., Harris, G., Sundet, P., & Lloyd, K. (2006). Understanding and responding to racial differences in drug court outcomes. *Journal of Ethnicity in Substance Abuse, 5,* 1–22.

Deschenes, E. P., & Greenwood, P. W. (1994). Maricopa County's drug court: An innovative program for first-time drug offenders on probation. *Justice System Journal, 17,* 55–73.

Dowden, C., & Andrews, D. A. (1999). What works for female offenders: A meta-analytic review. *Crime & Delinquency, 45,* 438–452.

Dowden, C., & Andrews, D. A. (2000). Effective correctional treatment and violent reoffending: A meta-analysis. *Canadian Journal of Criminology, 42,* 449–467.

Dowden, C., & Andrews, D. A. (2004). The importance of staff practice in delivering effective correctional treatment: A meta-analytic review of core correctional practice. *International Journal of Offender Therapy and Comparative Criminology, 48,* 203–214.

Dowden, C., & Tellier, C. (2004). Predicting work-related stress in correctional officers: A meta-analysis. *Journal of Criminal Justice, 32,* 31–47.

Drug Courts Program Office. (1997). *Defining drug courts: The key components.* Washington, DC: Office of Justice Programs, US Department of Justice.

Faul, F., & Erdfelder, E. (1992). *GPOWER: A priori, post-hoc, and compromise power analyses for MS-DOS* [Computer software]. Bonn: Bonn University, Department of Psychology.

Festinger, D. S., Marlowe, D. B., Lee, P. A., Kirby, K. C., Bovasso, G., & McLellan, A. T. (2002). Status hearings in drug court: When more is less and less is more. *Drug and Alcohol Dependence, 68,* 151–157.

Finn, P., & Newlyn, A. K. (1997). Miami's drug court: A different approach. In L. K. Gaines & P. B. Kraska (Eds.), *Drugs, crime, and justice* (pp. 357–374). Prospect Heights, IL: Waveland.

French, S. A., & Gendreau, P. (2006). Reducing prison misconducts: What works! *Criminal Justice and Behavior, 33,* 185–218.

Gendreau, P. (1996). The principles of effective intervention with offenders. In A. Harland (Ed.), *What works in community corrections* (pp. 117–130). Thousand Oaks, CA: Sage.

Goldkamp, J. (1999). Challenges for research and innovation: When is a drug court not a drug court? In W. C. Terry (Ed.), *The early drug courts: Case studies in judicial innovation* (pp. 166–177). Thousand Oaks, CA: Sage.

Goldkamp, J. S., & Weiland, D. (1993). *Assessing the impact of Dade County's felony drug court: Research in Brief.* Washington, DC: US Department of Justice.

Goldkamp, J. S., White, M. D., & Robinson, J. B. (2001). Do drug courts work? Getting inside the drug court black box. *Journal of Drug Issues, 31,* 27–72.

Gottfredson, D. C., Kearley, B. W., Najaka, S. S., & Rocha, C. M. (2005). The Baltimore City Drug Treatment Court: 3-year self-report outcome study. *Evaluation Review, 29,* 42–64.

Granfield, R., Eby, C., & Brewster, T. (1998). An examination of the Denver drug court: The impact of a treatment-oriented drug-offender system. *Law & Policy, 20,* 183–202.

Gray, A. R., & Saum, C. A. (2005). Mental health, gender and drug court completion. *American Journal of Criminal Justice, 30,* 55–69.

Hartman, J. L., Listwan, S. J., & Shaffer, D. K. (2007). Methamphetamine users in a community-based drug court: Does gender matter? *Journal of Offender Rehabilitation, 45,* 109–130.

Hedges, L. V., & Olkin, I. (1985). *Statistical methods for meta-analysis.* Orlando, FL: Academic Press.

Hora, P. F. (2002). A dozen years of drug treatment courts: Uncovering our theoretical foundation and the construction of a mainstream paradigm. *Substance Use & Misuse, 37,* 1469–1488.

Hora, P., Schma, W., & Rosenthal, J. (1999). Therapeutic jurisprudence and the drug treatment court movement: Revolutionizing the criminal justice system's response to drug abuse and crime in America. *Notre Dame Law Review, 74,* 439–538.

Huddleston, C. W., Marlowe, D. B., & Casebolt, R. (2008). *Painting the current picture: A national report card on drug courts and other problem-solving court programs in the United States.* Washington, DC: National Drug Court Institute.

Hunter, J. E., & Schmidt, F. L. (1990). *Methods of meta-analysis: Correcting error and bias in research findings.* Newbury Park, CA: Sage.

Kelley, G. A., Kelley, K. S., & Tran, Z. V. (2004). Retrieval of missing data for meta-analysis: A practical example. *International Journal of Technology Assessment in Health Care, 20*, 296–299.

Ley, P. (1972). *Quantitative aspects of psychological assessment.* New York: Harper & Row.

Lipsey, M. W., & Wilson, D. B. (2001). *Practical meta-analysis.* Thousand Oaks, CA: Sage.

Listwan, S. J., Cullen, F. T., & Latessa, E. J. (2006). How to prevent re-entry programs from failing: Insights from evidence-based corrections. *Federal Probation, 70*, 19–25.

Listwan, S. J., Jonson, C. L., Cullen, F. T., & Latessa, E. J. (2008). Cracks in the penal harm movement: Evidence from the field. *Criminology & Public Policy, 7*, 423–465.

Listwan, S. J., Shaffer, D. K., & Hartman, J. L. (2009). Combating methamphetamine use in the community. *Crime & Delinquency, 55*, 627–644.

Listwan, S. J., Sundt, J. L., Holsinger, A. M., & Latessa, E. J. (2003). The effect of drug court programming on recidivism: The Cincinnati experience. *Crime & Delinquency, 49*, 389–411.

Longshore, D., Turner, S., Wenzel, S., Morral, A., Harrell, A., McBride, D., . . . Iguchi, M. (2001). Drug courts: A conceptual framework. *Journal of Drug Issues, 31*, 7–26.

Lowenkamp, C. T., Holsinger, A. M., & Latessa, E. J. (2005). Are drug courts effective? A meta-analytic review. *Journal of Community Corrections, Fall*, 5–10, 28.

Lowenkamp, C. T., Latessa, E. J., & Holsinger, A. M. (2006). The risk principle in action: What have we learned from 13,676 offenders and 97 correctional programs? *Crime & Delinquency, 51*, 1–17.

Lowenkamp, C. T., Latessa, E. J., & Smith, P. (2006). Does correctional program quality really matter? The impact of adhering to the principles of effective intervention. *Criminology & Public Policy, 5*, 575–594.

Marlowe, D. B., Festinger, D. S., & Lee, P. A. (2004). The judge is a key component of drug court. *Drug Court Review, 4*, 1–34.

Marlowe, D. B., Festinger, D. S., Lee, P. A., Dugosh, K. L., & Benasutti, K. M. (2006). Matching judicial supervision to clients' risk status in drug court. *Crime & Delinquency, 52*, 52–76.

Marlowe, D. B., Festinger, D. S., Lee, P. A., Schepise, M. M., Hazzard, J. E. R., Merrill J. C., McLellan, A. T. (2003). Are judicial status hearings a key component of drug court? During treatment data from a randomized trial. *Criminal Justice and Behavior, 30*, 141–162.

Miethe, T. D., Lu, H., & Reese, E. (2000). Reintegrative shaming and recidivism risks in drug court: Explanations for some unexpected findings. *Crime & Delinquency, 46*, 522–541.

Office of Justice Programs Drug Court Clearinghouse and Technical Assistance Project. (2009). *Summary of drug court activity by state and county.* Retrieved from http://www1.spa.american.edu/justice/documents/2150.pdf

Orwin, R. G. (1983). A fail-safe *N* for effect size in meta-analysis. *Journal of Educational Statistics, 8*, 157–159.

Pearson, F. S., & Lipton, D. S. (1999). A meta-analytic review of the effectiveness of corrections-based treatments for drug abuse. *Prison Journal, 79*, 384–410.

Pearson, F. S., Lipton, D. S., Cleland, C. M., & Yee, D. S. (2002). The effects of behavioral/cognitive-behavioral programs on recidivism. *Crime & Delinquency, 48*, 476–496.

Peters, R. H., & Murrin, M. R. (2000). Effectiveness of treatment-based drug courts in reducing criminal recidivism. *Criminal Justice and Behavior, 27*, 72–96.

Pratt, T. C., Holsinger, A. M., & Latessa, E. J. (2000). Treating the chronic DUI offender "Turning Point" ten years later. *Journal of Criminal Justice, 28*, 271–781.

Roman, J., Townsend, W., & Bhati, A. S. (2003). *Recidivism rates for drug court graduates: Nationally based estimates, final report.* San Diego, CA: Caliber Associates and the Urban Institute.

Rosenthal, R. (1991). *Meta-analytic procedures for social research.* Newbury Park, CA: Sage.

Rosenthal, R. (1994). Parametric measures of effect size. In H. Cooper & L. V. Hedges (Eds.), *The handbook of research synthesis* (pp. 231–244). New York: Russell Sage Foundation.

Rottman, D., & Casey, P. (1999). Therapeutic jurisprudence and the emergence of problem-solving courts. *National Institute of Justice Journal*, July, 12–19.

Senjo, S. R., & Leip, L. A. (2001). Testing and developing theory in drug court: A four-part logit model to predict program completion. *Criminal Justice Policy Review, 12*, 66–87.

Shaffer, D. K., Hartman, J. L., & Listwan, S. J. (2009). Drug abusing women in the community: The impact of drug court involvement on recidivism. *Journal of Drug Issues, 39*, 803–828.

Shaffer, D. K., Listwan, S. J., Latessa, E. J., & Lowenkamp, C. T. (2008). The drug court phenomenon: Findings from Ohio. *Drug Court Review, 6*, 33–68.

Sloan III, J. J., & Smykla, J. O. (2003). Juvenile drug courts: Understanding the importance of dimensional variability. *Criminal Justice Policy Review, 14*, 339–360.

Spohn, C., Piper, R. K., Martin, T., & Frenzel., E. D. (2001). Drug courts and recidivism: The results of an evaluation using two comparison groups and multiple indicators of recidivism. *Journal of Drug Issues, 31*, 149–176.

Taxman, F. S., & Bouffard, J. (2002). Treatment inside the drug treatment court: The who, what, where, and how of treatment services. *Substance Use & Misuse, 37*, 1665–1688.

Vito, G. F., & Tewksbury, R. A. (1998). The impact of treatment: The Jefferson County (Kentucky) drug court program. *Federal Probation, 62*, 46–51.

Wells-Parker, E., & Bangert-Drowns, R. (1995). Final results from a meta-analysis of remedial interventions with drink/drive offenders. *Addiction, 90*, 907–927.

Wexler, D. (2000). Therapeutic jurisprudence: An overview. *Thomas M. Cooley Law Review, 17*, 125–134.

Wilson, D. B. (2002). *Meta-analysis macros for SAS, SPSS, and Stata.* Retrieved from http://mason.gmu.edu/~dwilsonb/ma.html

Wilson, D. B., Mitchell, O., & MacKenzie, D. L. (2006). A systematic review of drug court effects on recidivism. *Journal of Experimental Criminology, 2*, 459–487.

Winick, B. J., & Wexler, D. B. (2003). Drug treatment court: Therapeutic jurisprudence applied. In B. J. Winick & D. B. Wexler (Eds.), *Judging in a therapeutic key: Therapeutic jurisprudence and the courts* (pp. 106–100). Durham, NC: Carolina Academic Press.

Wolf, F. M. (1986). *Meta-analysis: Quantitative methods for research synthesis.* Beverly Hills, CA: Sage.

Wolfe, E., Guydish, J., & Termondt, J. (2002). A drug court outcome evaluation comparing arrests in a two-year follow-up period. *Journal of Drug Issues, 32*, 1155–1172.

Yeaton, W. H., & Wartmon, P. M. (1993). On the reliability of meta-analytic reviews: The role of intercoder agreement. *Evaluation Review, I*, 292–309.

▌2 Policy Analysis and Program Evaluation

In this chapter, I will focus on the two different types of applied research—policy analysis and program evaluation. Specifically, this involves researching and recommending new programs and policies and then evaluating their effectiveness once implemented. Regardless of what part of the criminal justice system you like and what you plan to do when you finish school, it is likely that what is discussed in this chapter will be relevant to your career. Either you will be directly involved in this type of work, or people whom you associate with will be doing it. That prediction might sound pretty far-fetched right now, especially if you anticipate going into a field with non-office jobs, such as law enforcement. Even if you do start out in the field, you should aim to work your way up the ranks. Law enforcement, corrections personnel, court administrators, victim-witness advocates, and just about every criminal justice and social service profession has people in the higher ranks making decisions all the time. They have to analyze problems and propose new policies and programs. Then, they either have to evaluate the new system put into place or work alongside those who are called in to do the evaluation (like me!). If you just turned to your aunt, uncle, or grandparent who is a retired officer or case worker, and that person said that this is all nonsense because their jobs did not involve any policy or evaluation work, they aren't lying to you. What you must realize is that the field is changing, so things are different today. When your relatives entered the field, they did not need to have a college education, but you do now. It is now common for agencies to require their leaders to have master's degrees, which was something unheard of years ago. Our field is going to continue to move in the direction of relying on evidence-based policies, so this kind of work is going to be part of your future.

Policy analysis and program evaluation are two very different jobs that occur at different times in the life of a policy or program. Policy analysis, also known as problem analysis, is the process of identifying potential solutions to a current or anticipated problem. Program evaluation comes after policy analysis and involves studying how well the policy or program was implemented and whether it had the predicted impact.

Policy Analysis

It might be useful to first distinguish between programs, policies, and projects. Welsh and Harris (2013) define a **policy** as "a rule or set of rules or guidelines for how to make a decision" (p. 4). Policies may or may not lead to the development of programs and projects. A department of corrections, for example, can establish a policy that no inmate is to ever leave custody straight from isolation. With that announcement would come the need for the department to establish a new step-down program that would integrate people from isolation back into a more congregate setting within the prison for several months before they complete their sentences. A **program** is "a set of services aimed at achieving specific goals and objectives within specified individuals, groups, organizations, or communities" (Welsh & Harris, 2013, p. 5). So, the step-down program would work toward fulfilling the policy objective of acclimating inmates to social settings prior to release. **Projects** are smaller than programs and include a "time-limited set of services provided to particular individuals, groups, organizations, communities, usually focused on a single need, problem, or issue" (Welsh & Harris, 2013, p. 5). A project within the larger step-down program might be offering 12 weekly one-hour anger management sessions to a group of 15 inmates.

In criminal justice, we are constantly working to develop new policies or modify existing ones. Ideally, these changes should be a product of careful consideration of the facts, with an eye on the impact that the proposed change might have on all constituents. We do this by trying to look into the future and predict possible outcomes. Patton and Sawicki (1993) noted that this type of work goes by many names, including ex ante, pre hoc, anticipatory, or prospective policy analysis (Patton & Sawicki, 1993).

Bardach and Patashnik (2020) identified eight steps to conduct policy analysis:

1. Verify and define the problem
2. Assemble evidence
3. Construct alternatives
4. Select criteria
5. Project outcomes
6. Confront trade-offs
7. Decide
8. Present the plan

The elements of policy analysis listed here make up a good formula for making a rational, evidence-based decision. Once analysts identify the problem and assemble evidence of a current or anticipated future problem, the next step is to consider our options. One possibility could be just staying the course and not changing the current trajectory. That can be used as a type of yardstick against which we can compare other ideas. After we identify alternatives, we need to list criteria that we will use to compare the viability of our options. Here, we might want to consider potential effectiveness of addressing the problem, financial cost, political feasibility, ethical considerations, and administrative robustness of the plan. For ethical considerations, one thing that we must consider is how the proposed policy might differentially impact certain populations. **Administrative robustness** refers to how resilient the proposed policy would be when faced with poor implementation (Bardach & Patashnik, 2020). Next, we try to project the outcomes to predict how each of our policy alternatives might play out in the future. A good historical example of our failure to carefully consider the future impact of our decisions is the war on drugs policies of the 1980s and 1990s. These laws had disproportionately negative impacts on minority communities and pushed criminal justice expenditures to the point that counties, states, and the federal government could no longer afford to keep incarcerating people. When those laws were passed, there was little thought about what the social or fiscal impacts would be. This is why some state governments now require fiscal or minority impact statements to accompany any punitive change to sentencing practices (Subramanian, Moreno, & Broomhead, 2014). Once we have those projections, we can compare our assembled evidence, consider how our policy alternatives rank on our selected evaluation criteria, select one, and then try to state our case to promote the proposed policy.

An unfortunate fact of life in criminal justice is that we do not always take this careful, logical approach to decision-making. Welsh and Harris (2013) discuss planned and unplanned change. **Planned change** is done more carefully and is likely to follow the aforementioned steps. **Unplanned change** occurs much more hastily and often without consideration of some important facts. Unplanned change and even ill-conceived planned change occur in criminal justice more often than they should. The reason for this goes back to something I mentioned in Chapter 1, and that is the belief among many that crime control is a "common sense" issue, so it is not necessary to

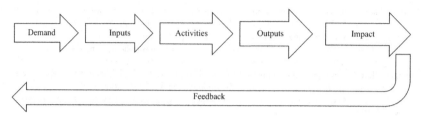

Figure 12.1 System Model
Source: Lineberry, R. L. (1977). *American Public Policy*. New York, NY: Harper Rowe. p. 43

consider research results or experts in the field when we make decisions. In criminal justice, there are numerous stakeholders, including criminal justice professionals, offenders, labor unions, politicians, special-interest groups, corporations, and voters who have an interest in criminal justice policy. The result is that sometimes politicians will advocate approaches that have been found not to work but would still appeal to certain groups of constituents. Corporations, lobbyists, and even labor unions may push for policies that might not be effective but will provide job security and profits for the people they represent. The unfortunate result is that we often see policy analysis that does not conform to the appropriate steps, or it is done properly but is then ignored by decision-makers.

Regardless of how well we adhere to the steps of policy formulation, we introduce new or modified criminal justice policies at the national, state, county, local, agency, and department levels all the time. Lineberry (1977), in his classic text on American public policy, presented the system model, displayed in Figure 12.1. This model explains the policy implementation process.

The policy process begins with individuals or groups demanding action. The response to that demand results in some type of **input**, which could include money, personnel, or other resources that are to be used to address the demand. Next, we have **activities**, and those consist of whatever is done with the inputs. As a result of those activities, the new policy or program generates outputs. The **outputs** lead to some sort of **outcome** or **impact**, hopefully a desirable one that addresses the original demand. As an example, we can consider the bail reform efforts that are taking place throughout the country. The demand for these programs came from prisoners' advocacy and racial justice groups concerned about the racial disparities that exist in our pretrial detention practices, especially since pretrial detention has been found to be associated with worse sentencing outcomes. Even groups such as fiscal conservatives, who historically have been less concerned about prisoners' rights, became amenable to change due to the financial impact of mass incarceration on county and state budgets. That demand for change produced bail reform policies in some states and counties, with pretrial detention decisions being made based on risk assessment models that heavily weigh the seriousness of the current charge. The inputs for this new policy include resources to make the risk assessment model and personnel to staff the pretrial services offices in the court and probation departments. Outputs include reduced jail populations and increased numbers of people released on recognizance or with pretrial supervision conditions. The outcome of bail reform is how much this is impacting the area's crime rates, the percentage of pretrial individuals who are failing to appear for court after release from jail, and the percentage of inmates subject to pretrial release who commit additional crimes while awaiting trial.

There are several different types of desirable impacts and outcomes in criminal justice that we might want to measure. Some of the most obvious ones are numbers of crimes, crime rates, and

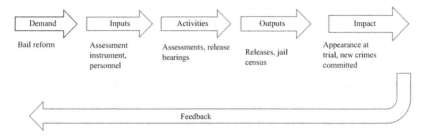

Figure 12.2 System Model Applied to Bail Reform

recidivism statistics. Following the recession of 2008, cost saving became an especially important outcome as governments were seeking ways to manage offenders with cheaper alternatives to incarceration. For juveniles, we might be interested in school attendance, suspensions, and graduation rates as outcomes.

Once we know about the impacts, we should provide feedback to influence what Lineberry (1977) calls tomorrow's inputs. Feedback is vital as it allows us to consider keeping, modifying, or shutting down the new policy or program, depending on its effectiveness. In New Jersey, police and prosecutor feedback following the initial months of bail reform implementation was used to modify the pretrial release procedure to make it easier to detain people charged with gun crimes, eluding the police, assault on a police officer, or crimes related to child pornography (Office of the Attorney General, 2017). Once state officials were able to see the program in practice, they were dissatisfied with some of the types of offenders who were being released, and that feedback prompted changes. The next section will address how we evaluate programs to generate that feedback.

Evaluation Research

As you have probably already guessed, the purpose of evaluation research is to evaluate programs or policies to determine whether they are achieving their stated goals. Obviously, this occurs after the policy has been created. There are two types of evaluation research, each of which is equally valuable. First, there are process evaluations. **Process evaluations** involve studies of the actual implementation of the program. In other words, we would be studying what Lineberry (1977) referred to as inputs, activities, and outputs from Figure 12.1. The question we ask ourselves at the outset of a process evaluation is whether the program was implemented as intended.

The second type of evaluation research is the **outcome** or **impact evaluation**. With this type of work, we are interested in the last part of Lineberry's (1977) system model—the impacts of our policy or program. With this, we look to establish a relationship, specifically a causal one, between the program's impact and the previous phases of the model, including the inputs, activities, and outputs. If the program is effective, the impact will be what the policymakers intended. If the impact evaluation reveals that the program was not effective, this is where the results of the process evaluation become really important. Due to funding and time restrictions, it is fairly common for researchers to just do outcome evaluations and skip the process evaluation. People are usually so anxious to get to the question of "Did it work?" that they want to skip over the process issues and focus on the impacts. The problem is that without a process evaluation, we will not be able to answer the question of why the program failed.

With a process evaluation, we observe all the moving parts while the program is being implemented. We need to know the extent to which implementation matched what was planned. Think of it this way: you make a new recipe, and when you taste the finished product, it is just horrible. You should throw out that recipe, right? Not necessarily. First, you should go read it again to make sure that you actually adhered to the directions. Did you leave out or substitute ingredients because you didn't have time to go to the store? Did you cook it on the right temperature for the correct amount of time? If it turns out that you did everything correctly and it was still terrible, then what you have is called **theory failure** (Suchman, 1969; Weiss, 1998). You carried out the plan (or policy or program) exactly the way it was intended, yet it still failed. That means that the entire premise was flawed. Throw out the recipe, discontinue the program, or change the policy.

But what if you did not follow the recipe? The recipe called for flour, but you were out of that and figured that baking soda looks like flour, so you used that instead. That is **implementation failure**, or a failure of the program due to lack of adherence to the program's plan. The recipe (theory) might be just fine, but we do not know for sure because you didn't actually make the recipe. It is not yet time to scrap the recipe, program, or policy. Another way to think of a process evaluation is that it is a check on treatment integrity. **Treatment integrity** is the extent to which the program or policy was implemented as intended. If the program called for staff to be properly licensed and for everyone to undergo 40 hours of training before interacting with clients, yet only one employee was licensed and training lasted 20 hours, that program lacks treatment integrity.

The use of an outcome evaluation in the absence of a process evaluation is known as the **black box** approach to program evaluation (Duwe, 2013). Of course, it is nearly impossible to see inside a black box, so if you are asked to describe that box to someone, you would be very limited in what you would be able to say. Applied to research, the inputs, activities, and outputs are located inside the box, while the impacts and outcomes are on the outside. Evaluators who only do outcome evaluations will be unable to explain whether a program failed due to poor implementation or if it was executed correctly and still fell short of expectations. Conversely, if a program does well, it may be a result of an unexpected input or activity and not at all because the program was implemented correctly. At minimum, we should try to do **gray box evaluations** that would provide some indication of how the program was implemented. Ideally, the organization running the program and the researcher should work together to allow for a **clear box evaluation**, which is one in which the researcher has complete access and a full view of how every aspect of the program is being implemented. Of course, this takes a lot of time and money, and that, combined with our interest in just finding out "Did it work or not?" often results in our forgoing the process evaluation.

Issues Unique to Evaluation Research

Carol Weiss (1998) has written extensively about evaluation research. She observed that researchers' experiences with applied research can be quite different from those involved in basic research. To start, the goal is different. For basic research, the objective is simply to produce knowledge with the hope of advancing the field. With program evaluation, we have a specific goal of helping an organization understand whether they are properly implementing a program and if it is producing the desired outcomes. Applied research work tends to come with its own set of research questions built into the program. The program has a set of goals and objectives, and the evaluator is expected to compare "what is" to "what should be." So, if the curriculum is supposed to be 60 hours over a 12-week period, we need to compare that objective to what actually happened during implementation. The researcher's obligation to examine the extent to which the program is being implemented as planned and producing positive outcomes has the potential to complicate the relationship between the researcher and practitioners. The arrival of researchers is not always met with enthusiasm as practitioners can be fearful that the evaluation results will embarrass the organization and/or its employees and even put careers at risk. I have been involved in situations in which staff members from the agency that hired me were uncooperative and even downright hostile. I was hired by an agency and was preparing to evaluate a cognitive-based intervention when all the course binders we were set to distribute to the clients "walked away" from a locked storage room that only the staff could access. This theft of our materials forced us to delay the start of the program. During another evaluation, I drove 90 minutes to a facility on a Saturday to conduct an observation. I had been visiting that facility for weeks, but all my previous visits had been during times when high-ranking administrators were present. When I arrived that Saturday, the officer in the control room, who had previously met me and knew that his agency hired me to do this specific job, claimed he knew nothing of the project. That officer had previously been cooperative with the evaluation, but on a day when his supervisors were not present to correct him, he blocked my access to the facility. While most practitioners are cordial and professional, there are unfortunate incidents when staff try to derail evaluations, either out of a desire to derail the research or just because people are mean spirited.

Practitioners might also think that the research is a waste of time, as they doubt the researcher's ability to learn more about the program than the staff already know themselves. This can lead to friction and an unwillingness of the staff to cooperate with the evaluator. Staff might be reluctant to participate in interviews or help the researchers collect data, even if ordered to do so by supervisors. In some circumstances, they might even try to work against the researcher by concealing negative information or trying to mislead them to put themselves or the program in a more positive light. The researcher must engage in a balancing act. While we do not want to harm anyone, we have an obligation provide the group funding the study with an honest evaluation, and we owe it to our profession to produce accurate work. The funding could be from a grant awarded by a private foundation or a government office. Funding can also come from the organization that is being evaluated, since the administrators may have decided to request the evaluation.

One unique aspect of evaluation research relates to the question of whether the results can be published. With evaluation research, the specific goal is to answer questions about one particular program, and since the researchers might be getting paid by the agency being evaluated, the agency might object to publishing the results. This is something that the researcher and the agency will have to negotiate. One possible work-around is that the researcher agrees to be vague about the agency that was subject to the evaluation. For example, the researcher can just state in the publication that the evaluation took place in a mid-Atlantic state and then not name the specific agency. Weiss (1998) remarked that, historically, evaluation research has not been published because some of the evaluations are of poor methodological quality. That is not necessarily due to a lack of effort and talent of the evaluator. Instead, it is likely due to data restrictions that I will discuss in greater detail later in this chapter.

Designs for Evaluation Research

Evaluations can take place at various times. We can do a **formative evaluation**, which is conducted while the program is being implemented and helps provide feedback to the designers so they can make improvements. This is essentially a process evaluation. **Summative evaluations** are conducted a bit later, such as after the program has been implemented, since the focus of summative evaluations is the program's outcomes. Weiss (1998) distinguishes the purpose of these two types of evaluations as follows: formative evaluations help improve the program in its early stages of development while summative work helps us decide whether to keep, modify, or discard the program.

The ideal plan is to conduct a summative or outcome evaluation with the classical experiment design. To review, classical experiments have three distinguishing characteristics: (1) the presence of an experimental and control group, (2) random assignment to the experimental and control groups, and (3) pre and post measurements. This design allows us to see how groups, organizations, or geographical areas were at baseline and then again after one is exposed to the experimental stimulus while the other is not. The random assignment increases our chances of having two groups that are similar in all respects except for the presence of the independent variable. If, after the posttest, we find a difference between the two groups on the variable of interest, we can confidently state that the independent variable contributed to that difference.

Unfortunately, it can be very difficult to conduct a classical experiment for several reasons, mostly having to do with the element of random assignment. There might be ethical concerns about with-holding something potentially valuable from the control group. This issue is likely to arise when evaluating rehabilitation programs, including drug and mental health treatment. Another reason could be that it is simply impractical, given the way the program must be implemented. I have been involved in evaluations of programs in juvenile training schools in which the determining factor of who would get the new curriculum versus treatment as usual (the control condition) was the housing unit where the students resided. Unfortunately, placement in housing units is not conducted ran-domly, as safety and security concerns outweigh the research goal of randomized assignment to the treatment condition. Due to the impracticality of randomization at times, researchers are often left with designing either a quasi-experiment or a one-group before-after design. If there is any way to come up with a comparison group, quasi-experiments are certainly preferable to any one-group design. As discussed in previous chapters, one-group designs leave us wondering what would have happened if time progressed without the introduction of the treatment stimulus? Would crime have decreased anyway? Would offenders have matured on their own and not recidivated? We can only answer those questions with either a control group, a matched comparison group, or a comparison group in which we also use statistical controls to account for the differences between the two groups.

Additional possibilities for evaluation research are cross-sectional or posttest-only designs with either one or two groups, but those should only be used if it is unavoidable. Without any pretest measures, we will have no way of knowing where the participants were at baseline. If I taught my students about ethics in criminal justice with the hope of making them better ethical decision-makers and then gave them a test at the end that shows the students scored an 80 percent, what did I really learn from my evaluation? Maybe they picked up ethics lessons in a previous criminal justice course. The only way I would know if my teaching impacted the students is if I had some sort of pretest to measure their knowledge *before* I began my instruction.

Should We Do the Evaluation?

Not every program should undergo an evaluation. There will be times when the program itself or the agency running it is just not at a state at which an evaluation would be worthwhile. Before we commit time and energy to evaluating a program, we should first consider an evaluability assess-ment. Weiss (1998) defines **evaluability assessment** as "a systematic way to examine the program both theoretically and empirically to determine whether full evaluation of the program outcomes is warranted" (p. 73). In this process, we should consider how plausible it is that this program, with its current setup, would achieve its goals. There have been times when I have looked at programs and known, right away, that they were being implemented in such a haphazard manner and so far removed from what constituted best practices that there was no way they could be effective. In those instances, I declined the opportunity to evaluate the programs. In one case, I quickly shared a few numbers with the director to illustrate my concerns and succeeded in getting the institution to discontinue the program in favor of something more evidence-based.

Weiss (1998) identified four circumstances in which the evaluation would not be worthwhile. First, the program has few routines and little stability. If we do conduct the evaluation, by the time we are ready to share our findings, they will be outdated because the program likely changed since we evaluated it. Second, those involved in the program cannot agree on the program goals. There's a relevant saying: "If you don't know where you are going, you might not get there." If there are no clear program goals, how do we set up a plan to determine whether goals are being met? At best, the researcher could offer to do a process evaluation, but any outcome research would be impossible. Third, the program administrator of the organization sponsoring the research imposes strict limits on what the researcher can or cannot study. Of course, no agency is going to throw open their doors and give you access to every file that they have ever written, nor should they. The evaluation needs to have structure, but if it appears from the start that there are going to be efforts to steer the evaluation a certain way, it would be best to walk away. I once lost an evaluation consulting job because one of the program providers wanted me to administer both the pre- and posttests on the last day of program implementation. She remarked that their agency had been doing evaluations this way, asking the students to imagine how they would have answered before learning all these new facts, and the results that they were getting were quite good. I explained why those results lacked validity and that, as a researcher I did not feel comfortable knowingly designing a problematic evaluation. Two days later, I was told that the agency had changed their mind about hiring me. While that was disappointing, I would rather lose that one opportunity in exchange for maintaining my integrity. Fourth, if there is not enough money or staff to do the evaluation, give very careful thought about moving forward. If it is something that really interests you and you can find the time to do it for little to no compensation, then that is okay. But if the budget constraints are such that you would not be able to do a good job or get the supplies or assistance that you need, it is probably not worth doing.

Will the Results Be Used?

No one likes to waste time. Imagine if you found out that your professors weren't actually reading the papers you wrote. If you procrastinated and then tossed a bunch of words on a paper right before it was due, you might be relieved. If you put a lot of time and effort into what you did, though, you would want that work to mean something. One of the frustrating parts of being involved in evaluation research is that the evaluation might have been requested simply to fulfill a requirement. Criminal justice and human service agencies frequently apply for grants to fund new initiatives. The grants frequently come with a stipulation that some of the money must go toward an unbiased evaluation, usually conducted by an outside consultant. That means that doing the evaluation was not the agency's idea, and they might not even consider it necessary. So they will comply for the sake of fulfilling the grant obligations, but the grant might not say anything about the agency's need to actually read and respond to the research findings. I was once called in to do a process and outcome evaluation by a state agency because their state Department of Education grant mandated that they hire an outside evaluator. As I did my work, I found out that the agency had already renewed the contract of the person who was facilitating the program, so regardless of my findings, the program was going to continue under the current leadership. My evaluation was not at all positive, and I think that had the agency waited to read it before making any decisions, they might have come to a different conclusion. Anyone who engages in evaluation research needs to be prepared to deal with the frustration and disappointment in the event that the research findings are ignored.

Finding What Works in Criminal Justice

Thanks to evaluation research, we have a good idea of what works in criminal justice. I am happy to report that our discipline is beginning to follow the medical field's lead in adopting evidence-based practice. As noted in Chapter 1, evidence-based practice (EBP) involves our use of only criminal justice interventions that have been found by multiple rigorous research studies to be effective. Criminal justice has several top-flight graduate programs, think tanks, and advocacy groups that are active in promoting EBP in our field.

Part of an early effort to introduce evidence into criminal-justice decision-making was the University of Maryland's 1998 publication *Preventing Crime: What Works, What Doesn't, What's Promising* (Sherman et al., 1998). Not only did this report present readers with examples of effective crime prevention strategies, but it also introduced the Maryland Scientific Methods Scale from Chapter 11. The scale provides a rating system to evaluate the quality of research. For researchers conducting systematic reviews and meta-analyses, the scale helps them determine which studies to exclude from their analysis.

One group that is working to disseminate research on the effectiveness of programs is the Campbell Collaboration Crime and Justice Coordinating Group (CJCG). Their mission is to encourage production of systematic reviews using only high-quality research designs on topics including prevention and control of crime and delinquency; programs designed to improve the criminal justice system; and issues relating to police, courts, corrections, criminal law, and civil law (Campbell Collaboration, 2020). The findings of these reviews can help inform decision-makers of good policies and programs to utilize. For example, Anthony Braga (2007) conducted a systematic review of **hot spots policing**. This is a patrol technique that first requires departments to analyze their crime patterns. Departments that engage in such fact-finding typically learn that disproportionate numbers of crimes occur in just a small number of areas around town. Armed with that knowledge, police can then concentrate their enforcement efforts on those locations. Braga studied previously completed classical and quasi-experiments of hot spot programs and found that seven of the nine studies reported substantial reductions of crime and disorder. While the Campbell Collaboration targets more academic readers than practitioners, other groups, such as the Community Oriented Policing Services (COPS), run by the National Institute of Justice, publish practitioner-friendly booklets on what works in policing (United States Department of Justice, n.d.). These publications summarize some of the best-practice research in a way that makes the information much more accessible to people who might not be interested in reading peer-reviewed research articles.

The two largest academic criminal justice organizations in the United States are the American Society of Criminology (ACS) and the Academy of Criminal Justice Sciences (ACJS). The two groups collaborated to create the Crime and Justice Research Alliance (CJRA), which aims to make policy experts available to the media, government officials, and practitioners who are seeking assistance with criminal justice matters. The goal of the alliance is to make experts and objective research more accessible so that sound research will be used as the basis of policy. CJRA has been working to publicize criminal justice research to increase media coverage of quality work so that it is more likely to reach the public.

Unfortunately, the effort to inject research into law and policy debates remains an uphill battle. As I have noted throughout the book, criminal justice is a field in which many people consider themselves proficient, regardless of their lack of knowledge or experience in the field. Political considerations also weigh heavily on decisions as crime has been used in numerous political campaigns. While we are making progress with injecting research and rational decision-making into criminal justice policy discussions, there is still much more work to do.

Some of this work involves something that I first mentioned in Chapter 4—replication of research. When we find some initial evidence that a new policy or program is effective, we need to resist the temptation to immediately place the "what works" tag on it and implement it across the country without doing careful replication first. I noted in Chapter 4 that the rush to anoint Project HOPE as an effective tool in community corrections based on evaluations in only one jurisdiction resulted in nationwide adoption of a program that now appears to be ineffective (Cullen, Pratt, Turanovic, & Butler, 2018). We witnessed a similar situation in the 1980s when Sherman and Berk (1984) published a study finding that arrest of domestic violence perpetrators was an effective deterrent. Multiple replications of that work in other jurisdictions revealed that the relationship between arrest and future offending is more complicated than initially thought (Schmidt & Sherman, 1993; Weisz, 2001). Some programs will work in one location but not others for a variety of reasons, including the size of the jurisdiction, the quality and dedication of staff, and the dynamics between different organizations that need to come together for the initiative to succeed (Cullen et al., 2018). As someone who tends to be extremely impatient, I understand the desire to rush to make a decision, particularly when we are excited about an innovation that we think can help people. We are better off waiting for the replications, though, as we run the risk of expanding programs that are ultimately harmful.

Summary

The focus of this chapter was applied research, which seeks to answer rather specific questions about policy issues and the effectiveness of existing policies and programs. Policy analysis is a type of forward-looking work in which analysts see a current problem, or one on the horizon, and identify policy alternatives. Analysts can then consider appropriate criteria to weigh the merits of each of the alternatives and then select one for recommendation. The criminal justice policy process is complicated by the presence of various stakeholders who are each promoting the interests of certain groups of constituents and by the fact that there is historical precedent for crafting criminal justice policy hastily and without careful and rational analysis.

Once a new policy or program is implemented, evaluation research can give us insight into whether it is being executed properly and producing desirable outcomes. Research that documents program implementation and its fidelity to the original program proposal is called a process evaluation. Outcome or impact evaluations seek to answer the question "Did the program work?" While process evaluations are frequently omitted to save time and money, they play a vital role in helping us understand the results of the outcome evaluation. Process evaluation data can tell us whether poor outcomes are a product of implementation failure or theory failure.

Evaluation research comes with a set of challenges that are different from what researchers engaging in basic research might experience. Evaluation researchers are almost certainly going to have to seek the cooperation of agency staff in order to complete the work. Navigating this relationship might be difficult at times as some practitioners view researchers as threatening and/or disruptive. Even if the researcher is fortunate enough to forge a positive and cooperative relationship with the agency staff, agency policies and program constraints might restrict the types of research designs that are feasible. Researchers also may not be at liberty to publish their findings. Researchers would be wise to conduct a short evaluability assessment before committing to participate in a program evaluation.

Our field is definitely moving in the direction of adopting more and more programs based on evidence-based practice. EBP allows policymakers to root their decisions in sound research rather than emotion, political influence, or anecdotal information. This is an important step in discontinuing ineffective policies and programs and replacing them with initiatives that have been subject to rigorous evaluation and are backed by evidence of their effectiveness. Evaluation research makes identification of effective programs possible.

Keywords

Policy
Administrative robustness
Inputs
Outcomes/impacts
Theory failure
Black box evaluation
Formative evaluation
Hot spots policing

Program
Planned change
Activities
Process evaluation
Implementation failure
Gray box evaluation
Summative evaluation

Project
Unplanned change
Outputs
Outcome/impact evaluation
Treatment integrity
Clear box evaluation
Evaluability assessment

Discussion Questions

1. What are black box, gray box, and clear box evaluations? Why are these important in helping us understand program success or failure?
2. What should we look for when conducting an evaluability assessment?
3. What additional challenges do researchers have to face when doing applied research compared to basic research?
4. What are some reasons we might make decisions in criminal justice that are not in line with evidence-based practice?

References

Bardach, E., & Patashnik, E. M. (2020). *A practical guide for policy analysis* (6th ed.). Los Angeles, CA: Sage Publications.

Braga, A. (2007). The effects of hot spots policing on crime. *Campbell Systematic Reviews, 1.* https://doi.org/10.4073/csr.2007.1

Campbell Collaboration. (2020). *Crime and Criminal Justice Coordinating Group.* Oslo, Norway: Campbell Collaboration. Retrieved from https://campbellcollaboration.org/contact/coordinating-groups/crime-and-justice.html

Cullen, F. T., Pratt, T. C., Turanovic, J. J., & Butler, L. (2018). When bad news arrives: Project HOPE in a post-factual world. *Journal of Contemporary Criminal Justice, 34*(1), 13–34.

Duwe, G. (2013). What's inside the "black box?" The importance of "gray box" evaluations for the "what works" movement. *Criminology & Public Policy, 12*(1), 145–152. https://doi.org/10.1111/1745-9133.12012

Lineberry, R. L. (1977). *American public policy.* New York, NY: Harper Rowe.

Office of the Attorney General. (2017). *Attorney general strengthens bail reform directive to better ensure that dangerous and recidivist criminals are kept in jail pending trial.* Trenton, NJ: State of New Jersey office of the Attorney General. https://nj.gov/oag/newsreleases17/pr20170524c.html

Patton, C. V., & Sawicki, D. S. (1993). *Basic methods of policy analysis and planning.* Upper Saddle River, NJ: Prentice Hall.

Schmidt, J. D., & Sherman, L. W. (1993). Does arrest deter domestic violence. *American Behavioral Scientist, 36,* 601–609.

Sherman, L., & Berk, R. S. (1984). The specific deterrent effects of arrest for domestic assault. *American Sociological Review, 49*(2), 261–272.

Sherman, L. W., Gottfredson, D. C., MacKenzie, D. L., Eck, J., Reuter, P., & Bushway, S. D. (1998). *Preventing crime: What works, what doesn't, what's promising?* Washington, DC: United States Department of Justice Office of Justice Programs.

Subramanian, R., Moreno, R., & Broomhead, S. (2014). *Recalibrating justice: A review of 2013 state sentencing and corrections trends.* New York, NY: Vera Institute of Justice.

Suchman, E. A. (1969). Evaluating educational programs. *Urban Review, 3*(4), 15–17.

United States Department of Justice. (n.d.). *Community Oriented Policing Services (COPS).* Washington, DC: United States Department of Justice. Retrieved from https://cops.usdoj.gov/

Weiss, C. H. (1998). *Evaluation* (2nd ed.). Upper Saddle River, NJ: Simon & Schuster.

Weisz, A. (2001). *Spouse assault replication program: Studies of effectiveness of arrest on domestic violence.* National Online Resource Center on Violence Against Women. Retrieved from www.vav.net

Welsh, W. N., & Harris, P. W. (2013). *Criminal Justice Policy & Planning* (4th ed.). Waltham, MA: Anderson Publishing.

Reading 12.1   The Cannabis Effect on Crime

Lu and colleagues' quasi-experiment with a multi-group interrupted time-series addresses a question that Americans have pondered for decades: what would happen to crime rates if we legalized marijuana? As of the time of this writing, 11 states have legalized marijuana while an additional 15 have decriminalized marijuana, and these are steps that were unthinkable in the 1980s and early 1990s. By using a multi-group interrupted time-series, the authors allow the readers to consider crime rates for a 17-year period for not only Washington and Colorado, two of the first states to legalize marijuana, but for states where marijuana remains illegal. The authors note that this is a complicated topic, and the impact of marijuana legalization needs to be examined at several different units of analysis. The authors conclude the article cautioning readers about the need for more research in this area. Marijuana legalization is new to the United States. They specifically call for replication, recognizing that this is one of the first, if not the first, time-series design that examines the impact of legalization on crime rates. Given all the rhetoric regarding the alleged dangerousness of marijuana and its assumed link to crime, the authors rightly encourage other researchers to continue to learn more about marijuana legalization and crime. They also caution that, as with alcohol following prohibition, it might take decades to fully understand the impact of legalization. Lu and colleagues chose to study legalization and crime at the state level, but the impact of legalization on crime could differ at the community level; therefore, future work should also consider different units of analysis.

The Cannabis Effect on Crime: Time-Series Analysis of Crime in Colorado and Washington State

Ruibin Lu, Dale Willits, Mary K. Stohr, David Makin,
John Snyder, Nicholas Lovrich, Mikala Meize,
Duane Stanton, Guangzhen Wu, and Craig Hemmens

Introduction

In many ways the legalization of cannabis by ten states and the District of Columbia, as of March 2019, constitutes a grand ongoing experiment into how a major public policy initiative does or does not accomplish its expected outcomes. One of the principal expectations of the proponents of Initiative 502, the voter-initiated bill authorizing the recreational sale of marijuana in Washington, was that crime would decrease. Crimes generally were expected to decline in number, but particularly those crimes associated with the use of marijuana (e.g., possession, black market production, sales and distribution of cannabis, burglaries or thefts believed to be committed to secure funds to purchase marijuana). Some preliminary studies released

shortly after legalization have intimated that crime rates have been going up rather dramatically in some of the states that have legalized recreational marijuana (Smart Approaches to Marijuana, 2018). In Washington State, early reports suggested that the number of marijuana-related offenses such as assault, theft, harassment, and vehicular offenses increased in Washington after the legalization (Northwest High Intensity Drug Trafficking Area [NHIDTA], 2016) but that "violent crime is down since Washington legalized marijuana" (Santos, 2017). Or, paradoxically, the article by Malcolm Gladwell in *The New Yorker*, claiming (based on a book by Berenson, [2019]) that violent crime had increased in Washington state post legalization.

As Garland (2001) has noted, there is a strong political demand for immediate answers to often quite complicated questions of public policy. In short, many politicians are inclined to make use of the earliest available data, and unfortunately, too often what is available for public consumption at the outset of a change in policy represents research employing limited pre/post analyses or misrepresentation of facts. Too often, the results reported from such analyses fail to take into consideration the context of practice. For example, consider headlines associated with increasing citations for public marijuana consumption, in and around major cities. In many ways, these headlines are interpreted to suggest that marijuana users are increasingly consuming in public, a practice which was explicitly banned in Washington law. However, to some extent, these increases may in fact relate to property ordinances and rental agreements banning smoking, where violation is an automatic qualification for termination of the lease. Such policy conundrums create an environment where it is illegal to smoke in public and essentially illegal for marijuana users to smoke in their residence. Additionally, pressure from retail establishments and other members of the public can create pressure on police officers to issue citations.

In the absence of more rigorous and robust types of analyses, policy discussions and decisions in those states considering the liberalization of their own cannabis laws are prone to believe the misleading conclusions disseminated about likely outcomes. A variety of claims regarding the deleterious effects of legalization have already been made in a number of instances, such as in Berenson's widely cited book (2019) about the purported dangers of marijuana and Vestal (2019)'s column for the *Spokesman Review*. Some politicians have also linked the legalization of marijuana with increases in violence, often without the support of empirical data (Adams, 2018). Advocacy groups, both for and against marijuana legalization, might also contribute to this problem. For example, the group Smart Approaches to Marijuana (2018) frequently presents anecdotal or single-site evidence about potential increases in crime, without a robust analysis to support assertions.

Recognizing the importance for public policy making of more robust research designs in this area, this study uses a quasi-experimental multigroup interrupted time-series design to determine if, and how, crime rates in Colorado and Washington State were influenced by the legalization of recreational marijuana in 2012 and the start of retail sales in 2014.

Literature Review

Background of Cannabis Laws in Colorado and Washington

In 1998 Washington State voters emulated action taken by voters in California in 1996 to pass Initiative 692, a law which legalized the use of cannabis for qualified patients with certain medical conditions (NHIDTA, 2016). Voters in Colorado continued this trend in 2000 with Amendment 20, which allowed physicians to recommend marijuana to patients and allowed patients to grow up to six plants with a registry identification card. Under Amendment 21, caregivers in Colorado were legally allowed to have minor grow operations for up to five patients (Salomonsen-Sautel, Sakai, Thurstone, Corley, & Hopfer, 2012).

Over the course of a decade, legislation was enacted loosening the restrictions on prescribing medical marijuana licenses and expanding qualifying conditions. In 2010, Colorado allowed for large-scale licensed medical marijuana dispensaries (Reed, Hilkey, Thome, & English, 2018). In the following year in Washington, Senate Bill 5073 authorized the use of "collective gardens" that allowed up to ten patients or providers to grow up to 45 plants and produce up to 72 ounces of usable marijuana. It is believed that this collective garden provision in the state's medical marijuana laws substantially expanded the state's black market for cannabis whereby largely unregulated marijuana "dispensary" storefronts were able to sell substantial amounts of cannabis both to properly qualified and to unauthorized consumers alike (NHIDTA, 2016).

During this period after the passage of Initiative 692, voters in Seattle and Tacoma, two of Washington's most populous cities, passed local ordinances by the initiative process that required that police officers regard the possession of marijuana as a low priority for enforcement (a policy known as *deprioritization*). The first such ordinance was passed in 2002 ("Seattle Municipal Code," 2003, 12 A.20.060, Sect. A), and the second was passed in 2011 (ReformAct.Org., 2017, p. 1). Citizens of the consolidated City/County government of Denver, Colorado, passed comparable legislation in the form of Question 100 in 2007. This measure made marijuana possession offenses the lowest priority for law enforcement officers. Although the initiative passed by a comfortable margin, Denver officials reiterated their right to enforce state and federal marijuana laws should public health and public safety require their action. Columnist Dick Kreck likened this action of the citizens of Denver to that taken to end prohibition (Amendment Seven) in 1934 by a vote of 2-to-1 once the federal government turned over alcohol regulation to the states and their local governments (Kreck, 2009).

The growing movement to decriminalize cannabis use led to the eventual legalization of recreational marijuana in both Colorado and Washington. In November 2012, Washington State voters passed Initiative 502 by a 56% to 44% margin, and Colorado voters passed Amendment 64 by a similar 55% to 45% margin; both pieces of legislation legalized the possession, consumption, and purchase of cannabis by individuals 21 years and older for recreational purposes, and allowed residents to start regulated licensed businesses that produce, process, and sell cannabis legally (NHIDTA, 2016; Washington State Liquor and Cannabis Board [WSLCB], 2014; Colorado Department of Revenue, 2019).

One of the core issues of concern for proponents and opponents of cannabis legalization was its likely effects on crime. Proponents believed that crime would decrease just by redefinition (possession of up to one ounce by adults would be legal), and that ancillary crimes attributed to black market drug dealing and acquisition, such as thefts and burglaries, would also decrease (Aalen, 2013; Contreras, 2017; Kepple & Freisthler, 2012). Those who opposed legalization were concerned that the prevalence of cannabis would lead to problematic consequences, including an increased crime rate as intoxicated and less inhibited adult and juvenile users engaged in index and traffic offenses and as adolescents found it easier to access cannabis for illegal use (Doherty, Tyson, & Weisel, 2015). In accord with these beliefs by both proponents and opponents, there is some research that indicates marijuana legalization and/or decriminalization can lead to: (1) increased marijuana use; (2) increased cash-based marijuana businesses; and (3) diminished black marijuana market and cannabis-related charges.

Cannabis Use

Perhaps the least debated direct consequence of permitting the sale and possession of marijuana for recreational purposes is increased marijuana use. While some researchers claim medical marijuana laws do not affect drug use (Harper, Strumpf, & Kaufman, 2012), most studies consistently demonstrate that after the passage of medical marijuana laws, marijuana use became more widespread in states which allowed its legal use (Cerdá, Wall, Keyes, Galea, & Hasin, 2012; Chu, 2015; Schuermeyer et al., 2014; Wall et al., 2011).

The passage of marijuana laws may also induce more cannabis use by altering people's perceptions about it (Schuermeyer et al., 2014; Wall et al., 2011). For example, Schuermeyer et al. (2014) compared the perceived risk of marijuana use by adults and adolescents living in Colorado with those who live in states without medical marijuana laws, using the *National Survey on Drug Use and Health* (NSDUH) statistics on self-reported attitudes toward cannabis use. They used 2010 to 2011 as the observation period because there was a series of policy changes in Colorado in 2009 that resulted in the rapid increase in the number of medical marijuana cardholders in Colorado. Their results indicated that compared to residents of non-medical marijuana states, Coloradans were less likely to disapprove of marijuana use and were less likely to perceive its use as a risky behavior in the time leading up to the legalization of recreational marijuana in Colorado in 2012.

Consequently, consuming cannabis for medical and/or recreational purposes may become a more popular choice if people perceive the legalization of this substance as indicating its use is acceptable conduct.

Crime and Cannabis Use

Whether increased cannabis use will ultimately affect crime rates, however, is far from a settled matter. Prior research provides mixed and inconclusive evidence on the effect of marijuana use on crime. On the one hand, a number of empirical studies find that marijuana use enhances the likelihood of engaging in violent and property crimes and other forms of serious delinquent behavior (Brook, Brook, Rosen, & Rabbitt, 2003; Pacula & Kilmer, 2003; Phillips, 2012; Reingle, Staras, Jennings, Branchini, & Maldonado-Molina, 2012; Reynolds, Tarter, Kirisci, & Clark, 2011).

Cannabis users' risk of offending is also confirmed by a meta-analysis that investigated the connection between drug use and crime (Bennett, Holloway, & Farrington, 2008). This meta-analysis reviewed 30 studies examining the effect of drug use on a broad range of violent and property crimes across the globe. Among these studies, 18 were conducted in the United States, and 10 investigated the relationship between marijuana use and offending. The average effect size of the meta-analysis suggested that the odds of marijuana users offending are about 1.5 times higher than the odds of non-marijuana users offending. Overall, based on these empirical studies, one would expect crime rates to increase after legalizing medical and recreational cannabis use because there would be more marijuana abusers. One important caveat here is that this line of argument assumes that the relationship between marijuana and crime is the same for individuals who chose to use it when illegal as for those who choose to use it once it is legal.

Importantly, some evidence suggests cannabis use either will not affect or may even ameliorate drug users' violent tendencies (Miller, 1990). In a study of spousal violence using a sample of parolees, Miller (1990) found

that when parolees report having an alcohol problem, but not a drug problem, their level of violence increased, whereas individuals who report having both alcohol and drug problems have a relatively steady violence level. Miller (1990) interpreted these results as possibly indicating drug use may suppress the violence induced by alcohol consumption. Another study examining the relationship between drug use and violent delinquency among adolescent Mexican Americans found that when this group incrementally increased their use of cannabis, their commission of violent crimes decreased, possibly because marijuana is often used as a substitute for other controlled substances more consistently related to violent behaviors, such as alcohol, cocaine, and amphetamines (Aalen, 2013). Hence, in light of this contradictory evidence, it is difficult to predict if, and to what extent, more frequent cannabis use is related to violent crimes.

Cash-Based Cannabis Business and Crime

There is also the concern that permitting state-licensed recreational cannabis production and sale will inevitably create booming businesses, inclusive of dispensaries, growers, and production facilities, in communities that by association may become attractive targets for crimes. This is due to commercial enterprises relying heavily on cash transactions and stolen products that can be readily sold and consumed (Contreras, 2017; Kepple & Freisthler, 2012). As cannabis remains a Schedule One drug that is prohibited at the federal level, banks have been unwilling to engage in transactions associated with marijuana businesses as they fear the risk of money laundering prosecution by federal authorities (Chemerinsky, Forman, Hopper, & Kamin, 2015). Therefore, cannabis business owners, especially in the early years of legalization, were forced to make cash transactions and to keep large quantities of cash on hand. Notably, in some communities there are now state-chartered savings and loan establishments that will handle cannabis business monies with a substantial surcharge fee.

Routine activity theory holds there are three elements necessary for a crime to occur, including motivated offenders, suitable targets, and capable guardians (Cohen & Felson, 1979). Based on this theory, cannabis businesses and customers are suitable targets for motivated offenders seeking cash and/or drugs. They are at risk of property crimes such as burglary and shoplifting, and economically oriented violent crimes such as robbery. More property and violent crimes may also occur in the neighborhoods where marijuana businesses are located because offenders are targeting customers who are forced to carry large amounts of cash. The increased presence of offenders may lead to additional crimes against other persons or businesses not related to marijuana, simply because offender presence may equate with opportunity. Of course, potential offenders' final decision to engage in crime might be influenced by the protective measures taken at the dispensaries and in the communities. If strong guardianship technology, such as security and monitoring systems, are present, then the businesses may not necessarily attract more motivated offenders because they are less accessible (Kepple & Freisthler, 2012).

The Marijuana Market and Crime

Scholars also argue that it is the systematic nature of illicit marijuana markets that causes violent crimes (Aalen, 2013; Goldstein, 1985). Because there are ample demands for marijuana and abundant profitable opportunities associated with marijuana businesses, the prohibition of this substance gives rise to black markets. However, those involved in marijuana businesses cannot resolve disputes through legal channels without risking incriminating themselves. They have to rely on alternative means, which usually involves corruption (payoffs) or violence, to address disputes (Aalen, 2013). By having a legalized market for cannabis transactions, growers, producers, sellers, and customers can operate in a safer and more predictable environment where transactions are transparent, open to scrutiny, and free from corruption. These newly lawful circumstances will necessarily depress the systematic violence

inherent in an underground cannabis market (Aalen, 2013).

Some scholars argue that the association between crime and marijuana is due to its illegality, which would not exist, or at a minimum, diminish significantly, in an environment where cannabis is legalized. Pedersen and Skardhamar (2010) followed 1,353 Norwegian adolescents over the span of 13 years and found that early cannabis use can only predict adolescents' future involvement in drug-specific crimes such as use and possession of drugs. They found little evidence indicating cannabis use is a stepping-stone to more general criminal involvement. Even though there was a robust association between cannabis use and subsequent criminal involvement in their study, Pedersen and Skardhamar (2010) report this relationship disappears when drug-specific charges are excluded. Their research indicates that if use and possession of recreational cannabis were legal, then adolescent abusers would not have been labeled as more prone to commit crimes.

At the same time, prior research on the effect of enacting medical marijuana laws on crime also provides mixed and inconclusive evidence about what could happen if recreational marijuana use is further permitted. Analyzing *National Crime Victimization Survey* (NCVS) data between 1992 and 1994, Markowitz (2005) finds violent crime rates are higher in states where marijuana use is decriminalized. In contrast, other empirical findings suggest permitting medical marijuana is associated with a significant drop in violent crime rates, especially homicide and assault rates (Aalen, 2013; Morris, TenEyck, Barnes, & Kovandzic, 2014; Shepard & Blackley, 2016), and a non-significant change in property crime rates (Morris et al., 2014; Shepard & Blackley, 2016). For example, a recent study conducted on the violent and property crime rates of 11 states in the Western US shows after controlling for state-level factors, states that adopted medical marijuana laws experienced a significant drop in the violent crime rate and a non-significant change in the property crime rate (Morris et al., 2014).

Summary of Research Findings and Limitations

In sum, the literature on cannabis use and legalization/decriminalization evinces two conflicting paradigms of how they affect use, abuse, and crime. Under the first paradigm, with research that supports a more malevolent view of legalization, loosening marijuana laws will motivate more cannabis use and alter people's attitudes toward this substance (Cerdá et al., 2012; Chu, 2015; Schuermeyer et al., 2014; Wall et al., 2011). The prevalence of cannabis use, particularly the early onset of youth cannabis use, will increase youths' risk of engaging in violence and delinquency (Brook et al., 2003; Phillips, 2012; Reingle et al., 2012). The growth in the number of marijuana abusers as a result of the legalization may also lead to more crimes because some research suggests marijuana users are more likely to commit violent and property crimes (Bennett et al., 2008). The vulnerability of cannabis businesses (i.e., cash-based businesses, with easily sold and consumed merchandises) may also incentivize crimes such as burglary, shoplifting, and robbery as these businesses are attractive targets for crimes. Hence, under the first paradigm, with a more malevolent view of the effects of legalization, there is theoretical support for an increase of violent and property crime rates post cannabis legalization.

An alternate paradigm, however, with research that supports a more benign view of the effects of legalization, suggests that cannabis legalization will not affect, or even lead to an increase in crime rates. Violent crime rates may decrease because some research suggests an individual's violent tendencies may be suppressed by the consumption of cannabis (Miller, 1990). There is also evidence that cannabis users are not more prone to commit general crimes than others; they are not more likely to violate the law if drug-specific conduct, such as use and possession of drugs, is legal (Pedersen & Skardhamar,

2010). Meanwhile, the systematic violence inherent in an underground cannabis market is expected to diminish as the marijuana market is legalized (Aalen, 2013).

Methods

This study aims to overcome the limitations of previous studies and address the conflicting malevolent and benign views about how cannabis legalization would affect crime rates. We conducted a series of multi-group interrupted time-series of monthly crime rates comparing Colorado and Washington to states which have yet to legalize marijuana. Interrupted time-series analysis has long been viewed as one of the strongest quasi-experimental approaches for understanding the short- and long-term effects of interventions (Bernal, Cummins, & Gasparrini, 2017; Cook & Campbell, 1979; Wagner, Soumerai, Zhang, & Ross-Degnan, 2002). The basic principle behind an interrupted time-series approach is to estimate the trend of some particular outcome before and after an intervention, with a focus on determining if there are immediate intervention effects and/or intervention effects over time (Linden, 2015). In a traditional interrupted time-series design, the period prior to the intervention serves as a counterfactual, and by controlling for this pre-intervention trend, interrupted time-series analysis is able to estimate the impact of interventions on a given outcome.

For our purposes, we are interested in the degree to which crime rates changed following the legalization of recreational marijuana and the start of recreational sales in Colorado and Washington State. Instead of examining each state in a single-group interrupted time-series approach, which is known to have limited ability to determine causality, we compare crime trends in these states to those with no marijuana laws on the books using a multi-group approach. Linden (2017) demonstrates that a multi-group interrupted time-series design can better detect immediate and over-time intervention effects. As such, for our models, we compare monthly crime rates in Colorado and Washington State to the 21 states that have not legalized marijuana use for recreational or medical purposes on a large scale.

Crime data for this project were obtained from the FBI's *Uniform Crime Report* for the period 1999 to 2016 for agencies which reported complete data over this time period. Specifically, yearly *Uniform Crime Reporting Program Data: Offenses Known and Clearances by Arrest* data from 1999 to 2016 were obtained from the Institute for Social Research at the University of Michigan (ICPSR) website. We calculated monthly violent, property, aggravated assault, auto theft, burglary, larceny, and robbery rates for Colorado and Washington and the monthly average of each of these crime rates for the control group. For aggravated assault, auto theft, burglary, larceny, and robbery, monthly crime rates are calculated by firstly summing up the total number of the corresponding type of crime cleared by the law enforcement agencies in a state each month. Next, the monthly crime rates per capita are calculated by dividing the total number of crimes by the state's population and then multiplying that number by 100,000. Monthly violent and property crime rates are calculated by the same procedures but include more types of offenses. Violent crime includes murder, manslaughter, aggravated assault, rape, and robbery. Property crime includes auto theft, burglary, and larceny. Though our primary focus is on examining the effects of legalized recreational marijuana, we include a longer time-series to better account for trends in violent and property crime prior to the legalization in both states in 2012. Table 1 displays each of the potential intervention points, and the date of each intervention.

Results

To better illustrate the trends of different types of crimes in Colorado and Washington and states that do not have broad laws legalizing marijuana, we present our results both visually and in table form. Table 2 displays the interrupted time-series results for Colorado for violent and property crime, as well as results disaggregated by crime type. Each of the models presented in Table 2 also includes a set of monthly dummy variables to account for month-to-month variation, but these results are not presented to improve the presentation of results. Table 3 presents the same set of models for Washington.

Overall, each of the fitted multiple-group interrupted time-series models fits well (all of the likelihood ratio tests indicate that the models are superior to null models). For both of the interruption points (the legalization of recreational marijuana and the start of recreational sales), multiple-group ITSA regressions produce coefficients for trends prior to the intervention, immediately after the intervention, and post-intervention effects over time. They also produce coefficients describing the differences in crime rates between treatment group (Colorado or Washington) and control group (states that have no broad laws legalizing marijuana) for immediate changes associated with each intervention, and for changes in trends between the treatment and control group following each intervention.

In general, the results suggest that marijuana policies and laws have had *little effect on crime* in Colorado or Washington State. The most important rows in this chart are those that describe the difference in immediate crime rate changes between the control states and Colorado/Washington, and those that describe the difference in trends between the control states and Colorado/Washington after a specific intervention. For example, for violent crime, there were no statistically significant immediate treatment effects of legalization in Washington

Table 1 *Major Marijuana Laws in Washington State and Colorado*

Intervention Date	Description
December 2012	Legalization of recreational marijuana in Washington State (I-502) and Colorado (Amendment 64)
January 2014	Date of legalized retail sales of recreational marijuana in Colorado
July 2014	Date of legalized retail sales of recreational marijuana in Washington State

Table 2 Colorado ITSA Results on Specific Crime Rates per Month

	Violent Crime	Property Crime	Agg. Assault	Auto Theft	Burglary	Larceny	Robbery
Difference between CO and control prior to interventions	-3.70** (.493)	-45.477** (3.978)	-2.825** (.350)	7.936** (.919)	-19.993** (1.002)	-33.419** (2.595)	-1.492** (.229)
Trend prior to legalization (Control)	-.051** (.004)	-.632** (.037)	-.030** (.003)	-.078** (.009)	-.050** (.008)	-.503** (.023)	-.018** (.002)
Trend prior to legalization (CO)	.049** (.005)	-.115** (.041)	-.030** (.003)	-.049** (.009)	-.061** (.010)	-.006 (.027)	.009** (.002)
Immediate effect after recreational legalization (Control)	-2.315 (1.414)	-9.490 (12.565)	-1.835+ (1.021)	-.363 (3.087)	-6.707* (2.812)	-2.348 (7.947)	-.685 (.542)
Immediate effect difference between control and CO after recreational legalization	.050 (1.750)	28.069* (14.178)	-1.364 (1.243)	1.656 (3.284)	6.016+ (3.552)	20.382* (9.238)	.827 (.800)
Trend after recreational legalization (Control)	.080 (.192)	.436 (1.702)	.074 (.139)	.111 (.418)	-.261 (.382)	.589 (1.077)	-.026 (.074)
Trend after recreational legalization (CO)	-.170 (.238)	-1.639 (1.928)	-.020 (.169)	-.065 (.447)	-.224 (.482)	-1.358 (1.256)	-.132 (.108)
Immediate effect after retail (Control)	-3.136+ (1.897)	-11.245 (16.936)	-2.322+ (1.371)	-.485 (4.179)	-6.250+ (3.770)	-4.674 (10.693)	-.603 (.726)
Immediate effect difference between control and CO after retail	.001 (2.345)	-23.055 (18.959)	1.129 (1.665)	-7.617+ (4.386)	.605 (4.762)	-15.911 (12.360)	-1.048 (1.082)
Trend after retail (Control)	.156 (.196)	-.037 (1.741)	.090 (.142)	.041 (.428)	.148 (.390)	-.227 (1.101)	.064 (.075)
Trend after retail (CO)	.091 (.243)	2.503 (1.968)	-.049 (.172)	.426 (.456)	.322 (.493)	1.759 (1.282)	.128 (.111)
Constant	35.367** (.593)	271.945** (5.307)	22.055** (.429)	16.157** (1.307)	67.565** (1.176)	188.820** (3.350)	9.619** (.219)
LRT	744.447**	577.188**	773.226**	555.870**	857.504**	744.991**	611.124**
AR(1) rho	.125	.202	.139	.246	.106	.179	-.059
Corrected Durbin-Watson	2.156	2.336	2.157	2.428	2.153	2.272	1.933

n = 432. Prais-Winsten corrected standard errors in parentheses.
+p < .1
*p < .05
**p < .01

(b = 2.132, p > .05) or Colorado (b = .050, p > .10). This trend of non-significant results held true for most models for both states.

There were, however, some statistically significant results suggesting that legalization may have had an immediate effect on crime. In Colorado, there was a statistically significant increase in the property crime rate (b = 28.069) at the point of legalization, which appears to be largely driven by a statistically significant increase in larceny (b = 20.382). In Washington, there was a statistically significant increase in property crime overall (b = 24.299), burglary (b = 14.112), and aggravated assault (b = 2.034) at the point of intervention. These coefficients correspond to a one-time increase in the crime rate per 100,000 of the coefficient values listed. In the segmented regression approach utilized here,

Table 3 Washington ITSA Results on Specific Crime Rates per Month

	Violent Crime	Property Crime	Agg. Assault	Auto Theft	Burglary	Larceny	Robbery
Difference between WA and control prior to interventions	−11.021** (.425)	12.396** (3.496)	−9.132** (.330)	14.354** (.705)	−1.267 (1.038)	−.717 (2.314)	−1.345** (.138)
Trend prior to legalization (Control)	−.051** (.003)	−.634** (.028)	−.030** (.002)	−.079** (.006)	−.050** (.007)	−.504** (.018)	−.018** (.001)
Trend prior to legalization (WA)	2.132+ (1.278)	−.152** (.036)	.002 (.003)	−.012 (.007)	14.117** (3.099)	−.112** (.024)	.011** (.001)
Immediate effect after recreational legalization (Control)	−2.654** (.894)	−7.238 (8.051)	−2.051** (.649)	−.412 (2.149)	−6.056** (2.009)	−.821 (5.338)	−.874* (.375)
Immediate effect difference between control and WA after recreational legalization	2.132+ (1.278)	24.299* (10.563)	2.034* (.987)	−1.374 (2.146)	14.112** (3.099)	11.565+ (6.992)	.498 (.418)
Trend after recreational legalization (Control)	.102 (.080)	−.123 (.721)	.076 (.058)	.143 (.192)	−.455* (.180)	.175 (.478)	.008 (.034)
Trend after recreational legalization (WA)	.008+ (.004)	1.184 (.947)	−.104 (.088)	.320+ (.193)	−.029** (.011)	1.075 (.627)	−.009 (.037)
Immediate effect after retail (Control)	−3.680* (1.627)	−16.577 (14.661)	−3.099** (1.183)	−1.681 (3.959)	−7.687* (3.664)	−6.892 (9.720)	−.396 (.687)
Immediate effect difference between control and WA after retail	.147 (2.331)	13.634 (19.217)	.410 (1.806)	−.695 (3.893)	3.627 (5.674)	10.865 (12.721)	−.100 (.758)
Trend after retail (Control)	.157+ (.089)	.596 (.806)	.114 (.065)	.044 (.217)	.360+ (.201)	.198 (.535)	.030 (.038)
Trend after retail (WA)	−.010 (.128)	−1.271 (1.058)	.018 (.099)	−.254 (.214)	−.003 (.311)	−1.014 (.700)	−.025 (.042)
Constant	35.628** (.427)	271.446** (3.915)	22.395** (9.303)	16.463** (1.057)	68.191** (.934)	187.365** (2.596)	9.356** (.185)
LRT	1132.253**	701.564**	1135.887**	727.398**	541.402**	559.434**	768.660**
AR(1) rho	−.015	.072	−.088	.286	−.106	.073	.209
Corrected Durbin-Watson	1.971	2.108	1.886	2.486	1.849	2.102	2.231

n = 432. Prais-Winsten corrected standard errors in parentheses.
+$p < .1$
*$p < .05$
**$p < .01$

this is equivalent to shifting the intercept for the second segment of the regression model. It is important to note that none of the coefficients represented the trends or long-term effects were statistically significant, suggesting that if marijuana legalization influenced crime, it was short-lived. In fact, our models did not produce any statistically significant positive results regarding the long-term effects of legalization or retail sales on any of our measures of crime for either state.

The only statistically significant result was a negative coefficient burglary in the Washington model, where burglary rates declined by .029 (per 100,000) per month following the legalization in Washington.

In summary, our results suggest that there may have been some immediate increases in crime at the point of legalization, yet there have been essentially no long-term shifts in crime rates because of legalization, aside from a decline in burglary in Washington. Though the short-term increases might appear to suggest that marijuana increased crime, we caution against this interpretation as the increases do not reflect permanent shifts (that is, these are shifts in intercepts, not slopes) and could be artificially induced by the small number of time units between legalization and sales.

Finally, we also display our results visually. Figures 1 through 4 illustrate the interrupted time-series results for violent crime and property crime in Colorado and Washington. Figures for the disaggregated crime models are available upon request. Specifically, each plot contains dots for observed values for the control states, triangles for the observed values for Colorado/Washington, solid lines for the predicted values for the control states, and dashed lines for the predicted values for Colorado/Washington. It is important to note that these figures are not generated using the exact same models presented in Table 2. Specifically, we estimated these models without the monthly dummy variables. Though fitted lines with the

monthly dummy variables show a pattern in which the predicted values track the observed values much more closely, these fitted values oscillate from month to month and make it difficult to visually track trends in crime rates. Figures accounting for monthly variation are available upon request.

These figures show an overall decline in crime for Colorado, Washington, and the control states over time with a potential uptick in violent crime in later years. This is perhaps reflective of the continuation of the crime drop of the 90s (Blumstein & Wallman, 2006), which largely continued until somewhere around 2015 (Gravert & Cullen, 2016). When interpreting these curves, it is important to note that they do not match up precisely to the results in Table 2. As mentioned, the models used to generate these fitted curves do not include monthly dummy variables. But more importantly, these predicted values are mapped to observed trends in crime rates, while the coefficients in the interrupted time-series models have to be interpreted in comparison to the prior time periods

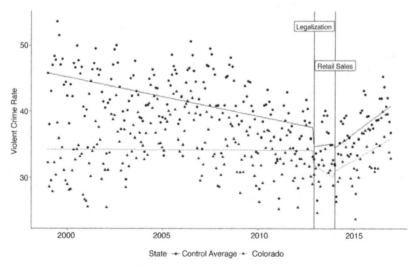

Figure 1 Violent Crime Rate per 100,000 in Colorado from 1999 to 2016

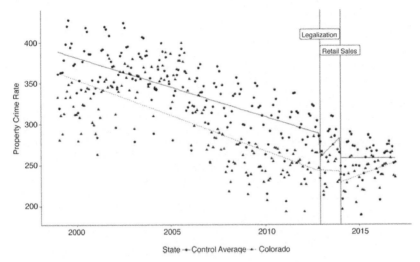

Figure 2 Property Crime Rate per 100,000 in Colorado from 1999 to 2016

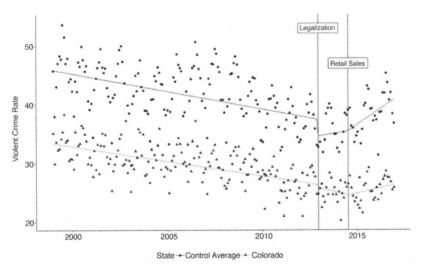

Figure 3 Violent Crime Rate per 100,000 in Washington from 1999 to 2016

in the model and, for Washington, in comparison to the control state coefficients.

For violent crime, Figures 1 and 3 show that this type of crime declines most steadily for Washington and the control states from 1999 to 2012 (legalization), while violent crime is relatively flat for Colorado. Following legalization and the start of retail sales (2014), Colorado and Washington follow the same basic pattern as the control states, suggesting that legalization did not result in any major increases or decreases in crime. For property crime, the same general results are found, though there is some evidence that property crime in Colorado increased after the start of retail sales. Though this finding did not reach the traditional cutoff for statistical significance, it is important to continue to track this trend in the future, as it is possible that with more time, property crime rates in Colorado may end up increasing since the start of retail sales.

Supplementary Analyses

Though the multi-intervention models presented above are a staple of the segmented interrupted time-series approach, there is some concern that the relatively short time period between legalization and sales makes it difficult to parse out the independent effects of policy. In essence, each interruption point forces a new intercept on that particular segment of the regression line, which, when dealing with short time periods, could affect the slopes. As a robustness check, we estimated the above models again with only a single interruption point (the start of retail sales). Though we estimated single interruption models using both the point of legalization and the start of retail sales, we present the models using the start of retail sales as the intervention point below. These models are substantively similar, but if marijuana policy is to have a large effect on serious crimes, using retail sales as the intervention seems somewhat more reasonable. While legalization made marijuana legal

Table 4 Colorado ITSA Results for Start of Retail Sales Only

	Violent Crime	Property Crime	Agg. Assault	Auto Theft	Burglary	Larceny	Robbery
Difference between CO and control prior to intervention	−3.614** (1.417)	−41.057** (3.463)	−3.189** (.295)	8.249** (.788)	−18.866** (.853)	−30.445** (2.251)	−1.089* (.536)
Trend prior to retail (Control)	−.055** (.004)	−.647** (.033)	−.033** (.003)	−.078** (.008)	−.069** (.008)	−.501** (.021)	−.020** (.001)
Trend prior to retail (CO)	.047** (.004)	−.075* (.037)	.032** (.003)	−.046** (.008)	−.051** (.009)	.021 (.024)	.009** (.002)
Immediate effect after retail (Control)	−4.981** (1.417)	−19.122 (12.301)	−3.787** (1.047)	−.934 (3.038)	−10.877** (2.867)	−7.401 (7.849)	−1.089* (.536)
Immediate effect difference between control and CO after retail	.298 (1.670)	.688 (13.887)	.134 (1.183)	−6.292* (3.164)	5.592 (3.418)	1.416 (9.027)	−.235 (.771)
Trend after retail (Control)	.240** (.043)	.415 (.371)	.166** (.032)	.152 (.092)	−.095 (.086)	.361 (.237)	.040* (.016)
Trend after retail (CO)	−.077 (.050)	.820 (.420)	−.066 (.036)	.359** (.095)	.086 (.103)	.377 (.272)	−.003 (.023)
Constant	34.864** (.570)	270.518** (4.948)	21.675** (.421)	16.222** (1.218)	65.447** (1.152)	189.206** (3.157)	9.415** (.209)
LRT	730.445**	571.157**	749.176**	554.935**	829.506**	734.460**	591.085**
AR(1) rho	.159	.192	.191	.246	.150	.178	−.022
Corrected Durbin-Watson	2.202	2.320	2.227	2.430	2.220	2.275	1.974

n = 432. Prais-Winsten corrected standard errors in parentheses.
$^{+}p < .1$
$^{*}p < .05$
$^{**}p < .01$

Table 5 Washington ITSA Results for Start of Retail Sales Only

	Violent Crime	Property Crime	Agg. Assault	Auto Theft	Burglary	Larceny	Robbery
Difference between WA and control prior to intervention	−10.671** (.339)	23.765** (3.072)	−8.787** (.266)	14.870** (.567)	2.699** (.921)	6.223** (1.960)	−1.213** (.110)
Trend prior to retail (Control)	−.056** (.003)	−.659** (.024)	−.034** (.002)	−.076** (.006)	−.081** (.006)	−.502** (.016)	−.021** (.001)
Trend prior to retail (WA)	.012** (.004)	−.048 (.033)	.005 (.003)	−.007 (.006)	.007 (.010)	.368 (.255)	.012** (.001)
Immediate effect after retail (Control)	−5.780** (1.428)	−21.023 (13.138)	−4.723** (1.037)	−2.422 (3.478)	−10.436* (3.504)	−7.840 (8.934)	−1.011 (.613)
Immediate effect difference between control and WA after retail	1.945 (2.005)	26.589 (18.160)	2.109 (1.562)	−2.669 (3.376)	13.083* (5.409)	15.462 (11.608)	.282 (.650)
Trend after retail (Control)	.264** (.041)	.495 (.375)	.193** (.030)	.185 (.099)	−.065 (.100)	.368 (.255)	.040* (.018)
Trend after retail (WA)	−.127* (.057)	−.192 (.518)	−.090* (.045)	.063 (.096)	−.235 (.154)	−.002 (.331)	−.036 (.019)
Constant	35.016** (.392)	269.044** (3.625)	21.928** (.278)	16.743** (.967)	64.894** (.926)	187.732** (2.495)	9.046** (.172)
LRT	1118.349**	664.296**	1119.074**	717.845**	452.847**	507.110**	755.982**
AR(1) rho	.006	.022	−.072	.299	−.104	.081	.241
Corrected Durbin-Watson	1.996	2.034	1.901	2.511	1.841	2.119	2.273

$n = 432$. Prais-Winsten corrected standard errors in parentheses.
+$p < .1$
*$p < .05$
**$p < .01$

to possess, it did not necessarily make marijuana more prevalent in the state, whereas the start of retail sales corresponded with the opening of several stores in both states and presumably increased the availability of marijuana in both states. These results are presented in Tables 4 and 5 below.

Put simply, these models further suggest that marijuana legalization has not statistically significantly affected serious crime in Washington or Colorado. The most noteworthy results from these models are the statistically significant increase in auto theft in Colorado following the start of sales and a statistically significant decrease in violent crime in general

and aggravated assault in Washington following the start of retail sales. Given the relatively high rho value, divergent Durbin Watson statistic, and non-stationarity results for auto theft, these results, while statistically significant, must be viewed cautiously. Lastly, we also estimated a pooled time-series regression model in which Washington and Colorado were included with the 21 states which had no marijuana legalization or mediazation laws. These results (available upon request) were substantively similar, showing no general effect of marijuana legalization or sales on index crime rates.

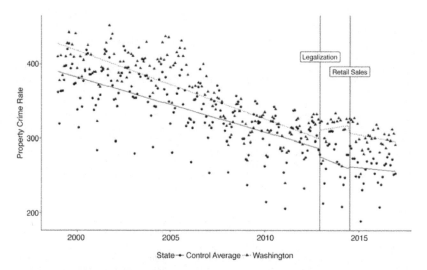

Figure 4 Property Crime Rate per 100,000 in Washington from 1999 to 2016

Conclusions

Authors of previous studies (Berenson, 2019; NHIDTA, 2016; Smart Approaches to Marijuana. (2018) argue that legalization is associated with an increase in crime. Our results suggest that cannabis laws more broadly, and the legalization of recreational marijuana more specifically, have had minimal effect on major crime in Colorado or Washington State. We observed virtually no statistically significant long-term effects of recreational marijuana legalization or retail sales on violent or property crime rates, except for a significant decline in burglary rates in Washington. There were some immediate increases in crime at the point of legalization, but these did not result in long-term effects. It is difficult to study trends for less serious crimes, as the UCR only includes arrest data for these offenses and not offenses known. Though NIBRS data presents an attractive alternative, not all of Washington is NIBRS compliant, and many of the agencies that are reporting NIBRS data have not done so for a

long enough period of time pre-legalization for time-series modeling to be examined. Still, the results related to serious crime are quite clear: the legalization of marijuana has not resulted in a significant upward trend in crime rates. Our results are robust in that we examined the first two states to legalize marijuana and compared them to states with no marijuana laws at all. Moreover, we estimated our models in a variety of manners, including models with different interruption points, single-group interrupted time-series analyses, and as a set of pooled cross-sectional models. None of our models revealed long term effects of marijuana legalization on serious crime rates.

In concert with recent research results from Makin et al. (2019), our results from Colorado and Washington suggest that legalization has not had major detrimental effects on public safety. Having said this, we would caution that it would also be premature to suggest that legalization renders substantial increases in public safety, as the rates of most crimes remained steady in this study in the post-legalization period and because crime is not the only measure of public safety. Additional work is needed to examine the effect of legalization on other public safety outcomes, including public and mental health measures.

Though our results are robust to modeling choices and control group specifications and the multiple-group interrupted time-series methodology is excellent for calculating estimated causal effects, these results are not without limitations. As previously mentioned, our results examine changes in serious crime, and it is possible that marijuana laws might be more likely to affect other types of crime, including cannabis-related DUIs. In addition to this, we cannot rule out the possibility that marijuana laws might have different effects on different types of communities within a state. Given that this is not a true experiment, it is important to acknowledge that these results are ultimately correlational in nature, though we have attempted to marshal as much comparative logic as possible to document changes that can be attributable to marijuana laws. In terms of specific limitations, the auto-theft models continue to exhibit issues related to autocorrelation and non-stationarity. As such, these results should be viewed as tentative.

Another broad shortcoming is that crime rates are also affected by criminal sanctions, law enforcement efforts, and a variety of other possible factors. For example, many states that have legalized recreational marijuana have earmarked tax revenue for increased law enforcement resources (Bryant, 2017), which, if effective, could be compensating for cannabis's tendency to increase criminality. Though we believe that state-level differences are an important starting point (indeed, our analysis echoes much of the prior work examining state-based medical marijuana laws), future work should examine individual jurisdictions to see if some communities are more or less affected by the legalization of marijuana. Indeed, a disaggregated approach is essential to fully understand the scope of marijuana laws and their effects on crime, law enforcement, and public safety.

As aforementioned, a lack of robust research studies and overreliance on limited pre-post analysis perpetuate a state of confusion concerning to what extent legalization influences crime. As we conclude, we believe it is an opportune moment to restate that this is but one study, and we would be remiss to offer to policymakers that it is proof/evidence that legalization did not affect crimes negatively. Rather, the present study is but one of many that are needed to provide the public and policymakers with results generated from more robust and rigorous research designs. Importantly, this design, and improved versions, must be replicated, because it is through replication that we will find an ultimate answer to the question of the impact of the legalization of marijuana on crime.

Given the likelihood of further liberalization of state and even federal marijuana laws, it is imperative that policymakers and research funders allocate the necessary resources to conduct these more rigorous and intensive types of contextualized studies. Large-scale policy shifts can take a considerable amount of time to produce stable and understandable effects. It took 40 years following the repeal of alcohol prohibition for alcohol consumption to reach pre-prohibition levels (Hall, 2010), and research to date on cannabis legalization suggests that it is likely too soon to fully understand the effects of marijuana legalization in the United States (Hall & Lynskey, 2016).

Discussion Questions

1. The researchers studied crime rates in two states that legalized marijuana and multiple states that had not. Besides legalization, think about what other factors could explain the results.

2. What are the arguments that suggest that crime would increase in the wake of legalization? What are the arguments suggesting a crime decrease?

3. If you worked as a policy analyst for a state considering legislation, what would you recommend to your state, given these results? What more information would you want to obtain before making a final decision?

References

Aalen, P. (2013). *The impact of medical marijuana legalization on violent crime.* (Master's thesis). University of Oslo, Oslo, Norway.

Adams, M. (2018, March 28). California officials say marijuana legalization causing more violent crime. *Forbes.* Retrieved July from www.forbes.com/sites/mikeadams/2018/03/28/california-officials-say-marijuana-legalization-causing-more-violent-crime/#467755382c3b

Bennett, T., Holloway, K., & Farrington, D. (2008). The statistical association between drug misuse and crime: A meta-analysis. *Aggression and Violent Behavior, 13*(2), 107–118. https://doi.org/10.1016/j.avb.2008.02.001

Berenson, A. (2019). *Tell your children: The truth about marijuana, mental illness, and violence.* New York, NY: Simon & Schuster.

Bernal, J. L., Cummins, S., & Gasparrini, A. (2017). Interrupted time series regression for the evaluation of public health interventions: A tutorial. *International Journal of Epidemiology, 46*(1), 348–355.

Blumstein, A., & Wallman, J. (Eds.). (2006). *The crime drop in America.* Cambridge, UK: Cambridge University Press.

Brook, J. S., Brook, D. W., Rosen, Z., & Rabbitt, C. R. (2003). Earlier marijuana use and later problem behavior in Colombian youths. *Journal of the American Academy of Child & Adolescent Psychiatry, 42*(4), 485–492. https://doi.org/10.1097/01.CHI.0000037050.04952.49

Bryant, A. R. (2017). Taxing marijuana: Earmarking tax revenue from legalized marijuana. *Georgia State University Law Review, 33*(3), 659–694.

Cerdá, M., Wall, M., Keyes, K. M., Galea, S., & Hasin, D. (2012). Medical marijuana laws in 50 states: Investigating the relationship between state legalization of medical marijuana and marijuana use, abuse and dependence. *Drug and Alcohol Dependence, 120*(1–3), 22–27. https://doi.org/10.1016/j.drugalcdep.2011.06.011

Chemerinsky, E., Forman, J., Hopper, A., & Kamin, S. (2015). Cooperative federalism and marijuana regulation. *UCLA Law Review, 62*(1), 74–122.

Chu, Y. W. L. (2015). Do medical marijuana laws increase hard-drug use? *The Journal of Law and Economics, 58*(2), 481–517. https://doi.org/10.1086/684043

Cohen, L. E., & Felson, M. (1979). Social change and crime rate trends: A routine activity approach. *American Sociological Review, 44*(4), 588–608. https://doi.org/10.2307/2094589

Colorado Department of Revenue. (2019). *MED laws and regulations.* Retrieved from www.colorado.gov/pacific/enforcement/med-laws-and-regulations

Contreras, C. (2017). A block-level analysis of medical marijuana dispensaries and crime in the city of Los Angeles. *Justice Quarterly, 34*(6), 1069–1095. https://doi.org/10.1080/07418825.2016.1270346

Cook, T. D., & Campbell, D. T. (1979). *Quasi-experimentation: Design & analysis issues for field settings* (Vol. 351). Boston, MA: Houghton Mifflin.

Doherty, C., Tyson, A., & Weisel, R. (2015). In debate over legalizing marijuana, disagreement over drug's dangers in their own words: Supporters and opponents of legalization. *Pew Research Center.* Retrieved from www.people-press.org/2015/04/14/in-debate-over-legalizing-marijuana-disagreement-over-drugs-dangers/

Freisthler, B., Gaidus, A., Tam, C., Ponicki, W. R., & Gruenewald, P. J. (2017). From medical to recreational marijuana sales: Marijuana outlets and crime in an era of changing marijuana legislation. *The Journal of Primary Prevention, 38*(3), 249–263.

Garland, D. (2001). *The culture of control.* Chicago, IL: The University of Chicago Press.

Goldstein, P. J. (1985). The drugs/violence nexus: A tripartite conceptual framework. *Journal of Drug Issues, 15*(4), 493–506. https://doi.org/10.1177/002204268501500406

Governing Magazine. (2018). *State marijuana laws in 2018 map.* Retrieved from www.governing.com/gov-data/state-marijuana-laws-map-medical-recreational.html

Gravert, A., & Cullen, J. (2016). *Crime in 2015: A final analysis.* New York, NY: Brennan Center for Justice at New York University School of Law.

Hall, W. (2010). What are the policy lessons of national alcohol prohibition in the United States, 1920–1933? *Addiction, 105*(7), 1164–1173.

Hall, W., & Lynskey, M. (2016). Why it is probably too soon to assess the public health effects of legalisation of recreational cannabis use in the USA. *The Lancet Psychiatry, 3*(9), 900–906.

Hall, W., & Weier, M. (2017). Has marijuana legalization increased marijuana use among US youth? *JAMA Pediatrics, 171*(2), 116–118.

Harper, S., Strumpf, E. C., & Kaufman, J. S. (2012). Do medical marijuana laws increase marijuana use? Replication study and extension. *Annals of Epidemiology, 22*(3), 207–212.

Jandoc, R., Burden, A. M., Mamdani, M., Lévesque, L. E., & Cadarette, S. M. (2015). Interrupted time series analysis in drug utilization research is increasing: Systematic review and recommendations. *Journal of Clinical Epidemiology, 68*(8), 950–956.

Kepple, N. J., & Freisthler, B. (2012). Exploring the ecological association between crime and medical marijuana dispensaries. *Journal of Studies on Alcohol and Drugs, 73*(4), 523–530. https://doi.org/10.15288/jsad.2012.73.523

Kreck, D. (2009, July 5). High, dry times as prohibition era sobered Denver. *The Denver Post.*

Linden, A. (2015). Conducting interrupted time-series analysis for single- and multiple-group comparisons. *The Stata Journal: Promoting Communications on Statistics and Stata, 15*(2), 480–500. https://doi.org/10.1177/1536867X1501500208

Linden, A. (2017). Challenges to validity in single-group interrupted time series analysis. *Journal of Evaluation in Clinical Practice, 23*(2), 413–418.

Makin, D. A., Willits, D. W., Wu, G., DuBois, K. O., Lu, R., Stohr, M. K., . . . Lovrich, N. P. (2019). Marijuana legalization and crime clearance rates: Testing proponent assertions in Colorado and Washington State. *Police Quarterly, 22*(1), 31–55. https://doi.org/10.1177/1098611118786255

Markowitz, S. (2005). Alcohol, drugs and violent crime. *International Review of Law and Economics, 25*(1), 20–44. https://doi.org/10.1016/j.irle.2005.05.003

Miller, B. A. (1990). The interrelationships between alcohol and drugs and family violence. In M. De La Rosa, E. Y. Lambert, & B. Gropper (Eds.), *Drugs and violence: Causes, correlates, and consequences use* (pp. 177–207). National Institute on Drug Abuse Research Monograph #103, DHHS Pub. No. (ADM) 91–1721.

Morris, R. G., TenEyck, M., Barnes, J. C., & Kovandzic, T. V. (2014). The effect of medical marijuana laws on crime: Evidence from state panel data, 1990–2006. *PLoS One, 9*(3), E92816. https://doi.org/10.1371/journal.pone.0092816

Northwest High Intensity Drug Trafficking Area (2016). *Washington state marijuana impact report.* Seattle, WA: Northwest High Intensity Drug Trafficking Area.

Pacula, R. L., & Kilmer, B. (2003). *Marijuana and crime: Is there a connection beyond prohibition?* (No. w10046). Cambridge, MA: National Bureau of Economic Research.

Pedersen, W., & Skardhamar, T. (2010). Cannabis and crime: Findings from a longitudinal study. *Addiction, 105*(1), 109–118. https://doi.org/10.1111/j.1360-0443.2009.02719.x

Phillips, M. D. (2012). Assessing the impact of drug use and drug selling on violent offending in a panel of delinquent youth. *Journal of Drug Issues, 42*(3), 298–316. https://doi.org/10.1177/0022042612456017

Prais, S. J., & Winsten, C. B. (1954). *Trend estimators and serial correlation* (Vol. 383, pp. 1–26). Chicago: Cowles Commission discussion paper.

Reed, J. K., Hilkey, S., Thome, J., & English, K. (2018). *Impacts of marijuana legalization in Colorado: A report pursuant to Senate bill 13–283.* Retrieved from Department of Public Safety Division of Criminal Justice website: https://cdpsdocs.state.co.us/ors/docs/reports/2018-SB13-283_Rpt.pdf

ReformAct.Org. (2017). *Complete text of Tacoma Initiative No. 1.* Retrieved from www.cannabisreformact.org/initiative-text/

Reingle, J. M., Staras, S. A., Jennings, W. G., Branchini, J., & Maldonado-Molina, M. M. (2012). The relationship between marijuana use and intimate partner violence in a nationally representative, longitudinal sample. *Journal of Interpersonal Violence, 27*(8), 1562–1578. https://doi.org/10.1177/0886260511425787

Reynolds, M. D., Tarter, R. E., Kirisci, L., & Clark, D. B. (2011). Marijuana but not alcohol use during adolescence mediates the association between transmissible risk for substance use disorder and number of lifetime violent offenses. *Journal of Criminal Justice, 39*(3), 218–223. https://doi.org/10.1016/j.jcrimjus.2011.02.002

Salomonsen-Sautel, S., Sakai, J. T., Thurstone, C., Corley, R., & Hopfer, C. (2012). Medical marijuana use among adolescents in substance abuse treatment. *Journal of the American Academy of Child & Adolescent Psychiatry, 51*(7), 694–702. Retrieved from https://doi.org/10.1016/j.jaac.2012.04.004

Santos, M. (2017). What actually happened to violent crime after Washington legalized marijuana. *The News Tribune.* Retrieved from www.thenewstribune.com/news/local/marijuana/article163750293.html

Schuermeyer, J., Salomonsen-Sautel, S., Price, R. K., Balan, S., Thurstone, C., Min, S. J., & Sakai, J. T. (2014). Temporal trends in marijuana attitudes, availability and use in Colorado compared to non-medical marijuana states: 2003–11. *Drug and Alcohol Dependence, 140*, 145–155. https://doi.org/10.1016/j.drugalcdep.2014.04.016

Seattle Municipal Code. (2003). *12A.20.060, Sect. A.* Retrieved from https://clerk.ci.seattle.wa.us/~public/initref/init75.htm

Shepard, E. M., & Blackley, P. R. (2016). Medical marijuana and crime: Further evidence from the western states. *Journal of Drug Issues, 46*(2), 122–134. https://doi.org/10.1177/0022042615623983

Smart Approaches to Marijuana. (2018). *Lessons learned from marijuana legalization in four U.S. states and DC.* Retrieved from https://learnaboutsam.org/wp-content/uploads/2018/04/SAM-Lessons-Learned-From-Marijuana-Legalization-Digital.pdf

Vestal, S. (2019). Rechecking the stats on pot and violence. *Spokesman-Review.* Retrieved from www.spokesman.com/stories/2019/jan/11/shawn-vestal-rechecking-the-stats-on-pot-and-viole/

Wagner, A. K., Soumerai, S. B., Zhang, F., & Ross-Degnan, D. (2002). Segmented regression analysis of interrupted time series studies in medication use research. *Journal of Clinical Pharmacy and Therapeutics, 27*(4), 299–309.

Wall, M. M., Poh, E., Cerdá, M., Keyes, K. M., Galea, S., & Hasin, D. S. (2011). Adolescent marijuana use from 2002 to 2008: Higher in states with medical marijuana laws, cause still unclear. *Annals of Epidemiology, 21*(9), 714–716. https://doi.org/10.1016/j.annepidem.2011.06.001

Washington State Liquor and Cannabis Board. (2014). *Annual report: Fiscal year 2018.* Retrieved from https://lcb.wa.gov/about/annual-report

Reading 12.2   Treatment Integrity and Recidivism Among Sex Offenders

Risk-need-responsivity is currently the dominant model for correctional interventions. Programs that target the highest-risk offenders, assess and respond to their criminogenic needs, and provide evidence-based treatment interventions have been found to have the greatest impact on reducing recidivism. The evidence-based Correctional Program Checklist (CPC) was designed to assist researchers conducting process evaluations of programs. The checklist prompts evaluators to look for evidence of 70 facets of programs that are associated with effective treatment. For this study, Makarios, Lovins, Myer, and Latessa (2019) used previously collected process and outcome data for sex offender treatment programs in Ohio. Their goal was to see if the CPC predicted outcomes of the programs, with the hope that the CPC would be found to be an effective tool for use in process evaluations. The authors did caution that, as a quantitative tool, the CPC is helpful but may not catch subtle differences between programs that qualitative research might be able to detect.

Treatment Integrity and Recidivism Among Sex Offenders: The Relationship Between CPC Scores and Program Effectiveness

Matthew Makarios, Lori Brushman Lovins, Andrew J. Myer, and Edward Latessa

A large body of research in the field of corrections has examined the effectiveness of different types of correctional interventions at reducing recidivism. This body of research suggests that there are specific types of interventions that are effective, others that are not, and even some that increase recidivism (for an overview, see Andrews & Bonta, 2010 or Cullen & Gendreau, 2000). The programs that have most consistently demonstrated positive treatment effects are based on the principles of effective intervention. These principles suggest that effective correctional programs target dynamic risk factors (Andrews et al., 1990; Lowenkamp Latessa, & Smith, 2006) in high-risk offenders (Lowenkamp, Latessa, & Holsinger, 2006) while using a cognitive-behavioral or social learning approach (Andrews et al., 1990; Drake, Aos, & Miller, 2009; Latessa, Brushman Lovins, Smith, & Makarios, 2010). The principles of effective intervention largely dominate the literature on evidence-based correctional programming (Cullen & Gendreau, 2000). An evidence-based correctional approach suggests that pro-

grams should model interventions that have been found to be effective in prior research and engage in ongoing evaluations to ensure that the interventions are achieving their desired goals (MacKenzie, 2000).

The Evidence-Based Correctional Program Checklist (CPC) is a tool designed to assess how well correctional programs align with "best practices" and the principles of effective intervention. The CPC is an actuarial instrument that is administered as an in-depth process evaluation and seeks to determine whether correctional programs ascribe to more than 70 different items that are theoretically driven and have been shown to be correlated to reductions in recidivism. Items in the CPC are grouped into five domains: leadership and development, staff characteristics, assessment, treatment characteristics, and quality assurance. Several studies conducted by researchers at the University of Cincinnati were used to develop and validate the indicators on the CPC. The results from these studies indicate that the CPC yields strong correlations with recidivism (Holsinger, 1999;

Lowenkamp, 2004; Lowenkamp & Latessa, 2003, 2005a, 2005b).

Although research on the CPC has shown that higher scores yield stronger treatment effects, no research to date has examined whether this finding applies to correctional interventions that serve sex offenders. The goal of the current research is to determine whether scores on the CPC are correlated with reductions in recidivism using process and outcome evaluations of community correctional facilities that serve sex offenders. The data from the current research come from a large study that examined the processes and outcomes of all community correctional facilities that received funding from the Ohio Department of Rehabilitation and Correction. The larger study consisted of 64 different community correctional facilities that sought to reduce offender recidivism. The current study uses data gathered from eight of these programs that served sex offenders. As a result, the current project extends prior research on evidence-based correctional programs by focusing on the effectiveness of community correctional facilities that serve sex offenders as well as the characteristics of successful programs.

Overview of Risk, Need, and Responsivity Model

The CPC is an actuarial instrument that is designed to determine how well treatment programs ascribe to the principles of effective intervention. The principles of effective intervention provide empirically based guidance to correctional agencies regarding who to treat, what factors to target for change, and how to administer treatment. The risk, need, and responsivity (RNR) principles are the focus of the principles of effective intervention. The risk principle of effective intervention suggests that programs should avoid treating low-risk cases and should instead target moderate- to high-risk clientele (Andrews & Bonta, 2010; Lowenkamp et al., 2006). This is because low-risk offenders have the least to gain because their odds of engaging in recidivism are already low (Lowenkamp & Latessa, 2004). On the other hand, moderate-

and high-risk offenders are more likely to recidivate as they have more dynamic risk factors driving criminal behavior, thereby making them more likely to see reductions in recidivism when their risk factors are appropriately targeted.

The need principle provides insight as to what offender needs correctional interventions should target. Targets for change should be dynamic risk factors, or criminogenic needs (Andrews & Bonta, 2010; Cullen & Gendreau, 2000). These are risk factors that are related to the odds of recidivism and, when changed, reduce the likelihood of further criminal behavior. The strongest criminogenic needs include antisocial personality characteristics, criminal peers, and antisocial attitudes; others risk factors include employment, family issues, and substance abuse (Gendreau, Little, & Goggin, 1996). When dynamic risk factors are addressed in moderate- or high-risk clientele, they experience a subsequent decline in the odds of recidivating because the factors that are encouraging their criminal behavior have been addressed (Labreque, Smith, Lovins, & Latessa, 2014; Raynor, 2007; Vose, Lowenkamp, Smith, & Cullen, 2009).

The responsivity principle is concerned with how programs attempt to change dynamic risk factors. It suggests that correctional interventions be responsive to how offenders learn and address barriers to treatment (Andrews & Bonta, 2010). There are two components to the responsivity principle: specific and general responsivity. General responsivity is concerned with ensuring that correctional interventions engage in therapeutic modalities that have been shown to work with offending populations. In particular, behavioral interventions that use social learning principles in group therapy have been shown to be an effective means of teaching offenders the skills they need to avoid recidivism (Andrews et al., 1990; Lipsey, 2009). Specific responsivity is concerned with removing barriers to treatment. Even evidence-based curricula will be ineffective at changing behavior if there are barriers that keep individual offenders from engaging in treatment. Responsivity factors such as language barriers, lack of transportation to treatment, lack of day care for children, or mental health issues make it difficult for clients to become engaged in treatment, thereby limiting the system's ability to address criminogenic needs.

Effectiveness of Sex Offender Treatment

Several major meta-analyses have been conducted that examine the impact of sex offender treatment on recidivism. Furby, Weinrott, and Blackshaw's (1989) early meta-analysis of sex offender treatment programs found little evidence the programs in their review reduced recidivism. Hall's (1995) follow-up to this study included 12 sex offender treatment studies and found a modest effect of treatment on recidivism. The research findings revealed that the most effective forms of treatment were cognitive-behavioral and hormonal treatments.

Hanson et al.'s (2002) research reported on the analysis of 43 treatment effects from the Collaborative Outcome Data Project. They found a recidivism rate of 12% for treated offenders and a recidivism rate of 17% for the control participants. Hanson et al. (2002) confirmed Hall's (1995) finding that cognitive-behavioral programs were more effective than other forms of treatment.

More recently, Hanson, Bourgon, Helmus, and Hodgson (2009) conducted a meta-analysis of 23 studies and found that the recidivism rates for treated sex offenders was lower than that of the control participants for sexual recidivism, violent recidivism, and general recidivism. They also found that cognitive-behavioral programming was associated with increases in program effect sizes. Of interest, they coded the methodological rigor of studies using a set of standardized criteria and found that larger effect sizes were associated with weaker methodological designs.

Finally, Losel and Schmucker (2005) conducted the most comprehensive meta-analysis of sex offender treatment studies by analyzing 69 different studies. The authors found a mean odds ratio of 1.70 that translated into recidivism rates of 11% for the treatment group and 18% for the control group. Losel and Schmucker (2005) also looked at the impact of different types of treatment. They found that surgical castration and hormonal treatments were associated with the largest reductions in recidivism, followed by cognitive-behavioral and classical conditioning approaches. Not related to reductions in recidivism were insight-oriented talk therapies or therapeutic communities.

Effectiveness of the RNR Model in Treating Sex Offenders

Although there has been a good deal of research that has examined the effectiveness of sex offender treatment, relatively little has examined the characteristics of effective programs. Olver, Wong, and Nicholaichuck (2009) examined the effectiveness of a high-intensity in-patient sex offender treatment program that ascribed to the principles of effective intervention. In particular, the program targeted moderate- to high-risk sex offenders while utilizing a cognitive-behavioral approach. Further, the program targeted criminogenic needs such as antisocial attitudes and family dynamics and addressed responsivity factors such as language ability and treatment readiness. Their results indicate that the program was successful at reducing recidivism, with treated sex offenders less likely to recidivate than controls.

Hanson et al. (2009) conducted a meta-analysis of 23 treatment programs for sex offenders. They found that overall, participants in the treatment programs were less likely to recidivate than those in the control groups. Furthermore, programs that ascribed to the principles of RNR were more effective than those that did not. Additionally, as programs adhered to more of the principles, effect sizes increased. That is, there was a linear relationship between ascribing to the principles of effective intervention and program effect size. These findings suggest that a better understanding of sex offender program effects can be gleaned by evaluating variation in program adherence to the principles of effective intervention. In particular, these findings suggest that measures of a program's adherence to the RNR model may correlate with program effectiveness at reducing recidivism in sex offenders.

Overview of CPC

The CPC is an actuarial assessment instrument that is designed to determine how closely correctional programs meet the principles of effective intervention. Studies by the University of Cincinnati were used to construct and validate the CPC using adult and juvenile treatment interventions. These studies found that individual items and domain areas of the CPC maintained moderate to strong correlations with program effect size (Holsinger, 1999; Lowenkamp, 2004; Lowenkamp & Latessa, 2003, 2005a, 2005b; Shaffer, 2006).

The CPC is divided into two areas that contain a total of five domains. The capacity area measures whether the treatment programs have the capability to deliver evidence-based interventions for offenders. There are three domains in the capacity area: program leadership and development, staff characteristics, and quality assurance. The content area examines the substantive services that are provided by the program and focuses primarily on whether the programs meets the principles of risk, need, and responsivity. It includes two domains: treatment and assessment.

Current Study

Given the research that suggests that that the principles of effective intervention apply to sex offender treatment, it is of interest as to whether the CPC is related to increases in program effectiveness in programs that serve sex offenders. Although research on the CPC has shown that it is related to significant reductions in recidivism at the program level (Holsinger, 1999; Lowenkamp, 2004; Lowenkamp & Latessa, 2003, 2005a, 2005b; Shaffer, 2006), no research to date has examined whether it applies to correctional interventions that serve sex offenders. The goal of the current research is to determine whether scores on the CPC are correlated with reductions in recidivism using process and outcome evaluations of eight halfway houses that serve sex offenders. As a result, the current project extends prior research on evidence-based correctional programs by examining whether factors that have been shown to be effective in general offending populations are also effective at reducing recidivism in sex-offending populations.

Method

Sample and Setting

The current research seeks to examine whether scores on the CPC are related to program outcome. Data were gathered as part of a larger project that sought to examine the process and outcomes of all community correctional facilities in Ohio. The current research utilizes a subset of the data and includes eight facilities that admitted sex offenders into their program. All of the current programs reported providing sex offender treatment as a major component of their program.

Separate outcome evaluations were conducted on eight community correctional facilities. The outcome evaluations involved a quasi-experimental matched-pairs design and was used to create program effect sizes. Measures from the CPC were gathered through process evaluations that involved site visits to each of the programs. As a result, data from the process evaluation provides scores on the CPC that can be used to predict program effect size. Measures of program effect size were gathered using a quasi-experimental design that matched a control group to a treatment group of sex offenders that were referred to the programs. The larger project utilized a treatment group that consisted of all offenders referred to the programs between February 1, 2006, and June 1, 2007. The current research utilizes only those offenders in the treatment group that were convicted of a sex crime as the instant offense. The control group consisted of sex offenders that were on community supervision during the same time frame and were matched on county size, gender, race, and risk level.

Measures Demographics

Demographic information was gathered for purposes of matching. These measures include offense type, gender, race, county of conviction, and risk in the treatment and comparison samples. These data, along with county size, were used to match the treatment and comparison groups. As the reader can see from Table 1, matching was successful as there were no differences across the groups for any of these measures. In total, there are 266 treated offenders distributed across eight community correctional facilities. The number of offenders in each program ranges from 10 to 72. Nearly three fourths of the sample is White. Approximately 15% of the sample is low risk, three fourths of the sample was considered moderate risk, and nearly 7% considered high risk. Table 1 also presents validation statistics for the risk instrument. For low-, moderate-, and high-risk cases, 22%, 46%, and 67% of the sample was arrested, respectively. This stepwise increase in the rates of recidivism produces a correlation of .21 with recidivism. Given the wide range of the sample size for each program, the relationship between program effect size and sample size was examined. These analyses revealed only weak and inconsistent relationships between program effects and program size, suggesting that program size did not play a role in the relationships examined here.

CPC Scores

Between August and December 2006, site visits and surveys were conducted at 64 of the community correctional facilities for the larger Ohio study. CPC site visits entailed conducting structured interviews with all treatment staff and administrators, observation of group sessions, interviews of selected participants who attended programs, file review of treatment cases, review of treatment protocols, and review of program materials. Researchers who conducted the site interviews held at least a master's degree in a human service profession and were trained on the administration of all data collection instruments. During this process, information was gathered that was used to score the programs on the CPC. Programs received overall scores as well as scores for each CPC domain. Score percentages for the overall instrument and subdomains were then classified into four categories: highly effective, effective, needs improvement, and ineffective. For further information on the CPC, see Blair, Sullivan, Lux, Thielo, and Gormsen (2016).

The first domain of the CPC is leadership and development. It consists of 14 items that measure factors such as the experience and education of the program director, the stability of funding, and whether the program is valued by stakeholders, to name a few. The domain of staff characteristics consists of 11 items that measure factors such as the education and experience of staff, frequency and consistency of staff meetings, and the amount of training

Table 1 Descriptive Statistics for the Offender Sample

	Tx Count (%)	Comp Count (%)
Halfway House		
Program A	66 (24.8)	66 (24.8)
Program B	20 (7.5)	20 (7.5)
Program C	18 (6.8)	18 (6.8)
Program D	72 (27.4)	72 (27.4)
Program E	57 (21.4)	57 (21.4)
Program F	13 (4.9)	13 (4.9)
Program G	10 (3.8)	10 (3.8)
Program H	10 (3.8)	10 (3.8)
Race		
Black	71 (26.7)	71 (26.7)
White	195 (73.3)	195 (73.3)
Risk Level		
Low	41 (15.4)	41 (15.4)
Moderate	207 (77.8)	207 (77.8)
High	18 (6.8)	18 (6.8)
Outcome		
Arrest	100 (37.5)	144 (54.5)
$\chi^2 = 14.65$, r = .166		
Incarceration	59 (22.1)	93 (34.9)
$\chi^2 = 10.65$, r = .141		
Sex Offense	62 (23.3)	66 (24.8)
$\chi^2 = .165$, r = .018		

	Not Arrested	Arrested
Risk by Arrest		
Low	64 (78)	18 (22.0)
Moderate	224 (54.1)	190 (45.9)
High	12 (33.3)	24 (66.7)
$\chi^2 = 24.32$, r = .214		

Note: Tx = Treatment Group; Comp = Comparison Group

that staff receive. The domain of offender assessment consists of 13 items that measure the programs assessment practices. Items include factors such as exclusionary criteria, the types of risk and need factors assessed, and whether validated instruments are used to determine risk and need level and responsivity concerns. The domain of treatment characteristics consists of 31 items that measure factors such as use of structured curricula, incorporation of rewards and punishments, whether structured skill building is taking place, and whether the program has aftercare as a component. The final domain of the CPC is quality assurance. It has 8 items that measure whether the program employs internal quality control mechanisms, whether it engages in quality assurance for outside treatment providers, and whether it works with an outside evaluator. Each domain of the CPC receives a rating based on the percentage of items exhibited by the program. All domains are totaled to give the program an overall score.

Outcome

Upon release from the program, offenders were tracked for recidivism for 24 months. Recidivism was measured in three ways: a new criminal arrest for any offense, a new incarceration, and a new arrest for a sex offense. These three outcomes were chosen because they were they were considered the most valid and reliable measures and follow previous research (Maltz, 1984; Hanson et al., 2009; Lowenkamp, Flores, Holsinger, Makarios, & Latessa, 2010). It is worth noting that two years is a relatively short follow-up period for sex offenses, and the findings from the analyses that examine arrest for a sex offense should be interpreted with this caveat in mind. The rates of recidivism of the entire sample (treatment and control groups combined) are 46% for any arrest, 29% for incarceration, and 24% for sex offense arrest. Table 1 provides the rates of recidivism for the treatment and control groups separately. Chi-squared analysis suggests significant differences between the treatment and control group in the percentage that experienced any arrest or incar-

ceration. There is not a significant chi-squared value for sex offense recidivism.

Effect Sizes

After follow-up data were gathered, program-level effect sizes were created by comparing the recidivism rates between treatment and control groups. This was done to examine the relationship between CPC items/domains and recidivism with sex offenders. Consistent with prior research (e.g., Lowenkamp, Makarios et al., 2010), the effect size for the current study represents the difference of the proportion of those offenders that recidivated between the treatment and control groups. Average effect sizes for programs serving sex offenders are compared by ratings on each CPC domain and by the overall CPC rating. Bivariate correlations between the CPC scores and effect sizes are also examined.

Results

Overall Effects

Table 2 presents mean effect sizes for all programs. The results for the arrest effect size suggest that overall, there was a 17 percentage point reduction in general recidivism for community correctional programs that treated sex offenders. The confidence interval does not fall around zero; that suggests that this is a significant reduction in recidivism. For incarceration the effect size of .128 suggests that the programs were modestly effective in keeping offenders out of prison. Again the confidence interval for this effect size does not include zero, which indicates

Table 2 Overall Effect Sizes

	Mean Effect Size	95% Confidence Interval
Arrest	.170	[.11, .32]
Incarceration	.128	[.04, .21]
Sex offense arrest	.015	[–.12, .19]

that overall, the programs were effective at reducing new incarcerations. For arrests for a sexual offense, the effect size of .015 is small, and the confidence interval does include zero; that suggests that overall, the programs did not significantly reduce sex offense recidivism.

Figure 1 presents the effect sizes for each of the eight programs by recidivism measure. This figure shows that six of the eight programs showed a positive treatment effect using arrest as the recidivism measure. Likewise, just one of the eight programs showed a negative treatment effect using incarceration as the recidivism measure; treatment effects did not reach as high a level, but they consistently demonstrated a moderate treatment effect. Fewer positive results were demonstrated when sex offense arrest was used as the recidivism measure; just three of the eight programs demonstrated a positive treatment effect.

Table 3 presents effect sizes by CPC rating and correlations between rating categories and

effect size. Positive correlations indicate that increases in ratings are corresponding to increases in effects size, and negative correlations indicate increases in ratings are corresponding with decreases in effect sizes. For the domain of leadership and development, the CPC rating has moderate to strong correlations for all three effect sizes. For arrest, the correlation is .482, for incarceration the correlation is .248, and for arrest for a sex offense the correlation is .355. For the domain of staff characteristics, the effect size for arrest has a correlation of .371; however, the correlation for incarceration and sex offense is –.265 and –.016, indicating that for these latter two effects, increases in categorization resulted in reductions in effect size. For the domain of quality assurance, correlations between CPC categorization and effect size are all positive and moderate to strong. For arrest the correlation is .365, for incarceration the correlation is .381, and for arrest for a sex offense the correlation is .467.

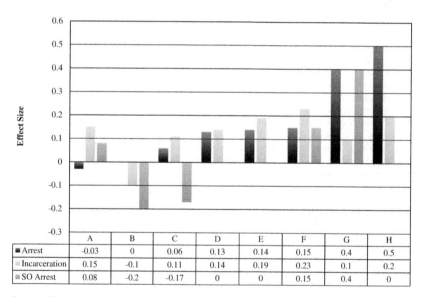

	A	B	C	D	E	F	G	H
■ Arrest	-0.03	0	0.06	0.13	0.14	0.15	0.4	0.5
Incarceration	0.15	-0.1	0.11	0.14	0.19	0.23	0.1	0.2
■ SO Arrest	0.08	-0.2	-0.17	0	0	0.15	0.4	0

Figure 1 Effect Sizes for All Programs
Note: SO = Sex Offense

Table 3 Effect Sizes by Correctional Program Checklist (CPC) Domain

	Number of Programs	Arrest	Incarceration	Sex Offense Arrest
Leadership and development				
Highly effective	2	.228	.106	.117
Effective	3	.265	.208	.051
Needs improvement	3	.032	.064	−.041
Ineffective	0	–	–	–
r value	8	.482	.248	.355
Staff characteristics				
Highly effective	6	.206	.114	.031
Effective	2	.055	.172	.038
Needs improvement	0	–	–	–
Ineffective	0	–	–	–
r value	8	.371	−.265	−.016
Quality assurance				
Highly effective	2	.228	.106	.117
Effective	3	.208	.194	.077
Needs improvement	1	.140	.193	.000
Ineffective	2	.063	.019	−.100
r value	8	.365	.381	.467
Assessment practices				
Highly effective	3	.203	.147	.129
Effective	2	.235	.176	.038
Needs improvement	0	–	–	–
Ineffective	3	.089	.077	−.067
r value	8	.315	.359	.477
Treatment practices				
Highly effective	0	–	–	–
Effective	1	.500	.200	.000
Needs improvement	1	.056	.111	−.167
Ineffective	6	.132	.119	.072
r value	8	.564	.237	−.270
Overall rating				
Highly effective	1	.056	.111	−.167
Effective	2	.450	.150	.200
Needs improvement	2	.062	.191	.115
Ineffective	3	.089	.077	−.067
r value	8	.390	.201	.157

Effects by CPC Domain Rating

For the domain of assessment, all of the correlations between CPC categorization and program effect size are positive and moderate to strong. The correlation for arrest is .315, the correlation for incarceration is .359, and for arrest for a sex offense the correlation is .477. For the domain of treatment practices, two of the correlations are positive and one is negative. The correlation for arrest is .564, for incarceration the correlation is .237, but for sex offense the correlation is −.270. It is worth noting that there is limited dispersion for the domain of treatment characteristics. That is, six of the eight programs scored in the ineffective category.

Effects by Overall CPC Rating

The last series at the bottom of Table 3 presents effect sizes by overall CPC rating. The correlations between CPC rating and effect size are all positive and modest to moderate in strength. The correlation for arrest is .390, the correlation for incarceration is .201, and the correlation for arrest for a sex offense is .157. Except of for the highly effective category, there are general increases in all three effect sizes as CPC rating increases. That is, as programs increase from ineffective to needs improvement to effective, program effect sizes also tend to increase. Worth noting, there was one program that scored highly effective, and it did not produce effect sizes that were larger than the programs that scored effective.

Discussion

Three important findings emerged from this research. The first finding is that the community correctional facilities that treated sex offenders displayed moderate reductions in general recidivism and weak reductions in sex-offending recidivism. New arrests were reduced on average by 16.8% overall, and new incarcerations were reduced by 12.8%. New arrests for a sexual offense were only reduced by 3.3%.

The relatively small reductions in sex offense recidivism should be discussed. The treatment group had just over three percentage points lower than their controls on community supervision. This reduction in recidivism for community corrections facilities is lower than those observed in other evaluations of sex offender treatment (see Hanson et al., 2009; Losel & Schmucker, 2005). As noted in the Method section, the current study had a follow-up time that was limited to 24 months. Other research that looks at sex-offending recidivism tends to have a longer follow-up (Hanson et al., report the median follow-up time for programs in their meta-analysis as 4.7 years). Traditionally, studies of sex offending tend to have a longer follow-up period than general offending because of the longer time it takes for sexual offending to occur (Brake, 2011). That is, several studies find that employing a follow-up period of fewer than 3 years finds very low recidivism rates, and that increasing follow-up time substantially increases these recidivism rates (see, e.g., Langan, Schmitt, & Rose, 2003). As a result most research suggests having follow-up periods of at least 5 years (for a discussion, see Przybylski, 2006). The current research was not able to use the longer follow-up times that prior research recommends, and this caveat should be kept in mind when interpreting the results because it is possible that a longer follow-up time could have yielded larger effect sizes.

The second noteworthy finding is that scores on the CPC were correlated with reductions in recidivism. Although the single program that scored highly effective only saw at best modest reductions in recidivism, moving from ineffective to needs improvement to effective was related to increases in program effect size. For example, for any arrest, the reduction in recidivism was .45 for effective programs and .06 and .09 for needs improvement and ineffective, respectively. The same results hold for those arrested for a sex crime; other than the highly effective category with one program, the sex offense effect sizes decreases as overall rating improves. This suggests that in most cases, the CPC was able to correctly classify programs in a manner that correlated with improved program outcome.

The above finding indicates that not only were the community correctional facilities in this study able to reduce recidivism, but those that were rated as effective saw moderate to large reductions in recidivism, those rated as needs improvement saw modest reductions in recidivism, and those rated as ineffective saw at best weak reductions in recidivism. This suggests that the positive relationship between CPC and outcome of general treatment programs found in prior research (Lowenkamp, 2004) can be generalized to community correctional facilities that treat sex offenders. This is consistent with prior research that has found that high-fidelity, cognitive-behavior programming is effective at reducing recidivism in sex offenders (see Olver et al., 2009). It also suggests that the CPC provides a valid measure of the likely effectiveness of these programs.

The third and final noteworthy finding is that the domains of the CPC were found to have varying correlations with recidivism. The domains of leadership and development, quality assurance, and assessment practices were consistently found to have the strongest effects on recidivism. For example, the domain of leadership and development was found to have a correlation of .48 and .36 with the arrest and sex offense arrest effect sizes, respectively. Quality assurance was correlated with arrest and sex offense arrest at .37 and .47, respectively. The domain of assessment practices was correlated with arrest and sex offense arrest at .31 and .48, respectively. The domain of treatment practices displayed some moderate to strong reductions in recidivism but not as consistently. That is there was a correlation of .56 with arrest and .24 with incarceration, but a −.27 with sex offense arrest. Finally the domain of staff characteristics only displayed modest reductions in effect size for arrest (.37) and actually made things worse with the other two effect sizes (incarceration = −.27 and sex offense arrest = −.16). It suggests that in these data, the most predictive domains of the CPC were leadership and development, quality assurance, and assessment practices.

The treatment domain is the largest on the CPC. Given this domain examines what criminogenic needs are targeted in treatment and how these needs are targeted (i.e., the model used, the services that support the program), it makes sense that when working with sex offenders, predictors of sexual recidivism should be targeted as part of the program if the hope is to reduce likelihood of sexual recidivism. Furthermore, given that most programs scored in the ineffective range, the bulk of programs in this study not only failed to incorporate aspects of RNR effectively, but may have also failed to incorporate sex offender–specific targets and treatment strategies.

Caution should also be taken in the interpretation of the findings for the domain of staff characteristics and treatment practices because both domains were marked by a reduced dispersion of cases. In the staff characteristics domain, only two categorizations are used (highly effective and effective), and most cases fall into only one (highly effective). The limited distribution of cases here may be the reason for the unstable/inconsistent estimates observed. The same holds for the domain of treatment practices, except the distribution is at the other end of the CPC categorization. As noted, six of the programs scored ineffective, only one scored needs improvement, and one scored effective. It could be that the negative effect size observed for sex offense arrest is due to having so many programs scoring poorly and few scoring very well because it created unbalanced estimates for the programs that did well.

It is, though, important to note that the program that scored the highest did not have the largest reductions in recidivism. That is, one program scored highly effective and yet only produced weak effects on recidivism. There are two possible reasons for this. First, it could be that the CPC is flawed and does not do a good job at ranking programs by effectiveness. This is unlikely given the findings from this research. Rankings of all other programs did produce moderate to strong correlations with recidivism, and there were stepwise changes in effect sizes for the other categories of the CPC. The second possibility is that the outcome evaluation did not produce accurate estimates of the program's effectiveness. It is worth noting that the sample size for this program was small (N = 36). It is reasonable to expect that if there were more cases included in the evaluation that the program effect size could substantially change. As a result, future research should seek to examine the relationship between CPC scores and programs that serve sex offenders using larger sample sizes.

Although the above findings are notable, it is also important to note the limitations of this research. The first limitation is the external validity or generalizability of this study. This research clearly identifies the population of offenders for this research as sex offenders that attended treatment in a community correctional facility in Ohio during the study period. As a result, replications of this research should be conducted in other areas, states, and regions before generalizations are made beyond those observed here. The findings of this research should be limited to sex offenders that attended community corrections facilities in Ohio.

Another limitation to the study findings is the small sample sizes observed here, in the number of programs and, in the some instances, the number of participants within each program. There are a total of eight community correctional facilities examined in the current study. Although this study is smaller than most major meta-analyses that report findings, it is important to remember that this analysis of eight individual programs is a substantial addition to the literature. It is also worth noting that in four of the programs, there are fewer than 20 treatment cases examined. The small sample size of these programs may bias the estimates, though no sample sizes with fewer than 10 treatment cases were allowed in this study. Although the findings from the current research are compelling, future research should seek to include more community correctional facilities with larger sample sizes.

It is also worth noting the quantitative nature of the data used for the current study. The CPC is an actuarial instrument that gathers largely quantitative data. Although quantitative data are necessary for the current analyses to examine correlations between program effect size and CPC score, qualitative data would be helpful to tease out more subtle differences between the programs and the services that they provide. Supplemental qualitative analyses could help to better understand differences between effective and ineffective programs, and future research should seek to incorporate qualitative and quantitative data to get a better picture of the differences between effective and ineffective programs that serve sex offenders.

Despite these limitations, the findings from this research indicate that the community correctional facilities in this study were able to reduce recidivism, and they performed the best when they scored in the effective range on the CPC. As a valid indicator of program success, the CPC thus provides agencies with an assessment which measures adherence to evidenced-based practices, identifying areas where the

programs are doing well and areas where there is need of improvement. Thus, from a program level, it provides an important baseline for programs, helping to guide action planning and determine future priorities.

Discussion Questions

1. The researchers used multiple measures of recidivism. What are the different ways that they measured that concept?
2. What types of programs were found to be most effective in reducing recidivism among sex offenders?
3. What suggestions did the researchers have for future research?

References

Andrews, D. A., & Bonta, J. (2010). *The psychology of criminal conduct*. Newark, NJ: Matthew Bender and Company.

Andrews, D. A., Zinger, I., Hoge, R. D., Bonta, J., Gendreau, P., & Cullen, F. T. (1990). Does correctional treatment work? A clinically relevant and psychologically informed meta-analysis. *Criminology*, *28*, 369–404. https://doi.org/10.1111/crim.1990.28.issue-3

Blair, L., Sullivan, C. C., Lux, J., Thielo, A. J., & Gormsen, L. (2016). Measuring drug court adherence to the what works literature: The evidence-based correctional program checklist—drug court. *International Journal of Offender Therapy and Comparative Criminology*, *60*, 165–188.

Brake, S. (2011). *Recidivism and reoffense rates of adult sex offenders*. Unpublished manuscript. Retrieved from www.stephenbrakeassociates.com/RR12.pdf

Cullen, F. T., & Gendreau, P. (2000). Assessing correctional rehabilitation: Policy, practice and prospects. *Policies, Process, and Decisions of the Criminal Justice System*, *3*, 109–175.

Drake, E. K., Aos, S., & Miller, M. G. (2009). Evidenced-based public policy options to reduce crime and criminal justice costs: Implications in Washington State. *Victims and Offenders*, *4*, 170–196. https://doi.org/10.1080/15564880802612615

Furby, L., Weinrott, M. R., & Blackshaw, L. (1989). Sex offender recidivism: A review. *Psychological Bulletin*, *105*, 3–30. https://doi.org/10.1037/0033-2909.105.1.3

Gendreau, P., Little, T., & Goggin, C. (1996). A meta-analysis of the predictors of adult offending: What works! *Criminology*, *34*, 575–608. https://doi.org/10.1111/crim.1996.34.issue-4

Hall, G. C. N. (1995). Sexual offender recidivism revisited: A meta-analysis of recent treatment studies. *Journal of Consulting and Clinical Psychology, 63,* 802–809. https://doi.org/10.1037/0022-006X.63.5.802

Hanson, R. K., Bourgon, G., Helmus, L., & Hodgson, S. (2009). The principles of effective correctional treatment also apply to sexual offenders: A meta analysis. *Criminal Justice and Behavior, 36,* 865–891. https://doi.org/10.1177/0093854809338545

Hanson, R. K., Gordon, A., Harris, A. J. R., Marques, J. K., Murphy, W., Quinsey, V. L., & Seto, M. C. (2002). First report of the collaborative outcome data project on the effectiveness of psychological treatment of sex offenders. *Sexual Abuse: A Journal of Research and Treatment, 14,* 169–194. https://doi.org/10.1177/107906320201400207

Holsinger, A. M. (1999). *Opening the 'black box': Assessing the relationship between program integrity and recidivism.* (Unpublished doctoral dissertation). University of Cincinnati.

Labreque, R. M., Smith, P., Lovins, B. K., & Latessa, E. J. (2014). The importance of reassessment: How changes in the LSI-R risk score can improve the prediction of recidivism. *Journal of Offender Rehabilitation, 53,* 116–128. https://doi.org/10.1080/10509674.2013.868389

Langan, P. A., Schmitt, E. L., & Rose, M. R. (2003, November). *Recidivism of sex offenders released from prison in 1994 (NCJ 198281).* Washington, DC: U.S. Department of Justice, Bureau of Justice Statistics.

Latessa, E. J., Brusman Lovins, L., Smith, P., & Makarios, M. (2010). *Follow-up evaluation of Ohio's community based correctional facility and halfway house programs: Program characteristics supplemental report.* Cincinnati, OH: University of Cincinnati.

Lipsey, M. (2009). Primary factors that characterize effective interventions with juvenile offenders: A meta-analytic overview. *Victims & Offenders, 4,* 124–147. https://doi.org/10.1080/15564880802612573

Losel, F., & Schmucker, M. (2005). The effectiveness of treatment for sexual offenders: A comprehensive meta-analysis. *Journal of Experimental Psychology, 1,* 117–146.

Lowenkamp, C. T. (2004). *Correctional program integrity and treatment effectiveness: A multi-site, program-level analysis.* (Unpublished doctoral dissertation). University of Cincinnati.

Lowenkamp, C. T., Flores, A. W., Holsinger, A. M., Makarios, M. D., & Latessa, E. J. (2010). Intensive supervision programs. Does program philosophy and the principles of effective intervention matter? *Journal of Criminal Justice, 38,* 368–375. https://doi.org/10.1016/j.jcrimjus.2010.04.004

Lowenkamp, C. T., & Latessa, E. J. (2003). *Evaluation of Ohio's Halfway Houses and community based correctional facilities.* Cincinnati, OH: University of Cincinnati, Center for Criminal Justice Research.

Lowenkamp, C. T., & Latessa, E. J. (2004). Understanding the risk principle: How and why

correctional interventions can harm low-risk offenders. *Topics in Community Corrections, 5,* 3–8.

Lowenkamp, C. T., & Latessa, E. J. (2005a). *Evaluation of Ohio's CCA programs.* Cincinnati, OH: Center for Criminal Justice Research, University of Cincinnati.

Lowenkamp, C. T., & Latessa, E. J. (2005b). *Evaluation of Ohio's reclaim funded programs, community correctional facilities, and DYS facilities.* Cincinnati, OH: University of Cincinnati, Center for Criminal Justice Research.

Lowenkamp, C. T., Latessa, E. J., & Holsinger, A. (2006). The risk principle in action: What have we learned from 13,676 cases and 97 correctional programs? *Crime & Delinquency, 52,* 77–93. https://doi.org/10.1177/0011128705281747

Lowenkamp, C. T., Latessa, E. J., & Smith, P. (2006). Does correctional program quality really matter? The impact of adhering to the principles of effective intervention. *Criminology and Public Policy, 5,* 575–594. https://doi.org/10.1111/cpp.2006.5.issue-3

Lowenkamp, C. T., Makarios, M. D., Latessa, E. J., Lemke, R. L., & Smith, P. (2010). Community corrections facilities for juvenile offenders in Ohio: An examination of treatment integrity and recidivism. *Criminal Justice and Behavior, 37,* 695–708.

MacKenzie, D. L. (2000). Evidenced-based corrections: Identifying what works. *Crime and Delinquency, 46,* 457–471. https://doi.org/10.1177/0011128700046004003

Maltz, M. D. (1984). *Recidivism.* Orlando, FL: Academic Press.

Olver, M. E., Wong, S. C. P., & Nicholaichuck, T. P. (2009). Outcome evaluation of a high-intensity inpatient sex offender treatment program. *Journal of Interpersonal Violence, 24,* 522–536. https://doi.org/10.1177/0886260508317196

Przybylski, R. (2006). Adult sex offender recidivism. In C. Lobanov-Rostovsky & R. Przybylski (Eds.), *Sex offender assessment and planning initiative: Office of sex offender sentencing, monitoring apprehending, registering and tracking* (pp. 89–110). Washington, DC: U.S. Department of Justice. Retrieved from www.smart.gov/SOMAPI/pdfs/SOMAPI_Full%20Report.pdf

Raynor, P. (2007). Risk and need assessment in British probation: The contribution of the LSI-R. *Psychology, Crime, and Law, 13,* 125–138. https://doi.org/10.1080/10683160500337592

Shaffer, D. K. (2006). Looking inside the black box of drug courts: A meta-analytic review. *Justice Quarterly, 28,* 493–521.

Vose, B., Lowenkamp, C. T., Smith, P., & Cullen, F. T. (2009). Gender and the predictive validity of the LSI-R: A study of parolees and probationers. *Journal of Contemporary Criminal Justice, 25,* 459–471. https://doi.org/10.1177/1043986209344797

Glossary

Accelerated/intensive longitudinal design: A type of research design that involves frequent measurements of multiple cohorts.

Activities: The third part of the system model of the policy process. Inputs are turned into outputs through activities. The combination of inputs, activities, and outputs produces impacts/outcomes.

Administrative robustness: The extent to which a program can remain successful in the face of poor implementation.

Aggregates: Groups or collections of items.

Anecdotal evidence: Evidence collected informally and largely based on personal experience.

Anonymity: The identity of the research participant is not known to anyone, including the researcher. It is not possible to link the research participants' responses to any of the data.

Applied research: Research that deals with a specific policy or program question. Includes program evaluation and policy analysis.

Arrestee Drug Abuse Monitoring (ADAM): Originally called Drug Use Forecasting. Researchers interviewed newly arrested individuals and asked them to self-report drug use and provide a urine sample. ADAM I data were collected from 1997–2003, while ADAM II data were collected from 2007–2014.

Attribute: A characteristic that describes something.

Basic research: Research conducted with the goal of contributing to academic knowledge and advancing science. Also called pure research or scientific research.

Belmont Report: Report published by the US Department of Health, Education, and Welfare in 1979. The report provided ethical guidelines for research involving human subjects, including three principles: respect for persons, beneficence, and justice.

Beneficence: A principle of the Belmont Report that requires researchers to maximize benefits to human participants in research while minimizing any possible harms.

Black box evaluation: A program evaluation that includes only the study of the program's impacts or outcomes.

Blind peer review: A process of reviewing research for publication that involves experts in the field reading manuscripts without knowing the identities of the authors.

Bounding: A technique used in panel studies to reduce telescoping. Researchers conduct a baseline interview, and then during the follow-up interview, the initial interview is used as a temporal reference point.

Cambridge Study in Delinquent Development: Prospective longitudinal design of delinquency including interviews of over 400 boys born in the early 1950s. The study began in the early 1960s, when most of the boys were eight or nine years old.

Causation: One event, specifically the independent variable, causes a particular outcome or impact on the dependent variable. To establish causation, one must demonstrate a relationship between the independent and dependent variables, that the independent variable precedes the dependent variable in time, and that all other possible explanations are explained away.

Certificate of confidentiality (CoC):   Certificate available through the US National Institutes of Health or the Department of Health and Human Services that allows researchers to protect the privacy of research participants. Researchers are prohibited from disclosing the identities or sensitive information of research participants to anyone outside the research project without their consent. This certificate is available for research funded through NIH or DHSS grants and for selected studies related to NIH or DHSS but not funded through them.

Cleaning: Preparing data for analysis by correcting mistakes, removing duplicates, and properly formatting the data.

Clear box evaluation: A type of program evaluation that involves both a full process evaluation and an outcome/impact evaluation. This is more informative than gray box and black box evaluations.

Close-ended questions: Survey items for which the answer options are provided for the respondent to select from.

Coding: Assignment of numerical values to items to facilitate data analysis.

Cohort studies: A prospective longitudinal design that involves tracking individuals who are part of the same group, such as same class in school or age.

Communities that Care Youth Survey: A panel study with repeated surveys of over 4,000 students, starting when they are in the fifth grade. The goal is to assess risk and protective factors associated with substance abuse.

Comparison group: A group monitored as part of research for comparison purposes. Individuals, groups, or organizations are non-randomly assigned to this group to compare to the experimental group being exposed to the independent variable. Researchers can then contrast the performance of the experimental group (exposed to the independent variable) to the comparison group (not exposed to the independent variable) on the outcome of interest (dependent variable). Used in quasi-experimental and some pre-experimental designs.

Compensatory equalization of treatment: A threat to internal validity that involves efforts to compensate for the control or comparison group's lack of exposure to the independent variable.

Compensatory rivalry: A threat to internal validity that involves members of the control or comparison group trying to improve their performance to keep pace with or outperform the experimental group.

Complete observer: A field researcher role in which the researcher makes observations without interacting with those being observed. The individuals being observed may not even be aware of the observer's presence.

Complete participant: A field researcher role in which the researcher participates in the daily lives of the individuals being studied while keeping his/her true identity a secret. Also known as covert observation.

Computer-assisted interviewing (CAI):   Interview protocol involving the use of a computer for data collection.

Computer-assisted survey instruments (CASI):   Interview protocol involving the use of a computer for data collection. Respondents can either take the survey independently on a device with the CASI software on it, or interviewers can read the questions while respondents key in their answers on the computer or tablet.

Computer-assisted telephone interviewing (CATI):   Telephone interview protocol in which the interviewer reads questions from a computer and types in the respondents' answers.

Concept: An abstract idea or conception.

Concurrent validity: A type of criterion validity. This is the extent to which a measure or set of measures produces the same outcome as another measure taken at the same time.

Confidence interval: Range of values in which the population parameter lies.

Confidence level: Probability that the population mean falls within a confidence interval.

Confidentiality: Researchers are aware of the participants' identity, but they agree to keep their research participation secret. While researchers will share the results of the research, they promise not to attribute any specific aspect of the data to an individual. If direct quotations are to be used, researchers will use a pseudonym instead of actual names.

Constant: Something that is not a variable.

Construct validity: The extent to which a measure or set of measures accurately reflects the theory and philosophy the concept aims to measure.

Content analysis: Objective, systematic, and generalizable description of communication content.

Content validity: The extent to which a measure or set of measures captures the full range of meaning of the concept.

Contingency questions: Survey questions that are asked only if the respondent provides a certain answer to the previous question. People who respond that they have not been victims of crime over the past six months would be asked to skip questions specific to recent victimization.

Continuous variables: Variables with an infinite number of answer options.

Control group: A group monitored as part of research for comparison purposes. Individuals, groups, or organizations are randomly assigned to this group to compare to the experimental group being exposed to the independent variable. Researchers can then contrast the performance of the experimental group (exposed to the independent variable) to the control group (not exposed to the independent variable) on the outcome of interest (dependent variable). Control groups are an element of experimental designs.

Control variable: A variable that is not the primary focus of research. Multivariate statistical analysis can account for the possible influence of control variables by holding them constant, allowing us to look at the relationship between X and Y independent of their influence.

Convenience sampling: Non-probability sampling plan that is based on what is convenient for the researcher. Also known as accidental sampling.

Correlation: A mutual relationship or association between two things.

Covert participation: A type of participant observation in which research subjects are not informed of the researcher's true identity or purpose. Also known as complete participant.

Creaming: Selecting only those most likely to succeed for a sample in a program evaluation.

Crime Mapping: Use of mapping software to analyze crime incidents.

Criterion validity: The extent to which a measure or group of measures predicts the outcome of another measure. Types of criterion validity are concurrent and predictive validity.

Cross-sectional design: A study involving observations/data collection at a single point in time.

Dark figure of crime: Crimes not known to the police.

Declaration of Helsinki: Statement developed by the World Medical Association that outlines ethical principles for medical research involving human subjects.

Deductive reasoning: Method of inquiry in which researchers start with what is already known, in the form of existing research and theories, then use that information to make predictions (hypotheses), followed by data collection. Deductive reasoning moves from more general ideas to examination of more specific issues.

Demoralization: A threat to internal validity in which the control or comparison group's experiences reduced morale or productivity due to its awareness that it is not receiving the experimental stimulus.

Dependent variable: The outcome or effect variable. Researchers hypothesize that changes in the independent variable will impact the dependent variable. Also known as "Y" or "DV."

Depth interview: Long interviews used in qualitative research. Researchers often approach these interviews with a topic list but no specific questions to be asked.

Diffusion of treatment: A threat to internal validity in which the experimental stimulus is applied to the comparison or control group in addition to the experimental group. Also called contamination.

Dimension: One particular aspect of a concept.

Discrete variables: Variables with a finite number of answer options.

Disproportionate stratified sampling: A type of proportionate sampling in which the population is first stratified into categories of interest (e.g., race), and then random samples are taken from each group, but disproportionately, to provide some groups greater representation in the sample.

Ecological fallacy: Drawing conclusions about individuals based on research findings from a larger unit of analysis.

Empirical evidence: Information acquired through systematic observation and experimentation.

Equal probability selection method (EPSM): Sampling procedure that provides all members of the population an equal probability of being selected, typically achieved through random sampling.

Equivalent groups posttest-only design: An experimental design that involves random selection into either the treatment or control group and then measurement of the dependent variable after the experimental group has been exposed to the independent variable.

Evaluability assessment: A systematic way to examine a program to determine whether a full evaluation is warranted.

Evidence-based practice (EBP): The use of methodologically rigorous research to inform decisions about which programs are effective and which should be discarded.

Exception fallacy: Generalizing findings from a few individuals or an exceptional circumstance to large groups. Also known as individualistic fallacy.

Exhaustive: Providing enough options for survey items to allow for every participant to truthfully and accurately answer the question.

Experimental group: The group in research that will be exposed to the experimental stimulus.

External validity: The likelihood of being able to replicate research findings in another time or place. A type of generalizability.

Face validity: The extent to which, by appearance, measures are accurately capturing what they intend to measure.

Factorial design: An experimental design that allows for comparison of multiple treatments. Also includes random assignment to groups and pre- and posttest measures.

Focus group: Type of in-person guided discussion, typically involving 8 to 15 people.

Forgiving introduction: A technique used to introduce self-report survey questions about socially undesirable, or even illegal, behavior by first assuring respondents that others have engaged in such behavior.

Formative evaluation: Program evaluation conducted while the program is being implemented with the goal of providing the implementation team feedback.

Gatekeeper: A known and well-respected member of a subculture who is willing to introduce researchers to informants and vouch for them.

Generalizability: The extent to which research results based on a sample are applicable to the population.

Going native: Ethnographers becoming too familiar with the group they are studying to the point that they start to identify with the study group.

Gray box evaluation: A type of program evaluation that involves an outcome/impact evaluation plus a partial process evaluation. This is more informative than a black box evaluation but less informative than clear box.

Grey literature: Unpublished research.

Grounded theory: Development of theory based on gathered data.

Hawthorne Effect: A threat to external validity that involves improved performance of individuals who realize that they are being observed. Named after the Hawthorne Plant where it was first noted.

Historicism: Belief that all historical and social events are unique and warrant chronicling.

History: A threat to internal validity that involves an event outside the study contributing to changes in the dependent variable.

Hot spots policing: Policing technique that starts with geographic analysis to identify locations experiencing disproportionate amounts of crime or calls for service and then conducting saturation patrols of those areas.

Hypothesis: Prediction of a relationship between variables.

Implementation failure: Failure of a program due to lack of adherence to the program's plan.

Inductive reasoning: Method of inquiry beginning with specific observations and then moving to more general concepts, such theory development.

Independent variable: The predictor or cause thought to impact the value of the dependent variable. Also known as "X," "IV," experimental stimulus, or treatment.

Index: A measure constructed by summing the items on a survey or data collection tool.

Informed consent: Agreement of individuals to participate in research after they have been fully informed of the elements of the study. Elements generally include the purpose, length of research participation, any potential risks or rewards, and the voluntary nature of participation.

Inputs: The second part of the system model of the policy process including resources allocated to address some type of demand.

Institutional Review Board (IRB):   A formal college or university board with the responsibility of reviewing and monitoring research involving human subjects. IRBs are tasked with ensuring that researchers are providing potential human research participants with necessary protections.

Instrumentation: A threat to internal validity that involves changes to data collection strategies for the same variables over time.

Inter-rater reliability: A measure of reliability across data collectors.

Interrupted time-series with non-equivalent comparison group: A type of quasi-experiment with several data collection points over time, a non-equivalent comparison group, and the introduction of the independent variable as the "interruption" that occurs after several data collection waves.

Interrupted time-series with treatment removal: A type of quasi-experiment with several data collection points over time and the introduction, and then removal, of the treatment stimulus, otherwise known as the independent variable.

Inter-university Consortium for Political and Social Research (ICPSR):   A consortium of academic institutions and research organizations that maintains a data archive of over 250,000 files pertaining to social and behavioral sciences.

Interval variable: A level of measurement with equal distance between the items.

Justice: One of three principles of the Belmont Report. Requires that the benefits and burdens of research be evenly distributed among research participants.

Kansas City Preventive Patrol Experiment: A study conducted in Kansas City in the early 1970s in which neighborhoods were randomly assigned to receive intensive police patrols, regular amounts of patrols, or only visits from the police if they needed to respond to a call for service. The researchers found no difference in crime rates between the three areas.

Latent content: Underlying meaning of content. Also known as context units.

Lehigh Longitudinal Study: A panel design that followed children and their parents to collect data on child abuse and children's exposure to domestic violence.

Likert scale: A scale, usually five to seven points, that allows respondents to indicate their level of satisfaction or agreement.

Longitudinal design: A type of research design with repeated measurements/observations over time.

Manifest content: Obvious, clearly measurable items. Also known as recording units.

Matching: A technique used in research designs with non-equivalent groups to pair individuals from treatment and comparison groups on theoretically relevant variables. Offenders split into treatment and comparison groups through non-random assignment might be paired on gender, age, offense history, and other offense- and treatment-related variables. Matching can be conducted manually or through using statistical procedures.

Maturation: A threat to internal validity in which the change observed in study participants is a result of individual maturation rather than the treatment stimulus.

Matrix: A set of close-ended survey items in which the same set of answer options appear in the columns while the survey questions or statements are listed in the rows.

Maryland Scientific Methods Scale (SMS): Scale that measures research on methodological vigor on a five-point scale.

Meta-analysis: A systematic review of research that also involves statistical analysis of the studies' results.

Mnemonic device: Rhyme or other verbal tool used to aid memory.

Monitoring the Future (MTF): Cohort design study, sponsored by the National Institute of Drug Abuse, that surveys adolescents to learn about their drug and alcohol use and attitudes.

Mortality: A threat to internal validity that involves research participants withdrawing from the research before completion.

Multiple treatment interference: A type of external validity that involves the inability of researchers to identify which of multiple treatments is producing a change in the dependent variable.

Multistage cluster sampling: A probability sampling technique that involves researchers dividing a location into segments and then taking random samples from each of those areas.

Mutually exclusive: Two events that cannot occur at the same time. For survey construction, this means that only one answer option will be an appropriate answer for each respondent.

National Crime Victimization Survey (NCVS): Longitudinal panel design of US households conducted by the United States Census Bureau to measure victimization. All members of the household over the age of 12 are surveyed about their victimization experiences every six months for 3.5 years.

National Incident-Based Reporting System (NIBRS): An incident-based, FBI-sponsored crime reporting system intended to replace the UCR. NIBRS provides crime data from participating federal, state, county, local, college/university, and tribal law enforcement agencies.

National Youth Survey (NYS): Longitudinal design of self-reported delinquent behavior of juveniles 11 to 17 years of age.

Nominal level: A level of measurement that places items into categories with no rank order.

Nonprobability sampling: Sampling techniques that violate the equal probability selection method.

Null hypothesis: A prediction of no relationship between the independent and dependent variables.

Nuremberg Code: A set of ethical principles written following the Nuremberg trial of Nazi war criminals. It includes ten rules for protecting human subjects involved in research.

Obedience to Authority Study: An experiment conducted by Stanley Milgram to study human behavior. Participants were given the role of teacher and told to review vocabulary words with a person identified as a learner. If the learner did not recite the correct words, a man in charge of the laboratory would order the teacher to administer a shock to the learner. The teachers were unaware that they were not actually shocking anyone.

Observer as participant: A role for field researchers in which the researchers do one-visit interviews with participants.

One-group before-after design: A pre-experimental design that includes observations of a sample before and after the introduction of the independent variable.

One-group posttest-only design: A pre-experimental design that lacks a comparison group and a pretest measurement.

Open-ended questions: Survey questions that require the respondents to answer using their own words.

Operationalization: Defining concepts to make them more specific, resulting in measurable variables.

Ordinal level: A level of measurement that rank orders the items.

Outcome evaluation: A type of evaluation research that studies the types of outcomes produced by the program's inputs, activities, and outputs. Also known as an impact evaluation.

Outcomes: The fifth part of the system model of the policy process. Outcomes (or impacts) are the product of the policy's inputs, activities, and outputs.

Outputs: The fourth part of the system model of the policy process. Outputs are the product of inputs and activities and lead to outcomes.

Panel study: A longitudinal design that involves data collection at least two times from the same individuals.

Participant as observer: A fieldwork role in which researchers perform participant observation by partaking in the daily lives of those being studied while making their identity and purpose known.

Peer review: A quality-control process used by many research and academic publications that involves manuscripts undergoing a review by experts in the field who will then determine whether the document should be published. Peer-reviewed journals are considered the best outlet for research.

Philadelphia Birth Cohort Study: Cohort study of nearly 10,000 boys born in Philadelphia in 1945. Researchers tracked the boys from their 10th birthdays through their 18th birthdays and measured their involvement in delinquent behavior. Notable results included the finding that 6 percent of the cohort was responsible for over half the group's offending and that the juveniles did not specialize in any particular type of criminal activity.

Plagiarism: Passing off someone else's work as one's own.

Planned change: Policy changes in response to a problem or perceived problem, characterized by careful research and analysis.

Policy: Rule or set of rules or guidelines for how to make a decision.

Policy analysis: Process of researching and identifying potential solutions to a current or anticipated problem. Also called problem analysis.

Population parameter: Summary description of a variable in the population.

Positivism: Approach to research common in the natural sciences that prioritizes using the scientific method.

Power: The probability of correctly rejecting the null hypothesis. Power can be increased by increasing the sample size.

Predatory journals: Publications that prioritize self-interest at the expense of scholarship and quality. These journals often publish articles, for a fee, without concern for quality control.

Predictive policing: A combination of policing tactics, including problem-oriented policing, intelligence-led policing, and crime mapping, to allow police to analyze data and prevent crime.

Predictive validity: A type of criterion validity concerning the extent to which a measure or a set of measures predicts an outcome.

Pre-experimental design: A research design that lacks two of the three elements of the classical experiment. These designs lack randomization of participants into experimental and control groups. They may also lack pretest measures and/or have a non-randomly selected comparison group.

Primary data sources: Raw data that researchers make available to other researchers for secondary data analysis.

Process evaluation: A type of evaluation research that involves studying program implementation.

Program: A set of services aimed at achieving specific goals and objectives within specified individuals, groups, organizations, or communities.

Program evaluation: Type of applied research that studies the extent to which a program was implemented as planned and produced the desired outcomes. Includes process and outcome/impact evaluations.

Project: Time-limited set of services provided to individuals, groups organizations, or communities that usually focuses on a single need, problem, or issue.

Proofs: Mathematical procedures demonstrating that stated assumptions logically guarantee a conclusion.

Propensity score matching (PSM):   Statistical technique that matches comparison group participants to experimental group members on variables relevant to the specific research project.

Proportionate stratified sampling: A type of probability sampling in which the population is first stratified by some characteristic of interest, and then proportionate random samples are selected from each stratum.

Prospective design: A type of longitudinal design in which researchers collect data at baseline and then follow participants for additional data collection to observe changes over time. A prospective study of delinquency might start by identifying a group of ten-year old children and interviewing them every two years.

Pseudonym: A fictitious name given to a research participant to protect his/her identify.

Publication bias: Tendency for studies finding support for the research hypothesis to have a greater chance of being published.

Purposive sampling: A non-probability sampling plan that is based on the judgment of the researcher.

Quackery: Application of interventions that are not based on knowledge of effective programs for reducing crime or changing offender behavior.

Quasi-experiment: A research design that is missing one of the characteristics of a classical experiment. Includes quasi-experiments with non-equivalent groups and time-series designs.

Quota sampling: A non-probability sampling plan in which the researcher selects proportions of individuals based on a characteristic of interest (e.g., race).

Randomized response technique (RRT):   An approach to asking participants sensitive questions in which the participant flips a coin and, based on the results, responds to one of two questions. The data collector records the answer but is unaware of which question was asked. The goal is to give the respondent a degree of privacy while participating in the interview.

Ratio level: A level of measurement with equal distance between the items. Similar to interval level but has a definite zero.

Reactivity: A research participant's change in behavior as a response to being observed.

Reliability: The consistency or stability of a measure or set of measures.

Replication: Repeating a study at a different time and/or place to see if the findings match earlier research results.

Research hypothesis: A prediction of a relationship between the independent and dependent variables.

Respect for persons: One of three principles of the Belmont Report. Requires that research participants be treated as autonomous agents who can make decisions for themselves free of coercion.

Respondent-driven sampling: A type of non-probability snowball sampling. Researchers try to limit the amount of sample bias by increasing the number of initial informants and limiting the number of referrals from each informant.

Retrospective design: A research design that measures past behavior by asking participants to recall events or by researchers collecting data memorializing past events.

Rival causal factors: Variables other than the independent variable that impact the value of the dependent variable. Also known as "Z" or threats to internal validity.

Sample: A subset of a population.

Sample statistic: Summary description of a variable in the sample.

Sampling error: The discrepancy between a sample and the population.

Sampling frame: A comprehensive list of all members of a population from which a sample is to be selected.

Scale: Ordered survey responses that allow researchers to increase the level of measurement from nominal to ordinal or possibly interval or ratio. Examples of scales are items from 1 to 5 with 1 = strongly disagree and 5 = strongly agree, or rating interest in an event from 1 = definitely will not go to 10 = definitely will go.

Scientific method: A blueprint for a way of doing empirical research that involves hypothesis formulation and testing, systematic observation, and precise measurements.

Scientism: An extreme form of positivism that suggests only concepts that can be measured are worth studying.

Secondary data analysis: Reanalysis of data that were originally gathered for other purposes. Sources of secondary data are raw data collected by others, publicly available official/agency reports, and non-public agency records.

Secondary data sources: Data that have already been analyzed and reported but then are used by other researchers for secondary data analysis.

Selection-maturation interaction: A threat to internal validity that involves the combination of selection bias in sample selection and differential maturation.

Selection (sample) bias: A threat to both internal and external validity that involves selection of nonequivalent groups.

Series victimization: Crimes that are similar in type but occur with frequency.

Semi-structured surveys: Surveys that contain a combination of close-ended and open-ended questions.

Skip logic: Computerized survey programming that moves the respondent to the next appropriate question based on their response to a contingency question.

Simple random sampling: A type of probability sampling that involves selecting subjects at random, usually by "picking out of a hat" or using a random number generator.

Simulation: Attempted replication of real-life scenarios in a laboratory setting.

Snowball sampling: A non-probability sampling method that involves researchers increasing their sample size by getting referrals from research participants.

Solomon four-group design: An experimental design including randomized assignment of participants into four groups. Group one is an experimental group that receives the pre- and post-test and is exposed to the independent variable. Group two gets the pre- and posttest but is not exposed to the independent variable. Group three is exposed to the independent variable and receives a posttest but not a pretest. Group four receives only the posttest.

Split-half reliability: A test of reliability that involves measuring the same construct on one survey by splitting the questions measuring that construct in half and then testing them for consistency.

Sponsor: A person or organization that can help researchers make connections with organizations they wish to study.

Spurious relationship: A relationship between the independent and dependent variables that is not genuine because both are related to an additional variable, known as a rival causal factor ("Z").

Stanford Prison Experiment: A simulation of prison conditions that occurred in the basement of an academic building at Stanford University. College-age males were randomly selected to act as either prisoners or guards. The two-week study ended after six days.

Statistical conclusion validity: A type of threat to internal validity that is the extent to which researchers are able to determine whether two variables are related.

Statistical regression: A threat to internal validity that involves those research participants with extreme scores regressing to the mean independent of the influence of the treatment stimulus.

Stratified random sampling: A probability sampling technique that involves dividing the population into different strata that are of interest to the study. After that division, the researchers take random samples from each stratum.

Structured surveys: Surveys with close-ended questions or items in which respondents choose from available answer options.

Summative evaluation: Program evaluation conducted after the program has been implemented that focuses on program outcomes.

Systematic random sampling: A probability sampling technique that involves selecting the nth (5th, 10th, etc.) element of the population.

Systematic review: Collection and summarization of empirical evidence that meets pre-specified inclusion criteria.

Tearoom Trade: Controversial book published by Laud Humphreys in the 1970s. Humphreys did covert observation of males engaging in secret homosexual activities and then tracked them to their homes so he could survey the men and their families under the guise of doing social health research.

Telescoping: Placement of an incident into an incorrect timespan when asked to recall events. An individual responds affirmatively to a question asking about being a victim of a property crime within the past six months when the victimization actually occurred eight months ago.

Testing effects: A threat to internal validity that involves the pretest sensitizing participants to the purpose of the study. This enhanced awareness then impacts the value of the dependent variable.

Test-retest reliability: A reliability check that involves surveying individuals and then surveying them again on some of the same variables to check for consistency of responses.

Theory: An attempt to construct a plausible explanation of reality.

Theory failure: When the theory underlying the creation of a program was flawed, resulting in the program failing. Researchers determine that theory failure has occurred when a program does not produce the expected outcomes despite the program having been implemented correctly.

Threats to internal validity: Factors other than the independent variable that might explain variation in the dependent variable.

Time-series: A type of longitudinal design that involves numerous data collection points, typically collected at equal time intervals.

Treatment integrity: The extent to which the program or policy was implemented as intended.

Trend study: A type of longitudinal design that tracks specific characteristics of a population over time.

Two-group posttest-only design: A non-equivalent groups design in which posttest measures are taken after the experimental group is exposed to the independent variable.

Uniform Crime Reports (UCR):   Nationwide program, with 18,000 participating police departments, to collect crime data from states, counties, cities, colleges and universities, tribal areas, and federal law enforcement departments.

Unit of analysis: Who or what is being studied.

Units of observation: Items or individuals from whom researchers collect data with the goal of learning about the study's unit of analysis. In some studies, the unit of observation and the unit of analysis are the same.

Unplanned change: Policy changes that occur quickly, in reaction to a problem or perceived problem, and with little consideration of consequences.

Unstructured surveys: Surveys consisting of open-ended questions or items that respondents answer using their own words.

Validity: The extent to which an item or set of items accurately measures what it is intended to measure.

Variable: A measurable concept that varies from case to case.

Verstehen: Means "understanding" in German." In the social sciences, it refers to ethnographers achieving a level of understanding of the culture that they are studying.

Victimless crimes: Crimes that lack a clear victim, including prostitution, drug dealing, and gambling.

Index

Made in the USA
Coppell, TX
28 August 2024

36553628R00275